An Introduction to Sociology

THE
SOCIAL
WORLD

Pg 422

SECOND EDITION

An Introduction to Sociology

THE SOCIAL WORLD

LORNE TEPPERMAN
University of Toronto

R. JACK RICHARDSON
McMaster University

McGraw-Hill
Ryerson
Limited

Toronto Montreal New York Auckland Bogotá
Caracas Lisbon London Madrid Mexico Milan
New Delhi Paris San Juan Singapore Sydney Tokyo

THE SOCIAL WORLD: *An Introduction to Sociology*

SECOND EDITION

ISBN: 0-07-549790-5

3 4 5 6 7 8 9 0   TRI   0 9 8 7 6 5 4 3 2

Printed and bound in Canada

Care has been taken to trace ownership of copyright material contained in this text. The publisher will gladly accept any information to rectify any reference or credit in subsequent editions.

SPONSORING EDITOR: CATHERINE O'TOOLE
SENIOR SUPERVISING EDITOR: ROSALYN STEINER
COPY EDITOR: WAYNE HERRINGTON
PERMISSIONS EDITOR: NORMA CHRISTENSEN
COVER DESIGN AND TEXT: SHARON MATTHEWS
TECHNICAL ARTIST: PAT CODE

Canadian Cataloguing in Publication Data

Main entry under title:

The Social world : an introduction to sociology

2nd ed.
Includes bibliographical references and index.
ISBN 0-07-549790-5

I. Sociology   I. Tepperman, Lorne, date .
II. Richardson, R.J. (Richard John), date .

HM51.S64 1991   301   C90-095601-1

contents

Acknowledgments

Compiling a multi-authored text can be difficult. However, we enjoyed putting this one together because of the excellent people we worked with.

Our greatest thanks go to the contributing authors. They are all fine scholars and, more than that, they have demonstrated that they are professionals. They took our criticisms and requests for revision with good humour and grace. Needless to say, the book could not have existed without their scholarship, creativity, hard work and co-operation. We also gratefully acknowledge the contribution of the many anonymous reviewers who commented on all the original drafts.

We are grateful to Catherine O'Toole, sponsoring editor at McGraw-Hill Ryerson who skilfully took command of the development of this second edition and shepherded it through the mass of administrative steps that accompany any project of this scope. Thanks, too, to Rosalyn Steiner who was tireless in supervising the production of the book with a cheerful dedication to quality and timeliness. Norma Christensen, permissions editor, somehow managed to track down and obtain permissions from the myriad of copyright holders of excerpts and visuals that our authors used to accompany their chapters. Michelle MacDonald, development editor, found several of the photos that enhanced the written text. Dennis Bockus, consulting editor, did a thorough and effective job in achieving continuity and consistency throughout the volume and in helping to make the book a "user-friendly" one for beginning sociology students. Wayne Herrington, the copy editor, took another run through our prose to iron out the wrinkles that remained.

Finally, we are extremely grateful to the growing number of instructors who have adopted the first edition of this book (and the students who have studied it) over the past four years. They made the text popular enough to justify this second edition. They also participated in an extensive survey conducted by Danelle D'Alvise of McGraw-Hill Ryerson. More than 50 respondents told us what they liked and what they disliked about the first edition. We took their advice seriously so we could build on the book's strengths and eliminate weaknesses. In doing this, we hope to repay the loyalty of these users—the survey was unable to uncover a single instructor who had used the first edition and then dropped it in favour of another text.

The resulting book is, of course, imperfect and we accept responsibility for the flaws that remain. We hope the book will achieve the purpose for which it was written: namely to better inform our students, a new generation of sociologists, about this challenging enterprise in which we share, the discipline of sociology.

LORNE TEPPERMAN / R. JACK RICHARDSON

part 1

Sociology and Society

Sociology teaches us things we did not know about our own everyday lives. In this respect, sociology is different from common sense, gossip or what you read in the newspaper. Sociology is full of surprises: contradictions, paradoxes and the non-obvious. Consider the following sociological findings:

- Crime is a normal and necessary condition for conformity.
- Ruling classes create the conditions for their own overthrow.
- A particular kind of religious belief—strict Protestantism—is best suited for capitalism and science to develop.
- Love and marriage are the result of a social exchange that must balance.
- Conflict with outsiders keeps group members loyal.
- Secret terrorist organizations work best if they are made up of friends and relatives.
- Informal groups produce similar kinds of leadership, including group "jokers."
- Political radicals see the world in pairs of opposites, while liberals see odd-numbered groupings.
- Families are "small societies," with their own politics, economies, value systems and means of resolving conflict.
- Sexual behaviour in North America mirrors our culture's concerns with mass production, efficiency, bigness, toughness and "getting the job done."

What, then, is this field of sociology that allows us to study such a rich variety of strange, yet familiar experiences?

Formal Definitions

Sociology is the science that makes theories about social relations. Let's consider what this means.

To sociologists, the word *science* means much the same as it does to physicists or biologists; namely, the construction and testing of theories about the real world. A science of social relations is more complex than other sciences, because people are more complicated than atoms and amoebae. But all sciences have the same goals.

For sociologists, just as for physicists, *theories* are tentative explanations of the world we can see or measure. These theories are the basis for predicting future events. Every theory is judged against competing theories in terms of how well it predicts the future and explains the present. A science tests its theories over and over to improve them. Theories that fail such tests are discarded in favour of better ones.

1

Social relations are relationships between people that are somehow binding. For this reason, the subject matter of sociology is the social bond that connects individuals to one another in groups and societies.

Societies are collections of social relations. A society is made up of all the understandings (including arrangements and rules) that its members share, all the bonds that are based on these understandings, and all the organizations (from friendships and families up through business and governments) that grow out of these bonds.

The boundaries of a society are hard to find. Many social relationships cross international borders, such as the one between Canada and the United States. Some writers have even wondered whether Canada and the United States, which are distinct nation-states, are really distinct societies. For similar reasons, others have wondered whether the two are distinct economies, since they are tied together by trade and the flows of capital and migrants. Yet, the idea of a Canadian society still has value. It helps us understand why life is different in Halifax and Boston, Toronto and Detroit, Winnipeg and Minneapolis, Vancouver and Seattle (to name only a few comparable cities).

The Character of Sociological Theories

Sociological theories have certain common characteristics. Good theories are always tentative, thorough and economical. They should also be true, as far as we can tell. In practice, sociologists sometimes lose sight of what is true and false. Personal interests and biases may mislead them. To reduce the risk of error, sociologists use agreed-upon methods of discovering, testing and communicating their findings and theories.

Sociological theories should not be circular by definition. A theory that "satisfied workers are happy with their jobs" is circular if what we mean by "satisfied" is "happy with their jobs." Such a theory, though true, has no value to science because it can never be proved false and adds nothing to our stock of knowledge.

A theory that is not circular can be tested for validity. Scientists, including sociologists, never prove a theory absolutely right; they only prove contending theories less right. The theory that best survives many attempts at disproof and shows itself most thorough and economical is considered the most valid, *for the time being*.

All sociological theories must be tested against the world we can observe or measure. Some of Einstein's theories in physics waited for decades until there was equipment that was sensitive enough to test his mathematically derived predictions. Likewise, some sociological theories are not immediately testable. But whatever the difficulties, sociologists must always seek validation for theories. Every theorist must sooner or later appeal to the evidence our senses offer, and to rely on reason over intuition, emotion and good intention. None but the court of empirical evidence will decide the theory's fate in the long run.

Two other aspects of sociological theories need mentioning. Sociological theories should be relevant to everyday life and they should not be obvious. All social relations are of interest to sociologists. But, as citizens, sociologists should and usually do pay special attention to the public problems of their times. Sociology's history shows that the most enduring work has been done by "middle-range" researchers moving back and forth between pure theory and an active concern with current events.

Sociology that immediately influences the way some portion of society functions is called *applied sociology*. Each year, more graduate sociologists take jobs outside universities and apply their knowledge to government and corporate decision making.

Sociologists apply their knowledge in a wide variety of ways. For example, political polling—one type of applied sociology—analyses the popular support for particular candidates or policies. By understanding the results of polls, political parties can modify their positions and the way they present these positions to the public.

Another type of applied sociology—market research—analyses consumer preferences and public perceptions of different products. With such information in hand, manufacturers and advertisers can better decide which new products to introduce, how to change old ones and where (and how) to focus their advertising.

Sociologists also carry out a wide variety of policy research, another kind of applied sociology. Policy research is aimed at determining the need for new policies and likely public reactions to new policies. One kind of policy research, social impact assessment, tries to anticipate the ways a policy will likely change society if put into practice. Another type of applied sociology, evaluation research, is used to assess whether a new policy is achieving what policy makers hoped it would and, if not, why not.

Good sociological theories are not obvious. The main activity of sociologists is not knowledge application, it is theory making. Without good theories, applied sociology can never achieve the results we desire. By connecting previously unconnected facts, a good theory yields insights no one anticipated, leading us *beyond* the obvious to the unexpected, the paradoxical and the contradictory. The more sociology succeeds in making non-obvious predictions, the more mature a science it has become.

Sociology Contrasted with Other Disciplines

Sociologist Kenneth Westhues has helped us understand sociology better by comparing it to other related disciplines. For example, sociology is different from journalism and history. Both journalism and history describe real events and usually base their descriptions on a hidden theory. Sociology is different. It reveals and states its theories, in order to test them. Sociology may be a good preparation for doing history or journalism (and vice versa), but it differs from these disciplines.

Sociology also differs from philosophy. Both sociology and philosophy use logic to make and test theories by means of logical deduction. However, theorizing is quite different in these two fields. Sociological theories must stand up logically, but they must also stand up to measurable reality in a way philosophical theories need not. A sociological theory whose predictions are not supported by evidence gathered in an agreed-upon way will not be accepted by sociologists, no matter how logical the theory.

Finally, sociology differs from psychology. Psychologists study the behaviour of individual humans (or, occasionally, animals) under varying experimental conditions. Sociologists study a social relationship or group of relationships observed in nature: for example, the family, club, organization or total society. Sociology and psychology come closer together in a field called social psychology, but sociologists and psychologists even define this subfield differently.

To repeat, sociology is concerned with making scientifically valid theories about social relations. These theories should be "scientific" in the usual meanings of the word. But certain methodological problems make the scientific study of social relations more difficult than the scientific study of atoms, amoebae or even individual monkeys and humans.

Some Methodological
Difficulties

First, sociologists can rarely, if ever, experiment on groups or families, let alone societies. Yet, experimentation is the common way of testing theories in physical science. Because experimentation is impossible, sociologists develop alternative methods, none completely satisfactory. The sociologist must know and use a large variety of research methods. Any sociological theory must withstand a battery of weak tests, using many approaches, since strong (experimental) tests are not possible.

A second problem making the scientific study of social relations difficult is the existence of competing paradigms in sociology. Paradigms are ways of thinking. Different paradigms define which problems are key to understanding social relations and also which research procedures are most appropriate and which evidence is most relevant.

Paradigms have multiplied in sociology for many reasons, including a strong philosophical (deductive) tradition in European sociology and an empirical (inductive) one in America and Britain; the rising and falling popularity of particular research techniques; and the ebb and flow of political ideologies in the university. The uncertainty of sociological evidence also contributes. If a sociological proof must consist of many weak approximations, room exists for many approaches, many paradigms.

A third main difficulty arises from the nature of the sociologist's object of study—people and their relationships. As sociologist W. I. Thomas argued, what people believe is real is real in its consequences. Social reality has its subjective, as well as objective, aspects. Therefore, to accurately explain and predict social relations, sociologists must understand actors' perceptions, beliefs and expectations, as well as their goals and opportunities.

Unfortunately, to reach such an understanding is very difficult. It must be done without calling attention to the researcher and research enterprise itself. Interfering with normal social relations in order to study them may change those relations drastically. Even more than in physics, which thanks to Heisenberg also recognizes the problem of measuring without interfering, research in sociology demands great sensitivity and creativity.

A fourth problem is the non-repetitiveness of history and the uniqueness of relations we study. Sociologists will never find two societies that are identical in every respect except the one of theoretical interest. Always, new kinds of societies arise in new historical contexts. Not even two families, two friendships or two marriages are the same. And no society is quite the same society a week, a year or a decade later.

Consider the Industrial Revolution. It will never be repeated. There never will be another Industrial Revolution of the kind that occurred in England between 1775 and 1850. For this reason, sociologists cannot test a theory about the Industrial Revolution in the way chemists might test a theory about chemical reactions at low temperatures or physicists test a theory about nuclear fission.

The Notion of a
Social System

These methodological problems may never be fully overcome. On the other hand, several other factors make the scientific study of social relations somewhat easier. As noted above, all sociologists study social systems, and all social systems, large and small, have certain common features. For this reason, an understanding of social systems in general can help us understand a particular case that is hard to study directly. Information about small social systems, systems that are nearer at hand, or better known, can be used to develop and test theories about larger, less accessible ones.

Research shows that people are often limited by the social relationships in which they participate, despite their own plans and wishes to the contrary. Whether alone or in groups, people are part of a larger, complex reality beyond their easy control. They are part of a *social structure*, as discussed in the first chapter and elsewhere in this book.

The chapters that follow develop some of the ideas discussed in this introduction. The first, "What is Sociology?," clarifies the discipline's competing paradigms and discusses their historical background. The second chapter, "Sociological Methods of Research," extends our understanding of experimental and non-experimental methods. These chapters come first in the book because they are fundamental. Understanding sociology means, first, understanding the discipline's outlook and methods.

CHAPTER 1

What Is Sociology?

ALFRED A. HUNTER AND
MARGARET A. DENTON

Introduction

Although it was late to develop as a distinct discipline, the science of society has been around at least since the French thinker Auguste Comte named it sociology in 1838. We can trace its origins back through history in the writings of the fourteenth-century Moslem historian Ibn Khaldun, the pre-Christian Greek historian Polybius, and much earlier scholars and thinkers, including Plato and Aristotle (Barnes and Becker, 1938). Despite its long history, however, sociology remains poorly understood, often misunderstood.

Why is sociology not better known? One reason is that it is the study of something that is quite abstract. Who has seen society? It is like the wind—as much an object for the mind's eye as for the naked one. Another reason is that it is seldom taught in Canadian schools in a form that most sociologists would recognize. The mission of sociology is to expose the nature of social life and point to how it might be changed. Such topics as child abuse, corporate crime, drug addiction, environmental pollution, poverty, racism, sexism and sexual deviance invite controversy. Sociology looks at the nature of these problems and at their causes, consequences and solutions.

Despite the general confusion about what it is, sociology is an integral part of our lives. We are all amateur sociologists. In our everyday lives, we continually add to and revise our factual knowledge about society and act upon and test our theories of how it works. Using common sense, however, differs from the discipline of sociology in that sociologists are more deliberate than ordinary people in gathering information and drawing conclusions from it.

Many decisions that affect our lives are made using sociological knowledge. Governments, private businesses, voluntary associations and other organizations increasingly rely upon it. Many economic, educational, employment, health, housing, welfare and other public policies are devised, carried out and evaluated using it. Commercial products and services are conceived and marketed, elections are called and political campaigns waged, and fund-raising and membership drives are conducted using it.

How does sociological knowledge enter into corporate and public decisions? First, sociological theories are increasingly employed by policy makers and others in framing questions for research. For example, we know that students from backgrounds with high socio-economic status (that is, well to do, well educated) are less likely to drop out of high school than are students from low-status backgrounds (Radwanski, 1987). Educational policy makers look to sociologists to tell them why, since they see this as a problem that needs to be addressed.

Second, sociological methods are more and more often used in research. In particular, by drawing upon developments in psychology and statistics, sociologists have polished the art and perfected the science of the *sample survey*. Sample surveys provide accurate descriptions of large populations (for example, all Canadians) by means of interviews or questionnaires administered to relatively few people (a sample of a few hundred or thousand Canadians). Sample survey data have shown that Ontario high-school students from high socio-economic backgrounds are much more likely than others to be placed in the advanced (or university-bound) stream (Radwanski, 1987). Students in university-bound streams are much less likely than others to drop out, apparently due in part to the higher quality of the classroom instruction that they receive. In response to these findings, the government of Ontario has announced an end to streaming in high schools, beginning in 1990.

Finally, popular culture has superficially absorbed bits and pieces of sociological theories. In J. D. Salinger's *The Catcher in the Rye* (1951), Holden Caulfield complains of *anomie*—the absence of rules governing behaviour in a society. This concept was introduced into sociology by Emile Durkheim, the first university sociologist in France. The term "significant other" was coined by George Herbert Mead, an early twentieth-century American philosopher whose ideas have been very influential in sociology. Does the prime minister lack "charisma"? Are fast cars part of your "life style"? These familiar concepts would certainly have been recognized by the turn-of-the-century German sociologist Max Weber, who created them.

Nature and Goals of Science

To the founders of modern sociology, including Comte (France, 1798–1857), Marx (Germany, 1818–1833), Spencer (England, 1820–1903), Durkheim (France, 1858–1917) and Weber (Germany, 1864–1920), sociology was a science. To see what a scientific study of society would involve, we need to look at what science is.

Science as we know it first took form in Europe in the eighteenth century. During this Age of Enlightenment, thinkers realized that observation and reason could reveal how the world works and that people might control nature, including human nature, to improve the quality of life. This way of thinking is based on the assumption that there is a world outside of our personal consciousness, that this world is knowable through our senses, that events do not occur at random and that *causal explanations* can provide the knowledge necessary to control events.

If there were only chaos in the universe, there would be nothing to explain scientifically or to manipulate purposively. There would be no quarks, atoms, molecules, cells or organs to make up people's bodies, much less the families, communities, societies and empires that people make up. Humanity is a highly organized form. There is a good deal of order in both nature and society and, therefore, much to understand and control.

Scientific Theories

A *scientific theory* is a set of beliefs about a relatively simple order that lies behind a large number of concrete things and seemingly unconnected events. Flowing water in a stream, the apple that bounced off Newton's head and the orbits of the planets in the solar system are all explained by the theory of gravity. The extra tingle of a winter kiss on a synthetic carpet, random access memory in a computer and a lightning storm in August are brought together in the theory of electromagnetism.

A scientific theory is an *idea*, and a fact to which a theory refers is a *perception*. No one theory is true in a final sense, but is only useful more or less in explaining perceptions. Some theories are widely believed in the scientific community, while others are dismissed. Some facts are generally agreed upon, while others are not. Theories and perceptions are, then, ultimately matters of belief and agreement, not truth. So it is that a panel of physicists at a meeting of the American Physical Society in May 1989 voted eight to zero, with one abstention, in favour of the proposition that Stanley Pons and Martin Fleischmann, two chemists working at the University of Utah, did not achieve cold fusion. Old theories are replaced by new ones, not necessarily because the former are overwhelmed by evidence, but because, as Kuhn (1970) points out, the people who believe the old theories eventually die.

A scientific theory describes the statements of cause and effect relationships between two or more aspects of things that can take on different values. These aspects are called *variables*. The particular "thing" is the *unit of analysis*. Using individual people as the unit of analysis, a physiologist might describe them in terms of the variables of height and weight. A sociologist might use the variables of wealth and power.

Causal statements can be depicted visually, as in Figure 1-1. "X" stands for a change in a cause. "Y" represents a change in an effect. The arrow indicates the direction of the causal flow. The theory must describe the form of the causal connection between the two variables; for example, increases in people's wealth cause increases in their power.

"*By God, for a minute there it suddenly all made sense!*"

FIGURE 1-1

Visual Representation of Causal Model, with Theoretical Variables and Empirical Indicators

Variables are abstractions. They can have many concrete manifestations. Therefore, we distinguish between variables and the particular *indicators* we use to measure them. In Figure 1-1, variables "X" and "Y" are measured using indicators "X^1 and Y^1." We do not actually see increases in molecular activity (variable) in pots of water on the stove. We only see bubbling, steaming or thermometers rising (indicators). And we do not directly observe people gaining in wealth or power (variables). We only see new Mercedes cars in their driveways or increases in the dollar values of their stock portfolios and that more and more people tend to see things their way (indicators).

Causal explanations are appealing because they point to how we might manipulate our environments for our own betterment. Are many people unemployed because they lack motivation, as some sociologists suggest? If so, then they must be inspired to seek work. Or, are they unmotivated because they lack job opportunities, as other sociologists argue? If so, then they must be given the chance to work for pay.

The Science of Sociology

What, then, is sociology a science of? To its founders, sociology was the science of human *social organization*. That is, it asks how the various parts of human society, including individual people and groups of people, are related to one another across space and time. It seeks answers through careful observations of people and groups. Weber (1947) elaborated a second definition, which has yet to be completely reconciled with the first: sociology is the interpretive understanding of *social action*—behaviour to which the actor attaches meaning. In the second definition, to explain social action is to adopt the viewpoint of the actor in imagination and, thereby, to connect the meanings that objects and events have for that person with his or her behaviours. This is sometimes called "taking the role of the other." It is also known as the method of *empathetic understanding* or *verstehen*.

When sociology was founded, there was one social science. Today, we usually speak of the social sciences, which include anthropology, economics, political economy, political science, sociology and, perhaps, history. The boundaries that separate these, however, are fuzzy or even non-existent. Consequently, the emphasis here will be on what sociology is, rather than on what the other social sciences are or are not.

Human Society

Great or small, all creatures must meet certain needs if they are to survive. One is for nourishment. Another is for protection from disease and injury. Beyond this, a species as a whole depends on biological reproduction for survival.

Members of many animal species meet their needs as individuals. They come together only for mating, as moths around a flame. Accidentally and occasionally, they may associate. They may even respond to one another's presence or behaviours; that is, they may engage in *social interaction*. These encounters are, however, transitory.

Members of many other species meet at least some of their needs *as* members of groups. They come together to give and receive goods, information or work. Systematically and regularly they commingle. They interact socially, and their interactions, being repeated over and again, become *social relationships*. Whether they are bees or wolves or chimpanzees or humans, these species form *societies*—collections of individuals living in close proximity who meet their survival needs to some extent through repeated exchanges with one another.

Life is organized around recurrent rituals. A child addresses valentines to members of his class.

Societies would not exist if there were no *division of labour*. In a division of labour, two or more members combine their efforts to accomplish what no isolated individual could do. The particular tasks that each performs is that member's *social role* or, in a metaphor from the theatre, the role that the member plays. The simplest form of the division of labour is where the work required to reach some end is distributed among two or more members, as when two people dig a ditch by starting at opposite ends and meeting in the middle. Here, the activities of each member are the same, and their roles are co-ordinated. In more complex forms of the division of labour, different members perform different tasks, as when a rock group performs at a festival or a high-wire troupe entertains under the big top. Here, the members' roles are not only co-ordinated, but also specialized. The overall pattern of relationships in the division of labour of a group or society is part of its social organization or social structure.

Social organization assists individual organisms, then, in exploiting the environment for nourishment and protection. It also aids the species by bringing the sexes together for reproduction and the generations together for care of the young. The Shakers are a religious sect who established several large and thriving colonies in the United States in the nineteenth century. They strictly segregate the sexes, forbid sexual intercourse and, because their rules prevent biological reproduction, survive only by recruiting new members from outside. Today, there are only a handful of Shakers, because the Shakers' celibate, pre-industrial way of life holds little appeal for contemporary Americans. Cowbirds do not build their own nests or sit upon their own eggs. Instead, they lay their eggs in the nests of other birds and only survive as a species because the others hatch the eggs and raise the young cowbirds as their own. Fortunately, for them, there are other species available to perform these tasks.

Human versus Animal Society

What distinguishes the worst architect from the best of bees is this, that the architect raises his structure in imagination before he erects it in reality. (Marx, 1967 : 178)

Bees and humans alike have highly organized social lives, with a specialized division of labour. The ways in which bees and babies develop into members of their respective societies, though, are very different. Bees do not gradually learn social skills. They arrive suddenly at an adult stage fully formed, able to fend for themselves and fit into society. The behaviours they need originate in their genes, with no learning required. While they can exchange certain kinds of information (for example, where pollen can be found), they have no real language (Mazur and Robertson, 1972 : 27). Adult humans mature in a process that takes almost twenty years, learning many or most of the necessary behaviours, including a language, from other humans.

Chimpanzees have complex social lives that are closer to the lives led by humans. The ways in which chimpanzees and humans become members of their respective societies are very similar. At birth, both chimpanzees and humans are highly dependent upon adults to meet their basic physical needs. There is a lengthy period (on the order of twelve years for chimpanzees) before maturity is reached. A large fraction of the behaviour of both chimpanzees and humans is learned from adults. Both chimpanzees and humans, for example, use and make tools. Chimpanzees also appear to use a language, although it is largely non-verbal.

The fundamental difference between bee and human society is that bees lack a culture. The principal difference between chimpanzee and human society seems to be that chimpanzee culture (including language) is simpler than human culture (Mazur and Robertson, 1972:38). With spoken language to accumulate knowledge and opposable thumbs to fashion and manipulate tools, human beings have fashioned the most complex societies of all animals.

The *culture* of a society is the sum and organization of its symbols, including values, norms, beliefs and expressive symbols (Peterson, 1979). *Values* are general criteria for judging what behaviours or ends are desirable. For example, Canadians profess equal rights and opportunities for all and freedom of speech as values. *Norms* are specific rules for behaviour. For instance, we think mashed potatoes should be eaten with a fork, but that fried chicken may be eaten with the fingers. *Beliefs* are acceptances of things as facts; for example, the belief that it is safer to walk the streets in a Canadian city than in an American city. *Expressive symbols* are the concrete products and practices of a society, including all of the artifacts and activities involved in commerce and industry, government, education, religion, the arts, the family and so on. When they use the word culture, sociologists do not mean the elite as opposed to the popular (for example, Stravinsky as opposed to Sting), but all of the values, norms, beliefs and expressive symbols of a society, sublime or otherwise.

Skytrain, a computer-controlled urban rapid transportation system in Vancouver, B.C., is an expressive symbol. It has no drivers or on-board attendants, including ticket takers. Passengers' tickets are checked at irregular intervals by inspectors who board the train and send any riders without tickets off at the next station.

Social Organization and Culture

Social organization is the network of relationships among individuals or groups. *Culture* is the system of symbols shared among members of society. There is always at least some correspondence between social organization and culture. In particular, the roles that people play are often represented in the culture as the positions that they occupy, such as their positions at work or in the family (husband, wife, daughter or son). *Positions* are collections of rights and duties—expectations—that others think the occupants ought to exercise or discharge in relation to the occupants of other positions. So, there are social roles on the one hand, and positions on the other. The former refer to what actually happens and the latter to what people think happens or what ought to happen.

Some sociologists see culture as a kind of instruction set for social structure. They often seek to unravel the secrets of social relationships through the study of culture. Sometimes, too, they analyse how powerful groups manipulate culture and how artists, scholars, scientists, religious figures and others create it. These sociologists might examine the effects of exposure to the print or broadcast media or the processes by which the contents of the media are created. Or they might seek to discover how people use symbols such as automobiles, food or clothing or speech accents to manage the impressions that others have of them in their day-to-day encounters (Goffman, 1959).

Other sociologists view culture as primarily a reflection of the social structure. They believe that the relationships among people and groups in a society effectively determine that society's symbolic production. These sociologists may study, for example, how the form and content of literature, music or the visual arts are determined by whether a society is capitalist or socialist, agrarian or industrial. Or they might look at what the legal systems of different societies reveal about which groups are powerful and which are not.

Bases of Social Order

How does social order develop? How does it break down? These are fundamental sociological questions. Sociologists disagree on the sources of social order (Dahrendorf, 1959). At one pole is the consensus argument, advanced by structural funtionalists (for example, Parsons, 1951) and others. This theory sees social order as originating largely from voluntary agreement on appropriate ways of behaving. At the other pole is the coercion argument, associated with Marxists and others. This theory sees social order as essentially involuntary obedience—conformity enforced on the powerless by the powerful.

Power and Status

In social relationships, the parties involved are typically unequal in power or status (Weber, 1947). *Power* is the capacity that a person or group has to influence other people or groups. *Status* describes how valued a person or group is. Power and status usually come from the roles that people play or the rights and duties attached to their positions. They rarely spring solely from force of personality, physical strength or personal ability. Power and status do not necessarily go together. For example, General

Manuel Noriega at one time wielded enormous power as president of Panama, declaring void a national election that would have removed him from office and making a fortune in the international drug trade. He was widely despised. In contrast, Mother Teresa is a Roman Catholic nun who has spent most of her life ministering to the poor. She is admired throughout the world and may be a future candidate for sainthood. However, in comparison with Noriega or other despotic rulers she is not very powerful.

Power that others recognize as the right of a person's position is *authority*. A company owner can shut down a plant or buy a new one, can hire or fire an executive. Those are an owner's legal rights. These actions are exercising authority. A Mafia family head who orders the murder of a subordinate or the bombing of a rival's business (Dubro, 1987), however, is exercising power without benefit of authority.

Sociologists have a more difficult time measuring power than measuring status. Sociologists can measure authority within certain kinds of organizations (for example, by examining the organizational chart for a business), but no measure of power that can routinely be applied to people generally has yet been developed. Peter C. Pineo and John Porter (1967) asked a sample of Canadians to rate the status ("social standing") of about two hundred different occupations. Among those that ranked high were county court judge, physician and university professor; intermediate were airline pilot, public grade school teacher and social worker; low were garbage collector, newspaper peddler and whistle punk.

A company borrows from the authority of science to advertise its "stop smoking program." Unfortunately, there is no scientific evidence that lasers are useful for this purpose.

Social Classes

Sociologists often find the concept of *social class* useful in analysing social organization and change. *Class* theorists, such as Marx, Weber and their followers, see people as divided into distinct categories, or classes, by whether they own or control the means of economic production, for example, the mines, mills and factories. Marx believed that there are three broad social classes in capitalist society: the bourgeoisie, the proletariat, and the petite bourgeoisie. The *bourgeoisie* own or control the means of economic production and employ workers at a salary or wage that is less than the value of what the workers produce. The *proletariat* are the workers—the exploited class of those who exchange their labour power for income. Finally, the *petite bourgeoisie* own and control productive private property, but employ at most only a very small number of people.

According to Marx and Weber, societies in which there is private ownership of the means of economic production are typically characterized by various forms and degrees of class conflict, such as strikes. The bourgeoisie are fewer in number, and they are usually a fairly solidaristic class whose members are conscious of their common cause; the proletariat are numerous and are often divided among themselves.

Marx considered class conflict to be *the* moving force of history. When the bourgeoisie are dominant, society is a bourgeois society. As the proletariat become more and more concentrated in cities and factories and their discontents deepen, class consciousness and organized resistance emerge and develop. This can culminate in revolution. For Weber, class conflict was one engine of social change, but not necessarily always the most important one.

Status Groups

In addition to social class divisions, Weber pointed to ethnic, occupational and other differences in status as bases for groups to organize and conflicts to develop. Whereas social classes are phenomena of industrial production, status groups result from differences in consumption, that is, in the styles of life people lead. Recognizing that class and status are distinct allows us more interpretive possibilities as we study society. For example, deaf people agitating for their own schools and the use of American sign language or the Innu protesting low-level military training flights over Labrador are not essentially class-based activities. If we try to explain everything in relation to class, such phenomena may be hard to understand.

Elites

In studying power in society, some sociologists use the concept of an elite (Mills, 1956; Porter, 1965). An *elite* is the group of people occupying the top positions of authority in an institution. An *institution* is a set of social positions organized in a division of labour that endures over time to meet some continuing or recurrent individual or collective need. For example, people require nourishment and protection from nature. The young need to be tutored. Social order must be maintained. Each of these needs is the basis for an institution—respectively, the economy, the educational system and the state. Consequently, there can be an economic elite, an educational elite, a political elite and so on.

Some elites are more powerful than others. In the United States in the 1950s, C. Wright Mills (1956) characterized the country as dominated by an alliance of the economic and military elites. In Canada at about the same time, John Porter (1965) described the economic elite as the dominant one.

The Individual and Society

The study of social organization includes the analysis of social behaviour and relationships of individuals. This is sometimes called social psychology. Social psychology studies the reciprocal connections between the individual and society; that is, it addresses questions of how culture and social structure influence individuals in their social relationships and of how individuals in turn influence culture and social structure.

Social Behaviour

Sociologists studying individual social behaviour disagree on the relative importance of self-interest on the one hand, and values and norms on the other (Wrong, 1959). At one pole, some sociologists see social behaviour as largely motivated by self-interest and pursued rationally. In Homans's (1961) exchange theory, for example, he argues that individuals maximize benefits and minimize costs in social interaction within a pre-existing context of social norms. This view is often criticized for conveying an image of human beings as insensitive to or unaware of their culture, that is, as "under socialized."

At the other pole, other sociologists see individual social behaviour as *directed* largely by ideas. Parsons (1951), for instance, argues that people, born into an ongoing social and cultural system, incorporate the norms and values of the culture as part of their personalities; that is, they *internalize* the culture. To the extent that the culture of a society is successfully internalized by the personalities of those in it, these individuals are subsequently able to function as conforming, contributing members of that society. This conception is often faulted for an "oversocialized" image of people.

The undersocialized view is clear on what moves people to act. They act to further their interests. However, it is not clear why they put boundaries on their range of permissible actions. Why don't people use wholesale force, fraud and war to achieve their aims? The oversocialized view is clear on how behaviour is directed. People behave as they do because they have incorporated the values and norms of the culture into their personalities. Here we are left to wonder why they do anything at all, where their motivation to act comes from.

Finally, neither the undersocialized nor the oversocialized conception of behaviour pays much attention to the *process* of individual social behaviour. *Symbolic interactionism*, however, does. Symbolic interactionism is a perspective closely associated with George Herbert Mead (1863–1931). According to it, people are able to interact socially when each can intuit the meanings that lie behind the other's actions or take the role of the other. Of course, a person may be mistaken in the meanings that are attributed to others, that is, in his or her *definition of the situation*. However, as W. I. Thomas, an early-twentieth-century sociologist, pointed out, "a situation defined as real is real in its consequences."

Cops Beat Blind Man They Thought Had Illegal Martial Arts Weapon

HAYWARD, Calif.—Two police officers beat a blind man with their batons when they mistook his collapsible cane for an illegal martial arts weapon.

"It bothers me to the core and I want to get to the bottom of this right away," said Acting Police Chief Dick Dettmer.

Eric Ristrim, a field training officer, was with trainee Marie Yin last week when they came upon David St. John, 37, at a bus stop.

Mr. Ristrim said Mr. St. John placed in his pants pocket what appeared to be nunchakus, a martial arts weapon that consists of two wooden dowels connected with a chain. Possession of the weapon is illegal in California.

The officers thought the man could see their uniforms so they didn't identify themselves when they demanded that Mr. St. John hand over the contents of his pockets, the report said.

Mr. St. John said later he thought he was about to be mugged and a struggle followed.

"I did what my self-defence training and my instincts told me to do," a bruised and swollen Mr. St. John said yesterday.

Mr. Ristrim said Mr. St. John's eyes were milky in color but were wide open "as if looking directly" at him.

The officers said they first hit Mr. St. John twice on the legs. Then, when he pulled the cane out of his pocket "and raised it to about face level," they struck him on the forearm in an attempt to get him to drop it.

It was then that someone yelled, "He's blind." The officers identified themselves, bringing an end to the struggle.

"It's a very regrettable incident," Mr. Dettmer said.

"They ought to be careful who they clobber with their night sticks," said Mr. St. John.

Associated Press.

Socialization

Much can be done with a Scotsman if he can be caught young. (Samuel Johnson)

Social psychology tries to explain how people become functioning members of society. Sociologists refer to this process as *socialization*. To appreciate the extent to which human behaviour is learned, examples of so-called feral ("wolf-raised") children are instructive.

Symbolic interactionism provides one of the few explanations of the process of socialization. In communication with parents or others, the human infant first learns to distinguish between itself and its environment, that is, to be a conscious actor. Mead referred to the conscious actor as the *I*. The infant then acquires the capacity to regard itself as an object, to be a self-conscious actor. Mead called the self-conscious actor the *me*. Taken together, the "I" and the "me" are one's identity or *self*. Chimpanzees and humans (perhaps gorillas as well) can recognize themselves in a mirror, that is, treat themselves as objects (Mazur and Robertson, 1972; Mowat, 1987).

Born illegitimate, Anna was confined by her grandfather to a room alone. She was fed, but not given much more attention than that required.

"When finally found and removed from the room at the age of nearly six years, Anna could not talk, walk, or do anything that showed intelligence. She was in an extremely emaciated and undernourished condition, with skeleton-like legs and a bloated abdomen. She was completely apathetic, lying in a limp, supine position and remaining immobile, expressionless, and indifferent to everything. She was believed to be deaf and possibly blind. She of course could not feed herself or make any move in her own behalf. Here, then, was a human organism which had missed nearly six years of socialization. Her condition shows how little her purely biologi-cal resources, when acting alone, could contribute to making her a complete person.

"Four and a half years later, she had made consider-able progress as compared with her condition when found. She could follow directions, string beads, identify a few colors, build with blocks, and differentiate between attractive and unattractive pictures. She had a good sense of rhythm and loved a doll. She talked mainly in phrases but would repeat words and try to carry on a conversation. She was clean about clothing. She habitually washed her hands and brushed her teeth. She would try to help other children. She walked well and could run fairly well, though clumsily. Although easily excited, she had a pleasant disposition."

From Kinglsey Davis. 1949. *Human Society*. New York: Macmillan, pp. 204–5.

Finally, the developing child learns how to take the role of the other, including the generalized other. The *generalized other* is the group or society to which the child belongs. Being able to take on the role of the generalized other entails incorporating culture into the personality, thus making social behaviour possible. The initial stages of socialization are complete, then, when a person is able to imagine how other people in the group will define a variety of different situations.

As part of the development of the self, infants learn to display behaviours appropriate to different roles in social interaction. One basic role is the gender role. Each person learns to see her or himself as female or male and, therefore, to act in ways expected of women or men. It is important to appreciate that even most gender-related behaviour is learned, not genetically determined. In cases where individuals are genetically of one sex but raised as if they were of the other (perhaps mistakenly, because of the misleading appearance of their genitalia at birth), their behaviours conform to their gender identity, not their genes (Mazur and Robertson, 1972 : 55).

Because we ordinarily take on a series of different roles throughout our lives, socialization usually ends only with death. What usually begins in the context of the family typically moves out into the school, the workplace, a family of one's own, etc. In each case, we are socialized to play new roles, which may include those of student, worker in an occupation, husband or wife, mother or father, aunt or uncle, grandfather or grandmother and retiree.

Canadian male in training. "I don't want any more of this kicking with skates, hooking with sticks, punching, or hitting from behind. This was a practice. Save it for the game." (Manager of team of ten- and eleven-year-olds in non-contact hockey league to his players.)

Deviance and Control

Once it was believed in Western society that children were born evil. We know now that concepts of right and wrong, while part of every culture, are learned, and that they vary from person to person, group to group, across societies and over time. Behaviours that are regarded as unacceptable by some may be perfectly acceptable to others. Examples include the ritual suicide of women upon their widowhood, as occasionally practised among lower-caste Hindus in India, and the "swarming" of pedestrians by skinheads and other youth gangs in Canadian cities.

Crime is behaviour that contravenes legal norms; *deviance* is behaviour that contravenes other norms. It is important to distinguish between these behaviours on the one hand, and *criminals* and *deviants* on the other. The latter are people (or organizations) who have been publicly labelled as rule violators in a social, perhaps formally legal, process (Lemert, 1967; Becker, 1963). Note that criminals and deviants are not simply or necessarily rule-breakers. Rather, they have been *socially stigmatized* or *labelled* as violators, which is not the same thing. Not all violators are publicly labelled and not all who are publicly labelled are violators.

Labelling occurs in a sometimes elaborate process whose outcome is never certain until it is over. For example, a driver stopped for speeding may or may not be charged, depending upon the police officer's discretion. If charged, the charge may subsequently be dropped or reduced, depending upon the prosecutor. If the case goes to trial, the defendant may or may not be convicted, depending upon the judge or the jury. At each stage in the process, the police officer, the prosecutor, the judge or the jury makes decisions based on such factors as the evidence and characteristics of the defendant (sex, race, occupation). Included in that decision is whether the label of criminal will be applied to the person. *Labelling theory* (Lemert, 1967; Becker, 1963), an offshoot of symbolic interactionism, describes how people come to be publicly labelled as criminals or deviants.

What Canadians usually think of as crime and delinquency are largely acts committed by young, working-class (often native) males convicted in the courts. Part of the reason for this conception is that the legal norms, along with the law enforcement and criminal justice systems in any society, operate to protect the interests of the powerful against incursions from the powerless (Turk, 1969). By and large, it is the underclass of society that is policed and, therefore, punished. One of the revelations of criminology, however, is that violations of the law may be no more common among the less privileged in society. Another is that organizations, such as business firms, commit many crimes. *White-collar crime* consists of legal violations that occur when a person

People in many cultures use signs to ward off evil.

fails to keep a trust that is part of his or her occupation (for example, the accountant who embezzles company funds); *corporate crimes* consist of crimes committed by companies (Sutherland, 1949). Yet, only a fraction of those who commit crimes and deviant acts end up being publicly labelled as criminals or deviants.

How, then, do we account for crime and deviance? At the level of social structure and culture, the problem has at least two sides. First, how is it that some behaviours have come to be defined as criminal or deviant and others not? Second, how do some people come to be publicly labelled as violators and others not?

At the level of the individual, to account for crime or deviance may be to explain how it is that some people violate certain rules and others do not, although most of us violate rules from time to time. *Primary deviation* is the occasional violation of rules (Lemert, 1967). *Secondary deviation* is the occurrence of persistent, career-like crime or deviance undertaken by people who have developed deviant self-concepts. According to labelling theory, the transformation of a person from a primary to a secondary deviant is made much more likely by public labelling.

Criminals and deviants do not generally differ from other people biologically or because their socialization was unsuccessful or incomplete. First, norm-violating behaviour is learned just like other behaviour. According to the theory of *differential association* (Sutherland, 1947), the appropriate attitudes and skills are learned from others who already possess these attitudes and command these techniques. If we wish to understand how some people have become criminals or deviants, therefore, we should look to how they were socialized. Perhaps, lacking strong ties to conventional institutions, they were socialized to the *subculture*, a culture within the larger culture, of a criminal or deviant group, for example, skinheads (Hirschi, 1969). Second, most people commit crimes and deviant acts fairly often; only some people, however, end up being publicly labelled as criminals or deviants.

Methods of Social Research

> You can observe a lot by just watching. (Yogi Berra, former catcher and manager, New York Yankees)

Sociologists gather data in a variety of different ways. Interviewing people or having them fill out questionnaires and observing people directly in laboratories or in their everyday comings and goings are standard techniques (Bulmer, 1984). Analysing the contents of documents produced for some purpose other than research, such as city and telephone directories, magazines and newspapers, voting lists, city tax rolls, corporate or judicial or law enforcement agency files, biographical dictionaries, letters or diaries, can also turn up valuable information. A wealth of evidence is to be found, too, in the traces that people leave in the courses of their lives, such as the amount and pattern of wear on carpets, steps and grassy areas, inscriptions on tombstones, even the contents and volume of garbage or sewage (Webb et al., 1966).

The choice of a particular data-gathering technique is typically a compromise dictated by such considerations as the type and quality of the evidence it produces relative to what the solution to the problem requires; how expensive it is in time and money; and whether it is ethical. Does the solution require detailed, minute-by-minute information on people's social contacts? If so, then a direct observational study might be the best choice. Is it important that the results apply to all Canadians? Then a survey with face-to-face or telephone interviews or mail questionnaires might be advised. Ethically, it is important that people's anonymity be protected and that they not suffer from being or having been studied. Ethical considerations can be difficult if, for example, a researcher observes some criminal activity. Canadians—social researchers included—are required by law to inform the police of criminal acts that they have witnessed, and they are not protected by law from having to reveal their sources of information in the courts.

When data are to be used to test a causal theory, they should be gathered in a way that models the causal process. In other words, changes in a particular cause will affect some units and not others; and causes precede effects. Well-designed social research intended to test a causal theory, then, will always try to observe at least two groups, one that has been exposed to a change in a causal variable and another that has not. The units should ordinarily be observed both before and after a causal change. Finally, care must be taken to ensure that the units exposed to a causal change and those not exposed do not differ systematically to begin with. For example, if Boy Scouts were found to be, on the average, more law abiding than other youth, this could be because Scouting induces conformity or because conformist adolescents are more likely than others to join Scouts in the first place. A fair test of Scouting and conformity would have to take any such initial difference between Scouts and others into account. These principles are basic to the logic of research design for causal inference, first systematically enunciated by John Stuart Mill, a nineteenth-century English philosopher and economist. In social science research, they are best exemplified in *longitudinal studies*—research where the same people or groups are studied over time.

The logic of research design is nicely illustrated in the following proposal by Handsome Lake, an eighteenth-century North American Indian, arguing the evils of alcohol among his people:

"Good food is turned into evil drink. Now some have said there is no harm in partaking of fermented liquids.

"Then let this plan be followed: Let men gather in two parties, one having a feast of food, apples and corn, and the other cider and whiskey. Let the parties be equally divided and matched and let them commence their feasting at the same time.

"When the feast is finished you will see those who drank the fermented juices murder one of their own party but not so with those who ate food only."

From Anthony F. C. Wallace, 1962. "Culture and Cognition." *Science* 2 : 356.

Finally, it is often important in social research that the units observed be selected in such a way that the results obtained from them are also likely to apply to units that have not been observed. The best way to ensure this is through probability sampling from a population. A *population* is a complete collection of some kind of object or event, such as all Canadians or all societies or all revolutions. *Probability sampling* involves choosing units from a population in such a way that the probability of any particular unit's being selected is known.

Bias Seen in AIDS Studies

Special to The New York Times

NEW YORK, Dec. 17—An AIDS organization has charged that trials for experimental drugs at three medical schools here have excluded the poor, members of minority groups and women, and praised one of the schools for taking remedial steps.

The organization, Act Up, said the research at the New York University, Albert Einstein and Mount Sinai medical schools had the effect of denying potentially helpful medications to the excluded groups.

The federally financed drug trials enrolled most of their more than 500 patients from private hospitals, but only a few dozen patients from affiliated municipal hospitals, said Act Up, which stands for the AIDS Coalition to Unleash Power. AIDS patients at private hospitals are generally white, middle-class males, while those at municipal hospitals tend to be members of minority groups and include most of the women and babies with AIDS, the group said.

An Act Up leader, James J. Eigo, made the accusation. He praised New York University for belatedly submitting its drug trials for approval by the city hospitals, a preliminary step to enrolling patients.

An N.Y.U. spokesman, John Deats, said, "We are enthusiastic about the opportunity to enroll more people with AIDS in drug protocols." A Mount Sinai spokeswoman said her medical school did not discriminate among patients. An Albert Einstein spokesman did not have an immediate comment.

Suzanne Halpin, a spokeswoman for the City Health and Hospitals Corporation, which runs the municipal hospitals, said her agency had been working to improve the schools' performance in making the drug trials available to city patients.

"There has been some progress," she said. "We would like to see more, and we think we will see more."

Theory and Research in Practice

Having discussed sociological theory and social research methods, it would be instructive to go through an example of a research project from the initial idea that prompted it to the practical implications of its results. The particular research discussed here began with the observation that positions of political authority in every society, including democratic ones, are largely held by men. How does this occur? To investigate this question, we looked at the national political elite in Canada (Hunter and Denton, 1984).

From sociological theory, we concluded that there are several reasons why women might be underrepresented as elected members of political elites in democratic societies such as Canada. First, women may not compete in equal numbers or on an equal basis with men for party nominations. This could arise because the subordinate position of women in the larger society has left them less inclined or less well equipped than men to compete or because political parties tend to prefer male candidates. Second, among those nominated, women candidates may tend to be selected to contest seats that the party is unlikely to win. Third, voters may prefer male candidates. We decided to concentrate our research on those women who received nominations, investigating for party and voter discrimination.

From official data, we assembled information on the sex of each candidate in the general elections of 1979 and 1980 in Canada. As well, for each candidate, we recorded the party represented, whether the candidate was nominated to run against an incumbent, how often the party had been successful in that constituency in previous elections and the number of votes received.

The logic behind the analysis was as follows. To begin with, the men and women candidates can be compared to see if the males received more votes on the average than the females. If not, it would be unlikely that the women tended to be selected to contest unwinnable seats or that the voters discriminated. If so, the men and women candidates can then be compared in the kinds of nominations that they received. Specifically, were women more likely than men to be nominated to run against an incumbent or in a constituency where their parties had not won recently or often? If not, then any vote differential between the sexes would likely be due to voter discrimination. If so, then men and women running under similar circumstances (that is, men and women contesting winnable seats and men and women contesting unwinnable seats) could be compared to see if they differed in the number of votes received. If not, then party discrimination would explain the vote differential between the sexes. If so, then at least some voter discrimination would seem indicated.

We found that the women candidates received far fewer votes on average than the men. At the same time, the women candidates were much more likely than the men to be nominated to contest seats against incumbents or seats that the party had not won in the recent past. Such candidates received many fewer votes than did candidates who contested seats where they were not running against incumbents or in which their party had done well previously. These two factors entirely accounted for why the women candidates were less successful at the polls. That is, the men and women contesting winnable seats did not differ in the numbers of votes received; likewise, the men and women contesting unwinnable seats received comparable numbers of votes. The results, then, seem to be clear: the parties discriminated, the voters did not.

This research has practical implications for the elimination of sex discrimination. Specifically, activities devoted to increasing the representation of women in the political elite in Canada are probably better directed at changing political party practices than at transforming voters' attitudes. Future research should show whether the same is true for other democratic societies.

Summary

Confined to a room alone, fed, but not much more, you would likely be "completely apathetic, lying in a limp, supine position and remaining immobile, expressionless, and indifferent to everything" (Davis, 1949:204). But you're not, and that difference makes all the difference. For the first six years of her life, Anna was only a human being. You are a person.

As a person, you are a creature of history. You are also a creator of history, both your own day-to-day, face-to-face history and the history of the species. As such, you bear a responsibility, not only for yourself, but also for those you love, like, live out the parts of your life with or only know about from television, radio or the newspapers. Better that these responsibilities be discharged in knowledge than in ignorance.

The study of sociology can make you a conscious participant in history, rather than an unwitting victim of it. It can also enlighten you. Knowledge of sociological theories and techniques should alert you to the social nature of what you may think of as personal problems: school, divorce, unemployment, substance abuse and so on. Perhaps one day sociology will show you how to take better command of your life and to question unwise decisions that affect you. Why did the government of Ontario decide to end streaming in high schools, for example, when the poor quality of classroom instruction was the factor cited for the high dropout rate in the non-university streams? Why do we gather criminals together in large groups when we know that this practice reinforces existing bad habits and teaches new ones? Perhaps some day sociology will help us learn how to prevent students from dropping out of high schools and show us how to rehabilitate criminals. The study of sociology can assist us in leading fuller and happier lives in a more just society.

Suggested Readings

Bulmer, Martin, ed.
  1984. *Sociological Research Methods: An Introduction*. London: Macmillan. Collected essays on social research methods.

Collins, Randall, and Michael Makowsky
  1972. *The Discovery of Society*. New York: Random House. Important contributors to the history of sociology in their times and in perspective.

Gould, Stephen Jay
  1981. *The Mismeasure of Man*. New York: W. W. Norton. Abuses of science in the study of race.

Hearnshaw, L. S.
1979. *Cyril Burt: Psychologist*. London: Hodder and Stoughton. Classic study of how a scientist can go wrong.

Kuhn, T. P.
1970. *The Structure of Scientific Revolutions*. Chicago: University of Chicago Press. Influential perspective on the philosophy and history of science.

Discussion Questions

1. Skytrain is an expressive symbol of Canadian culture. What do you think the existence of a technology such as Skytrain tells us about social relationships in the economy?

2. Using the concepts of socialization and deviance, discuss cheating on examinations in school.

3. In research on potentially useful drugs in the treatment of AIDS, the criticism by the group Act Up is that the sampling procedures proposed would under-represent members of minority groups, women and babies. What ethical problems might this pose? How might this also present scientific problems? How would you have designed the sampling procedures to meet this criticism?

Data Collection Exercises

1. What sociologists have most influenced Canadian sociology? Introductory sociology textbooks contain information that can be used to address this question. As a group project, you might use data from the bibliographies (or footnote references) or name indexes of two or more introductory textbooks to measure how influential different sociologists have been. In this project, you will have to draw a probability sample of textbooks. Describe the steps involved, and then draw the sample. You will also have to develop one or more indicators of influence. Indicate the steps involved in indicator construction and the reasons why you think that the indicators yield the necessary information. Finally, collect the data and use them to draw conclusions about which sociologists have been the most influential. Note how the information from one textbook is not exactly the same as that from another. Why might this be? Does this cause you to qualify your conclusions in any way?

2. People are generally very skillful at taking the role of the other, that is, at attributing meaning to other people's gestures and utterances. Compile a list of phrases or short sentences that refer to nothing in particular (for example, "It could get worse," "It all depends upon the person"). Write them down on separate pieces of paper and shuffle the pieces. Then, after you have begun a conversation with someone, simply respond to whatever that person says

by using the first phrase or sentence in the pile, then the second, and so on. How many of these are you able to use before the conversation breaks down? Describe your feelings as the other person attempts to give meaning to what you say.

3. Many cities now have recycling programs for paper, glass and metal waste that include a regular curbside pickup of these materials. There is much information to be gained here about the occupants of the houses. How much paper they discard may give clues to their reading habits. Empty pet food tins tell of the presence of cats or dogs. Liquor or wine bottles speak to drinking habits. Information can also be gleaned on aspects of the houses or neighbourhoods (for example, telephone calls to realtors to find out the asking prices of houses for sale, the presence of "Block Parent" signs in the windows or "Neighbourhood Watch" signs at the end of the block, children's possessions and so on). Design and carry out a research project in which you use two or more pieces of this kind of data to examine the relationship between two variables (for example, affluence and alcohol consumption). Be careful not to disturb the materials to be recycled or to trespass on private property. (And expect some people to notice that you are examining what they have discarded!)

Writing Exercises

1. The division of labour depends upon two or more people co-ordinating their activities and, perhaps, specializing in some of the tasks that need to be performed if the collective goal is to be reached. A lack of such co-ordination is the basis for a certain brand of physical comedy. Outline a comedy routine indicating some of the things that could go wrong when two people are unco-ordinated in attempting to carry out a task. (As an example, two labourers were given sledgehammers and asked to demolish a stone jetty. Each started at one end. They had to be rescued by a coast guard vessel when they ended up stranded twenty-five metres from shore with a storm blowing up.)

2. Describe in detail an incident in which you were involved that might have ended with you being publicly labelled as a criminal or deviant, but did not. What do you think terminated the social construction before the label was successfully applied? Also describe an incident in which you were actually labelled and indicate the various factors that you think kept the process going to the end.

3. Construct a partial family tree including yourself, your parents, your grandparents and your great-grandparents, including birthdates, wedding dates, divorce dates and death dates as best you can determine them. Then, note the dates of the major wars in which Canada has been involved, along with the years of the Great Depression. Using concepts in this chapter, speculate how the tree might have been different if the First World War, the Great Depression, the Second World War or the Korean War had not happened.

Glossary

Authority: *the power that one person or group exercises over another that is regarded as appropriate or right by those subject to it.*

Belief: *accepting something as a fact.*

Bourgeoisie: *the social class of individuals who own or control the means of economic production and who employ others to work for them.*

Causal explanation: *accounting for the occurrence of some event by reference to the occurrence of some prior event that led to it.*

Corporate crime: *violations of laws by companies.*

Crime: *behaviour that violates laws.*

Criminal: *a person publicly labelled as a law violator.*

Culture: *the shared values, norms, beliefs and expressive symbols of a group.*

Definition of the situation: *the meanings that an individual attaches to objects or events.*

Deviance: *behaviour that is inconsistent with the norms of a group.*

Deviant: *a person publicly labelled as a breaker of norms.*

Division of labour: *co-ordinated activities of two or more individuals to complete a task.*

Elite: *those persons in positions of high authority in an institution.*

Empathetic understanding: *the act of explaining social action by identifying the meaning that a behaviour has for the actor or actors involved; verstehen.*

Expressive symbol: *the concrete products and practices of a society.*

Generalized other: *the group or society to which a person belongs.*

Indicator: *the observations used to measure a variable.*

Institution: *an enduring set of social roles organized in a division of labour around some continuing or recurrent individual or social problem, for example, government, economy, family, education.*

Labelling theory: *a perspective on the processes through which people are attributed a certain kind of identity by the members of a group or society.*

Longitudinal studies: *research in which the events or objects investigated are observed at more than one point in time.*

Norm: *specific rule for behaviour.*

Petite bourgeoisie: *the social class of persons who own the means of economic production but who employ few, if any, workers.*

Population: *a complete collection of objects or events.*

Position: *a collection of rights and duties that a person is expected to discharge.*

Power: *the influence that one person or group exercises over another.*

Primary deviation: *the irregular, non-systematic breaking of norms.*

Probability sample: *a subset of a population in which each member of the population has a known probability of being selected.*

Proletariat: *the social class of persons who exchange their capacity to work for a salary or a wage.*

Sample survey: *interviews or questionnaires administered to some members of a population.*

Scientific theory: *set of beliefs about a relatively simple order that lies behind a large number of concrete things and seemingly disconnected events.*

Secondary deviation: *the regular, systematic breaking of norms.*

Social action: *behaviour to which the actor attaches meaning.*

Social behaviour: *people systematically orienting their activities to the presence or activities of others; social interaction.*

Social class: *a group of individuals similarly situated in regard to ownership of the means of economic production.*

Social interaction: *social behaviour.*

Socialization: *the process through which an individual becomes a functioning member of a group or society.*

Social organization: *the relationships among individual people and groups in a society.*

Social relationship: *recurrent social interaction.*

Social role: *a particular set of activities repeatedly carried out by one individual in relation to other individuals.*

Sociology: *the scientific study of the relationships among individuals and groups.*

Status: *how valued a person or group is.*

Status group: *a collection of individuals with a similar style of life.*

Subculture: *the values, norms, beliefs and expressive symbols of a group within a larger group or society.*

Symbolic interactionism: *a social psychological perspective on the process in which people come to be able to attribute meanings to objects and events.*

Unit of analysis: *the object or event whose characteristics a theory describes.*

Value: *general criterion for judging what behaviours or goals are desirable.*

Variable: *an aspect of an object or event that can take on different characteristics.*

Verstehen: *see Empathetic understanding.*

White-collar crime: *illegal violations of trust by people in occupations with high socio-economic levels.*

References

Barnes, Henry Elmer, and Howard Becker
1938. *Social Thought from Lore to Science.* Boston: D. C. Heath.

Becker, Howard S.
1963. *Outsiders: Studies in the Sociology of Deviance.* New York: Free Press.

Bulmer, Martin, ed.
1984. *Sociological Research Methods: An Introduction*, 2nd ed. London: Macmillan.

Dahrendorf, Ralf
1959. *Class and Class Conflict in Industrial Society.* Stanford: Stanford University Press.

Davis, Kingsley
1949. *Human Society.* New York: Macmillan.

Dubro, James
1987. *Mob Rule.* Toronto: Totem Books.

Durkheim, Emile
1956. *Suicide*. New York: Free Press.
1964. *The Rules of the Sociological Method*. New York: Free Press.

Goffman, Erving
1959. *The Presentation of Self in Everyday Life*. Garden City, N.Y.: Doubleday.

Hirschi, Travis
1969. *Causes of Delinquency*. Berkeley: University of California Press.

Homans, George C.
1961. *Social Behavior: Its Elementary Forms*. New York: Harcourt, Brace and World.

Hunter, Alfred A., and Margaret A. Denton
1984. "Do Female Candidates 'Lose Votes'?: The Experience of Female Candidates in the 1979 and 1980 Canadian General Elections." *Canadian Review of Sociology and Anthropology* 21:395–406.

Kuhn, T. S.
1970. *The Structure of Scientific Revolutions*, 2nd ed. Chicago: University of Chicago Press.

Lemert, Edwin
1967. *Human Deviance, Social Problems and Social Control*. Englewood Cliffs, N.J.: Prentice-Hall.

Marx, Karl
1967. *Capital*, vol. 1. New York: International Publishers.

Mazur, A., and L. S. Robertson
1972. *Biology and Social Behavior*. New York: Free Press.

Mills, C. Wright
1956. *The Power Elite*. New York: Oxford University Press.

Mowat, Farley
1987. *Virunga*. Toronto: Seal Books.

Parsons, Talcott
1951. *The Social System*. New York: Free Press.

Peterson, Richard A.
1979. "Revitalizing the Culture Concept," pp. 137–66. In Alex Inkeles, ed., *Annual Review of Sociology*. Palo Alto, Cal.: Annual Reviews.

Pineo, Peter C., and John Porter
1967. "Occupational Prestige in Canada." *Canadian Review of Sociology and Anthropology* 4:24–40.

Porter, John
1965. *The Vertical Mosaic*. Toronto: University of Toronto Press.

Radwanski, George
1987. *Ontario Study of the Relevance of Education and the Issue of Dropouts*. Toronto: Ministry of Education.

Salinger, J. D.
1951. *The Catcher in the Rye*. Boston: Little, Brown and Company.

Sutherland, Edwin
    1947. *Principles of Criminology*. New York: Lippincott.
    1949. *White Collar Crime*. New York: Dryden.

Turk, A.
    1969. *Criminality and the Legal Order*. Chicago: Rand McNally.

Wallace, Anthony F. C.
    1962. "Culture and Cognition." *Science* 2:356.

Webb, E. J., D. T. Campbell, R. D. Schwarz and L. Sechrest
    1966. *Unobtrusive Measures: Non-reactive Research in the Social Sciences*. Chicago: Rand McNally.

Weber, Max
    1947. *The Theory of Social and Economic Organization*. New York: Oxford University Press.

Wrong, Dennis
    1959. "The Oversocialized Conception of Man in Modern Sociology." *American Sociological Review* 26:183–93.

CHAPTER 2

Sociological Methods of Research

HARVEY KRAHN

Introduction

When you look closely at how sociologists do research, it is apparent that their methods are often little different from those used in the natural sciences. However, the subject matter of sociological research is unique in one important respect: people can think and react. Since social researchers are themselves thinking and acting human beings, they can try to understand and interpret the behaviours of their subject matter. While the majority of sociological researchers stick closely to the principles of the *scientific method*, some place more emphasis on *interpretive methods*.

The Scientific Method

Opposite page:
In order to adequately reflect diversity in a population of university students, a random sample must be selected.

OFFICE OF PUBLIC AFFAIRS, UNIVERSITY OF ALBERTA.

If we observe that police officers are laying fewer marijuana charges today compared to five years ago (as did Johnson, 1988), we might be tempted to explain this phenomenon without doing any research because we think we know something personally about the subject. Are we entitled to rely on our own experiences, on common sense, to address sociological questions such as these?

Common sense helps us make many everyday decisions and gets us safely through most days. But common sense is really only accumulated personal experience. It begins to fail us when we move into areas where our personal experience and knowledge are limited. Hence, we need a method that accents the clarity and logic of those features of common sense that are useful and eliminates those features that often lead to incorrect conclusions. Those features include a tendency to overgeneralize, to rely on faulty and incomplete information, to ignore evidence that does not support our beliefs and to reason illogically (Babbie, 1986:10–16).

The solution is the *scientific method*, defined as the "systematic and controlled extension of common sense" (Kerlinger, 1973:3). Science proceeds, not by a selective search for evidence that supports a particular position, but by examining as much of the relevant evidence as possible. In fact, scientists feel most confident with their explanation or theory when they deliberately set out to look for disconfirming evidence and find none. Such a systematic approach ensures that contrary evidence will not be ignored, and that the research can be replicated by others. If replications lead to similar conclusions, the evidence for a particular explanation accumulates. If they do not, the theory has to be changed to accommodate the contrary evidence. Thus, the scientific method is self-correcting.

Theories, Hypotheses and Research Questions

What do scientists do? They seek solutions to human problems, according to Kerlinger (1973:34). Some of these problems are worldwide, such as the absence of a cure for AIDS. Others may be more unique: for example, the kind of training programs most likely to improve the labour market chances of Canadian high-school dropouts. To argue, then, that a primary goal of science is to develop theories might seem somewhat odd. Our image of science is generally that of a very practical enterprise with concrete results. We probably think of theories as less useful.

In considering this argument, an example of a theory would be helpful. We note that younger workers typically report less job satisfaction than do their older peers. After some thought, we propose an explanation. Education levels have been rising steadily in North America over the past several decades and so young workers are generally more educated. Higher education brings with it higher expectations. Therefore, younger workers are more often dissatisfied because their jobs are less likely to meet their expectations.

This is an example of a *formal theory*, which consists of several initial axioms and a final proposition deduced from them (Babbie, 1986 : 37). *Axioms* are statements presented as givens that describe a pattern of events. In this case, one axiom is that younger workers experience less job satisfaction than older workers. The *proposition* attempts to explain why events occur in this regular pattern. Not all social science theories can be presented this formally. However, all begin with a description of some systematic pattern of events, and all contain an explanation. The word "because" invariably appears, since theories are accounts of cause and effect relationships. In our example, job satisfaction is said to be influenced (or caused) by the match between one's education and one's job.

Specific predictions deduced from a theory are called *hypotheses*. The overall account of youth, education and job satisfaction, both description and explanation, is our theory. The specific prediction that "the greater the mismatch between education and job requirements, the greater the job dissatisfaction" is a hypothesis.

This theory does not claim that all young people are dissatisfied with their work. Instead, like other social science theories, it is a probabilistic explanation. It proposes that younger people are "more likely" to express job dissatisfaction. Human beings are thinking and acting subjects, each with his or her own unique history of experiences. Thus, while our theory might suggest that certain behaviours would be expected of certain types of people under a certain set of conditions, some degree of original, non-patterned behaviour should also be expected. It should not surprise us, for example, that some well-educated individuals might report satisfaction with a boring job. Thus, the question becomes whether we find evidence of high education being associated with low satisfaction often enough to convince us that it is not merely a randomly occurring phenomenon. The rules that determine what we mean by "often enough" are the rules of probability theory and the science of statistics, something beyond the scope of this chapter.

A theory that adequately explains a recurring pattern of events can be very useful since it allows us to predict where we could expect to observe that pattern again. If we can predict with any accuracy, we may gain more control over the events in question. Convinced that younger workers are less satisfied because their education has raised their expectations, we might try to redesign the jobs so that they provide more opportunities for skill development.

The Research Cycle

Science does not claim to produce ultimate truths. If we find relevant data to be in line with our hypotheses, this evidence becomes support for our theory. But it does not prove, finally, that the theory is true. It is always possible that some other theory would be supported equally well by these facts, or that some contrary evidence might be discovered.

Scholarly research reports leave the impression that scientific research always begins with a theory and hypotheses. One then designs a study that will test these hypotheses, undertakes the testing and matches the results against the predictions. This particular sequence is frequently followed, but equally often sociologists begin their study with a more general research question. Examples would include our question above about why police forces are charging fewer people with marijuana offences. This is not a theory, since it offers no explanation, and it is not an hypothesis, since it does not involve a prediction. It is, however, a useful starting point for research.

The research process is better seen as a cycle, with various possible starting points. On noticing a decline in marijuana offences, a criminologist might be reminded of previous research on the discretionary behaviour of police officers. When confronted with evidence of a relatively minor crime, officers do not always charge the offender. To lay a charge in every case would keep police officers from completing other tasks required of them and would overburden the criminal justice system. Hence, officers must use their own discretion in deciding when to lay a charge. Among the factors influencing the decision might be the severity of the offence, the characteristics and behaviour of the offender and also general community values.

On the basis of this theory and the evidence of a decline in marijuana charges, the researcher might then hypothesize that: (a) public opinion today is less condemning of marijuana use; and (b) compared to a few years ago, police officers are less likely to charge someone they find in possession of marijuana.

To test the first hypothesis, the researcher might compare responses to questions about the severity of the "marijuana problem" in current and past public opinion polls conducted in the community. The second hypothesis might be tested by surveying local police officers and asking them how frequently they decide not to charge someone possessing marijuana, and whether they make such decisions more often now than they did in the past. Results showing less public concern about marijuana use, and more police discretion, would be supportive evidence.

If the results showed more discretionary behaviour but no shift in public opinion, the researcher would be forced to reassess the theory. Perhaps police officers believe (incorrectly) that public opinion has changed, and are acting accordingly. If so, "officers' perceptions" might become an important explanatory concept. The researcher might now test a new hypothesis: police officers believe that the public is more tolerant of marijuana use.

This example demonstrates the cyclical nature of scientific research. A research question led to several hypotheses being deduced from a theory. After the researcher decided how to measure the concepts, the hypotheses were tested. Since the data supported only one of the hypotheses, the generalizations from these hypotheses (that is, public opinion has not changed, but police officers are acting as if it has) led to a revision of the theory, new hypotheses and further research.

FIGURE 2-1

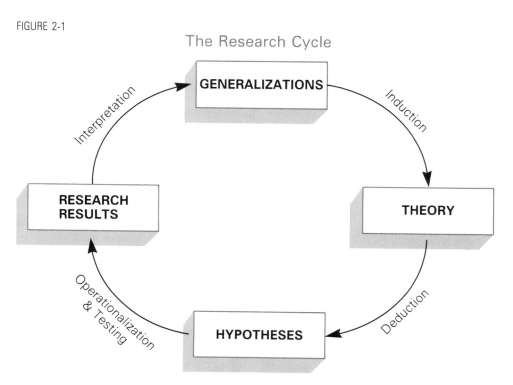

The Research Cycle

Testing the original hypotheses might have shown that public opinion had not changed, and that police officers were not admitting to more discretionary behaviour. In fact, when questioned, the police officers' explanation might be quite simple: fewer people are using marijuana. Such research results would provide no support for a theory of police discretion affecting the decrease in marijuana charges. Hence, revisions to the basic theory would be of little value, and the criminologist would be forced to seek a new explanation for the decline in marijuana offences.

Compared to a decade ago, there are now relatively fewer people in the fifteen to twenty-four age category, while the number of people in the twenty-five to thirty-four age category is somewhat larger. Perhaps this larger and slightly older group prefers alcohol or cocaine over marijuana. If so, an explanation of the decline in marijuana arrests that focuses on changing population distributions may be better than the police discretion theory. Thus, we sometimes find that more than one theory can logically account for an observed regularity. Given competing theoretical explanations, a scientist must deduce hypotheses and devise tests, the results of which could show one theory to be better than the other.

Measurement: Linking Concepts and Variables

Concepts are verbal generalizations used to describe phenomena that resemble each other in important ways (Labovitz and Hagedorn, 1976: 27–34). They are of great value because their shared meaning makes them an efficient form of communication. For example, having defined the concept "police discretion," we can now use it without having to explain the types of behaviour that are encompassed by the term. Terms such as "stratification," "norm," "deviance" and "fertility" are among the many other sociological concepts used in this textbook to assist us in our efforts to generalize about the social world.

While theoretical concepts are essential parts of the research enterprise, they need to be *operationalized* before research can proceed; that is, the measurement standards need to be clearly specified (Labovitz and Hagedorn, 1976: 31). General concepts such as "job satisfaction" must be made much more specific before a researcher can determine whether the behaviour just witnessed is really an example of this particular phenomenon. We might decide to operationalize this particular concept with the question: "On a scale of one to five, with five meaning 'very satisfied' and one meaning 'very dissatisfied,' how satisfied are you with your job?" We could then make the rule that answers of "four" or "five" would indicate job satisfaction.

Researchers have noted that this question typically reveals a very high proportion of satisfied job-holders (Krahn and Lowe, 1988: 160), so some critics question these results. They argue that most people are conditioned to answer positively to such general questions. In addition, some people might be unwilling to say they are dissatisfied for fear this would reflect negatively on themselves ("If you don't like the job, why do you stay?"). In other words, these critics believe that this is not a valid operationalization of the concept "job satisfaction."

Although there are several distinct types of *measurement validity* (Carmines and Zeller, 1979), we generally use the term to question whether an indicator is really measuring what it is supposed to be measuring. We operationalized "police discretion" by asking police officers how frequently they decide against charging someone with marijuana possession. But perhaps police officers can avoid a difficult decision by simply staying away from places where marijuana users might congregate. In other words, discretionary behaviour might be occurring, but long before a decision about laying a charge has to be made. In addition, police officers might be reluctant to admit to discretionary decisions since, while common, such behaviour would not receive official approval. In short, we should probably question the validity of this indicator. We might eventually decide to undertake a different type of study where we would personally observe the decisions officers make while on duty.

While measurement validity refers to the match between operational and conceptual definitions, *reliability* is an issue of measurement stability. A reliable measure is one that would provide the same answer if we were to use it again under exactly the same conditions, or if someone else were to use it. If we were using the general question about job satisfaction, we would expect that individuals who said they were dissatisfied with their jobs today would answer the same way tomorrow (about the same jobs). We would also expect them to give two different researchers the same answer. If not, we would have to conclude that our indicator of satisfaction was not very reliable.

When specifying the types of subjects they are studying, researchers use the term *unit of analysis*. In this particular example, our unit of analysis is the individual worker. We are focusing on characteristics of specific individuals, including their age and their level of job satisfaction. We might also undertake a different study in which we compared workplace morale across a range of work organizations. Here our unit of analysis would be the organization, and our key concepts would describe important organizational characteristics.

When operationalizing concepts, we are constructing *variables*, measurable character-istics of a unit of analysis that vary across units (Loether and McTavish, 1988 : 5). Age (in years) and job satisfaction (operationalized in some specific way) are both variables since they vary from individual to individual. In this study, age is our *independent variable* (the cause), and job satisfaction is treated as our *dependent variable* (the effect). We are arguing that job satisfaction depends on age. Thus, our theory determines which measure should be labelled as the independent and which as the dependent variable.

If we look more closely, we can see that we are relying on some other variables to explain the link between age and job satisfaction. Specifically, we reasoned that younger workers would be more highly educated, and that higher education leads to higher expectations from one's job. This, in turn, increases the probability of one's job not matching one's expectations. In this particular study, then, education and job expectations (as yet not operationalized) are *intervening variables*. They are the link between the independent and dependent variables.

When operationalizing variables, we have some choice among levels of measurement (Stevens, 1951). *Nominal measures* merely classify units of analysis. Examples are sex (female, male) and voting preference (Liberal, New Democrat, Progressive Conserva-tive, other). With *ordinal measures*, we can simultaneously categorize and rank the subjects in our study as exhibiting low, medium and high satisfaction, for example, or as being members of the lower, middle or upper class. We could rank education similarly, but we might prefer a more precise level of measurement. *Interval measures* have equal distances between the possible values of a variable. If, in response to a question about number of years of completed education, one respondent answered "ten" and another replied "twelve," the interval between these two values would be identical to that between nine and eleven years. Age (in years), income (in dollars) and number of children are other examples of variables measured at the interval level. As well as categorizing and ranking units of analysis, interval measures allow a researcher to undertake more sophisticated mathematical analyses of the data.

Experimental Research

While researching imitative behaviour, we might hypothesize that seeing violent behaviour on television encourages children to play aggressively. To test this hypothesis, we could engage in *participant observation*, spending time with children as they play and watch television to see if we can observe the predicted effects. Alternatively, we might undertake a *survey*, interviewing children about their television viewing and playtime preferences. Or we might complete an *experiment* in which we show one group of children a violent television show and a second group a non-violent show, and then observe them both at play.

These alternative approaches demonstrate basic differences between these three research methods. In an experiment, the researcher deliberately alters, or *manipulates*, the values of the independent variable in order to see the reaction in the dependent variable, in a setting where the effects of other less important factors can be minimized (Kerlinger, 1979:111). A survey systematically collects information from subjects allowing the researcher to examine patterns in the data. In participant observation, data collection also occurs, but less systematically and less often for the explicit purpose of hypothesis testing. Instead, much more of the emphasis is on understanding and interpreting attitudes and behaviours. Survey research and participant observation will be discussed more fully later in the chapter.

Most of us would be more convinced by evidence from the experiment than from the other two methods because we could see exactly what happened when the independent variable was manipulated. In survey and other forms of non-experimental research, we are forced to draw such conclusions from patterns in the data. Experimental results are also more convincing because the researcher has greater control over other variables that might be influencing the results. Hence, alternative explanations can be eliminated more easily (Kerlinger, 1979:110).

For example, critics of our participant observation might suggest that, given all the other things influencing children's behaviour, we cannot really prove that television is a cause of aggression. Or the validity of children's responses in our survey might be questioned. Will children provide accurate information about what they watch on television, or about how aggressively they play? In an experiment, we could ensure that all children in the one group and none in the other watched the violent show. We could also carefully observe and record the actual playtime behaviours of all children in both groups.

In addition, we could strengthen our research strategy by introducing a playtime observation period before exposing the children to the television programs. If our results showed that children who generally played non-aggressively before watching the violent show became more aggressive after seeing it, and that no such change occurred for the other group, it would be harder to dispute our conclusions.

Types of Experiments This last modification to our experiment made it a classic experimental design. A *classic design* involves one independent variable and one dependent variable. (Other more complex experimental designs could consider the combined effects of several independent variables.) A second important feature of the classic design is the use of *treatment* and *control* groups. Only one group viewed the violent television show (received the treatment). The other group is the control group. Without it, we would be open to at least one alternative explanation: simply watching television, whatever the content, leads to more aggressive play activity (after sitting still for a while, children are more energetic). However, if we can demonstrate that children who watched a non-violent television show do not play aggressively later, we have eliminated this explanation.

A third characteristic of the classic design is the use of a *pre-test* and a *post-test*. By measuring our dependent variable before and after we manipulated the independent variable, we can clearly show how the two groups were similar at the outset, and how one of them changed.

Finally, in a classic experimental design, subjects are randomly assigned to the treatment and control groups. With *random assignment*, each subject has an equal chance of being placed in either group. While this does not guarantee that the two groups are similar, it is an unbiased method of distributing potentially important subject differences, such as individual levels of aggressive behaviour, across the two groups. Random sampling techniques, which are discussed in more detail later in the chapter, take this process one step further by ensuring that all possible subjects have an equal chance of being chosen to participate in a study. However, most social science experiments do not employ random sampling. Instead, they rely on random assignment of subjects, frequently university students who volunteered or were requested to participate.

The classic design is the ideal experiment, but for a variety of reasons, many research questions must be addressed with less complex designs. Concerned about

FIGURE 2-2

Classic Experimental Design

	PRE-TEST	Manipulation of Independent Variable	POST-TEST	Hypothesis Test
TREATMENT GROUP ↑ [randomly assigned subjects] ↓	Observation 1	Treatment	Observation 2	O_2-O_1
CONTROL GROUP	Observation 3	———	Observation 4	O_4-O_3

unemployment problems among its graduates, a school board hires a sociologist to test the effectiveness of a program instructing graduating students in job search techniques. The sociologist proposes to present the program to half the students and to use the rest as a control group. The effectiveness of the instructional package will be tested with a short "How to Find a Job" quiz administered immediately before and again a month after the presentation. But fearing a negative reaction from parents, the school board insists that all graduating students must participate in the program. The pre-test/post-test comparisons show that students have learned more about the labour market. However, the absence of a control group leaves the researcher open to criticism: perhaps the learning would have occurred anyway, since students about to leave school might make an effort to learn about the labour market. This experiment is modelled on a *one group pre-test/post-test* design.

If the sociologist providing the job search instruction had not done a pre-test, a *one-shot case study* would have been conducted. With this experimental design, there would have been no defence against a criticism that the participants, while scoring well on the post-test, had learned little or nothing from the presentation. They might have known it all before. Thus, less complex designs cannot eliminate as many alternative explanations of research findings.

These examples demonstrate that experiments need not be completed in a laboratory, although most social science experiments have been done in such a setting. Milgram (1974), for instance, conducted a series of elaborate experiments in which male subjects were instructed to administer electric shocks to another individual to "help him learn" a memorization task. Milgram's subjects were unaware that the learner was an accomplice and that the shocks were not real. As Milgram manipulated his independent variable (the characteristics of the authority figure), many of his subjects administered "shocks" strong enough to injure someone seriously. Milgram went on to theorize about the extent of obedience to authority, and the conditions under which people will obey authority even though doing so involves going against their own moral principles.

Field experiments are completed outside of a laboratory setting and, hence, allow less control over the research setting. A provocative field experiment conducted by Rosenthal and Jacobson (1968) examined the effect of teachers' expectations on grade-school students' performance. Teachers were told that certain students could be expected to make considerable intellectual gains during the coming year. The researchers compared beginning-of-the-year pre-test results with year-end post-test results and concluded that the designated children had, in fact, made above-average progress. Since these pupils were really randomly selected and no different from other children, the intellectual gains must have been a product of the way in which teachers had treated these children.

Quasi-experimental designs (Campbell and Stanley, 1963) differ from real experiments in one critical respect—the independent variable is not manipulated by the researcher. Instead, the occurrence of some event produces an experiment-like situation where one group of people is affected and another is not. In 1981, parallel public opinion surveys in Edmonton and Winnipeg showed Edmonton residents less likely to agree that labour unions provided their members with economic benefits (Krahn and Lowe, 1984). Since Edmonton's economy was booming at the time, the researchers reasoned that easily available jobs and high wages in this city might be one of the explanations of the city differences in union attitudes.

Several years later, the Alberta economy was devastated by the recession and dropping oil prices. In comparison, the Manitoba economy remained more stable. When the two surveys were repeated in 1987, Edmonton residents were now more likely than citizens of Winnipeg to agree that there might be economic benefits to union membership (Lowe and Krahn, 1989). In this quasi-experiment, the presumed effects of the independent variable (the economy) on the dependent variable (attitudes) could be documented, but the absence of direct control over the experiment meant that conclusions could be drawn with less certainty.

Internal and External Validity in Experimental Research

As we have seen, measurement validity is a conceptual concern over whether a variable is really measuring what it is intended to measure. We can also speak about validity of research results: Do they really prove what we think they are proving? Many social science experiments are done with convenient samples of university students, and generally the special characteristics of this kind of sample may not be problematic. If our study is examining the effect of political propaganda messages on behaviour, however, the reactions of university students may not be like those of the larger public. Hence, even if students are randomly assigned to treatment and control groups, the non-representative sample may be a source of *external invalidity*. In other words, we might be led to conclude that political propaganda has a certain type of effect on behaviour. However, our research results may not really support this unqualified conclusion. Propaganda might only have the observed effect on university students.

External validity may also be threatened by the experimental setting itself. The advantage of experiments done in a laboratory is that they can be custom designed to test a theory, while potentially disruptive variables are controlled. The disadvantage is that this controlled setting seldom resembles the real world, and one may not be able to generalize the results. Subjects in an experiment may be more sceptical of political propaganda in the laboratory than they would be outside the laboratory.

Concerns about *internal invalidity* reflect the possibility that changes in the dependent variable that were attributed to the independent variable were, in fact, caused by something else. In our propaganda experiment, pre-test/post-test differences might be a result of *maturation*, or changes in the subjects themselves over the course of the experiment (they might get bored or tired). Changes could also simply be due to *testing*, that is, to subjects catching on to the intent of the experiment and giving the predicted results. In an effort to counter the testing problem, we might design our experiment with a week between the pre-test and the post-test. The time delay could reduce the possibility that subjects would catch on to the experiment and, even if they did, that they would remember how they responded in the pre-test. Now, *history* could be a source of internal invalidity. Some outside event, such as a series of pre-election ads on television, might have influenced our experiment results.

In addition, internal validity can be threatened by problems of *instrumentation*, which in experimental terms means unreliable measurement. If measures of our central concepts cannot be trusted, we have no way of knowing whether the changes in our dependent variable are caused by our independent variable.

Experimental researchers must remain conscious of these and other potential sources of internal invalidity (Campbell and Stanley, 1963). However, they can be avoided. Careful design of an experiment will frequently eliminate much of the problem. For example, *selection bias* is a possible source of internal invalidity. It describes differences in the dependent variable that can be traced to differences between the subjects in the treatment and control groups. But random assignment of subjects should limit its effect, as could *matching*, a procedure where members of the control and treatment groups are deliberately matched on age, sex, education and other variables. Similarly, with effort, experimenters can avoid many problems of testing, maturation, history and instrumentation.

While experiments can lead to more convincing conclusions, they are not appropriate for many sociological questions. Experiments are much easier to design when the unit of analysis is the individual person. Researchers who study population characteristics, organizations or social movements can rarely use experiments, since the causal factors that influence countries and organizations can seldom be manipulated. Even when individuals are the unit of analysis, experiments are of little value if our goal is to understand the meanings behind individuals' actions, if our subjects are spread around the country or if we want to look at gender, age or racial differences in attitudes or behaviours. In these cases, sociologists must choose a research method more appropriate to their research question or theory.

Survey Research

Survey research, in which data are systematically gathered from the units of analysis via interviews or self-administered questionnaires (Li, 1981:81), is the most common sociological method. Individuals are typically the units of analysis. Surveys of the adult residents of Montreal or of nurses in British Columbia would be examples. But sociologists also survey groups or organizations. A recent survey of hundreds of large Canadian firms focused on the introduction of new micro-electronic and robotic technologies (Betcherman and McMullen, 1986). Individuals within each company answered the questions, but the information collected described the firms.

The emphasis on systematic data collection (trying to obtain exactly comparable information from each of the subjects) helps distinguish surveys from other more interpretive research strategies. Unlike the experimental method where independent variables are manipulated in order to see if dependent variables react as predicted, the survey method is an *ex post facto* (after the fact) method (Kerlinger, 1979:116). Researchers are measuring variation in the independent and dependent variables that is already present in the subjects.

In a survey of Montreal adults, the subjects would include both women and men. A minority would be unemployed, the rest would have jobs. We would find additional variation in age, ethnic origin, voting behaviour, job satisfaction, education and preference for large families. Adapting the logic of the scientific method to the survey approach, we now examine the data for the patterns that were predicted by our hypotheses. Do our results show less job satisfaction among the young, a preference for larger families among certain ethnic groups or that the unemployed are more inclined to vote against the party in power? Our theory might have predicted the latter *relationship* between the two variables. We might explain this relationship by stating that the unemployed will vote against the party in power because they attribute their personal misfortune to the failings of the government.

However, there could be alternative explanations. Younger people are more likely to be unemployed, may be less inclined to support the status quo in general and, so, might more often vote for opposition parties. Hence, age, and not employment status, may be the critical causal variable. When experimental researchers are uncertain as to whether variable A or variable B is responsible for changes in variable C, they might alter their experimental design to eliminate the effects of one of the two possible causal variables. If variable B is age, they might ensure that all the subjects in the experiment are the same age. Thus, they would *control* the variation in B, allowing a clearer look at the effects of A on C.

But survey researchers cannot alter their research design directly to control additional variables. Instead, they must manipulate the data they have already collected. Thus, survey researchers use *statistical controls*, rather than the direct controls of an experimental design, to counter competing explanations. By separating the data from younger and older subjects, and then seeing if the relationship between employment status and voting remains within each group, the researcher controls for the potential effects of age.

Compared to experimenters, survey researchers have more difficulty proving the existence of cause and effect relationships. Imagine devising an experiment where you randomly assigned one group of subjects to be unemployed and allowed members of the control group to hold a job. If a pre-test/post-test design showed more people in the unemployed group changing their voting behaviour away from the party in power, you could speak fairly confidently about cause and effect relationships. Survey research results showing that the unemployed were less likely to support the governing party would not be as convincing, since they would not be the result of your own manipulation of the independent variable. Hence, we need some guidelines for identifying cause and effect relationships in survey research results.

At a minimum, we must be able to demonstrate a significant relationship between the independent and dependent variable in question. If unemployed people are no more likely to vote against the party in power, there is little value in arguing further about the causal effects of unemployment. We must also be able to argue that the cause preceded the effect. To suggest that anti-government voting increases one's chances of unemployment makes much less sense than the reverse—that unemployment influences people to vote against the party in power. Finally, we must be able to counter suggestions that the relationship is *spurious* (not genuine), that it is caused by some prior variable that is affecting both our independent and dependent variable. If younger people experience more unemployment and also tend to vote against the party in power, then there is probably a spurious relationship between employment status and voting patterns.

Types of Surveys

Most surveys are *sample surveys*—they target a subset of all the elements within a specified population. A *population* could be all residents of a city, all university undergraduates in Canada or all nurses in Nova Scotia. Sometimes a *census* (a survey of the complete population) is useful, but for most research purposes this type of all-inclusive survey is much too expensive.

Most surveys are also *cross-sectional*; that is, they collect data only at one point in time. Immediately after the 1988 federal election, Canadian social scientists completed the National Election Study. This cross-sectional sample survey asked thousands of Canadians how they had voted, why they voted as they did and what their opinions were on a variety of political and social issues. It allowed analysts to examine the effects of age, gender, income and ethnicity, among other things, on voting behaviour.

But given the manner in which public opinion shifted during the election campaign due to the free trade issue, a panel design would have been a more powerful research tool. Using a *panel design*, a sample of potential voters would have been regularly reinterviewed in the weeks before the election, and then again after it was all over. Because they cover a span of time, panel studies are a form of *longitudinal research*. Panel surveys are very useful for studying changing behaviour and attitudes, but are also much more costly and difficult to complete than cross-sectional surveys.

Trend analyses, comparisons of the results from a series of cross-sectional surveys, are an alternative form of longitudinal research. Public opinion polls that repeat questions at regular intervals can demonstrate changes in behaviour and attitude of the population. Unlike a panel design, however, they cannot track changes at the individual level, since each new poll involves a new sample drawn from the population.

Sampling in Survey Research

The external validity of sample survey research depends on whether the sample is representative of the population from which it was drawn. No matter how clearly our data support our hypotheses, we cannot generalize beyond them unless we have some confidence that our sample adequately reflects the characteristics of the population. Given a research interest in the sexual attitudes and activity of high-school students in Toronto, for example, how could we ensure that the varieties of family backgrounds, personal beliefs and other individual differences are represented in our sample?

Probability (random) sampling techniques are the solution. A random sample is not a sample put together in a haphazard manner. Instead, random sampling methods are used to ensure that each element in the population (each high-school student in Toronto) has an equal (and known) chance of appearing in our sample. If we use them, we can have more confidence that our sample is representative. Random sampling does not guarantee that all of the population diversity will be reflected in the sample, but it does reduce the possibility of biased samples.

Even if our sample was randomly selected, it is unlikely that it would be representative of the population if it contained only ten individuals. A random sample of two hundred would be more representative, and a sample of one thousand even more so. Explanation of just how large a sample must be in order to reduce random sampling error to a specified level requires a more advanced discussion of probability theory than can be covered in this chapter. It should be remembered, however, that both the sampling technique and the size of the sample play an important part in ensuring that the sample is representative.

The most commonly used probability sample is the *simple random sample* where every element has an equal probability of being chosen. If we wished to select a simple random sample of 1000 Toronto students, we would need a complete list of all the students in the city. Such a list of all the elements in a population is called a *sampling frame*. Given a population of 250 000 students, the probability of any one student being chosen would be 0.004. We would draw the actual sample by numbering the names on the list and then using a computer or a table of random numbers to select the sample.

A *systematic sample*, which chooses every *nth* element in the population (every 250th student in our example) is not technically equivalent to a simple random sample. For those appearing second, third, and so on in this list, the probability of being chosen would be zero. However, systematic samples generally provide a reasonable approximation of a simple random sample.

Sociologists frequently use more complex probability sampling designs. A *stratified random sample* is obtained by dividing the population into several discrete groups (or strata) on the basis of some important variable, and then randomly selecting a predetermined number of subjects from each group. For example, we might decide to survey 250 Toronto students from each of grades nine through twelve. The advantage of this approach is that we are not relying on chance, but are ensuring that each grade is proportionately represented (assuming that Toronto high-school students are equally distributed across the four grades). Thus, stratified sampling improves our ability to generalize accurately to the population.

Social researchers are sometimes forced to rely on *non-probability sampling* techniques, methods of obtaining a sample in which the probability of any one population element being chosen is unequal (and unknown). One non-probability sampling technique is *quota sampling*. When using quota sampling, interviewers might be instructed to find a sample with equal proportions (quotas) of women and men and certain proportions of individuals in different age categories. This technique attempts to create representativeness, but it is impossible to account for all the variation within a population in this manner.

When using *snowball sampling*, researchers rely on information provided by respondents to locate other potential subjects. Since sample members would probably identify people like themselves, this method can introduce a distinct bias into the final results. Researchers can counter this tendency to some extent by getting several "snowballs" rolling, and by using a quota system. Samples that depend on volunteers are even more prone to bias, since people with an interest in the subject are generally most likely to volunteer.

Data Collection Strategies

Some surveys are completed by interviewers in a face-to-face setting or over the telephone. Interviewers use an *interview schedule*, questions previously written by the researcher. Face-to-face interviews can generally be longer than telephone interviews. An interviewer can explain problematic questions, especially to those who might have difficulty reading and writing. A face-to-face interview may also build enough rapport to allow questions about potentially sensitive subjects. On the other hand, the anonymity of a telephone may encourage more frank answers from respondents. Telephones also provide easier access to samples spread across a wide area and to individuals who might not allow an interviewer into their home (Frey, 1983).

Personal interviews have long provided the sociological data analysed by survey researchers.

New data collection techniques, such as computer-assisted telephone interviewing (CATI), allow social scientists to interview respondents who might otherwise be unwilling to participate in the research.

Other surveys are completed via *self-administered questionnaires*, which may be sent through the mail or distributed in a group setting, such as a classroom. Self-administered questionnaires provide even more anonymity, since the respondent records his or her own answers. They also eliminate some of the tendency for respondents to answer in a socially desirable manner. But their biggest advantage is the cost savings realized by not hiring interviewers. On the negative side, self-administered questionnaires are problematic for less literate populations (children, the elderly and recent immigrants are examples). Questionnaires arriving through the mail are easy to ignore, so researchers relying on this approach must work much harder at convincing potential respondents to participate.

Face-to-face interviews were generally preferred in the past. However, telephone and mail survey techniques have improved, and a greater societal emphasis on privacy and personal security may be making it more difficult to complete face-to-face interviews (Goyder and Leiper, 1985). Hence, sociologists must think carefully about the questions they wish to ask, the characteristics of their sample and their budget before choosing among alternative data collection strategies. They must then convince the sample members to participate. A large random sample is of little value if only a minority actually answer the questions. The *response rate*, the percentage of subjects in the sample who complete the survey, can be raised by rewarding respondents for their participation (either materially or through acknowledging their contribution). Persistence on the part of the researcher (reminder letters and telephone calls, for example) is even more effective.

Questionnaire Design   The physical appearance of self-administered questionnaires and the length of time it will take to complete an interview or questionnaire could both have a significant effect on response rates. Writing good questions is equally important, and much more difficult than most people believe (Converse and Presser, 1986). Imagine yourself developing questions for our survey of Toronto high-school students. Should we begin by asking whether respondents are "sexually active"? Will they know what we mean? What *do* we mean? Will students be offended by this personal question? How can we convince them that their answers will be treated confidentially? Should we ask about their knowledge of AIDS? How many questions? Will respondents be tense and resentful because they feel as if they are taking a test?

– 19 –

54. In the past year, has any <u>member of your immediate family</u> (not counting yourself) been <u>unemployed</u> (out of work and looking for work)?

    No 1

    Yes .... ②

55. In the past year, how many of your <u>friends</u> have been unemployed (out of work and looking for work)?

    ___5___ (number of friends unemployed)

56. In your opinion, how likely is it that <u>you will be unemployed</u> at some time during the next 12 months?

    Very likely 4

    Somewhat likely 3

    Not very likely 2

    Not at all likely .... ①

57. What do you think is the <u>most important cause</u> of unemployment in Canada today?

GOV'T IRRESPONSIBILITY. GOVT SPENDS MILLIONS OF $$$ WHERE IT SHOULDN'T, YET DOESN'T HAVE MUCH INTEREST IN CREATING NEW JOBS.

58. What is the <u>most important advice</u> you would offer a young person about <u>looking for a job</u>?

START YOUR OWN BUSINESS AND MOVE BACK IN WITH YOUR PARENTS TO CUT YOUR EXPENSES TO MINIMUM, WHICH WILL HELP YOU GET STARTED !

Many question-writing problems are a function of conceptual confusion and inadequate theorizing. But even with a clearly defined set of concepts, operationalization difficulties can lead to biased results. Asking high-school students whether the government should do something about the "problem" of teenage pregnancy will almost certainly increase the number of students calling for government action. Questions about topics with which respondents are unfamiliar can lead to very unreliable results. Asking high-school students about their parents' premarital sexual experience would be an example.

Survey researchers must also take specific characteristics of their sample members into account. Can the respondents understand the question or the instructions for answering questions? Will they be willing to answer an *open-ended question* (one in which the respondent is free to make any reply), or would a *forced-choice question* (which offers a set of alternative answers) be more appropriate? Will the questions, and their order, keep the respondents' interest? Are the questions offensive or, equally problematic, likely to strike the respondent as silly? Finally, the survey researcher must look ahead to the data analysis stage of the research. Have measures of all the necessary control variables been included? Could a higher level of measurement be used for operationalizing some of the concepts?

Well-trained interviewers will improve the quality of data obtained in face-to-face and telephone interviews. Equally important is the pre-testing of questionnaires and interview schedules on a small sample of typical subjects. The pre-test will identify questions that are difficult to understand or overly sensitive. It will also indicate how long an interview might last. By examining the data obtained from the pre-test, the researcher can also determine whether this set of questions will provide clear answers to the research questions.

Participant Observation

Max Weber, a German sociologist writing early in the twentieth century, made many theoretical contributions to sociology. His classic analyses of stratification, bureaucracy and religion are introduced in later chapters. But Weber is also remembered for his discussion of appropriate research methods for studying the social world (Weber, 1922).

Weber clearly recognized that the behaviour of human beings is influenced by external social and economic forces. However, he was also very aware of the degree to which human actors make decisions on the basis of individual goals, values and beliefs. As social researchers, he argued, it is not enough simply to document patterns of regularity in our data. We must also try to uncover the meanings behind the actions, to understand why our subjects would act in this manner. We could do this by asking about these meanings in a survey. Or we could put ourselves in our subjects' place, literally (by observing and questioning them at length in their own social environment) and figuratively (by trying to imagine ourselves in their place). The German word *verstehen* means "understanding," and is often used to describe this research orientation. Sayer (1984 : 37) provides the helpful analogy of "understanding" a book, something we do by interpreting the meaning behind the words, not by counting the words or analysing their placement on the pages.

Surveys and experiments are often called *quantitative research methods. Qualitative methods* are less systematic, more descriptive and less statistically oriented. They tend to focus on small groups and the social dynamics within them and are less inclined toward sweeping theoretical generalizations. Unfortunately, strict use of the terms quantitative and qualitative ignores the degree to which survey and experimental researchers try to interpret the meanings behind the patterned behaviours they observe, and the extent to which qualitative researchers quantify their findings. In fact, many of the most interesting sociological studies combine these different but complementary research methods.

Participant observation is the most common qualitative method. Participant observers attempt to gain an understanding of the meanings behind behaviours, and of the social dynamics of a particular group, by observing the day-to-day lives of the group members at close range over an extended period of time. This method was not invented by sociologists, but by nineteenth-century anthropologists writing *ethnographies* (detailed descriptions of unique cultures) about the primitive tribes with which they lived. The "Chicago school" of sociology, at its peak in the 1920s and 1930s, continued this tradition with its many in-depth studies of the poor and the deviant in that city. Today, ethnography continues to be the main method of anthropology, but also remains a respected sociological research tool. Because of its emphasis on doing research in the subjects' own social environment, it is also called *field research* (Shaffir et al., 1980).

Although a number of useful resource books do give practical advice (Hammersley and Atkinson, 1983; Lofland and Lofland, 1984), it is not easy to list the various steps involved in this less structured research approach. Participant observation studies seldom begin with a theory or a testable hypothesis. However, generalizations about patterned behaviour, reasons for such behaviours and outcomes of group processes do emerge in the course of the study. These may be the source of *grounded theory* (Glaser and Strauss, 1967), which is developed slowly and inductively through participating in or observing the group. Whyte's (1943) famous study *Street Corner Society* is a good example. His description of the day-to-day lives of a small group of young working-class men highlights many of the relationships from which a theory of small-group power structures can emerge.

Survey researchers may have problems convincing respondents to participate in a hour-long interview. But imagine the difficulties in gaining entry to a group for several months or more when your intention is to watch what everyone is doing and to ask questions continually. Some researchers have handled this problem by becoming covert or "undercover" observers. For example, Festinger et al. (1956) had several sociology students infiltrate a group that believed that the world was going to end on a specified day to see what would happen when the prophecy failed. The ethical implications of this approach are discussed in the last section of this chapter.

However, there are many groups, particularly those whose members have some unique characteristic or skill, that sociologists would have trouble infiltrating. Identifying oneself as a researcher is the only alternative. Having done so, the sociologist must work on gaining acceptance by the group. For example, Gallmeier (1988) spent eight months as an open participant observer of a semi-professional hockey team. He had to rely on personal contacts to get permission, and then work extremely hard to develop the rapport necessary to be accepted as a member of the group.

Participant observers do more than observe; they also ask many questions. Covert observers must be more cautious since too many questions might look suspicious. Generally, researchers come to rely on some group members more than on others. The choice of these *key informants* is critical, because it is through them that the explanations for behaviours are obtained. If these individuals are not representative of the group, the interpretations based on their information may be faulty. Thus, in participant observation, reliability of measurement can refer directly to the reliability of informants. Participant observers typically use more than one informant and try to cross-check information received. Nevertheless, measurement reliability remains problematic. However, measurement validity (the certainty that one is measuring what one intends

The collective behaviour exhibited in this student protest over university fee increases might be best studied through participant observation.

OFFICE OF PUBLIC AFFAIRS, UNIVERSITY OF ALBERTA.

to measure) may be higher because of the natural research setting and the chance to observe group processes at length.

Participant observation can make a number of unique contributions to the study of the social world. Researchers within this tradition begin with the premise that patterned behaviours within social groups reflect important systems of meaning shared by group members. Participant observers seek to uncover these shared values and beliefs, rather than to explain the behaviours from the perspective of the observer. Hence, this approach is less likely to result in an inappropriate theoretical explanation. It is an ideal method for examining the social dynamics and the belief systems of small groups. And, as anthropologists have often demonstrated, it allows access to groups and settings where surveys and experiments would be impossible.

But the focused nature of such a study may also mean that its results can be generalized to other settings only to a limited degree. It is not a method that easily allows the testing of general theories and hypotheses. Non-systematic approaches to data collection introduce additional sources of measurement error, and researchers must be on guard against their own values and beliefs biasing their interpretations. Relatively unstructured research procedures also mean that replication of the study may be difficult. But there are also flaws in other research methods. Sociologists must choose methods that suit their research questions, and in many cases participant observational approaches are very useful.

Other Research Methods

Case Studies A *case study*, simply defined, is a detailed analysis of a single example of some phenomenon (McNeill, 1985 : 87). A year-long observational study of a primitive tribe could be called a case study. Whyte's (1943) account of male working-class culture in *Street Corner Society* has been described in this manner (Yin, 1984 : 15). So too could Clairmont and Magill's (1974) analysis of the relocation of a black community in Halifax during the 1960s. In this particular study, the researchers examined historical documents, completed interviews, distributed questionnaires and took the role of participant observers in the community (1974 : 32). In short, the term *case study* does not describe a method so much as a commitment to examine a single case at length, and often using multiple sources of information (Yin, 1984 : 23).

Some case studies are mainly descriptive, while others are more explanatory, seeking answers to questions about why something happened. For example, Gouldner's (1954) account of a wildcat strike in a gypsum mine attempted to identify the primary causes of the work stoppage. Researchers may even develop theories on the basis of case studies. Gouldner went beyond the single strike he observed to discuss a theory of "group tensions" (1954 : 124). While evidence from a single case is not as convincing as one might like, replicated findings in other case studies could provide additional support for a theory.

Theories can also be tested through analysis of a single *critical case*. If a theory predicts that certain outcomes should be observed under specific conditions, and if detailed examination of a single case under precisely these conditions fails to reveal the predicted outcomes, the theory must be questioned (Yin, 1984:42). Smith (1988) tested the theory that worker militancy is a cause of inflation with data from the province of Quebec. He reasoned that if there were any place in Canada where militant workers might have pushed wages upwards, it should be in this province. Finding no support for the theory, he concluded that worker militancy might be a consequence rather than a cause of inflation.

Historical Comparative Research	Historians writing the political history of the province of Alberta would document significant pieces of legislation and noteworthy events, while describing the people and groups that figured prominently in them. However, historians might also comment on why something occurred. For example, a historical study of the 1935 defeat of the United Farmers of Alberta by the Social Credit League might explain that the winning party reflected the concerns and values of a class of self-employed farmers struggling through the Depression (Macpherson, 1953). But as the province became more prosperous and urbanized in the post-war years, and as the oil industry grew in strength, the Conservative Party, promoting different values and reflecting different interest groups, took power in 1971.

There is an implicit theory in this explanation: urbanization and a decline in agriculture lead to a shift in values that, in turn, can result in dramatic changes in the fortunes of political parties. What distinguishes historical sociology from the discipline of history is the explicitness of its theorizing. Historians emphasize the detail and sequence of historical events, but are less likely to generalize beyond such a case to other times and places. Sociologists typically reverse the emphasis, generalizing beyond the historical details.

When sociologists focus on a single historical event or set of events (what social conflicts led to the 1919 Winnipeg General Strike?) or on a single country or society (what social and economic forces lay behind the Quiet Revolution in Quebec?), they are engaging in a historical case study. But sociologists may go on to compare several historical cases, using the *historical comparative method* to draw theoretical conclusions. For example, Laxer's (1989) study of the origins of foreign ownership of Canadian industry also examines other countries, such as Sweden, Australia, and even Japan, that began to industrialize at about the same time. Laxer systematically compares the social, economic and political characteristics of these cases, trying to answer his main question: Why did Canada come to have a heavily foreign-owned, resource-based economy while some other countries did not?

Over a hundred years ago, John Stuart Mill outlined the logic used in the historical comparative method (Skocpol, 1984:378). When demonstrating that the phenomenon to be explained and the presumed causes are both present in two (or more) cases, a researcher is using the *method of agreement* to draw a conclusion. Alternatively, when showing that the outcome (extensive foreign ownership, for example) is present only in the case(s) where the cause is observed, the *method of differences* is being employed.

By combining the two methods (Sweden and Canada resembled each other in several ways, but differed in one or more crucial respects), we can begin to eliminate alternative explanations.

This is, of course, the same deductive logic used in experimental and survey research designs. In the former, we ask whether the treatment leads to the predicted outcome, and if its absence results in no change. In a survey we examine our data to see if the presence of some hypothesized cause (unemployment, for example) is associated with some effect (voting against the party in power). The difference is that historical analyses seldom involve more than a handful of cases (Skocpol, 1984 : 378).

Historians obtain their information from a wide range of public and private documents, the accuracy of which can vary considerably. Sociologists using the historical comparative method are less likely to go to these primary sources. Instead, they often rely on secondary sources, that is, on the writings of historians who have themselves examined the primary sources. The potential for error (facts ignored or reported incorrectly) and misinterpretation is, consequently, even greater (Teevan, 1989 : 133). The only recourse of sociologists is to search for as many alternative information sources as possible and to question seriously the reliability of each. If one has confidence in the sources used, the historical comparative method can be a powerful research tool for explaining the social past.

Official Statistics   Primary sources for historians include official statistics from an earlier era. Governments have been counting their citizens for taxation and military purposes for centuries. Many have also preserved various kinds of economic data, voting records, crime reports, birth and death records and other sorts of information. Churches, unions, businesses and other formal organizations may also have extensive records that might interest historical sociologists. But historical sources are limited compared to today's official data sources. As societies become larger and more bureaucratic, more information is collected by governments. This trend has been strengthened by the rapid spread of computers, which have multiplied data storage and retrieval capacities.

The government of Canada undertakes a national census every five years, attempting to collect demographic information (age, sex, marital status, ethnicity, occupation, income, home ownership and a limited number of other variables) from all households in the country. These census data are of great value to demographers. So too are vital statistics (data on births, deaths and marriages) collected by provincial governments in a uniform manner allowing across-province comparisons.

Analyses of demographic data may be primarily descriptive, profiling population characteristics in a very precise manner. However, more interesting theoretical conclusions about Canadian society emerge when analyses are done over time. This sort of analysis reveals that we are having fewer children, that people are living longer and that divorce rates have increased. Comparisons across population groups can also be enlightening. Trovato and Jarvis (1986) linked census and vital statistics data to compare suicide rates of Canadian immigrants. They showed that immigrants from predominantly Catholic countries were more integrated into their communities and had lower rates of suicide, a finding in line with Durkheim's original explanation of variations in suicide rates.

Every month, the federal government collects information on unemployment, hours worked and other labour force concerns via a large survey of Canadian households. Since these surveys also record demographic characteristics of respondents, researchers can use the data to compare the labour market experiences of men and women, of different age groups and of people living in different parts of the country.

Crime and justice statistics may also be of interest to sociologists, providing them with an opportunity to test theories about criminal behaviour and about the operation of the justice system. Unlike census or national survey data, crime data are collected by individual police forces. Hence, the procedures for dealing with complaints, laying charges and recording information can vary greatly, and comparisons across police jurisdictions may be problematic (Silverman and Teevan, 1986:77).

While some types of official data are less prone to comparison problems, all users of official data must concern themselves with measurement validity (Slattery, 1986). Do the definitions employed in data collection and processing adequately match the

FIGURE 2-3

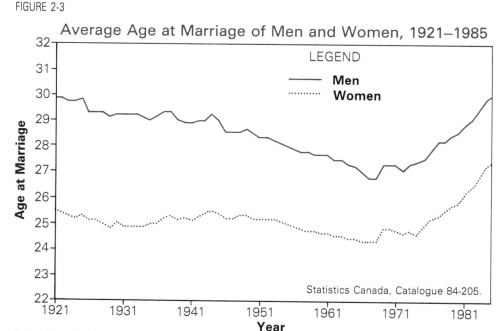

Official statistics allow sociologists to explore questions such as: "Why are Canadian youth today marrying later than at any point in this century?"

key theoretical concepts? Decisions about what type of information to collect and about how it will be collected are made long before most users of official data have focused their research questions. Hence, the data often dictate the types of questions that can be answered. The advantages of official data lie in the precise population descriptions they provide, and in the fact that most researchers could never afford to collect such data on their own.

Content Analysis

Observing that fewer immigrants to Canada are arriving from Europe than in the past, we might hypothesize that Canadians have become more tolerant of non-European immigrants. Comparison of public opinion surveys from earlier decades with contemporary survey results would be one way of testing this hypothesis. Alternatively, we might decide to examine the content of Canadian newspaper editorials from several decades for opinions about non-European immigrants. If we set up explicit rules for classifying editorial content, and if we attempted to obtain a representative sample of newspapers across the time period in question, we would be following standard research procedures for a *content analysis*, a study of the content of a communication medium to draw conclusions about the people and society who produced it.

Content analysis has been used to document, among other things, gender stereotyping in school textbooks, the treatment of trade unions in news reporting and violence in television programming. It can also be used to examine the content of movies, advertisements, paintings, graffiti and other communication media. For example, Grayson (1983) analysed the images of women found in a random sample of over one hundred novels written by major Canadian writers in the two hundred years up to 1976. He concluded that contemporary authors portrayed women no more progressively than did earlier writers.

Sociologists often use content analysis to generalize about the values and beliefs of a society. With such a research goal, measurement validity can be a major concern. Do newspaper editorials really reflect the values of average Canadians? Sometimes, researchers undertake a content analysis because they are concerned about the effects of images and ideas presented. Analyses of gender stereotypes in school textbooks, or of violent scenes in television programming, are examples. In such studies, the tendency of the researchers to assume, rather than demonstrate, that these images and ideas have negative effects on those exposed to them is a common problem.

Who Benefits from Sociological Research?

The respect of other scholars, career advancement and personal satisfaction are among the benefits that individual sociologists obtain from their research. Society in general also benefits through increased information about, and improved understanding of, social patterns and population characteristics, but it is difficult to quantify such benefits. In other cases, the societal advantages are more obvious. The results of social psychological studies of learning and communication processes have had an important impact on our education system. The social research techniques employed in government surveys are clearly useful for policy and program development in the areas of education, health and labour markets.

On a smaller scale, we find that social research methods are frequently used by a wide range of community groups and organizations. *Evaluation research* is a term that refers to the use of experimental and other research designs to assess the effectiveness of some new program, policy or other organizational innovation (Singleton et al., 1988 : 225). It might take the form of a survey of employee satisfaction before and after a new management approach has been introduced. It could involve observations of the interview skills of a group of young job-seekers before and after they have taken a course in job-search techniques.

Sociologists have also used their research skills to attack a broad range of social problems. Studies examining work opportunities available to women (Armstrong, 1984) have been instrumental in highlighting and removing some of the workplace barriers they face. In fact, sociologists sometimes begin a study precisely because they wish to do something about a social problem. Leyton's (1975) description of Newfoundland fluorspar miners dying from work-related lung diseases was a deliberate attempt to make this individual problem into a public concern. In such cases, sociological research certainly acts to provide benefits for society.

Do the subjects in experiments, the respondents in surveys and those observed and questioned in more qualitative studies benefit from their participation in the research? More important, might they be negatively affected? We will conclude with a few comments on research ethics, a topic addressed at greater length in most research methods textbooks.

Most Canadian universities require that all research involving human subjects be approved by a research ethics review committee. These committees insist that the researchers think carefully about the possibility of physical or psychological harm to subjects. Will participation in an experiment lead to excessive stress? Will respondents be annoyed, angered or insulted by questions asked in a survey? Will the presence of an observer in a group lead to conflict? Is the use of a court observer in a group justified? If such possibilities exist, it is up to the researcher to find ways to avoid them.

It is also imperative that sociologists obtain the *informed consent* of all their subjects. In other words, participants must have a chance to refuse to participate, must be told what their participation will entail and that any information they provide will be treated confidentially, and must have some understanding of the purpose of the study. Such ethical guidelines would clearly restrict the scope of many participant observation studies, as well as some experiments where it is important that the subject not know what is being tested. In situations such as these, a researcher should be able to demonstrate that the potential social value of the research is sufficient to justify a bending of the rules.

Social researchers generally agree about these basic ethical guidelines. Some would go on to argue that any active participants in a sociological study (a survey or an experiment) should be rewarded in some way for their assistance. This might mean paying them for their time, or giving them a gift. Clairmont and Magill (1974:34) took another approach in their study of the relocation of Africville. They became involved in the community's struggle with city officials, reasoning that any assistance they might provide was only a fair trade for the opportunity to study the community.

Some sociologists would view such blending of social action and social research as totally appropriate, while others would insist on a distinct separation of the two activities. But whatever one's position in this debate, it is essential that social researchers carefully consider the ethical implications of their research activities.

Summary

Sociologists use a variety of different methods to address their research questions. The logic underlying most of these approaches is that of the scientific method. However, the unique nature of their subject matter means that sociologists must go beyond explanation and prediction to try to understand the beliefs and behaviours of their subjects.

Social science experimental research designs most clearly reflect the logic of the scientific method. Surveys are much more common and equally useful. Observational studies, historical analyses, the examination of official data and content analyses are other major alternative research strategies. There is no single best way to do sociological research. Instead, one's theory or research question will determine the most appropriate research approach.

Suggested Readings

Babbie, Earl
1986. *The Practice of Social Research*, 4th ed. Belmont, Cal.: Wadsworth. This textbook treats the topics covered in this chapter, and many other topics, in great depth, but does so in a very readable manner.

Fowler, Floyd
1984. *Survey Research Methods*. Beverly Hills: Sage. Fowler discusses sampling, data collection strategies, questionnaire design and ethical concerns relating to survey research in a somewhat more concise and more complex manner than the several chapters devoted to this topic in Babbie's textbook.

Hammersley, Martyn, and Paul Atkinson
1983. *Ethnography: Principles in Practice*. London: Tavistock. These authors provide a useful and interesting discussion of how to do observational research, an approach that is often difficult to describe systematically.

Jackson, Winston
1988. *Research Methods: Rules for Survey Design and Analysis*. Englewood Cliffs, N.J.:

Prentice-Hall. Jackson combines an overview of the logic of survey research with practical advice on doing a survey, processing survey data with a computer and analysing the data with a major social science statistical package.

Northey, Margot, and Lorne Tepperman

1986. *Making Sense in the Social Sciences*. Toronto: Oxford University Press. This very helpful book combines chapters on social science research design and measurement with others providing advice on how to write essays, exams, book reports and research reports.

Reynolds, Paul Davidson

1982. *Ethics and Social Science Research*. Englewood Cliffs, N.J.: Prentice-Hall. Reynolds presents a reasoned discussion of ethical concerns in experimental, survey, observational and other social science research methods, as well as several codes of ethics adopted by social science professional associations.

Discussion Questions

1. Some groups argue that "bad" books should be removed from schools and public libraries since such books can encourage "bad" behaviour in those who read them. Restate this argument as a testable hypothesis and describe several different ways it might be tested.

2. The field experiment by Rosenthal and Jacobson (1968) examined the manner in which teachers' expectations influence the performance of students. Identify the independent, dependent and any intervening variables, as well as their level of measurement. What kind of experimental design were the researchers using? On the basis of our brief description of the study, would you have any concerns about internal or external validity?

3. "Younger people are less inclined to support the status quo." Operationalize the concepts in this statement and describe two non-survey research designs that could be used to see whether age and status quo supportive behaviour are related.

4. "What are some of the effects of an aging Canadian population on post-secondary educational institutions in Canada?" Discuss several research designs that might be useful for addressing this research question.

5. What types of information might you collect and analyse if you decided to use a case study approach to learn about how senior citizens adjust to life in a nursing home?

6. What are the ethical implications of completing a national random sample survey of adults that asks questions about sexual activity and exposure to AIDS?

Data Collection Exercises

1. Photocopy a page from a novel and attach a short questionnaire that asks questions about the quality of the writing. Prepare two versions of a fictitious biography of the author, one that says the author is an award-winning writer and another that states the author is unpublished. Distribute this material. Did your intervention have an effect on evaluations of the quality of the writing? Discuss the sources of internal and external invalidity in your experiment.

2. Construct a short questionnaire that asks university students about how they interact with members of the opposite sex when drinking in a bar. After spending an evening observing such interactions in a local student bar, redraft your questionnaire. Did your participant observation experiences assist you in any way?

3. Construct and distribute to a sample of students a short questionnaire that asks about the most important problems they face while attending university. Complete a content analysis of student problems identified in letters to the editor of the campus newspaper. Account for any differences in conclusions reached by the two methods.

4. Interview some of your friends, family members and fellow students, asking them about the number of immigrants admitted to Canada over the past decade, and about their countries of origin. Find the official statistics that tell you the real story and develop a theoretical explanation accounting for the difference between perceptions and reality.

Writing Exercises

1. Write a two-page letter to the dean of your faculty requesting financial assistance for a survey to determine how many graduates were successful in finding jobs related to their training. Explain how you will locate these people and convince them to participate. Comment on the types of questions you plan to ask.

2. Prepare a two-page handout, appropriate for distribution in an undergraduate sociology class, that describes the major differences between experimental, survey and observational methods of research.

3. Write a two-page letter to the Canadian president of Alcoholics Anonymous requesting permission to attend the organization's annual convention as a participant observer. Discuss the types of questions you wish to answer with your research and explain how you will handle any ethical concerns that might arise.

4. Write a research proposal to be submitted to community officials in which you

offer to do an evaluation of a new television ad campaign intended to reduce shoplifting among teenagers.

Glossary

Hypothesis: *a specific prediction, deduced from a theory, that can be empirically tested.*

Operationalization: *specifying of the standards to be employed when measuring a theoretical concept.*

Reliability: *degree of measurement stability, over time, or across observers.*

Survey: *research method in which data are systematically gathered via interviews or self-administered questionnaires.*

Theory: *an account of a recurring pattern of events that explains and predicts this pattern.*

Validity: *extent to which an operational definition matches a conceptual definition.*

Variable: *a measurable characteristic of a unit of analysis that varies across units.*

References

Armstrong, Pat
   1984. *Labour Pains: Women's Work in Crisis.* Toronto: Women's Press.

Babbie, Earl
   1986. *The Practice of Social Research*, 4th ed. Belmont, Cal.: Wadsworth.

Betcherman, Gordon, and Katheryn McMullen
   1986. *Working with Technology: A Survey of Automation in Canada.* Ottawa: Supply and Services Canada.

Campbell, D. T., and J. C. Stanley
   1963. *Experimental and Quasi-Experimental Designs for Research.* Chicago: Rand McNally.

Carmines, Edward G., and Richard A. Zeller
   1979. *Reliability and Validity Assessment.* Beverly Hills: Sage.

Clairmont, Donald H., and Dennis W. Magill
   1974. *Africville: The Life and Death of a Canadian Black Community.* Toronto: McClelland and Stewart.

Converse, Jean M., and Stanley Presser
   1986. *Survey Questions: Handcrafting the Standardized Questionnaire.* Beverly Hills: Sage.

Festinger, Leon, H. W. Riecken and S. Schachter
   1956. *When Prophecy Fails: A Social and Psychological Study of a Modern Group that Predicted the Destruction of the World.* New York: Harper.

Frey, James H.
   1983. *Survey Research by Telephone.* Beverly Hills: Sage.

Gallmeier, Charles P.
   1988. "Methodological Issues in Qualitative Sport Research: Participant Observation Among Hockey Players." *Sociological Spectrum* 8 : 213–35.

Glaser, B. G., and A. L. Strauss
   1967. *The Discovery of Grounded Theory: Strategies for Qualitative Research.* Chicago: Aldine.

Gouldner, Alvin W.
  1954. *Wildcat Strike: A Study in Worker-Management Relationships*. New York: Harper.

Goyder, John, and Jean McKenzie Leiper
  1985. "The Decline in Survey Response: A Social Values Interpretation." *Sociology* 19(1): 55–71.

Grayson, Paul
  1983. "Male Hegemony and the English Canadian Novel." *Canadian Review of Sociology and Anthropology* 20(1): 1–21.

Hammersley, Martyn, and Paul Atkinson
  1983. *Ethnography: Principles in Practice*. London: Tavistock.

Johnson, Holly
  1988. "Illegal Drug Use in Canada." *Canadian Social Trends* (Winter): 5–8.

Kerlinger, F.
  1973. *Foundations of Behavioral Research*, 2nd ed. New York: Holt, Rinehart and Winston.
  1979. *Behavioral Research: A Conceptual Approach*. New York: Holt, Rinehart and Winston.

Krahn, Harvey, and Graham S. Lowe
  1984. "Community Influences on Attitudes Towards Unions." *Relations Industrielles/Industrial Relations* 39(1): 93–112.
  1988. *Work, Industry and Canadian Society*. Toronto: Nelson.

Labovitz, Sanford, and Robert Hagedorn
  1976. *Introduction to Social Research*, 2nd ed. New York: McGraw-Hill.

Laxer, Gordon
  1989. *Open for Business: The Roots of Foreign Ownership in Canada*. Toronto: Oxford University Press.

Leyton, Elliott
  1975. *Dying Hard: The Ravages of Industrial Carnage*. Toronto: McClelland and Stewart.

Li, Peter
  1981. *Social Research Methods*. Toronto: Butterworths.

Loether, Herman J., and Donald G. McTavish
  1988. *Descriptive and Inferential Statistics: An Introduction*. Boston: Allyn and Bacon.

Lofland, John, and Lyn Lofland
  1984. *Analyzing Social Settings*. Belmont, Cal.: Wadsworth.

Lowe, Graham S., and Harvey Krahn
  1989. "Recent Trends in Public Support for Unions in Canada." *Journal of Labor Research*.

Macpherson, C. B.
  1953. *Democracy in Alberta: Social Credit and the Party System*. Toronto: University of Toronto Press.

McNeill, Patrick
  1985. *Research Methods*. London: Tavistock.

Milgram, Stanley
  1974. *Obedience to Authority: An Experimental View*. New York: Harper and Row.

Rosenthal, R., and L. Jacobson
  1968. *Pygmalion in the Classroom*. New York: Holt, Rinehart and Winston.

Sayer, Andrew
1984. *Method in Social Science: A Realist Approach*. London: Hutchinson.

Shaffir, W. B., R. A. Stebbins and A. Turowetz
1980. *Field Experience: Qualitative Approaches to Social Research*. New York: St. Martin's Press.

Silverman, Robert A., and James J. Teevan, eds.
1986. *Crime in Canadian Society*, 3rd ed. Toronto: Butterworths.

Singleton, R., B. C. Straits, M. M. Straits and R. J. McAllister
1988. *Approaches to Social Research*. New York: Oxford University Press.

Skocpol, Theda
1984. "Emerging Agendas and Recurrent Strategies in Historical Research," pp. 356–91. In T. Skocpol, ed., *Vision and Method in Historical Sociology*. Cambridge: Cambridge University Press.

Slattery, Martin
1986. *Official Statistics*. London: Tavistock.

Smith, Michael
1988. "Wages and Inflation in Quebec." *Canadian Review of Sociology and Anthropology* 25(4): 577–602.

Stevens, S. S.
1951. "Mathematics, Measurement, and Psychophysics," pp. 1–49. In S. S. Stevens, ed., *Handbook of Experimental Psychology*. New York: Wiley.

Teevan, James J.
1989. "Research Methodology," pp. 111–38. In J. J. Teevan, ed., *Introduction to Sociology: A Canadian Focus*, 3rd ed. Scarborough: Prentice-Hall.

Trovato, Frank, and George K. Jarvis
1986. "Immigrant Suicide in Canada: 1971 and 1981." *Social Forces* 65(2): 433–57.

Weber, Max
1922. "The Theory of Social Action," pp. 7–32. In W. G. Runciman, ed., *Weber: Selections in Translation (1978)*. Cambridge: Cambridge University Press.

Whyte, William F.
1943. *Street Corner Society*. Chicago: University of Chicago Press.

Yin, Robert K.
1984. *Case Study Research: Design and Methods*. Beverly Hills: Sage.

part 2

Processes of Social Organization

What ties people together in groups? What makes them behave in predictable ways? How do people assimilate into communities and social organizations? These questions are addressed in this second section of the book, in chapters that examine the basic processes of social organization.

In sociology, the problem of order is a central one. For example, English political theorist Thomas Hobbes (1588–1679) wrote that in a society without government, people's selfish desires would run wild. People's lives would be "solitary, poor, nasty, brutish and short." To prevent this unhappy result, people needed a sovereign ruler. They could not rely on good nature or "society" to protect them: only a strong, even autocratic, ruler could do so, Hobbes believed.

Events following the French Revolution of 1789 seemed to justify this bleak prediction. In particular, the French Revolution made way for a short reign of popular democracy and a longer reign of terror, political intrigue and despotism. But the earlier American Revolution of 1776 had a different result. The revolution installed a government that could be peacefully changed by election, and the Constitution did indeed protect certain rights to life and property. (Of course, it was not a democratic government of the modern kind: no women or slaves could vote; nor could many poor white men, at first.)

French sociologist Alexis de Tocqueville came to study democracy in America firsthand. He discovered that at the root of this peaceful yet vital new society there lay enlightened self-interest, community involvement and national pride. The American "experiment" proved Hobbes wrong: self-interested people had created a fluid new kind of society that was neither despotic nor brutish.

In the late eighteenth century, the connection between society and state began to change dramatically, and so did the connection between society and economy. The notion of an "economy" as distinct from a state or society, and of "economics" as a type of social accounting, emerged around this time. The year 1776 saw the American Revolution, the publication of economist Adam Smith's classic *The Wealth of Nations* and the first industrial use of James Watt's steam-powered engine: thus, the start of the Industrial Revolution. For these reasons, we can think of 1776 as the year when modern societies really began.

With industrialization and the growth of cities that accompanied it, social relations changed markedly. No longer based on tradition and blood ties, social relations became ever more temporary, impersonal and limited in scope. But though social, political and economic life were all changing, they were changing at different rates. This fact of uneven change proved further that social, political and economic life are all distinct, though related. This realization stimulated a systematic study of social order, what establishes and what disrupts it; in short, it set the stage for sociology to emerge as a discipline.

Culture and Acculturation

In the nineteenth and twentieth centuries, the culture of the entire Western world modernized. By *culture* we mean the entire collection of values, behaviours and shared symbols that characterize life in a society. *Modernization* is a complex concept. It grows out of industrialization, urbanization, the increased complexity of science and technology, secular religion, mass literacy and a new public awareness of the world. A modernized culture is one that accommodates these new developments.

According to such researchers as sociologist Alex Inkeles, a modernized culture produces new kinds of personalities: people who are more inclined to plan, reason, treat others as equals and interest themselves in other parts of the world. Modernization expands human horizons beyond past and present to future, beyond narrow interest in self, family and community to an interest in nation, world and cosmos.

Other images of modernization are less rosy. Karl Marx (1818–1883) and Max Weber (1864–1920) depicted modern society as exploitive, alienating, impersonal, over-organized, lacking concern for human beings, obsessed with technology and efficiency, faddish and overcrowded with meaningless gadgetry. Modernity, in this view, is a worldwide consumer's market obsessed with the need for material possessions as a proof of personal value.

Whichever assessment seems more accurate, and both seem to apply, Western culture has changed significantly in the last two centuries. Culture is an important part of the context within which a society changes or maintains order. Accordingly, along with cultural modernization, the social relations that make up societies in the West have also changed significantly.

Acculturation is the process by which members of a society learn their culture. It often occurs without planning or awareness, the way people learn a language. Babies learn to speak their society's language without knowing they are learning it. They practise, imitate, use trial and error. Likewise, newcomers to a culture learn cultural values this way.

For example, research by sociologists Bernd Baldus and Verna Tribe has shown that, by an early age, Canadian school children have learned to associate good manners and morals with symbols of high social standing—a nice car, large home, expensive clothes. Said simply, if they see someone rich, they assume he or she is also nice. But where and how did they learn this? Was it from mass media portrayals of rich and poor people, or from unintended hints their parents, teachers and other adults have provided?

Socialization

The second related process is *socialization*, by which people learn the social rules defining relationships into which they will enter. Socialization goes on throughout life, but in childhood the changes are most dramatic and visible. A child is born without any knowledge of social rules. By the time he or she begins school, the child has learned to follow the orders given by people in authority (chiefly adults), to co-operate (chiefly with peers), to accept certain responsibilities and to carry out assigned tasks at home.

Typically, the rules children learn in socialization are suited to values learned in acculturation. For example, in our society children are taught to believe that they must obey authority. They are trained to associate authority with adults, and particularly with specific adults: parents, grandparents, teachers and police officers, among others. By contrast, peers must establish their authority. Since none of the learned bases for authority seem to apply, children often establish authority and rules among themselves by fighting, just as animals do. Once they have established a rough hierarchy, children "know their place" in the playground just as they do at home. For the time being, social order is assured.

Like schoolyards, many social situations lack a clear "definition of the situation." Rules must be hammered out by the interacting group, then learned and obeyed. In other cases, rules already exist, and players must follow the rules even if they conflict with earlier experiences. In this instance, people must be "resocialized."

For example, the worker promoted to supervisor experiences a conflict of values. The worker may have felt loyal to the union and opposed to management, but as supervisor he or she might be more loyal to management and, equivalently, opposed to the union. The very nature of the worker/supervisor relationship creates this conflict. People solve such conflicts through resocialization, and research shows they generally make the change satisfactorily, if not always smoothly. This fact reminds us that socialization goes on throughout life and people prove almost infinitely capable of learning and relearning social roles.

Aging and the Life Process

School children, newlyweds, young parents and elderly retired people lead quite different lives and fill quite different social roles. Maintenance of the social order depends on people learning different age-specific roles; yet, the requirements of these age-specific roles are often quite unclear.

Paradoxically, we usually receive the least preparation for these important and complex roles we play as adults. No one is educated for retirement. Few take courses in being a good spouse or parent. Who needs to pass an examination or get a licence (except a marriage licence) to pass from one of these roles to another? This lack of preparation has serious consequences. High divorce rates illustrate, among other things, many people's inadequacy as spouses, while high rates of child abuse attest to the strains of parenthood without preparation.

The problems of aging and the life process go well beyond marriage and parenthood. Aging brings many life crises in its wake: changes in a person's sense of self-worth or life purpose, for example. We must find our way through the problems of young adulthood, full maturity and old age largely on our own. Many people seek social supports and form groups to help them cope. Some cannot cope socially with these strains and, isolated, retreat into alcohol, drugs or even suicide. Their lonely failure attests to the importance of social bonding for a happy and productive life.

Control and Deviance

Social relations bring restrictions. Social life requires rules. Rules imply control, and control in turn usually implies authority, the right to impose and enforce rules. Unequal authority creates other types of social inequality. As a result, no society, whether capitalist, socialist or communist, can ever be wholly egalitarian, for no society can operate without rules and authority. This theme will be developed at length in other chapters.

An early, surprising discovery by Emile Durkheim (1858–1917) is that every society needs deviance. This statement seems paradoxical, since every society also needs order and deviance implies disorder. Yet, deviance offers an opportunity to reaffirm order by reminding society's members of the limits of proper behaviour. Like warring with outsiders, punishing deviants strengthens social solidarity and group cohesion. In this way, it is a process of social organization.

Criminologists study why particular people break particular rules and give many reasons for deviant behaviour, ranging from chemical, physiological, psychological, up through social and cultural factors. What is surprising is not that deviance happens so often, given the tremendous number of reasons for its occurrence, but rather that it happens so rarely.

Of course, everyone deviates in some way, at some time or another. In this sense, deviance is amazingly common, the norm and not the exception in human societies. Yet, most deviance is minor and hidden. Moreover, deviance is often prevented, minimized or hidden, but not for the reason Hobbes thought. People mainly conform to rules because of acculturation, socialization and an unwillingness to risk exposure to ridicule, criticism or ostracism. It is society, not the state, that is maintaining order.

To say this is not to idealize conformity; often we conform for crass material reasons. We all depend upon the good will and cooperation of others for money, information and other kinds of assistance. Without these, we would find it hard to carry out our social roles, hold jobs or participate in social life. For these reasons, a wide variety of organizations have used excommunication, communal expulsion, the "silent treatment" and other forms of banishment to control their members. The suffering of an expelled member helps to keep other group members in line.

As well, we must remember the importance of formal social controls. These include laws and law enforcement agencies, which punish serious deviations. We shall never know whether informal social controls would be sufficient without formal ones backing them up, because no societies of any complexity have lacked formal social controls. But we should not underestimate the importance of socialization, interdependence and informal control in maintaining social order. Recognition of this fact is one of sociology's central contributions to knowledge.

A Summary and Look Ahead

To summarize, people are gathered into social relationships by processes of social organization. These include acculturation, socialization, progress through the life stages, control and deviance. These processes are similar in social organizations of differing size and complexity. All social systems require that these processes function smoothly. Yet, social organizations of different sizes and complexity differ in important ways. Thus, the science of society cannot be reduced, as some would wish, to a science of human individuals or groups. To move from individuals to groups to societies, sociologists must understand a great deal more than they do about the effects of size and complexity on social functioning.

Opposite page:
Culture in Canada often reflects the ideas of a predominant anglo group, which has often misunderstood the culture of native peoples. As well, native peoples feel distanced from this dominant culture. Native groups have struggled to maintain and assert their culture in the midst of a modern setting.

CALGARY HERALD
COLLECTION/GLENBOW
ARCHIVES.

CHAPTER 3

Culture

HARRY HILLER

Introduction

One of the most popular prizes that is awarded to winners of contests is a trip for two to a distant destination. Even for those not fortunate enough to win, it is not unusual for people to save their money over a period of years to enable them to visit a part of the world that has always intrigued them. For many, travel is an exciting adventure.

What makes travel so exciting? The idea of escaping our usual routines may be one reason, and the prospect of taking in beautiful scenery may be another. Probably the most interesting part of our travel experience will be to observe how people live in some other environment, how they express themselves, what they eat and how they do things. In other words, we want to experience their culture.

Experiencing another culture is rewarding because of the comparisons we continually make with our own culture. Our reaction of astonishment ("Did you see what they were eating!") or intrigue ("Did you see how they reacted when that happened?") or bafflement ("What did they mean by that?") are the result of becoming more aware of how our culture differs from theirs. Upon returning home from the trip, we might spend more time telling our friends about these cultural differences than describing the scenery.

Retelling tales of distant journeys has not only been a favourite pastime of the returning traveller, but has provided unending fascination for listeners and readers for thousands of years in societies everywhere. Explorers and traders were valued and revered because they exposed people to previously unknown aspects of culture and human life. As new worlds were discovered through curiosity, commercial expansion, empire extensions and military aspirations, the desire to catalogue and describe these cultural differences created a climate favourable to the beginning of scientific disciplines to understand culture.

The discovery of new cultural groups by European powers, in particular, created an awareness of peoples at different levels of technological advancement. Furthermore, the influence of Social Darwinism implied that different peoples existed at different levels in the evolutionary process. From these observations, value-laden terms such as "primitive culture" emerged to describe the cultural contrasts that were perceived. Anthropology became the discipline that focused on primitive and non-industrial societies and attempted to understand each society as a totality, from language to food to kinship. It was not surprising that countries with flourishing colonial interests, such as Britain, also had active anthropological interests in global cultures.

Whereas early anthropologists were primarily interested in whole cultures, sociologists, while sharing much in common with anthropologists, were primarily interested in parts of cultures and in cultural differences between societies. Emile Durkheim, for example, attempted to explain differences in suicide rates between various societies by examining cultural expectations in social relationships. Max Weber sought to explain why capitalism thrived in northern Europe but failed in India, and he found an explanation in religious cultural differences.

Global variations in culture may have initially prompted social science interest, but modern sociology received its most prominent impetus from a different type of intercultural contact that occurred in the United States. As a country of immigrants representing many cultures, the United States needed sociologists to help explain and interpret intergroup conflicts that occurred in large American cities such as Chicago and New York. Consequently, sociological analysis addressed not only the cultural differences that existed between peoples physically distant from one another, but also people co-existing in the same society but culturally or socially distant.

What Is Culture?

Culture is the total of human-produced values, behaviours and symbols that a group of people share. It includes morals, laws, customs, beliefs, knowledge, symbols, art, tools, organization or, in sum, the way of life of a people. When people who interact share a culture, the result is a society. A society cannot exist without a culture, and a culture cannot exist unless people interact with one another and form a society.

To understand the difference between culture and society, think of what takes place in a drama. First, actors are needed, people who will play the various parts and interact with each other as required. This is society. But what do they say to one another? How do they dress? What is expected of them? How does the plot change? Culture, then, is the way things are done on the set: the props, the words, the dress as laid out by the script. For a society, the script is the culture, which is determined by custom and tradition. It is "the way we do things here" and is recognized and acknowledged by all. A society, then, is a group of people whose interaction is organized and structured by a culture.

We frequently think of culture as a given—as something that has always been that way. Why is an engagement symbolized by the female partner wearing a diamond ring given to her by the male partner? That is an important tradition in our culture that we may take for granted because that is the way we learned it. But this custom is not found in every society, nor did it exist two thousand years ago. So where did it come from?

It is difficult to trace the origin of most customs, though numerous myths have been suggested to do so. Peter Berger (1966) has proposed what he calls a dialectic to explain how it is that humans can both create culture and follow culture. He says that most of us view our culture as an object that we inherit and make our own. Because its elements have existed for many years, we see culture as the way things are. We then think it is our duty to internalize cultural meanings and traditions so that they become our own. But what this side of the process ignores is that humans create culture. Customs, tradition and language appear fixed and permanent, and yet we are constantly creating new culture through fashion, inventions, new vocabulary and slang and other means of self-expression adopted by people in a society. Berger notes that it is this dialectic of creating new culture and internalizing existing culture that ensures both continuity and change within a society.

Characteristics of Culture

What distinguishes human life from animal life is that we possess a culture. A flock of birds in North America is no different from a flock of birds of the same species in Africa because birds are genetically programmed through instincts that determine their behaviour. Human beings, in contrast, have drives or needs rather than instincts. These drives include the need to satisfy hunger or thirst, sexual drives or the need for rest. What makes human life unique is that we have the capacity to modify these needs and even suppress them. Consider the paradox of living in a society where food is in abundance, yet valuing thinness, as evidenced by a preoccupation with dieting. In other societies, large body size may be valued. Our culture determines how we choose to satisfy our drives or needs. All human beings may require nourishment, but what we eat and how we eat it and even when we eat is framed by our culture. The British may prefer afternoon high tea; Americans may eat an early supper at five-thirty; Chinese may dislike milk but enjoy dog meat; Canadians are likely to enjoy milk but dislike dog meat; and the Japanese eat with a bowl and chopsticks, whereas we prefer a plate with knife, fork and spoon. All of these examples suggest that human beings create their culture. The fact that different groups of people decide to resolve their needs in different ways produces cultural variations.

In spite of the global variations in culture, there is a tendency for patterns of behaviour *within* a given society to be more or less uniform. The young and those who move to a new culture must *learn* the behaviours acknowledged by that culture. Those behaviours are not inborn, but must be acquired either consciously or unconsciously. We learn by watching others and following their example or through formal instruction.

If culture is learned, then it is also *shared*. We learn about our culture by interacting with others. We create our culture in interaction with others. Culture is not something an individual possesses alone, but is engendered and sustained through group interaction. For example, females in some Middle Eastern societies learn to cover all of their bodies with a garment, including their heads and faces, when in public. This fundamental characteristic of that culture is reinforced through mechanisms of social approval or disapproval. If someone violates these cultural expectations, she may be formally punished by the group or experience an informal sanction aimed at correcting her behaviour.

Culture is also *adaptive*. It responds to changing circumstances and conditions. Culture is dynamic in spite of the fact that sometimes it appears static. In this century, we have seen women obtain the right to vote as well as enter the labour force in large numbers. We have witnessed changes in transportation from the automobile to jet travel to space flight. We have observed a shift from an agricultural economy to a manufacturing economy to a service economy. Our culture has undergone enormous changes.

In spite of change, culture at any given moment is not a new creation. Culture builds from a legacy of experiences and ways of doing things that are part of a cultural heritage that is never totally erased. For example, women may have recently entered the labour force, but numerous studies have shown that women are still expected to do traditional household chores and that many men have resisted moving beyond their traditional roles (Lupri and Mills, 1987). Laws, customs and traditions that are part of the earlier eras stay with us over many generations, though their relative importance may change. The meaning of the practice of throwing rice at a bridal couple after the ceremony escapes most of us, and yet the practice continues. It is this *cumulative* aspect of culture that allows us to identify ourselves as part of an ongoing social unit with both a history and a future. It helps us understand ourselves by making us aware of our roots and gives us the guidelines to instruct the next generation. It means that every generation does not start anew, but builds on the culture of its forebears of which it is a product.

Components of Culture

While we speak of cultures as though they are integrated units, they can be broken down into their constituent parts. For example, if we are examining the eating habits of people within a culture, we may focus on what they eat and how they eat it. This emphasis may tell us about their economy and technology (are they hunters, fishers, gatherers or do they grow their own crop?) and reveal what utensils they use (wooden chopsticks and a bowl or metal cutlery and a plate). These aspects of culture are tangible items referred to as material culture. But studying eating practices may also tell us what foods are taboo, who is allowed to eat with whom, and how one is expected to behave while eating. These non-material aspects of culture are less tangible, but just as important to understanding people.

The purpose of this section is to point out that there are many aspects to culture. After exploring the material basis of culture, we will discover that how we communicate (the symbols we use), what we think is important (our values) and how we act (our behaviour patterns) are also expressions of culture.

Material Aspects of Culture

Culture can be usefully divided into material and non-material aspects. *Material culture* is made up of the artifacts, the technologies and physical items such as food that is consumed or tools that are manipulated by the members of a society.

Technological determinism is the assumption that the material or physical traits that predominate in a society will shape its culture. Cultures that use primitive tools are clearly different from cultures that use machines. The invention of the automobile changed our culture, as have the television set and, more recently, the photocopy machine. A technological determinist argues that we become what our technology makes us, for it changes how we think, act and interact with others. One influential form of this argument is expressed in French sociologist Jacques Ellul's (1967) position that technology unconsciously controls us with its demands for efficiency, rationality and know-how. The fact that your car failed to start this morning or your automated banking machine ran out of cash only reminds us how dependent we are on our technology.

There is perhaps no better illustration of concerns over technological control of human life than the computer and its powerful computer chip. Sociologist Sherry Turkle (1984) has studied the impact of the computer and suggests that instead of viewing the computer instrumentally in terms of the work it will do, we should understand the computer subjectively in terms of how it enters our social life and psychological development. While we all realize that a computer is a piece of hardware composed of wires, silicon chips and metal, we are more likely to be impressed by its interactive capacity, for it knows things, it tells us things, it speaks and it wins. Even though we remind ourselves that computers only do what we program them to do, we anthropomorphize these machines so that they take on a life of their own. For example, when things go wrong, we blame the computer as though it was capable of being blamed. The computer may bill us twice or delete us from the payroll, and its apparent lack of flexibility may aggravate and even threaten us: "I'm sorry, sir, but the computer does not list you for this flight." For others, the computer becomes a companion with whom they regularly interact. Some "hackers" are totally absorbed by the computer. Turkle argues that the computer provides a sense of companionship with no emotional demands. "You can be a loner but never alone. You can interact but never feel vulnerable to another person."

Turkle rejects technological determinism because she sees that computer technology must be understood in terms of the social meanings people give it. But she also sees computers as a second self because they are on the border between mind and not-mind and between life and not-life. Some people indeed appear to be mechanically driven by the computer, while others find new freedom and creativity in computer technology. Turkle argues that computers have forced us to think clearly about what it means to be human and what it means to be free.

By examining the reactions of people to computer technology, we learn a lot about our culture. Other material aspects of culture also serve as a useful index of the nature of a culture. Examining housing technology (for example, a thatched house built on stilts in the jungle or an insulated house resting on permafrost in the North), food preparation technologies (crushing wheat in a bowl or extracting blubber from a whale), or resource technologies (plowing fields with oxen or extracting oil from tar sands) all tell us important things about a culture. But they are not sufficient indicators of what makes that culture work.

Non-Material Aspects of Culture

Sociologists regard the material artifacts of a culture as less important than the particular meaning the artifacts hold for participants in that culture. Sociologists ask what beliefs and values those artifacts represent. Or, to shift the focus away from the objects to the people, how do people structure their lives in relation to the material aspects of culture? What agreements order their behaviour, how do they communicate shared meanings and how do they organize themselves to get things done? These are the aspects of *non-material culture* that are its backbone and character: communication, behaviour patterns and values.

Communication: Non-Verbal and Verbal

One of the unique things about the human species is our capacity to reason. This ability allows us to evaluate what goes on around us and to form our own judgments. Because we are social creatures, we do not just keep our thoughts, evaluations and observations to ourselves. Sharing them with others requires a system of communication. In order for communication to occur, we require a common set of symbols that can convey our interpretations of reality. Animals are capable of communicating messages, but they repeat the same message over and over. Humans, in contrast, are able to shape (using tone of voice, facial appearance) and change messages (by the order of words, using gestures rather than words) in a way that reflects their own meanings.

Every culture has its own symbol system, that is, words, objects and gestures to which specific meaning is given. In the Middle East, it was traditionally unacceptable to smile at people in public. A smile was a special act reserved for special occasions and indicative of intimacy and warmth. Imagine the interpretations given to the smiles in public of Western (particularly women) visitors. Other forms of non-verbal communication occur with our eyes and especially with our hands. We can call for help (raise one hand), indicate we are being searched (raise two hands), point in a direction or to a place or person (pointed index finger), indicate to stop (put our palm out in front of us), hitchhike (hand out with thumb extended), give the peace sign (two middle fingers raised) and so on. Some of these signals may not be culturally specific and may help us communicate in a foreign land when we do not know the language. Or they may reveal attributes of our own culture. For example, when travelling in Europe or Japan, North Americans are sometimes frowned upon because of our casual intimacy when meeting strangers. Many Europeans and Japanese are offended when we say "Hi" instead of "Hello," are too willing to shake hands with people in status-superior positions or too quickly try to establish a first-name basis with people.

While non-verbal communication allows for shared meanings and interpretations to occur, it is the verbal form of communication that allows for an unlimited number of unique messages to be transmitted between people. As members of a culture, we are handed a code of symbols (which we call words) that have established meanings. We learn which word to use in which situation and therefore are able to communicate how we feel, what we think and how we interpret something that just occurred. Our language is so refined that we can talk about the past, the present and the future. We can distinguish our intentions from what we actually did, and we can project our interpretation to the actions of others, as well as understand how they interpreted their own actions.

Culture, then, includes both non-verbal and verbal symbols. These symbols have little meaning outside of the significance our culture gives to them. Two lines intersecting may lead people in one culture to think of the religious symbolism of the cross.

In another cultural group, the primary symbolism may be that of the unknown quantity in science, while still others may see the symbolism of Nazism in the swastika. Every culture creates its own symbols and interprets their meanings. As an indication of cultural change, it is interesting to see that the word "wicked," which formerly meant immoral or evil, has now been redefined by youth to mean great or fantastic. Someone who entered our culture for the first time using a dictionary to interpret our language would misunderstand, because the socially shared meaning of that word may vary with who used it and where it was used.

Language, both in its written and verbal form, is the keystone of culture. It is composed of learned symbols that evolve and change. Some symbols develop special significance or special meanings to a social group. If you really want to understand another culture, you must know its language, because it frequently conveys nuances of meaning that are virtually untranslatable.

What is the relation of language to culture? A number of years ago, a principle of linguistic relativity was proposed that became known as the Sapir-Whorf hypothesis (Pinxten, 1976). In short, it suggested that the cultural behaviour found within a society is directly influenced by the language people use, which then shapes their understanding of reality. For example, in the language of the Hopi, time is not

These Croatian Canadians are demonstrating in support of Croatian independence. As Yugoslavia is made up of several different cultural groups, their argument is that Croatians have a distinct language and self-identity that must be preserved as a distinct culture.

CALGARY HERALD
COLLECTION/GLENBOW
ARCHIVES.

objectified as it is in English where time has both an objective existence and is linear. Consequently, this native American group has no conception of punctuality or preciseness. Hopi behaviour, then, is very different from that of the dominant North American society where time is expressed in a diversity of ways in the English language. Darnell (1981) has argued that among the Cree in northern Alberta, speaking is less important in communication than listening, pausing or being silent and that this produces considerable misunderstanding in interacting with other groups.

Clearly, the structures of different languages do exert some influence on the thinking of speakers, but it is also possible to note that language interprets and expresses the experience of a cultural group. In fact, sociologists tend to emphasize that language is the product of group life. We create new words with new meanings when our experiences change. So it is that computer programmers have a whole new vocabulary of jargon to describe their activities.

An analysis of language tells us important things about the nature of a society. Language reveals our sexual biases (for example, postman, fireman, policeman), but

The Language of the Computer Culture

Computers not only reshape our culture by changing the way people work and how they live (such as working at terminals or allowing computer surveillance of our work habits, providing home security, or even telephone screening), their frequent users also form a culture around computers with their own status symbols, values, operational norms, and, above all, a language with specialized meanings not understood by someone who stands outside the culture. Words like mouse, monitor, dumb terminal, peripherals, modem, menu, or dot matrix express the material aspects of the culture. "Mouse" and "menu" clearly have an entirely different meaning outside computer culture. Other words like bits and bytes, dialects, virus, down-time, or acronyms like CPU or CRT reflect language pertaining to the operation of the computer culture. Further specialization of language occurs with programming languages, such as BASIC, C, and PASCAL that programmers use to "talk to" computers. These make it clear who is part of the culture and who is not.

The wave of new language brought in by the global spread of the computer culture led the government of France to seek French neologisms or equivalents to English words as a means of preserving the French language. Once established, these terms became mandatory for all government agencies and all those doing business with the French government. Just as the computer created new words or new meanings in English, so a similar process was required in French. A few examples of this mandated French terminology follow:

computer—ordinateur
hardware—matériel
spreadsheet—tableur
off line, stand-alone—autonome
keyword—mot clé
hard copy—tirage
office automation—bureautique
software package—progiciel
to debug—deboquer
joystick—manche à balai

Eric A. Weiss. 1988. "An Informatique Vocabulary Mandated For Official Use," pp. 161–65. In Kathryn Schellenberg, ed., *Computers in Society*, 2nd ed. Guilford, Conn.: Dushkin Publishing.

the changes in language reflect changes in our thinking and practices (the growing use of letter carrier, firefighter, police officer). Language usage tells us that certain words are considered crude (breast, cock, sex, toilet) because of the way they are interpreted, whereas other words that essentially mean the same thing are acceptable (bosom, rooster, went to bed together, restroom). Inuit have a variety of words for snow because the interpretation of its quality is important to their daily life, whereas such is not the case for us. Women tend to use a greater variety of specific terms for colours (mauve, taupe, etc.), which reflect their traditional tasks. People who are caught between two cultures reflect that condition in their language. In Africa, for example, pidgin is the word used to describe the mixture of two or more languages that serves as the means of communication between cultural groups.

In sum, language is a verbal code or set of symbols that we learn in order to communicate with others who are part of our social group. The only reason that we can communicate is that we agree on what these symbols mean. While French and English are the names of the symbol system of France and England, it is interesting that both languages underwent changes as they were adapted to Canada. For example, Parisian French differs from Quebec French and an Englishman is readily identified in Canada as having a British accent. Even within a nation, language usage, idioms and accents may vary, expressing important cultural variations. *The Dictionary of Newfoundland English* suggests that the people of Newfoundland have a unique modification of English that reflects the Anglo-Irish and West Country–English background of settlers who lived for many years in relative isolation from other North American settlements. Other words such as toque, separate school and "eh?" represent societal adaptations and idioms that are particularly characteristic of Canadian society as a whole and not found in other cultures.

Language as a Symbolic Cultural Code

Have you even taken a language course? Have you ever thought of it as learning the secret code of a culture? Why should an apple be an "apple" and not a "pomme" or an "apfel"? You can recognize which cultural group a person belongs to by recognizing the special code that is used.

Australia and Canada have a lot in common. Both countries have significant British influences and use the same symbol code—English. Yet if you had a friendship with an Aussie, would you understand this letter?

Dear André:

How are things in Canada? It's been pretty hot here. Just had a cut lunch and a spider and I feel better now. This avo I'll have either a cuppa with a bikkie or a tinnie. Will put my togs and jumper in the boot and drive down the bitumen quick smart to look for a beach. Better watch out though for those sleepers and that panel beater on the way. Got a stitch and a cork last time I went. Coming home I'll pick up a joint or silversides and maybe a capsicum or two. When are you coming to visit? Soon, I hope. Good on you, mate!

Without a means to communicate, a culture could not exist. The meanings that are given to symbols are critical to understanding a culture and interaction within that culture. The sociological perspective that studies human behaviour as a complex web of interpreted communication is known as *symbolic interactionism*. The primary focus of this perspective is on the meanings people give to their own actions and the actions of others. By understanding both the symbol system and the interpretations given to action within that system, we understand more clearly what a culture is about.

Patterns of Behaviour   If communication within a culture is ordered and not random, and serves as the basis for action, then it is also important to understand what structures behaviour within a society. Behaviour as well is not random and unpredictable; rather, each society expects its members to act in certain accepted ways that are typical of that culture.

As discussed in Chapter 1, sociologists use the term *norms* to refer to the guidelines that a society gives to its members about what is considered acceptable behaviour. Norms do not always reflect how people *do* act, but they do make explicit how people *should* act. For example, the norm in your class is that students are expected to concentrate on what the professor is saying and to take notes of appropriate points. That norm will not prohibit some students from daydreaming or talking or writing notes to their neighbour. Nevertheless, the expectation is clear about what is considered normative behaviour (behaviour according to the rules). Without norms, our society would disintegrate.

Some norms are so important to the structure of a society that we create institutions around them. For example, our expectation that learning is necessary to our culture is reflected in the establishment of educational institutions that all children are required to attend. An *institution* is an orderly, enduring mechanism for ensuring greater uniformity of behaviour by perpetuating norms learned in the broad interests of a society. Our society has political, religious and economic institutions. Even the family can be considered an institution. Individually or together, they form a normative structure that shows our shared expectations of what behaviour should be like.

Not all norms are of equal importance in a society. Some norms, such as excusing yourself when you belch, may be considered good manners, but are not of the same substance as norms about murder. Consequently, we distinguish two types of norms: mores and folkways. A *more* (pronounced mor-ay) is a norm that is essential for the survival of a society. Conformity to these types of norms is usually not optional but is severely sanctioned with harsh punishment. Mores are usually enacted into laws as a society attempts to clearly structure the obligations and responsibilities of its members. A society would soon be chaotic if there were not strict norms about taking other people's lives or taking their possessions. The survival of our society may also be directly related to the responsibility parents take for raising their children properly. We do have high-order norms to clarify our expectations about child rearing (some of which are codified into law), but we do not bring sanctions or punishments to bear for these mores as often as we could.

A lower-order norm is referred to as a folkway. A *folkway* is a typical or traditional form of conduct of minor moral significance to which conformity is not imperative. Folkways are customs that we learn as children or through experience. If we violate a folkway, people may laugh or turn away or even be offended, but the violation does not normally threaten society. After a sneeze, in our society, we learn to say excuse me, whereas we seldom say anything when we cough. Why are our norms different when both actions have similar effects? We do not belch loudly in the presence of a host after a meal as a way of showing our appreciation, although this is the custom in other societies. When students finish certain levels of their schooling, they dress up in special gowns and caps and a graduation ceremony is held. As a custom, it is a folkway that is looked upon with favour, but it is certainly not imperative for the survival of the society.

Table Manners

"Put your food on a thick slice of bread [plates are not typical]. Cut your meat with the cleaned knife which you carry with you but which is placed on your right by your goblet. When eating, it is most refined to use only three fingers. Everyone from the King and his court to the peasants eat with the hands. If you cannot swallow a piece of food, turn around discreetly and throw it somewhere. Do not be afraid of vomiting but it is foul to hold the vomit in your throat. Fools who value civility more than health should repress natural sounds."

This passage is adapted from a short treatise on manners by Erasmus that appeared in 1530 and had enormous circulation. (It is discussed in Norbert Elias, *The History of Manners: The Civilizing Process*, vol. 1. New York: Pantheon, 1978, pp. 56–58.) Elias is concerned with the question of how social standards of etiquette

have evolved and notes that contemporary behaviour may later arouse the same kind of embarrassment or repugnance that we feel about the behaviour of our forebears. Traditions that were oral during the Middle Ages were codified into manners in the transitional period to the modern era, which was characterized by social regrouping and increasing individualization. These courtesies represented the imposition of upper-class modes of behaviour on society as a whole as individuals of different social origins began to intermingle. As a form of self-discipline with social sanctions, Elias argues that manners are a form of social control in which feelings of shame and embarrassment lead to conformist habits. Eventually, eating with the fingers became an offensive sight, regarded as unhygenic, and forks were adopted. (Are forks any cleaner than fingers?)

In a society that is dynamic, one of the difficulties may be in determining precisely what the norms are or in at least clarifying them. *Normative confusion* refers to the uncertainty that may exist in a society when its rules of conduct are not clear or are in a state of change. Syndicated newspaper columnists such as Ann Landers or Miss Manners frequently deal with people's uncertainties about what is appropriate behaviour in certain circumstances. Codes of etiquette that were once clear have now been eroded and, in some instances, are being revised. Other more important norms have

In our society, we have mores prohibiting violence against other persons. Yet considerable normative confusion exists over whether violence should be tolerated in hockey because it is "part of the game." In this instance, the referees were trying to separate players while policemen were called in to control the crowd. Should established mores be set aside in hockey games?

CALGARY HERALD
COLLECTION/GLENBOW
ARCHIVES.

been challenged by new ideas about individual rights and personal freedoms so that considerable variation in behaviour is now tolerated and sanctions are difficult to invoke. Changing codes of behaviour in wearing apparel (for example, shifting hemlines or varying tie widths) occur, but they are clearly of a different order than behaviour codes pertaining to sexuality, drug use or discipline and punishment.

In spite of these variations, behaviour in every society takes place within a framework that is unique to that culture. The methods used in Sweden, the Soviet Union and the United States to resolve these ambiguities are shaped by cultural traditions that are transmitted from one generation to another and are therefore at least somewhat specific to the culture of each country. Therefore, a very important requirement in understanding a culture is that we understand the expectations for behaviour or the norms that guide how people relate to one another.

Values   Values form the third of the non-material aspects of culture that stand behind the choices people make regarding their behaviour. In Chapter 1, you saw that values are the criteria for judging the rules and actions within a society. While it might be possible to think of small-scale societies as having a uniform set of values that inform all activity, it is not possible to identify such value consensus in complex societies. There may be some core values such as democracy or justice or human dignity to which most people pay allegiance, but the values become less defined and the norms that result from the values become more diverse as the society becomes more complex. The values of an Old Order Mennonite group in Ontario are clearer and more distinct than the values of Canadian society as a whole.

In attempting to identify the differences between American and Canadian society, S. M. Lipset (1986) outlined values that he thought explained the essential contrasts between the two societies. While Canada and the United States have much in common, Lipset sees a different set of values in Canada as a consequence of this country's early history. For example, the British conquest of an existing French settlement in Canada required an accommodation between these two ethnic groups that caused francophones to withdraw into rural Quebec away from centres of power. Perhaps most important, however, the Canadian rejection of the American War of Independence meant that Canada embraced British values and traditions, whereas the United States charted a new set of values as reflected in the Declaration of Independence and the Constitution. According to Lipset, both of these experiences prompted more conservative values to exist in Canadian society. In comparison to liberal values such as achievement and individualism, which became central ideals in the United States, Canada has been more elitist, law abiding, statist (more power given to governments) and collectivity oriented (sharing resources). In other words, Canada was a more traditional society because it retained Old World values and then modified them to the Canadian situation.

Lipset's argument is frequently considered unsatisfactory because it deals with values, which are often regarded as less important than realities such as economic factors. Furthermore, to try to identify overarching values for a society as diverse and far-flung as Canada could be compared to "whistling into the wind." There is also debate over whether the terms "conservative" and "liberal" are really the appropriate labels for the two countries since, depending on the definition utilized and the issues at hand, the labels might be more appropriately reversed. But Lipset has raised an intriguing question about how societal experiences may shape different values and how these values then serve as principles for societal action. Are there a core of society-wide values embraced by members of this society, which we may even hold unwittingly? Or is it more accurate to identify competing values held by different groups in Canada, each of which clamours for pre-eminence?

There are substantial value differences within Canadian society. Values may be different depending on region, social class position, ethnicity or religious affiliation. Values may be personally idiosyncratic, may be shared with others in an organized group or informal group, or may be carefully articulated in a belief system. Regardless of where these values originate, we do know that they affect the behaviour choices we make, and that the values we share form, in combination, the cultural quilt that is characteristic of our society.

Culture as a Mirror of Society

If symbols, behavioural patterns and values are the backbone and substance of culture, it appears that culture can be analysed as an independent commodity, that is, that culture stands above a society informing its members how to act. From this point of view, culture shapes society. This is the *idealist view of culture*. It emphasizes the impact downward from the culture to the society. The idealist view regards culture as a creative product that influences the lives of people. What is the effect of rock music on society? When the followers of Martin Luther King sang "We Shall Overcome," how did that song move them to action? What is the impact of computers? How do they enable a society to get things done more efficiently? These impact-type questions are typical of the *functionalist* understanding of culture, which looks for the influence that cultural products have on the social order.

The opposing position is that, as a product of society, culture is a mirror of that society (Peterson, 1979). It reveals underlying tensions and represents the ideals of the dominant group in that society. This approach is more *materialist* in nature and is typical of the *conflict* perspective. If a society is composed of groups with different and competing ideas, then the dominant culture will reflect the ideas of the dominant group, which is known as cultural capital. Or, to put it another way, cultural products will be shaped by the social context in which they are produced. Conflict theorists are interested in how the popularity of particular comics, music or movies (who likes them? what is it about them that is preferred? what message do they convey?) reflects underlying tensions found within a society. Who sang "We Shall Overcome" and why was it meaningful to them? Why are the lyrics of a rock song popular and for whom is it popular, and who decided what songs should be promoted? The important thing about such music, then, is not so much how it affects people, but what its popularity says about the nature of that society, and why it is popular with a particular segment of society. All of these questions suggest that an analysis of culture reveals important aspects of the state of a society and, particularly, the relationships of power that exist among its constituent groups.

Probably the most helpful way to resolve the disagreement between the functionalist and conflict approaches is to combine them in a way that embeds the culture within a society and yet gives it considerable autonomy once it is placed in a context. Marvin Harris (1979) has proposed a theory of cultural materialism that roots culture in a specific environment where concern for subsistence and survival serve to organize activities. The focus on production (economic subsistence) and reproduction (ensuring the population can be supported) leads to an economy supported by orderly relationships. The sociocultural practices that result are restricted by the needs to produce and reproduce, but apart from those restraints, people respond with considerable creativity.

To illustrate, Harris (1981) argued that families once had a very strong procreative function because, for agriculturalists, children were economically valuable. However, in urban industrial society, large families are an economic cost, so a shift took place toward a new emphasis not on procreation but on personal sexual gratification. Thus, our ideas about families as a cultural form began to change in response to different conditions. But the cultural practices that emerge from that situation are diverse. For example, some may retain the traditional family form with the father as the wage earner and the mother as the caregiver. Others may modify this form through dual parental careers or even choose to be childless. Still others may redefine marriage more as a friendship to be discarded when the friendship pales. The possibilities are numerous within the same set of circumstances, and this is where choices are made.

Clearly, our culture is rooted in the society from which it emerges and reflects the conditions found therein. But culture also reflects the human capacity for creativity amid those conditions. Recognition of this duality is lost unless we take a balanced approach toward understanding culture.

Evaluation of Culture

We learn about our culture through daily social contacts, so we normally take our culture for granted. It is not until we are exposed to other cultures that we even become aware of the distinctive aspects of our own culture. Reading accounts of life in other cultures or travelling to distant lands not only helps us to understand other cultures, but also makes us aware of how different our culture is from the cultures of other nations.

Culture is what makes you a stranger away from home. Being with people who share your culture means that you act automatically within the range of options your culture specifies. However, when you are in a different culture, you struggle to understand what the expectations are. Direct exposure to an alien society can produce a disturbing feeling of disorientation and frustration known as *culture shock*. The bewilderment that results from being unfamiliar with customs and expectations and of feeling different or foreign can produce considerable discomfort.

The severity of culture shock experienced depends on how wide the *cultural distance* is between your culture and the foreign culture. An anglophone Canadian who travels to Great Britain is not likely to experience as much culture shock as one who travels to Japan, where unfamiliarity with the language and its script and cultural practices pertaining to eating and bathing may prove disorientating. The severity of culture shock also depends on how limited our experiences are with other cultures. The more a person travels abroad, the less culture shock is experienced. The longer we are exposed to a new culture, the more familiar we become with it and the more we are able to adapt our behaviour accordingly. *Acculturation* is the process of acquiring new cultural traits through the course of cultural contact.

Travel in itself is not necessarily broadening. Tourist hotels and tour buses do not necessarily mean the tourist has really experienced anything different in spite of the rolls of film brought home. It is possible for people to insulate themselves from the real substance of another culture by constantly evaluating that foreign culture in terms of the premises and practices of their own culture. Quick judgments that are made about how other people do things often reflect a disposition to evaluate the other culture by the standards of our own culture. This is known as *ethnocentrism*. We are all ethnocentric to an extent. Whether we like it or not, our own cultural values predispose us to preferring cultural practices with which we are familiar.

In an attempt to control ethnocentrism, social scientists frequently advocate the idea of *cultural relativity*, that each culture should be understood and accepted on its own terms and not evaluated by some external standard. This is particularly difficult when a culture engages in a practice that we find abhorrent. For example, the Yanomamo of northern Brazil place the old and seriously ill in a cave and then barricade the entrance leaving the people to die (Shalinsky and Glascock, 1988). This is not considered murder in their culture, but is defined as a ritual transition. While we cannot avoid our own cultural biases, we should try to understand the meaning of beliefs and practices within a culture and to exercise care in projecting our own interpretations on the behaviour of people from other cultures.

Subculture and Counterculture

We frequently speak as if culture is defined by national boundaries, but it is clear that as societies increase in size they encompass variations in cultural themes from dialects to life-style practices, to beliefs and values. Furthermore, as the result of migration and other population movements, people take their cultural practices and identities with them. The implication of both of these observations is that as human diversity increases within a society, so also will cultural diversity increase.

While we may look for an overarching culture that ties all members of a society together, considerable national fragmentation exists. Consider South Africa with its race and class divisions into two cultural groups. Consider the sense of ethnic and regional distinctiveness among the Basques in Spain, the French and the Dutch in Belgium, or ethnic communities or even motorcycle gangs in Canadian cities. Contrast the life style, language and beliefs of a business executive with those of a blue-collar auto-assembly worker. Each of these illustrations suggests that a singular national culture, if it exists at all, may be highly fragmented by smaller social groups with their own norms, language or values.

When a segment of society possesses its own distinctive language, values or social norms, we speak of it as a *subculture*. A subculture is still part of the larger cultural system. When the beliefs, values and behaviour of a group differ radically from those of the dominant culture and, indeed, imply rejection of the dominant culture, the result is a *counterculture*. Subcultures can be based on differences such as ethnicity, occupation, age or social class. Countercultures can range from hippie communes to Marxist/Leninist groups to Hutterites. In general, subcultures and countercultures both reflect a society's increasing complexity.

Wolf and Young (1983) studied an outlaw motorcycle club in western Canada known as the Rebels. Categorizing them as a deviant subculture, the researchers

Graffiti and Street Subculture

Graffiti contains profound social, psychological, and cultural information worthy of serious attention—not triviality to be ignored. Nowhere is this fact better illuminated than in the graffiti of homeless youth . . . .

For 6000 years humans have been known to communicate through graphic imagery. Cuneiform characters on clay in Mesopotamia, writings on stone in Assyria, Babylonia, and Persia, and dendroglyphs on trees in Europe and North America provide specific examples. Generations of archaeologists have provided perspectives on the wall writings of the past back to the stylus of Pompei; social scientists have only recently focused on contemporary graffiti. Sociologists, for example, consider graffiti to be evidence of social change and unrest, a representation of shifting conditions. Psychologists believe it is a communicative process whereby people give form to their thoughts. It is also seen as a substitute for more violent actions . . . .

To understand the graffiti of street teenagers, we first have to understand the plight of homeless youth . . . . Many were cast out of their homes or thrown away by parents or other family members . . . .They flee turbulent households racked by conflict, violence, indifference, and, in a large number of cases, social abuse . . . .

We best understand a culture or social organization within its ecological setting and with reference to the milieu in which it operates. The graffiti are the most graphic expressions and by-products of the culture of the street. We confront what street youth reveal about their lives in the marks they leave.

Excerpted from G. Cajetan Luna. 1987. "Welcome To My Nightmare: The Graffiti of Homeless Youth." *Transaction: Social Science and Modern Society* 24(6) : 73–78.

discovered that the Rebels maintained their image as a tightly knit group in spite of the diversity that existed among the members. While outlaw bikers can be viewed as symbolic of individual freedom and the rejection of middle-class ideals, they are considered outlaw only in the sense that they are not registered with the Canadian Motorcycle Association. Tattoos, black jackets and Harley Davidson motorcycles provide a sense of in-group solidarity as a brotherhood that is perpetuated during gatherings at the clubhouse. Biker language such as "riding a hog," "leathers" or "colours," nicknames such as "Terrible Tom" and "Wee Albert," and values regarding group decision making and the role of women help us identify a biker subculture that at times borders on a counterculture. Because they are not self-sufficient or self-contained and allow considerable individual diversity, they must participate regularly in the surrounding society. But when the group felt threatened by external challenges, Wolf and Young observed that internal diversity was camouflaged to present an image of cultural solidarity to the public.

Some subcultures are *convergent* in that they appear to be in the process of being assimilated into the dominant culture. The Italian community in Canada, for example, could be viewed as a transitional subculture for recently arrived immigrants, and after one or two generations the subculture could disintegrate. In general, convergent subcultures lack a sense of hostility to the dominant culture. On the other hand, a subculture can be *persistent* in that its very existence depends on maintaining one or more points of substantial difference from the dominant society. The Rebels provide an example of a persistent subculture, for the moment they lose that element of rebellion they become no different than a conventional motorcycle club.

The Hutterites, in contrast, provide an illustration of a changing counterculture. Built on the presupposition that the evilness of the world required total withdrawal from it in order to maintain their own pristine beliefs, values and social organization, Hutterites formed colonies in agricultural areas based on communal principles. In his study of the dynamics of Hutterite society, Karl Peter (1987) speaks of Hutterite culture as a culture of work performance. Work is a duty performed for personal satisfaction with religious implications. It is not done for material benefits, but for the good of the group. In restricting consumption while rationalizing their economic activities, Hutterites have become successful farmers. But with advanced technologies that they readily adopt to enhance their productivity, a smaller labour force is needed. Consequently, important shifts in their society are occurring, such as a declining birth rate, a drop in the average size of the colonies and a redefinition of traditional roles. Peter argues that the transformation of work patterns from co-operation in social groups to the technology of machines has weakened the fabric of the group and enhanced individualization. This transformation may enhance the productivity of the commune, but may be the seed of destruction of the culture. In fact, it may already be lowering the barriers of the group so that what was once a counterculture may now be taking on some attributes of a subculture.

Status Cultures

The idea that a society may possess a variety of subcultures is known as *cultural pluralism*. A cultural pluralist model assumes that people who possess similar social characteristics will create a similar culture. We will examine pluralism in more depth when we discuss ethnicity. The concept of *status culture* refers to a group that develops around a common social position, prestige level and style of life. A status culture possesses its own preferred forms of activities and behaviour, such as sports, hobbies or music styles (Peterson, 1979 : 147–49). Sociologists used to think that these subcultural groups were synonymous with class-divided societies. Now, it is commonly thought that interests need not be economically based. People may be intensely committed to their corporate work group, a distinctive leisure pursuit or an age group such as youth culture in which class position may be relatively meaningless. People who are devoted to a common interest may possess similar values, norms and language regardless of their class position.

One influential argument tying culture to similarity of condition is known as the culture of poverty thesis. In his study of poor Mexican families, Oscar Lewis (1966) proposed the idea of a *culture of poverty* that is perpetuated from one generation to

As both an expression of ethnic and class position, members of the Austrian Canadian Society illustrate status culture at a Viennese Grand Ball.

CALGARY HERALD
COLLECTION/GLENBOW
ARCHIVES.

another as a rather persistent and distinctive way of life. Children absorb value and behaviour patterns that involve alienation and cynicism about the basic institutions of society, and these ideas become so ingrained that such persons cannot take advantage of changing conditions or opportunities if they do occur. In other words, the culture of poverty perpetuates enduring poverty from which there is no escape.

The culture of poverty thesis sparked considerable debate (Waxman, 1983) because it implied that poverty was the fault of the poor. Perhaps the poor share the dominant cultural values, but cannot attain them due to the structure of society. Or, maybe poor people are not as passive as the culture of poverty thesis suggests and only need supportive opportunities. In any case, there is less disagreement about whether a culture of poverty exists than there is about what should be done about it. Just as elites have their own norms and cultural attributes, so do the poor, and Lewis has sensitized us to how these status cultures can have an impact upon behaviour.

Culture and Society in Canada

We have already demonstrated that culture and society are interrelated. People who interact with one another develop a way of life in common that forms a culture. It is now useful to apply what we have learned to an examination of Canadian culture. Is there such a thing as a distinctive Canadian culture? If so, what are its constituent elements? The question of Canadian culture is problematic because of the structural features of Canadian society. These characteristics need to be examined in order to understand why the matter of Canadian culture is open to such debate.

Understanding Culture: Yekcoh Ritual Among the Snaidanac

Just when field workers think they have visited all tribal peoples and been exposed to all types of cultures, new discoveries are made of poorly understood or previously unexplored cultures. This report represents a first attempt by our research team to provide a summary of some of our initial observations about the Snaidanac culture.

What first drew the attention of our research team to this culture was the discovery of a ritualistic practice relatively unknown in other cultures. The practice primarily occurs at a particular time of the year when the ecosystem undergoes a fundamental metamorphosis, which our field team has labelled "froide" conditions. For conceptual clarification, we refer to the contrasting conditions in the annual cycle as "chaude." When chaude prevails, this practice seldom occurs. However, when froide prevails, the practice reaches unusual intensity. As froide begins to encroach on chaude (a type of overlap period), the practice sometimes produces severe eruptions of boisterous behaviour which is still to be fully understood. At that point, the ritual ends until a new cycle begins.

The ritualistic practice appears to have its earliest symptoms in the behaviour of the young. Children are all issued a type of colour-coded leather foot covering (females wear white, males wear black) which acquaints them with elementary forms of the ritual that, in contrast, primarily involves adolescents and adults. The pre-pubescent phase involves attaining a euphoric consciousness by propelling oneself around translucent surfaces

which are diligently maintained in every village. As far as we can tell, these rectangular surfaces and their enclosed structures are a type of temple which include small cubicles for secret meetings and places for the preparation of the body (such as water purification and the administration of magical lotions). No one lives at these temples, but the devout make pilgrimages to the temple several times a week.

At an early age, the young are given an elongated wooden hammer (actually their shape is difficult to describe), and, almost as preparation for warfare, they are issued head ballasts. It at first appeared to our field personnel that the tribal group was expecting an imminent battle, but rather than use these armaments as a defence against invasion (such as warriors encountered in other cultures), much to our surprise, they use this battle gear in combat against each other.

As the young males mature (females appear to be excluded from the ritual), those who are most successful at this ritualistic type of combat become cultural heroes and are known not just in one village but in all villages. We confirm that their bravery and heroism is incredible, and many lose teeth, break their bones, or have exposed cuts on their skin as a consequence of the intensity of their flagellation against other bodies on the translucent altar. The most successful ritualist combatants are given sainthood through a lottery system that determines the combatant group to which the promising combatant will belong. These combatant groups are often given names from the naturalistic world such as a part of a tree, underground liquids, bush fires, or the names of animals found in their ecosystem.

The most important forms of the ritual take place in enormous temples where many people are present. Generally speaking, the rich and the privileged attend, but physical presence during the ritual is not necessarily important and others participate vicariously. In fact, rumour and gossip seems to carry the ritual to all corners of the society. At the beginning of the ritual, the unity of the culture is celebrated through a song which reaffirms the determination of its members to guard the society from external attack. The combatant-priests (or warriors) themselves seldom sing but wait for a respected deity to blow a mouth-piece signalling the commencement of the ritual in earnest. The significant part about this ritual is that it involves not only the priests of the ritual itself (as in all cultures), but also those observing the ritual. Behavioural responses vary from clapping hands, whistling, glum dejection, or even throwing objects at the combatant-priests. As in all rituals, the locals seem to leave the ritual site feeling much better.

Oblations are usually available throughout the ritual for ingestion to enhance the sense of well-being.

The ritual has a rather uniform duration and occurs several times a week. However, Saturday night is the traditional ritual night, particularly for those away from the ritual centre. The ritual is projected via electronic impulses (a technology which they have perfected) to boxes in dwellings and village centres where adults only are allowed. Here adults sip a brown intoxicating liquid and respond in various ways as the ritual unfolds. As the result of their dedication to this ritual, members of the society willingly give significant portions of their currency so that the ritualist performers can sustain their role as warriors and live a life of ease when away from the ritual field.

The ritual is known to exist elsewhere, but clearly is of much less importance in other societies. A careful linguistic analysis of the phonetic sounds used to describe the ritual has led us to refer to it as the Yekcoh ritual. Further comparisons of this and other rituals need to be made with other societies.

Adapted from Harry H. Hiller. 1989. "Understanding Culture: The Discovery of the Yekcoh Ritual." *Canadian Journal of Sociology* 14 : 225–28.

A society requires people to interact with one another in order for them to have a feeling of belonging together. That means they must share a common territory (locality), distribute tasks and roles so as to develop a web of interrelationships (organization), develop durable patterns of interaction (durability) and be aware of themselves as a distinct and independent entity (self-identity) (Hiller, 1986 : 4–7).

Just because Canada is a politico-geographic unit does not mean that its population automatically forms a society. In the first place, the Canadian territory is so large and its population so dispersed that the societies of Newfoundland and British Columbia, for example, each have their own sense of history and cultural attributes. This suggests that regionalism may be a divisive factor. Second, immigration has been an important factor in the development of the society, and each wave of immigrants has been from a difference source. For example, Germans were a significant immigrant group in the immediate post–Second World War period, Italians in the 1960s and Asians and Latin Americans in the 1970s and 1980s. The changing nature and composition of the society is also demonstrated by the fact that emigration, or out-migration, has also been a significant factor for much of Canada's history until the 1960s. Third, the duality of Canadian society, as expressed by the history of conflict and accommodation between anglophones and francophones, has produced unresolved issues that imply Canada is composed of two societies rather than one. Fourth, Canada's proximity to the United States, a larger society with a more dominant culture, has led to repeated debate about the appropriate level of integration and independence for Canadian society. This problem is further compounded by the fact that even though the national territory is a vast one, most of the Canadian population resides adjacent to the American border, which encourages considerable transborder interchange. Canadian society, then, is not a homogeneous, tightly knit society where it is easy to identify a national culture.

It has already been noted that complex societies are more likely to produce subcultures. In Canada, regional or ethnic subcultures combine with class and status cultures to produce a highly diverse society. What is of particular significance is that as a relatively young society, Canada is struggling to formulate and defend its own culture. It is because the factors mentioned above make it difficult to identify a national culture that the quest for, and analysis of, a Canadian culture becomes so intriguing. Some of the specific cultural ambiguities that Canada must wrestle with are examined below.

The Issue of Bilingualism

Earlier we spoke of the importance of a shared pattern of communication as the basis of culture. Language, in particular, plays a vital role in fostering interaction among people within a society. If there is one feature of Canadian society that perplexes us more than others, it is the issue of bilingualism. Anglophones like to think of Canada as a country where English is the dominant language and other languages are essentially for private use because the British were the controlling group at the time of Confederation. Francophones, on the other hand, tend to think of Confederation as a pact between two founding ethnic groups in which the French language could be preserved along with other facets of Quebec culture. While francophones in other parts of Canada may have experienced varying degrees of assimilation to the English language, the concentration of francophones within the territory of Quebec allowed the French language to be retained there. Symbolic of the acknowledgment of the two language groups, the Canadian Broadcasting Corporation has both an English language and French language network with totally different programs and even different presentations of the news. In other words, programming is not simply translated into the other language.

Have you ever been part of a conversation with a group of people when two or three people in the group begin to carry on a conversation of their own in a language that the others do not understand? Should this carry on for more than a few sentences, the group is then likely to break up. Why? Because if we cannot communicate with them, our interaction must cease. If you have ever experienced this phenomenon, then you will know what it means to be an outsider. When groups of people in a society cannot talk to one another, then we strongly suspect that the basis for a single culture has been eroded. It is for this reason that Canada's two language groups are frequently referred to as "two solitudes."

As an attempt to bridge this gulf, the federal government passed the Official Languages Act in 1969 to make both French and English the official languages of Canada (Waddell, 1986). In other words, Canada declared itself a bilingual society. But what does bilingualism mean? Because the government supported instruction programs in the language of the other language group, many interpreted this federal policy to mean *personal bilingualism*, that is, that everyone should become fluent in both languages. But the government's primary objective was *institutional bilingualism*, the right to service by both language groups in their own language when dealing with any federal agency. However, the reality of what was occurring in Canadian society was an increasing shift toward *territorial unilingualism*. Francophones assimilated to the anglophone majority in most parts of Canada with the exception of northern New Brunswick, and Quebec, particularly after the passing of Bill 101 in which French was made the only language of that province, became more unilingually French. Thus, the reality of bilingualism based on territorial unilingualism clashed with federal ideas about what bilingualism was, and the result has been considerable confusion and alienation.

From the point of view of a national culture, personal bilingualism by all citizens would be the ideal. From the point of view of the realities of social life, territorial unilingualism within a federal framework of institutional bilingualism is probably most workable. But this latter option does nothing to avoid the two solitudes and what is essentially two cultures. For a society concerned about nation-building, personal bilingualism as expressed through immersion programs is clearly a preferred option, but is not without opposition in both Quebec and the rest of Canada. In sum, the issue of a common form of communication remains contentious and problematic for Canadian culture.

Multiculturalism

When the Royal Commission on Bilingualism and Biculturalism released its report in 1967, it admitted that its hearings had brought an outcry from other cultural minorities who felt ignored and discriminated against. Consequently, the federal government declared support for a multicultural social framework in 1971, but it did so while supporting only two official languages. To assume that Ukrainians, for example, could maintain their culture without maintaining their language violates a basic principle of cultural survival. The policy of multiculturalism must be seen as a political compromise with other ethnic minorities while at the same time implicitly requiring conformity to the two language groups. Minorities may be encouraged to maintain trivial aspects of their cultures (for example, folk dancing or celebrations), but this is not really retaining or building a separate culture. Most social scientists view the realities of multicultural-ism as a type of symbolic ethnicity (the ethnic culture is not part of everyday behaviour) where the real objective is for the minority fragmented culture to serve as a transitional device or a building block in the building of a national culture (Roberts and Clifton, 1982).

Cultural Diffusion

If francophones in the province of Quebec have the capacity to sustain their culture (including language) because they control a political territory (province), then the notion of two cultures rather than one possesses considerable meaning. But does this preclude a Canadian culture from developing? Cultural dominance perspectives suggest that since the anglophone culture has more adherents than the francophone culture, anglo conformity among all cultural groups is the way to build a national culture. This prospect continually threatens the francophone culture. Indeed, the fear of assimilation is at the root of many francophone policies.

The Reality of Bilingualism

A study of Grade 6 students in the bilingual community of Châteauguay, Quebec, attempted to determine the children's ability to confront a world of two languages beyond home and school. Even though both languages were heard just about everywhere in the community, few students were able to recount a real-life situation where they had been forced to try to use their second language outside school. And even when they did have such an experience, the research concluded that it was more likely to occur while outside the community on visits. Few children, then, are forced to speak the other language in any regular or frequent fashion. These children also reported a reluctance to speak the other language as long as bilingual adults were present who served as mediators for them. The study concluded that this version of the two solitudes shows how it is possible to intermix without interacting.

Linda J. Hubbell. 1981. "Coping in a Bilingual Community: Six Graders in Châteauguay, Quebec." *Culture* 1 : 42–47.

There is an alternative to the idea of cultural dualism and cultural dominance. *Cultural diffusion* means that existing cultures exchange cultural traits. In other words, through both deliberate and unconscious sharing in the course of routine activities, a blend of two or more cultures develops. The fact that the school system provides instruction in the language of both cultural groups, as one example, provides the basis for intercultural contact and shared understanding. The existence of two languages on product containers means that we absorb aspects of the other language, even if we do so unconsciously. It is this kind of cultural sharing that has the potential of producing a unique Canadian culture.

Cultural Penetration

Cultural diffusion implies a two-way interchange of cultural traits. But cultural dominance implies that such exchange is unlikely to be equal because some cultural groups are stronger than others. Nowhere is this issue clearer than in Canada's relationship with American society. Because of the economic strength of the United

Oktoberfest is a German tradition that has been adopted throughout the world. Many Canadian communities have begun their own Oktoberfest celebrations either as a response to their residents of German descent or merely as an excuse to celebrate. Both processes of cultural diffusion and cultural change are illustrated.

CALGARY HERALD COLLECTION/GLENBOW ARCHIVES.

States and its influence in various sectors from technology to entertainment, the question is whether it is possible to build and sustain a Canadian culture more or less independent from the United States. This unequal exchange in a one-way direction from the more dominant culture is known as *cultural penetration*. We watch American movies, prefer American entertainers and watch American television to such an extent that cultural differences between the two societies are blurred. Therefore, one of the repeated issues in Canadian society is the impact of Americanization on an independent Canadian identity.

Cultural Change

No modern society is static; rather, change is continually occurring as adaptations are made to new stimuli, as innovations are instituted and as groups within a society advocate alternative cultural forms. *Cultural change* refers to any alterations in the elements and patterns of culture.

Raymond Breton (1984) has argued that one of the reasons Canadian society is in such turmoil in the current era is that our cultural symbols are in a state of considerable change. In the post-war era, it became increasingly clear that the vision of a "British-type society" was unrealistic as a consequence of the growing multicultural character of Canada and in particular the emergence of more carefully articulated francophone interests. Therefore, changes in the symbolic system began to occur in areas such as language, the devaluation of the British monarchy, the desire for minority representation in the civil service, the adoption of a national flag, the decision about metrication and the repatriation of the Constitution, each of which contributed to significant changes in the definition of what Canadian society and its culture was all about. Breton observes that these changes threatened to reallocate status among segments of the society and resulted in conflicts over whose conceptions of the national identity would prevail. Cultural change may take many forms, such as the impact of new technologies or new economic practices (for example, free trade), but it is clear that the change over what constitutes Canadian identity at the symbolic level is one change that will have great significance for Canadian culture.

By raising the idea of Canadian culture as problematic, this certainly does not imply that the residents of Canada have no culture. We have already established that when people interact in a society, they will create a culture. However, we have identified some special factors that make it difficult to speak of a national culture that is unique and collectively shared. At the same time, it is in the way we deal with these problems that the uniqueness of our culture is expressed. Cultural dualism, bilingualism, Americanization and regionalism, for example, all cause debate and controversy, which in turn produces a cultural response that is distinctively this society's solution to these vexing issues. It may be that Canadian culture will always possess this elusiveness, but at the same time, it clearly represents the Canadian way of life.

Summary

Culture is formed through the interaction of people in a society. Culture is not inborn, but is learned, socially shared, adapted and cumulative. It has both material and non-material aspects, of which latter group communication, behaviour patterns and values are of particular sociological significance. Our own culture provides us with a lens to filter the social practices and customs of other cultures when we are exposed to them. Furthermore, even in our own society, we encounter cultural differences, which are identified as subcultures. While it is frequently difficult to speak of a national culture when numerous subcultures exist, people who share a geographic and political territory do develop their own way of life. The idea of a Canadian culture encounters a number of special problems, and Canadians have evolved their own unique way of dealing with these problems, thereby producing a society with cultural distinctiveness.

Suggested Readings

Audley, Paul
    1983. *Canada's Cultural Industries*. Toronto: Lorimer. This book presents a discussion of the broadcasting, publishing, recording and film industries in Canada.

Brake, Michael
1980. *The Sociology of Youth Culture and Youth Subculture*. London: Routledge and Kegan Paul. This book examines British youth culture as the expressive use of style, focusing on special language and appearance from teddy boys to skinheads.

Crean, S. M.
1976. *Who's Afraid of Canadian Culture?* Don Mills: General. Crean presents a spirited argument in favour of Canadian culture and attacks the forces that threaten it.

Harris, Marvin
1978. *Cows, Pigs, Wars and Witches: The Riddles of Culture*. New York: Random House. This is an interesting attempt to explain distinctive elements of cultures, such as the sacred cow in India. Harris uses an environmental model to explain them.

Mandel, Eli, and David Taras, eds.
1987. *A Passion for Identity*. Toronto: Methuen. This book is a compendium of essays dealing with issues fundamental to Canadian culture from cultural dualism to continentalism to regionalism.

McLuhan, Marshall
1965. *Understanding Media*. New York: McGraw-Hill. McLuhan develops his famed thesis about the world becoming a global village by showing how electronic connections are changing the nature of our culture.

Discussion Questions

1. How do you react when you encounter another language or cultural group? How acceptant are you of cultures different from your own? Why?

2. What does the content and nature of rock music tell you about your society? Why do you think it is popular? Is it an important part of our culture?

3. To what extent is there a subculture of poverty? Does your interpretation of the existence of such a subculture blame the victim or excuse the victim?

4. Do you think there is such a thing as a Canadian culture, or has the combination of our ethnic diversity, Americanization, our colonial ties and our regional identities made a mockery of the idea? Do you think the federal government should do more to create a Canadian culture? If so, what?

5. How would you resolve the issues of trying to build Canadian culture in a society with two language groups? How can two languages be simultaneously maintained without offending anyone?

Data Collection Exercises

1. Analyse any subcultural group in your community. Interview its participants for evidence of the non-material aspects of their subculture and engage in observation for evidence of the material aspects of their subculture.

2. Find evidence of the Americanization of some aspect of Canadian culture. For example, analyse the range of television programs and their contents in a given evening available to viewers in your community. Does the evidence of Americanization that you discover make any difference to Canada?

3. Interview five people in each of two different age groups and ask them whether they think it is important to be fluent in both of Canada's official languages. Analyse the reasons given in their responses. What does this tell you about the prospects for a society in which both language groups will understand each other?

4. List all the ways cultural diffusion has taken place between francophone culture and anglophone culture. For example, how have anglophones even unwittingly become more knowledgeable about French language and culture?

Writing Exercises

1. Assuming you are anglophone, read any book about Quebec or francophones and write an essay discussing the extent to which francophones have a distinct culture.

2. Read the *Report of the Royal Commission on Bilingualism and Biculturalism*. Write a summary of its conclusions, describe what you find most interesting, and assess whether the report has really had an impact on our daily life from the perspective of twenty years later.

3. Write a report of your experience with cultural shock or ethnocentrism in another country or perhaps even in another part of Canada where you have travelled. If you have not travelled yourself, interview someone who has had such an experience.

4. Read a syndicated columnist such as Ann Landers over a two-week period and write an essay of the norms that are represented in the letters and advice given. Why would people want to clarify norms through such a column?

Glossary

Acculturation: *the process of acquiring new cultural traits through cultural contact.*

Counterculture: *a social group in clear rejection or rebellion from the dominant culture.*

Cultural change: *any alterations in the elements and patterns of an existing culture.*

Cultural diffusion: *the exchange of cultural traits between societies of different cultural characteristics.*

Cultural distance: *the degree of unfamiliarity one feels when encountering another culture.*

Cultural penetration: *the unequal exchange of cultural traits in a one-sided direction from a more dominant culture.*

Cultural relativity: *understanding and accepting each culture on its own terms rather than imposing an external standard.*

Culture: *the total of human-produced values, behaviours and symbols that a people share who interact with one another.*

Culture shock: *feeling of disorientation, bewilderment or frustration that results from exposure to an unfamiliar society.*

Ethnocentrism: *evaluating another culture by the standards of our own culture, which is deemed superior.*

Folkway: *a typical form of conduct of lesser moral significance to which conformity is not imperative.*

Institution: *an orderly, enduring mechanism for perpetuating norms considered in the broad interests of society.*

Institutional bilingualism: *the right to service by both official language groups in their own language when dealing with any federal agency.*

Language: *learned symbols, both written and spoken, shared by a cultural group that allow communication to occur.*

Material culture: *the artifacts created by members of a society.*

More: *a norm essential for the well-being or survival of a society.*

Multiculturalism: *an official policy tolerating and encouraging all cultural groups as vital to the fabric of the broader society.*

Non-material culture: *the meanings, expectations and beliefs shared by members of a society.*

Normative confusion: *the uncertainty existing in a society when its rules of conduct are not clear or are in a state of change.*

Personal bilingualism: *all members of a society display reasonable fluency in the two official languages.*

Status culture: *a social group that develops around a common social position, prestige level and/or style of life.*

Subculture: *a segment of a society with its own normative system, but subsumed under the larger cultural system.*

Symbolic ethnicity: *retaining fragments of a culture by an ethnic people whose culture is not really part of everyday behaviour.*

Technological determinism: *the assumption that the material or physical traits that predominate in a society will shape or determine its culture.*

Territorial unilingualism: *the tendency for one language to dominate all others in an area and thereby serve as the primary means of communication.*

References

Berger, Peter
   1966. *The Social Construction of Reality.* New York: Doubleday.

Breton, Raymond
   1984. "The Production and Allocation of Symbolic Resources: An Analysis of the Linguistic and Ethnocultural Fields in Canada." *Canadian Review of Sociology and Anthropology* 21 : 123–44.

Ellul, Jacques
1967. *The Technological Society*. New York: Random House.

Harris, Marvin
1979. *Cultural Materialism: The Struggle for a Science of Culture*. New York: Random House.
1981. *America Now: The Anthropology of a Changing Culture*. New York: Simon and Schuster.

Hiller, Harry H.
1986. *Canadian Society: A Macro Analysis*. Scarborough: Prentice-Hall.

Lewis, Oscar
1966. *La Vida*. New York: Random House.

Lipset, Seymour Martin
1986. "Historical Traditions and National Characteristics: A Comparative Analysis of Canada and the United States." *Canadian Journal of Sociology* 11 : 113–55.

Lupri, Eugen, and Donald L. Mills
1987. "The Household Division of Labour in Young Dual-Earner Couples: The Case of Canada." *International Review of Sociology* (New Series) 2 : 33–54.

Peter, Karl A.
1987. *The Dynamics of Hutterite Society*. Edmonton: University of Alberta Press.

Peterson, Richard A.
1979. "Revitalizing the Culture Concept." *Annual Review of Sociology* 5 : 137–66.

Pinxten, Rik, ed.
1976. *Universalism and Relativism in Language and Thought: Proceedings of a Colloquium on the Sapir-Whorf Hypothesis*. The Hague: Mouton.

Roberts, Lance W., and Rodney A. Clifton
1982. "Explaining the Ideology of Canadian Multiculturalism." *Canadian Public Policy* 8 : 88–94.

Shalinsky, Audrey, and Anthony Glascock
1988. "Killing Infants and the Aged in Non-Industrial Societies: Removing the Liminal." *Social Science Journal* 25 : 277–87.

Turkle, Sherry
1984. *The Second Self: Computers and the Human Spirit*. New York: Simon and Schuster.

Waddell, Eric
1986. "State, Language and Society: The Vicissitudes of French in Quebec and Canada." In Alan Cairns and Cynthia Williams, eds., *The Politics of Gender, Ethnicity and Language in Canada*. Toronto: University of Toronto Press.

Waxman, Chaim
1983. *The Stigma of Poverty*. New York: Pergamon Press.

Wolf, Daniel R., and David E. Young
1983. "Intra-Group Diversity and How It Is Managed by an Outlaw Motorcycle Club." *Culture* 3 : 59–71.

*S*ocialization

SUSANNAH WILSON

During childhood, members of our family have the greatest influence on our socialization. But beginning sometimes at an early age, child care workers, teachers, friends, and the mass media also help shape our basic beliefs and values.

Introduction

Peter Berger (1975 : 55) called *socialization* the process by which we learn to become members of society. For all of us, this process starts at birth and continues throughout our lives. Because of the importance of early learning, sociologists distinguish primary from secondary socialization. *Primary socialization* occurs from birth to adolescence. And, as Berger points out, because children have less power than adults and because they are unaware of alternatives, early socialization is largely imposed. In satisfying a newborn infant's needs—even such a basic need as food—parents respond within a framework of culturally defined expectations. If an infant is fed according to a schedule, the baby will learn to be hungry at "feeding time." "The same observation applies to elimination, to sleeping and to other physiological processes that are endemic to the organism" (Berger, 1975 : 50). Consequently, while we will all develop individual likes and dislikes, even our early experiences of hunger, pain and comfort are mitigated by the social world into which we are born.

While sociologists have been most concerned with primary socialization, socialization continues throughout the life cycle. *Secondary socialization* is the ongoing process of learning to adjust to new situations. At key transition points, such as entering or leaving the labour force or becoming parents or grandparents, we learn new role expectations and adjust our behaviour to these expectations. Socialization is not a single process, but a series of processes. Because adults bring to new situations the accumulated learning of their previous experiences, including certain preconceptions about each new role, secondary socialization differs from primary socialization in both context and content.

Socialization establishes boundaries of behaviour. Because of this, there are similarities in the way individuals in certain cultural settings mature. But we are all individuals, so people react differently to similar experiences. Some children thrive on routine; others resent it. Some grow up wanting to be like their parents; others react against them. There are fundamentally different behavioural expectations for men and women, old and young. Despite the influence of individual differences, the research cited throughout this chapter shows that there are some interesting patterns in socialization practices and outcomes.

Differences in language, customs and values reflect differences in how we have been socialized. Parents have specific individual goals and expectations for their children, and the socialization of the child will be influenced by these goals. Parental and societal influences combine to form the context of socialization. The context of socialization includes macro-level factors such as class and ethnicity, family structure variables (birth order, number of siblings) and our own and our parents' predispositions. Consequently, how we are socialized will be affected by whether we grow up in Vancouver or Moncton; whether we speak English or Ukrainian at home; whether we worship at a church or a synagogue; whether we grow up in a single-parent or two-parent household and whether our parents are strict or lenient in their discipline.

During childhood, members of our family have the greatest influence on our socialization. But beginning at an early age, child care workers, teachers, friends and the mass media also help shape our basic beliefs and values. The family, schools, peer groups and the mass media are the most important *agents of socialization*. Other agents include the church, community agencies, summer camp and athletic teams. The influence of these groups will vary from child to child, depending on the particular conditions of their individual lives (Elkin and Handel, 1989: 206). In most cases, agents of socialization reinforce what children have first learned from their families. For example, schools support family goals of preparing children for responsible adult roles. Sometimes the messages will be contradictory. The peer group may influence adolescents to question certain family beliefs and values.

In many ways socialization is a reciprocal process. Because early socialization is largely imposed, young children will learn more from their parents than vice versa. Reciprocity increases with age and maturity. Later in this chapter we will look at a study by Peters of the reciprocal socialization between parents and adolescents. Much of adult socialization involves reciprocity as we adjust to new relationships and changing circumstances. Identities and self-concepts are altered by social interaction throughout life.

In summary, we can make four general points about socialization. First, socialization continues throughout the life cycle. Second, socialization occurs in a social context. How we are socialized will depend largely on our sex, our social class, our ethnicity, our religion and so on. Third, it is a reciprocal process. Finally, although we normally refer to parents, the media, education and peer groups as the most important agents of socialization, socialization involves all of our interactions, whether formal or informal, consciously perceived or not.

Primary Socialization

Theoretical Perspectives   As you become more familiar with sociology, you will see sociologists often disagree about the best way to analyse any social situation. This, of course, is not unique to sociology, although it has been argued that sociology differs from other sciences in that no one perspective dominates. In the first section of this book, you read about several theoretical points of view within sociology and learned that the questions sociologists ask, and often the research methods they use, depend on their theoretical orientation. Not all sociologists make the same distinctions when categorizing the extensive body of theoretical and empirical work done in their field.

Some sociologists begin with social structure as the unit of analysis, and others begin with individuals. The difference between them largely depends on what assumptions are made about human nature and the nature of social organization. Dawe (1970: 214) called these two approaches (1) the sociology of social system and (2) the sociology of social action. "One views action as the derivative of system whilst the other views system as the derivative of action." The "action is derivative of system" approach sees socialization as a process whereby individuals learn socially approved norms and values. This approach to socialization is best represented in the work of Talcott Parsons (1902–1980). According to Parsons, socially approved norms and expectations are embodied in social roles.

Socialization in a particular social environment involves learning behaviours associated with myriad social roles—the interactions between which constitute a particular social structure. This view of socialization underplays the extent to which individuals are actively engaged in the process of socialization. The emphasis on individual conformity to group norms amounts, as Wrong (1961 : 183–93) pointed out, to "an oversocialized view" of people. To say that we are all socialized does not imply that we have been completely moulded by the norms and values of our culture.

Symbolic interactionism focuses on the processes of socialization and the ways individuals actively participate in this process. George H. Mead (1863–1931) and Charles H. Cooley (1864–1929), two American sociologists, were instrumental in developing the symbolic interactionist perspective. Perhaps more than any other theorists, these two men have influenced the way most sociologists understand socialization. Both Cooley and Mead were interested in how individuals develop a sense of self and in the importance of family interaction in this process. Cooley believed children were born with an instinctive capacity for self-development and that this matured in interactions in primary groups. Cooley defined *primary groups* as "characterized by intimate face to face association and cooperation" (1902 : 23). These interactions Cooley called "nurseries of human nature." Once infants have gained control over their immediate environment, they begin to develop a sense of self, or what Cooley called an "I-feeling."

Adults communicate their attitudes and values to their children primarily through language, and children understand themselves based on these interactions. In other words, we begin to see ourselves as we imagine others see us. This feeling, "I feel about me the way I think you think of me," Cooley called the *looking-glass self*, which he said has three elements. This awareness involves "the imagination of our appearance to the other person; the imagination of his judgment of that appearance; and some sort of self-feeling, such as pride or mortification" (1902 : 184). Cooley was pointing out the importance of the perceptions of others' reactions to us in determining how we feel about ourselves.

This dependence on the perceptions is not limited to children. Miyamoto and Dornbusch (1956) asked students in a professional school to rate themselves and others in terms of intelligence, self-confidence, physical attractiveness and likeableness. Each student was also asked to indicate how they thought others would rate them. The researchers found more similarity between the students' ratings of themselves and their perceptions of how others would rate them than between their perceptions and the actual ratings given by their peers. The perceived views of others, not their actual opinions, shape our self-concepts.

One important problem raised by Mead deals with how we become sensitive to the responses of others. How do we learn to present ourselves in different social situations? According to Mead, we learn symbolically, through role taking. At first, a child's behaviour is a combination of instinctive behaviour and imitation. This Mead called the *pre-play stage*. Later, during the *play stage*, children learn to assume the roles of others and to objectify that experience by seeing themselves from the others' point of view. In the next stage, the *game stage*, children learn to handle several roles at once and thus to anticipate the behaviour of others. Finally, children learn to internalize general social expectations by imagining how any number of others will act and react. At this *generalized other stage*, the child has a sense of self and can react in a socially approved way. Nevertheless, because social meanings are based on assumptions of others' understanding and intentions, they are always more or less ambiguous and subject to ongoing interpretation and reinterpretation.

Piaget (1932), whose interest was the cognitive development of children, argued that children come to understand with difficulty the perceptions of others. However, recent research shows that children are far more perceptive in interpreting the emotions and intentions of family members, at an earlier age, than the cognitive development theorists say is the case. Dunn (1986) argues that children have an early and sophisticated sense of the emotional states of members of their family and respond appropriately. Based on her research of British families, Dunn (1986:112) argued that by two years of age children have developed "powers to anticipate the feelings and intentions of other family members" and "powers to recognize and transgress social rules and to understand that jokes about such transgressions can be shared with other people."

All socialization takes place in a social context. For most of us, the enduring and intimate nature of family relations makes socialization in the family the most pervasive and consequential experience of childhood. Parent/child interactions occur within a complex web of interactions between other family members, and are framed by the relationships between family members and those outside the family. These are further affected by family size, birth order, family structure and household composition. Patterns of influence are extremely complex and become more so as the child increases his or her contacts to include neighbours, friends and schoolmates.

At a more abstract level, historical circumstances, ethnicity, class and gender affect parental values and child-rearing techniques. For example, it has only been within the last one hundred years that we have come to define childhood as a unique stage of development, and to show as much concern for children's emotional and psychological well-being as their health and safety. So when we refer to the role of the family, the schools and the peer group in the socialization of children, we are talking about twentieth-century conceptualizations. On the other hand, as the discussion later in the chapter will show, anthropologists have found child-rearing values and practices in pre-literate societies are in some ways comparable to modern North American patterns.

Socialization is complex and multidimensional. In many ways it is an umbrella concept because it takes in all of our social contacts and continues from birth to death. Analysis is made more complex because socialization is not directly observable, nor are the effects of parental practices, gender, class and so on readily partitioned. So while some socialization theories begin with the individual and some with the social environment, the relationship between the two is more than accounting for ways one shapes, or is shaped by, the other. Individuals do not experience the separation between self and society the way it is described analytically.

Three determinants of status in most cultures are gender, age and class. In the next sections we will look at (1) how children learn to make gender and class distinctions and to understand the implications of these and (2) the effects of gender and class on socialization practices. For children, adolescents and adults, gender identity and perceptions of socio-economic status are fundamental aspects of the development of self-concept. Gender and class infuse social interaction as children develop physically, cognitively and emotionally and anticipate adult family and economic roles.

Learning Gender   Individuals develop an understanding of gender and a sense of the behavioural implications of this awareness through a complex interweaving of individual and environmental factors, expectations and predispositions. Children as young as two years of age know their own sex and can identify others as being either male or female. Kohlberg (1966) argued that children first learn to identify themselves as boy or girl because they are so labelled. At the same time, they learn to apply the labels consistently to others and to associate physical, social and personality characteristics with gender. However, the connection between this awareness and subsequent behaviour is not clear.

Gender socialization focuses on the processes by which boys and girls acquire different personality characteristics, skills and preferences. Socialization theory assumes that parents and other agents of socialization reinforce sex-specific attitudes and behaviours. However, the relationship between biological predisposition, socialization and consequent gender differences in behaviour is elusive.

Some sociologists argue that gender differences develop because parents react to innate differences. In other words, girls become more verbal because girls are more receptive to verbal interaction. Boys become more physically aggressive because very young boys respond positively to aggressive play. Others argue that parents reinforce behaviour in a way that is consistent with their perception of their child's future.

Hundreds of studies reporting gender differences have been published. Much of the research has focused on the behaviour of infants and young children. Reviews of this body of research, including Maccoby and Jacklin's review (1974) of 1400 studies, find few behaviours that consistently differentiate males and females. The main differences are greater verbal ability in girls and greater mathematical ability in boys. That these differences do not appear until at least mid-childhood suggests that there is a learned component to these skills. In many cases, studies investigating similar behaviours have contradictory results. For a number of reasons this body of research needs to be read with a critical eye (see Wilson, 1986; Henshall and McGuire, 1987). In the first place, there is a bias in the selection process. Studies that establish gender differences are more likely to be published than studies of "no difference" (Henshall and McGuire,

1987 : 137). Typically, studies report behaviour differences without regard to social context. For example, consistent gender differences have been reported in aggression and in a preference for certain toys. In fact, in most of these studies the actual differences between groups are small. Most children are not aggressive, and children spend most of their time playing with toys that are not gender related (Henshall and McGuire, 1987). Furthermore, since boys are handled more roughly from birth, it is predictable that there will be some sex differences in behaviours such as level of activity or aggressive behaviour, which may have more to do with socialization practices than biology. Most adult behaviours do not have clear antecedents in early childhood. The important differences in adults—for example, status differences—are unrelated to the differences typically found in children.

If, as the body of research on gender differences implies, young boys and girls are more alike in behaviour and aptitude than different, why do we find such clear indications of gender inequality in adults? One of the keys to the puzzle is the pervasiveness of gender stereotyping. Despite the efforts of the women's movement to debunk gender stereotypes, most people continue to hold rather firm beliefs about gender differences. Many of these beliefs have little factual basis. Gender stereotyping begins even before birth. The size, activity and position of the fetus are presumed to be clues to the infant's sex, although these assumptions are clearly based on folklore. Male children continue to be more desired than female children. Oakley (1981 : 95) asked British women expecting their first child what sex they preferred. Fifty-four percent said boys, 22 percent said girls and the rest didn't care. After the children were born, 93 percent of those who had boys were pleased, but 44 percent of those who had girls were disappointed. Strong reinforcement of gender stereotypes takes place from birth on. Rubin, Provenzano and Luria (1974) interviewed parents of newborn children within twenty-four hours of the birth. Although the babies were similar in size and other physical characteristics, they were described very differently by their parents. Daughters were described as "softer, finer featured, weaker, smaller, prettier, more inattentive, more awkward and more delicate." Sons, on the other hand, were described as "firmer, larger featured, better co-ordinated, more alert, stronger and hardier." Thus, the stage for gender stereotyping is set within the first hours of life.

Gender stereotypes continue to frame our understanding of the social behaviour of males and females from infancy through childhood, adolescence and adulthood. Small behavioural and attitudinal differences in childhood are reinforced through adolescence and become pronounced in adults. However subtly, people react to boys and girls, men and women, differently, and in the process encourage different behavioural responses. These reactions may be quite unintentional. Parents say they have similar expectations for their children concerning dependency, aggression, school achievement and so on, although fathers are typically more concerned than mothers about gender-typed behaviour in their children. Socialization is in many ways based on nuance and subtlety, and as we argued above, children are perceptive readers of their social environment. They observe patterns of interaction in the home and the gender relatedness of household tasks. Even in homes where two adults are gainfully employed, children will observe that women do more of the routine caring for children than men.

The process of gender socialization is complex. Children are exposed to many models of behaviour and gain a sense of masculinity or femininity from a variety of sources. Furthermore, individuals receive inconsistent messages even from the same sources. In an extensive study of sex-role socialization in Canada, Fischer and Cheyne (1977) concluded that the media are far more consistent in stereotyping women than either parents or the educational system. Hundreds of studies of media content have shown the extent to which women are underrepresented, stereotyped and trivialized by the media. And because children spend more time watching television than they do in school, the media may have a greater impact on subsequent self-concepts. Interestingly, viewers who watch television a lot are more rigid gender stereotypers than viewers who watch only a little (Losh-Hesselbart, 1987:457).

Gender stereotyping of occupational choices has important implications for a young woman's future. Occupational stereotypes frame educational, occupational and interpersonal choices of women, and are the basis of discriminatory practices in education and work organizations. Children have clear views of which jobs are more likely to be done by men and women. Nemerowicz (1979) found that primary-school children had internalized stereotypes that associated men with paid work and women with housework. The children thought that men didn't know how to cook or do housework. Boys tend to have stronger stereotypes, even when their own mothers are gainfully employed. When asked about future occupational plans, young girls typically aspire to a limited range of occupations, most of which are stereotypically female.

WOMEN'S BUREAU, LABOUR CANADA. *WHEN I GROW UP . . . CAREER EXPECTATIONS OF CANADIAN SCHOOL-CHILDREN.* P. 41. CATALOGUE NO. L31-69, 1986 E. REPRODUCED WITH PERMISSION OF THE MINISTER OF SUPPLY AND SERVICE CANADA.

—"WOMEN CAN'T BE MINISTERS BECAUSE WOMEN'S VOICES ARE TOO SOFT TO BE HEARD AT THE BACK OF THE CHURCH."

Ellis and Sayer (1986) questioned over seven hundred Canadian school children about their future occupational plans. They found that most of these children felt that many occupations were open to both men and women. Not surprisingly, the children more readily envisioned women in traditionally male occupations than vice versa. In small-group discussions the children revealed some classic misunderstandings. One boy thought women could not become ministers because their voices were too soft to be heard at the back of the church. Another explained that women could not become fire rangers because if the fire got too close they would have trouble running in high heels!

Traditional Career Choices of Boys and Girls

A very large sex difference was found in the traditionality of children's first choice of career. In the case of the girls, 32 per cent identified occupations that are traditionally feminine, 25 per cent picked occupations in which neither sex currently makes up more than 60 per cent of the participants, and a surprising 43 per cent said that their first choice was an occupation which currently has fewer than 40 per cent women. How about the boys? Their pattern of responses was quite different; 93 per cent have traditionally masculine occupations as their first choice of career, 6 per cent mentioned occupations in which neither sex currently dominates, and only 1 per cent chose traditionally feminine careers.

From Women's Bureau, Labour Canada. 1986. *When I Grow Up . . . Career Expectations and Aspirations of Canadian Schoolchildren*. Ottawa: Minister of Supply and Services Canada, p. 43.

The fact that a majority of young Canadians feel a wide range of career opportunities are open to both men and women speaks well of attempts by the schools to change gender stereotypes. However, while young girls seem to understand that women can do a variety of jobs, they continue to choose traditional female occupations for themselves. "Many of them seemed to be saying, 'Yes women can become doctors, but I expect to be a nurse,' 'Bank managers can be women as well as men, but I am going to be a teller,'" (Ellis and Sayer, 1986:55). Furthermore, the girls' primary focus was marriage and parenthood, responsibilities they did not expect to combine with paid employment. "There do not seem to be any unmarried mothers, deserted wives, widows, or divorcees among the imaginary women Canadian schoolchildren expect to become" (Ellis and Sayer, 1986:56).

Traditionally, it was assumed that gender differences were related to biological capacities and predispositions. However, contradictory findings in studies of gender differences have suggested that male–female differences may have more to do with social learning than biology. It is clear that there have been significant changes in the economic and family responsibilities of adult men and women over the last thirty years.

These changes indicate that behaviour can be modified, even for those whose primary socialization was very traditional. We should, however, as Losh-Hesselbart (1987 : 543) points out, be equally wary of the "socialization copout":

> With the socialization copout, the onus for changes related to gender is placed on the younger generation. Our girls will be raised to be more assertive, our boys more expressive. At some vaguely defined future point, the sexes will be as "equal" as physiology or other restrictions allow them to be. How the gender-typed adults of today will raise the less gender-typed adults of tomorrow is never quite explained.

Much of the research on gender differences is framed in the language of roles. Sociologists take male and female roles for granted, although a number of feminist critiques (see, for example, Stacey and Thorne, 1985) have pointed out that it makes no more sense to talk in such determinist terms about gender than it does to talk about class or race roles:

> The notion of "role" focuses attention more on individuals than on social structure, and implies that "the female role" and "the male role" are complementary (i.e., separate or different but equal). The terms are depoliticizing; they strip experience from its historical and political context and neglect questions of power and conflict. (Stacey and Thorne, 1985 : 307)

Social Class and Socialization

Another important context of socialization is socio-economic class. The kinds of work adults perform and the coping strategies they employ to make sense of their work have fundamental implications for the socialization of children. And, as with the learning of gender, children begin at a very young age to absorb the implications of class in our society. They learn early "who counts" and where they themselves fit in the social hierarchy.

How do children perceive and understand social-class differences? An American study (Lauer, 1974) discovered that even children in grade two could rank occupations by prestige. Furthermore, the children's ranking closely resembled the rankings established in national studies, and the accuracy of the ranking increased with the ages of the children.

> By the time we reach grade six, the rank correlation is nearly .9 and the children are quite capable of legitimating the ranking by reference to occupational functioning, prerequisites, and rewards . . . . Thus beginning in the home and continuing in the school, these children have been socialized to accept the inequalities implied in the rankings and to perpetuate them through legitimating reasons. (Lauer 1974 : 179, 181)

Goldstein and Oldham (1979 : 172) found that while children have little perception of the actual incomes associated with different occupations, even children in first grade have a good understanding of the *relative* rewards associated with different occupations. "With age, correlations improved to the point at which children must be regarded as comparable to adults with respect to their knowledge of such matters."

In a study of Toronto area children, Baldus and Tribe (1978) used pictures and stories to assess young children's perceptions of social inequality. The pictures were presented in sets. The first set showed two men, one well dressed and one casually dressed. The children were also shown pictures of two houses (one taken in a high-income area of the city, one in a working-class area), two different living rooms, and two cars (one old and one new and expensive). Children in grades one, three and six played a game matching the sets of pictures. Children's ability to match correctly increased with age, but was not affected by the children's sex, their school environment or their parents' social class. The children also provided ready evaluations of the two men. The well-dressed man was described as cheerful, nice, intelligent and well liked. They described the casually dressed man as tough, lazy, likely to swear, steal or drink and not caring much about his family.

The researchers felt one of their most important findings was the similarity of response despite social-class differences among children, for these evaluations are keys to the children's self-concepts as well as to their evaluations of others. The results of these three studies indicate the extent to which very young children recognize and evaluate class and occupational differences.

Child-rearing practices and socialization contexts change over time and reflect cultural, ethnic and social class differences. Kohn (1977) was a pioneer in researching the relationship between social class and socialization values and practices. His research has important implications for understanding cross-cultural variations as well. Kohn argued that attitudes to child rearing will vary by social class because of important class differences in occupational experiences. According to Kohn, the key variables are closeness of supervision, routinization and the substantive complexity of work. Blue-collar workers are more closely supervised, perform more routine tasks and work primarily with physical objects rather than people or ideas. Parents with these kinds of jobs emphasize conformity, neatness and orderliness. Typically, middle-class parents are more permissive and place greater emphasis on self-reliance. White-collar parents focus on behavioural intentions; blue-collar parents on consequences.

Anthropologists have used Kohn's model to explain cross-cultural variations in socialization values and practices. It seems that self-reliance is valued in hunting and fishing societies, whereas conformity is valued in agricultural societies (Lee, 1987). Like the middle-class Americans described by Kohn, fishing societies depend on individual skill, initiative, creativity and independence. Work in societies based on agriculture is routine and repetitive and depends on co-operation and conformity: conditions found in blue-collar work. Data from 122 cultures support the assumption that the relationship between autonomy for adults and self-reliance in children is a universal phenomenon (Lee, 1987).

Remley (1988) argues that there has been a general shift in North American parental values over the past several decades. Whereas parents used to want their children to be obedient and conforming, they are now more inclined to want to instil a sense of independence. Alwin's research supports this assumption. Alwin (1984) found that parents place a higher value on autonomy than they did a generation ago. Public opinion surveys done in Detroit in 1958, 1971 and 1983 revealed some interesting differences. Parents were asked, "If you had to choose, which thing would you pick as the most important for a child to learn to prepare him for life?" and were given the following five choices: (a) to obey; (b) to be well liked or popular; (c) to think for himself; (d) to work hard; (e) to help others when they need help. Respondents were asked to rank their top four choices. Alwin found "To think for himself" was the most preferred quality and that the number of parents citing this as most important increased over time. Being well liked was the least preferred, and this became less important over time. Obedience decreased in importance, but hard work increased. The number of parents who valued being helpful remained stable. Studies in Germany, Italy, England and Japan show a similar parental concern for developing independence in children (Remley, 1988).

While parental values may be changing, they are only one part of the equation. A number of factors combine to influence children's behaviour. The fact that parents claim to value self-reliant behaviour does not necessarily imply that children will respond accordingly (Lee, 1987 : 76).

Adolescent Socialization

Childhood, adolescence and adulthood are social constructs broadly defining periods of social, psychological and biological development. These are generally, but not absolutely, determined by age. Adolescence, as Campbell (1975) describes it, involves a period of unlearning as young people develop a sense of autonomy and independence and prepare for adult responsibilities. According to Campbell, the most significant experience of adolescence is "the demise in relative influence of the family as a reference group and the central emotional pillar" (1975 : 34). This does not mean that the family becomes unimportant, but the influence of peers, the media and the school is greater than ever before. Although adolescence has been characterized as a period of rebellion and turbulence, the majority of teenagers experience adolescence positively. Daniel Offer's (1988) study of six thousand adolescents from ten countries found surprising similarities in the experience of growing up. Most adolescents (about 80 percent in each country) were well adjusted, confident, enjoyed life, had a positive self-image and liked their parents. They had positive expectations about the future, and felt emotionally able to cope with the future.

Generally, there will be considerable correspondence between parental and adolescent values (Campbell, 1975). Because parents want their children to be well liked and because they want good relationships with their children, they are generally supportive of their children's activities. The peer group's influence is tempered because parents control "scarce and valued resources," including their approval. Also, early socialization created important cultural boundaries. "By virtue of membership in a family, one is assigned to a social class, to a residential area, to a race, to a moral system, to a religion, to an ethnic tradition, to a social space" (Campbell, 1975 : 43). This is not to say that adolescents are entirely moulded by their upbringing, or that they have little influence on their parents. In fact, many parents may be said to be socialized by their children.

The mutual effects of parent/child interaction is an example of reciprocal socialization. According to Peters (1985), parental socialization (the socialization of parents by their children) will be optimal in families where respect is good and where excessive parental power is not exercised. He also believes that parents' self-image will be influenced by their children's reactions to them as parents. Peters used a sample of parents of undergraduate students to test how adolescents socialize their parents. While several parents responded to questions by saying, "I learned nothing from my adolescents," others said that their children influenced them. The area of greatest influence was sports, although adolescents also influenced parental involvement in politics, leisure and personal care. They also influenced their parents' attitudes to sexuality, handicapped persons, minorities and drugs.

During adolescence, the influence of peers, the media, and the school is greater than in childhood.

As children mature, they increase their contacts and experiences, but these will not be random events or associations. By and large, they will be compatible with earlier experiences. It is, therefore, unlikely that the school environment will be very different from the environment the adolescent already knows. Middle-class children will attend a high school with other middle-class children, who will for the most part value school achievement. Certainly, some students will rebel, but for most young people learning to be independent adults, adolescence is not a particularly turbulent time.

Schools are explicitly charged with the responsibility of socializing young people. High school is probably the most important locus of adolescent socialization because it is central to an adolescent's social life and a screening place for future occupational choice. Yet, much of what is learned in school is implicit. The greater the disjunction between the behaviours reinforced at school and those reinforced by the family or the peer group, the less likely that success in school will be seen as relevant from the adolescent's point of view. For example, young women, particularly if they have been socialized in a traditional way, may feel ambivalent about their future occupational commitment, and thus may not make educational choices that will maximize their future economic security. While adolescent women typically aspire to a more limited range of occupational futures than adolescent men (see Baker, 1985), middle- and upper-class girls are more likely to consider pursuing professional occupations.

Teenage Gangs

At 17, Willy is a veteran of the gang life. A white student at Toronto's Danforth Technical School, Willy already has a criminal record for theft, assault, attempted theft and possession of a deadly weapon—a .38-calibre revolver that he says he never used. He spent two weeks in jail for two of those convictions and is scheduled to appear in court this month on a new charge. He is also missing two front teeth as the result, he said, of being head-butted by a skinhead who picked a fight with him in the school yard two weeks ago.

Willy also said that he was one of the first of The Untouchables and that founding members now called themselves The Originals. Although he is no longer an active member, Willy still has the characteristic Untouchables look—Vuarnet-style sunglasses, black Doc Marten boots, a stylish hooded sweatshirt and a crew cut. "We were immature," said Willy of his days as an active gang member. "It's the young kids who are causing the trouble now because they want to be like us. We're their idols. But we get blamed for everything because we are known as gang members."

From Paul Kaihla. 1989. "Violence is Nice. Honestly. Life in the Ganglands of the Young." *Maclean's* (May 22): 40. Reprinted with permission.

For some young people, however, adolescence is a troublesome time. Lyell (1973) argues that adolescent feelings of ambivalence and low self-esteem occur because, until people enter the labour force, their activities are not generally highly regarded. She used a semantic differential scale to test this assumption. She asked young people to score themselves on twenty-five adjective pairs (for example, active–passive, strong–weak, good–bad), first as they would like to be and, second, as they really are. A high correspondence between these two ratings was taken to indicate high self-esteem. The four groups in the study were: young adult working males and females and similar aged males and females who were not employed. Lyell found that working

Ceremonies such as marriage signal the transition to adulthood.

adult males felt more positively about themselves than the other three groups, all of whom showed considerable evidence of low self-esteem. Thus, Lyell argues, when adolescents are aloof, indifferent or apathetic, we should understand that these feelings result from their subordination to and exclusion from the formal occupational system.

To summarize, although adolescence is a period of turbulence and rebellion for a few, the majority acquire cognitive, emotional and physical maturity with relative confidence. Because life-cycle stages do not follow a predictable or orderly tack, there is no specific point at which an adolescent is declared to be an adult. Some young people will have assumed adult roles of marriage, parenthood or economic independence long before their eighteenth birthday. Others remain in school and financially dependent on parents well into their twenties. Ceremonies such as graduation or marriage may be more appropriate than age as signals of the transition to adulthood.

Adult Socialization

While the assumption that socialization is a lifelong process meets with little argument, adult socialization has not been a major focus of research. Adult socialization differs from childhood socialization because it is based on accumulated learning and previous experience. As we change jobs, marry, have children, cope with middle age and so on, we are continually engaged in the process of socialization. As with adolescents, adult rituals such as fortieth birthday parties signal changes in status.

Many of the changes of adulthood are life-cycle changes, although the fact that we can predict childbirth, retirement or widowhood does not mean that the adjustment will be easy. Adjusting to the changes brought about by divorce, remarriage, step-parenting, grandparenting and widowhood can all be seen as part of the ongoing process of adult socialization. When these changes occur, individuals go through a period of *disengagement* as they change roles. The idea of disengagement has been used to describe the experience of widowhood and divorce, although it can describe any role change.

Socialization for Dying

The final and inevitable step for the elderly, as well as for younger people with terminal illnesses, is death. Until recently in our North American society, death was surrounded by numerous taboos and was a topic to be avoided in conversation, if not in thought. Those who were dying were encouraged to think they would recover, and when they died, others spoke of their "passing away" and "breathing their last." Children were "protected" by excluding them from attendance at funerals and the emotional experiences of surrounding adults. In recent years, however, for social scientists and many in the public at large, the taboos have been lifted. Researchers and popular writers now openly discuss the fear of death; the grief of the dying and those who feel close to them; and the relationships among the dying, their families, and the attending medical personnel. Socialization for death and dying has been given a legitimacy unknown a generation ago.

From Frederick Elkin and Gerald Handel. 1989. *The Child and Society: The Process of Socialization*, 5th ed. New York: Random House, p. 281.

In most cases we cannot anticipate what it will mean to our sense of self to experience the sudden death of someone we love, our parents' divorce or being fired. When we encounter these situations we have to learn new rules. There are, however, occasions when people choose to, or are required to, change their behaviour in rather dramatic ways. This process is called *resocialization*. For example, when families or individuals relocate for school or work, they may find that their previous world view is fundamentally challenged. Companies often expend considerable energy preparing employees for this kind of culture shock. Sometimes resocialization is occasioned by social changes that individuals cannot control, as when the nature of a job is completely altered by technology. Some institutions (for example, prisons or psychiatric hospitals) are specifically designed to resocialize "deviants."

In some cases we can learn to adjust to new situations because our previous experiences gave us the capacity to imagine what new experiences will be like. Sociologists call this preparation *anticipatory socialization*. "Anticipatory socialization refers to training in skills and values that is oriented to a new role that one will enter at some future time" (Campbell, 1975 : 47). The effectiveness of anticipatory socialization will depend on how ambiguous the new situation is and how similar to our previous experience.

The assumption underlying the anticipatory socialization concept is that if the individual is prepared ahead of time for the new role, the sense of understanding the norms associated with the role, having the necessary skills to carry out the role, and becoming aware of expectations and rewards attached to the role, that he or she will move into the new role easily and effectively. (Bush and Simmons, 1981 : 147)

Socialization for Adult Family Responsibilities

Parenthood is an important experience of adulthood, yet many parents are ill prepared for the time and energy demands of caring for a newborn. Not surprisingly, Steffensmeier (1982) found anticipatory socialization had a significant effect on the transition to parenthood. The more previous experience new parents had, or the more they were prepared by training for the experience of parenting, the more satisfying they found it. Belsky (1985) found women more likely to find a disjunction between their expectations and their experiences regarding childbirth, and consequently reported less satisfaction. Given that women assume the greatest responsibility for infant care, this is hardly surprising. While the household division of labour tends to become more traditional following birth, mothers in Belsky's sample were more involved in infant care relative to fathers than either had anticipated, and this was a major source of dissatisfaction. While most men marry, and attitude surveys indicate that men give high priority to family life, early socialization does little to prepare men to be fathers.

Fathers have little preparation for the possibility of caring for infants and young children.

Why are fathers so minimally involved in infant and child care? To some extent, low involvement by fathers is a self-fulfilling prophecy. Fathers have very little preparation for the possibility of caring for infants or young children, and are likely to feel awkward, and thus experience failure in their attempts to help. Research investigating the interactions of fathers and infants suggests that men "tend to avoid high involvement in infant care because infants do not respond to their repertoire of skills and men have difficulty acquiring the skills needed to comfort the infant" (Rossi, 1984 : 8). For Rossi (1984), the solution is to teach fathers about parenting and so encourage their participation. She assumes that men are not more active parents because they have not been socialized to anticipate this role. Recently it has become customary for fathers to attend prenatal classes, assist during labour and be present during the birth of their child. High divorce rates mean an increase in the number of weekend fathers— divorced fathers who have periodic responsibility for their children. These experiences seem to pave the way for their increased involvement in child care.

Socialization for Employment

Professional schools are important socializing agents for adults, and medical schools in particular have been studied in this regard. What students learn during their years in medical school goes beyond acquiring technical skills. They are learning to *behave* like doctors. Some researchers feel that the similarity of attitudes and values among graduates of medical school has more to do with selective recruitment of middle- and upper-class students than the training they receive. In their panel study of Canadian medical students, Chappell and Colwill (1981) found that students recruited to medical schools shared certain attitudes at the outset. Interestingly, these seemed unrelated to social class or sex. Although these researchers do not describe their findings in terms of anticipatory socialization, it seems that a medical student's orientation to the profession begins long before she or he enters medical school.

Seiber and Gordon (1981) introduced the idea of "socializing organizations" as a way of understanding socialization. Socializing organizations include total institutions, as well as schools, job-training programs, counselling centres and voluntary associations. Goffman (1961) defined a *total institution* as "a place of residence and work where a large number of like-situated individuals, cut off from the wider society for an appreciable period of time, together lead an enclosed, formally administered round of life." These organizations are formally chartered to bring about some change in their members, but often the explicitly stated aims are less important than the latent messages they send. "As recruits participate in the organization they learn its social and speech etiquettes, modes of self-presentation, rituals, routines, symbolic codes of deference, and other patterns of social relations" (Seiber and Gordon, 1981 : 7). For example, newly recruited employees must learn what the organization and its members consider to be normal patterns of behaviour. Sometimes there is a formal period of orientation designed to facilitate this kind of learning. An extreme example is the introduction to military training usually referred to as "boot camp." Universities customarily hold orientation weeks where "recruits" are introduced to the informal side of university life.

Much of adult socialization is self-initiated. Some is formal, as in the training we receive in professional schools or in work-related courses; some is informal. Increasingly, formal training is available in areas previously left to the family, the schools or to other agents of socialization, or for which socialization was once taken for granted. Thus, new parents may feel inadequate without training in childbirth and later in child care, and people anticipating retirement sign up for courses in retirement training. When adults join organizations such as Weight Watchers, Parents without Partners or homophile groups, they do so because they seek the social support the groups provide. It is during transition periods that this support is most needed. The consciousness-raising groups that characterized the women's movement in the 1960s provided a supportive environment wherein women could discuss the kinds of changes they were experiencing. Whether adults change as a result of these experiences will depend on the extent of the changes sought and the other demands placed upon them (Mortimer and Simmons, 1978).

Summary

This chapter has introduced concepts used by sociologists to describe the process of socialization and a number of studies that develop these concepts. Generally, sociologists view socialization as a process that continues throughout life, a process that is influenced by all of our social interactions. In the past, some sociologists described socialization as if it were imposed on individuals. Cooley and Mead both helped to shed light on ways individuals are actively engaged in their own socialization. Now, we believe that socialization is not something that simply happens to us. The messages we receive are inconsistent and sometimes contradictory, and we all draw our own conclusions from these competing influences as we establish a life course.

Individual life chances are strongly influenced by structural variables, the most important of which are gender and social class. Gender and social class shape socialization and the development of the self-concept throughout life. The socialization of children and adolescents anticipates their adult work and family responsibilities. The competencies people develop in primary socialization enable them to anticipate, prepare for and deal with the exigencies of adulthood.

Suggested Readings

Baker, Maureen

1985. *What Will Tomorrow Bring? A Study of the Aspirations of Adolescent Women*. Ottawa: Canadian Advisory Council on the Status of Women. A rich analysis based on in-depth interviews of adolescent women and a smaller sample of men. Findings describe the young women's feelings about school and their future employment and relationship expectations.

Brake, Michael
    1985. *Comparative Youth Culture*. London: Routledge and Kegan Paul. A study of youth culture in the United States and Great Britain, with a chapter on youth culture in Canada, and a concluding chapter on adolescent women's expression of youth culture.

Ellis, Dormer, and Lyz Sayer
    1986. *When I Grow Up . . . Career Expectations and Aspirations of Canadian Schoolchildren*. Ottawa: Labour Canada. A Study based on a sample of over seven hundred Canadian children about their stereotypes of a range of occupations and how these opinions shape their own employment expectations.

Hess, Beth, and Myra Ferree
    1987. *Analyzing Gender*. Newbury Park, Cal.: Sage. A synthesis of current social science issues of gender, including chapters on gender and the family and women's family roles in life course perspective.

Richards, M., and P. Light, eds.
    1986. *Children of Social Worlds*. Cambridge: Polity Press. This book contains fourteen articles by British social scientists, who share the belief that children's social development cannot be understood outside the social context in which it occurs.

Sussman, M. B., and S. K. Steinmetz, eds.
    1987. *Handbook of Marriage and the Family*. New York: Plenum Press. An excellent and comprehensive resource for students of marriage and the family. This book includes review chapters on parent–child socialization, the development of gender roles and sections on cross-cultural patterns of socialization.

Discussion Questions

1. Talk to your parents about what they considered to be important values in your early development. What differences do you anticipate in raising your own children?

2. What social changes do you think explain the shift in parental values from obedience to conformity?

3. Ask students who have come to your university from another country what resocialization they experienced in making the transition.

4. Feminists object to the use of the generic "he" or "man" because they argue that people hearing these terms envision a male referent. Alwin's 1984 study, referred to on page 115, contains examples of such usage. Do you think Alwin's results would have been different if a non-sexist term had been used? What if "she" was substituted for "he" in the questionnaire?

5. Generate a list of stereotypes about a designated group (women, sociologists, Scots, etc.) Critically consider each belief. How did the ideas originate? Whose interests are served by their perpetuation?

6. What are the implications of the research finding that there are few characteristics that consistently differentiate very young males and females?

Data Collection Exercises

1. Arrange to observe a group of young children in a day care centre, nursery or play group. Study their interactions during periods of unstructured play. Analyse their behaviour in terms of Mead's stages of social development.

2. Replicate Alwin's study (see page 115) using a sample of students. Prepare a questionnaire using the five values in Alwin's study and at least three independent variables (age, sex, socio-economic status, major course of study, i.e., business, music, etc.). Consider whether to use non-sexist referents ("him/her" or "their") when you adapt Alwin's study. Analyse and interpret your results.

3. Some people argue that the entertainment media provide lessons in "who counts" in our society. When you are watching television, note what power relations are implied in your favourite programs.

4. The underrepresentation of minority groups (including women) in educational materials is a subtle means of socializing students. Compare textbooks and document the extent to which minority groups are underrepresented in the pictures used. You might compare several current introductory sociology texts; changes over time; or comparisons between texts used in various disciplines.

Glossary

Agents of socialization: *socialization influences, the most important of which are the family, school, the peer group and the mass media.*

Anticipatory socialization: *explicit or implicit training in preparation for a future role.*

Disengagement: *the process of adjusting to a sudden change in role, through divorce, for example, or the death of a parent or spouse.*

Gender stereotypes: *beliefs held about the natural capacities of men and women, often with little basis in fact.*

Generalized other: *the final stage in Mead's conceptualization of self-development at which point a child has learned to internalize general social expectations by imagining the reaction of others.*

Looking-glass self: *a concept introduced by Cooley to emphasize how our self-concepts are based on our perceptions of others' opinions about us.*

Primary groups: *groups characterized by face-to-face association and personal co-operation.*

Primary socialization: *the early socialization of children, much of which takes place in a family setting.*

Resocialization: *the process of learning new social roles in responses to changes in life circumstances.*

Secondary socialization: *the ongoing and lifelong process of socialization, based on the accumulated learning of childhood and adolescence.*

Total institution: *a place where a large number of people are cut off from a wider society for an appreciable period of time and where they lead an enclosed, formally administered existence.*

References

Alwin, Duane F.
1984. "Trends in Parental Socialization, Detroit, 1958–1983." *American Journal of Sociology* 90(2): 359–82.

Baker, Maureen
1985. *What Will Tomorrow Bring? A Study of the Aspirations of Adolescent Women*. Ottawa: Canadian Advisory Council on the Status of Women.

Baldus, Bernd, and Verna Tribe
1978. "The Development of Perceptions and Evaluations of Social Inequality Among Public School Children." *Canadian Review of Sociology and Anthropology* 15(1): 50–60.

Belsky, Jay
1985. "Exploring Individual Differences in Marital Change Across the Transition to Parenthood: The Role of Violated Expectations." *Journal of Marriage and the Family* 47 (November): 1037–44.

Berger, Peter, and Brigette Berger
1975. *Sociology: A Biographical Approach*, 2nd ed. New York: Basic Books.

Bush, D. M., and R. G. Simmons
1981. "Socialization Processes Over the Life Course," pp. 133–64. In M. Rosenberg and R. Turner, eds., *Social Psychology: Sociological Perspectives*. New York: Basic Books.

Campbell, Ernest Q.
1975. *Socialization, Culture and Personality*. Englewood Cliffs, N.J.: Prentice-Hall.

Chappell, Neena L., and Nina L. Colwill
1981. "Medical Schools as Agents of Professional Socialization." *Canadian Review of Sociology and Anthropology* 18(1): 67–79.

Cooley, Charles H.
1902. *Human Nature and Social Order*. New York: Scribner.
1962. *Social Organization*. Glencoe, Ill.: Free Press.

Dawe, Alan
1970. "Two Sociologies." *British Journal of Sociology* 21: 207–18.

Dunn, Judy
1986. "Growing Up in a Family World: Issues in the Study of Social Development in Young Children," pp. 98–115. In M. Richards and P. Light, eds., *Children of Social Worlds*. Cambridge: Polity Press.

Elkin, Frederick, and Gerald Handel
1989. *The Child and Society: The Process of Socialization*, 5th ed. New York: Random House.

Ellis, Dormer, and Lyz Sayer
1986. *When I Grow Up . . . Career Expectations and Aspirations of Canadian Schoolchildren*. Ottawa: Labour Canada.

Fischer, Linda, and J. A. Cheyne
1977. *Sex Roles*. Toronto: Ontario Ministry of Education.

Goffman, Irving
1961. *Asylums*. New York: Anchor Books.

Goldstein, Bernard, and Jack Oldham
1979. *Children and Work: A Study of Socialization*. New Brunswick, N.J.: Transaction Books.

Henshall, Chris, and Jacqueline McGuire
1987. "Gender Development," pp. 135–66. In M. Richards and P. Light, eds., *Children of Social Worlds*. Cambridge: Polity Press.

Kohlberg, L.
1966. "A Cognitive-Development Analysis of Children's Sex-Role Differences." In E. Maccoby, ed., *The Development of Sex Differences*. Stanford: Stanford University Press.

Kohn, M. L.
1977. *Class and Conformity: A Study of Values*, 2nd ed. Chicago: University of Chicago Press.

Lauer, Robert
1974. "Socialization into Inequality: Children's Perception of Occupational Status." *Sociology and Social Research* 58(2): 176–83.

Lee, Gary
1987. "Comparative Perspectives," pp. 59–80. In M. B. Sussman and S. K. Steinmetz, eds., *Handbook of Marriage and the Family*. New York: Plenum Press.

Losh-Hesselbart, Susan
1987. "Development of Gender Roles," pp. 535–63. In M. B. Sussman and S. K. Steinmetz, eds., *Handbook of Marriage and the Family*. New York: Plenum Press.

Lyell, Ruth
1973. "Adolescent and Adult Self-Esteem as Related to Cultural Values." *Adolescence* 8: 85–92.

Maccoby, Eleanor, and Carol Jacklin
1974. *The Psychology of Sex Differences*. Stanford: Stanford University Press.

Miyamoto, Frank, and Sanford Dornbusch
1956. "A Test of Interactionist Hypotheses of Self-Conception." *American Journal of Sociology* 61.

Mortimer, Jeylan, and Roberta Simmons
1978. "Adult Socialization." *Annual Review of Sociology* 4: 421–54. Palo Alto, Cal.: Annual Review.

Nemerowicz, G. M.
1979. *Children's Perceptions of Gender and Work Roles*. New York: Praeger.

Oakley, Ann
1981. *Subject Women*. New York: Pantheon Books.

Offer, Daniel
1988. *The Teen-Aged World*. New York: Plenum Press.

Peters, John
1985. "Reciprocal Socialization." *Adolescence*.

Piaget, Jean
1932. *The Language and Thought of the Child*, rev. ed. London: Routledge and Kegan Paul.

Remley, Anne
1988. "From Obedience to Independence," *Psychology Today* (October).

Rossi, Alice
　　1984. "Gender and Parenthood." *American Sociological Review* 49(1): 1–18.

Rubin, J., F. Provenzano and Z. Luria
　　1974. "The Eye of the Beholder: Parents' Views on Sex of Newborns." *American Journal of Orthopsychiatry* 44(4): 512–19.

Seiber, Timothy, and Andrew Gordon
　　1981. *Children and Their Organizations.* Boston: G. K. Hall.

Stacey, Judith, and Barrie Thorne
　　1985. "The Missing Feminist Revolution in Sociology." *Social Problems* 32(4): 301–16.

Steffensmeier, Renee
　　1982. "A Role Model of the Transition to Parenthood." *Journal of Marriage and the Family* 44(2): 319–34.

Wilson, S. J.
　　1986. *Women, the Family and the Economy*, 2nd ed. Toronto: McGraw-Hill Ryerson.

Wrong, Dennis
　　1961. "The Oversocialized Concept of Man in Modern Sociology." *American Sociological Review* 26: 183–93.

CHAPTER 5

Roles and Interactions

NANCY MANDELL

BORIS SPREMO/ *THE TORONTO STAR.*

Social Order

The Individual and Society

Among girls age fifteen in 1981, Planned Parenthood estimated one in six, or 17 percent, would experience a first pregnancy before her twentieth birthday in 1986 (Orton and Rosenblatt, 1986). The remainder of female teenagers have taken measures to shape and control their sexual activity. Once pregnant, a variety of alternatives are available, choices that profoundly affect young women's life styles and financial futures. For example, female-headed single-parent households end up being overrepresented among the poor in Canada. How are we, as social scientists, to explain the social behaviours of female adolescents? Two interpretations prevail. Either we can see teenagers from a *voluntarist perspective* as freely acting individuals creating and organizing their own social responses, or we can adopt a *determinist perspective*, viewing young adults as prisoners of society, controlled and driven by social forces beyond their control.

While determinists or structuralists minimize the efficacy of individuals, voluntarists or interactionists overemphasize the significance of individual actions and decisions in predicting outcomes. In fact, teenagers both create their own futures by realizing the consequences of their decisions and respond to constraints and possibilities presented by the social environment within which they live. The "social construction of reality" approach (Berger and Luckmann, 1966) and what is sometimes called the "duality of structure and agency" perspective (Giddens, 1976) both recognize that individuals have the "power of agency" to act, to create and to achieve things, but that these actions take place within structures and institutions that provide us with the cultural rules and knowledge, the social motivation and even the desire to design and carry out action (Sharrock 1987). For example, even though we are born with unique capacities to create and sustain interaction with others, the ways in which we work, socialize, make love and play reflect routine and culturally patterned arrangements. Even our emotional displays of love, hate and anger reflect, to some extent, socially conditional responses.

Individuals both produce social organizations, varieties of interactional patterns found in society, and are acted upon by them. The family is an example. Couples who establish a joint residence, have children and both contribute to the household have created a social unit called a nuclear family. Thus, organizations arise from the day-to-day conduct of their members. Yet, once in existence, organizations can affect the behaviour of their members. Most people in families insist on fidelity, nurturing of children and financial provision for dependants. Organizations are thus objective entities that help determine our behaviour. Macro-order analyses reveal how large organizations shape our behaviour. In contrast, micro-order studies examine the interpersonal bonds among organizational participants.

While individual and societal behaviours are inextricably linked, too often studies proceed as if the micro and macro levels of analyses acted separately. How determinists on the macro level and interactionists on the micro level study the relationship between social class and educational achievement illustrates their differences. For *structuralists*, particularly Marxists, an individual's educational achievement is said to be determined by his or her social class. Social class is seen as a static concept defined according to the individual's relationship to the means of production. Hence, the bourgeoisie own, control and manage the factories that employ the working class, or proletariat. Middle- or upper-class students have access through their families to cultural capital advantages that facilitate their advancement through the educational system. Their use of language and books and their extensive background experience, acquired through exposure to foreign travel, museums, art galleries, sports events and so on, mark these students as bearers of cultural capital.

While not denying the influence and weight of social class in affecting educational achievement, interactionists or subjectivists are more interested in the day-to-day process in which the effects of ambition and achievement are shown. How we eat, talk, maintain friendships, join social clubs, organize children's leisure time, interact with teachers and monitor children's educational progress are a few ways we create and maintain social class. Documenting how the parents' experiences in school affect their relationships with their children's schools and how children create school careers over a period of time are just two interactional processes shaping children's educational futures.

Essentially these two perspectives differ on the question of *constraint* (Sharrock, 1987). As Sharrock (1987 : 146) explains, everyone recognizes that people find themselves in situations they did not create, situations such as unwanted pregnancies, boring jobs, abusive dating relationships, unstimulating classes. Sociologists disagree about the extent to which people are able to alter such situations. Determinists suggest that what happens in a situation is due to the operation of the forces or structures that govern it. Determinists think that people's capacities to alter the course of action are negligible in affecting outcomes. Interactionists suggest individuals always maintain the ability to alter their own social histories and emerge with creative strategies to cope with current dilemmas.

The Macro Level of Analysis

A macro level of analysis focuses on the functioning of large organizations and their relationship to other institutions. Institutions perpetuate the stable cluster of values, norms, roles and expectations that decide how the needs of a society should be met. Through socialization strategies, bureaucratic rules and informal practices, institutions transfer cultural beliefs, norms, values and roles to new generations. For example, in Canadian medical studies, we see that the socialization of doctors (Shapiro, 1978), residents and interns (Haas and Shaffir, 1978), midwives (Benoit, 1989) and chiropractors (Kelner et al., 1980) in formal, institutional settings and in informal collegial networks ensures that new recruits will emerge with shared attitudes toward peers, clients and the public. Institutions act as the bridge between what people believe and what people do. Institutional studies concentrate on roles, status and social groups.

The Micro Level
of Analysis

The micro approach is associated with three common sociological approaches: interactionism, phenomenology and ethnomethodology. These approaches concentrate on analysing daily exchanges among individuals. Three elements in the ways individuals and groups create social structure are usually identified. These are situational definitions, continuity and change and conflict.

Situational Definitions

Situational definitions include all the ways that people organize their perceptions of objects, meanings and other people (Hewitt, 1988 : 148). They have been seen as co-ordinating sets of ideas and actions that a person or group uses in dealing with ordinary and problematic situations. They are ways of thinking, feeling and acting (Becker et al., 1961). How people act depends upon how they view and interpret the situation. Or, as the famous W. I. Thomas (1966) dictum states, "If people define situations as real, they are real in their consequences." Situational definitions are also referred to as perspectives.

Perspectives vary across history and across society. Medieval notions of appropriate childhood behaviour differ substantially from modern ones. Situational definitions vary by race, class and gender. Middle-class black women may espouse different views on parenting than working-class white men. Within a social context, perspectives often clash; for example, undergraduates and professors may disagree on the relative importance of partying and studying in college.

Continuity and
Change

Interactional studies centre on continuity and change. Social order exists not only because participants perceive it, but also because members actively construct society. Everywhere in social life we see bargaining, working agreements and the use and misuse of rules to accomplish social order and co-ordinate activity (Hewitt, 1988 : 209). Situational definitions are constantly changing. Rules of conduct, agreements and bargains shift, requiring participants to adjust. This behavioural fluctuation is referred to as *negotiation*.

Wilfred Martin, in a Canadian field study of the schooling process, employed the concept of negotiation to explain how teachers view students. Martin (1976 : 6) defined negotiation as the "total set of processes whereby actors, in pursuit of common interests, try to arrive at a settlement or arrangement with each other or with a third party." The teachers Martin observed classified student role performance according to three categories. The "non-negotiable" students were those the teachers viewed as problems. Hence, the teachers refused to bargain with them and instead issued explicit directives and stated explicit consequences of disobeying these directives. The second group was labelled "continuously negotiable." These "teacher's pets" joined in open negotiation with the teachers and were often successful in gaining their ends. The third group, the "intermittently negotiable," represented the silent majority whose participation in open or closed negotiation depended on how legitimate their demands were seen to be.

The collective activities of people within bounded social situations working out temporary and more permanent social arrangements constitute *negotiated orders*. The concept negotiated order was originally developed by Anselm Strauss (1963) to account for how the ongoing activities of a complex institutional organization, a hospital, are co-ordinated. More recently, Peter Hall (1982) has applied the concept to an analysis of political life on the societal level. In all cases, the concept is intended to capture the dual nature of social interaction as a co-ordinated social structure.

Negotiation order studies have proved among the most fruitful for interactionists in Canada. Research topics have ranged diversely from examining negotiation processes among teachers and students (Stebbins, 1976), professional wrestlers and the public (Turowetz and Rosenberg, 1978), Hasidic Jews and the community (Shaffir, 1978), children and teachers in day care centres (Mandell and Duffy, 1988), customers and salespeople (Prus, 1989) and street children and hustlers (Visano, 1989). In a classic American study, Glaser and Strauss (1965) build on their concept of negotiated order when analysing the emergence of awareness contexts to describe the complex interactions among terminally ill patients and the hospital staff.

Awareness of Dying

The phenomenon of awareness is central to the study of interaction. Barney Glaser and Anselm Strauss (1965) introduced the concept of awareness contexts. Any act of communication contains varying degrees of understanding or awareness between the participants. Awareness context refers to the combination of what each person knows about the identity of the other and his own identity in the eyes of the other. Any interaction contains four possible types of awareness. An open awareness context occurs when each participant knows his own and the other's true identity. In a hospital, an open awareness context prevails when a patient knows he is dying, identifies himself this way and is defined and treated by the hospital staff as dying. The patient might finalize his will, take care of business and financial matters and settle personal scores. The medical staff, in turn, makes no attempt to disguise the diagnosis.

The complete opposite to this is the closed awareness context. In such cases, the patient does not know he is dying and is not aware that the hospital staff has identified him in this way. As Glaser and Strauss state: "The hospital is magnificently organized, both by accident and design, for hiding the medical truth from the patient." Records are not available for scrutiny, the staff conceals information, and the family makes constant reference to future events.

The third context, the suspicion awareness context, is a modification of the closed awareness context. One participant suspects the true identity of the other or the other's view of his own identity or both. For example, the patient may suspect he is dying, yet the physician may believe the patient does not know.

Finally, in the pretence awareness context, both participants realize that the patient is dying but pretend not to know.

Conflict   The final element interactionists assess captures the problematic or conflictual aspects of exchange. While most role enactment takes place in routine and familiar settings, a great deal of social life is unpredictable, problematic and conflictual. According to a prominent social psychologist, George Herbert Mead (1938:79), confusions and misunderstandings between people often arise in the course of interaction and effectively end the exchange. Participants cannot continue to act until these problems are solved. Resolution occurs when individuals reflect on their situation and devise alternative ways of behaving. These reflections can occur within several minutes in a conversation or can take many years to resolve.

In solving interactional problems, people actively construct social reality. People create social reality, new roles and new ways of behaving for individuals and groups in their attempts to devise interactional strategies. This quality of social life is what provides people with novelty, excitement and feelings of efficacy and mastery as they actively control their own destinies.

Interpersonal negotiation is central, then, to most decision making and problem solving. In most studies, degrees and types of bargaining can be identified. Working agreements broadly outline how individuals should interact. These general agreements are not as specific or constraining as rules. Rather, any agreement can be "stretched, negotiated, argued, ignored and applied at convenient moments" (Strauss, 1963:153). When people encounter problems in social relationships, they try to negotiate solutions. Understanding this process of conflict resolution is essential in analysing social situations.

Social Roles and Social Identities

Social Roles and Everyday Life

Both macro- and micro-level studies examine the connection between roles and interactions. By participating in collective activities, human beings learn how to behave in particular social situations. Roles provide normative expectations and standards for anticipating how strangers will act and for judging how we should adjust our responses.

The smooth transaction of society's daily affairs is greatly facilitated by role playing. In fact, we often do not realize how much we rely on roles to predict others' behaviour until someone violates our expectation of how their role should be played. Confronting "out of role" behaviour confuses and frustrates us. Harold Garfinkel (1967), an American ethnomethodologist, demonstrated how much humans rely on roles by having his sociology students deliberately break norms in familiar social settings. By breaking customary and unspoken expectations, Garfinkel and his students were scraping below the surface of social behaviour to discover how people understand daily routines. One of Garfinkel's more popular experiments was to have his students act as guests in their parents' home. They asked permission to use household facilities and equipment, addressed their parents formally as Mr. and Mrs. and displayed impeccable manners. This behaviour so violated the norms of usual family interaction that neither the students nor the family members could tolerate it for very long.

The Structuralist Approach to Roles

All sociologists, it seems, want to know about the origin and transmission of social roles. Macro-level role analyses take a structuralist approach, which stems from the work of Talcott Parsons (1951), Robert Merton (1967) and Ralph Linton (1936). These sociologists viewed society as organized according to a system of roles. For them, the concept of social role became the conceptual link between individual activity and social organization. All individuals have scripts to enact. These scripts are organized into systems of roles; hence, we have family roles, workplace roles and friendship roles. Their followers often analyse social organizations by examining their role structure.

The structuralist sees roles as the prescribed pattern of behaviour expected of a person in a given situation by virtue of his or her position in the transaction. Roles refer to observable behaviour, to what the individual actually does in a given social situation. All roles are socially defined according to the position or status an individual occupies in the social structure. Every social status carries with it a set of norms and expectations that specify how the role it defines ought to be played. The status of doctor suggests a set of behaviour, obligations and privileges that we can all agree upon. Doctors should always act in their patients' best interests. They are obligated to prolong and save lives. In exchange for their dedication and long working hours, they receive the societal privileges of professional autonomy, elevated prestige and high wages. A *role* is generally defined, then, as a cluster of duties, rights and obligations associated with a particular social position (Hewitt, 1988 : 70).

Roles involve both prescribed behaviours and reciprocal claims and obligations specifying what activities the actor is entitled to expect from others. Patients expect doctors to make every effort to heal them. Reciprocally, doctors expect patients to contribute to the healing process by following their orders. While the patient role specifies ideal role behaviour, our actual role performance often deviates from the norm. For example, studies indicate that over half of all patients ignore their doctor's advice. It is the nature and extent of such deviation that the interactionists study.

We are not always free to choose the parts we play in society. Some scripts, called *ascribed roles*, are assigned to us whether we like it or not. These ascribed roles are given to us at birth on the basis of biological characteristics such as race and sex and on the basis of some characteristics of our parents, such as religion, caste or social class. Other parts, called *achieved roles*, require individual choice or talent before they are assumed. Occupational, marital and friendship roles are achieved.

Both ascribed and achieved roles can be ones we accept but do not enjoy. The role of mental patient may be partially ascribed and partially achieved, but is not likely to be a role that is joyfully accepted. Other roles are less clearly differentiated according to their voluntary or involuntary assignment. For example, are sex and gender ascribed or achieved? Sex is usually seen as physiological, an ascribed status, while gender role behaviour is achieved. *Gender* refers to the cultural, social and psychological characteristics assumed appropriate to one's sex. Thus, gender represents learned behaviour that is acquired over a lifetime.

Merton (1967) outlined how roles are systematically organized. Each social status involves not just a single associated role, but an array of roles. Physicians play the roles of primary care consultant, scientific researcher, hospital administrator, government consultant and medical school teacher. Upon entering a new status, individuals are confronted with a *role set*, an array of roles to be played in order to meet the expectations of a variety of people.

Role sets differ from multiple roles. Multiple roles refer to the fact that each person simultaneously enacts many different roles through her or his life. Hence, a physician may also be a mother, a wife, a daughter, a professional weightlifter and a community worker.

Anxiety and stress are pervasive experiences in twentieth-century life. This pressure to succeed, achieve and conform can be analysed as role strain or conflict. Our actual behaviour does not match our definition of the normative expectations contained in our role prescriptions. We often feel pulled apart by the competing demands within role sets. The role of primary care consultant, for example, may make time claims on physicians that make it difficult for them to fulfil their teaching and research commitments. Peer discussion regularly revolves around strategies for coping with the pressures of role-set demands.

The Role of Anorectics

Anorexia nervosa is perhaps the most dramatic outcome of the culture's obsession with regulating body size. In the last ten years this psychological syndrome has risen to epidemic proportions. Anorexia nervosa—self-starvation—is both a serious mental condition affecting thousands upon thousands of women, and a metaphor for our age. Like the psychological symptom of hysteria that Freud described so well in late-nineteenth-century Vienna, anorexia nervosa is a dramatic expression of the internal compromise wrought by Western women in the 1980s in their attempt to negotiate their passions and desires in a time of extraordinary confusion. But whereas hysteria was an "imagined" physical response to emotional distress caused by the imprisoning feminine role of the Victorian period, what occurs in anorexia nervosa is the excruciating spectacle of women actually transforming their bodies in their attempts to deal with the contradictory requirements of their role in late-twentieth-century America and England.

Women today are presented with an apparently bewildering number of social role options. One only has to choose what one wishes and the world is open. Where narrow role-definition previously imprisoned women, now variety, opportunity and unlimited possibilities exist. Or rather, so goes the myth. At the heart of the new possibilities for women, anorexia illuminates the difficulties of entry into a masculinist world. The anorectic woman encompasses in her symptom a way of being entirely at odds with the phlegmatic response of her nineteenth-century hysterical sister. Not for her the fainting, falling or flailing fits; her protest is marked by the achievement of a serious and successful transformation of her body, that same body that her great-great-grandmother used as a weapon in her own time. Rather than collapsing because of "feminine frailty," the anorectic woman today, in losing the defining curves of femininity and in ceasing to menstruate, does away with the explicit marker of her reproductive capacities. In essence she defeminizes her body.

Another source of role strain is the attempt to fulfil multiple roles. Individuals often play two or more roles, each governed by conflicting norms. Consider the working mother. The norm of a wage labourer may periodically conflict with the norm of a domestic labourer. Which norm do women adhere to when their children are sick? Do they stay home and care for the child or go to work? Conformity to one role (staying home) may require deviating from another (going to work).

How individuals perform their roles provides another source of potential strain. Role performance can produce conflict when we disagree with others about how we or they ought to behave. Often the norms associated with roles are merely blueprints providing general behavioural guidelines. There are many ways to father, for example. Most of us will find that our definitions of good parenting are sometimes in contradiction to others' definitions. Prolonged discrepancy between actual and situational expectations can cause guilt feelings, frustration and anger. One way to cope with this is to recognize that these feelings result not from personal inadequacies, but from competing role definitions.

Role performance can also produce strain when the role itself requires inconsistent and diverse conduct. The role of teacher contains a potential conflict in that it requires satisfying both administrators and parents. Educational administrators want teachers to cover all the material outlined by the Ministry of Education for their grade level. Parents may expect a more individualized program tailored to meet the academic and social needs of their child. Teachers sometimes "burn out" as a result of the frustration they experience in juggling conflicting role demands.

Ambiguous roles create role conflict. The more unclear the role requirements, the more likely it is individuals will disagree over how to play the role. Typically, newly created roles and changing roles are unclear. Alice Rossi (1968) has discussed how women are prepared, through anticipatory socialization and gradual acquisition, to take on occupational and marriage roles. In contrast, transition to the parenting role occurs abruptly with the birth of a child. Isolated, fatigued and suddenly immersed in twenty-four-hour child care, the role of caretaker often feels overwhelming to new mothers.

The structuralist perspective employs the blueprint approach when discussing roles and interactions. Individuals are perceived as learning a set of roles in the course of their socialization, which determines their interactional behaviour. Roles are conceptualized as standard, rule-governed actions that individuals automatically and appropriately enact in various settings. Since other organizational members have internalized the same rules, predictable relationships occur. This unified and orderly pattern of interaction becomes codified into characteristic structures.

The Interactionist Perspective on Roles

While the structural perspective views roles as passive constructions, interactionists emphasize the dynamic aspect of activity formation, performance and conflict. For symbolic interactionists, the important thing about the concept of role is not that it completely constrains our behaviour, but that it provides a way for people to grasp how situations are structured (Hewitt, 1988:79). As Hewitt (1988) explains, our current knowledge of roles, and our past experience with role sets, allows us both to anticipate and predict behaviour and to make sense of the behaviour of others in terms of our understanding of roles. For interactionists then, roles are both predictive and sense-making devices. Knowing, for example, that basic to the definition of a job interview is the expectation that applicants will behave politely, dress appropriately and appear fascinated with the company, interviewees can enter job interviews with routine role behaviour expectations.

Interactionists do not analyse events solely in terms of roles. Rather, they consider the type of experience individuals are having at a particular moment, in a particular place in their social lives. Interactionists ask, "What is it that's going on here?" (Goffman, 1974:8) and, "How are these situational definitions different for various groups in this setting?" Discerning group perspectives means understanding what social acts individuals engage in to create distinct activities, how these activities coalesce into regular patterns and what external or internal forces lead to behavioural changes.

According to Gregory Stone (1981), all interaction entails two components: we observe and respond to others' *discourse*, to others' words and deeds, and to *appearance*, to manners of dress, demeanour and physical appearance. To understand group perspectives, researchers must discern both the verbal and non-verbal cues of the participants. In conversations, adults rely on a host of non-verbal cues to tell their partners to elaborate, repeat, hurry up or finish talking. By nodding one's head, shifting one's eyebrows, making eye contact and shifting one's posture slightly forward or back, interactants transmit symbolic messages.

Appearance and manner of dress strongly affect the way we perceive people.

NATIONAL ARCHIVES OF CANADA/PA 129838.

Role Taking and Role Making

Rather than discussing role playing as consisting of living up to the obligations of the role one assumes and insisting that others meet these expectations, interactionists distinguish between two concepts that capture the essence of interaction as influenced by roles: role taking and role making. Following Mead, Ralph Turner (1962) defines *role taking* as the process wherein the person imaginatively occupies the position (role) of another and looks at the situation from that vantage point. *Role making* refers to the process wherein the person constructs his or her own activity in a situation. It is consonant with the person's own role and meshes with the activity of others.

All social interaction would be impossible without role taking. To take on a role, you have to understand how others might react to you. You gain this understanding by imaginatively projecting yourself into the point of view of others. Patients, for example, imagine how their complaints will sound to the physician and state their situations vigorously or diffidently, depending on the length and severity of the illness. Mead called this "taking the role of the other toward self" (1938 : 374). Role taking refers to empathizing with others by symbolically assuming their point of view. We observe their behaviour, learn how they think and feel and, simultaneously, see how others are interpreting our behaviour.

We take roles of others into account so naturally that we never reflect upon this process unless an interactional problem arises. A problem, according to Mead, is some action, word, gesture, thought or physical obstacle that stops the smooth flow of interaction and causes us to think about our situation. When problems arise, we realize that we must put ourselves in the other's shoes and imagine his or her thoughts and feelings. Greeting friends is done with no reflection, unless one of them snubs you. Most daily exchanges occur on this customary, habitual level. Life would be too exhausting and stressful otherwise. The role of tourist in a foreign country is often tiring because we have to work so hard at comprehending the new cultural system. Similarly, one reason new students at university feel so lost and anxious is the alarming array of new problems they confront. Meeting the demands of professors, finding student hangouts, making new friends and securing dates are all difficult in a strange situation. For the most part, students behave as most people do in new situations. They appear nonchalant, remain silent and closely follow the ways of more experienced students. Often neophytes find people to inform or coach them on how to behave in an unfamiliar setting.

The exercise of power is a central element in interpersonal relations affecting how we behave and manage others. Generally, the individual or group within a social situation with the most power or ability to control the actions of others controls the prevailing definition of the situation. Negotiation theorists acknowledge that most relationships are unequal and that individuals do not possess identical power and ability to determine outcomes.

Role making refers more generally to the process in which individuals shape their behaviour so as to fit in with prevailing situational definitions. This concept does not presume that individuals mechanically act out prearranged scripts in routine situations, but rather that individuals carve out unique responses within a range of possible behaviours. In order to mesh their situational perspectives with ongoing activity, individuals align their conduct with others. *Aligning actions* (Stokes and Hewitt, 1976) through role making is one way individuals co-ordinate social acts with others while at the same time taking account of ongoing cultural knowledge, belief and norms (Hewitt, 1988 : 199).

Structuring Inequality Through Language

From early socialization experiences within the context of ascribed social environments, people form deeply held self-concepts and acquire a variety of interactional skills. Different ascribed positions are associated with identifiable linguistic and communicative expressions (Nash, 1985 : 203). Women's speech is seen as reinforcing their subordinate status. Some features of female language are listed below.

1. *Inappropriate Question Intonation.* The use of the rising voice or question intonation for assertive utterances is frequently attributed to female speech. When asked how many children she has a woman replies, "Three?"

2. *Tag Questions.* A tag question is a question appended to a declarative sentence and indicates the need of the female speaker to solicit agreement or acquiescence from the listener. "It's very hot in this room, isn't it?"

3. *The Use of "He" and "Man" as Generic Terms.* For example, policeman and chairman are used to indicate both males and females.

4. *Vocabulary Items Indicating Fine Colour Discriminations.* The lexical repertoire of females includes many words for making fine colour discriminations. Examples include taupe, mauve, turquoise, burgundy and off-white. Using these words is seen as an obsession with trivia.

5. *Complimentary Vocabulary Items.* Adjectives such as "adorable," "sweet," "cute," "lovely" and "divine" are associated with females and seen as trivializing, sugar-coated words.

6. *Extensive Use of Qualifiers.* Women use more qualifiers such as "generally," "fairly," "quite," "really" and "perhaps." Qualifiers are perceived as hedging, weakening terms which allow the speaker to avoid taking full responsibility for what is being said.

7. *Extensive Use of Modals.* Women use more modal verbs such as "can," "could," "shall," "should," "will," "would," "may" and "might." These are perceived as signalling doubtfulness or uncertainty and having a softening effect on a statement.

8. *Interruption Patterns.* In cross-sex conversations, the interruption of female by male speakers is consistent, systematic and largely independent of idiosyncratic features relating to the nature and disposition of the participants.

9. *Interaction Patterns.* The speech of women is more supportive, makes an effort to elicit and encourage the contributions of the other speaker, asks more questions and intersperses questions with supportive "ums" and "ahs."

10. *Silence Patterns.* Contrary to the popular myth, women talk significantly less than men do. Women's silence is a function of their exclusion from making and validating language and reflects their curtailed power in the world.

Maryann Ayim. 1987. "Wet Sponges and Band-Aids: A Gender Analysis of Speech Patterns," pp. 418–30. In Greta Hofmann Nemiroff, ed., *Women and Men: Interdisciplinary Readings on Gender.* Toronto: Fitzhenry and Whiteside.

Role Taking and
Social Acts

Role taking and role making are discussed by interactionists as active, reflective processes in which individuals try to figure out their parts in the social exchange and to ascertain how others expect them to behave. In his discussion of how individuals co-ordinate activity, Mead (1938 : 8–25) identified four phases individuals go through in carrying out social acts.

The first involves an identification with self. The individual asks who he or she is or ought to be in that particular situation. Second, an individual must then behave in a manner appropriate to this identification. We do not simply play roles as puppets; we explore possibilities and choose those most suitable. These decisions are relatively simple when the social norms governing action are clearly defined. Our interactions with shopkeepers and post office workers are based on distinct rules. However, choosing an appropriate stance becomes difficult in ambiguous situations. When we are unsure of someone's sex, considerable confusion results. People greeting new babies always want to know the child's sex because this information determines how they will treat the child.

Third, individuals use the behaviour of others as cues to guide their own behaviour. Through their actions, other people convey to us what they expect us to do. By symbolically communicating their expectations, people create a collective definition of the situation. In devising any role performance, we consider the expectations of others. These shared expectations provide countless regulations that we hardly ever think about.

The final element integral to the enactment of roles is an evaluation by us and by others of our performance. An individual's part in an exchange provides a distinctive position from which to evaluate his or her own performance and those of others.

A *social act* for Mead, then, represents a functional unit of conduct with an identifiable beginning and end that is related to the organism's needs and purposes and that is oriented toward one or more social objects (Hewitt, 1988 : 66). *Social objects* represent symbolically designated things that individuals take into account and that constitute the focus of their joint act. Social objects include the actor, others, concrete or material things and ideas. In every joint encounter, whether talking to oneself out loud about a problem or talking in hushed tones to a friend, the focus of joint involvement revolves around social objects.

Impression
Management

In all sorts of exchanges, people employ interactional strategies designed to help them control and impose their definition of the situation on the group. Since group definitions often become self-fulfilling prophecies, we recognize the importance of controlling how others interpret our behaviour.

The late Erving Goffman, an American sociologist, investigated how people manage their self-impressions. Self-impressions include impressions the self makes on others and impressions that others make on the self. (In the course of interaction, selves act, others respond, and selves incorporate these responses into their next act. People are

Altercasting, Disclaimers, Accounts and Motive Talk

The complexity of social life has forced interactionists to devise certain concepts for analysing social reality. Among these, altercasting, disclaimers, accounts, motive talk and impression management are terms widely used in field studies.

Altercasting is the conceptual opposite of role taking. While role taking emphasizes the individual's control of interaction by empathetically imagining what the other is meaning, thinking or feeling, altercasting refers to the effects of this role taking on the other. Often, one person's acts actually constrain what the other can do. This process of casting the other (the alter) into a particular role emphasizes the limiting consequences of role taking by demonstrating how people are sometimes forced to act in a certain way because they are treated as if they are already acting this way. Parents and teachers, for example, often use altercasting to control children's behaviour. Informing a child that you assume she or he is bright and has the correct answer often leads to positive increases in children's classroom behaviour. Somehow, continually telling children they are smart leads children into behaving in intelligent ways. Altercasting can lead to self-fulfilling prophecies in which people act on the basis of a given definition of a situation and actually bring about conditions that confirm the definition on which they have acted, even if events were not originally as they thought them to be (Hewitt, 1988 : 156).

Disclaimers (Hewitt and Stokes, 1975) refer to verbal devices people employ when they want to ward off the negative implications of something they are about to do or say. Many conversations begin with, "I know this sounds weird but . . ." or, "I don't want you to think I'm sexist but . . . ." These key phrases are then followed by a statement that completely contradicts the disclaimer. Thus, "I don't want you to think I'm sexist but women really are better suited to household cleaning and cooking" is an inherently contradictory statement. People use disclaimers in an attempt to keep others from forming a negative evaluation of them without actually modifying their conduct.

Accounts (Scott and Lyman, 1968) refer to the verbal process in which actors demand and provide explanations for social interaction that has been disrupted by inappropriate behaviour, by unexpected or inconvenient activities or by rule violations. Accounts include both excuses and justifications. Excuses acknowledge the act is inappropriate, but deny individual responsibility. Students offer excuses for late papers such as deaths in the family, car accidents and illness. Justifications are accounts in which the individual does assume responsibility, but denies that the act itself should be seen as wrong. Student protestors assert that since no individual is harmed by demonstrations, there is nothing wrong with destroying school property.

Motive talk was a term coined by C. Wright Mills (1981) to explain the connection between what people do and what they say. One of the ways we make sense of others' behaviour is to ask for and impute motives. A large part of gossip involves motive talk in which we question and reveal the rationale for and consequences of an individual's behaviour. Children are depressed because their parents divorced. Fathers are grumpy because they haven't had any recreation time all week. *Vocabularies of motive* develop when people learn to use certain words to describe their purposes and intentions. These words contain all the information we need to assess their motives for various actions (Nash, 1985 : 143). Religious groups, for example, refer to "serving God" or attaining a "state of grace" as appropriate motives, while politicians often suggest their actions are "in the interests of the public." Most occupational groups develop specific vocabularies of motive to explain and legitimize group conduct (see Mills in Stone and Faberman, 1981 : 326).

constantly evaluating their own behaviour and that of others.) Goffman's approach is called dramaturgical, as in an idea expressed by Shakespeare: "All the world's a stage, and all the men and women merely players."

Building on Mead's notion of role taking, Goffman suggested that actors both empathize with their fellow participants in creating joint social acts and actively strive to manage and control how these others will interpret their behaviour. In all interactional exchanges, we consider our audience expectations and characteristics and attempt to present ourselves favourably. In *The Presentation of Self in Everyday Life* (1959a), Goffman outlined two ways an individual manages impressions. The individual deliberately gives some impressions. These consist of the information or sign activity an actor wants the audience to receive. An individual also gives off some impressions unwittingly. Goffman calls attempting to convey a specific impression front-stage behaviour. Deliberately concealing information from our audience is called back-stage behaviour. Goffman uses a waiter in a restaurant to illustrate. The front-stage scene for waiters is the formal dining area of the restaurant. Waiters try to convey a sense of sincerity in serving their customers. As in any successful front-stage performance, the actor stages a good performance by acting out an expected role and by manipulating the situational props (the setting, lighting, food). In some social encounters, such as those that take place in a restaurant, performance teams co-operate in staging a successful and convincing routine for the audience. (Do you remember the bartenders in the movie *Cocktail*?)

However, according to Goffman, if we really wanted to know what the waiter was like, we would also have to observe his back-stage, or out-of-role behaviour. Kitchens are back-stage areas for waiters, where the audience does not normally enter. The information a waiter discloses about himself in the kitchen when discussing his customers or arguing with the chef is far more instructive in providing us with a well-rounded picture of this person than the image he presents to his customers.

Gender Displays   While we do sometimes willfully manage gender-type impressions, many gender behaviours are not consciously manipulable. Learning appropriate gender displays is a central lesson in childhood socialization, so these behaviours become habitual. However, in one of his last works (*Gender Advertisements*, 1979), Goffman suggests several ways individuals deliberately use gender-related strategies to control and manage social encounters.

Gender displays are the culturally established gender behaviours that are so stereotypical they can be recognized in almost any social context. Gender displays include the coy smile, the leer, the seductive posture and the feminine touch. Each display represents typically masculine and feminine behaviour. These displays are part of our everyday life and are easily recognized in television and magazine advertisements.

Using Goffman's analytical frame, Posner (1982) looked at sex-role stereotyping in Canadian magazine advertisements. By examining body postures, facial expressions, eye contact and relationship to physical objects, Posner shows how these advertisements reinforce stereotypical images of women and men. Women are portrayed as childlike,

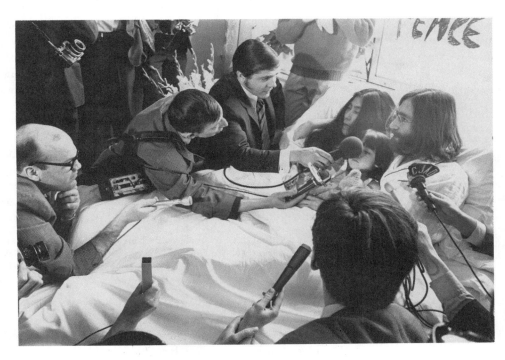

John Lennon and Yoko Ono illustrate that "All the world's a stage."

NATIONAL ARCHIVES OF CANADA/PA 152444.

tactile, mentally drifting and passive. Men are aggressive, active, alert and in control. Our uncritical acceptance of these images indicates that we agree that men and women present themselves to others in fundamentally different ways.

Roles and Self-Identity Sociologists have linked the concepts of self and role. Through social interaction, we develop a self-identity. Our self-image is closely linked to the roles we enact and reflects how we imagine others characterize us. Just as we perform many diverse roles during our lifetimes, we also have many selves or ways of viewing ourselves.

A classic field-work study by Erving Goffman (1959b) dramatically reveals how roles and situational expectations affect self-behaviour and the behaviour of others. Goffman analysed the effect of being labelled mentally ill and treated as such within the institutional setting of a mental hospital. Mental patients go through a regular sequence of changes in their self-definitions and their definitions of others. In the first stage, as pre-patients, they typically feel betrayed and sceptical of those who committed them. Once committed, patients are stripped of their rights and liberties. Tension arises between the patients and the staff and family who try to convince the patients that this help is "for their own good."

In the second stage, as in-patients, the patients' self-definitions undergo a transformation. Confronted with unacceptable views of themselves and with isolation, humiliation and stark living conditions, patients present favourable explanations for their past and current behaviours. Patients suggest they were misdiagnosed, overworked or suffer from bad nervous systems. However, the staff and other patients create a social environment that denies these agreeable self-images and forces the patients constantly to review who they are. Over time, patients take on the selves the others present to them. Adopting these self-images is also a more efficient way of coping with their demoralizing situations.

How, then, do we define the self? The self is a social product, an outgrowth of our interaction with others. According to Lindesmith et al. (1977:324), the self is an organization or integration of behaviour imposed upon individuals by themselves and by societal expectations and demands. Selves do not exist except in a symbolic environment from which they cannot be separated. As we move through life, we acquire a succession of selves. William James, the noted American social psychologist, commented on the social and multifaceted nature of self-identity (1890:294):

> The individual has as many different social selves as there are distinct groups of persons about whose opinion he cares. Many a youth who is demure enough before his parents and teachers, swears and swaggers like a pirate among his "tough" friends.

Given the situational and changeable nature of self-concepts, is there one true or real self, a unique identity that persists despite the variety of experiences we encounter? Sociologists disagree on this question. But the majority have used role enactment as an explanation for multiple selves. Role enactment allows for a wide variety of acts within a permitted range. Despite individual differences in personality, temperament and life experiences, sociologists emphasize the similarities in role performance. What role variations do exist are seen as resulting from an individual's prior experience or from immediate situational pressures.

Not only do we appear to others as many different people, but often the performance of one role is interrupted by the encroachment of other roles. Given this role diversity, what unifies an individual's behaviour is his or her controlling conception of what he or she is doing. This self-direction comes from the ongoing, private dialogues individuals have with themselves. By talking with themselves, reviewing their behaviour in different situations and evaluating their diverse performances, individuals maintain a consistent sense of self.

Recognition of the situational self, the concept that the self adopts different behaviours in different situations, has led to research on how various environments affect individual and group behaviour. Phillip Zimbardo (1971), a social psychologist, demonstrated the effect of the situation on the self in his Stanford County Prison experiment. Zimbardo designed a realistic mock prison in the basement of one of Stanford's buildings. Through a newspaper advertisement, he solicited volunteers who were willing to spend two weeks playing the role of either a prisoner or a guard. The experiment had to be abandoned after six days due to the emotional strain the prisoners were under. Five prisoners had to be released, four because of severe emotional depression or acute anxiety attacks, one because he developed a psychosomatic rash.

The prisoners were behaving like "servile, dehumanized robots who thought only of escape, of their individual survival and of their mounting hatred of the guards" (Zimbardo, 1971:3). This happened because, soon after the experiment started, the guards began abusing their power. They made the prisoners obey petty and meaningless rules, forced them to do tedious and useless work, demanded that they laugh and sing on command and ordered them to humiliate each other publicly. In less than a week, ordinary, mature, emotionally stable, middle-class college students became caught up in the traditional prisoner and guard roles.

Hockey Aggression

Hockey is known as a violent game. Coaches, players and owners are sensitive to questions about fighting and concerned with the image of the game. In the past twenty years, programs in youth hockey have proliferated. Children as young as six are now playing organized hockey. Critics point to the violence of pro hockey and caution parents and organizers about the deleterious effects of hockey on children.

Nash and Lerner (1981) conducted a study to assess the extent to which violence in professional hockey constitutes a model for youth hockey. They discovered that young hockey players are aware of hockey violence but they act on the basis of their understanding of the pros as a model for interpreting their own game. Children's version of what the pros do serves as their guideline. Even though the boys' version of "good" hockey contrasts with the pros', certain indirect effects of the pro model can be identified.

First, boys regard hockey as fun. It is the playing that matters, not the fact of winning or losing. To play and play a lot is their prime objective. The appeal of hockey is its action. A puck in the corner provides the opportunity to kick, flail, elbow, push and collide with the other boys, all of which the boys regard as fun.

Second, boys do not believe they will be injured while playing or fighting. Like their pro counterparts, the children believe there are no serious injuries in hockey.

Third, the discipline required to play hard or aggressively is within the range of ability for most boys. This means the rules referees evoke, the judgements coaches and parents make about the appropriateness of aggression during the game take into account the level of skill and motivations of the players.

The code the young players abide by consists of six tenets:

1. Play hard.
2. Skate fast.
3. Do not complain about ice time or the position the coach wants you to play.
4. Control your emotions and express them appropriately through aggressive play.
5. Do not give "cheap" shots unless in retaliation.
6. Play hockey in kind, clean for clean, cheap for cheap.

A description of how children model their play after the pros tells us that modeling is never a direct imitative process. Children simplify and accentuate themes of available adult models in terms of their own needs and social relationships. By virtue of the organization of the game itself, interaction with coaches, parents and fellow players, boys learn the meanings of situational violence, that is, the time, place and form of aggression.

From Jeffrey Nash. 1985. *Social Psychology: Society and Self*. St. Paul, Minn.: West Publishing, pp. 261–67.

How do we reconcile an individual's controlling sense of self with the presentation of various and often unpleasant selves? Individuals resolve this tension by talking to themselves about their seemingly discrepant behaviours, assessing the origin of these behaviours and evaluating their impact on others. This private self-reflection allows an individual to explain current behaviours within the context of his or her own historical account of past and present acts.

The Influence of Groups

What Is a Social Group?

Throughout this chapter, we have stressed the social character of interaction. People have always formed associations and most social interaction occurs within groups. Our behaviour, personality and character are moulded by the groups to which we belong. Moreover, most changes in our lives result from alterations in our group membership. Entering university, working in our first job, getting married, having children and aging are experienced as group events. How we interpret our university life varies tremendously according to our group participation. Women's studies, athletic teams, debating societies, chess clubs and musical societies are examples of different groups in which students can become involved and which can colour their university experience.

But what is a social group? What, for example, distinguishes a random collection of people at a hockey game from a neighbourhood street gang? Generally, a *social group* is any collection of two or more people interacting in an orderly way on the basis of shared understanding about how they and other group members ought to behave. Just because people are together in the same place does not mean that they constitute a social group. For the crowd at a hockey game to be regarded as a social group, its members must interact. Instead, crowd members react individually to a central stimulus (the game) and only subliminally to each other. In contrast, neighbourhood gangs develop group consciousness and a sympathetic identification with similar groups. Social groups vary in size, organization, durability and flexibility of action.

Sociology contains two distinct approaches to studying group behaviour. The first, a structuralist interpretation, focuses on the structural characteristics that distinguish groups from non-groups. Often, only stable groups with a readily identifiable membership, a clearly defined central activity and the binding of one member to another in well-established relationships are studied (Shibutani, 1961:33). This definition of groups includes everything from small peer groups to all members of the Moslem faith, for example.

The second approach, the interactionist perspective, defines groups according to their central activity. Interactionists focus on group processes—how the group members work together. They regard a group as more than a collection of individuals who happen to be at the same place at the same time. Social groups are units of interacting individuals who have a common sense of identity and a "capacity for common endeavour" (Shibutani, 1961:33).

Incorporating both the structuralist and the interactionist views, groups can be said to have the following characteristics:

1. Group members share a sense of identity, co-operation and consciousness of themselves as a group.

2. This identity is established through repeated patterns of interaction, in which group members evolve stable and predictable ways of accomplishing group goals.

3. These interactional patterns are based on shared understandings about definitions of situations, expected situational responses, goals, plans of action and rules of appropriate conduct.

4. Interactional patterns are further differentiated according to the division of labour within the group. The allocation of various group tasks creates a degree of member interdependence and integration within the collective enterprise.

5. Interactional patterns are further differentiated according to the degree of ongoing negotiation, in which group members adjust to situational demands.

Each group has its own norms, roles, status arrangements, rules, shared beliefs, negotiation limits and lines of action. Sociological investigation reveals the internal dynamics of group processes and explores the group's external relationships to other social organizations.

Reference Groups and the Generalized Other

In discussing role taking, Mead distinguished between taking the role of a *significant other* such as a peer, family member or teacher and taking the role of the generalized other. The *generalized other* represents Mead's term for the general standpoint or perspective of the group or society as a whole. The generalized other refers not to a concrete, specific other person, as significant other often does, but rather to an abstract other, a conception of the ideal expectations to which one is subject.

There are many generalized others in society. Reference groups provide generalized others whose perspective individuals can assume even if they are not necessarily group members (Hewitt, 1988:86). *Reference groups* are associations that provide generalized others to whom individuals refer their conduct when formulating and evaluating their own beliefs and actions. Reference groups are powerful organizing influences in shaping individuals. They are groups to which people aspire and do not necessarily belong. For example, nursing students and law students may look to practising professionals for their standards of conduct rather than to their fellow students.

Collective Behaviour

Collective behaviour includes a wide range of phenomena from rumours and gossip to organized efforts of large numbers of people trying to change societal values (Nash,

1985 : 280). Most often, collective behaviour studies focus on crowds, panics, mass hostility, riots, fashions, fads, cults, emergency responses to national disasters and social movements. In all of these situations, conduct appears as a novel, unpredictable and innovative response to a set of social conditions.

A *social movement* represents a collective effort to bring about some kind of change in society by restructuring the society, altering its values, beliefs, practices and modes of organization (Hewitt, 1988 : 223). The women's movement, the peace movement, the civil rights movement and the anti-poverty movement are collective responses to specific societal conditions that many people think need to be changed.

Social movements become well organized with a program of objectives, a set of organizations with distinct members, leaders, resources and strategies. Some social movements such as *scenes* represent urban, leisure-oriented and youthful forms of collective behaviour from which members derive self-esteem and a sense of uniqueness (Irwin, 1977). The Toronto gay scene, the California beach boy scene and the thirty-something scene are leisure arrangements producing profound social change and altering social conventions. Increasingly, people are participating in small activity systems in ways that allow them to think of themselves as doing important things. Scenes are territories within which action is sought that provides people with excitement and novelty (Nash, 1985 : 294). According to Irwin, the increases in leisure time and disposable income as well as increased job alienation and boredom have contributed to people's search for identity and uniqueness by participating in social scenes.

Summary

In this chapter, we have discussed the differences between macro and micro analyses and their approaches to the study of roles and interactions. Macro-level studies stress the objective conditions that influence the interpersonal bonds that develop. The social structure or environment within which interaction takes place encourages some types of interaction more than others. Micro-level studies focus on interactional activities in which individuals learn new behaviours, express their interpretations and adjust to the demands of others.

The structuralist, or blueprint, approach to roles and interactions sees individuals as passive; they merely learn prescribed patterns through the socialization process. Successfully socialized individuals perform in situationally appropriate ways. Thus, role sets, multiple roles and role strain are defined according to prevailing norms.

In contrast, the interactionist, or process, perspective emphasizes the dynamic quality of social structure. Individuals are seen as active agents who bring their own meanings to social encounters. Within a general framework of consensus, individuals continually negotiate definitions of legitimate behaviour. Roles and interactions are negotiable social acts, patterns that coalesce into group perspectives.

Social roles and social identities are constructed in accordance with expectations and standards of different social situations. While structuralists conceptualize roles and identities as pre-given behaviours that individuals acquire, interactionists view roles and identities as active creations conforming only broadly to prescribed standards. While the role of doctor requires adherence to principles of healing, the methods of treating vary from doctor to doctor and from culture to culture. In constructing identities, individuals rely on words and deeds, physical appearance, manners, dress and demeanour to portray the images they want others to discern. Role taking and role making are constitutive processes in social behaviour. Through social interaction, we develop a self-identity. Our self-esteem and self-image are tied both to the roles we play and to our conceptions of how others view us. The self is thus a social product that changes over time and in various situations.

Social groups are an intermediate level of social organization linking the macro and micro orders. Primary relations are the most intimate interpersonal bonds. It is from these affiliations that we derive our sense of identity, and in them we experience relationships most intensely. The influence of reference groups, one type of primary group, as a source of values and actions attests to the significance of primary relations.

However, most of our behaviour occurs within larger, more impersonal secondary groups. We co-operate with larger numbers of people in institutions to accomplish group goals. Analyses of collective behaviour reveal the influence of organizational settings in delineating interactional processes. Focusing on social movements and scenes reveals the novel or emergent aspect of social interaction in contrast to the more predictable and routine behaviour emanating from institutional settings.

Suggested Readings

Becker, Howard S., Blanche Geer, Everett C. Hughes and Anslem R. Strauss
1961. *Boys in White: Student Culture in Medical School*. New Brunswick, N.J.: Transaction Books.

Denzin, Norman
1977. *Childhood Socialization*. San Francisco: Jossey-Bass. Denzin presents a challenge to traditional psychological studies of child development by studying children's discovery of social worlds, the genesis of self-development and children's culture from children's points of view.

Goffman, Erving
1959. *The Presentation of Self in Everyday Life*. New York: Doubleday/Anchor. This classic text traces the shaping and development of self-concept and self-esteem as individuals confront and challenge others in group contexts.

Hewitt, John P.
1988. *Self and Society: A Symbolic Interactionist Social Psychology*. Boston: Allyn and Bacon. This concise summary of basic ideas, concepts and studies in symbolic interactionism provides students with an invaluable resource.

Spradley, James P., and Brenda Mann
1975. *The Cocktail Waitress: Women's Work in a Man's World*. New York: Wiley. Focusing on the experiences of waitresses, the authors provide a vivid analysis of the frustrations and triumphs of women's work under male authority.

Stack, Carol
1974. *All Our Kin*. New York: Harper and Row. Stack ties the social organization of black family and community life to interactional strategies adopted by those at the bottom of America's status system.

Discussion Questions

1. Accounts, disclaimers and motive talk are forms of talk significant in maintaining social order. Discuss when these devices are used and provide examples of various types.

2. In what ways does a social scene, such as the singles bar scene, differ from a social movement such as the women's movement?

3. Studies reveal that many of our racial attitudes and behaviours are rooted in our reference groups. In conversation with your colleagues, discuss how your reference groups define and maintain racism.

4. By impression management we try to create an image that will lead others to act as we wish them to act (Goffman, 1959). Analyse a recent social situation in which you have applied impression management and altercasting.

5. Role strain is a characteristic feature of modern life. Discuss how conflicting role requirements exacerbate personal anxiety.

6. Choose a social structure with which you are familiar. Apply a negotiated order analysis by analysing different group perspectives and awareness contexts. Be sensitive to physical setting, institutional rules and their deviations, working agreements among participants and the implementation of change.

Data Collection Exercises

1. Buy a set of index cards and carry them with you for a period of time as you visit a specific social location such as your dorm, class, a bar or health club. Jot down in short phrases your daily impressions of these visits until you have one hundred cards. Then sort these cards into categories that make sense to you. Write a short paper in which you explain your reasoning for the sorting. This field-work exercise will uncover many implicit features of the social construction of your research site.

2. Unobtrusively observe a group of children at play in a natural setting (park, outdoors, back alley) or in an institutional setting (child care centre, schoolyard). Make notes on the activities of the children you watch. Record details about their gestures, verbal exchanges, play patterns, age and sex groupings and their interactions with adults. Analyse these patterns using concepts of role, definition of the situation, role taking, role making and perspective.

3. Tape record male and female conversations with members of their own sex and members of the other sex. Try to be conscious of inequality in interaction as indicated by interruptions, voice inflections, turn taking, time spent talking, topics pursued.

4. Select four of five popular men's or women's magazines. Cut out examples of gender displays in advertising and arrange these according to themes, such as madonna/whore or gay/straight images. Write a brief account of why you regard these as illustrations of such displays. Check your findings with those of other content analyses.

Glossary

Achieved role: *behavioural patterns that depend on individual choice or talent such as friendship, marital and occupational roles.*

Altercasting: *the process of casting another into a particular limiting role.*

Ascribed role: *a part that is assigned to a person on the basis of characteristics such as race, sex, religion or social class.*

Collective behaviour: *an unpredictable and innovative group response to a set of social conditions.*

Determinist perspective: *people are seen as controlled and driven by social forces beyond their control.*

Negotiated order: *the temporary and permanent solutions that are worked out by people in a social situation to resolve and minimize conflicts.*

Role: *a cluster of duties, rights and obligations associated with a particular social position.*

Role making: *the construction of an activity in a situation.*

Role set: *an array of roles related to a particular social status.*

Role taking: *the imaginative adoption of another's point of view on a situation.*

Situational definition (also called perspective): *the way that people organize their perceptions of objects, meanings and other people in dealing with a situation.*

Social group: *people interacting according to a shared understanding about how group members ought to behave.*

Social movement: *a collective effort to bring about some kind of change by restructuring society, altering its values, beliefs, practices and modes of organization.*

Social object: *anything that shapes a social act.*

Voluntarist perspective: *people are seen as freely acting individuals, creating and organizing their own social responses.*

References

Ayim, Maryann
1987. "Wet Sponges and Band-Aids: A Gender Analysis of Speech Patterns," pp. 418–30. In Greta Hofmann Nemiroff, ed., *Women and Men: Interdisciplinary Readings of Gender*. Toronto: Fitzhenry and Whiteside.

Becker, Howard S., Blanche Geer, Everett C. Hughes and Anselm L. Strauss
1961. *Boys in White: Student Culture in Medical School.* New Brunswick, N.J.: Transaction Books.

Benoit, Cecilia
1989. "Traditional Midwifery Practice: The Limits of Occupational Autonomy." *Canadian Review of Sociology and Anthropology* 26(4):633–49.

Berger, Peter, and Thomas Luckmann
1966. *The Social Construction of Reality.* Garden City, N.Y.: Doubleday.

Garfinkel, Harold
1967. *Studies in Ethnomethodology.* Englewood Cliffs, N.J.: Prentice-Hall.

Giddens, Anthony
1976. *New Rules of Sociological Method.* London: Hutchinson.

Glaser, Barney A., and Anselm L. Strauss
1965. *Awareness of Dying.* Chicago: University of Chicago Press.

Goffman, Erving
1959a. *The Presentation of Self in Everyday Life.* Garden City, N.Y.: Doubleday.
1959b. "The Moral Career of the Mental Patient." *Psychiatry* 22:123–42.
1974. *Frame Analysis.* New York: Harper and Row.
1979. *Gender Advertisements.* New York: Harper and Row.

Haas, Jack, and William Shaffir
1978. *Shaping Identity in Canadian Society.* Toronto: Prentice-Hall.

Hall, Peter D.
1982. *The Organization of American Culture.* New York: New York University Press.

Hewitt, John P.
1988. *Self and Society*, 5th ed. Boston: Allyn and Bacon.

Hewitt, John P., and Randall Stokes
1975. "Disclaimers." *The American Sociological Review* 40 (February):1–11.

Irwin, John
1977. *Scenes.* Beverly Hills: Sage.

James, William
1890. *The Principles of Psychology in Two Volumes.* New York: Holt.

Kelner, Merrijoy, Oswald Hall and Dan Coulter
1980. *Chiropractors: Do They Help? A Study of Their Education and Practice.* Toronto: Fitzhenry and Whiteside.

Lindesmith, Alfred R., Anselm L. Strauss and Norman K. Denzin
1977. *Social Psychology.* New York: Holt, Rinehart and Winston.

Linton, Ralph
1936. *The Study of Man: An Introduction.* Englewood Cliffs, N.J.: Prentice-Hall.

Mandell, Nancy, and Ann Duffy
1988. *Reconstructing the Canadian Family: Feminist Perspectives.* Toronto: Butterworths.

Martin, W. B. W.
1976. *The Negotiated Order of the School.* Toronto: Macmillan.

Mead, George Herbert
1938. *The Philosophy of the Act*. Edited by Charles Morris. Chicago: University of Chicago Press.

Merton, Robert K.
1967. *On Theoretical Sociology*. New York: Free Press.

Mills, C. Wright
1981. "Situated Actions and Vocabularies of Nature," pp. 325–32. In Gregory Stone and Harvey Farberman, eds., *Social Psychology Through Symbolic Interaction*, 2nd ed. New York: Wiley.

Nash, Jeffrey
1985. *Social Psychology: Society and Self*. St. Paul, Minn.: West Publishing.

Orbach, Susie
1986. *Hunger Strike: The Anorectic's Struggle as a Metaphor for Our Age*. New York: W. W. Norton.

Orton, Maureen Jessop, and Ellen Rosenblatt
1986. *Adolescent Pregnancy in Ontario: Progress in Prevention*. Report #2. Planned Parenthood of Ontario, McMaster University, Hamilton, Ontario.

Parsons, Talcott
1951. *The Social System*. New York: Free Press.

Posner, Judy
1982. "From Sex Role Stereotyping to SadoMasochism." *Fireweed* 14.

Prus, Robert
1989. *Making Sales: Influence as Interpersonal Accomplishment*. Beverly Hills: Sage.

Rossi, Alice
1968. "Transition to Parenthood." *Journal of Marriage and the Family* 30:26–39.

Scott, Marvin, and Stanford Lyman
1968. "Accounts." *The American Sociological Review* 33 (December):46–62.

Shapiro, Martin
1978. *Getting Doctored: Critical Reflections on Becoming a Physician*. Kitchener, Ont.: Between the Lines Press.

Sharrock, W. W.
1987. "Individual and Society," pp. 126–56. In R. J. Anderson, J. A. Hughes and W. W. Sharrock, eds., *Classic Disputes in Sociology*. London: Unwin.

Shibutani, Tamotsu
1961. *Society and Personality: An Interactionist Approach to Social Psychology*. Englewood Cliffs, N.J.: Prentice-Hall.

Stebbins, Robert A.
1976. *Teachers and Meanings: Definitions of Classroom Situations*. Leiden: E. J. Brill.

Stokes, Randall, and John Hewitt
1976. "Aligning Actions." *The American Sociological Review* 46 (October):838–49.

Stone, Gregory P.
1981. "Appearance and the Self: A Slightly Revised Version," pp. 187–202. In Gregory

Stone and Harvey Farberman, eds., *Social Psychology Through Symbolic Interaction*, 2nd ed. New York: Wiley.

Strauss, Anselm, et al.

1963. "The Hospital and Its Negotiated Order," pp. 147–69. In Eliot Freidson, ed., *The Hospital in Modern Society*. New York: Free Press.

Thomas, W. I.

1966. *On Social Organization and Social Personality*. Chicago: University of Chicago Press.

Turner, Ralph H.

1962. "Role-taking: Process vs. Conformity." In Arnold M. Rose, ed., *Human Behavior and Social Processes*. Boston: Houghton Mifflin.

Turowetz, Alan, and Michael Rosenberg

1978. "Exaggerating Everyday Life: The Case of Professional Wrestling," pp. 87–100. In Jack Haas and William Shaffir, eds., *Shaping Identity in Canadian Society*. Toronto: Prentice-Hall.

Visano, Livy

1989. "Street Children." In Patricia Adler and Peter Adler, eds., *Sociological Studies of Child Development*. Greenwich, Conn.: JAI Press.

Zimbardo, Phillip

1971. "The Psychological Power and Pathology of Imprisonment." Unpublished paper. Stanford University.

CHAPTER 6

Control and Deviance

AUSTIN T. TURK

A punk rocker.

TORONTO.

155

Introduction

Against any form of determinism, social and behavioural scientists have accumulated an enormous fund of empirical and logical evidence showing that deviance is socially defined and that deviant behaviour patterns are learned. The purpose of this chapter is to introduce some of this evidence and to examine some of its implications. Sociological researchers have used many approaches to study deviance and social control, but they converge from various directions on certain key topics:

1. how society constructs its ideas of what is right and wrong (social definitions of deviance);
2. how and why individuals violate social norms (sources and patterns of deviant behaviour);
3. how and why organizations engage in illegal and ethically questionable conduct (organizational deviance);
4. how society controls its members and why moral orders change (social control and social change).

These topics will be the focus of attention in this chapter.

Social Definitions of Deviance

What is deviance? We are not born knowing how to "read" people. But every one of us does it, one way or another; so somewhere and somehow we learned to do this. We *know* what *deviance* is—whatever disturbs, frightens, threatens us, whatever doesn't seem right. Sociologists begin from this basic idea. They then try to discover the social factors that determine how we learn to draw lines between what is respectable, legal, good, beautiful and right and what is disreputable, illegal, bad, ugly and wrong. The general term for these social factors, whatever they are, is *social control*. However, this general usage is too broad: it could include anything that happens to us, from studying art to being imprisoned, from winning a prize to being fired.

Perhaps the best definition of social control is whatever some people do, more or less consciously, to influence how other people define deviance and react to it. Parents, teachers, religious leaders and political-legal authorities are generally sure of what they want us to learn. Friends, advertisers, newspeople, actors, musicians and artists may or may not be as overt about what points of view they are supporting. All, however, are *control agents*—they encourage some ways of thinking and behaving and discourage, even penalize, others.

Over time, some views win out over others, at least for a while; these are the norms by which we judge one another. People may not realize that their norms have histories, or even be aware that they have norms. We have a very human tendency to take the familiar for granted and an equally human tendency to distrust the unfamiliar. Our tastes in food, clothes, music; our conceptions of truth; our customs and laws—these come to be the standards by which alternatives are judged.

Our capacity to accept diversity and change in norms varies. *Absolutists* find it hard to accept norms other than those that they themselves hold. They consider themselves to be superior because their norms are "right." *Relativists* reject the idea that any one viewpoint can be legitimately used to evaluate other people's norms and behaviour. They often condemn the use of coercion to prevent, eliminate or punish deviance. Deviance, they argue, is merely difference. Most of us are neither so intolerant nor so tolerant. We are absolutist about some things, accept diversity of opinion about other things and are fairly indifferent toward most normative issues.

Because moral issues, almost by definition, concern most people more than other right/wrong, better/worse issues, deviance and control research has focused mainly upon moral and legal questions, rather than such questions as, for instance, "What is good/bad art?" One of the first questions a sociologist asks about morality is, "How are particular moral boundaries established?"

To answer that setting moral limits is "natural" or "inevitable" does not explain anything, but it does remind us that every human relationship generates its own characteristic pattern of norms and controls. People have to read one another's signals, reach some agreement on meanings and priorities in what they do with one another, and commit themselves to making the relationship work in terms of that agreement. Lovers must learn how to love one another; parents and children must learn how to be a family; leaders and followers, bosses and workers must learn how to give and take direction and supervision. None of this happens automatically: maintaining any social relationship is an ongoing task. As we move from person-to-person relationships to more complex and distant groupings and organizations, the task of describing and explaining norms becomes more complex.

Creating Moral Order: The Functions of Deviance and Control

When bad, illegal, improper, anomalous and generally disturbing human behaviour began to be studied scientifically in the nineteenth century, investigators shared the common assumption that deviation is pathological and conformity is healthy. They believed that societies as well as individuals could be "sick." Their aim was to learn how to eliminate deviation, especially in what they perceived as its most disturbing forms: violence, insanity, perversion, dishonesty and idleness. Research since then has led to the initially startling conclusion that the meaning of such concepts is largely subjective. It has also shown, however, that concepts of deviance are, nonetheless, "essential to the very organization of society . . . functioning to establish and maintain behavioural boundaries and to affirm the value of conformity" (Farrell and Swigert, 1982 : 27).

Concepts of deviance vary from one individual to another and change over time. People tend to reject and stereotype deviants in general, but there is considerable variation in the particular images of them and their attributes. In Simmons's

(1969:25–38) survey research on public stereotyping, respondents were asked to use five words each to characterize "marijuana smokers, adulterers, homosexuals, beatniks, and political radicals." The term "deviant" was not used in presenting the categories. Analysis revealed a fair degree of stereotyping, but the inclination to stereotype was significantly correlated with low education. All categories were seen as "irresponsible," and all except the political radical were described as "lonely and frustrated." The more specific images were as follows: marijuana smoker—"an insecure escapist, lacking self-control and looking for kicks"; adulterer—"immoral, promiscuous, and insecure"; homosexual—"perverted and mentally ill"; beatnik—"a sloppy, immature nonconformist"; political radical—"ambitious, aggressive, and dangerous" (Simmons, 1969:28).

One might downplay such findings by suggesting that stereotyping by the general public has no effect on the way deviance is officially defined. Given that people with education are less likely to stereotype, it could be that the most highly informed—that is, professional control agents—accurately identify "real" deviants on scientific, not stereotypical, grounds. However, studies of the classification of "mentally ill" and "criminal" individuals do not support this argument. Numerous studies "demonstrate that the behaviour or 'condition' of the person alleged to be mentally ill is not usually an important factor in the decision of officials to retain or release new patients from the mental hospital" (Scheff, 1984:105). From a flood of research on the criminalization process, "sufficient evidence has accumulated to reject the traditional assumption that distinguishing crime from not-crime merely involves the fitting by competent specialists of legal concepts to observed facts" (Turk, 1984:319). Deviance as professionally and officially defined is the outcome of a complex series of problematic interpretations and discretionary actions.

Historical and comparative studies have revealed that perceptions of specific forms of deviance are not constant. Demon possession, sin, witchcraft and werewolves, once regarded as ordinary forms of deviance, are taken less and less seriously. Our conceptions of the nature and causes of mental illness have become increasingly controversial as the "medical model" of deviance as disease has been challenged from within and without the "psy-professions" (Ingleby, 1983; Scheff, 1984). Blasphemy, mopery (exposing one's genitalia in the presence of a blind person), abortion and lottery gambling are no longer crimes in Canada. However, new crimes, such as the improper disposal of toxic waste and unauthorized entry to computer files, are constantly being created. In short, our conceptions of deviance are subjective and they vary over time.

Yet, though it is always the target of control efforts, some amount and form of deviance is present in any relationship, in any time and place. Some theorists have suggested that anything so universal must somehow be needed, that is, that deviance performs certain functions, contributing to the process of organizing and maintaining social relationships.

Cohen (1966:6–11) discusses seven ways in which deviance is functional. First, an organization may require the bending or breaking of its own rules (getting around bureaucratic "red tape") in order to achieve its goals. Second, some kinds of deviance may act as safety valves for the tensions built up in any ongoing relationship. Every culture seems to include "norms of patterned evasion" and "moral holidays" that permit at least occasional and/or ritual rule-breaking, for example, legalized prostitution, licensed casinos or holiday season partying. Third, a specific act of deviance resolves ambiguities about whether a rule exists or what it means. For example, the meaning of plagiarism becomes clear when a student is penalized for copying someone else's work.

Fourth, the occurrence (real or rumoured) of a crime or other violation may promote group solidarity, as people join forces to deal with the threat. Fifth, the opposite can happen: people sometimes unite to protect "their own" deviant. Workers and soldiers, for example, have been observed to cover for their less competent or responsible fellows. Sixth, badness and abnormality provide reference points for measuring goodness and normality. Examples of people who are "bad" help greatly to make clear what it means to be "good." This process seems to be at work in the cultural invention of the traditional Tahitian village *mahu*—a male who as a child is selected to spend his life as a woman (Levy, 1971). A village has only one *mahu*, who is expected to have sexual relations with the other men. In a culture marked by the minimal differentiation of gender roles, the *mahu* serves to remind everyone of their appropriate roles as "men" and "women."

Finally, deviance may be a signal that something is wrong with the rules, that the organization or society has a problem. For example, serious crime rates may be escalating despite all-out efforts to catch and punish the offenders.

Merton's Anomie Theory

Robert Merton's (1957 : 131–44) famous *anomie* theory of deviance locates the sources of deviance in the "means-ends discrepancy"—the contradictions between culturally encouraged goals and structurally available means for achieving them. A society that teaches people to value themselves and others according to how much material success has been attained, but maintains class and racial barriers to legitimate success, can expect the disadvantaged to turn to illegitimate means such as robbery, theft and drug trafficking. "Double failures" denied illegitimate as well as legitimate opportunities are likely to "retreat" into alcoholism, drug addiction, sexual deviance, mental illness or suicide. This once dominant particular theory has not stood up well under empirical testing (Clinard, 1964). However, the general proposition remains compelling—that deviance may signal defects in social organization and possibly lead to needed social changes.

Observing that deviance can be functional does not imply that it is always functional. The harmful consequences of some forms of deviance (for example, mass terrorism, sadistic murder) may outweigh their functional payoffs, and less harmful forms may serve just as well in contributing to social organization and moral order. It is also true that the *amount* of deviance required to establish and sustain particular norms is debatable.

Erikson (1966:181) has speculated that "societies somehow 'need' their quotas of deviation and function in such a way as to keep them intact." His study of the seventeenth-century New England Puritans focused upon the three "crime waves" the Massachusetts Bay Colony experienced. The Antinomian (1636) and Quaker (late 1650s) theological challenges to Puritan orthodoxy, and later the Salem witchcraft outbreak in 1692, violated the normative demands of the theocratic state, which brutally but clearly asserted its supreme authority. Erikson's evidence does not directly support his interpretation. Furthermore, his extremely functionalist idea that some distinct quota of deviance is needed in society has been severely criticized. In fact, it has been shown that the forms and amounts of deviance identified and processed by control institutions are enormously variable—depending largely upon political-legal policies and economic contexts (Cohen and Scull, 1983; Currie, 1985; Turk, 1982).

Labelling: How Deviance Is Defined and Controlled

The view that deviance is more a socially or politically created reality than an objective and somehow functional reality is advanced by labelling and conflict theorists. Labelling theorists concentrate on describing the labelling process and showing its effects on individual deviants. Conflict theorists are mainly concerned with demonstrating the association between labelling, on the one hand, and class, ethnic and other intergroup power differences and struggles, on the other. Both perspectives emphasize the importance of power in producing, as well as defining, deviance.

Moral boundaries are drawn by defining and stigmatizing (labelling) particular individuals as deviant, not merely or necessarily by announcing explicit rules. Variations in the labelling process, and in its impact upon those being processed, are associated with the scale and formality of the social order. There are significant differences as well as similarities in labelling within small groups and across group boundaries.

Though deviance is a socially constructed reality, it is not constructed on the spot. What has already occurred becomes a framework within which later interpretations and responses are made. Because members of a small group share understandings of "how we do things," its norms are generally unspoken. Friends, for instance, do not usually tell each other what the "rules" are in their relationship. In contrast, where people from different backgrounds and groups try to control one another, the norms are likely to be explicit, written in laws or contractual agreements. The process of labelling may be viewed as having five phases: *identification, justification, negotiation, enclosure* and *disposition* (Grimes and Turk, 1978:41).

Identification   How do we identify deviance? The first step is that we feel something is wrong; we react to observed or imputed behavioural, anatomical, mental or spiritual attributes. Initial perceptions of deviance are based on very little information and are interpreted largely in accord with stereotypes. Within a small group, the criteria for feeling something may be "out of line" are generally understood without having to be spelled out. In a larger social context, or when members of a small group are dealing with outsiders, the criteria generally have to be clearer so everyone will understand what is going on. Whether in small or large social contexts, the initial identification of a possibly or probably deviant "case" marks the beginning of a process that makes it increasingly hard for the accused to challenge the perceptions and assumptions of the accusers.

Justification   People who identify cases of deviance almost immediately begin marshalling arguments and facts justifying their perceptions. Inside small groups, justification depends upon the common-sense knowledge that people share about right and wrong and about one another. There are no technical restrictions upon the gathering of evidence. Labelling across groups, however, is a potential source of conflict, as common understandings cannot be assumed. Therefore, more limiting formal procedures are ordinarily used to "build" cases in the absence of intimate knowledge.

Negotiation   Accused persons are under pressure to help confirm the accuracy of the labels pinned on them. They are expected to confess, thus "proving" their guilt—which assures the labellers that no mistake has been made. Within groups, the controlling members typically exert pressure by emphasizing what the individual ought to do and want as a fellow member of the group. The value of continued participation in the group's life (friendship, marriage, team) is emphasized. Across groups, control agents tend rather to emphasize the fact that the accused is subject to "the law" as a subject or citizen of the state. Of course, the accused deviant may plead innocence or admit only to a lesser offence. The outcome may be a deal ("negotiated plea") that both helps justify the initial labelling and yet reduces the seriousness of the label.

Enclosure   While negotiation is underway, the labelled deviant is controlled within physical, social and/or symbolic restraints. Opportunities for normal interaction are closed off, and pressure to accept a "deviant identity" become increasingly hard to resist. Enclosure is more often symbolic and social within a group (for example, ostracism, transfer to a lower position, stripping of medals and insignia). It is more often and sooner physical in cross-group labelling (for example, pre-trial detention).

Disposition   The final disposition of a case may be rehabilitation, termination or institutionalization (in a sociological, not a physical, sense). Rehabilitation to normal participation in social life seems to be more genuinely desired and more likely to happen when the deviant and the control agents belong to the same group. Termination (exile or execution) tends to occur only when the group has given up hope of rehabilitation. In cross-group cases, because real desire for rehabilitation is far less likely to be present and because termination may be politically risky or economically impractical, deviants are most likely to be relegated to a permanently inferior status. Modern societies, it is often argued, have underworlds to which many deviants are consigned through labelling, and where they may be expected by much of the public to provide illicit goods and services.

Coping and Identity: The Individual as Deviant

Though deviance may be functional for constructing moral boundaries and preserving social order, labelling is nearly always intended not to create but to eliminate or reduce deviance. And deviance is usually understood to be conduct beyond a group's range of tolerance. Non-behavioural attributes—whether observed (skin colour, clothing, hair style) or imputed (genetic tendencies, magic powers, secret or unconscious desires)—are ordinarily of concern only because they are presumed to be associated with or causes of intolerable behaviour. Accordingly, most theorists and researchers have focused upon the problem of explaining deviant behaviour.

The search for explanations of deviant behaviour has led scientists to consider many different biological, psychological and social factors. Some forms of behaviour, notably violence, unconventional sexual activities and habitual non-medical drug use, have typically been assumed to be deviant without worrying much about the origins of such assumptions, or taking into account the problematic nature of labelling. Most criminological studies aim to explain why people commit crimes—with little or no attention to such questions as why some acts are legally defined as crimes but others even more harmful are not, and why some people are more likely than others to be labelled as criminals even when their behaviour is the same. For example, why is it illegal for one individual to rob another individual, but legal for a company that takes over another to terminate the second company's pension program and keep the money that was in the pension fund?

Specific efforts to account for deviant conduct have tended to dissolve into a general effort to explain all human behaviour. Although some investigators continue to look for causally significant biopsychological factors, the great majority of researchers remain convinced that the patterning of deviant and other human behaviour has far more to do with social learning.

Learning and Labelling: Becoming Deviant   The basic principles of social learning theory have been summarized by Akers (1985:39–70), who has led the way in applying them in the study of deviant behaviour. A basic assumption is that deviant and conforming behaviours are learned the same way. Specifically, behaviour is learned through conditioning—the repetition of certain experiences and consequences following an act—and by imitating other people. A behaviour pattern is strengthened by being rewarded (positive reinforcement) or by avoiding punishment (negative reinforcement), and weakened by being punished (positive punishment) or not being rewarded (negative punishment).

Whether a form of behaviour persists or changes depends upon *differential reinforcement*—the ratio of reinforcing to punishing experiences. Evaluations of behaviour are similarly learned: the more a person learns to define an act as good or justified rather than wrong, the more likely is the act to occur and reoccur. Reinforcers and punishers may be non-social (for example, the physiological effects of drugs, foods, odours, air temperature and pressure), but by far more crucial are social ones, that is, experienced or anticipated reactions from other people. Most important are those who "control sources and patterns of reinforcement, provide normative definitions, and expose one to behavioral models" (Akers, 1985 : 58).

The Think-Drink Effect

The experimentally demonstrated "think-drink effect" (Akers, 1985 : 142–43) is a good example of a learned behaviour pattern. Social drinkers as well as alcoholics drink more if they believe they are drinking alcohol instead of a non-alcoholic beverage—even when drinking tonic water with no alcohol! The tremors and cravings of alcoholics are lessened if they believe they are drinking an alcoholic beverage, and persist if they believe the beverage is non-alcoholic—when in each case the opposite is true! Learned expectations about "what happens when people drink" match changes in measures of anxiety, aggression and sexual arousal. Men become less anxious, women more so. Men become more aggressive. Women and men feel more aroused. And all this as a result of believing they are drinking, whether or not they are! Men even become less aggressive if they think the beverage is non-alcoholic even when it is! Query: If the effects of so powerful a drug as alcohol depend heavily upon learned assumptions instead of its pharmacological properties, how can violent crimes such as rape, murder and robbery be blamed on the effect of drugs?

Becoming a deviant is neither inevitable nor easy. Learning who one is and how to behave is a matter of coping with all the "reinforcers" and "punishers" encountered as one moves through life. For example, whether a child becomes an abusive parent depends upon the whole sequence of experiences through which that individual moves. If a child is abused repeatedly over a long time, if co-operation and keeping silent are rewarded, if the abuse is not countered by other more loving and supportive experiences, if no alternative role models to the abusive parent are provided, then learning theory predicts that the child will be an abusive parent. However, it is not always easy to track a life course in terms of the reinforcement model offered by social learning theory.

The problem facing those who hope to improve people's social behaviour is to figure out which kinds of experiences will punish or reinforce the kind of deviant behaviour in which one is interested. Consider stealing. If one learns that one's family comes first no matter what, then love and loyalty toward family can reinforce stealing to ensure the family's welfare. A poor man may steal bread, a rich one may embezzle trust funds, and each may believe his behaviour is necessary to take care of family needs. But if one learns that it is wrong to steal no matter what, then morality may require—as in the Islamic *shari'a*—that even a beloved family member's hand be cut off. On the other hand, if one learns to care for no one but oneself, then one may steal whenever given the chance, or refrain from stealing as one learns that it leads too often to unpleasant consequences.

Perhaps the labelling experience is still the most promising focus for developing a learning theory of deviance. Being treated as a deviant, as someone who deserves punishment, is certainly one of the most obvious punishers. But does labelling deter or produce further deviation? The question has provoked fierce debates (Gove, 1975). The answer is that labelling may have either effect, depending upon the circumstances in which it takes place. Labelling is more likely to deter when (1) it occurs early in the person's life; (2) the deviant has not yet been disposed of by social institutionalization; (3) the labeller's opinion matters to the person being labelled; (4) labelling ends when the deviation ceases (unlike the plight of the "ex con"); (5) genuine efforts are made to help the deviant, for example, by rewarding attempts to do better (positive reinforcement). Insofar as such conditions are more often found in small groups than in larger social organizations, deterrence is more likely to result when labelling is between intimates rather than between strangers.

Lemert's Labelling Theory

One of the most influential attempts to give research on deviant behaviour a theoretical focus has been that of Edwin Lemert over the past forty years. Lemert's (1972:62–92) proposal is that we concentrate on the task of explaining "secondary" rather than "primary" deviation. He sees *primary deviation* as an essentially unpredictable "polygenetic" occurrence,

arising out of a variety of social, cultural, psychological, and physiological factors, either in adventitious or recurring combinations. While it may be socially recognized and even defined as undesirable, primary deviation has only marginal implications for the status and psychic structure of the person concerned. (Lemert, 1972:62)

Secondary deviation refers to the patterned responses of individuals to being subjected to labelling. The personal problems created by "societal reactions" to their deviation "become central facts of existence for those experiencing them, altering psychic structure, producing specialized organization of social roles and self-regarding attitudes" (Lemert, 1972:63). The eventual outcome is the "secondary deviant," whose life and identity are organized around the experience of being a deviant in his own and others' eyes. Like Merton's anomie theory, the labelling perspective has fallen short of providing an adequate theory of deviant behaviour. But the idea that labelling is likely to affect one's self-concept and behaviour is consistent with social learning theory.

Learning to be deviant involves more than labelling at the hands of others. Some forms of deviation can only be practised if the requisite equipment and skills are available and if there are opportunities to acquire and use them. The less equipment (weapons, tools, computers, vehicles, costumes, substances, sales records, etc.) a deviant act requires, the more likely it is to occur and recur. Many forms of deviance, such as casual promiscuity, disorderly public conduct and incidental assault, require no equipment, so are easy options available to anyone. But to become a professional thief, robber, fence, prostitute, drug dealer or terrorist, one must acquire the necessary equipment and learn how to use it.

Road hustlers advance from the haphazard, crude operations of rough hustling to professional standing only after surviving a hard apprenticeship (Prus and Sharper, 1977 : 47–59). Much like a professional musician, the road hustler not only uses equipment (dice, cards, cash, appropriate clothing), but also develops extremely complex skills to the point where "the ability to manipulate cards or dice is rather commonplace and taken more for granted" (Prus and Sharper, 1977 : 47). Only a true virtuoso is considered a "mechanic," and few reach this level.

Physical and social skills aside, not everyone has the opportunity to learn how to be a road hustler. Places vary greatly in the extent to which they facilitate or inhibit deviant behaviour. It is easier to carry on many forms of deviant behaviour in private than in public, or else in places formally or tacitly set aside for deviant activities.

Cities offer a much greater diversity of scenes and experience than do small towns.

CATHERINE JOLLY,
TORONTO.

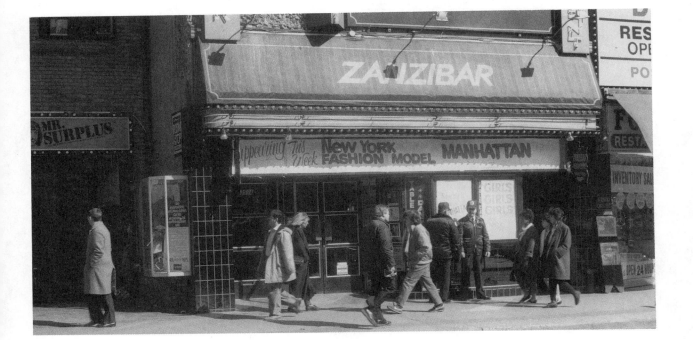

The "strip" is found in cities all over the world. Toronto's Yonge Street, Montreal's "The Main," New York's Times Square are well-known examples. In such areas, opportunities are present for all sorts of deviant experiences. Socially institutionalized deviants constitute a significant part of the population in such places, where they serve as guides and providers to those looking for illicit goods and services—especially drugs and sex. In contrast, small towns—where individuals are widely known and expected to be in particular places at specific times—offer fewer opportunities to experiment or persist in violating local or legal standards.

Facilities for enclosing and "correcting" deviants are themselves places where deviants are under heavy pressures to accept a deviant identity, that is, to be socially institutionalized. In one controversial study (Rosenham, 1973), "pseudopatients" feigned hearing voices to gain admission to the psychiatric wards of twelve hospitals on the East and West coasts of the United States. All were admitted for observation, then immediately ceased any pretence to abnormality. Eleven were diagnosed as schizophrenic, one as manic-depressive psychotic (a more favourable prognosis, given by the only private hospital in the sample). The major findings were that the phony patients were never detected, and that the initial diagnosis persisted no matter what they did. Observation periods ranged from seven to fifty-two days, averaging nineteen days, and were determined by staff decisions. Despite the absence of any unusual or symptomatic personal history information (all true excepting names and occupations) and of any observed symptomatic behaviour, all the pseudopatients were discharged with a diagnosis of "in remission"; that is, they were still perceived as being insane.

Punk Subculture

The punk subculture may be viewed as either a cultural expression or a form of politics (Tanner, 1988 : 341–46). From the cultural perspective, punk originates in the rejection of conventional values by British youth who find themselves unemployed and unwanted. Defying adult standards of decorum and responsibility is a way of rejecting what cannot be had anyway. The political perspective sees in punk not merely a rejection, but a revolution. Punkers are out to subvert a prevailing morality and class structure that condemns them to poverty and insignificance. But as Tanner (1988 : 345–46) observes, such "erudite explanations" fail to consider that only a minority of working-class youth are punkers in any meaningful sense. Moreover, they do not explain the attraction of punk for middle-class youth. As a more or less temporary life style chosen by some "culturally adventurous" young people, punk—and youth culture in general—is perhaps being given more attention than it deserves. If

we narrowly concern ourselves with the corrupting influences of popular culture, we need never raise more fundamental questions about the limited range of social and economic roles available to youth in the context of contemporary social structures. (Tanner, 1988 : 355)

Deviant Worlds and Straight Ways: Subcultures, Evasions and Holidays

Social scientists and other observers have produced thousands of reports describing the infinite variety of ways in which learning, labelling, equipment and opportunities have combined to form deviant "subcultures." These worlds of deviance are usually pictured as alien, exotic or erotic islands cut off from the rest of society. Though by no means commonplace to most of us, deviant worlds are nonetheless linked (whether or not "functionally") to the straight world of moral evasions and holidays.

Deviant worlds usually incorporate several forms in a kind of symbiotic relationship with one another and to the straight world. Such "vices" as illicit drug use and transactions, pimping and prostitution and illegal gambling tend to go together, along with stealing, mugging and various hustles. The "underworld" so comprised is the habitat of socially institutionalized deviants. They live partly off one another, but mostly off the "straights" who visit them seeking fun, relaxation, adventure, information or more sordid gratifications. In this uncertain and often dangerous world, few total commitments are possible; relationships are typically ephemeral and expedient.

Inhabitants of the underside world openly deviate from the prevailing norms of prosperity, appearance, competence, and hopefulness.

CATHERINE JOLLY, TORONTO.

Overlapping the underworld of pimps, thieves, pushers, informers and other "criminal elements" is the "underside" world of the assorted "bums, dropouts, freaks and losers" who openly deviate from the prevailing norms of prosperity, appearance, competence and hopefulness. They are "the disreputable poor," the dregs and junk of society, who are an affront to "decent people"—who are prone to explain social failure on moral shortcomings, blaming the victims instead of the social environments that produce them.

Adjunct to the losers' world is the "fringe" world of the semi-respectable whose occupations or other attributes make them suspect, and who are largely excluded from normal participation in straight, respectable society. Carnival workers, circus performers and those who perform some of the more gruesome and unpleasant services for society deviate from norms of stability, appearance, smell and work (productive, honest, clean, etc., as commonly defined). Among the denigrated occupations are gravediggers, executioners, "night soil" (human feces) removers in Asia—as well as surgeons and police in many countries throughout history. You may be able to think of other examples.

An irony of police work is that the respectable people who expect protection often feel disturbed or frightened in the presence of police officers, who find themselves more or less isolated and looked down upon by those they try to "serve and protect." Demands for "dirty work" are not necessarily matched by appreciation of those who have to do it.

Labelling of the Physically Handicapped

Many of those who inhabit the "fringe world" are afflicted with "abominations of the body" (Goffman, 1963:4). "Deformed," blind, deaf, and mentally retarded people typically find themselves relegated to discredited and inferior social statuses. Well-meaning people frequently though inadvertently push the handicapped toward accepting deviant identities (hopeless abnormal, not a real person, helpless loser, etc.). Attempts to behave as normally as possible may be officially and consciously encouraged, but sabotaged by the overly protective and helpful behaviour of concerned others—as well as the distant, depersonalizing behaviour of insensitive others. Intimate relationships with normals (for example, as friends, lovers, spouses or adoptive parents) are generally discouraged and sometimes legally prohibited. The more stringent the definition of normalcy, the less able are abnormals such as retarded children to resist labelling. Mercer (1973), for example, found that higher-status parents were less accepting of their afflicted children than were lower-status parents, less hopeful for their children, and readier to institutionalize them.

Respectability and normalcy presumably mean the absence of deviance. But do they? The straight world tolerates and may even encourage deviations in some exceptional circumstances. New Year's Eve and Mardi Gras, for instance, are traditionally "moral holidays" when the usual rules are relaxed. Business and professional people may be expected to enjoy "time-outs" at conventions; vacationers may enjoy "shipboard romances" without censure. Moreover, deviance is often "hidden" within the most sacred bastions of the straight world: child molestation in nurseries and schools; sexual misconduct among seminarians and religious leaders; alcoholism, abuse and violence within families. Bryant (1973:396) has even concluded that

> a family may be considered a social collusion system for the maintenance of internal secrets and the concealment of stigma, scandal, and inappropriate behavior on the part of its members.

The pervasiveness of deviance throughout the underworld, underside, fringe and straight parts of the social world has led sociologists to reject the common assumption that deviance is concentrated at the bottom of society.

Elite Deviance: Upperworld Offenders   Since Edwin Sutherland coined the term "white-collar crime" in the 1930s, the patterns and rates of deviant behaviour by high-status people have been of growing interest. Most research has focused upon deviance related to their occupational activities. Illegal or unethical conduct by business people, politicians, lawyers and physicians has been extensively studied—and there is mounting evidence of cheating, plagiarism and fraud in the world of scientific research.

Deviant Scientists

Scientists are trained and expected to meet the highest standards of objectivity and truth in doing and reporting their studies. Not all do. Falsifying, trimming (to fit a pet theory), and cooking (selectively reporting and suppressing) data; plagiarism (stealing others' ideas); and the unethical or illegal use of human subjects are serious deviations because they undermine the scientific enterprise itself. If scientists cannot trust one another, and the public cannot trust what is reported to be "knowledge," the door is left open for all sorts of non-rational and untestable subjective claims. Insofar as such claims result in wrong political decisions and social policies, the welfare of humanity itself is threatened.

The most famous case of falsification is Charles Dawson's "Piltdown Man," a supposed anthropological discovery of prehistoric human remains in Sussex that was eventually proven to be a hoax. Less well known but potentially more consequential are the several recent instances of fraudulent research in major centres of medical and psychological research—for example, Mark Spector's spurious work at Cornell University on how viruses cause cancer; John Darsee's fraudulent research at Harvard Medical School; Sir Cyril Burt's repeatedly falsifying data during his distinguished career at Oxford, Cambridge and University College, London, to support his assertion that higher IQ is strongly correlated with higher social class. (For detailed analyses of these and many other cases, see Ben-Yehuda, 1987:168–207.)

Among high-status occupational groups, doctors have generally been the most highly esteemed and handsomely rewarded. Yet, fraudulent and even physically harmful activities by medical professionals have been documented in numerous investigations by private researchers and governmental agencies. Studies of medical program fraud in the United States (Geis et al., 1988; Jesilow et al., 1986) have shown not only that fraud is common, but also that doctors are virtually immune from prosecution and punishment.

Detection of Medicare and Medicaid violations is extremely difficult. Physicians are reluctant to police and expose one another, and are often sympathetic to violators because reimbursement schedules under the programs are viewed as inadequate. Federal and state enforcement programs are underfunded, have only limited powers and are oriented more to encouraging compliance than to prosecution. The U.S. criminal justice system is so overloaded that only a handful of cases can be thoroughly investigated and prosecuted. Excepting the rare "most blatant" case, the most severe penalty upon conviction is partial or full repayment.

> All of the above, combined with the possibility that the defendant may well be politically influential and affect the reelection chances of the prosecutor, put a severe damper on prosecutorial zeal in regard to physician fraud. (Jesilow et al., 1986:19)

Why do advantaged people break the rules? Traditional common sense says that their learning experiences would tend to reinforce conformity, not deviance. They are trained for legitimate success, given ample opportunities and support, and rewarded with wealth and status for their contributions as the leaders of society. In a sense, they are breaking their own rules, in that they have more influence than lesser citizens upon the making, interpretation and enforcement of their society's norms.

Speculations that high-status deviants are extremely rare, typically mentally disturbed or otherwise abnormal or usually newly arrived from the lower class or alien cultures do not fit the evidence. The known and suspected rates of elite deviance are anything but insignificant. Most high-status offenders are indistinguishable from their presumably normal peers. Neither humble class origin nor immigrant background is present in the vast majority of cases. Accordingly, explanations of elite deviance tend increasingly to focus upon cultural and structural contexts.

Radicals blame the aggressive egoism and competition fostered by capitalism; conservatives blame the breakdown of traditional morality. Social scientists tend to look beyond cultural sources to the institutional and organizational settings in which normative beliefs are formed and modified. Market and career demands are often cited as forcing even basically moral high-status individuals to commit deviant acts. Even though many people still reject pressures and opportunities to deviate, it appears that most succumb when organizational or political interests are at stake. This leads some theorists and researchers to question whether moral boundaries really exist independently of political ones; that is, whether the moral boundaries merely reflect the interests of the people who hold power in a society.

Competition and Power: The Organization as Deviant

Legal and moral boundary construction has long been viewed by many as a "conflict process" or "game" in which the creation and application of norms depend upon how power is distributed. Different categories and groups of people are assumed to be in open or implicit competition for "the means and opportunities to realize their respective visions of the good life" (Turk, 1982:12). Deviance becomes, then, not so much a matter of whether and how individuals violate norms as of whether and how groups exercise power over one another. The sociologist's problem shifts from explaining individual deviance to explaining collective deviance, also called organizational deviance.

Many of us find it hard to think of *collective* behaviour as something other than the sum total of *individual* acts. While it is deceptively easy to see individuals as deviants, the deviance of organizations and other collectivities—up to and including whole societies (Nazi Germany? Stalinist Russia?)—is not as readily visualized. A little thought, however, shows that the only real problem is getting used to the idea. Governments, armies, corporations and even social classes and ethnic populations are frequently regarded as acting units, and stigmatized for their actions or attributes. In fact, since the Middle Ages churches, towns and kings ("the Crown")—and eventually "free corporate actors"—have been understood to be "juristic" or legal people, though not "natural" ones (Coleman, 1974:13–31). For the most part, analysts of organizational deviance have limited their attention to deviance and control within societies, specifically to "organized crime" and "corporate deviance."

Criminal Organizations

Bandit and outlaw gangs have existed all over the world. Pirates have been known since the invention of sailing ships. Wherever political-legal boundaries have been drawn, there have been those who banded together in defiance of them. In our times, terms such as "Mafia" and "syndicate" have been used in reference to many kinds of ongoing associations created to profit from deviance. Providing illicit goods and services has been a route to fortune and power, and the foundations of later respectability have often been laid in the earlier predations and dubious exploits of ancestral heroes.

Efforts to differentiate criminal from non-criminal organizations analytically rather than legally have not been successful. When access to legitimate markets is limited, or when such markets are not sufficiently profitable, both "respectable" and "criminal" organizations are likely to seek alternative opportunities for profit. As Sacco (1986) has observed, the emergence and operations of so-called criminal organizations are in response to markets—especially to markets created by attempts to prohibit goods and services for which there is widespread demand. If the potential profits are high enough, organized lawbreaking will ensue—as in the international trafficking in drugs. How is one to differentiate between the trafficking of Colombian drug kings, or of the Crips and Bloods black street gangs of Los Angeles, and of CIA agents in Southeast Asia and Central America?

If our focus becomes organized lawbreaking, the problem becomes even more difficult. Not only do presumably respectable corporations and other organizations frequently violate ethnical and legal norms, they also have considerable impact (for example, through political campaign contributions) upon how the norms are created and applied.

Corporate Deviance   Ermann and Lundman (1982:9–11) observe that corporate entities can produce deviant behaviour in at least three ways. First, leaders may deliberately use their positions to bring about collective actions in violation of legal or other norms. Second, administrative coalitions and compromises may lead to unintended deviant collective behaviour. Third, organizational complexity itself may result in deviant behaviour even though no individual deviance occurred.

Corporate Deviance

Clinard and Yeager (1980) systematically analysed administrative, civil, and criminal actions started or completed by twenty-five American federal agencies against the 477 largest publicly owned manufacturing corporations during 1975 and 1976. In addition, they did a more limited study of the 105 largest wholesale, retail and service corporations. Sixty percent of the 582 corporations had 1553 cases begun, an average of 2.7.

Of the 350 corporations against whom at least one action was begun, the average was 4.4 cases. The violations included *administrative* violations (for example, failing to provide required information, file reports or obtain permits); *environmental* violations (pollution, failures to install required controls); tax, currency and other *financial* violations; *labour* violations (employee health and safety, discriminatory practices, exploitative wages and hours); *manufacturing* violations (of product safety regulations); and *unfair trade practices* (false advertising, price fixing, rigging bids, collusion to control markets). Manufacturing, environmental and labour violations accounted for more than three-fourths of the total; financial and trade violations were the least frequent.

Violating firms tended to be larger, less financially successful, more diversified and showing poorer growth rates. However, the relationships were too weak to predict corporate involvement in illegal activity. Clinard and Yeager (1980:132) conclude that

economic pressures and other factors operate in a corporate environment [e.g., the oil industry] that is conducive to unethical and illegal practices. On the other hand one may find extensive corporate violations where no financial pressures or structural characteristics are evident.

Elite manipulation of organizational resources to violate legal norms has been described in a large number of studies of corporate and governmental deviance. The Lockheed Corporation, for instance, has at various times been in trouble with the law, most notably for bribing foreign officials to buy their airplanes (including the Starfighter jet that the American Air Force had rejected as unsafe). One of the best documented examples of governmental deviance is the "Watergate" scandal—the series of crimes (breaking and entering, obstructing justice, perjury and several others) engineered by then President Richard Nixon and his top aides. The "Iran-Contra Affair" of Ollie North and other figures in the Reagan government suggests that there is a pattern of secretly organized violation of the laws that are intended to limit American political and military activities abroad.

The Ford Pinto story illustrates how administrative procedures can result in organizational deviance (Ermann and Lundman, 1982 : 10, 17–18). Lee Iacocca was eventually successful in pushing for a crash program to develop a small fuel-efficient car to meet the foreign competition. The Pinto was rushed through design to production in record time, with a clear sense of urgency, if not desperation. When evidence of a potentially hazardous fuel tank was found, it was shelved because the design engineers were keenly aware of Iacocca's decree that the car could not exceed 2000 pounds in weight or $2000 in cost. (It was later calculated that the cost of correcting the problem would have added about eleven cents per unit!) Over the next several years, the Pinto fuel tank ruptured in numerous crashes and several people died in the resulting fires. Ford tried to deny responsibility, but lost a number of suits. In 1978 the company was ordered to repair the nearly two million Pintos, and achieved the distinction of being the first corporation ever to be indicted for criminal homicide (by an Elkhart, Indiana, grand jury). No one ordered or desired an unsafe vehicle, but organizational policies and hierarchical division of responsibilities produced one.

It is not easy to find other than hypothetical examples of entirely inadvertent organizational deviance. Still, many researchers have found that corporate deviance is often better explained as a product of insensitivity or ignorance than intent. Clinard and Yeager's (1980) monumental study of corporate lawbreaking suggests that both executives and lower-level supervisors are socialized to be dedicated "organization men" who do not look past "the bottom line" and their particular assignment (see also Clinard, 1983). Responsibility is diffused through a complex and dehumanizing system, and any lingering personal doubts tend to be discounted as irrelevant.

Given such findings, it is not surprising that many people see organizations as inherently deviant. Anarchists have developed an ideology condemning all varieties of formalism, legalism and hierarchy. Critics of "bureaupathology" and "bureaucratic justice" have advocated the dismantling of organizations and their replacement with informal and equalitarian associations. Social theorists have uncovered "dysfunctions" and insoluble "dilemmas" believed to characterize all formal organizations. And attitude surveys have consistently revealed high levels of hostility toward bureaucracies.

Whether complex organizations of diverse people and groups can ever be fully "legitimate" seems doubtful. As long as collective demands and goals take precedence over individual and local ones, organizations must inevitably deviate from the norms of those who do not control them but are nonetheless constrained by them. Regardless, the large-scale organization of social life is a fact and a continuing process with which human beings will have to come to terms.

Merely to condemn organizational deviance as a function of what organizations are and do is equivalent to imputing original sin to every person. Criteria must be developed that recognize variations in the human and environmental casualties associated more with some organizational forms than others. As was learned in the long search for the causes of individual deviance, the causes of organizational deviance are most likely to be found in the interactions between organizations and their changing social environments.

Social Control and Social Change

Environments are not constant. It follows that the sources of organizational as well as individual deviance will change as environmental conditions change. Technological innovations, discovery or depletion of natural resources, economic development or decline, internal and international political realignments—all such factors generate pressures upon whatever social and moral orders have been constructed. Norms change as their social and cultural foundations change in response to environmental changes.

Whether the scale and pace of change are revolutionary or evolutionary, people experiencing the change are forced to revise the norms that enable them to relate to

Christian morality was a strong force in medieval Europe, where the church became a symbol of a stable moral order.

CATHERINE JOLLY, TORONTO.

Protest demonstrations are signs of a changing moral order.

CATHERINE JOLLY, TORONTO.

one another. The alternative is to lose all sense of life as meaningful. To some observers, this is what has been happening. They see a "return to anarchy," a "legitimation crisis" and "the end of the world." To others, humanity is going through the often painful process of adapting the traditional religious moralities to new economic, political and cultural environments that are emerging.

Jacques Ellul (1969) discerns three great historical transformations in the basic moral order of the Western world. *Christian morality* developed in the Middle Ages and was refined during the sixteenth and seventeenth centuries. It extolled an otherworldly orientation over the material concerns of this world, especially political and economic concerns. The inner soul of the individual was the only significant reality, its salvation the only important goal.

Bourgeois morality, originating in the Reformation, was an adaptation to the industrial and commercial revolution. It retained the preoccupation with an individual's inner state, but developed a new conception of its relationship to the material world. Success in this world became the outward sign of inner virtue. Attending to one's proper business and rejecting idleness, unproductive pleasures and undue levity became the identifying characteristics of a good man or woman. Industriousness and propriety were assumed by the prevailing ideology to be the moral preconditions of success. Material success in competition with others became the measure of one's worth as a human being. Poverty was evidence of moral weakness and lack of character.

Today, says Ellul, the once-dominant bourgeois morality is crumbling as individualism is made meaningless by the large-scale organization of social life. Entrepreneurial orientations and skills are becoming irrelevant and unwanted. Individuals perceive themselves to be cogs in massive and complex economic and political machines. The emerging new order is reflected in the *technological morality* of the fully bureaucratized person. Whatever is required to perform one's assigned role is good. Normalcy and morality are defined by organizational interests and demands, not by any otherworldly or personal standards. "In the last analysis, it appears as a suppression of morality through the total absorption of the individual into the group" (Ellul, 1969:198).

There are, of course, reasons to disagree with Ellul. The demise of individualism and religion may not be as imminent as he believes. Resistance to governmental and corporate regimentation is widespread, even in the most dictatorial societies. Individualism and religious zeal have acquired new vigour. The moral relativism and irresponsibility fostered by technological morality are increasingly under attack, as people all over the world are demanding both freedom and meaning in their lives. Against Ellul stand people like Orrin Klapp (1969), who argues that people always seek moral order—a "symbolic balance" enabling them to achieve personally meaningful identities.

Summary

Conceptions of right and wrong are developed in the ongoing process of constructing social relationships. Variations beyond what has come to be expected tend to be regarded as not just different, but somehow *wrong*. At the extremes, *absolutists* reject anything contrary to what they believe, while *relativists* are indiscriminately tolerant.

Although images of deviance vary among individuals and groups and change over time, deviations in some form are always present. This has led some theorists to conclude that deviance and control are somehow *functional*, benefiting groups in such ways as promoting unity and giving concrete meaning to norms.

When people fail to meet the expectations (norms) of others, a process of *labelling* occurs. The others try to place (label) and control the deviant within their particular framework of norms (the *prior normative context*). The labelling process begins with an initial *identification*, then goes through *justification* of the labelling, *negotiation* of the particular label and symbolic or physical *enclosure* of the deviant as the others become more convinced they are right. When a deviant has been fully processed, the final step is *disposition*. Disposition may take the form of termination (ending the person's group membership), rehabilitation (resocializing the person) or social institutionalization (relegating the individual to permanent deviant status).

Labelling is an important element in social learning. Patterns of deviant behaviour are learned, like any other behaviour, through exposure over time to various combinations of reinforcers and punishers. Imitation also plays a part in social learning.

Deviant worlds are not sharply separated from the straight world, but vary in the degree to which they are a part of it. The *underworld* of socially institutionalized deviance blends into the *underside* world of society's losers, which in turn overlaps the *fringe* world of the semi-respectable and the *hidden* and *holiday* deviance of the straight world. Because deviations are so widespread, particularly among elite and respectable members of society, some analysts have concluded that variations in rates of deviance depend more upon power differences among groups than upon real differences in their behaviour.

Studies that look at organizations as deviant actors have focused upon organized crime and corporate deviance. Criminal and legitimate organizations are in many ways similar, notably in their responsiveness to market opportunities and political pressures. Governmental and corporate actors frequently engage in illegal or unethical actions, but they have considerable influence upon the creation and enforcement of legal and other norms so their exploitative and predatory behaviour may at times be legal. If illegal, it is less likely to be punished.

Both individual and group deviance are the products of responses to, and interactions with, their environments. As environments change, so do individual behaviours and group behaviours. Consequently, patterns of deviance and social control shift as people try to adapt to the changing conditions of their lives. Against the notion that a "technological morality" of the fully regimented individual is ascendant, there is much evidence supporting the opposite view that the world's peoples are rejecting bureaucratization—reasserting the values of individual freedom and a meaningful life.

Suggested Readings

Ben-Yehuda, Nachman
  1987. *Deviance and Moral Boundaries*. Chicago: University of Chicago Press. Richly detailed natural histories of the growth and survival of several forms of rarely studied deviance: witchcraft, the occult, science fiction, deviant sciences and deviant scientists.

Cohen, Stanley, and Andrew Scull, eds.
  1983. *Social Control and the State*. Oxford: Martin Robertson. A definitive collection of historical and comparative essays summarizing current knowledge about how crime, insanity and other forms of deviance have been defined and treated in North America and Europe.

Goffman, Erving
  1963. *Stigma: The Management of Spoiled Identity*. Englewood Cliffs, N.J.: Prentice-Hall. Sensitive and insightful analysis of the social meaning of deviance and the social pressures upon the stigmatized to accept deviant identities.

Sacco, Vincent F., ed.
  1988. *Deviance: Conformity and Control in Canadian Society*. Scarborough: Prentice-Hall. Up-to-date reviews of Canadian studies of various forms of deviance, with an excellent introductory overview of the basic issues and major theories in the field of deviance and control research.

Scheff, Thomas J.
  1984. *Being Mentally Ill: A Sociological Theory*, 2nd ed. New York: Aldine. The authoritative study of mental illness from a sociological perspective. Detailed review of the relevant literature and a commendable demonstration of how a non-deviant scientist revises theoretical propositions in light of further research.

Turk, Austin T.

1982. *Political Criminality: The Defiance and Defense of Authority*. Beverly Hills: Sage. A major statement of the conflict perspective on deviance and social control. Critically reviews what is known about the legal definition of political deviance, the attributes and behaviour of political deviants, tactics and consequences of political policing, and problems in measuring the survival chances of political authority structures.

Discussion Questions

1. What are some examples of moral *absolutism* and *relativism*?

2. How can we know when deviance is "functional"?

3. In what ways is a university class a moral order?

4. Are there some forms of deviant behaviour *not* learned?

5. What is insanity? Who is insane?

6. Is it really possible to differentiate individual and organizational deviant behaviour?

Data Collection Exercises

1. Using some or all of Simmons's labels, as well as more current ones you can think of, make up a questionnaire (a) listing some deviant labels and (b) asking your respondents to use at least five words each to describe what they think each kind of deviant is like. (Try for a sample of 100.) Do your respondents use the same words to characterize deviants? Do they see Simmons's types the same way his respondents did?

2. Are elite deviants punished less often and less severely? Review a major newspaper's reports over the past few months of illegal activities by high- and low-status actors. Compare the dispositions of the high-status and low-status cases.

3. What are the norms of your friendship? One way to find out is to do something that your friend(s) may find odd. Try something like carrying around a teddy bear for several days, wearing very dressy instead of ordinary clothes or being unusually polite.

4. Have you ever been labelled? Describe your experience in terms of the labelling process.

Writing Exercises

1. Is the straight world really a deviant world? Write an essay showing how this question might be answered differently by a functionalist, a labelling theorist and a conflict theorist.

2. The labelling perspective has been severely criticized and rejected by a number of leading social scientists. Write a critical review of the book edited by Walter Gove (1975), indicating whether you think the labelling approach was accurately described and adequately defended.

3. Policy analysis: If a major corporation, employing thousands of workers, is found guilty of polluting the environment, what should be done? Consider the possibilities and consequences of using various control strategies, with different combinations of reinforcers and punishers.

4. Construct a questionnaire for interviewing people on how they define "normal." Do they have universal criteria, or does it depend on who, what, when, where? Are some things more deviant than others? Consider such questions in explaining why you think your questionnaire would be a good one.

Glossary

Anomie: *the theory that deviant behaviour is a way of trying to cope with the discrepancy between the "goals" people are socialized to seek and the "means" available to attain those goals—that is, deviance is caused by unequal "opportunity structures."*

Deviance: *the violation of a norm; that is, whatever someone finds disturbing, frightening or threatening.*

Deviant world: *a place or sector of society where deviant activities are expected, or tolerated, and perhaps even encouraged.*

Differential reinforcement: *the ratio of reinforcing to punishing experiences.*

Elite deviant: *a high-status person who violates occupational norms.*

Labelling: *the theory that deviance is a "socially constructed reality"—that right and wrong are decided by the power of some people to impose their norms on less powerful people.*

Norm: *any rule or standard, explicit or implicit, by which people judge one another.*

Social control: *whatever people do, more or less consciously, to influence how others perceive and react to deviance.*

Social learning: *the theory that deviant behaviour is learned from exposure over time to reinforcers and punishers, and from role models.*

References

Akers, Ronald L.
    1985. *Deviant Behavior: A Social Learning Approach*, 3rd ed. Belmont, Cal.: Wadsworth.

Ben-Yehuda, Nachman
   1987. *Deviance and Moral Boundaries*. Chicago: University of Chicago Press.

Bryant, Clifton D.
   1973. "The Concealment of Stigma and Deviancy as a Family Function," pp. 391–97. In Clifton D. Bryant and J. Gipson Wells, eds., *Deviancy and the Family*. Philadelphia: F. A. Davis Co.

Clinard, Marshall B.
   1983. *Corporate Ethics and Crime: The Role of Middle Management*. Beverly Hills: Sage.

Clinard, Marshall B., ed.
   1964. *Anomie and Deviant Behavior*. New York: Free Press.

Clinard, Marshall B., and Peter C. Yeager
   1980. *Corporate Crime*. New York: Free Press.

Cohen, Albert K.
   1966. *Deviance and Control*. Englewood Cliffs, N.J.: Prentice-Hall.

Cohen, Stanley, and Andrew Scull, eds.
   1983. *Social Control and the State*. Oxford: Martin Robertson.

Coleman, James C.
   1974. *Power and the Structure of Society*. New York: W. W. Norton.

Currie, Elliott
   1985. *Confronting Crime: An American Challenge*. New York: Pantheon.

Ellul, Jacques
   1969. *To Will and To Do*. Philadelphia: United Church Press.

Erikson, Kai T.
   1966. *Wayward Puritans*. New York: Wiley.

Ermann, M. David, and Richard J. Lundman
   1982. *Corporate Deviance*. New York: Holt, Rinehart and Winston.

Farrell, Ronald A., and Victoria Swigert
   1982. *Deviance and Social Control*. Glenview, Ill.: Scott, Foresman.

Geis, Gilbert, Henry N. Pontell and Paul Jesilow
   1988. "Medicaid Fraud," pp. 17–39. In Joseph E. Scott and Travis Hirschi, eds., *Controversial Issues in Crime and Justice*. Newbury Park, Cal.: Sage.

Goffman, Erving
   1963. *Stigma: Notes on the Management of Spoiled Identity*. Englewood Cliffs, N.J.: Prentice-Hall.

Gove, Walter R., ed.
   1975. *The Labelling of Deviance: Evaluating a Perspective*. New York: Wiley.

Grimes, Ruth-Ellen M., and Austin T. Turk
   1978. "Labeling in Context: Conflict, Power and Self-Definition," pp. 39–58. In Marvin D. Krohn and Ronald L. Akers, eds., *Crime, Law, and Sanctions: Theoretical Perspectives*. Beverly Hills: Sage.

Ingleby, David
   1983. "Mental Health and Social Order," pp. 141–88. In Stanley Cohen and Andrew Scull, eds., *Social Control and the State*. Oxford: Martin Robertson.

Jesilow, Paul, Henry N. Pontell and Gilbert Geis
1986. "Physician Immunity from Prosecution and Punishment for Medical Program Fraud," pp. 7–22. In W. Byron Groves and Graeme Newman, eds., *Punishment and Privilege*. Albany, N.Y.: Harrow and Heston.

Klapp, Orrin E.
1969. *Collective Search for Identity*. New York: Holt, Rinehart and Winston.

Lemert, Edwin M.
1972. *Human Deviance, Social Problems, and Social Control*, 2nd ed. Englewood Cliffs, N.J.: Prentice-Hall.

Levy, Robert I.
1971. "The Community Function of Tahitian Male Transvestism: A Hypothesis." *Anthropological Quarterly* 44 (January): 12–21.

Mercer, Jane R.
1973. *Labeling the Retarded*. Berkeley: University of California Press.

Merton, Robert K.
1957. *Social Theory and Social Structure*, rev. ed. New York: Free Press.

Prus, Robert C., and C. R. D. Sharper
1977. *Road Hustler*. Toronto: Gage.

Rosenham, D. L.
1973. "On Being Sane in Insane Places." *Science* 179 (January 19): 250–58.

Sacco, Vincent F.
1986. "An Approach to the Study of Organized Crime," pp. 214–26. In Robert A. Silverman and James J. Teevan, Jr., eds., *Crime in Canadian Society*, 3rd ed. Toronto: Butterworths.

Scheff, Thomas J.
1984. *Being Mentally Ill: A Sociological Theory*, 2nd ed. New York: Aldine.

Simmons, J. L.
1969. *Deviants*. Berkeley: Glendessary Press.

Tanner, Julian
1988. "Youthful Deviance," pp. 323–59. In Vincent F. Sacco, ed., *Deviance: Conformity and Control in Canadian Society*. Scarborough: Prentice-Hall.

Turk, Austin T.
1982. *Political Criminality: The Defiance and Defense of Authority*. Beverly Hills: Sage.
1984. "Criminology and Socio-Legal Studies," pp. 309–34. In Anthony N. Doob and Edward L. Greenspan, eds., *Perspectives in Criminal Law*. Aurora, Ont.: Canada Law Book.

CHAPTER 7

Aging: The Middle and Later Years

BARRY D. McPHERSON

Introduction

Since the 1960s scholars, practitioners and policy makers have increasingly recognized that aging is not just a biological process that leads to medical and housing problems. Rather, how we age, how society adapts to increasing numbers of elderly people and how members of different generations interact with each other can only be understood by viewing aging as a social process. In this chapter you will learn that aging is a complex social process that involves the interaction of individual and population aging, and that not every society, or every individual in a specific society, ages in the same way. More specifically, you will be introduced to the theory, methods, social processes and social issues that must be understood and addressed if we are to understand and change, if necessary, how we and future generations will age in Canada.

Social Illusions (Myths)

Opposite page:
Aging together after more than sixty-five years of marriage.

REPRODUCED FROM THE BOOK *PRESENT FACES OF WATERLOO PAST*, WITH PERMISSION OF DR. W. FORBES, EDITOR, AND MR. M. GREEN, PHOTOGRAPHER. THIS BOOK IS PUBLISHED BY THE PROGRAM IN GERONTOLOGY, UNIVERSITY OF WATERLOO, WATERLOO, ONTARIO: NOVEMBER 1988.

When asked to identify older adults, you probably think about your parents and grandparents, and about middle-aged and elderly persons you see in the neighbourhood and on campus. You may also think about those who are physically frail and must live in nursing homes or other long-term care institutions. When you are then asked to describe the life situation or life style of elderly people, you may respond, as many do, by reporting one or more of the following beliefs: namely, that they are isolated, alone and lonely; depressed; asexual; weak and physically inactive; less intelligent than younger people; senile or mentally confused; abandoned by their family; forgetful; dependent on others; living in institutions; heavy users of prescription drugs; poor and unemployed; or ultra-conservative in thought and behaviour.

These beliefs, and the subsequent accompanying attitudes, portray and perpetuate a negative image of aging and being old, often because the source of our information is the media or is based on our limited experience with elderly persons, especially outside the family. Our beliefs and attitudes are highly influenced by news reports, jokes in greeting cards, or personal observations of one or two elderly relatives or neighbours. Based on this limited information we may then generalize these life situations or characteristics to all elderly people. Furthermore, because of the phenomenon of *age homophily*, whereby people tend to socialize with those of about the same age, we often believe that the elderly comprise a homogeneous group wherein all older people have the same abilities, interests, needs or characteristics.

Because these unfounded beliefs and generalized attitudes have been accepted as facts, negative myths about aging are perpetuated. As a result, the presence of these social and biological myths in a society may influence the behaviour of middle-aged and elderly persons. That is, a self-fulfilling prophecy is created; elderly people either adopt inappropriate beliefs and behaviours in order to fit with social expectations, or they engage in coping strategies to avoid the expected behaviour. Moreover, these stereotypes, myths and inaccurate beliefs also influence the behaviour and attitudes of younger people regarding the elderly and regarding anyone who happens to look, dress or act aged. This can lead to direct or indirect forms of discrimination against the elderly, sometimes referred to as *ageism*, and to the further perpetuation of stereotypes, prejudices and fears about aging. To illustrate, men who are prematurely bald or grey at about age thirty may be viewed as old. A woman of about thirty-five may be considered unemployable if she has not been in the labour force during the previous decade.

Social Reality

In this chapter, you will learn that aging is a lifelong process characterized by a continuity in personal life style; that most of our stereotypes about aging are myths; that the elderly are characterized by a wide range of individual differences on a number of health, social, emotional, economic and psychological factors; and that aging is as much a social as a biological process. Indeed, individuals age differently both within a society (for example, Newfoundland vs. British Columbia; northern Quebec vs. southern Ontario; rural Saskatchewan vs. metropolitan Toronto) and across societies (for example, Canada vs. the Soviet Union; China vs. Japan; Pakistan vs. the United States; or, in more general terms, in developed vs. developing nations; in northern vs. southern climates; or in nations with low vs. high mortality or longevity rates).

Population Aging

Although the human *life span* has remained relatively stable since the last century, since the early 1950s birth rates have declined and *life expectancy* has increased in most modern industrial societies. For example, the life expectancy for Canadians at birth is eighty years for women (up from seventy-four in the early 1960s) and seventy-three years for men (up from sixty-eight in the early 1960s). By age sixty-five, a woman can expect to live nineteen more years and a man fifteen more years (Canada, 1988:7). As a result of the combined demographic processes of declining birth rates, increasing life expectancy and lower immigration rates, Canada's population of adults over sixty-five increased from 6 percent of the population in 1931 to 11 percent (2.7 million) in 1986. It is projected that this segment of the population will increase to 15 percent by 2011 and 22 percent by 2031 (Canada, 1988:6).

This phenomenon, where an increasing percentage of the population is comprised of older people, is known as *population aging* (McDaniel, 1986). This is a universal process that is occurring at different rates throughout the world. Thus, depending on the proportion of the population over sixty years of age, nations are viewed as "young" (less than 4 percent over sixty), "youthful" (between 4 percent and 6 percent over sixty), "mature" (between 7 percent and 9 percent over sixty), or "aged" (10 percent or more over sixty). To illustrate, Nicaragua and Kenya are classified as young, Mexico and Peru as youthful, China and Jamaica as mature, and Canada, Japan, the United States and the Soviet Union as aged. Note the positive relationship between a higher degree of industrialization in a nation and a greater proportion of adults over sixty years of age. Some sociologists predict that as developing nations become more industrialized, life expectancy will increase, birth rates will decline, emigration will decline and the number of elderly persons will increase dramatically.

Thus, nations experience population aging in different ways and at different times in history. There are also different social definitions of "old" because of the variation in life expectancy within and among nations. To illustrate, the life expectancy of the Inuit and of many North American Indians is only about fifty years compared to seventy to eighty years for the majority of North Americans. An important policy question that follows from this demographic fact is whether native Canadians should be eligible for old age assistance programs before the traditional and legal criterion of sixty-five years of age.

Canada's Older Population

In order to better understand the social world in which Canadians are aging, we need to understand the size, composition and distribution of Canada's older population (see also Chapter 19, Population Processes). In the previous section we learned that the percentage of Canadians over sixty-five is projected to double between 1986 and 2031. The most rapid increase will occur in the years from 2010 to 2025 when the baby boom generation (the large post-war group born from 1945 to 1960) reaches age sixty-five. At that time, nearly one in every five Canadians will be at least sixty-five years or more. This large increase in the number of older adults will be preceded by an increase in the percentage of all adults who are over eighty-five years of age (from 8 percent in 1986 to an estimated 13 percent in 2010). There will be a large number of those over eighty-five who will become dependent, to some degree, on others for assistance. In 1986, only 2 percent of seniors between sixty-five and sixty-nine lived in institutions, compared to 37 percent of those eighty-five and over (Canada, 1988 : 11).

As noted earlier, the elderly population is *not* a homogeneous group with respect to a number of sociodemographic factors or life experiences. First, the number of women compared to men (the *sex ratio*) increases with age. The current sex ratio for those sixty-five to seventy-nine years of age is 124 women for every 100 men. By age eighty, the ratio increases to 134 women for every 100 men. Clearly, as age increases, issues such as housing and social and economic support become increasingly women's issues. As a result of this changing sex ratio, most older men are married (75 percent), whereas most older women are not (59 percent), and few older men live alone (14 percent) compared to older women (34 percent). More significantly, only 28 percent of men over eighty-five are institutionalized, compared to 40 percent of women.

Contrary to popular belief, most older adults are reasonably healthy and live active and independent lives; in fact, 64 percent of Canadian seniors own their homes. Moreover, 67 percent of people aged sixty-five to seventy-four report that their health is good or excellent, while 57 percent of those over seventy-five have the same belief. However, women over sixty-five report somewhat poorer health than men over sixty-five. Although 85 percent of adults over sixty-five report at least one chronic health problem, most older adults still participate actively in society. For example, 60 percent report that they exercise regularly. In one month, 58 percent travelled outside their community, 61 percent visited movie theatres or restaurants and 24 percent went to

Aging: A Women's Issue

Women, because of a greater life expectancy, constitute a larger proportion of the elderly population, especially among the oldest surviving age cohorts. This imbalanced sex ratio is further compounded in the later years because women tend to marry men approximately two years older than themselves. Hence, elderly women may outlive their spouse by ten or more years. Moreover, given changing life styles, there are more divorced or never-married elderly women.

These demographic facts suggest that many elderly women live their later life alone, and are more likely than older men to experience economic, housing and transportation problems in the later years. As Gee and Kimball (1987 : 54) conclude: "It is a virtual certainty that more than one-third of Canada's elderly women are poor." Much of this poverty results from not having a private pension plan because they have not participated regularly in the labour force, or because they do not have access to survival benefits in the pension plan of their deceased spouse. Elderly women are also more likely to enter institutionalized housing at some stage when they lose the informal social support of friends and family, thereby becoming dependent on the formal support system. This likelihood of becoming dependent on the formal support system is compounded if they cannot drive or do not have easy access to public transportation; if they can no longer, physically or financially, care for an aging home; if they are widowed or never-married; if they live in a neighbourhood that generates fears of being victimized; if one or more of their children do not live nearby; or if they are discovered to be the victim of overt or subtle physical or psychological abuse.

In spite of these social, economic and mobility constraints, most women seem to cope well with the challenges of aging, primarily due to a strong bond of interpersonal ties with family and other women. Nevertheless, considerable social and economic change is needed to enhance the quality of life for older women. Given the biological evidence, women are likely to continue to outlive men. Therefore, attitudes must change and policies and programs must be initiated to ensure that the majority of the elderly population, namely women, are provided with the necessary resources to maximize their life chances and life styles in the later years.

---

bingo or card games or took courses. Moreover, 17 percent of the men and 16 percent of the women report that they do volunteer work (Canada, 1988 : 19–23).

The extent of population aging also varies from region to region. To illustrate, in 1986 Prince Edward Island had the highest percentage of people over sixty-five (12.5 percent), while Newfoundland (8.5 percent) and Alberta (8 percent) had the lowest percentages. These patterns are partially the result of the interprovincial migration patterns of young adults who leave one region and move into another region in search of employment or a new life style (Northcott, 1988).

There are also common urban/rural living patterns for Canada's older adults. The largest concentration of older adults can be found in villages with populations of 1000 to 2499 people (they often constitute 15 percent or more of the residents). The next largest concentration (11.2 percent) is in small urban centres with a population less than 30 000; followed by urban centres (10.5 percent) of 30 000 to 100 000 residents. The smallest percentage (5.4 percent) is found in rural farm areas, probably because

A senior "Volunteer of the Year" who is actively involved in the production of cable programs.

REPRODUCED FROM THE BOOK *PRESENT FACES OF WATERLOO PAST*, WITH PERMISSION OF DR. W. FORBES, EDITOR, AND MR. M. GREEN, PHOTOGRAPHER. THIS BOOK IS PUBLISHED BY THE PROGRAM IN GERONTOLOGY, UNIVERSITY OF WATERLOO, WATERLOO, ONTARIO: NOVEMBER 1988.

a large percentage of former farm dwellers have moved to the nearest small village of less than 2500 people.

Individual Aging

As we age, we all experience structural, sensory, motor, behavioural, biological, physiological and cognitive changes. This process is known as *individual aging*. Individual changes influence our social interactions, our life chances and our life styles at particular stages in our life cycles. However, these changes, and the resulting adaptations, do not occur in a vacuum. The process is influenced by such sociocultural and environmental factors as gender, social class, ethnicity, race, income (past and present), education, nationality and place of residence. We all age in different and constantly changing social contexts.

Many social processes significantly influence how we, as individuals, behave throughout our personal life cycle. Some of the more important processes include the changing age structure of the society, age stratification, social differentiation, socialization, ageism, migration and mobility, and social change. In summary, individual aging involves adapting to structural and behavioural changes within the individual. But the aging individual also interacts with, and is influenced by, population aging, social processes and sociocultural and environmental factors unique to a given culture or subculture.

Aging as a Social Process   The *age structure* of a society is comprised of subgroups known as *age cohorts*. These groups include all persons born during a particular time period, often a five- or ten-year period. Most members of a cohort enter societal institutions (such as university, marriage, the labour force, retirement or homes for the aged) within approximately the same time period.

Aging is a dynamic and complex social process whereby a changing individual interacts with a changing age structure. This age structure, in turn, is part of a society that may be experiencing varying degrees of economic, political or social change. Unlike biological aging, which is relatively similar for all humans, social aging involves reciprocal interaction between the social system and the aging individual. If identical twins were separated at birth and raised in different families, regions or societies, later in life they would likely exhibit age-related patterns of social behaviour more influenced by their separate histories than by their common biological heritage. Yet, both siblings would also be members of a specific age cohort and would, therefore, exhibit some similarities in experiences and behaviour because of the stages in the life cycle they had both completed. That is, within the age structure of most modernized societies, individuals occupy a number of status positions at socially determined stages in the life cycle. Within most cultures, *age norms* and social timetables define which behaviours are appropriate for various age levels, and the approximate chronological age when one should enter or leave various stages (childhood, adolescence, adulthood, retirement). Age norms also influence certain social positions (for example, spouse, parent, retiree). Thus, age norms contribute to members of an age cohort sharing some similar experiences. However, there is also considerable variation in values, beliefs and experiences within a particular age cohort and between age cohorts.

Age structure changes in terms of gender. Each age cohort, as it passes through the life course, decreases in size and increasingly comprises a larger percentage of females. Generally, most members of a cohort are influenced by major social events (for example, the Great Depression or a major war) in a similar way. As a result, the life chances and experiences of a specific cohort may be quite different from that of previous or succeeding age cohorts. In the extreme case, the unique values, beliefs, needs or experiences of one age cohort may lead to generational conflict with an older or younger cohort, especially where the two cohorts are competing for scarce resources (jobs, housing, income, for example). For the most part, however, there is a process of *cohort flow*, wherein emerging cohorts interact with, learn and adopt the general goals and values of preceding cohorts. In effect, there is considerable negotiation and co-operation between existing and emerging age cohorts, which prevents serious or prolonged age-related conflict.

Individual and group differences result in different patterns of aging. To illustrate, consider the views and behaviours of women with respect to participation in the labour force. When the current cohort of senior citizens were in their twenties to forties, neither social norms nor employment opportunities encouraged women to seek higher education or to pursue a career. Rather, they encouraged marriage, child rearing and home care. Today, many women in the twenty to forty age cohort are encouraged by both social norms and social opportunities to seek and pursue a career—either instead of or while raising children. Clearly, the economic status and life styles of women in these two cohorts are different during the middle-aged and later-life years. To carry this example further, the attitudes of women toward working outside the home vary considerably within a given age cohort according to factors such as class background, ethnicity, race and geographical region. Women in different age cohorts and women within the same age cohort may disagree about whether a career and marriage are desirable and compatible goals.

To summarize, aging is a social process that involves individual and population aging, biological and psychological aging, individual and societal change, individual and cultural differences within and between age cohorts, and cross-cultural and subcultural differences in values, beliefs and norms. Because this process involves so many factors, aging as a social process is relatively difficult to understand. To help you understand this multifaceted social process, this chapter discusses methodological and theoretical issues; the age stratification system; social and cultural differentiation; social processes; and social problems and policy issues concerning aging in Canada.

Understanding Aging Phenomena

As a field of study, the sociology of aging seeks to describe and explain patterns of behaviour in individuals and groups in a variety of social settings across the life cycle. These settings may constitute a micro social system, such as the family, or a macro social system, such as Canada. For the sociologist, aging is a complex social process that involves describing and explaining patterns of interactions among individuals and age cohorts. Sociologists consider aging in a variety of social systems and in a changing age structure. They examine specific cultural and subcultural norms pertaining to chronological age or stage in the life cycle, and they analyse historical events that may have a unique impact on specific age cohorts. Moreover, they look at the influence on life chances and life styles of ascribed (e.g., age, sex) and achieved (e.g., education, occupation) attributes common to individuals or segments of age cohorts. How we age is greatly influenced by our sociodemographic attributes; by the age structure of our society and the social organizations in which we interact; and by a variety of social processes (for example, ageism, socialization, age stratification) within particular social systems (family, work, leisure).

Toward an Explanation of Aging Phenomena

To simplify our approach to understanding aging from a sociological perspective, we can focus on one of two levels of analysis—the micro or the macro levels. The micro level concerns behavioural changes and adaptations in the individual across the life cycle. In contrast, the macro level involves the study of the age structure, social processes and social problems as they relate to age cohorts or the aging population.

To assist us in this analysis, we use theories and research methods unique to the fields of sociology and gerontology. The purpose of a theory is to provide a summary of existing or anticipated explanations for some complex social phenomena. Many competing theories seek to provide a more valid and complete explanation of some aspect of aging. As you will discover throughout your university career, sociologists have derived a variety of competing theoretical perspectives that are based on different assumptions, concepts and views of the social world. It is these "differences" that stimulate thinking and creativity in a field of study. Eventually, on the basis of research evidence, some theories are found to be more complete and valid than others in explaining a specific pattern, process or problem.

In reality, and certainly in the sociology of aging, one theory cannot explain all social phenomena. It is for this reason that the following sections briefly describe some of these micro and macro theories. As a novice sociologist, it is important for you to understand the variety of theoretical perspectives that are available to study various aging phenomena. As you will note, many of the theories were derived in the 1960s and 1970s. More recently, there are a number of emerging theories (Birren and Bengtson, 1988) that will be tested, revised and either discarded or adopted over the next decade.

Micro Theories of Aging

Many general micro-level theories from sociology and social psychology have been used to explain aging phenomena, including role theory, reference group theory, socialization theory, social exchange theory and labelling theory. In addition, four micro-level theories specifically explain how older people adapt or age successfully: activity theory, disengagement theory, continuity theory and the life course perspective. These theories do not provide a complete explanation of aging, but the concepts they provide are often used in research studies that seek to explain why some older people report higher levels of life satisfaction or well-being than others.

Activity Theory

In the search for an explanation of how to age successfully, Havighurst and Albrecht (1953) argued that adaptation to aging involved continuing an active life style to maintain the self-concept and, hence, a sense of well-being or life satisfaction. Individuals should slow down but remain active in their retirement years. Thus, according to activity theory, individuals should maintain a high level of social activity by replacing lost activities (work) with new activities (leisure or a new occupation).

Disengagement Theory

In 1961 Cumming and Henry challenged the validity of activity theory by proposing that adaptation to old age requires meeting the needs of both the aging individual and the society. Thus, they argued, normal aging involves the inevitable and necessary voluntary withdrawal, or disengagement, of the individual from societal responsibilities. It also involves the disengagement of the society from the individual. This voluntary disengagement permits younger members of the society to enter functional roles, and relieves the older members from pressures to perform or behave as they did when they were younger. This decreased role involvement and social interaction enhances life satisfaction and morale in the later years. To date, there is little, if any, research support for this theory of aging. Indeed, one only has to scan the media or look around the community to observe many older adults who demonstrate high levels of satisfaction and morale *because* they have not disengaged from social interaction or previous social roles.

Continuity Theory   Continuity theory (Atchley, 1971) argues that successful adjustment to aging involves maintaining continuity in one's life style. Thus, interests, habits and values expressed earlier in life should be continued in the later years. This theory has generally been supported by research evidence. As a result, pre-retirement planning often involves identifying highly valued personal interests and activities that can be pursued in greater depth following retirement. For some, continuity may even involve paid or volunteer work past the normal age of retirement, although the location or type of work may change.

The Life Course Perspective   Neugarten (1985) conceptualized the life course as a sequence of roles that individuals experience throughout their life. According to this perspective, human development

Some older Canadians, like this farm couple, still work full-time.

REPRODUCED FROM THE BOOK *PRESENT FACES OF WATERLOO PAST*, WITH PERMISSION OF DR. W. FORBES, EDITOR, AND MR. M. GREEN, PHOTOGRAPHER. THIS BOOK IS PUBLISHED BY THE PROGRAM IN GERONTOLOGY, UNIVERSITY OF WATERLOO, WATERLOO, ONTARIO: NOVEMBER 1988.

is a lifelong dynamic process whereby we move from one age stratum to another within the age structure. The events, experiences and roles of one stage are influenced by those at earlier stages. However, there are considerable individual differences in opportunities and experiences within a stage, and succeeding cohorts may face different opportunities and experiences at a given stage. This perspective clearly illustrates the interaction between the micro and macro levels of analysis. That is, to fully understand aging phenomena we must consider historical and personal events earlier in the life cycle, as well as demographic changes in the age structure of a society.

Macro Theories of Aging

The behaviour of individuals is also influenced by the social environment or social structure in which they age. Again, concepts from some general macro-level theories have been used to study aging phenomena, including structural-functionalism, the conflict perspective and social systems theory. Within the field of social gerontology, three macro-level theories of aging have been proposed to help us understand the sociological aspects of how cohorts age: age stratification theory, modernization theory and the political economy of aging.

Age Stratification Theory

Age stratification theory studies the interaction of age cohorts at different stages in the life cycle. It stresses the interaction, and possible conflict, between age cohorts (Riley, 1971). Society is divided into numerous age cohorts, each with different characteristics and life experiences because of a common social history. As we pass through different age strata, we gain or lose access to specific social roles and to their accompanying rewards.

The interaction between various age cohorts can involve co-operation or conflict (for example, if mandatory retirement is eliminated, younger members of a society may be prevented from entering the labour force if older adults do not retire and thereby permit entry into the labour market). Conflict may also arise if there are perceived age-related inequalities in a society. A recent example is the rise of the "grey power" movement whereby retired persons are demanding greater benefits and a larger voice in political and policy decisions affecting their life styles and economic situations.

Modernization Theory

According to modernization theory (Cowgill and Holmes, 1972), the status of the elderly changes as a society evolves from an agricultural to an industrial society. In an agricultural society, the elderly own the land and thus control the economic resources. Also, their experience and wisdom are needed and valued. However, as a society becomes more modernized, older people may lose these functional roles, become devalued and lose status and security.

Today, there is still considerable debate as to how and to what extent modernization leads to a loss of status for the elderly. While those over sixty-five years of age certainly have less power and status in the industrialized nations, some of this loss may have occurred prior to industrialization. Moreover, there are exceptions to the modernization theory. For example, although the pattern is changing, the elderly in Japan still have

Seniors as Advocates

As the proportion of older adults has increased, this segment of the population has become more vocal, active and powerful. This growing social movement has been called "grey power." As a heterogeneous cohort, the elderly have experienced different life situations and have not tended to vote as a block. However, with the emergence of elderly activists as leaders and the formation of voluntary organizations (for example, the United Senior Citizens of Ontario, One Voice, the National Advisory Council on Aging, Fédération de l'age d'or du Québec), Canada's older adults are making their concerns known to politicians and younger voters. This political awareness and activism reached its highest level in 1985 when the Mulroney government introduced legislation to partially de-index Old Age Security payments. An organized media campaign, the writing of letters to MPs by thousands of senior citizens, and marches on Parliament Hill led to a quick withdrawal of the proposed changes. For the first time, the government had listened to seniors. Following this show of "grey" power, the government created a Seniors Secretariat in 1987, headed by a Minister of State for Senior Citizens. The purpose of this agency is to provide information to seniors, and to keep the government informed about policies and issues that are of concern to older Canadians.

Advisory councils concerning senior interests and needs have been created, as well, at the provincial and local levels. Totally staffed by volunteer senior citizens, many of these councils have conducted studies and generated reports in which they advocate social, political and economic changes to better meet the needs of seniors. To illustrate, the Ontario Advisory Council on Senior Citizens conducted a two-day public consultation meeting in January 1988. As a result of this process, the following areas of need and concern were identified as priorities for seniors in their annual report to the government: health and related services; long-term care; mental health services; social services; education services; family care and elder abuse; ethnicity and aging; financial concerns; transportation; housing; rural mail service; homemakers' programs; and financial affairs. This organization also publishes a quarterly newsletter, *Especially for Seniors,* to inform the 937 000 recipients about senior issues and benefits. This publication stimulates seniors to become involved at the local and provincial level and to express their needs and concerns in public forums. Clearly, senior citizens no longer are willing to quietly accept their disadvantaged situation. Elderly Canadians have come out of the "rocking chair" to become active and articulate advocates of their particular and unique needs and concerns.

relatively high status, both within the family and in society. Also, the elderly in some primitive societies have never been accorded high status, and may, indeed, be abandoned when they can no longer physically contribute to the survival of the group.

Political Economy of Aging   Faced with an aging population within the welfare state, political theorists and economists have become interested in the institutions and processes that influence the elderly (Myles, 1984; Estes et al., 1984). Specifically, this approach is concerned with public expenditures on the elderly (for example, health, pensions, housing); the social, political and economic rights of the elderly; how population aging changes the process of distributing public income; and the issue of voluntary versus mandatory retirement. In short, this theoretical approach focuses on social power, economic demands and inequality among age groups. According to this view of social reality, crises or problems associated with an aging population are not the result of demographic changes. Rather, they are due to "social, political and economic forces" (Myles, 1984:120) that define and label the elderly and that create public policies such as mandatory retirement and government-funded pensions.

Studying Aging Phenomena

In order to obtain valid and reliable information about the aging process and older adults, and to accurately interpret information presented to us by the media, we must understand the following unique methodological issues that apply to this area of study.

Cross-Sectional versus Longitudinal Research

Cross-sectional research involves studying individuals of different ages and then reporting the results by age groups (for example, reporting the percentage of Canadians, by age, who voted in the last federal election). These results might show that a relatively small percentage of older people voted. However, this type of study would not allow us to conclude that voting declines with age. Rather, it only shows that, at the time of the survey, people in the older age groups were less likely to vote. A similar survey taken twenty years ago, or twenty years in the future, might indicate that those in the older age groups were more likely to cast a vote than those in the younger age groups.

Longitudinal studies conducted over a number of years can provide information about how behaviour, values or attitudes change with age. This type of study follows the same cohort for a number of years as it moves from one age stratum to another. Longitudinal studies are very expensive, and subjects are prone to drop out because they move, die or no longer wish to participate. Also, they may focus on only one age cohort, which may be atypical, as it moves through the life cycle. Thus, this type of study also has limitations with respect to the validity of the information that is derived.

Selecting a Sample

It is important that research be based on representative samples of the population being studied. Unfortunately, many studies of aging adults tend to be based on volunteers, on males, on those from the middle class and on those from urban centres. Thus, we can not be assured that the findings of one study can be generalized to the entire population of older Canadians. For example, volunteers are generally healthier, more mobile and better educated. Similarly, males may respond to questions about retirement, health, leisure or social interaction quite differently than females. Thus, depending on the research question(s) being asked, a representative heterogeneous sample of older respondents must be selected from across Canada to reflect accurately the older population.

Collecting
Information from
Elderly
Respondents

Many older people may have had little experience with social science research and may be suspicious of interviewers or hesitant to participate in a study. Thus, it is essential that they understand the purpose of the research, that their responses will be confidential and that only the researcher will have access to their responses. Many researchers now use elderly interviewers when completing studies of older adults. This use of age peers seems to increase response rates, and it may also increase the validity of the information provided.

The interview itself must consider the special characteristics of older respondents. Older adults may require more time to complete an interview, questionnaire or task. Moreover, extra time may be needed to compensate for visual or auditory deficiencies. Investigators must also make sure that elderly respondents understand how to complete a questionnaire or how to respond to an experimental task. Finally, the investigator should make a special effort to determine whether older adults are responding in socially approved or misleading ways, rather than with honest, objective responses. For example, they may exaggerate the positive state of their economic or health status in order to maintain the image of being independent. They may even fear that certain responses could lead to institutionalization. An elderly respondent may be more likely to respond honestly to an age peer who has had similar life experiences.

Cultural and Social Differentiation and Aging

Cultural
Differentiation

The status of the elderly and the experiences of aging vary within and between cultures. Even in modernized societies, where there tends to be greater homogeneity across societies in terms of the status of the elderly, there are still subcultural variations. Just as biologists have sought to discover, describe and explain similarities and differences in the aging process among different species, social scientists have sought to compare the status of the aged and the process of aging in different cultural contexts. These studies have focused most often on a comparison of pre-literate, pre-industrialized and industrialized societies, or on a descriptive account of a particular primitive or developing society (McPherson, 1983 : 37–55). The findings of these field observations show that the status of the elderly can vary between societies, depending on the period in history and on the rate of social, political and economic change in a society. For example, in nomadic tribes, the elderly were often left behind when they could no longer contribute to the survival of the tribe. In contrast, in non-nomadic tribes they were usually revered and cared for because they were a source of needed information, or because they were perceived to have special powers or functions (McPherson, 1983 : 44–45).

The process of aging and the status of the elderly can also vary within a society due to subcultural variations in beliefs, values and norms about the elderly. Examples are a high commitment to support and care for the elderly among Jews, self-segregation from mainstream society among Mennonites and native Canadians and age discrimination by the dominant cultural group. The cultural background or unique life history of specific subcultural groups can influence the aging process for members of that subculture. Subcultural values and beliefs, inadequate lifetime incomes, lack of pension rights, lower life expectancy, language differences and substandard housing can create handicaps that influence life chances and life styles in the later years. Other societal factors may strengthen the status and treatment of the elderly within the ethnic group. For example, many religious and ethnic groups in Canada accord special attention and care to the elderly. These groups may even build and operate long-term care facilities for elderly persons, especially those without family support. In this way, elderly Chinese single males who have always lived in Toronto's or Vancouver's Chinatown have facilities that have been provided for them by their communities.

Social Differentiation

In virtually every society, the composition of the population represents a heterogeneous group of individuals who vary according to a variety of ascribed or achieved attributes (gender, class, race, age, ethnic background). Some of these social characteristics are assigned differential values by the dominant social group so that people with certain characteristics are perceived to be more valuable, worthy or desirable than those with other characteristics. This social differentiation influences life chances and life styles so that all citizens are not treated equally.

As students of aging phenomena, we must understand how the various systems of social differentiation interact with the age stratification system to influence life chances and life styles throughout the life cycle. More specifically, we must recognize that each age cohort is comprised of a heterogeneous mix of individuals who vary along gender (Gee and Kimball, 1987), racial, ethnic (Driedger and Chappell, 1987), religious, educational or social class dimensions that can influence the process and product of aging (cf. McPherson, 1983 : 23–29). Individuals who are located near the least-valued end of one or more of these stratification systems may be disadvantaged throughout life, and may encounter considerable discrimination, segregation or isolation in the later years, especially if they are neglected by their extended families.

Race and class influence an individual's life chances at a particular stage in the life cycle. That is, an elderly, black, lower-class female experiences a different aging process than an elderly, white, upper-class female. Although both women belong to the same age cohort, the influence of the social and racial stratification systems creates a different social world for each woman. Thus, the interaction of age with one or more stratification systems can increase the disadvantaged status of an elderly person.

Multiple jeopardy occurs when racism, sexism and ageism interact to increase or compound the level of inequality for some members of an older cohort (for example, a poor, elderly, black or native female.) This situation does not constitute an aging event since the attributes of being black or native and poor and female have been present throughout the life course. However, this multiple jeopardy may make it more

The Ethnic Experience of Aging

As a multicultural society, the elderly population of Canada represents a diverse mix of individuals with a variety of lifelong experiences, values, beliefs, customs and practices that vary among ethnic and cultural groups (Driedger and Chappell, 1987).

The size of the elderly population in specific ethnic groups and its visibility varies by how long the group members have lived in Canada, by the fertility rates for the group, by where they live and whether they live in concentrated areas and by the size of the group that immigrated to Canada. The elderly in the Chinatowns of large cities tend to be very visible, for example. How, and in what way, older members of a particular ethnic group adapt to the later years often depends on their degree of cultural and structural assimilation into mainstream society, particularly with respect to whether they speak and read English or French; whether they have been able to move upward on the socio-economic scale with respect to education and income; and whether they age in an extended family (for example, Japanese) or religious (Jewish, Mennonite) environment that values and cares for the elderly members of the ethnic or religious group. This latter factor is especially important for older widows who may lack pension benefits, other than minimal government payments. These elderly women are especially vulnerable if they do not speak English or French.

Because of low levels of education, language problems and lack of job skills, many elderly members of ethnic groups, especially those who immigrated to Canada in the 1940s, now are retired without a pension. While many have savings, they may be more dependent than the non-immigrant elderly on their children for economic support. They may also be dependent on their children for social support and health care. This support is especially important since health care and long-term care facilities are designed to meet the language and cultural needs of the dominant culture. Elderly persons in some racial and ethnic groups underutilize social and health care services. This may occur because of a lack of knowledge about the availability of services and programs or because they cannot be served or assisted in their own language. At the present time, the elderly from some ethnic groups are unwilling or unable to enter long-term care institutions because differences in language, in customs, in beliefs about medical practices and death, in food preferences and in the need for privacy would make it difficult for them to use the services or adapt to the environment. Because of the potential influx of ethnic patients, hospitals in large urban centres now hire staff with the capacity to speak languages other than English or French.

For the above reasons, the burden of caring for an aged parent often falls upon the family. Fortunately, especially among some ethnic groups, there is a deep and genuine sense of filial responsibility to care for one's aging parents. In other groups, however, as members of subsequent generations become more acculturated within the dominant society, traditional values, beliefs and practices with respect to the elderly may be abandoned. This may be happening among the Asian-Canadian ethnic communities, where traditional respect for, and obligation to, elderly parents seems to be waning (Ujimoto, 1987).

In summary, aging in Canada represents a different and, sometimes, troublesome experience for the members of some ethnic groups who have not been assimilated into mainstream society. When elderly persons from these ethnic groups become frail and dependent, the presence of committed family resources or institutionalized support from the ethnic community are essential. For elderly members of an ethnic group who have been more assimilated, aging represents an experience similar to that experienced by non-ethnic Canadians. Thus, given the considerable influx of immigrants to Canada, those who design policies and programs for the elderly must be sensitive to the heterogeneous values, beliefs, needs and present and past life styles of older Canadians with strong ethnic roots.

difficult to adapt in the later years, especially for a widow with no pension rights and few, if any, lifetime savings.

Social Processes and Aging

In this section, social processes that influence individual and population aging, as well as the status of the aged, are introduced. These macro and micro social processes define the rights, responsibilities and power of different age groups; facilitate or inhibit interaction among individuals and groups of different ages; promote conformity to dominant age-based values and norms or create conflict within a society or a family; and integrate individuals and cohorts into the age stratification system.

Socialization   Socialization is a complex process that integrates each new individual and cohort into the society by transmitting prevailing cultural behaviours, beliefs and values. This process insures stability and maintains the existing social order. At the same time, the process integrates the individual into specific institutions or positions within a society. While most socialization occurs during infancy, childhood and adolescence, socialization continues during the middle and later years as we learn how to behave in new social positions (for example, spouse, parent, widow, retiree, divorced man or woman, a dependent resident of a long-term care institution).

An indirect outcome of the socialization process is that attitudes, beliefs or stereotypes about aging and the aged may be produced and internalized. Through social interaction with others and through exposure to the mass media, greeting cards, jokes and cartoons, we are exposed to a variety of attitudes and images about aging and the aged. Many of these images are myths, but they become accepted as facts or beliefs. Many of them portray a negative image of aging or the elderly (loss of sexuality, intelligence, memory, vision, hearing). These stereotypes, if accepted as fact, can influence our expectations about, fear of, and reactions to aging and the aged. They can also negatively influence the behaviour, beliefs and attitudes of the elderly toward aging, lower or destroy an older adult's self-concept, and lead to isolation and a labelling of oneself as "old." A self-fulfilling prophecy occurs wherein the elderly begin to think and behave as expected, thereby further reinforcing the stereotype. Thus, a self-perpetuating cycle is created through socialization unless these negative myths and stereotypes are refuted.

Negative stereotypes can contribute to a devaluation or a lowering of the status of older people in a society. This, in turn, can decrease the frequency and quality of social interaction between younger and older people, and result in fewer societal and personal resources such as social services being allocated to the elderly compared to those allocated to other age groups. On a more positive note, recent research and educational programs indicate that children, adolescents and young adults who have frequent and meaningful contact with elderly persons report more positive attitudes toward aging and the aged. Fortunately, recent research evidence is dispelling the myth of the senile, asexual, dependent elderly person. Moreover, the visibility of active elderly role models shows younger people that the later years can be characterized by significant accomplishments in a variety of fields and by a physically active life style, including competition in marathon running, cycling or cross-country skiing events.

Role Transitions   Throughout the life course, as individuals and cohorts move from one stage in life to another, they experience *role transitions*: student to worker to retiree; single to married to divorced or widowed. For many of these roles, there are appropriate times or ages by which a transition is expected to have occurred, for example, marriage by thirty or retirement at sixty-five. Often, we expect these role transitions (such as marriage, parenthood, retirement) and can initiate planning to adjust to them. However, others

Vigorous physical activity is possible and desirable in the later years.

REPRODUCED FROM THE BOOK *PRESENT FACES OF WATERLOO PAST*, WITH PERMISSION OF DR. W. FORBES, EDITOR, AND MR. M. GREEN, PHOTOGRAPHER. THIS BOOK IS PUBLISHED BY THE PROGRAM IN GERONTOLOGY, UNIVERSITY OF WATERLOO, WATERLOO, ONTARIO: NOVEMBER 1988.

can be unexpected (widowhood or a divorce in mid-life; becoming a father at fifty). Still others, while expected, can be stressful (the empty nest when children leave home; the onset of middle age; retirement; widowhood in later life) and can lead to an identity crisis, loneliness and a decreased quality of life.

Adaptation to later-life role transitions can be facilitated by anticipatory socialization, by the social support of friends and family, by developing personal coping skills, and by the presence of age peers who serve as role models on how to adapt (George, 1980). Through this process of adaptation, an individual often develops new patterns of social interaction and a change in identity (Martin Matthews, 1989).

Widowhood as a Role Transition

The process of aging involves change—in friendships, in health, in economic status, in role relationships and in other areas. The changes in daily routine often generate stress and the need to cope and adapt to a new life situation. Widowhood represents a major loss in later life for one member of nearly every married couple. While expected, the event often occurs suddenly and the surviving spouse must adapt to living as a single person. What is the impact of this transition on personal well-being and on interpersonal relationships?

In 1981 there were 153 000 widowers and 754 000 widows in Canada over sixty-five years of age. However, the picture changes by age. To illustrate, whereas there were 27 000 male and 150 000 female widowed persons between sixty-five and sixty-nine years of age, the numbers increase to 59 000 for males and 261 000 for females among those eighty years of age and over (Stone and Frenken, 1988 : 39–41). Thus, this later life event provides yet another example of why aging needs to be studied as a women's issue. The major reasons for this sex difference include: the greater life expectancy of women; the fact that husbands are generally two to three years older than their wives and therefore may die first; and the greater propensity for men to remarry following divorce or widowhood. Not only do more women experience this expectable life event, but they also live longer in this role. Even a woman who becomes a widow at age eighty can expect an average of almost nine more years of life as a single person.

A large body of research literature has documented that the death of a spouse is one of the most stressful role transitions throughout the life cycle, and certainly the most stressful in the later years (Martin Matthews, 1987). Most of this literature has focused on the experience of women. However, the few studies of widowers suggest that, while they are not often faced with economic burdens, they apparently have more difficulty in adapting as evidenced by higher suicide rates and higher rates of mortality following bereavement. For most older adults, widowhood occurs suddenly and unexpectedly. There is little opportunity to prepare for the transition from spouse to widow, unless the spouse has been terminally ill for a number of years. The process may also be somewhat easier if the widowed person has a friendship group in which some of the age peers have experienced widowhood already.

The transition or adjustment period begins with a stage of mourning, which may last up to two years. Unlike earlier times, a formal mourning period and the wearing of mourning clothes to signify the new status are seldom practised. Rather, the widowed person is left to find or develop a social support network. It is for this reason that community-based "widow-to-widow" programs have been created to provide emotional and social support from a role model who has previously experienced the transition to "widowhood" in later life. Following the immediate and acute period of grief and mourning, the widowed person must begin to reconstruct a new identity and life style—living alone; no one to share thoughts and feelings with; cooking for one person; loss of friends who were more closely tied to the deceased spouse; handling financial matters; and living on a reduced income if a widow who loses the pension rights of the deceased spouse. One of the more difficult adaptations for older widows is the initiation of heterosexual relationships, especially if female friends, children or siblings discourage or disapprove of the behaviour. This can be particularly stressful with respect to attendance at family events.

In summary, while the initial process of adjustment to widowhood is difficult, the majority of older adults do, eventually, make a successful transition. However, while they may adjust to the loss of the spouse, they may not adjust as well to the consequences of being widowed—loss of income; loss of companionship; loss of friends; and, for men especially, the loss of a homemaker. For widows, many become closer to their children or move into a social circle comprised of other widows. In recent years, as societal values and norms have changed, cohabitation or remarriage has become a more socially acceptable option for the elderly widowed person, especially males. However, with the onset of the women's movement, fewer older women are willing to remarry merely to play the role of nurse, cook and homemaker! Moreover, future generations of older widows should have more personal economic and social resources that will not require them to remarry for "survival." On the other hand, with a greater sharing of domestic tasks throughout the married years because of dual careers, widowers may be less likely, as well, to remarry mainly to acquire domestic assistance.

Intergenerational Family Relations: Solidarity or Conflict?

With increased life expectancy and the existence of larger extended families, the need for informal support for aging parents or grandparents has increased. Similarly, the need for social support from aging parents to middle-aged sons or daughters who become widowed or divorced is also increasing. For older adults, the frequency and quality of these relationships are influenced by their need for independence and support, by the intergenerational interaction patterns established early in life, by social class, by the gender of the offspring and by the location and type of their living arrangement (see Connidis, 1989).

The pattern of interaction among parents, children and grandchildren varies at different stages in the life cycle. The interaction between generations in the extended family can vary in frequency, quality and type depending on the age, interests and needs of the generations. During adolescence, the relationship may be characterized by conflict concerning values, beliefs or behaviours. As children reach adulthood and establish their own nuclear families, the relationship may decrease in frequency and intensity as the demands of child rearing and careers leave little time for interaction with parents. However, as the child enters mid-life and the parents enter the later years, interaction may increase, especially if an elderly parent becomes partially or totally dependent on a child for support. This shift from an independent parent to a dependent parent represents a shift in power and responsibility from the parent to the offspring. Depending on the quality of the relationship throughout the childhood and adult years, the onset of dependency can provide an opportunity to repay a parent for past debts, or to seek revenge for real or imagined parental injustices imposed on the offspring in earlier years. This revenge is more likely to occur when other family problems (such as poverty, alcoholism and stress) are present, thereby leading to abuse of the elderly parent.

Intergenerational friendship and support—a grand-daughter helps her grandfather sell the products of his craftsmanship at a local market.

In reality, the parent/child role relationship in later life is seldom characterized by conflict or abuse. Rather, the extended family serves as an informal support system to provide aging parents with physical, financial or emotional assistance. The type and amount of support directly provided by an offspring varies by geographical proximity, by whether daughters or daughters-in-law are employed, and by racial, ethnic or class-based values concerning the care of aging parents. Clearly, there appear to be gender differences in the type of support offered to aging parents. Whereas daughters are more likely to provide direct, primary care, sons are more likely to provide financial assistance. Often it is a daughter who feels more filial responsibility for a parent, perhaps because of a strong and long-standing mother-daughter tie. In short, contrary to popular myths, the relationships between aging parents and adult offspring are not characterized by conflict. Rather, in most extended families, offspring respond to the needs of aging parents and provide as much informal social, emotional and financial support as possible given the time, distance, work and fiscal constraints in their own social lives.

Mobility and Migration

For the older adult, retirement represents a choice between "aging in place" and relocating. Those who opt to relocate may choose a new residence in the same community, a new community or a new geographical region of the country. Until institutionalization very late in life, most Canadians age in place. However, increasingly, elderly Canadians, especially those who are healthy and of the middle or upper class, make seasonal or permanent moves in their retirement years (Northcott, 1988).

While most moves after retirement are local or seasonal, some elderly adults migrate to other parts of the country. When significant numbers of elderly people migrate, the demographic composition of the sending or receiving area can change dramatically. This has happened in Florida, where whole communities are inhabited by people of retirement age. In Canada, interprovincial migration by the elderly tends to be westward, with the most popular destination regions being British Columbia, Alberta and southern Ontario. The regions experiencing net losses of older residents are Quebec, the Prairie provinces and large cities across Canada. Cities experiencing net gains of older persons include Victoria and the St. Catharines—Niagara Falls region, two areas with reasonably temperate climates.

While less than 10 percent of the elderly population live in an institution at any one time, studies have estimated that anywhere from 25 to 75 percent of the elderly population may be housed in an institutional setting at some point in their later years. A move to an institution is more likely for women; for those who experience physical or mental health problems that increase their level of dependence; for the very old (aged eighty-five plus); for those without family or community-based support; and for those who have been financially or socially disadvantaged throughout life.

Relocation from independent, private living to an institution in the later years is seldom voluntary and is frequently traumatic (Forbes, Jackson and Kraus, 1987). The relocation seldom involves advance preparation or socialization, so adjustment to a restricted personal space, loss of privacy and personal possessions and a depersonalized, regulated life style can be stressful. For many, if they are not provided with adequate preparation and counselling, the move to an institutionalized setting is perceived as the last stage in life and can lead to feelings of abandonment. These feelings are compounded if friends and family visit less often. However, a move to an institutionalized setting, especially if voluntary, can lead to an increased activity level and an increased life satisfaction if a higher quality of life is offered.

Life in the Later Years: Social and Policy Issues

For many years, *gerontologists* viewed aging as a major personal and societal "problem." They thought of older people as being in poor health, impoverished, lonely, abandoned by friends and family, victimized and abused, roleless and dependent. This negative view of aging, largely exaggerated by the perpetuation of myths and by the media highlighting specific case studies of an older person at risk, fostered interest in the study of gerontology. These factors also generated considerable policy development and policy evaluation by the public and private sector.

As noted throughout this chapter, the elderly constitute a heterogeneous population with considerable diversity on a number of social, physical, health and economic factors. It is this considerable variation that constitutes a dilemma for programmers and policy makers who seek to ensure that social resources are distributed fairly and equitably. Should resources (for example, family allowance, old age security) be distributed to everyone as a right, regardless of need—the principle of universality? Should they be distributed solely on the basis of need, as we now do with the guaranteed income supplement and unemployment insurance? Or should a combination of universality plus need prevail (a guaranteed minimum old age security payment to everyone, plus a guaranteed income supplement to those in need)?

While it is beyond the scope of this chapter to discuss these policy debates in detail (cf. Neysmith, 1987), it is important to become familiar with some of these issues. They affect you and your family, now or in the future, and they affect us collectively, as residents of a particular province, city or town, or as employees or employers. These issues represent a debate over conflicting values and beliefs about the social responsibility of the state versus the individual and about the individual and collective rights of older Canadians. They are frequently compounded by an interesting debate as to whether the responsibility for the social welfare of older Canadians lies with the federal government (income security), a provincial government (health programs), a regional or municipal government (transportation, social services), the private sector (pensions) or the individual and his or her family (savings and investments for income security, housing).

Gender and Aging: A Women's Issue

Social policies and programs must take into account that the aged population is increasingly composed of women. Canada's gender imbalance is projected to increase by the year 2000 from the current ratio of 124 women per 100 men to 134 per 100 men for the sixty-five to seventy-nine age cohort, and from 134 to 218 women per 100 men for the eighty years and over age cohort (McDaniel, 1986). Many of these women are more vulnerable than men to the social, economic and health outcomes of the aging process. We see that age-related problems, such as widowhood, poverty, loneliness, drug abuse, illness, elder abuse, crime, the expression of sexuality and the empty nest, are increasingly becoming women's issues.

A close examination of the literature on women and aging, however, reveals that "women, in spite of their social and economic powerlessness, cope well with aging" (Gee and Kimball, 1987 : x). Indeed, not all older women experience the dual stigma of being old and being female. Rather, such factors as education, social class, ethnicity, race, wealth and marital status contribute to the diversity among women in the older age cohorts. Nevertheless, given the devalued status of women in our society, social policies designed to assist older women to cope with past and present injustices are needed. Policy changes are particularly necessary with respect to preventive health care, pension reform, gender desegregation of job opportunities, pay equity, assistance in the care of aging parents, housing for single elderly women and community-based social and health care services.

Economic Status: Adequate versus Poverty

Should people expect a lower standard of living following retirement? Is the support of the retired person the responsibility of the state, the former employer, the individual or a combination of these three sources? These two issues are the topics of perennial debates because many older adults, particularly elderly widows, are impoverished and because of the fear that public old age security funds and private pension plans may become bankrupt in the future.

The amount of income an individual receives after retirement depends on the pattern of employment (regular or sporadic), the place of employment (whether there is a private pension plan or not), the level of income while in the labour force and the pattern of savings, investments and expenditures over the life course. Society needs to ensure an adequate retirement income, especially for those with an irregular work history—the poorly educated, immigrants, women. But what is adequate? Is it the same annual income as prior to retirement, a minimal percentage decrease (15 to 20 percent) from the pre-retirement level of income, or the average income of those who retire in a given year? These amounts would all constitute objective definitions of an adequate income. In reality, people have subjective perceptions of financial adequacy, based on their particular life styles, needs, priorities and debts. Some individuals are able to survive on less income in the retirement years than they had when they were younger, while others cannot. Many older adults, especially members of minority groups or the poorly educated, report that inflation, the high cost of living and a reduced income are the greatest problems facing retirees. To cope, many retirees must dramatically change their spending patterns, especially with respect to the type and quality of goods they purchase. Also, they must often reduce the relative proportion of their income allocated to such items as clothing, leisure and transportation and increase the proportion allocated to food, health care and home maintenance.

Given the irregular participation in the labour force, their lack of private pensions and their greater life expectancy, older women are more likely to be impoverished than men, especially if they are widowed or divorced. In response to this problem, homemaker's pensions have been proposed to compensate women for their lifelong labour in the home—cooking, cleaning and child rearing. While this proposed policy has yet to gain the support of our political leaders, it does raise an important question as to who is responsible for the economic welfare of older women, especially those who are widowed and without the benefits of a private pension plan.

Retirement: Voluntary versus Involuntary

From both an economic and a human rights perspective, the issue of mandatory versus voluntary retirement has become an important policy debate. At present, mandatory retirement at age sixty-five is the legal and social norm in many provinces. However, a number of cases before provincial or federal courts are arguing that mandatory retirement is a form of age discrimination that violates provincial human rights codes or the Charter of Rights and Freedoms. As a result of the impending decisions, the mandatory retirement age could be raised to seventy, as it has been in the United States, or it could be declared unconstitutional and discriminatory at any age.

Many arguments for or against mandatory retirement have been presented (see McPherson, 1983:385). Support for the abolishment of mandatory retirement is increasing. A compromise position may be to require the periodic review of performance, based on valid tests, for employees beyond a certain age. This test would be similar to the mandatory driver's test at age eighty that is required by some provinces.

In reality, not all older adults need to, or want to, keep working beyond sixty-five years of age. Indeed, an increasing percentage of workers are opting for early retirement, and some companies offer incentives to employees who leave the labour force early so that young people can enter. Nevertheless, most employees are physically and mentally able to continue working long after they reach the age of sixty-five. If they so desire or need to work for economic or psychological reasons, they should have this option, especially women who have had a brief or irregular pattern of labour force involvement.

Victimization: Fear versus Reality

Newspaper reports periodically highlight savage crimes against elderly people, many of which occur near or within their home. At the same time, surveys report that an increasing number of elderly persons report a fear of being victimized, often to the extent that they become prisoners in their home, fearing to go outside at any time of day. These situations inhibit social interaction and lead to a decreased level of life satisfaction because of the real or imagined unsafe environment.

In reality, except for purse snatching, pickpocketing and home burglary, there are fewer crimes committed against the elderly than against other age groups. The elderly are not victimized as frequently as we think, nor are they personally assaulted more frequently than people in other age groups. Those elderly persons who are most vulnerable to criminal victimization are men; those who live alone; those who live in urban areas, particularly in older, lower-class neighbourhoods; those who are less physically mobile; and those who lack social support (Brillon, 1987). One reason for this lower rate of victimization is that the elderly go out less often at night.

Despite the lower than imagined crime rate against elderly persons, older people are more afraid of crime than other age groups, and this fear seems to increase with age. Not surprisingly, women and those who live in the centre of large cities report higher levels of fear. Yet, at the same time, many studies indicate that despite a fear of crime, the elderly take little action to protect themselves from crime. Some communities have initiated educational programs and social services to protect the elderly person. These programs include volunteer escort services, Dial-A-Bus transportation services, neighbourhood watch, postal watch and home security advice.

The neglect and abuse of elderly persons living in their homes or in an institution by those close to them (family, caregivers) also seems to be increasing. Many of these forms of abuse are subtle or unconscious acts, and therefore do not always constitute a "crime." Moreover, many incidents are not reported by the victims. Thus, elder abuse constitutes a "silent crime." Some of the more frequent forms of abuse or neglect by caregivers include cashing and keeping pension or old age security cheques; fraud; physical attacks; inadequate feeding, which leads to malnutrition; lack of attention; verbal intimidation; confinement or isolation; lack of medical care; and excessive use of medication. The excerpt "The Family and Elder Abuse" illustrates some incidents of abuse reported in interviews with six people working with the elderly in Quebec (Lamont, 1985, as cited in Brillon, 1987:83).

The Family and Elder Abuse

Although difficult to document because many victims are afraid to report incidents of elder abuse, or do not understand that they are being abused, an increasing number of incidents of elder abuse are being reported. Many of these incidents involve either family members with their own personal problems, or family members who can no longer cope with the stress of providing care to an older relative. A common reaction to personal stress is psychological or physical aggression against the elderly person. The following examples are based on four of the thirty histories compiled by Lamont (1985) following in-depth interviews with six people working with the elderly in Quebec.

- Madame A had her pension cheque taken from her regularly by an alcoholic son. Furthermore, when he was drunk, he would hit her. With almost no resources, she could barely feed herself and look after her needs. She had to be placed in a home in order to be protected from the son.

- Madame D, seventy-five years old, asked her niece to take her in. The latter tried to get rid of her. She insulted her. She frequently abused her. Sometimes she even doused her with water. She finally beat her, and stabbed her with a screwdriver.

- An elderly couple was manipulated by a son who had no resources and had to find money to pay his rent, buy food and look after his personal expenses. By threatening his parents, he got everything he wanted out of them. He entered their home without warning. He stripped them of their belongings, and stole whatever he wanted.

- Madame K lived alone. A nephew came to do light work and some messages for her. Little by little, the nephew became more and more demanding and more aggressive. One day when he was on drugs, he beat her, hit her with a hammer and raped her.

Yves Brillon. 1987. *Victimization and Fear of Crime among the Elderly.* Toronto: Butterworths, p. 83. Adapted by permission of the publisher.

To prevent abuse or neglect of the dependent elderly person, special services to assist the caregiver and the elderly person need to be provided. These include information about care, abuse and assistance; financial support to caregivers; day care centres for the frail, home-bound elderly; temporary housing services to give the caregiver some relief and a vacation; and more home services by non-family members.

While actual rates of victimization among the elderly are lower than commonly believed, reported fear of victimization is quite high (Brillon, 1987). This fear may be induced by media reports, but is also likely closely related with a sense of insecurity and vulnerability, which may be part of the aging process. Thus, older adults are more likely to report fears about having an accident, about becoming ill, about being alone and about not having enough money. Fears are also more likely to be present when mental health declines, such as with the onset of depression or loneliness.

Housing: Community versus Institutionalized Settings

The location and type of housing environment influences the quality of life and social interaction patterns of older adults. Sooner or later, because of declining health, alternative sources of housing may have to be considered. In the past, the primary alternative to living in one's own home was living in an institution. This practice led to the "warehousing" of the elderly, which was not appropriate for all elderly persons (Forbes, Jackson and Kraus, 1987). Inappropriate placement occurs more frequently than is necessary, particularly where there are few alternative options for the housing of older adults who are not fully independent.

More recently, because of private sector and government initiatives, a broader range of housing options have been provided in some communities, preventing or delaying institutionalization. Members of our society have begun to realize that total institutional care is frequently an inappropriate, inhumane and expensive way to provide the needed level of support. Many older people can be supported in their own home, with relatives, or in a quasi-family setting. These options, designed to house the elderly person within the community for as long as possible, provide some degree of institutionalized services in the home (for example, laundry, cleaning). Other options include apartments, condominiums, low-rent town houses, communal housing, retirement community housing, congregate housing and granny flats.

According to the 1981 census, an estimated 209 000 Canadians aged sixty-five and over reside in long-term care institutions (Forbes, Jackson and Kraus, 1987 : 31). These institutions range from residential care homes, for those who are relatively well, to homes for the aged and nursing homes, which provide chronic care facilities for the more severely disabled and dependent elderly. Interestingly, there are provincial variations in the rate of institutionalization, with Alberta having the highest rate (9.4 percent) and Newfoundland the lowest (5.6 percent). Part of the reason for this provincial variation is that the availability and co-ordination of services in the community and within institutional settings varies from province to province. Specifically, the cost of providing various types of institutions varies. As well, and more significantly, jurisdictional responsibility between a ministry of health and a ministry of social services and the type and level of support provided by municipal agencies differs. These jurisdictional variations often create disputes and problems with respect to the responsibility for the placement of elderly dependent persons, and in the co-ordination of services available to older persons at various stages of dependency.

In order to increase the availability of appropriate options and to improve the quality of institutional care, society needs alternative models of care and new assistance policies. Forbes, Jackson and Kraus (1987 : 83–121) stress that there is an urgent need to provide policy makers with valid and reliable data on the following topics: the needs and abilities of the independent and dependent elderly; attitudes toward institutionalization; the quality of life within institutions; the problems arising from excessive medication; the frequency and outcomes of inappropriate housing placement; the existence of funding and staffing problems within institutions; the problems resulting from divided or neglected jurisdictional responsibility for the care and support of elderly persons; and the need for financial incentives to enhance the quality of care within and outside institutions.

Social and Health Care: Informal versus Formal Support

The traditional method of caring for the frail elderly has been a medically based model that forces them to enter institutional settings. In response to accelerated population aging, policy makers are seeking alternatives to the medically based model to avoid the inappropriate placement of semi-independent elderly persons in chronic care institutions. This search has led to the development of informal and formal social support systems to assist older people to cope with health and daily living problems. These systems should not be viewed as a dichotomy (that is, either/or), but rather as a continuum from informal to formal support within a broad social network (see Corin, 1987).

Most elderly individuals are not isolated from family and friends. Rather, their network of relationships provides various degrees of informal care and assistance as needed. Indeed, most assistance to older adults is provided by family and friends, and especially by a spouse. Even where some assistance is provided by the formal care system, this assistance often complements that provided by the informal network. Informal assistance includes: financial aid; chores and errands; nursing and domestic care for temporary or long-term illness; transportation; emotional support; and personal care.

Formal support in the areas of health care, housing and income security is traditionally provided by society. More recently, however, the formal support system has focused on providing a continuum of social services for the elderly, including homemaker domestic assistance, transportation, home nursing, therapy services, senior centres, meals-on-wheels, congregate housing, bereavement counselling, geriatric day care and household repair services. All of these services are designed to increase the ability of older adults to live independently, thereby reducing the probability of needing expensive hospitalization or chronic-care housing. In short, a heterogeneous cohort of older adults needs more than two options—independent living in one's home or dependent living in an institution. The creation and co-ordinated amalgamation of informal and formal support systems in a community provides a continuum of care that can enable aging adults to remain in the community, and thereby maintain or improve their quality of life (see Chappell, Strain and Blandford, 1986 : 139–56).

Summary

This chapter has introduced some of the patterns, processes and problems of individual and population aging in Canada. It is important that the people of Canada become more sensitive to the inappropriate beliefs, attitudes and behaviours generated and perpetuated by the many myths that persist about aging and about the elderly. Contrary to prevailing views, this age group is characterized by considerable diversity on a number of social, physical and psychological factors. Each age cohort consists of a heterogeneous mix of people who vary on such factors as ethnicity, race, socio-economic status, education, marital status, employment history and geographical and urban-rural place of residence.

Throughout the chapter, aging has been described as a complex social process that involves the interaction of aging individuals and other age cohorts within a changing social, political and economic world. Each age cohort interacts with other age cohorts, which may be comprised of individuals with different values, beliefs and life experiences. Each age cohort diminishes in size and increasingly is comprised of a larger percentage of females. In modern societies such as Canada, the population itself is aging. All of these factors influence our life chances and life styles as we move across the life cycle, and as we interact with members of other age cohorts.

Since the 1960s, there has been considerable growth in the amount and quality of research on aging and the aged. Sociologists have been among the leaders in this new field of social gerontology. As a result, we now have a greater understanding of aging as a social process. However, large gaps in our understanding of aging phenomena still exist, and better policies and programs for older adults are still needed. Specifically, further research, policy analysis and practice is urgently needed with respect to such issues as gender and aging; the financial status of older Canadians, at present and in the future; mandatory versus voluntary retirement; fear of victimization; informal and formal support for aging individuals; elder abuse; housing an elderly population; the use and abuse of drugs; and transportation, mobility and migration. Thus, there is plenty of opportunity for further research and policy work by future generations of sociologists.

Suggested Readings

A. *Textbooks, Readers and Monographs*

Butterworths Series on Individual and Population Aging (1986+)

Each monograph in this series includes a review of the Canadian literature on the topic, as well as a discussion of policy and program implications for students, seniors and practitioners. To date, monographs on the following topics have been published:

- The Demography of Aging (S. McDaniel, 1986)
- Aging and Ethnicity (L. Driedger and N. Chappell, 1987)
- Drugs and Aging (W. McKim and B. Mishara, 1987)
- Victimization and Fear of Crime (Y. Brillon, 1987)
- Women and Aging (E. Gee and M. Kimball, 1987)

- Institutionalization of the Elderly (W. Forbes, J. Jackson and A. Kraus, 1987)
- Geographic Mobility and Migration (H. Northcott, 1988)
- Family Ties and Aging (I. Connidis, 1989)
- Work and Retirement (L. McDonald and R. Wanner, 1989)
- Widowhood (A. Martin Matthews, 1990)
- Aging in a Rural Environment (N. Keating and R. Coward, 1990)

Chappell, N., L. Strain and A. Blandford

1986. *Aging and Health Care: A Social Perspective.* Toronto: Holt, Rinehart and Winston. This book provides a discussion of the social context of aging and health care in Canada. Specific chapters address such issues as: health status and aging, informal support networks, the formal care system, community health and social services.

Marshall, V., ed.

1987. *Aging in Canada: Social Perspectives*, 2nd ed. Markham, Ont.: Fitzhenry and Whiteside. This reader includes thirty chapters grouped in the following major sections: theory and aging; the meanings of age and aging; aging workers and the labour force; aging, leisure and retirement; family structure and social relationships; health and well-being in relation to age; health care; and political, economic and social implications of population aging.

McPherson, B.

1990. *Aging as a Social Process: An Introduction to Individual and Population Aging*, 2nd ed. Toronto: Butterworths. This comprehensive Canadian text introduces the undergraduate student and practitioner to the many social aspects of individual and population aging. Specific chapters discuss aging as a social phenomenon; aging from a historical and comparative perspective; demographic aspects of aging; scientific methods and theories for understanding aging as a social process; the social consequences of adapting to physical and psychological changes; the social structure and social processes; social policy and social support systems; the physical environment; family dynamics; work, retirement and economic status; and aging and leisure.

Myles, J.

1984. *Old Age in a Welfare State: The Political Economy of Public Pensions.* Boston: Little, Brown. This book describes and analyses the economic responsibility of the state for the income and social security of the elderly in Canada.

B. *Journals*

Canadian Journal on Aging
The Gerontologist
The Journal of Gerontology
Research on Aging
Journal of Aging Studies

C. *Government Publications*

Canada, Government of

1988. *Canada's Seniors: A Dynamic Force.* Ottawa: Seniors Secretariat.

Statistics Canada

1984. *The Elderly in Canada.* Ottawa: Minister of Supply and Services Canada.

Stone, L., and S. Fletcher, eds.
    1986. *The Seniors Boom*. Ottawa: Statistics Canada.

Stone, L., and H. Frenken
    1988. *Canada's Seniors*. Ottawa: Minister of Supply and Services Canada.

Discussion Questions

1. Indicate how and why Canada's population is aging.

2. Identify five social myths about the elderly or about the process of aging. How and why have these been created and perpetuated? How might they be eliminated?

3. Other than the fact that their numbers are increasing, why is it essential to initiate research and policy planning for middle-aged and elderly women?

4. Compare the process of aging and the status of the aged in Canada with the situation in a developing country.

5. Discuss how and why aging should be studied as a social process rather than as a biological process.

6. "There is a constant interplay between individual and population aging. This is aptly illustrated by the process of retirement." Provide an argument to support or refute this statement.

Data Collection Exercises

1. *Participant Observation*
    Visit a public place (a park, a shopping mall, a movie theatre, a restaurant, a downtown street) on a Saturday and observe and record the following.
    (a) Identify the various age cohorts who visit the social setting, and indicate the approximate proportion of attendees by age group.
    (b) Do people attend with others of about the same age, or are most groups age integrated?
    (c) Do people of different ages use the social setting in similar or different ways? Identify any similarities or differences.
    (d) Do representatives of different age cohorts interact with each other in any way? If yes, indicate how they interact—formally or informally.
    (e) Record any observations about behaviour or interactions in the social setting that suggest age homophily or ageism is a common pattern.

2. *Social Survey*
    In co-operation with your minister/priest/rabbi, or your family physician, design a one- or two-page questionnaire that focuses on the leisure habits and attitudes of elderly (sixty-five plus) members of the religious group or medical

practice. Determine whether these habits and attitudes vary by gender, education and by age (65–70; 71–75; 76–80; 81+); and whether they have changed since the respondents were middle aged (that is, about forty-five to fifty-five years of age).

3. *Secondary Analysis*
   Visit the government documents section of your university library. Request the following provincial data about those sixty-five and older from the 1981 or 1986 census, for your province and any two other provinces:
   (a) gender;
   (b) urban-rural place of residence *or* size of community of residence;
   (c) employment status;
   (d) marital status;
   (e) educational attainment.
   Once you have retrieved the basic information, develop comparisons between your province and the other two provinces, noting similarities and differences. Present these comparisons in tables, figures or graphs, and propose possible explanations for any significant patterns (similarities or differences) you find.

4. *Case Study*
   Interview a friend, stranger or neighbour (not a relative) who is over sixty-five years of age. Ask them to discuss what life was like when they were your age. As they talk, probe with specific questions concerning education, family interaction, employment, dating patterns, music and movies, sports, etc.

5. *Content Analysis*
   Observe television commercials and shows for a week, *or* read a variety of popular magazines for a month, and document the frequency and situations in which elderly adults appear in these various forms of the media. On the basis of your documented observations, identify any patterns that appear and try to explain, using sociological concepts and theories, why these patterns exist.

Writing Exercises

1. Select a piece of fiction, preferably by a Canadian author, about aging or the aged. Critically review this book by summarizing the content and indicating how, and in what way, the book reinforces or refutes scientific evidence about aging.

2. You have decided to run for political office. Your campaign chairperson notes that a high percentage of your potential constituents are fifty-five years of age and older and recommends that you target your platform to appeal to this age group. Write a draft of a major campaign speech in which you outline the policies and programs you would initiate or support if you were elected.

3. Interview an elderly adult and write a case study focusing on a real or perceived problem experienced by this person in the last few years. In the case study, indicate all pertinent background information about the individual, how the problem occurred and how it has been or might be resolved.

4. At a future meeting of gerontologists, a panel discussion is to be held on the theme "Aging Differently." You have agreed to be one of the panelists. Write a draft of your proposed talk, being sure to include ideas relevant to both individual and population aging, and the interaction between these two levels of analysis.

Glossary

Age cohort: *a group comprised of all persons born during a particular year, five-year or ten-year period. This group proceeds through the life course together.*

Age homophily: *the tendency of people to socialize and interact with others of about the same chronological age.*

Ageism: *a form of social behaviour based on negative attitudes, stereotypes or a lack of knowledge about aging or the aged. This form of prejudice may lead to discrimination, usually against older adults, on the basis of actual or perceived chronological age.*

Age norms: *socially constructed rules or guidelines that define socially appropriate behaviour at different ages or stages in life, that define status through ascription, that regulate social interaction and that define when and in what order life events should occur.* Ascriptive age norms *are determined by a specific chronological age (for example, driving at sixteen, voting at eighteen, drinking at twenty-one, retiring at sixty-five), while* consensual age norms *provide an approximate age range in which specific roles or behaviours are acquired or relinquished (for example, leaving the parental home, marrying, having children, dressing in a certain style, regularly visiting discos).*

Age structure: *the population in any society is comprised of subgroups known as age cohorts. These groups form an age stratification system ranging from the very old to newborns. These age strata, each made up of members who are at the same chronological stage in the life cycle, are interconnected. Associated with each age stratum are age-related norms, expectations and rights that can influence our life styles, life chances and interaction patterns.*

Cohort flow: *a demographic process whereby a series of succeeding birth cohorts, varying in size and composition, interact and pass through the life cycle over a period of time.*

Generation: *within the extended family, grandparents, parents and grandchildren are referred to as belonging to different generations. Within society at large (that is, outside the family context), a generation refers to adjacent age cohorts that have experienced a similar life event (for example a depression, war) that subsequently makes their life experience different from other generations.*

Gerontologists: *scholars, policy makers and practitioners who focus their study and work on older adults and on the process of aging in the later years.*

Individual aging: *a process whereby individuals experience and adapt to physical, social and psychological changes as they proceed through the life cycle. These changes, and how we interpret and adapt to the changes, influence our life chances, our social interaction, our life styles and our quality of life at different stages in the life cycle.*

Life course: *a sequence of roles, opportunities and experiences unique to individuals or age cohorts as they age from birth to death. Some scholars refer to this as a life script.*

Life expectancy: *the* average *number of years of life remaining for an individual at a given age.*

Life span: *the theoretical* maximum *number of years an individual can live. For humans, this life span is about one hundred years. However, most die before this limit is reached, although in each society a few attain centenarian status.*

Multiple jeopardy: *a situation where age interacts with social class, race, ethnicity and gender to create a devalued social status and a disadvantaged social position. Usually, multiple jeopardy refers to an elderly female who is also poor and a member of a racial or ethnic minority group.*

Population aging: *a process whereby an increasing proportion of the population is over sixty or sixty-five years of age. This process occurs in those provinces or countries where birth rates or fertility rates are declining, where life expectancy is increasing, and where immigration rates of young people are decreasing (in Western, industrialized nations) or where emigration rates of young people are increasing (in developing nations).*

Role transitions: *the process whereby individuals gain or lose a status position (for example, single to married; married to divorced or widowed; employed to unemployed). As a result of the transition, individuals must learn new, or abandon old, role behaviours, rights and responsibilities. The process may create role conflict for some individuals and may be perceived as an event that enhances or detracts from their quality of life.*

Sex ratio: *the number of males per one hundred females in a given population at a given point in time. A ratio of 1.0 indicates an equal number of males and females, while a ratio less than 1.0 indicates that there are fewer males than females in a particular age cohort. For those sixty-five and over, the sex ratio in Canada is .86, but is projected to decline to about .78 by the year 2000.*

References

Atchley, R.
   1971. *The Social Forces in Later Life*. Belmont, Cal.: Wadsworth.

Birren, J., and V. Bengtson
   1988. *Emergent Theories of Aging*. New York: Springer Publishing.

Brillon, Y.
   1987. *Victimization and Fear of Crime among the Elderly*. Toronto: Butterworths.

Canada, Government of
   1988. *Canada's Seniors—A Dynamic Force*. Ottawa: Seniors Secretariat.

Chappell, N., L. Strain and A. Blandford
   1986. *Aging and Health Care: A Social Perspective*. Toronto: Holt, Rinehart and Winston.

Connidis, I.
   1989. *Family Ties and Aging*. Toronto: Butterworths.

Corin, E.
   1987. "The Relationship Between Formal and Informal Social Support Networks in Rural and Urban Contexts," pp. 367–94. In V. Marshall, ed., *Aging in Canada: Social Perspectives*, 2nd ed. Markham, Ont.: Fitzhenry and Whiteside.

Cowgill, D., and L. Holmes, eds.
  1972. *Aging and Modernization*. New York: Appleton-Century-Crofts.

Cumming, E., and W. Henry
  1961. *Growing Old: The Process of Disengagement*. New York: Basic Books.

Driedger, L., and N. Chappell
  1987. *Aging and Ethnicity*. Toronto: Butterworths.

Estes, C., L. Gerard, J. Sprague Jones and J. Swan
  1984. *Political Economy, Health and Aging*. Boston: Little, Brown.

Forbes, W., J. Jackson and A. Kraus
  1987. *Institutionalization of the Elderly in Canada*. Toronto: Butterworths.

Gee, E., and M. Kimball
  1987. *Women and Aging*. Toronto: Butterworths.

George, L.
  1980. *Role Transitions in Later Life*. Monterey, Cal.: Brooks/Cole Publishing.

Havighurst, R., and R. Albrecht
  1953. *Older People*. New York: Longmans, Green.

Lamont, C.
  1985. La violence à domicile faite aux femmes âgées. Travail présente pour le Cour EAN
  6670: Condition féminine et éducation continue," Université de Montréal.

Martin Matthews, A.
  1987. "Widowhood as an Expectable Life Event," pp. 343–66. In V. Marshall, ed., *Aging in Canada: Social Perspectives*, 2nd ed. Markham, Ont.: Fitzhenry and Whiteside.
  1989. *Widowhood*. Toronto: Butterworths.

McDaniel, S.
  1986. *Canada's Aging Population*. Toronto: Butterworths.

McPherson, B.
  1983. *Aging as a Social Process: An Introduction to Individual and Population Aging*. Toronto: Butterworths.

Myles, J.
  1984. *Old Age in a Welfare State: The Political Economy of Public Pensions*. Boston: Little, Brown.

Neugarten, B.
  1985. "Interpretive Social Science and Research on Aging," pp. 291–300. In A. Rossi, ed., *Gender and the Life Course*. New York: Aldine.

Neysmith, S.
  1987. "Social Policy Implications of an Aging Society," pp. 586–97. In V. Marshall, ed., *Aging in Canada: Social Perspectives*, 2nd ed. Markham, Ont.: Fitzhenry and Whiteside.

Northcott, H.
  1988. *Changing Residence: The Geographic Mobility of Elderly Canadians*. Toronto: Butterworths.

Riley, M.
  1971. "Social Gerontology and the Age Stratification of Society." *The Gerontologist* 11(1): 79–87.

Stone, L., and H. Frenken

   1988. *Canada's Seniors*. Ottawa: Minister of Supply and Services Canada.

Ujimoto, V.

   1987. "The Ethnic Dimension of Aging in Canada," pp. 111–37. In V. Marshall, ed., *Aging in Canada: Social Perspectives*, 2nd ed. Markham, Ont.: Fitzhenry and Whiteside.

part 3

Types
of
Social
Organization

All societies are made up of social organizations. These include small ones and large ones, simple and complex ones, temporary and permanent ones, informal and formal ones.

Some societies are very small and simple. The earliest human societies, hunting and gathering societies, may have numbered mere dozens of people. They were really just extended families, with everyone related to everyone else by birth or marriage. In this sense, what was good for the family was good for society. Kinship groups and communities were bound together by marriage and rituals and exchanges associated with marriage, such as dowry and bride-price. For this reason, marriage then was an even more central process of social organization than it is today.

Today, modern societies are large and made up of many organizations, and many of these, in turn, are large. How are large organizations like smaller ones, and large societies like smaller ones? At first glance, many similarities are evident. For example, all organizations are composed of roles, interactions and relationships. Here we see a similarity between social and physical reality. All physical objects are composed of similar, though not identical, atoms. They are distinguished by the way these atoms join together. In exactly the same way, social organizations are made up of similar, though not identical, social building blocks, joined together to make different forms.

Large social organizations are composed of smaller ones. For example, social classes, ethnic groups and urban communities all contain families, genders and roles. In many cases they also include social movements and formal organizations (for example, clubs, church groups and political associations). Thus, smaller organizations are the blocks with which people build larger ones.

Just as large organizations contain smaller ones, so formal organizations include informal ones; permanent organizations, temporary ones; and complex organizations, simpler ones. In a sense, a large, complex organization is merely the sum of its small, informal, shorter-lived organizations. Take the Toronto Jewish community, which has existed for well over a century. It is made up of many large, formal organizations (schools, synagogues, newspapers, clubs). It also includes all Jewish individuals, families and temporary groupings who identify or interact with members of the community.

But beyond a certain point, a difference of degree becomes a difference of kind. A large, complex, fairly permanent and formal organization will turn into something that is more than the groups that make it up. Increasing size and complexity bring enormous organizational changes. For this reason, Max Weber (1864–1920) took modern organizations, especially modern bureaucracy and the modern city, as the defining feature of modern societies.

In a modern society, people live more and more of their lives under the umbrella of large, enduring and complex social organizations. Of these, the state, the labour union and the multinational corporation are prime examples. Their size, complexity, wealth, power and permanence allow them to amass greater resources than smaller organizations and mere individuals could ever do. In the end, it is the *power* these resources command that distinguishes the large, complex organization from the small, simple one. A change of size becomes a change of kind.

The strength of a complex organization is based on more than just material things such as money, land and buildings. It is also more than special rights written into law and protected by expensive lawyers. Cultural legitimacy also supports the organization's power and permanence.

Processes of legitimation shape the processes of social organization that were discussed in the last section; specifically, they influence how children are socialized (in school and by the mass media) and what laws are enacted and enforced. Large organizations can act to persuade people to accept a view of life that supports and even glorifies the organization. People—as consumers, workers, students and media watchers—are trained to love (or hate) communism, private property, war, gender and racial inequality and so on. What the organizations teach depends on who is in charge and what goals the organization wants to promote. The major conflicts of our time—class conflict, gender conflict and racial and ethnic conflict—are fought out in these organizational contexts.

Racial and Ethnic Conflict

Two Solitudes is a classic Canadian novel by Hugh MacLennan (1945). It captures in fiction the fact of Canada's two main, very different cultures, francophone and anglophone, as they co-existed in mid-century Quebec. The book's title implies that these culture groups are isolated from one another and unable to communicate meaningfully.

Conquest by the British, and the subsequent domination of French Canadians by anglophones, hardened New France's (later, Quebec's) commitment to tradition. Every political fight in Quebec since 1760 has been, at bottom, a fight about the English conquest. But the major forces of modern life, chiefly, urbanism and industrialism, have affected francophone Canadians just like other Canadians.

Cultural differences remain today, but anglophones and francophones communicate more, share more values and interests than in the past, and intermarry more. The traditional, self-protective French Canadian culture may have been very useful when Anglo-Saxons and the Catholic Church dominated French Canadians. Since 1960, Quebeckers have thrown off these twin yokes. They enjoy new social and economic opportunities, and can take advantage of these at little risk. Increasingly, they change their behaviour in the direction of the North American norm. They continue to identify strongly with their own unique, historic culture—as their licence plates say, "Je me souviens"—but the political consequences of this cultural identification remain unclear at the time of this writing. (Such, indeed, is the case wherever cultural and regional identities are being asserted against the worldwide assimilating tendencies of multinational capital.)

The more often anglophones and francophones interact, the more often they intermarry, a clear sign that social distance between the groups has diminished. This fact certainly questions the persistence of "two solitudes." Rather, opportunity (in this case, for intermarriage) seems to produce social and cultural assimilation. Even more dramatic instances of francophone assimilation can be found. With increasingly liberal divorce laws, birth control, abortion opportunities and chances for a single life, francophones have deserted the traditional large French Canadian family in record numbers. Only twenty-five years ago, sociologist Norman Taylor (1964) claimed that modern capitalism in Quebec could not take hold because of traditional francophone loyalties to family life. Yet, today, francophones have the lowest marriage and fertility rates in the country. They have even outdone the traditionally less family-oriented anglophones. What is more, capitalism is doing fine in the French-speaking province.

On balance, the francophone culture, its position in Canadian society and the relationship between francophones and anglophones has changed dramatically in the last thirty years. Similar changes can be seen in the relations between other racial and ethnic groups and the dominant culture. However, it should not be assumed that all ethnic and race relations in Canada are variations on the francophone/anglophone theme. All ethnic and race relations go through stages of faster and slower change, more co-operation and more conflict.

During periods of conflict, ethnic groups strengthen their internal cohesion by increasing "institutional completeness"—that is, by adding to the range of communal organizations that serve ethnic group members (usually in their own language). Community members form and strengthen large organizations to demand more money from the federal government (to support multiculturalism) and a greater voice in political affairs. Here is one clear example of "bottom-up" organizations influencing the larger society.

Gender Conflict

In any office, bank or department store, we find large numbers of women working in jobs that pay poorly, command no respect or authority, may soon be eliminated by new technology and hold little prospect of career advancement. Clerical, sales and service occupations are the job "ghetto" in which we find a majority of employed Canadian women.

Several facts about this ghetto are particularly ominous. First, the potential for "ghettoization" is growing. With the development of what Daniel Bell (1973) has called the "post-industrial society," more and more work in our society is of the kind that overwhelmingly employs women. So, as more women enter the labour force, more work of the kind women typically do is becoming available.

Second, efforts to improve the status of working women—their pay, job security, and chances for promotion—have met with little success. Unionizing the employees of banks, offices and stores has proved very difficult. As a result, women's paid work continues to be insecure, poorly paid and with little prospect of improvement. Upgrading the status of part-time work, which women do much more commonly than men, has also been slow. Moreover, affordable, good quality care facilities for the children of working mothers remain few and are increasing only slowly.

New technology poses a final problem. New technology eliminates jobs in agriculture and manufacturing, traditionally male-dominated work; but it also eliminates jobs that women traditionally do. New computer technology significantly reduces the need for large numbers of (female) clerical workers and stenographers. New communication technology may largely reshape sales and service occupations, eliminating many (female) workers. An example is the job of bank teller, which employs many fewer (female) cashiers since the money machine was introduced.

"Patriarchy"—the domination of women by men—is part of our cultural heritage (Fox, 1988). It has a very long history, and some part of the male domination that persists today is simply a holdover from earlier times. Where work was primarily agricultural, a sexual division of labour may have been more necessary; in any event, it was more easily imposed.

Not only do men and women lead different work lives; they also lead different married lives. As sociologist Jessie Bernard (1973) put it, every marriage is actually two marriages, *his* marriage and *her* marriage. The husband's marriage is full of *provided* support, nurturance and physical caring. The wife's marriage is made up of *providing* support, nurturance and physical caring. As well, wives see to the children, the shopping, the cleaning and other domestic chores.

Thus, wives experience marriage differently from husbands, they experience parenthood differently from husbands, and they experience paid work differently from husbands. Because their daily experience is different from men's in every important particular, their consciousness—or perception of the world—is different. They "live" in a different world, one that is subordinate, alien and captive: they live in a "double ghetto," as Pat and Hugh Armstrong have referred to it.

Again, we see the intertwining of small organizations and large. Disadvantages in the work world—for example, discrimination in hiring and promotion—keep many women in disadvantageous marriages that can be abusive, exploitive or unhappy. Equally, disadvantageous marriages keep women from advancing in the work world, which assumes that employees will receive (unpaid) home support, spousal energy and time commitment.

Class and Stratification

Women and ethnic/racial minorities are two categories of Canadians who have traditionally experienced unequal *life chances*—the chances people have to get what they need for a happy, healthy, secure life.

Social class also determines a person's life chances. Whatever your gender or ethnic origin, you will have more choices and better chances in life if you are born into a prosperous upper-class or middle-class home than into a working-class or impoverished home. This is an enduring fact of all human societies. Accordingly, the study of social inequality, and of social classes, has been one of the basic, classic preoccupations of sociology (see, for example, Brym, 1988).

Just as gender and race relations shape the struggle for dominance in all organizations, so do class relations. From this perspective, ethnicity, gender and class are not merely social categories or social groupings. They are dimensions of opposition within Canadian society. We have seen that understanding how *power* operates is crucial in sociology. The chapters in this section focus on the exercise of power in a variety of institutional contexts.

CHAPTER 8

Class and Stratification

GORDON DARROCH

Nineteenth- and twentieth-century workplaces.

ARCHIVES OF ONTARIO.

Introduction

> Order is Heaven's first law; and, this confessed,
> Some are, and must be, greater than the rest.
> (Alexander Pope, *Essay on Man*, 1733)

Stephen Jay Gould in his perceptive *The Mismeasure of Man* (1981:30) cites Pope to illustrate the argument that "appeals to reason or to the nature of the universe have been used throughout history to enshrine existing hierarchies as proper and inevitable. The hierarchies rarely endure for more than a few generations, but the arguments, refurbished for the next round of social institutions, cycle endlessly."

This chapter has three main objectives. First, we will consider the three basic traditions of social thought that influence the way we still think about social hierarchies and social inequality. Second, we will see how social hierarchies are sustained or reproduced by specific social processes; they do not merely continue of their own accord, nor are they in the "nature of things." Third, we will review some of the main patterns of inequality in condition and in opportunity in contemporary Canadian society and relate these to a specific interpretation of the rise of proletarianization and of the Canadian middle class. Our study of class and socio-economic stratification touches, but largely leaves unexplored, many related topics, such as the concentration of economic power, gender inequality, educational mobility and inequality among racial, ethnic, age or regional groups. These subjects are dealt with in their own chapters.

Perspectives on Inequality

There are two distinct ways of thinking about inequality. One considers differences among individuals or social groups in terms of some scale, such as the amount of income, education or status they possess. People with this view see social inequality as a ladder with individuals standing on different rungs, some higher than others. We say that social processes and barriers that tend to hold individuals in those positions over their lifetimes—or possibly over generations—generate *structured inequality*, or *stratification*. When movement up or down the ladder does occur, we refer to it as social mobility.

A second concept emphasizes *dichotomous* relations (sharp *class* distinctions) between a dominant group and a subordinate group (Ossowski, 1963). The divisions between such groups are *class* divisions and imply conflict in their interests. This perspective entails explicit political and moral judgments. People with this view see the interests of the two classes as conflicting and the dominant class exploiting the class that depends on it.

Class analysis and, in particular, Marxist theory, has set the terms of reference for the analysis of stratification. The latter has frequently been a response to class analysis—or as Albert Salomon called it, a "debate with Marx's ghost" (cited in Zeitlin, 1981:127).

The Marxist Theory of Class

The Marxist theory of social classes is the most elaborate, challenging and radical perspective on social inequality. It is most provocative because it carries a political and, ultimately, revolutionary message. Marx's theory commands attention because it is a complex theoretical system built from detailed historical analyses of the rise and expansion of Western capitalism.

Somewhat curiously, Marx did not formally define class, though there are clarifying remarks at the end of his major work, *Capital*. Marx, like the nineteenth-century economist Ricardo, considered the three great classes of the emerging industrial order in England to be landlords, capitalists and wage labourers (Zeitlin, 1981 : 114). These three groups can be distinguished by their main sources of income, that is, rents for land, profits from production and wages. But Marx found a more fundamental difference. He claimed that what divides these social groups is their relationship to and control of the basic economic resources of society. Landowners control major blocks of land, emerging *capitalists* own and control industrial production and wage labourers' livelihoods depend entirely on selling their capacity to work.

Pressing the analysis further, Marx recognized an even more fundamental division, the division between those groups that privately owned and controlled the basic economic resources of society and those who were excluded from ownership and control. In this respect, landowners and manufacturers shared common interests and were sharply divided from the workers. Marx did *not* suggest the real social world was divided neatly into two competing classes. Rather, he saw many class interests and many segments of classes—there are miners and dock workers, clerks and professionals, small farmers and artisans, financiers, merchants and industrialists and so forth. What he did recognize was that, within this social hierarchy of occupational, income and political groups, there was the fundamental division between the propertied and not-propertied. This fundamental division was at the root of class exploitation and class conflict.

"Exploitation" in Marxist theory means a process of extracting *surplus value* from a population. Surplus value is a familiar concept when we are thinking about slave-based societies. As part of their rights, slave owners claim all the products of the slaves' labour. The difference between the value of slave production and the cost of maintaining the slaves was the owners' surplus value. In the feudal society of medieval Europe, surplus value was extracted from the main producers in society—the peasants—in the form of surplus products. The peasant simply gave over a portion of his harvest in return for "services" of the landowner, for example, for protection from marauders and some assurance of help in lean years (Moore, 1969).

Marx was born in the early 1800s. Living in England (where he was in exile from 1849 to 1883) and in Germany, he witnessed the development of early industrial capitalism. Thus, Marx focused on how capitalism is also an exploitative mode of production. His explanation is complex, though we can see the nub of the matter in a brief passage from *Capital*. In Marx's words, in capitalism "two very different kinds of commodity-possessors must come face-to-face and into contact; on the one hand, the owners of money, means of production, means of subsistence, who are eager to increase the sum of values they possess, by buying other people's labour-power; on the other hand, free labourers, the sellers of their own labour-power and therefore the sellers of labour" (Marx, *Capital* I : 714).[1]

The enormous productive power of capitalism as a mode of production is unleashed in this historically unique meeting of private ownership and the legally free and competitive labour market. There is, however, a basic conflict in this meeting. The surplus value produced in capitalism (taking the form of profits) primarily benefits the capitalists; it is not distributed among its producers. In what way is this a "free and competitive" system?

Marx's answer begins with the labour theory of value, which in his formulation recognizes that only one commodity sold in the market actually creates value—that commodity is human labour-power. All other materials and commodities exchanged in the course of production are essentially inert; they embody or carry value, but do not create it. Moreover, as a result of the *private* ownership and control of the means of production,[2] only the capitalist class, or *bourgeoisie*, can claim the value that is added in the labour process. The class of owners also primarily determines the uses of labour and its products. Exploitation takes this "hidden" form in capitalism and is the basis of the inherent antagonism between capital and labour, as classes.

Capitalists and workers are, thus, inherently opposed to one another in a struggle over the distribution of capitalism's "social product"; that is, all that is produced by workers collectively. The struggle goes beyond wages and profits. The capitalists' drive for profits leads them to try to control the length of the working day, to set the rhythm and pace of production and, in general, to impose their authority over all aspects of people's working lives. Workers increasingly lose control of the tools and process of production and become merely wage employees. Marx expected this fundamental conflict of class interests to show itself in various forms. Some of these forms, such as social and labour movements, are discussed in Chapter 21. Ultimately, the conflict causes social revolution.

Marx's theory of class and class conflict is too complicated for us to attempt a major evaluation of it here. The major changes in capitalist societies over the last century, however, have had important implications for Marxist class theory. A variety of

---

[1] Marx came to use the term labour-power, rather than labour, in his analysis. Labour-power refers to the human capacity to create and to work *treated as a commodity in capitalism*, which workers sell on the labour market to make a living. I have appreciated useful comments on this and related issues by Tony Williams of Okanagan College.

[2] Note that private property is not simply the ownership or possession of things (pencils and pens, clothes or cars), but a social institution, entailing enforceable claims or rights to use. As C. B. Macpherson says, "What distinguishes property from mere momentary possession is that property is a claim that will be enforced by society or the state, by custom or convention or law" (1978 : 3). In contemporary society, both social convention and the state enforce property rights.

interpretations of Marx's work have emerged. In some cases there are deep divisions and lively debates *among* Marxist authors (Althusser, 1969; Poulantzas, 1973; Thompson, 1979). Some critics of Marx have turned the twentieth-century developments of capitalism into major revisions or rejections of Marx's core ideas (Dahrendorf, 1959; Nisbet, 1959; Bell, 1961; Porter, 1965). Some argue, for example, that the growth of social services and state welfare systems insulate the working class from hardship even if wages are low. Others say the increased standards of living and the growth of "middle-class" occupations (white-collar jobs) have transformed capitalism, so it is no longer a society divided between owners and workers over the control of the work process.

Others recognize the changes are fundamental, but argue that they do not render Marx's work irrelevant. After all, Marx was mainly concerned to establish a method of analysis that revealed the basic contradictions within capitalism and lent itself to the analysis of actual, historical tendencies. Class, as E. P. Thompson has taught us, is not a thing or a set of categories or a structure, but *relations* that emerge historically in experience as social groups face exploitation, inequality and crises within capitalism.

Class: A Historical Phenomenon

If we stop history at a given point, then there are no classes but simply a multitude of individuals with a multitude of experiences. But if we watch these men over an adequate period of social change, we observe patterns in their relationships, their ideas and their institutions. Class is defined by men as they live their own history, and, in the end, this is its only definition.

By class I understand an historical phenomenon, unifying a number of disparate and seemingly unconnected events, both in the raw material of experience and in consciousness. I emphasize that it is an *historical* phenomenon. I do not see class as a "structure," or even as a "category," but as something which in fact happens (and can be shown to have happened) in human relationships.

More than this, the notion of class entails the notion of historical relationship. Like any other relationship, it is a fluency which evades analysis if we attempt to stop it dead at any given moment and anatomize its structure. The finest-meshed sociological net cannot give us a pure specimen of class, any more than it can give us one of deference or of love. The relationship must always be embodied in real people and in a real context.

Reprinted from E. P. Thompson. 1963. *The Making of the English Working Class*. New York: Pantheon Books.

Weber and Status Groups

Max Weber (1864–1920) was the most influential of those who "debated with Marx's ghost." He has been called "the bourgeois Marx" (Salomon, 1945). Weber's understanding of the central institutions of capitalism was much like Marx's, emphasizing the concentration of the means of production in the hands of a few and the spread of a labour market of legally free individuals who hire themselves out to employers (Weber, in Roth and Wittich, 1968:I:300ff.; Gerth and Mills, 1958:180–81).

Despite these common points of analysis, two positions clearly distinguish Weber's perspective from Marx's. First, for Weber, twentieth-century capitalism was not a society divided between two main classes, even at its core. Rather, there were a variety of *class situations*, determined by differing relations to property and by differing positions in the labour market. Second, Weber analysed forms of power or domination, rather than relations of production and conflict. Weber is perhaps best known as the master theorist of the growth of modern bureaucracy. It is the growth of bureaucracy that led Weber to reject a Marxist focus on the separation of workers from the means of production as a specifically capitalist phenomenon. In fact, he saw the separation as only one example of a more general historical process of the concentration of power in the hands of the few (Weber, 1968:980ff.). Economic ownership is one form of power. "Also (and especially) every rational socialist economy would retain the expropriation of the workers and would only complete it by expropriating private owners" (Weber, in Mommsen, 1977:381). In other words, for Weber, private property is not a key to exploitation, since replacing it by state ownership would just deepen and extend the loss of control by individuals over their work and over the means of production.

In contrast to Marx, Weber was concerned to specify precisely the concept of class (Weber, 1968:II:926ff.). He begins with the claim, "Now: 'classes,' 'status groups' and 'parties' are phenomena of the distribution of power within a community" (Gerth and Mills, 1958:181). These different ways in which the interests of individuals and social groups can be pursued in market societies will be our focus of attention over the next few paragraphs.

For Weber, a *class* is a group that shares the same economic relation to markets whether these are commodity markets, labour markets or credit markets. Class situations, then, result from similar kinds of control over goods or skills that produce income. Weber accepts possession of property is one, but only one, critical determinant of class position—of one's chances on the market and therefore of life chances (Gerth and Mills, 1958:181–82). There are many other forms of marketable skills and, indeed, more than one type of property. Ownership may be of natural resources, of money or investment funds, of labour, of warehouses, stores, mills, factories, corporations. Each generates a significantly different class situation for the owners. Thus, for example, those people who only have their skills and energy to sell on the labour market are all in the same class position, while those who trade in wholesale goods or grain are in other class positions. A person might be simultaneously involved in several class situations, depending on his or her control of economic resources, though most will be in only one.

Thus, in the Weberian tradition, class entails no underlying theory of exploitation or value. In direct contrast to the Marxist tradition, Weber did not think that people who belong to the same class necessarily share a common purpose or are historically destined to organize and to act together as a class (Giddens, 1973:43).

For Weber, *status groups* are also understood as interest groups. But status is determined by the regard in which people are held by society or, in Weber's terms, by the "social estimation of honour." A status group maintains its position by claiming privileges at the *expense* of others. In contrast to social classes, they are based directly on shared "styles of life," forms of consumption and on prestige or honour accorded by the larger community, for example, landed elites or contemporary ethnic groups. Weber distinguishes between class and status group to stress that forms of stratification do not rest on property or position in economic markets alone. As Giddens has emphasized, economic control is not the only form of power Weber considers: "The theorem informing Weber's position here is his insistence that power is not to be assimilated to economic domination—again, of course, a standpoint taken in deliberate contrast to that of Marx" (1973:44).

Finally, Weber saw status groups as specifically social communities in which membership is conferred by social criteria, such as language, colour, ethnic heritage or family line. Membership criteria that distinguish who is to be included in, or excluded from, the community tend to generate shared ways of life, social interaction and values (Gerth and Mills, 1958:186–87). Social classes in Weber's view are seldom this kind of shared community. Thus, class consciousness and class politics are historically rare and fragile in comparison to the status group consciousness and politics, such as those of ethnic or racial groups.

Parties, Weber's third way in which power is socially organized, are forms of planned political action and are phenomena of the modern world, since they require a staff and modern organizational apparatus. As Weber used it, the term includes a range of political organizations, such as unions and lobby groups. For Weber, parties may either represent class interests or status interests or a combination of both (Gerth and Mills, 1958:194–95).

Despite his concern with analytic precision, Weber did not formulate a systematic theory of class and stratification. There is, however, a theoretical core to the definitions developed elsewhere in his work, centred on the concept of *social closure* (Weber, 1968:342). Social closure refers to any process by which a group defines social boundaries, thereby "restricting access to resources and opportunities to a limited circle of eligibles" (Parkin, 1979:44). In effect, closure is a strategy for monopolizing social and economic opportunities or positions. Ethnic and racial discrimination are obvious forms of social closure, but so is property ownership itself. Apartheid in South Africa is one particularly vicious form of closure; exclusive residential neighbourhoods are a more subtle form.

One major criticism of the Weberian tradition concerns its arid and formal definitions. Specifically, Weber's various distinctions seem to be difficult to apply to actual cases of class and status conflict or to the rise of class consciousness, as he intended (Giddens, 1973:79). Others argue that his work lacks a theoretical core that accounts for the realities of class exploitation and power (Stedman Jones, 1976).

The Functional
Theory of
Stratification

The third major perspective on class and stratification is a *functional theory*. In contrast to Marxist and Weberian thought, it suggests that social *class* divisions and conflict are largely irrelevant in contemporary, industrial societies, although it accepts that some inequality is both universal and useful (that is, *functional*). There are two key premises to functional theory.

The first premise is that social class divisions of an earlier era have been dissolved in the mid and late twentieth century since, functionalists argue, the material and social circumstances of the non-owning classes have greatly improved and the power of capitalists, as a class, has diminished.

A second premise is that social inequality is an *essential* feature of any complex society. Kingsley Davis stated the premise this way: "Social inequality is, thus, an unconsciously evolved device by which societies insure that the most important positions are conscientiously filled by the most qualified persons" (1949:367).

There are three separate parts to the second premise. First, certain positions or jobs in society are essential to its orderly functioning. It follows that some positions are more important than others; they require more skill and they impose more onerous responsibilities. Second, only a limited number of people have the talent and are willing to pay the costs of being trained to accomplish society's essential tasks. That is, there is a scarcity in the supply of talented and trained personnel. Third, there must be incentives or *differential rewards*, which motivate the talented and trained people to fulfil the "needs" of the society. Inequality is, thus, a mechanism of motivation— filling and fitting society's demand for labour from its limited supply of talent (Tumin, 1953; Wesolowski, 1962). Despite its simplicity and familiarity, the criticisms of the theory have been pointed and numerous.

One criticism questions the key functionalist assumption that positions in the occupational world can be ranked by importance. How do we compare the importance to society of, say, farmers and army generals, of lawyers and nurses, of teachers and politicians, of baseball players and those who keep house and raise children. Yet, these occupations differ widely in terms of prestige, in income and in various "perks" of the job (Tumin, 1953; Stinchcombe, 1963). Critics ask why it is that physically hard, dirty and dangerous work is usually much less well rewarded than safe, clean and physically undemanding work (Wesolowski, 1962). Is the work women do (including unpaid domestic labour) less functional for society than men's work? Certainly, it is less well rewarded.

Regarding the theory's second central premise, there is a question whether Western society may not be more wasteful of potential human talent than efficient in using it (Tumin, 1953). Some critics point to the relatively few women recruited to managerial positions or to the professions. Others point to the barriers to occupational mobility faced by visible minorities in all Western countries.[3]

---

[3] Mark Twain is credited with quipping: "Let us be thankful for fools, but for them the rest of us could not succeed." He might have had the functional theory of stratification in mind.

Class Formation in Canadian History

Both the Marxist and Weberian perspectives view class as a historical phenomenon. They theorize that class relationships and structures are maintained and changed according to specific historical patterns. This connection between social class and history promises an understanding of social change, but the promise is often unfulfilled.

Marx and Weber were mainly concerned with Europe. Their analysis centres on the emergence of capitalist relations out of feudal ones. That model does not necessarily fit other situations. For North America, and for Canada in particular, we need to know how a society dominated by small property owners—on the land or in their own shops and homes—is transformed into a society divided between big capital and wage-labour. As Greer neatly puts it: "If most producers in early Canada worked 'for themselves,' how and when did the practice of 'working for anyone but themselves' come to be the norm?" (1985 : 21). Although the answer to this question may provide a key to understanding Canada's class formation, we do not yet have a carefully researched answer.

Proletarianization is this historical process in which people increasingly come to depend for their livelihood on the sale of their labour-power (in exchange for wages or salaries) and capitalists increasingly control the means of production. The two aspects are directly related. This broad conception follows Marx's meaning in his historical work.[4]

Most analysis of proletarianization in Canada relies on a single interpretation of the changes gathering force after the middle of the last century. Before mid-century, wage labouring was relatively limited; it grew with industrialization, especially in the major cities of Montreal, Toronto and Hamilton (Burgess, 1977; Palmer, 1979; Kealey, 1980). Three factors are usually cited as the basis of this transformation (Palmer, 1984; Pentland, 1959; Teeple, 1972 : 43–66; Rinehart, 1975). First, the railway system grew rapidly from a mere seventy-two miles of track in 1850 to over 2000 in 1865, expanding the local economic market (Palmer, 1984 : 61). Second, some of the hundreds of small producers—the owners and operators of saw and grist mills, iron forgers, brewers, cabinet-makers, and so forth—began consolidating into larger operations that would be the backbone of industrial capitalism. Only a few succeeded; they increased wage employment for both men and women from the countryside, especially in Quebec (Robert, 1982) and absorbed large numbers of skilled immigrants from Great Britain. These men and women formed the first substantial wage labour force—

---

[4] Tilly (1981 : 179–81) has drawn attention to the several meanings of the term. Proletarianization often refers to a process in which wage and salary workers are subjected to a general degrading of the skills required in their work and to increasing discipline and intensification in the labour-process, as in Braverman's important work (1974). More narrowly, the term may refer to the increase in numbers of manual wage workers doing unskilled work in factory settings. Following Tilly, the meaning adopted in this chapter is broader than either of these.

ARCHIVES OF ONTARIO.

ARCHIVES OF ONTARIO.

Canada's industrial proletariat (Pentland, 1959). Third, the land for farming became more and more restricted after 1840. The restrictions are said to result from government land policy (Johnson, 1971), land speculators and the expansion of the more successful farmers (Gagan, 1978; McCallum, 1980).

Some version of this interpretation has been at the centre of virtually every historical and sociological account of how the capitalist class was formed in Canada (Teeple, 1972; Kealey, 1980; Palmer, 1979; Johnson, 1972; Rinehart, 1975; Hunter, 1981; Heron and Storey, 1986). Important as it is, the explanation has not been conclusively documented. Recent historical evidence suggests this prevailing view has exaggerated the significance of proletarianization at the time of Confederation. The process may have been much slower and uneven. For example, community studies have indicated

TABLE 8-1

Work Force by
Occupation, Canada,
1891–1961
(percentages)

Year	Owners & Managers	Profes- sions	Clerical & Sales	Farmers & Farm Workers	Labourers	Others & Oper- atives*	Total	Total Work Force
1891	4.9	3.4	5.3	45.7	6.8	32.9	100.0	1 607 945
1901	4.7	4.7	6.2	40.1	7.1	37.2	100.0	1 782 621
1911	8.0	3.1	8.3	34.1	12.2	34.3	100.0	2 275 148
1921	8.3	5.5	12.3	32.8	9.7	31.4	100.0	3 173 169
1931	5.7	5.9	11.9	28.7	11.6	36.2	100.0	3 927 230
1941	5.4	6.7	12.4	25.8	6.3	43.4	100.0	4 195 951
1951	8.1	7.3	16.3	15.9	6.7	45.7	100.0	5 218 596
1961	8.6	10.0	19.7	10.3	5.0	46.4	100.0	6 305 630

*"Others & Operatives" is a catch-all category that includes all members of the labour force not classified in the other categories. See Leacy's comment on the original table.

FROM F. H. LEACY, ED. 1983. HISTORICAL STATISTICS OF CANADA. OTTAWA: STATISTICS CANADA, TABLE D86-106. REPRODUCED BY PERMISSION OF THE MINISTER OF SUPPLY AND SERVICES CANADA.

family farming expanded in the 1860s and 1870s (Gagan, 1981) and that land speculation and land policies posed few barriers to acquiring farm land (Akenson, 1984). One historical study of occupational change in Ontario at the time of Confederation found there was a great deal of occupational change in just the ten years 1861 to 1871. A great many men still were becoming independent family farmers, despite restrictions, including nearly 40 percent of common labourers (Darroch and Ornstein, 1985). Thus, at the time of Confederation, Canada was a social formation still dominated by small property owners, with limited concentration of capital and limited proletarianization.[5] So the key question remains: How long did this social formation persist? Social and historical research does not yet provide us with a clear answer. We can, however, piece together some of the puzzle.

Table 8-1 provides some relevant data, showing changes in Canada's occupational structure between 1891 and 1961, the period in which the change is most dramatic. The data include both men and women in the labour force. In 1891, over 45 percent of the labour force was in farming. In 1921, one-third of the labour force was still in the farm sector (the majority again were small farm owners). It is not until after 1941 that farming engages less than a quarter of the labour force. The Great Depression of the 1930s and the demands for industrial production of the Second World War brought about the first dramatic decline of family farmers. By 1971 they are greatly

[5] That Canada was a land of small property does *not*, however, mean that this was an egalitarian society. Class structure, class experience and stratification are related, but separate, phenomena. Inequalities in wealth and property were deeply etched in the last century. For example, the best evidence indicates that at any one point in time 40 to 50 percent of the families owned *no* property whatsoever about 1871 (Katz, 1975; Darroch, 1983). Many people did, however, acquire farmland or a home in their lifetimes, even if the *structure* of inequality remained largely in place (Darroch, 1988).

reduced (Leacy, 1983 : Table M12-22). Of course, there were other small independent producers and shop owners. Despite the reduction, these groups have persisted as a significant element of the Canadian class structure to the present (Cuneo, 1984). Proletarianization in Canada has been a *relatively* slow and uncertain process both in terms of changes in class structure and in terms of the everyday experiences of Canadians over the last five generations.

Class and Stratification in Contemporary Canada

Has contemporary Canada become more deeply divided by the concentration of the control of capital in fewer and fewer hands and the increasing dependence of most people on wages and salaries? Or, as functionalists claim, have class divisions and conflict largely dissolved? In more direct terms, is our society characterized by inequality of condition or by equality of opportunity? We argue that in some respects it is both, and this very *duality* is crucial to understanding the Canadian class experience.

The Concentration of Capital and Wealth

One side of the process of proletarianization is the concentration of economic power in the hands of fewer and fewer people. That power means the capacity to control much of the organization of production, including the nature of jobs and, therefore, of people's working lives. The Canadian economy is dominated by a relatively small number of large capitalist enterprises; that is, corporate concentration is increasing (Naylor, 1972; Clement, 1977; Brym, 1985; Coyne, 1986). Corporate concentration is discussed in Chapter 17 of this book. We will only note here that the evidence of enormous concentration of power is unequivocal. A relatively small number of firms and families dominate the Canadian economy. The one hundred largest industrial firms in Canada, cited by the *Financial Post* in 1979, had total sales exceeding the combined sales of all the other businesses. These one hundred constituted only 0.3 percent of all firms in Canada (Osberg, 1981 : 27–28). In 1970, nearly 90 percent of all Canadian families reported owning *no* publicly traded stock at all; only about 3 percent owned shares worth $5000 or more in 1970 dollars (Osberg, 1981 : 36). In 1984, 80 percent of the firms listed on the Toronto Stock Exchange 300 Index were controlled either by a single family or by a small group. Only nine families in all of Canada controlled about half of the value of these companies (Coyne, 1986).

Despite some differences in interpretation, there is no doubt that this small group is sufficiently interconnected and powerful to be called a bourgeoisie—the "big" bourgeoisie—a small, dominant class. What does the power and social closure of a bourgeoisie imply for the Canadian system of stratification, especially for the distribution of wealth? Table 8-2 shows one estimate of the distribution of wealth measured as family assets.

The table shows the proportion of total assets or net worth in 1970 and 1977 held

TABLE 8-2
The Wealth Distribution of Canada (as Measured by the Survey of Consumer Finance), 1970 and 1977

	Family Units Ranked by Wealth					
	Financial Assets		Total Assets		Net Worth	
Decile	1970	1977	1970	1977	1970	1977
poorest 10%	0.0	0.0	0.0	0.0	−1.0	−0.6
2	0.1	0.1	0.2	0.3	−0.0	0.1
3	0.3	0.4	0.6	0.9	0.3	0.6
4	0.7	0.9	1.4	2.3	1.3	1.7
5	1.2	1.5	3.2	5.0	3.0	3.6
6	2.2	2.6	6.3	7.4	5.4	6.0
7	4.0	4.5	9.6	9.6	8.3	8.6
8	7.3	8.0	12.7	12.2	11.8	12.0
9	15.1	15.0	17.5	16.8	17.6	17.5
richest 10%	69.1	67.0	48.5	45.6	53.3	50.6

Financial assets = deposits, cash, bonds, stocks, mortgages, etc.
Total assets = financial assets, business equity, real estate, automobiles
Net worth = total assets − debts

ADAPTED FROM GAIL OJA. 1980. "INEQUALITY OF WEALTH DISTRIBUTION IN CANADA 1970 AND 1977." IN REFLECTIONS ON CANADIAN INCOMES. OTTAWA: ECONOMIC COUNCIL OF CANADA, P. 352. REPRODUCED BY PERMISSION OF THE MINISTER OF SUPPLY AND SERVICES CANADA.

by each 10 percent (decile) of the family units, starting with the poorest decile and ending with the richest decile. The poorest 10 percent of the families had no measurable assets and a small debt (-1.0 and -0.6, in 1970 and 1977). The wealthiest 10 percent of families were exceedingly wealthy; they had about 69.1 and 67 percent of all financial assets, just less than 50 percent of total assets and a little over 50 percent of net worth in the two years. To recognize how much inequality this represents, consider that the less wealthy half of the Canadian families (first to fifth deciles) together had just over 5 percent of the net worth of all families in 1977 and only 3.6 percent in 1970. The inequality is even more extreme for people not living in family units. Moreover, the table shows that in the seven years from 1970 to 1977 there was almost no change in these distributions. Indeed, it is unlikely that there has been any significant reduction in wealth inequality since the Second World War. As we shall see, inequalities in earned incomes, which are distinct from wealth-holding *per se*, have also been very stable for several decades.

Class Structure and the Occupational Division of Labour

The concentration of capital and economic power means that large numbers of people in the labour force have lost control of workplaces and the actual work process. Since the Second World War, the economy of small, rather independent producers has largely disappeared, replaced by an economy of blue- and white-collar *employees*. Table 8-3 provides a picture of this change through conventional census tabulations.

TABLE 8-3

Percentage
Distribution of
Labour Force
Fifteen Years and
Over by Occupation
Division, for
Canada: 1901, 1921,
1941, 1961, 1971
and 1981

Occupation Division	Percentage					
	1901[a]	1921	1941	1961	1971[c]	1981[d]
White-Collar	15.3	25.3	25.3	37.9	42.3	49.8
Proprietary, managerial	4.3	7.3	5.4	7.8	4.3	6.8
Professional	4.6	5.4	6.7	9.8	12.6	15.1
Clerical	3.2	6.9	7.2	12.7	15.9	18.3
Commercial, financial	3.1	5.7	6.0	7.6	9.5	9.6
Blue-Collar	27.8	25.8	27.1	26.6	24.3	23.9
Manufacturing, mechanical	15.9	11.4	16.1	16.1	17.7	17.5
Construction	4.7	4.7	4.7	5.2	6.6	6.4
Labourers[b]	7.2	9.7	6.3	5.3	—	—
Primary	44.3	36.2	30.5	12.8	7.5	5.8
Agricultural	40.3	32.6	25.7	10.0	5.9	4.2
Fishing, hunting, trapping	1.5	0.9	1.2	0.6	0.3	0.3
Logging	0.9	1.2	1.9	1.2	0.7	0.7
Mining, quarrying	1.6	1.5	1.7	1.0	0.6	0.6
Transportation, communication	4.4	5.5	6.4	7.7	3.9	3.8
Service	8.2	7.0	10.5	12.4	11.2	11.9
Unknown	—	0.2	0.2	2.6	10.3	4.8

[a] Ten years and over in 1901.
[b] Except those in Primary.
[c,d] Divisions not identical to previous years.

DERIVED FROM OSTRY (1967 : 50–51); HUNTER (1981 : 79); CENSUS OF CANADA 1981, HIGHLIGHT INFORMATION ON LABOUR FORCE, MARCH 1, 1983, PP. 29, 30. REPRODUCED BY PERMISSION OF THE MINISTER OF SUPPLY AND SERVICES CANADA.

Consider the general trends. First, blue-collar work has been very stable or actually *declined* slightly as a proportion of the labour force. Second, the proportion of primary workers (including the traditional independent producers) declined precipitously after 1941. Third, the decline in the primary sector has been mainly offset by the growth of the white-collar sector, notably in professional, technical and clerical jobs. This growth signals the rise of a service economy, oriented to the provision of services, rather than production of commodities. Most of the Canadian labour force is now part of this service economy, with a recent shift from growth in the social services to growth in business services (Myles, 1988).[6]

---

[6] For a recent recasting of census data, see Wallace Clement (1988), Tables 4.2 and 4.3, which show labour force shifts between 1931 and 1971 for men and women separately.

The census data show the extent to which wage and salary work has replaced self-employment. They do not, however, reveal much about how class structure is reflected in the labour process itself. Some information on this question is provided by a national survey conducted in 1982. Black and Myles (1986) reported on this study. The study surveyed a large number of Canadians in order to determine whether they were owners or employers, supervisors or employees, and how much control they exercised over their work and that of others. Researchers assigned each individual to one of five main classes. The first category is made up of employers, the true bourgeoisie or capitalists. The second group are the owners and operators of small businesses, the petite bourgeoisie, who work for themselves. The third level is composed of the working class, those who have no effective control over their work or others. The fourth group are the managers and supervisors, who help owners establish their policies or who have direct authority over other workers. The final category is for semi-autonomous employees, wage and salary workers who have no power over the uses of capital, the means of production or the work of others, but who do have significant control over their own work. In the latter category are various professional and semi-professional groups—lawyers, engineers, social workers, teachers and so forth (Black and Myles, 1986:159–60).

The largest of the categories used by Black and Myles (1986: Table 1) is the working class, comprising 43 percent of the labour force. More surprising, managers and supervisors are the second largest group, 25 percent of the labour force, followed by the "semi-autonomous" workers, 16 percent. Finally, the self-employed (*petite bourgeoisie*) are 12 percent, and all employers are just 4 percent. The last figure again indicates how concentrated the control of capital has become in Canada, as elsewhere in the Western capitalist world.[7]

The study also reveals Canada's unique class structure in comparison with two other Western countries, Sweden and the United States. Strikingly, Canada has the smallest capitalist class (the owner-employers), the largest class of the self-employed and, as a result of a relatively large group of supervisory and semi-autonomous workers, the smallest working class (Black and Myles, 1986:162).

Two features of the evidence are particularly interesting. First, Canada has an unusually large middle sector between the capitalist and the working classes. It is a diverse group, composed of the self-employed, supervisors and managers and the "semi-autonomous" workers. Second, a great many white-collar workers, represented in the conventional categories of Table 8-3, are actually members of the working class,

---

[7] In a similar analysis, based on a 1981 national survey, Ornstein (1983) uses somewhat different criteria of class location to report that some 13 percent of the Canadian employed labour force were self-employed, about twice as many (25 percent) were employed by government agencies or Crown corporations and 6 percent were owners or part owners of capitalist firms. The residual "working class" of salaried and wage workers employed by private firms comprise a full 56 percent of the labour force.

since they have no effective control over their product or service, their labour or the labour of others.

If the concentration of capital and the proletarianization of labour have been the dominant processes affecting Canadian life in this century, why do most Canadians *not* identify themselves or our society mainly in these terms? The principal reason is because more readily visible and experienced changes have occurred *simultaneously*. For a great many Canadians, these changes have brought a widening sense of participation in a middle-class society. Increased wage dependence and loss of autonomy in work take the *form* of increased prospects for white-collar service jobs, the promise of shorter hours and more stable incomes, greater family security and wider consumption alternatives. The changes have also been accompanied by widely shared aspirations for education and new definitions of social respectability based on residential locations and house styles, household technology, forms of recreation, clothing and child-rearing practices.

The Making of the Twentieth-Century Middle Class

The notion of the middle class was a nineteenth-century creation. In England, it arose as a self-conscious label used by the emerging business and industrial groups to distinguish themselves both from a landed elite and from the increasingly vocal "lower orders" of propertyless and labouring poor (Briggs, 1960). To be middle class in nineteenth-century England was to be propertied, acquisitive, industrious and socially respectable. Later in the century, the term came to be identified mainly with the small producers, master artisans, shopkeepers and even richer peasants—the small producers situated between the emerging capitalist and working classes.

In the early twentieth century, the term took on a wider and more ambiguous meaning in referring to those who did white-collar work in the growing bureaucracies of corporations and the state (Mills, 1956.) As the century progressed, the term became even more common in everyday language and political discourse. By the end of the Second World War, a great many ordinary Canadians, like people elsewhere in the Western world, began to think of themselves as members of a middle-class society. The idea was engendered by their experience of modestly increased disposable incomes, somewhat reduced working hours and deepened involvement in a consumer-oriented culture. It was anchored in family-centred lives, emphasizing women's domestic roles, urban residence and home ownership. These material and social changes were no mirage, though they were actively fostered in the interest of commerce, not least by advertising. Still, there was quite concrete "middle-class" reality to having indoor plumbing, modern heating and lighting and automobile transportation within the reach of large numbers, and eventually of a majority of people. The material changes were accompanied by an extension of the earlier middle-class culture, seen in a pervasive respect for individual effort, for property and political order. The nineteenth-century

The early twentieth century witnessed the rise of female clerical work.

ARCHIVES OF ONTARIO.

cultural roots were stretched, but remained intact. How did this encompassing meaning of the middle class emerge in Canada?

Not until the late 1920s, perhaps, were the wages of the average North American manufacturing worker sufficient to raise a family on one income. And only in the same decade were the wages of women workers sufficient to allow some women to be independent of their own or other families (Palmer, 1984:192). In the last century and early in this one, ordinary families survived by pooling several sources of income. Women's unpaid work and strategies for managing limited resources in and around the household were vital to family survival (Bradbury, 1984). In terms of notions of independence and respectability, the sense that one was "middle class" first depended on establishing minimum economic security. Reliance on the single male wage became coupled with the pervasive idea of the "cult of true womanhood," urging women to be responsible only for the home as a haven against the competitive, male world outside.

The Depression of the 1930s cut severely into the economic security of many families, but the post-war years saw greater gains in real incomes (purchasing power) and in consumer expenditures. And this economic trend continued through to the 1970s. The trend strengthened the nuclear family unit, its reliance on consumer goods, including the growth of home-centred entertainment, the spread of automobile transportation and suburbanization.

FIGURE 8-1

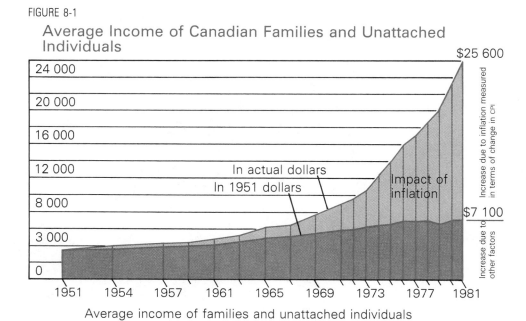

Average Income of Canadian Families and Unattached Individuals

Average income of families and unattached individuals

Charting Canadian Incomes, 1951–1981. March 1984. Ottawa: Statistics Canada, p. s. Reproduced by permission of the Minister of Supply and Services Canada.

Figure 8-1 shows the general pattern of family incomes in Canada over a thirty-year period. The figure plots the average incomes of families and unattached individuals from 1951 to 1981 and distinguishes actual dollar income from real income, measured in 1951 dollars (that is, income adjusted to account for inflation). Incomes include earnings from employment and from investments, as well as from social benefits and pensions.

The incomes people actually received rose throughout the entire period on average, and grew steeply from about 1965, although inflation accounted for a huge portion of the growth over the last twenty years. Real incomes grew more slowly to 1976 and then stagnated. The recent stability of average real incomes (and, hence, declines in income for some segments of the population) is a reversal of a quite long-term trend. The fact is that the middle-class ideal of the one-earner family was most closely approximated by 1951, encompassing 60 percent of all Canadian families. The proportion has progressively been *reduced* since: to 57 percent in 1961, 41 percent in 1971 and to just 29 percent in 1981 (Statistics Canada, 1984 : 11). In 1981, 60 percent of families had two or more earners.

These changes affected women more than men. The women's movement has been a key source of changing attitudes and a stimulus to women's labour force participation.

At the same time, the *return* to multiple earners in families has been one response to economic stagnation and higher unemployment, as a means of sustaining purchasing power and middle-class standards of family living. The proportion of *married* women in the work force has grown hugely since 1967, from 35 to 63 percent. Moreover, women have doubled their contributions to family income (Statistics Canada, 1984 : 11).[8]

It is in their paid work that class relations are *most* immediately experienced by people, in the organization of the labour process, its supervision and control.[9] For the most part, however, public and scholarly attention has focused on broadly changing occupational patterns and the question of occupational mobility of individuals. It is these trends that often have been interpreted as responsible for the demise of a class-divided society and the emergence of an increasingly homogeneous "middle-class" one.

We turn to this debate, but not in the usual "either/or" terms. Rather, we argue that to understand the class experience is to recognize that individuals live simultaneously in the context of class relations and of occupational and income mobility. Or, in our preferred terms, for large numbers of Canadians the class experience is a dual experience—they are distinctly proletarian, in the historical sense, and "middle class" in terms of the dominant cultural definition of their social and economic circumstances, life style and aspirations.

If the growth of the numbers who feel themselves part of a Canadian middle class accompanied the trends to increased income, suburbanization and expenditures on consumer goods, what about *inequality* in income throughout the period? Has increased purchasing power of the average family and involvement in consumption of goods and services reduced actual stratification of incomes? In a word, no. The distribution of wealth that we saw in Table 8-2 has remained constant. Table 8-4 shows the distribution of earned income as distinct from wealth, over a thirty-year period.

Five income groups are compared in Table 8-4. Each represents 20 percent of the population (quintiles) ranged from the fifth of the population with the lowest income to the fifth with the highest. The distributions over the post-war period seem virtually unchanged. The great stability in income distributions comes as some surprise. It flies in the face of the considerable rhetoric about the redistribution of income from upper-

---

[8] Although women have moved into all segments of the labour force, they have been overwhelmingly segmented in a few occupations: in 1984 over 30 percent were in clerical work, and nearly 40 percent more in a limited number of service, health and sales jobs. The average earned income of full-time women workers in 1984 was just 60.2 percent of men.

[9] This is so even for those who are not wage earners, such as children, the retired, the unemployed and unpaid domestic workers. Their living conditions and life chances are normally tied closely to their earlier wage-earning experience or to the labour force experience of those on whom they depend for income.

TABLE 8-4
Income
Stratification:
Percentage
Distribution by
Quintiles, Canada,
1951–1981

Families and Unattached Individuals	1951	1961	1971	1981
Poorest Quintile (20%)	4	4	4	4
Second Quintile	12	12	10	11
Third Quintile	18	18	18	18
Fourth Quintile	23	25	25	25
Richest Quintile	43	41	43	42

STATISTICS CANADA. MARCH 1984. CHARTING CANADIAN INCOMES 1951–1981. OTTAWA: MINISTER OF SUPPLY AND SERVICES CANADA, P. 6. REPRODUCED BY PERMISSION OF THE MINISTER OF SUPPLY AND SERVICES CANADA.

income to lower-middle earners and the poor through progressive taxation, social benefit and unemployment insurance programs and the welfare net. This notion of redistribution through progressive social policy is, as Gillespie (1980) aptly called it, one of the great myths perpetuated by politicians and the mass media.

Our vision of life in the capitalist society assumes that earned income is the most concrete reward for individual effort and talent in a fair and open competition. Belief in rewards of this kind were central to the bourgeois and liberal democratic revolutions that assaulted the privileged position of the European aristocracies. In contemporary capitalist societies, the adherence to competitive, individualistic values seems to have taken on a particular importance for middle-class families, especially as a way of trying to protect and improve the life chances of their children. Because of the effects of proletarianization, most Canadians no longer expect to ensure their children's futures through bequeathing property or establishing them in an independent craft or small business. They may, at least, hope to give their children *cultural capital* in the form of the credentials and social graces of the educated and hope that these qualities allow them to secure jobs that provide economic security and social respectability.

The research on educational trends and patterns of inequality is discussed in Chapter 13. It need only be noted here that enrolments at all levels of education have steadily increased from even before the establishment of a public school system in the 1870s. They continue to increase today at the post-secondary level. But the fact is, increased enrolment has not greatly reduced educational inequality. The children of low-income and working-class families remain strongly underrepresented in higher education (Guppy, Mikicich and Pendakur, 1984). Still, education does count. A host of studies of occupational mobility and status attainment document that people's education is the crucial link between their parents' social positions and the jobs they attain.

If education is the most important characteristic affecting job attainment, what have the trends in occupational mobility been over the last several decades? There is a large research literature, but for Canada a particularly useful, if somewhat dated, study was conducted in 1974. It examines occupational mobility over four generations in Canada (Goyder and Curtis, 1977).

TABLE 8-5
Occupational
Mobility: Four
Generations, Canada

Intercorrelations of Occupational Status Scores Among Grandfathers, Fathers, Respondents, and Sons

Generation	G	F	R	S
Grandfather (G)	1.00	.49	.22	.05
Father (F)	.50	1.00	.38	.13
Respondent (R)	.27	.33	1.00	.26
Sons (S)	.03	.09	.22	1.00

A 1.00 indicates the total sample; lower numbers show the farmers excluded in each generation.
JOHN GOYDER AND JAMES E. CURTIS. 1977. "OCCUPATIONAL MOBILITY OVER FOUR GENERATIONS." CANADIAN REVIEW OF SOCIOLOGY AND ANTHROPOLOGY 14(3) : 308.

Table 8-5 shows the correlations between the occupational status scores of survey respondents, their fathers and grandfathers and their eldest sons.[10] The data show that the occupational status of a man's grandfather or great-grandfather is almost entirely irrelevant to his own job status, whereas the status of his father's main job is more closely related. This is hardly surprising, and one can conclude it represents a very open or mobile society. On the other hand, the *structure* of occupations has altered so greatly over these generations that we might also say the individual mobility is more apparent than real: there are so few farming jobs left that not many young people could become farmers, even if they wanted to be.

The study illustrates one of the most important results of mobility research. Once the structural changes in the economy, such as the decline in farming and the increase in service jobs, have been accounted for, then *little if any* changes in mobility patterns can be detected (Hauser and Featherman, 1977 : 15; McRoberts and Selbee, 1981). What can we make of this? One implication is simply that changes in the whole economy account for much of the occupational mobility *experienced* by individuals between generations. Another is that those who begin with low socio-economic origins have not improved their *relative chances* to move up the occupational ladder in comparison to those whose parents are in the middle or top of the scales. In other words, the structure of unequal occupational status remains largely intact, despite individual mobility. The social ladder of occupational rank and prestige shifts as fast as people can climb it. Those who start at the bottom must climb fastest just to keep up or to keep from falling off.

---

[10] As was the custom in mobility research, only men were surveyed. Only "main" occupations were recorded. All sons over age twenty-five are included in these data. Women have been included in more recent mobility surveys (see Boyd et al., 1981). There are some important differences in men's and women's patterns of occupational mobility and job attainment, but the general issues discussed here apply to both. The occupational status scores are derived from a combination of average income and educational achievement of job-holders in the occupational categories. They are closely related to the prestige rank of occupations held by Canadians as expressed in surveys.

TABLE 8-6
Distribution of
Responses to Class
Identification
Questions
(National Survey
1965; Four Cities,
1971)

Open-ended Question: "What social class do you consider yourself a member of?"

	Upper	Upper Middle	Middle	Working	Lower	N/A
	%	%	%	%	%	%
1965	1.1	3.9	63.3	10.5	4.4	16.8
1971	0.8	5.9	53.7	16.4	1.2	22.0

Closed Question: "If you had to pick one, which of the following five social classes would you say you were in—upper class, upper middle class, middle class, working class, or lower class?"

	Upper	Upper Middle	Middle	Working	Lower	N/A
	%	%	%	%	%	%
1965	2.0	12.9	48.9	30.4	2.1	3.7
1971	1.0	13.4	46.9	27.4	0.3	11.0

JAMES CURTIS AND WILLIAM SCOTT, EDS. 1979. SOCIAL STRATIFICATION IN CANADA, 2ND ED., P. 434, J. GOYDER AND P. PINEO, "SOCIAL CLASS SELF-IDENTIFICATION," TABLE 1. TORONTO: PRENTICE-HALL. PERMISSION GRANTED BY PRENTICE-HALL CANADA, INC.

Occupational mobility experiences between generations have powerfully reinforced the notion of Canada as an increasingly middle-class society. How many Canadians do think of themselves as middle class? There are two useful studies of the self-identification of social classes in Canada. Table 8-6 shows the distribution of responses on two related questions from a national survey in 1965 and a survey of four major cities in Ontario and Quebec in 1971 (Goyder and Pineo, 1979). The differences in response patterns indicate that any interpretation of survey questions on this topic requires special caution, since results are heavily influenced by the exact wording of the questions and the nature of the survey (see Goyder and Pineo, 1979). In any case, between 60 and 70 percent of the Canadians surveyed consider themselves "middle class" or "upper middle class."[11] Despite their limits, the studies confirm the common impression that most Canadians, from every walk of life, think of themselves as middle class.[12]

[11] Another interesting study found that manual workers tend to have a rather more politicized view of Canadian society than non-manual workers; that is, manual workers in this study more often viewed themselves in a society divided by power than non-manual workers. Here again, however, the exact wording of the questions seems to have been crucial to the responses elicited (Rinehart and Okraku, 1974 : 200).

[12] It is significant that one study aimed at determining class positions in Marxist terms also reports that, with one exception, between 50 and 70 percent of each of the class fractions identified themselves as middle or upper middle class. The exception was the manual working-class group, among whom 54 percent called themselves working class and 40 percent middle class. The result confirms the more general and earlier surveys (Ornstein, 1988 : Table 8).

Most Canadians identify with the middle class because of their experiences of increased economic security, mass consumption and, crucially, of an increased sense of upward mobility generated largely by the changes in the organization of Canadian society, especially since the 1930s. They seem less aware of the persistent structures of inequality, the enormous concentration of capital and economic power and the progressive proletarianization of labour.

The reason for this relative invisibility of the main structural changes of the century is not a mystery. We attribute educational accomplishments, occupational "success" and increased family earning power to our own efforts, whatever social structural base may foster them. More damaging is our tendency to blame ourselves for our apparent failures when we achieve only limited gains. This is the hidden injury of a class society that idolizes individual achievement and largely ignores structural change (Sennett and Cobb, 1972). C. W. Mills (1959) insisted some years ago that the "sociological imagination" requires an understanding not just of personal experiences and the milieux of everyday life, nor of structures alone, but of the connections between these two social realities.

Contemporary working-class and upper-class housing.

Unfinished Business: The Two Faces of Class Experience

Make no mistake, what we experience as the emergence of middle-class patterns of income, consumer spending, life style and values is, at the same time, the growth of the modern working class. This is not a contradiction. Rather, they are the two faces of contemporary class experience—proletarianization, looking one way, the rise of middle-class life style and culture, looking the other. An understanding of contemporary Canada requires an understanding of how both processes are working. There are two views about the political implications of this dual experience. One reasons that the experience of proletarianization has the potential to give rise to a modern, mass political movement (Westergaard and Resler, 1975:401ff.). The other view argues that relative affluence and the emphasis of middle-class culture on social mobility, individualism and the private sphere of family life will effectively inhibit a broad class movement or forceful reform coalitions in the foreseeable future (for example, Runciman, 1966; Parkin, 1974: chs. 2 and 3; Mann, 1973).

At the same time it is essential to recognize the increases in real incomes and the extension of social services, from unemployment insurance to medicare and pensions, are gains for wage and salary workers that are very much the result of their own political responses and of an active labour movement. They are political gains. They did not occur merely as natural consequences of economic expansion, the growth of the state or of modernization. In this regard, central features of middle-class life in Canada can themselves be understood as responses to proletarianization.

Summary

Despite its importance, the process of proletarianization has received little serious analysis. The process moved unevenly from the middle of the last century into the early years of this one and then quickened greatly after 1920 and especially after the Second World War. The last three decades have witnessed both the increasing concentration of capital and wealth and the extension of wage and salary dependence for most Canadians. The more obvious and immediate experiences of Canadians over the post-war period have been those of increased real incomes and consumption paralleled by occupational and educational mobility. These experiences encourage people to think of themselves as belonging to the middle class. A majority of Canadians display a deep attachment to distinctive middle-class values (social order, propriety, the sanctity of property and rewards for individual effort). Relative affluence and mobility opportunities for many have masked the processes of property concentration and proletarianization in Canada, as elsewhere in the West. Social class and stratification theory have not been particularly adept at addressing the dual reality of middle-class society. The need for both historical and contemporary analysis is pressing if we are to understand the implications of the fact that some of the major structural changes in the making of the contemporary middle class have run their course.

Suggested Readings

Black, Don, and John Myles

1986. "Dependent Industrialization and the Canadian Class Structure: A Comparative Analysis." *Canadian Review of Sociology and Anthropology* 23(2): 157–81. A recent journal article presenting a systematic and thoughtful Marxist assessment of the Canadian class structure and comparing it to Sweden and the United States.

Bourdieu, Pierre

1964. *La Reproduction*. Paris: Editions de Minuit. The classic work on the notion of cultural capital, arguing that repression in capitalist societies rests on the inheritance of cultural trappings and the discrimination of the school system.

Carroll, William K.

1986. *Capital Accumulation and Corporate Interlocking in Post-War Canada*. Vancouver: University of British Columbia Press. This is the most recent and compelling contribution to the debate over the social and political implications of corporate concentration and the closure of a capitalist class for Canada. A finely researched and densely written monograph.

Linteau, Paul-Andre, Rene Durocher and Jean-Claude Robert

1983. *Quebec: A History, 1867–1929*, trans. Robert Chodos. Toronto: James Lorimer. An exemplary social and political history of Quebec, yet unmatched for any other region, with a clear emphasis on class and class relations. A companion volume of the same name for the years after 1930 was translated in 1987.

Palmer, Bryan D.

1983. *Working Class Experience: The Rise and Reconstruction of Canadian Labour, 1800–1980*. Toronto: Butterworths. A sweeping historical overview of the development of class relations in Canada over two centuries. A provocative, if simplified, history of labour–capital relations with an emphasis on working-class culture and on class struggle.

Tilly, Charles

1981. *As Sociology Meets History*. New York: Academic Press. A somewhat uneven, but clearly written look at the recent growth of social history bridging both of the traditional disciplines, arguing for the centrality of class theory and a historical perspective in all sociological interpretation.

Discussion Questions

1. The concepts of class and stratification refer to different social phenomena. What is the significance of the distinction?

2. Both Weberian and functionalist theory focus on occupational stratification. One is concerned with power and the other with societal needs. Discuss this latter statement and its implications.

3. Why are the size and character of the small-property-owning class (petite bourgeoisie) so important to understanding the emergence of the Canadian class system?

4. How can we explain that there are very deep and stable structures of inequality in Canada (in wealth and income for example), and yet a sense of equality of opportunity is widely shared?

5. Canada is often called a middle-class society. What does this mean? How can it be argued that most Canadians are both middle class and proletarianized? Has the working class disappeared because affluence and mass consumption have drawn them into a bourgeois way of life?

Data Collection Exercises

1. Tabulate and compare occupational distributions for two provinces from published statistics from 1901 to 1981. Interpret the differences in the growth of the working class in each province and offer an explanation of why these differences occurred.

2. Design an unstructured interview (organize about five or six questions) to determine the knowledge and views of fellow students (not in this course) on the degree of wealth and of income inequality in Canada. Probe further to assess their interpretation of the reasons for the inequality and its widespread public acceptance.

3. Select one month of a daily national or regional newspaper. Scan the lead stories and editorial pages to identify *all* articles referring directly or indirectly to social class in Canada. Develop a classification of the articles in terms of different meanings given to the terms *class, middle class* or *class society*. Compare these to the major sociological perspectives developed in this chapter.

4. Using data from local real-estate board publications (multiple listing services) or from land transfer records (public archives and local library holdings), map the residential divisions of your community in terms of housing costs and rental values. Discuss the implications in terms of social class.

Writing Exercises

1. Assume that you are an investigative reporter for a local newspaper. Your editor asks you to provide a two-page outline of an article on the nature and social implications of the concentration of corporate ownership in Canada.

2. You are asked to become a citizen member of a provincial planning commission. The commission's task is to assess inequality of access to post-secondary education in the province. You are asked to provide a preliminary outline of the main issues to be addressed.

3. Develop a three-page research proposal for an investigation of the differences between Canadians' "subjective" class identification and their "objective" class positions.

4. Assume you are an instructor in this course. Design three questions for an essay-type, take-home examination. The questions should be no more than three sentences in length.

Glossary

Bourgeoisie: *the social group who form a capitalist class; owners and effective controllers of productive property and its prerogatives, including benefits in wealth and income. Distinguished from the petite bourgeoisie.*

Capital: *the machinery, plant, raw materials and money for wages used in capitalist production.*

Capitalist class: *a group of employers or major investors who effectively own and control industrial production, make investment decisions and employ wage and salary workers for the purpose of making profits.*

Exploitation: *in Marxist theory, the extraction by a dominant class of the value or product of surplus labour from a subordinate class.*

Ideology: *a relatively articulate set of ideas and beliefs that serves to describe and justify existing institutions or their change by interpreting the past and prescribing future action.*

Labour-power: *the human capacity to work sold as a commodity on labour markets and purchased by capitalists for wages.*

Middle class: *in general use, the large group who view themselves as socially respectable and self-sufficient, but unexceptional in terms of power, wealth and life style. In Marxist theory, referring to salaried employees whose jobs entail some element of capitalists' rights and functions, such as supervision or policy advising.*

Occupational mobility: *the movement of individuals or groups up and down scales of occupational prestige and reward; also called* social mobility.

Petite bourgeoisie: *those who are effectively self-employed, usually owning their own productive property, such as farmers or shop owners, and providing most or all of the productive labour from their own families.*

Proletarianization: *the historical process in which people increasingly come to depend for their livelihood on the sale of their labour-power* and *in which capitalists increasingly control the means of production. See Labour-power.*

Social closure: *in Weberian theory, the process in which groups maximize their benefits by restricting access to rewards and opportunities to a limited circle of socially defined eligible people.*

Social mobility: *see Occupational mobility.*

Status group: *a group distinguished by social approval, esteem, prestige or respect—or the lack of them.*

Stratification: *social processes that tend to hold people in given social positions over their lifetimes, or families over generations.*

Surplus value: *in Marxist theory, the difference between the value of the product produced by workers and the value of the means of production and the labour-power used in the production process.*

Working class: *those who neither own nor control productive property and, hence, must make a living by selling their labour-power for wages or salaries; the term is variously defined. See also Proletarianization.*

References

Akenson, Donald
1984. *The Irish in Ontario: A Study in Rural History*. Kingston and Montreal: McGill-Queen's University Press.

Althusser, L.
1969. *For Marx*. Harmondsworth: Penguin Books.

Bell, Daniel
1961. *The End of Ideology*. London: Collier Books.

Black, Don, and John Myles
1986. "Dependent Industrialization and the Canadian Class Structure: A Comparative Analysis of Canada, the United States and Sweden." *Canadian Review of Sociology and Anthropology* 23(2): 157–81.

Boyd, Monica, John Goyder, Frank Jones, Hugh McRoberts, Peter Pineo and John Porter
1981. "Status Attainment in Canada." *Canadian Review of Sociology and Anthropology* 18(5): 657–73.

Bradbury, Bettina
1984. "Cows, Pigs and Boarders: Nonwage Forms of Survival among Montreal Families, 1861–1881." *Labour/Le Travailleur* 17 (Spring): 9–46.

Braverman, Harry
1974. *Labor and Monopoly Capital: The Degradation of Work in the Twentieth Century*. New York: Monthly Review Press.

Briggs, Asa
1960. "The Language of 'Class' in Early Nineteenth-Century England." In J. Saville and A. Briggs, eds., *Essays in Labour History*. New York: St Martin's Press.

Brym, Robert, ed.
1985. *The Structure of the Canadian Capitalist Class*. Toronto: Garamond Press.

Burgess, Joanne
1977. "L'Industrie la chaussure à Montréal, 1840–1870. Le Passage de l'artisanat à la fabrique." *Revue d'Histoire de l'Amérique Française* 31 (September): 187–210.

Clement, Wallace
1977. *Continental Corporate Power*. Toronto: McClelland and Stewart.
1988. *The Challenge of Class Analysis*. Ottawa: Carleton University Press.

Coyne, Deborah
1986. "Corporate Over-Concentration." *Policy Options* 7(3).

Cuneo, Carl
1984. "Has the Traditional Petite Bourgeoisie Persisted?" *Canadian Journal of Sociology* 9(3): 269–301.

Dahrendorf, Ralf
1959. *Class and Class Conflict in Industrial Society*. Palo Alto, Cal.: Stanford University Press.

Darroch, Gordon
1983. "Early Industrialization and Inequality in Toronto, 1861–1899." *Labour/Le Travailleur* 11 (Spring): 31–61.

1988. "Class in Nineteenth-Century, Central Ontario: A Reassessment of the Crisis and Demise of Small Producers during Early Industrialization, 1861–1871," pp. 49–72. In Gregory Kealey, ed., *Class, Gender, and Region: Essays in Canadian Historical Sociology*. St. John's: Committee on Canadian Labour History.

Darroch, Gordon, and Michael Ornstein
1985. "Ethnicity and Class, Transitions Over a Decade: Ontario, 1861–1871." Canadian Historical Association, *Papers, 1984*, pp. 111–137.

Davis, Kingsley
1949. *Human Society*. New York: Macmillan.

Gagan, David
1978. "The 'Critical Years' in Rural Canada West." *Canadian Historical Review* 59(3): 293–318.
1981. *Hopeful Travellers: Families, Land and Social Change in Mid-Victorian Peel County, Canada West*. Toronto: University of Toronto Press.

Gerth, H., and C. W. Mills
1958. *From Max Weber: Essays in Sociology*. New York: Oxford University Press.

Giddens, Anthony
1973. *The Class Structure of the Advanced Societies*. London: Hutchinson.

Gillespie, Irwin
1980. "On the Redistribution of Income in Canada," pp. 22–53. In John Harp and John R. Hofley, eds., *Structured Inequality in Canada*. Scarborough, Ont.: Prentice-Hall.

Gould, Stephen Jay
1981. *The Mismeasure of Man*. New York: Norton.

Goyder, John, and James E. Curtis
1977. "Occupational Mobility Over Four Generations." *Canadian Review of Sociology and Anthropology* 14(3): 303–19.

Goyder, John, and Peter Pineo
1979. "Social Class Self-Identification," pp. 431–47. In James E. Curtis and William G. Scott, eds., *Social Stratification: Canada*. Scarborough, Ont.: Prentice-Hall.

Greer, Allan
1985. "Wage Labour and the Transition to Capitalism." *Labour/Le Travail* 15 (Spring): 7–22.

Guppy, Neil, Paulina D. Mikicich and Ravi Pendakur
1984. "Changing Patterns of Educational Inequality." *Canadian Journal of Sociology* 9(3): 319–31.

Hauser, Robert, and David L. Featherman
1977. *The Process of Stratification*. New York: Academic Press.

Heron, Craig, and Robert Storey, eds.
1986. *On the Job: Confronting the Labour Process in Canada*. Kingston and Montreal: McGill-Queen's University Press.

Hunter, Alfred A.
1981. *Class Tells: On Social Inequality in Canada*. Toronto: Butterworths.

Johnson, Leo A.
1971. "Land Policy, Population Growth and Social Structure in the Home District,

1793–1851." *Ontario History* 67 (March): 41–60.

1972. "The Development of Class in Canada in the Twentieth Century," pp. 141–83. In Gary Teeple, ed., *Capitalism and the National Question*. Toronto: University of Toronto Press.

Katz, Michael
1975. *The People of Hamilton, Canada West: Family and Class in a Mid-Nineteenth Century City*. Cambridge, Mass.: Harvard University Press.

Kealey, Gregory S.
1980. *Toronto Workers Respond to Industrial Capitalism, 1867–1892*. Toronto: University of Toronto Press.

Leacy, F. H., ed.
1983. *Historical Statistics of Canada*. Ottawa: Minister of Supply and Services Canada.

Macpherson, C. B., ed.
1978. *Property: Mainstream and Critical Positions*. Toronto: University of Toronto Press.

Mann, Michael
1973. *Consciousness and Action among the Western Working Class*. London: Macmillan.

Marx, Karl
1967 [1887]. *Capital: A Critique of Political Economy*, vol. I. New York: International Publishers.

McCallum, John
1980. *Unequal Beginnings: Agriculture and Economic Development in Quebec and Ontario until 1870*. Toronto: University of Toronto Press.

McRoberts, Hugh, and Kevin Selbee
1981. "Trends in Occupational Mobility in Canada and the United States: A Comparison." *American Sociological Review* 46(4): 406–21.

Mills, C. Wright
1956. *White Collar: The American Middle Classes*. New York: Oxford.
1959. *The Sociological Imagination*. London: Oxford.

Mommsen, Wolfgang, J.
1977. "Max Weber as a Critic of Marx." *Canadian Journal of Sociology* 2(4): 373–98.

Moore, Barrington
1969. *The Social Origins of Dictatorship and Democracy: Lord and Peasant in the Making of the Modern World*. Boston: Beacon Press.

Myles, John
1988. "The Expanding Middle: Some Canadian Evidence of the Deskilling Debate." *Canadian Review of Sociology and Anthropology* 25(3): 235–64.

Naylor, R. T.
1972. "The Rise and Fall of the Third Commercial Empire of the St. Lawrence," pp. 1–41. In Gary Teeple, ed., *Capitalism and the National Question*. Toronto: University of Toronto Press.

Nisbet, Robert A.
1959. "The Decline and Fall of Social Class." *Pacific Sociological Review* 2: 11–17.

Ornstein, Michael D.
1983. "The Development of Class in Canada," pp. 216–59. In Paul Grayson, ed., *Sociology: An Alternative Approach*. Toronto: Gage.

1988. "Social Class and Economic Inequality," chapter 7. In James Curtis and Lorne Tepperman, eds., *Understanding Canadian Society*. Toronto: McGraw-Hill, Ryerson.

Osberg, Lars
1981. *Economic Inequality in Canada*. Toronto: Butterworths.

Ossowski, S.
1963. *Class Structure in the Social Consciousness*, trans. S. Patterson. New York: Free Press.

Palmer, Bryan D.
1979. *A Culture in Conflict: Skilled Workers and Industrial Capitalism in Hamilton, Ontario, 1860–1914*. Montreal: McGill-Queen's University Press.
1984. "Social Formation and Class Formation in North America, 1800–1900," pp. 229–309. In David Levine, ed., *Proletarianization and Family History*. New York: Academic Press.

Parkin, Frank
1971. *Class Inequality and Political Order*. London: Macgibbon and Kee.
1979. *Marxism and Class Theory: A Bourgeois Theory*. New York: Columbia University Press.

Pentland, Clare H.
1981 [1959]. *Labour and Capital in Canada, 1650–1860*. Toronto: University of Toronto Press.

Porter, John
1965. *The Vertical Mosaic: An Analysis of Social Power and Class in Canada*. Toronto: University of Toronto Press.

Poulantzas, N.
1973. *Political Power and Social Classes*. London: New Left Books.

Rinehart, James W.
1975. *The Tyranny of Work*. Don Mills, Ont.: Longman.

Rinehart, James W., and Ishmael O. Okraku
1974. "A Study of Class Consciousness." *Canadian Review of Sociology and Anthropology* 11 : 197–213.

Robert, Jean-Claude
1982. "Urbanisation et population. Le Cas de Montréal en 1861." *Revue d'Histoire de l'Amérique Française* 35 (March).

Runciman, W. G.
1966. *Relative Deprivation and Social Justice*. London: Routledge and Kegan Paul.

Salomon, A.
1945. "German Sociology." In George Gurvitch and Wilbert E. Moore, eds., *Twentieth-Century Sociology*. New York: Philosophical Library.

Sennett, Richard, and Johnathan Cobb
1972. *The Hidden Injuries of Class*. New York: Knopf.

Statistics Canada
1984. *Charting Canadian Incomes, 1951–1981*. Ottawa: Minister of Supply and Services Canada.

Stedman Jones, Gareth
1976. "From Historical Sociology to Theoretical History." *British Journal of Sociology* 27(3) : 295–305.

Stinchcombe, Arthur
1963. "Some Empirical Consequences of the Davis-Moore Theory of Stratification." *American Sociological Review* 28 : 805–8.

Teeple, Gary
1972. "Land, Labour and Capital in Pre-Confederation Canada," pp. 43–66. In Gary Teeple, ed., *Capitalism and the National Question in Canada*. Toronto: University of Toronto Press.

Thompson, E. P.
1963. *The Making of the English Working Class*. New York: Pantheon Books.
1979. *The Poverty of Theory and Other Essays*. New York: Monthly Review Press.

Tilly, Charles
1981. *As Sociology Meets History*. New York: Academic Press.

Tumin, Melvin M.
1953. "Some Principles of Stratification: A Critical Analysis." *American Sociological Review* 18 : 387–93.

Weber, Max
1968 [1908]. *Economy and Society*, 3 vols. Edited by Guenther Roth and Claus Wittich. New York: Bedminster Press.

Wesolowski, W.
1962. "Some Notes on the Functional Theory of Stratification." *Polish Sociological Bulletin* 3–4 : 28–38.

Westergaard, John, and Henrietta Resler
1975. *Class in a Capitalist Society: A Study of Contemporary Britain*. London: Heinemann Educational Books.

Zeitlin, Irving M.
1981. *Ideology and the Development of Sociological Theory*, 2nd ed. Englewood Cliffs, N. J.: Prentice-Hall.

CHAPTER 9

Race and Ethnic Relations

PETER S. LI

INTRODUCTION

FORMATION OF THE CANADIAN MOSAIC
Historical Roots of French Canada
Native Peoples
Immigrants to Canada

THEORETICAL PERSPECTIVES
What Are Race and Ethnicity?
Assimilation and Pluralism
Dominant and Subordinate Groups

THE VERTICAL MOSAIC
Bilingualism and Language Maintenance
Multiculturalism
Racism and Inequality

SUMMARY

An immigration train brings immigrants into downtown Saskatoon in 1903 to settle the Prairies. All Canadian citizens or their ancestors, except for native Indians, were originally immigrants.

SASKATOON PUBLIC LIBRARY—LOCAL HISTORY ROOM.

Introduction

With the exception of the *indigenous peoples*, or native peoples, Canada is made up of immigrants from different parts of the world. Initially, most of the immigrants to Canada came from Britain, France and other European countries. Since the end of the Second World War, Canada has become more willing to receive immigrants from other regions.

Today, like many industrial nations of the West, Canada is a *multi-ethnic society*— a society composed of peoples from a variety of ethnic and racial origins. Sociologists are interested in understanding the ethnic and racial mix of modern societies: how intergroup relationships among ethnic and racial groups influence the way societies are arranged and changed and, in turn, how particular social arrangements, or structures, affect race and ethnic relations.

There is substantial evidence to indicate that Canada is indeed a multi-ethnic society, or a mosaic as it is commonly referred to. Perhaps the best evidence is the census of Canada, which asks respondents to indicate which ethnic or cultural group they or their ancestors belonged to on first coming to this continent. According to the published information from the 1981 census of Canada, Canadians reported that they originated from a total of forty-one major ethnic origins (*Canada Year Book*, 1985 : 59–60). The largest group was the British, amounting to about 40 percent. The French, about 27 percent, came second in number. Other Canadians, that is, those who came from neither British nor French origins, made up about 33 percent of Canada's population. The majority of this 33 percent were Europeans, with Asians, Africans and native peoples making up most of the racial minorities. In 1981, for example, less than 2 percent of Canada's population were native peoples; and about 2.5 percent of Canadians came from African and East Asian origins. (The distinction between ethnicity and race will be discussed later in this chapter.)

Linguistically, Canadians also show many variations. The 1981 census indicates that English was the mother tongue for 60 percent of Canadians—*mother tongue* is the language a person learned in childhood and is still able to speak in adulthood. A quarter of Canadians reported French as their mother tongue. About 85 percent of these Canadians lived in Quebec. Like the ethnic composition of Canada, the language behaviours of Canadians tend to change over time. For example, according to the 1981 census, more than two million Canadians spoke a language at home that differed from their mother tongue. About 3.7 million Canadians were officially bilingual—they spoke both French and English—but bilingualism was more common among those whose mother tongue was French.

There are many social features of Canada that reflect its ethnic, linguistic and racial diversities. To better understand how ethnicity and race have shaped the social arrangements of Canada, it is useful to look back to the historical roots to see how the Canadian mosaic evolved.

Formation of the Canadian Mosaic

Historical Roots of French Canada

Before the British Conquest of 1760, New France was a French colony. Although the language among the 90 000 inhabitants was French, and the religion was Catholic, the life style was distinct from that of France (Milner, 1978). Under the seigneurial system, land titles were granted by the French Crown to seigneurs, or landowners, who in turn parcelled out land to settlers. The social structure reflects the colonial rule. The fur trade was monopolized by the French regime, while the *habitants* of New France were engaged in subsistence farming. The Catholic Church provided both the spiritual and administrative stability to the French settlement.

The conflict in the colony between Britain and France was over control of the fur trade and not a result of linguistic differences between the French and British settlers. The French defeat resulted in the Treaty of Paris of 1763, which gave Great Britain control over New France. With the immigration of English-speaking merchants, the English Protestants, although numerically a minority in Quebec, gradually assumed the majority power in Montreal and Quebec. The French population remained largely rural. Although the Quebec Act of 1774 recognized the religious and linguistic rights of the French, it also upheld the feudal legacy of the colonial system and the authority of the church.

The American Revolution of 1776 brought thousands of British Loyalists to Canada. In Montreal, the English Protestant minority became the elites of a unified financial, transportation and staples cartel that dominated subsequent economic development (Milner, 1978). By the time of Confederation, the English financial power that was based in Montreal was well entrenched. Although the British North America Act of 1867 recognized the status of French in the Parliament of Canada and the legislature of Quebec, commercial enterprises were firmly in the hands of the English.

The dominance of the Protestant English in Quebec persisted through the first half of the twentieth century unchallenged. A high birth rate, low education and submission to clerical authority were characteristic of the French peasantry in rural Quebec. The Roman Catholic Church perpetuated a rural mythology that was conservative, fatalistic and passive.

The victory of the Parti Québécois in the 1976 provincial election indicated the strength of French nationalism in the province, but changes really began earlier during the Quiet Revolution of the 1960s. Industrial expansion after the war, the increased migration to cities as a result of a high birth rate and the reform of the educational and welfare system contributed to a new consciousness among the young French intelligentsia (Milner, 1978; Guindon, 1978). Quebec nationalism can be seen as a response to the historical inequality between the British and the French and to the exploitation of French Canadians by English capitalists. Consequently, the independence movement was closely tied to labour politics and the political left (Milner, 1978).

As the Quiet Revolution of the 1960s was transforming the social order of Quebec, and Quebec nationalism was gaining momentum, the federal government responded by striking the Royal Commission on Bilingualism and Biculturalism in 1963. One of the outcomes of the Royal commission was the enactment of the Official Languages Act in 1969, which made English and French both official languages of Canada.

Despite the recommendations of the Royal Commission on Bilingualism and Biculturalism to promote French Canadians, English Canadians were able to maintain economic and cultural dominance in Quebec (Guindon, 1978). In fact, the Official Languages Act failed to address the fundamental problem of economic underdevelopment of Quebec and Québécois. It only created institutional bilingualism, bilingualism practised in public institutions, that was irritating to English Canadians and irrelevant to French Quebeckers (Guindon, 1978).

Shortly after the Parti Québécois came to power in Quebec, it passed the controversial language bill, Bill 101, or the Charter of the French Language, which was intended to make French the official and legal language of education, business, work and other public sectors. The defeat of the Parti Québécois by the Liberal Party in 1985 in Quebec opened a new opportunity for language conflicts to surface; some anglophones in Quebec are demanding repeal of some of the Parti Québécois legislation and the restoration of the right to use English in public sectors.

In many ways, the language struggle of French Canadians symbolizes their struggle against economic and political oppression (Jackson, 1977). Generally, when language serves to maintain group boundaries, language conflicts, as Jackson puts it, "also become the focus of class, status and power conflicts" (1977:63).

Native Peoples

The history of native peoples in North America dates back thousands of years before the founding of Canada as a confederation in 1867. Their history with Europeans since 1500, however, can be understood in four major phases.

According to Patterson (1972), the first phase of this history was the initial contact between the native peoples and Europeans, which often led to a period of prosperity as the two groups voluntarily exchanged technology and goods. Shortly after, however, hostility developed between the two groups in most cases. In the second phase, native peoples became increasingly drawn into the economy of the white people as they became more involved in fur trading and less reliant on their traditional means of making a living. The end result was a weakening of their political autonomy and a reliance on Europeans for military aid. Increasingly, native peoples were subjected to economic, political, military and religious domination by whites. The third phase of this history began with the creation of reserves for the natives. Agriculture was expanding and natives were removed to clear the way for white settlement. With the passage of the first Indian Act in 1876, the colonial status of the native people was legally confirmed. In terms of power, Europeans had become the charter group, or dominant group, while the natives had been transformed into a minority in the ethnic mosaic of Canada. The last phase began in the period after the Second World War, as more native people became aware of their plight and oppression and demanded autonomy and equality.

The Indian Act of 1876 was a comprehensive legislative bill to control every aspect of native life. It legally defined who were Indians and what they could and could not do on reserves. Status Indians are under the legislative and administrative control of the federal government, a status defined by the British North America Act and regulated by the Indian Act. Non-status Indians are broadly defined as those with partial Indian ancestry; among them are the Métis. The Inuit, on the other hand, have been defined by the federal government in different ways at different times. For example, when Canada began to develop the North, the government assigned a "disc" number to each Inuk, or member of the Inuit; only people with "disc" numbers were officially classified as Inuit (Frideres, 1988).

Hence, the classification of status and non-status Indians in Canada was the result of decisions made by government departments in charge of Indians, and not by native peoples themselves (Frideres, 1988:97). Besides the Indian Act, there were eleven numbered treaties signed with native people in western Canada between 1871 and 1921. These treaties forced the native people to give up their rights to land in exchange for small areas of reserves and yearly provisions.

Today, there are about 370 000 registered or status Indians, 460 000 Métis and 35 000 Inuit in Canada, making up about 2 to 3 percent of the country's population

S. L. McDonald (right), Indian agent at Battleford, retired in 1950. Chief Yahyahnum of the Sweetgrass reserve and his son, Andrew Swimmer, attended his retirement ceremony. Status Indians still come under the administrative control of federal government representatives.

SASKATOON PUBLIC LIBRARY—LOCAL HISTORY ROOM.

(Frideres, 1988). Over 90 percent of registered Indians live on reserves. The Indians in Canada have many of the symptoms of colonized people. They suffer from low educational and economic opportunities, poor health and housing conditions and a low social status.

Immigrants to Canada

Except for native peoples, Canada's population is made up of immigrants who came in different waves. The history of immigration may be divided into four periods. During the first period, from 1867 to 1895, Canada was quite free in accepting immigrants, especially from Europe and the United States. Between 1867 and 1895, about 1.5 million immigrants came, mostly from Europe. The second period of immigration ranged from 1896 to the beginning of the First World War in 1914. Canada was in favour of massive immigration for agricultural settlement. When the supply of emigrants from England and Western Europe was depleted, Canada began recruiting people from Eastern and southern Europe, such as Poles, Ukrainians, Hutterites and Doukhobors. Over three million immigrants came to Canada during this period. In the third period, from 1915 to 1945, Canada continued to follow the policy of recruiting immigrants for land settlement. British and American immigrants were considered the most desirable, followed by North Europeans. Other Europeans were tolerated and non-whites were not welcome (Manpower and Immigration, 1974). In total, about two million immigrants came in this period. After the Second World War, Canada made many changes to its immigration policy, and began the recruitment of skilled labour. In this process, Canada also opened up its historical policy of excluding non-white immigrants and began to accept them. In the four decades (between 1946 and 1986) after the war, about 5.5 million immigrants landed in Canada. These post-war immigrants have altered the ethnic and racial composition of Canada and brought other changes to Canadian society.

Table 9-1 provides a glimpse of the changing ethnic composition in Canada in the three decades after the Second World War. In 1951, about 48 percent of the total population were of British origin. By 1971, they declined to 45 percent. Those of French origin also decreased slightly from about 31 percent in 1951 to 29 percent in 1971. In contrast, the non-British and non-French population increased from 21 percent to 27 percent during the same period.

The increase in population among the ethnic and racial minorities is mainly attributed to the changing immigration patterns, especially in the post-war years of industrial expansion. The demand for technical labour led the Canadian government in 1962 and in 1967 to change the immigration policy to widen the recruitment of skilled workers from sources beyond the United Kingdom, northern continental Europe and the United States (Hawkins, 1972). The demand for skilled labour from these countries as a result of the post-war economic boom meant that Canada had to compete with other industrial nations for immigrants with professional and technical skills. For example, between 1953 and 1963 there was a net outflow of 41 263 professional workers and 38 363 skilled workers from Canada to the United States (Parai,

TABLE 9-1
Population by Ethnic Group, 1951, 1961 and 1971

Ethnic Group	1951		1961		1971	
	No.	%	No.	%	No.	%
British Isles	6 709 685	47.9	7 996 669	43.8 ⎫		
English	3 630 344	25.9	4 195 175	23.0		
Irish	1 439 635	10.3	1 753 351	9.6 ⎬	9 624 115	44.6
Scottish	1 547 470	11.0	1 902 302	10.4		
Welsh and other	92 236	0.7	145 841	0.8 ⎭		
French	4 319 167	30.8	5 540 346	30.4	6 180 120	28.7
Other European	2 553 722	18.2	4 116 849	22.6	4 959 680	23.0
Austrian	32 231	0.2	106 535	0.6	41 120	0.2
Belgian	35 148	0.2	61 382	0.3	51 135	0.2
Czech and Slovak	63 959	0.5	73 061	0.4	81 870	0.4
Danish	41 671	0.3	85 473	0.5	75 725	0.4
Finnish	43 745	0.3	59 436	0.3	59 215	0.3
German	619 995	4.4	1 049 599	5.8	1 317 200	6.1
Greek	13 966	0.1	56 475	0.3	124 475	0.6
Hungarian	60 460	0.4	126 220	0.7	131 890	0.6
Icelandic	23 307	0.2	30 623	0.2	27 905	0.1
Italian	152 245	1.1	450 351	2.5	730 820	3.4
Jewish	181 670	1.3	173 344	1.0	296 945	1.4
Lithuanian	16 224	0.1	27 629	0.2	24 535	0.1
Netherlands	264 267	1.9	429 679	2.4	425 945	2.0
Norwegian	119 266	0.8	148 681	0.8	179 290	0.8
Polish	219 845	1.6	323 517	1.8	316 425	1.5
Portuguese	—	—	—	—	96 875	0.4
Romanian	23 601	0.2	43 805	0.2	27 375	0.1
Russian	91 279	0.7	119 168	0.7	64 475	0.3
Spanish	—	—	—	—	27 515	0.1
Swedish	97 780	0.7	121 757	0.6	101 870	0.5
Ukrainian	395 043	2.8	473 337	2.6	580 660	2.7
Yugoslavic	21 404	0.2	68 587	0.4	104 950	0.5
Other	35 616	0.2	88 190	0.5	70 460	0.3
Asiatic	72 827	0.5	121 753	0.7	285 540	1.3
Chinese	32 528	0.2	58 197	0.3	118 815	0.6
Japanese	21 663	0.2	29 157	0.2	37 260	0.2
Other	18 636	0.1	34 399	0.2	129 460	0.6
Other	354 028	2.5	462 630	2.5	518 850	2.4
Eskimo	9 733	0.1	11 835	0.1	17 550	0.1
Native Indian	155 874	1.1	208 286	1.1	295 215	1.4
Negro	18 020	0.1	32 127	0.2	34 445	0.2
West Indian	—	—	—	—	28 025	0.1
Other and not stated	170 401	1.2	210 382	1.2	143 620	0.7
Total	14 009 429	100.0	18 238 247	100.0	21 568 310	100.0

CANADA YEAR BOOK, 1980–81, P. 137. REPRODUCED BY PERMISSION OF THE MINISTER OF SUPPLY AND SERVICES CANADA.

1965 : 47–57). Canada was able to maintain a net gain of 125 242 professional and skilled workers for the same period only because of a larger volume of those workers immigrating to Canada from around the world. In the process of what some referred to as the "brain drain," Third World countries became the main suppliers of skilled labour to Canada and other industrial nations (Parai, 1965). Table 9-2 shows the changing sources of immigrants to Canada. Before 1961, the ten leading sources of immigrants were European countries and the United States, with the British Isles accounting for nearly 30 percent of all immigrants. Between 1971 and 1981, however, the ten leading countries included India, the Philippines, Jamaica, Vietnam, Hong Kong and Guyana. The British Isles, still the largest supplier of immigrants to Canada, accounted for only 13.8 percent of all immigrants entering the country between 1971 and 1981. During the mid-1970s, the Canadian government admitted fewer immigrants in response to high unemployment and economic recession, but encouraged the immigration of entrepreneurs as a means to create more jobs. As the economic conditions improved in the 1980s, the Canadian government raised the annual intake of immigrants to about 150 000 a year.

Theoretical Perspectives

What Are Race and Ethnicity?   Up to this point, we have used the terms ethnicity and race somewhat loosely without defining them. There are two basic ways to define *ethnicity* and *race*, each reflecting a difference in theory.

Traditionally, sociologists have used identity as a basis for defining ethnicity and race. *Identity* refers to a feeling of attachment to a group based, presumably, on common individual characteristics. Accordingly, ethnicity is determined at birth. Members of an ethnic group share a sense of peoplehood, or identity, based on descent, language, religion, tradition and other common experiences (Weber, 1968 : 385–98). Ethnic identity provides a basis for members of an ethnic group to develop social boundaries (Weber, 1968 : 388) within which ethnic institutions, neighbourhoods, beliefs and cultures are developed and maintained. In the case of a racial group, there is an added feature of an observable physical trait, such as a different skin colour, that makes its members distinguishable from others.

More recently, some sociologists have defined race and ethnicity in the context of intergroup relations. For example, Wilson (1973 : 6) says that "racial groups are distinguished by socially selected physical traits; ethnic groups are distinguished by socially selected cultural traits." Physical and cultural traits define social groups only insofar as they are socially recognized as important. In other words, race and ethnicity take on a social meaning only when physical and cultural traits are paired with social attributes, such as intellectual, moral or behavioural characteristics. For example, although there is little scientific basis for relying on superficial physical traits such as skin colour to classify population groups, skin colour takes on a social significance when it is consistently paired with social privileges and rewards. Hence, in Canada,

TABLE 9-2
Ten Leading Countries of Birth of Immigrants for Each Period of Immigration, Canada, 1981

Before 1961 Country of birth	Number	% of total
Great Britain	524 900	29.8
Italy	214 700	12.2
United States	136 900	7.8
Poland	118 000	6.7
U.S.S.R.	112 600	6.4
Netherlands	112 400	6.4
Federal Republic of Germany	107 200	6.1
Yugoslavia	39 100	2.2
German Democratic Republic	28 400	1.6
Austria	28 300	1.6
Ten leading countries as a percentage of all immigrants who arrived before 1961		80.8

1961–1970 Country of birth	Number	% of total
Great Britain	195 300	21.1
Italy	141 000	15.2
United States	67 000	7.2
Portugal	57 300	6.2
Greece	40 700	4.4
Yugoslavia	33 200	3.6
Federal Republic of Germany	31 400	3.4
India	28 200	3.0
Jamaica	23 600	2.5
France	19 100	2.1
Ten leading countries as a percentage of all immigrants who arrived during the 1961–1970 period		68.7

1971–1981 Country of birth	Number	% of total
Great Britain	158 800	13.8
United States	97 600	8.5
India	75 100	6.5
Portugal	66 400	5.8
Philippines	55 300	4.8
Jamaica	49 900	4.3
Socialist Republic of Vietnam	49 400	4.3
Hong Kong	42 200	3.7
Italy	29 100	2.5
Guyana	27 500	2.4
Ten leading countries as a percentage of all immigrants who arrived during the 1971–1981 period		56.6

1981 CENSUS OF CANADA, CATALOGUE 99-936, CANADA'S IMMIGRANTS. *REPRODUCED BY PERMISSION OF THE MINISTER OF SUPPLY AND SERVICES CANADA.*

native people being non-white is socially important because it is associated with poor health status, low education and high unemployment. But whether such associations are alleged or real is often irrelevant. Attaching a social meaning to the physical or cultural characteristics of a group implies rewards and resources in society are, to some extent, divided along racial and ethnic lines, and that the dominant or privileged group can use physical and cultural features of people as a basis of stratification.

Ethnic Inequality in South Africa

In many ways, South Africa is clearly at one extreme . . . among most contemporary multiethnic societies. The economic, political, and social inequalities among ethnic groups, specifically, between whites and nonwhites, are unmatched. What is perhaps most peculiar about the South African system in comparison with the others is the officially proclaimed justification of these inequalities and the openly declared intention of dominant whites to sustain them. . . . But in contrast to South Africa, there is official acknowledgment in Brazil, Canada, Northern Ireland, and the United States of the desirability of reducing interethnic disparities. Equally anomalous is the shape and degree of institutional separation among South Africa's ethnic groups. In none of the other four societies is the segregation of groups so rigid, and nowhere is it so legitimized. The overwhelming issue of South Africa is thus unambiguous: how will the ethnic disparities in power and privilege be transformed?

Despite the resolve of dominant whites to preserve their supremacy, the forces of change today are drawn unmistakably in South Africa. The end of European colonialism and the assertion of self-determination on the part of indigenous African peoples after World War II marked a power shift in which black political elites replaced white. South Africa has tenaciously resisted this historical drift. Although white South Africans at this point may quite reasonably claim to be indigenous Africans, their objectives and policies seek the perpetuation of white supremacy. Thus, they find themselves portrayed by black Africans as well as Third World peoples everywhere as the sole anachronism of a past colonial era. In a very broad sense, the South African case represents symbolically the confrontation of white and nonwhite peoples globally. The ethnic issues of South Africa today, therefore, have implications not only for South Africa itself or for the larger African continent but also for the entire world.

From Martin N. Marger. 1985. *Race and Ethnic Relations: American and Global Perspectives.* © 1985 by Wadsworth, Inc. Reprinted by permission of the publisher.

Sociologists sometimes use the term social races to emphasize that races are not *genetic groupings*, or *genotypes*; that is, racial groups as socially defined do not correspond to biological groupings based on genetic structures. Rex (1983) cites the findings of a series of conferences organized by the United Nations Educational, Scientific and Cultural Organization (UNESCO), which concluded that the genetic variation within any one population group is probably as great as that between that group and other groups. Hence, skin colour, although carrying a social meaning, has little scientific use for classifying human beings into genetic groups. Consequently, race and ethnicity are social constructs based on unequal relations between ethnic groups, and not biological types based on superficial features. We can see this principle operating in South Africa, where a person's race is legally defined not by skin colour, but by ancestry. In South Africa, a person may have fair skin and be classified as black because one of the parents is legally black. Even in this society, which tries to define its members by race, there is no direct correspondence between skin colour, genetical grouping and social classification.

How ethnicity and race are defined affects the questions sociologists ask about ethnic groups and race relations. For example, if we define ethnicity on the basis of what group people identify themselves as belonging to, it would be logical to question how this identity might change as people become more assimilated into another culture. In contrast, defining race and ethnicity as being based on unequal relations leads to questions about differential power between dominant and subordinate groups.

Assimilation and Pluralism

The theme of assimilation dominated race and ethnic studies until the 1960s. *Assimilation* is the process whereby people of diverse origins conform to a single or amalgamated culture. This concept has been applied to the study of immigrant groups in North America to see how, over time, they become incorporated into the cultures, behaviours and institutions of the dominant group.

There are many versions of the assimilation theory. Park (1950) develops the notion of a race relations cycle that takes the form of contacts, competition, accommodation and assimilation. Through migration or conquest, people of different origins make contact. After the initial contact, the second stage of the cycle is characterized by conflicts arising from competition over scarce resources. Over time, conflicts are resolved as the competing groups accommodate each other. The final stage is assimilation, out of which a single culture emerges. According to Park, this process is progressive and irreversible. Immigration restrictions and racial barriers may slow down the process, but they can neither stop nor reverse it.

This theory of assimilation has been refined by many sociologists, notably Gordon (1964). He distinguishes several versions of the assimilation model as applied to the United States. Anglo-conformity refers to the process by which immigrant groups and racial minorities conform to the language, behaviours and institutions of the dominant Anglo-Saxon group. A second model of assimilation is the melting-pot thesis, which sees all groups as contributing to the American culture as people of every stock are amalgamated into a new nation. The term "triple melting pot" is sometimes used to suggest that assimilation in America takes place within the three major religious groups of Catholics, Protestants and Jews.

Pluralism, the third model, describes situations where ethnic groups may share some aspects of a common culture and participate collectively in its economic and political life, while retaining unique cultural aspects in their social networks, residential areas, churches and languages. Gordon (1964) distinguishes between two types of pluralism: cultural and structural. Cultural pluralism is the retention of ethnic tradition in primary

This cartoon from Canada: The Granary of the World, *1903, shows an example of anglo-conformity.*

SASKATCHEWAN ARCHIVES BOARD/R-A 12402.

group relations, while participating with other ethnic groups in secondary group relations. Structural pluralism, on the other hand, refers to the existence of separate ethnic subsocieties along with a massive trend of assimilation to a common culture. Insofar as racial and ethnic groups in American society maintain ethnic distinctiveness through religious ties and informal social networks, America is more accurately seen as a pluralist society then as a melting pot (Glazer and Moynihan, 1970).

The assimilation models have been criticized on several grounds (Li and Bolaria, 1979). Park's race relations cycle is simplistic and mechanical. Its prediction of irreversible assimilation is too rigid and is not supported by the experiences of many racial and ethnic groups. A more fundamental objection is that assimilation is too loosely defined. It implies a standard of behaviours and values that immigrant groups have to acquire to become assimilated, yet such a standard is often absent. For example, what does it mean if a person eats spaghetti more often than hamburger? Does it mean that immigrants are less assimilated if they work and live like their neighbours, but maintain their ethnic friends? Unfortunately, the concept of assimilation is a biased outlook calling for Americanization or anglicization rather than a description of immigrants' actual experiences. Thus, assimilation models have been branded *ethnocentric* because they reflect the belief that one race or ethnic group is the centre of all cultures.

Critics of pluralism, however, maintain that pluralism often assumes a basic equality for all ethnic and racial groups (Steinberg, 1981). In a society that has structural inequalities between ethnic groups, pluralism can only be an ideal for some ethnic members; most ethnic members will find it difficult to preserve a strong ethnic identity because there is little concrete societal basis to do so. They are more prepared to

Income Achievement and Adaptive Capacity

The historical facts show . . . that prior to the end of the Second World War, the Chinese were subjected to a discriminatory immigration system which sought to exclude them. One of the consequences of such exclusion was to produce a highly unbalanced sex ratio among the Chinese, even long after the legislative control was removed in 1947. This largely delayed the birth of a second generation which did not begin to emerge in sizable numbers until the sixties. In contrast, the immigration system permitted the Japanese to bring their wives as early as 1908, and this resulted in a much more balanced sex ratio among the Japanese community as compared to the Chinese. Furthermore, the experience of relocation and subsequent repatriation of the Japanese in Canada resulted in a large drop in population among the Japanese in Canada. The small volume of Japanese immigration to Canada in the postwar years greatly altered the demographic and social characteristics of the Japanese community. These historical factors, and not cultural adaptability, are important in understanding the present demographic structures of the Chinese and the Japanese in Canada.

Historically too, the Japanese and the Chinese entered different occupations in Canada, in part because of different opportunities available to the two groups. The heavy concentration of the Chinese in the service industry as laundrymen and restaurant workers, for example, was largely a result of restricted opportunities in the non-ethnic sector. The damage to the Japanese ethnic business during the relocation of the Second World War probably resulted in many Japanese having to seek employment in other sectors after the war. These historical experiences must be considered in explaining the differences of the two groups in the occupational structure of today.

What is understood as the adaptive capacity of minority groups, then, may be no more than different responses under various constrained situations. Ethnic differences in economic achievements in many cases are probably more related to unequal opportunity structures to which these groups are subjected than to the adaptive capacity of their old world cultures.

Peter S. Li. 1980. "Income Achievement and Adaptive Capacity: An Empirical Comparison of Chinese and Japanese in Canada." In K. V. Ujimoto and G. Hirabayashi, eds., *Visible Minorities and Multiculturalism: Asians in Canada.* Toronto, Butterworths.

maintain their ethnic distinctiveness through symbolic ethnicity. Ethnicity is symbolic if the ethnic language is not recognized in the school system as a language of instruction and if the cultural heritage is expressed mainly at the level of song and dance. Even among the upwardly mobile groups who have the resources to preserve their ethnic identities, ethnicity remains expressive or symbolic (Gans, 1979). In other words, there is little reason for someone to preserve ethnic distinctiveness while participating in mainstream economic and political activities that do not reward that distinctiveness, or that even penalize it.

The pluralist perspective has also been criticized for emphasizing the original culture from the old country as the defining characteristic of ethnic groups (Yancey, Ericksen and Juliani, 1976). In doing so, cultural pluralists overlook how the host society shapes ethnicity in urban life. Ethnicity changes as old cultures die and new ones evolve, change being constantly influenced by the need to survive. Valentine (1968) argues that there is a difference between the material conditions under which people live and the cultural responses they develop. The key question is not so much whether immigrants maintain their Old World culture, but under what conditions ethnicity becomes particularly relevant (Yancey, Ericksen and Juliani, 1976). Hence, the emergence of ethnic businesses among some ethnic groups may have more to do with discrimination and opportunity restrictions than a cultural tendency to engage in certain lines of work (Ward and Jenkins, 1984; Li, 1988a). For example, the Chinese in Canada before the Second World War did not naturally congregate in service occupations, but were forced to be cooks, waiters, and to operate laundries because they were excluded from other lines of work (Li, 1988a). Differences in historical and structural conditions help to explain why ethnic groups with similar cultural backgrounds and physical appearances evolve in different ways.

Dominant and Subordinate Groups

An approach to race and ethnic relations that differs from pluralism is to examine them as unequal relationships, produced and maintained by differential power between a dominant group and a subordinate one. From this point of view, the majority group is the ethnic or racial group with the greatest power, not necessarily the group with the largest number of members. This approach treats race and ethnicity as concepts about relationships, not as descriptive categories. The focus is on the institutional framework within which groups become defined as racial or ethnic and on how social interactions are organized accordingly (Bolaria and Li, 1988). For example, it was not differences in skin colour that produced the slavery system in America. Rather, it was the structure of slavery and the relationship between slave owners and slaves that produced the social importance of racial groups known as "black" and "white."

There is a close relationship between labour exploitation and the division of people into races (giving superficial physical traits social meanings) (Rex, 1983; Miles, 1982). This relationship is best illustrated by capitalist economies, under which labour cost is maintained as low as possible in order to maximize profit. The basic structural dilemma in such societies is how to maintain a pool of subservient labour to do menial tasks. Eventually workers accumulate the resources that allow them to become upwardly mobile. This diminishes the available labour. One solution is to choose physical and cultural attributes as a rationale for assigning a group of socially defined undesirables to undesirable jobs. Over time, the cultural and physical characteristics of a subordinate group become inseparable from its work role and its subservient position (Bolaria and Li, 1988). There are two models that are useful to study the dominant/subordinate relationships of racial and ethnic groups: the colonial model and the split labour market model.

The *colonial model* describes how race and ethnic relations develop under colonialism. The most significant aspect of colonial economies is the massive deployment of non-white labour (Rex, 1983). European colonizers privatized previously public resources. They actively developed some regions and resources of the colonies at the expense of other sectors. By importing slaves or indentured labourers and inviting in white settlers, they gradually replaced the indigenous social structure with a new social order in which dominant and subservient groups were defined by race (Bolaria and Li, 1988).

The colonization process has seven parts (Frideres, 1983). These are: (1) the incursion of the colonizing group; (2) the social, economic and cultural destruction of the colonized people; (3) the taking of external political control by the colonizers; (4) the establishment of the economic dependence of the colonized people; (5) the provision of low-quality social services for the colonized people; (6) the emergence of racism; and (7) the development of a colour line that becomes the social basis for excluding people from privileged positions.

Different aspects of the colonial model have been applied to explain race relations in advanced capitalist societies. For example, Rex (1983) argues that immigrants that move from ex-colonies to urbanized societies such as Great Britain carry the stigma of colonial workers, which places them in a disadvantaged position. Many immigrants are part of an underclass, a bottom stratum below the working class. Another extension of the colonial model argues that racism leads to the exploitation of immigrants and workers in developing countries, as advanced capitalist countries extend their investments to peripheral markets, and transform these countries to neo-colonies (Portes and Walton, 1981). Finally, the term internal colony has been used to describe the situation of some racial groups in America, such as the blacks, the Mexicans, and the natives (Frideres, 1983; Patterson, 1972) because of their similarity to colonized people. Internal colonization refers to the political and economic domination of minorities within a country who suffer from exploitation and oppression similar to that endured by indigenous people under classical colonization. Frideres (1983) shows that native people in Canada suffer from internal colonization. As a result of legal and social controls, the native people are second-class citizens in Canada, experiencing restricted opportunities and a poor quality of life.

The *split labour market model* was developed by Bonacich (1979) to explain racial and ethnic conflicts. She claims that the source of antagonism is not race and ethnicity, but differences in the price of labour between two groups that are often divided along racial and ethnic lines. The split labour market refers to the price differentials between two groups performing the same task; or in a submerged form in which the higher-paid group monopolizes certain positions and the lower-paid group is restricted to marginal participation. Historically, this economically based antagonism surfaced as racial conflicts between non-white and white labour. The real issue, however, had to do with white workers resisting their replacement by the cheaper labour of non-white workers as capitalists tried to lower their labour costs. Such racial antagonism may be "resolved" by excluding non-white workers, for instance by hiring only white people for certain jobs, or by assigning work by racial groups, as in a caste or near-caste system. A caste system rigidly determines social positions on the basis of ascribed characteristics.

The emergence of a split labour market is related to two conditions, both of which arose from the development of capitalism in Western Europe (Bonacich, 1979). The first was the rise in labour cost of white workers, and the second was the availability of non-white labour from Third World countries as imperialism accelerated their underdevelopment. The theory of the split labour market has been applied to explain racism against the blacks in the United States (Bonacich, 1976), and anti-orientalism in Canada (Li, 1988a) and Brazil (Makabe, 1981).

The split labour market implies there is a relationship between class and race. Bonacich's theory also suggests a close tie between capitalist expansion and labour recruitment. Indeed, there are grounds to suggest that the Canadian immigration policy, like that of other advanced capitalist countries, is designed to regulate the volume and type of immigrants to suit the country's labour needs. Historically, Canada favoured immigrants from Britain, the United States, and northern Europe and excluded others from non-white countries except in times of severe labour shortage (Li and Bolaria, 1979). A preferential system based on country of origin was maintained until 1967, when a universal point system was introduced (Hawkins, 1972). Under this universal point system, prospective immigrants are evaluated on the basis of skills, credentials, language proficiency and other criteria, irrespective of their countries of origin. The change facilitated the recruitment of skilled labour from other countries, as the economic prosperity in post-war years increased the demand for technical labour. Despite these changes, the post-war Gallup polls show Canadians most favour immigrants from the United Kingdom and northeastern Europe, and least from Asia (Tienhaara, 1974). Another study shows Canadians are more willing to accept the services of immigrants in lower-prestige occupations than higher-prestige occupations (Jones and Lambert, 1965). During economic hard times, immigrants are often seen as competitors, taking away jobs from native-born Canadians. These findings give further credence to the split labour market theory.

The Vertical Mosaic

Since the publication of *The Vertical Mosaic* (Porter, 1965), the term *vertical mosaic* is used popularly to describe the ethnic and race relations in Canada. Sociologists are interested in studying why some racial and ethnic groups do better than others. Obviously, there are different ways of comparing the performance of racial and ethnic groups. We can look at occupational status, income and membership in the elite. The explanations of this inequality, however, are more complex. To varying degrees, historical, cultural and institutional factors account for why certain ethnic groups occupy privileged positions in society, while others are deprived of an equal opportunity for advancement.

John Porter, in *The Vertical Mosaic*, offers several explanations of how ethnicity and class intersect in Canadian society. The title of his book refers to the intimate relationship between ethnicity and class. First, he argues that the historical process of immigration and labour recruitment has a lot to do with the social statuses of various ethnic groups. He compares the charter status of the British and French with the entrance status of later immigrants. The charter group is the society's founding group. It retains many privileges and prerogatives and lays down the conditions and rules under which other groups are admitted. Entrance status implies lower occupational status. Over time, some groups may improve their entrance status, while others may not. The concepts of charter group and entrance status are useful in understanding the privileged positions enjoyed by the British throughout the history of Canada, as compared to the disadvantaged status of the later immigrant groups recruited for various economic developments, for example, in the case of the Irish who built canals and railways in Upper Canada, the Asians who opened mines and constructed railways in the West and the Ukrainians who homesteaded in the Prairies.

Porter's second point is that, within the charter groups, the British are doing much better occupationally than the French. His analysis of the 1931, 1951 and 1961 censuses shows the French were underrepresented in professional and financial occupations and overrepresented in the agricultural and primary sectors. By comparison, the British were increasingly overrepresented in the professional and financial occupations. The occupational inequality between the British and French has been supported by many other studies. For example, Hughes (1943), in his study of an industrial town of Quebec, describes a general pattern of stratification typical of Quebec, with the English occupying the management positions and the French making up the rank and file. In a study of francophones and anglophones in the federal public service in 1965 and 1973, Beattie (1975) reports that francophones received less pay and had a lower chance of promotion than anglophones. Milner (1978) shows that in Quebec, the grande bourgeoisie, or owners of multinational institutions, are still largely Americans and English Canadians. Guindon (1978) discovers that despite the emergence of middle-class Québécois in the decade after the Quiet Revolution, they were mainly accepted in the public sector, but not in the large private corporate economy.

Perhaps Porter is best known for his analysis of the economic elite of Canada, in which he shows that the British had overwhelming control. The economic elites are those who hold directorships in dominant corporations in Canada. Of the 760 individuals in the economic elite in 1951, 92.3 percent were British, 6.7 percent French and 1 percent other, mainly Jewish in origin. In the same year, the British represented 47.9 percent of the total population in Canada, the French 30.8 percent and those of other origin 21.3 percent. The British were clearly overrepresented in the corporate upper echelon. Porter's findings are supported by Clement's more recent study of the Canadian corporate elite (Clement, 1975). Clement's data show that in 1972, 86.2 percent of the 775 individuals in the economic elite were English, 8.4 percent French and 5.4 percent other origin. The underrepresentation of the French goes back, as we have seen earlier, to the British Conquest of 1760, after which the British took over the economic and political institutions of New France. Subsequent generations of English Canadians maintained an economic empire, largely by relying on British markets and capital, and more recently, through ties with industrial capitalists in the United States (Clement, 1975).

The "vertical mosaic" also deals with the relationship between ethnic groups and occupational structure. Porter (1965 : 73) suggests that "immigration and ethnic affiliation have been important factors in the formation of social classes in Canada . . . (and) ethnic differences have been important in building up the bottom layer of the stratification system in both agricultural and industrial settings." His analysis of the 1931, 1951 and 1961 censuses shows that people of British and Jewish origins were persistently overrepresented in the professional and financial occupations and underrepresented in agricultural, primary and unskilled jobs. All other racial and ethnic groups were underrepresented in the professional and financial occupations, with the exception of Asians in 1961. Porter's conclusion is that, over the twenty-year period, the British maintained their overrepresentation in the white-collar sector, while the French barely maintained their level of representation relative to other ethnic groups. With the exception of the French, the rough occupational ranking of various groups had remained virtually the same, with the Germans, Scandinavians and Dutch close to the occupational levels of the English, and the Italians, Poles and Ukrainians near the lower end of the occupational structure.

More recently, Porter's thesis that some ethnic groups are blocked from upward occupational mobility has been questioned (Darroch, 1979), because a reanalysis of Porter's data indicates a trend of decreasing occupational dissimilarity among ethnic groups. However, using a more detailed analysis, Lautard and Loree (1984) show that despite declines since 1931, occupational dissimilarity among ethnic groups remained large. Lautard and Loree (1984) argue that although the average or mean ethnic inequality declined, the relative ranking of ethnic groups over the two decades remained stable. In other words, the ethnic groups at the top of the occupational structure stayed at the top and the groups that started in lower positions have stayed there throughout this period. On the basis of their reanalysis, Lautard and Loree (1984 : 342) conclude that the "relationship between ethnicity and occupation remains a durable feature of Canadian society."

There are several aspects of the Canadian mosaic that deserve special attention. They are: bilingualism, multiculturalism and inequality.

Bilingualism and Language Maintenance

The problem of linguistic inequality is central in understanding the British/French relationship in Canada. As we have seen earlier, it has historical roots that stretch beyond cultural and linguistic differences.

Although Canada is officially bilingual as a result of the Official Languages Act of 1969, there are marked regional differences in the linguistic patterns in Canada. Data from the 1981 census indicate that those who are officially bilingual represent 15.3 percent of the total population. About one-third of those whose mother tongue is French are bilingual, in contrast to 8 percent of the English. Bilingualism is less common among the English in Quebec than among the French in the rest of Canada. Figure 9-1 shows the bilingual population as a percentage of each region.

The 1981 census reports ten major home languages of Canadians. A *home language*

FIGURE 9-1

Bilingual Population as a Percentage of the Total Population, Canada, Provinces and Territories, 1981

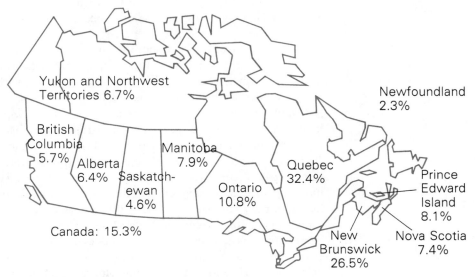

Yukon and Northwest Territories 6.7%

Newfoundland 2.3%

British Columbia 5.7%

Alberta 6.4%

Saskatchewan 4.6%

Manitoba 7.9%

Ontario 10.8%

Quebec 32.4%

Prince Edward Island 8.1%

Nova Scotia 7.4%

New Brunswick 26.5%

Canada: 15.3%

1981 Census of Canada, Catalogue 99-935, *Language in Canada*. Reproduced by permission of the Minister of Supply and Services Canada.

is the language spoken by the respondent at home at the time of the census. English is the home language for 68 percent of Canadians, and French is the home language for 25 percent. The remaining 7 percent of Canadians speak a home language other than English or French.

Language maintenance or retention has to do with whether an ethnic or racial group retains a language over time. *Language shift* refers to the change from the habitual use of one language to another. There are two types of shifts: ancestral and current (de Vries and Vallee, 1980). Ancestral shift occurs when the mother tongue of a person does not correspond to the person's ethnic origin, as in the case of an Ukrainian who learns English rather than the Ukrainian language as a mother tongue. Since the "loss" of the original mother tongue occurs some time in the past generations, it is called ancestral shift. In contrast, current shift occurs in the current generation. It refers to adopting a home language other than the mother tongue, as for example a person who has a French mother tongue but now speaks mainly English at home. In other words, the person has shifted, in the current generation, from speaking French as a mother tongue to English as a home language. Anglicization in language research refers to the extent to which a linguistic minority has adopted English as a mother tongue or a home language.

The data from the 1981 census indicate that there are more people speaking English as a home language than people whose mother tongue is English, thus indicating that anglicization is occurring. Other language groups have a varying tendency to shift to another home language. Although the French have a strong tendency to use French as a home language, language maintenance is strongest for French in Quebec and New Brunswick and weakest in the Prairies.

The ability of linguistic minorities to maintain their languages is affected by how large the minority is relative to the majority (Lieberson, 1970). In regions where the minority is small relative to the majority population, there is greater pressure for minority members to learn the language of the majority.

Language maintenance is sometimes seen as an aspect of ethnic identity, and language shift as an indication of assimilation. A number of factors influence whether a group will retain its mother tongue. Ethnic communities vary according to what Breton (1964) calls *institutional completeness*, or the extent to which an ethnic community can offer its members various services through their own separate institutions. The more institutionally complete an ethnic community is, the easier it is for members to maintain their language. Lieberson (1970) has suggested ethnic minorities that have a high degree of segregation have a greater chance of maintaining their languages. The degree of ethnic segregation or cohesion may be measured by in-group interaction, ethnic identification, endogamy or in-group marriage, ethnic language retention, ethnic neighbourhood residence and ethnic church affiliation (Reitz, 1980).

Multiculturalism

On October 8, 1971, Prime Minister Pierre Trudeau, in announcing to the Canadian Parliament the policy of multiculturalism, said:

> A policy of multiculturalism within a bilingual framework commends itself to the government as the most suitable means of assuring the cultural freedom of Canadians. Such a policy should help to break down discriminatory attitudes and cultural jealousies. . . . It can form the base of a society which is based on fair play for all. (House of Commons, *Debates*, October 8, 1971 : 8545)

Despite this intention, there is little indication that racial prejudice has been less prevalent or ethnic inequality less evident. The policy has failed to combat effectively racism and discriminatory practices, especially in the work force. The failure became evident in 1983 when the federal government had to appoint a Royal commission on equality in employment to deal with the problem of unequal opportunities for minority Canadians.

Roberts and Clifton (1982) argue that most ethnic groups in Canada do not have the resources to promote their cultural heritage, and the policy of multiculturalism simply reinforces the concept of symbolic ethnicity. Canada's multicultural policy may just provide the *appearance* of pluralism. As Li and Bolaria (1983 : 1) put it, "the irony of multiculturalism is that it furnishes Canadian society with a great hope without having to change the fundamental structures of society. Multiculturalism is the failure of an illusion, not of a policy."

With the entrenchment of the Canadian Constitution and the Charter of Rights and Freedoms, there should be a greater prospect for implementing the individual and collective rights of Canadians. However, Kallen (1982:230) suggests "individual human rights will take precedence over collective (ethnocultural) rights, except in the case of securing the linguistic and religious (cultural) rights of the English and French charter groups."

Racism and Inequality

The vertical mosaic thesis suggested that *structured inequality* is associated with ethnic and racial origin. Structured inequality refers to the institutional arrangements by which rewards and privileges are distributed and maintained. The idea of structured inequality is opposite to the notion of an open society in which everyone is believed to have the same chance of mobility. One aspect of structured inequality is institutional racism. *Racism* is an ideology of racial supremacy used to justify racial exploitation on the grounds that members of a subordinate group are inferior. Under institutional racism, racial inequality has become part of social institutions. For example, the Indians and Chinese were once legally disallowed to vote in Canada. Hence, they were excluded from participating in the political institutions of Canada. Wilson (1973:34) argues

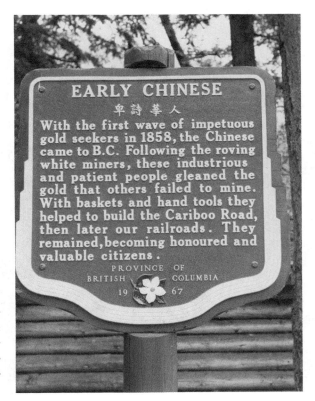

Early Chinese immigrants to Canada suffered from structured racism. They did not have access to the same jobs as non-visible minorities.

that institutional racism exists "when the ideology of racial exploitation gives rise to normative prescriptions designed to prevent the subordinate racial group from equal participation." This form of racism differs from individual racism, which may be manifested in various prejudiced dispositions.

There is substantial evidence to suggest that many racial minorities in Canada experience a double jeopardy in the labour market as a result of their recent immigrant status and racial origin. The 1981 census indicates that with the exception of those of Japanese origin, a high proportion of visible minorities in the labour force are foreign born (Abella, 1984). For example, 88.9 percent of black males and 91.5 percent of black females in the labour force were born outside of Canada. Over 90 percent of people of Indo-Pakistani, Indo-Chinese, Korean, Pacific Islands, and Central and South American origins in the labour force are foreign born. Many of them immigrated to Canada after the 1967 change in the Immigration Act. In a recent Royal commission report entitled *Equality in Employment*, Abella (1984) concludes that there is a definite occupational concentration of some racial origins in certain job categories. For example, Indo-Chinese males are largely employed in blue-collar and service occupations, and close to 50 percent of Indo-Pakistani women are in clerical and service jobs.

TABLE 9-3

Participation Rates and Unemployment Rates of Selected Ethnic Groups by Gender, 1981*

	Males		Females	
	Participation Rates	Unemployment Rates	Participation Rates	Unemployment Rates
British	77.8%	5.6%	51.4%	7.7%
French	76.2	9.7	47.9	12.4
Other European	80.9	3.9	54.0	5.9
Indo-Pakistani	85.7	4.5	60.3	10.0
Indo-Chinese	77.6	8.3	58.9	12.3
Japanese	82.4	3.1	58.6	5.0
Korean	82.2	4.9	63.7	6.6
Chinese	79.0	4.2	61.0	5.4
Pacific Islands, including Philippines	84.8	3.4	75.3	4.3
Black	83.0	7.3	65.2	9.5
Native People	60.7	16.5	36.7	17.3
Central/South American	86.2	6.9	57.9	7.1
Total Labour Force	78.2	6.5	51.8	8.7

*Single ethnic origin only.

REPORT OF THE ROYAL COMMISSION ON EQUALITY IN EMPLOYMENT, *1984, P. 82. THE ORIGINAL SOURCE IS FROM STATISTICS CANADA, UNPUBLISHED DATA FROM THE 1981 CENSUS. REPRODUCED BY PERMISSION OF THE MINISTER OF SUPPLY AND SERVICES CANADA.*

Native people have the highest unemployment rate (see Table 9-3). Other groups with high unemployment rates are French females (12.4 percent), Indo-Chinese females (12.3 percent) and Indo-Pakistani females (10 percent).

Table 9-4 shows the income levels of various ethnic and racial groups from the 1981 census. The income level of each group is expressed first as a gross deviation from the grand mean, or national average, and then as a net deviation controlling for sex, nativity, occupation, age, number of weeks worked and education. In other words, the net deviation measures the amount of income inequality associated with an origin when variations in other factors are controlled for. The table indicates that the lowest income groups are black, Chinese, Greek, "other" and French. That their low income positions do not change despite controlling for other factors suggests market discrimination on the basis of origin (Li, 1988b).

TABLE 9-4
Gross and Net Effect[1] of Racial and Ethnic Origin on Annual Income

	N	Gross Effect as Deviation from Grand Mean ($)	Net Effect, Controlling for Sex, Nativity, Occupation, Age, Number of Weeks Worked and Education ($)
Jewish	159 250	+ 6 261.6	+ 2 936.0
Scandinavian	176 650	+ 1 859.8	+ 1 034.6
Portuguese	104 200	− 2 001.9	+ 626.5
Croatian & Serbian	71 600	+ 458.6	+ 378.3
German	708 750	+ 652.4	+ 274.6
Ukrainian	325 350	+ 794.7	+ 212.7
Italian	443 100	− 509.4	+ 148.5
British	5 365 250	+ 355.8	+ 103.7
Dutch	251 800	+ 311.3	+ 76.6
Czech & Slovak	42 500	+ 2 136.9	+ 62.9
Hungarian	71 750	+ 1 901.6	+ 20.4
Polish	161 500	+ 720.8	− 222.7
French	3 333 800	− 501.1	− 240.3
Other[2]	1 610 400	− 1 113.3	− 277.9
Greek	83 750	− 1 893.9	− 796.3
Chinese	168 100	− 1 294.6	− 931.1
Black[3]	85 900	− 1 588.0	− 1 679.5
Canada (all groups)	13 163 650	14 044.9	14 044.9

[1]Gross and net effects are measured as deviations from the grand mean income, using Multiple Classification Analysis (Andrews et al., 1976).
[2]Includes other single responses and multiple responses of ethnic origin.
[3]Includes African, Caribbean, Haitian and other Black.

COMPILED FROM 1981 CENSUS OF CANADA PUBLIC USE SAMPLE TAPE, INDIVIDUAL FILE. CALCULATIONS WERE BASED ON THOSE FIFTEEN YEARS OF AGE AND OVER, WHO WERE EMPLOYED IN THE CANADIAN LABOUR FORCE, EXCLUDING INMATES.

In addition to structured inequality, racial minorities also suffer from racial prejudices and stereotypes held by the Canadian public. Berry, Kalin and Taylor (1977) show that, in ranking twenty-six ethnic groups, respondents from a national survey indicate a clear preference for some ethnic groups over others. The English and the French are favoured most. Other North European groups appear near the top of the hierarchy, while all the non-white groups, except the Japanese, appear near the bottom.

Summary

Canada is a multi-ethnic society. Its members show tremendous diversity in ethnic and racial origins as well as differences in the languages they speak. In studying race and ethnic relations, sociologists are interested to know how relationships among ethnic groups are structured, and how they influence the way societies are organized.

Much can be learned from the history of Canada about how the Canadian mosaic was formed. The conflicts between the French and the British can be traced to the eighteenth century when the British established their political and, later, economic control in New France. Likewise, the low social status of the native people can be attributed to a historical policy that was aimed at colonizing and controlling the native population. Recently, the Canadian mosaic has undergone major changes as a result of increased immigration to Canada after the Second World War.

There are two ways to define race and ethnicity: as cultural groups, and as conflict groups. The first definition leads to questions of assimilation and pluralism, whereas the second is mainly concerned with domination and subordination. Many views of assimilation and pluralism have been developed by sociologists, including the melting-pot thesis, anglo-conformity and cultural and structural pluralism. The assimilation models have been criticized for their mechanical and evolutionary overtone, and pluralism for unduly focusing on the transplanted culture. From the vantage of the approach that emphasizes unequal relationships, race is not based on hereditary or physical traits. Superficial physical traits, such as skin colour, are only seen as meaningful by sociologists when social meanings are being attached to those traits. The relationship between a dominant group and a subordinate group is developed in the colonial model and the split labour market model. Both models relate racial and ethnic relations to the process of production.

In *The Vertical Mosaic*, John Porter makes several points about the relationship between social class and ethnic origin in Canada: (1) the charter group retains many privileges and lays down the rules under which other immigrant groups are to be admitted; (2) within the charter groups, the British are doing much better than the French; (3) the British have the overwhelming control in the Canadian economic elite; and (4) there is a close relationship between ethnic origin and occupation.

There are other features in the Canadian mosaic that reflect structured inequality. Despite the Official Languages Act of 1969, Canadians show a trend toward anglicization, and French language maintenance is weak outside Quebec and New Brunswick.

Evidence suggests that visible minorities, mostly recent immigrants, encounter a double jeopardy in the labour market because of their immigrant status and racial origin as far as job opportunity is concerned. Despite the multicultural policy and its stated goals to accomplish greater equality, the available data indicate that opportunities in the labour market are affected by racial and ethnic affiliations.

Suggested Readings

Abella, Rosalie S.
1984. *Report of the Commission on Equality in Employment*. Ottawa: Minister of Supply and Services Canada. This is a Royal commission report about employment inequity in Canada as encountered by various minority groups. The report provides many useful data regarding racial minorities.

Bolaria, B. Singh, and Peter S. Li
1988. *Racial Oppression in Canada*, 2nd ed. Toronto: Garamond Press. This book challenges the myths associated with race and racism and provides a theory to explain how social groups become racialized. The book contains case studies of various racial groups in Canada: the native people, Chinese, Japanese, East Indians, blacks, etc.

de Vries, John, and Frank G. Vallee
1980. *Language Use in Canada*. Ottawa: Statistics Canada, Catalogue 99-762E. This is an analysis of the language behaviours in Canada using the 1971 census as a data base. There are numerous tables and statistics in the book concerning bilingualism and language maintenance. It also has an excellent discussion of past research on language in Canada.

Milner, Sheilagh H., and Henry Milner
1977. *The Decolonization of Quebec*. Toronto: McClelland and Stewart. This book provides an excellent analysis of Quebec society. It uses the colonial model to show how Quebec society has been under the control of the American metropolis, and how the events in recent decades have brought about a greater level of national consciousness among French Canadians.

Patterson, E. Palmer
1972. *The Canadian Indian*. Toronto: Collier Macmillan. This is one of the best accounts of the history of the native people in Canada from 1500 to the present. The relationship between the natives and Europeans is summarized under four historical phases. The book provides sound historical facts and succinct sociological analysis for each of the periods covered.

Porter, John
1965. *The Vertical Mosaic*. Toronto: University of Toronto Press. This is an important study that analyses the relationship between ethnicity and class in Canada. The major findings of the book greatly influence subsequent research in Canada in the area of ethnic relations.

Discussion Questions

1. Why is it meaningful to consider the dominant/subordinate group relationship, and not just physical traits, as defining characteristics of race and ethnicity?

2. What are the similarities and differences of the following models: melting-pot, cultural pluralism and anglo-conformity?

3. Is the colonial model applicable to the native people in Canada?

4. Why are some ethnic groups better able to maintain their language than others?

5. What are the basic arguments of the vertical mosaic thesis?

6. To what extent does institutional racism impede the achievements of visible minorities in Canada? How successful has multiculturalism been in combating racism?

Data Collection Exercises

1. Use the published data from the 1981 census to show which ethnic group in Canada is most likely to be officially bilingual.

2. Compare the native and non-native population in terms of educational level, unemployment rate, life expectancy and health conditions. What explanations can you provide to account for the differences?

3. Use data from the 1971 and 1981 censuses to assess whether Canadians of French origin are doing just as well as those of British origin.

4. Use the annual statistics provided by the Department of Employment and Immigration to construct a table showing the occupational level and country of origin of immigrants coming into Canada for the past five years.

Writing Exercises

1. How has the ethnic composition of your home province changed in the past thirty years? What are the factors that account for this change?

2. Develop an argument to show what would happen to Canada if it did not allow immigrants or refugees to enter the country for the next ten years.

3. As Canada is becoming more and more of an advanced industrial society, do you think that ethnicity and race will become less and less relevant to Canadian society? What are the bases of your prediction?

4. Why do you think French Canadians are more likely to be bilingual than English Canadians?

Glossary

Assimilation: *the process whereby people of diverse origins conform to a single or amalgamated culture.*

Colonial model: *describes how race and ethnic relations evolve under colonialism.*

Ethnicity/ethnic group: *there are at least two perspectives. The first treats ethnicity as a common feature of people, usually based on the same heritage, language and religion, which gives them the sense of being distinct. The second perspective sees ethnicity or ethnic grouping resulting from certain cultural traits being socially selected as bases to differentiate people.*

Ethnocentric: *the belief that one's own race or ethnic group is the centre of all cultures.*

Genotype/genetic grouping: *biological groupings based on the genetic constitutions, as opposed to the physical appearances, of people.*

Identity: *a feeling of attachment to a group based, presumably, on common individual characteristics.*

Indigenous people: *the native people or original people of a country.*

Institutional completeness: *the extent to which an ethnic community can offer its members various services through their own separate institutions.*

Language maintenance: *the retention by an ethnic or racial group of a language over time.*

Language shift: *refers to the change from the habitual use of one language to another.*

Mother tongue: *the language a person learns in childhood and is still able to speak in adulthood.*

Multi-ethnic society: *a society composed of peoples from a variety of ethnic and racial origins.*

Pluralism: *refers to the co-existence of many cultures. In a pluralistic society, ethnic groups may share some aspects of a common culture and participate collectively in its economic and political life, while retaining unique cultural aspects in their social networks, residential areas, churches and languages.*

Race: *there are at least two perspectives. The first sees race as a group of people bounded by a common heritage and origin. The second perspective uses race to mean a category of people that has been socially defined in a given society on the basis of superficial physical traits, such as skin colour.*

Racism: *an ideology of racial supremacy used to justify racial exploitation on the grounds that members of a subordinate group are inferior.*

Split labour market model: *explains that racial conflicts are based on differences in the cost of labour between two groups: white and non-white.*

Structured inequality: *refers to the institutional arrangements by which rewards and privileges are distributed and maintained.*

Vertical mosaic: *A term adopted by Canadian sociologists to describe the intimate relationship between ethnic origin and occupational differentiation in Canada.*

References

Abella, Rosalie S.
   1984. *Report of the Royal Commission on Equality in Employment.* Ottawa: Minister of Supply and Services Canada.

Beattie, Christopher
   1975. *Minority Men in a Majority Setting.* Toronto: McClelland and Stewart.

Berry, John W., Rudolf Kalin and Donald M. Taylor

1977. *Multiculturalism and Ethnic Attitudes in Canada*. Ottawa: Minister of Supply and Services Canada.

Bolaria, B. Singh, and Peter S. Li

1988. *Racial Oppression in Canada*, 2nd ed. Toronto: Garamond Press.

Bonacich, Edna

1976. "Advanced Capitalism and Black/White Race Relations in the United States: A Split Labor Market Interpretation." *American Sociological Review* 41 : 34–51.

1979. "The Past, Present, and Future of Split Labor Market Theory," pp. 17–64. In C. B. Marrett and C. Leggon, eds., *Research in Race and Ethnic Relations*, vol. 1. Greenwich, Conn.: JAI Press.

Breton, Raymond

1964. "Institutional Completeness of Ethnic Communities and Personal Relations to Immigrants." *American Journal of Sociology* 70: 193–205.

Clement, Wallace

1975. *The Canadian Corporate Elite*. Toronto: McClelland and Stewart.

Darroch, Gordon A.

1979. "Another Look at Ethnicity, Stratification and Social Mobility in Canada." *Canadian Journal of Sociology* 4 : 1–25.

de Vries, John, and Frank G. Vallee

1980. *Language Use in Canada*. 1971 Census of Canada, Catalogue 99–762E. Ottawa: Statistics Canada.

Frideres, James S.

1983. *Native People in Canada: Contemporary Conflicts*, 2nd ed. Scarborough, Ont.: Prentice-Hall.

1988. "Institutional Structures and Economic Deprivation: Native People in Canada," pp. 71–100. In B. Singh Bolaria and Peter S. Li, eds., *Racial Oppression in Canada*, 2nd ed. Toronto: Garamond Press.

Gans, Herbert

1979. "Symbolic Ethnicity: The Future of Ethnic Groups and Cultures in America." *Ethnic and Racial Studies* 2 : 1–20.

Glazer, Nathan, and Daniel P. Moynihan

1970. *Beyond the Melting Pot*. Cambridge, Mass.: MIT Press.

Gordon, Milton M.

1964. *Assimilation in American Life*. New York: Oxford University Press.

Guindon, Hubert

1978. "The Modernization of Quebec and the Legitimacy of the Canadian State." *Canadian Review of Sociology and Anthropology* 15 : 227–45.

Hawkins, Freda

1972. *Canada and Immigration: Public Policy and Public Concern*. Montreal: McGill-Queen's University Press.

Hughes, E. C.

1943. *French Canada in Transition*. Chicago: University of Chicago Press.

Jackson, John D.
1977. "The Functions of Language in Canada: On the Political Economy of Language," pp. 59–76. In W. H. Coons, D. M. Taylor and M. Tremblay, eds., *The Individual, Language and Society in Canada*. The Canada Council.

Jones, Frank E., and Wallace E. Lambert
1965. "Occupational Rank and Attitudes Towards Immigrants." *Public Opinion Quarterly* 29:137–44.

Kallen, Evelyn
1982. *Ethnicity and Human Rights in Canada*. Toronto: Gage.

Lautard, Hugh E., and Donald J. Loree
1984. "Ethnic Stratification in Canada, 1931–1971." *Canadian Journal of Sociology* 9(3):333–43.

Li, Peter S.
1988a. *The Chinese in Canada*. Toronto: Oxford University Press.
1988b. *Ethnic Inequality in a Class Society*. Toronto: Wall and Thompson.

Li, Peter S., and B. Singh Bolaria
1979. "Canadian Immigration Policy and Assimilation Theories," pp. 411–22. In J. A. Fry, ed., *Economy, Class and Social Reality*. Scarborough, Ont.: Butterworths.
1983. *Racial Minorities in Multicultural Canada*. Toronto: Garamond Press.

Lieberson, Stanley
1970. *Language and Ethnic Relations in Canada*. New York: John Wiley.

Makabe, Tomoko
1981. "The Theory of the Split Labor Market: A Comparison of the Japanese Experience in Brazil and Canada." *Social Forces* 59:786–809.

Manpower and Immigration Canada
1974. *The Immigration Program*. Ottawa: Information Canada.

Miles, Robert
1982. *Racism and Migrant Labour*. London: Routledge and Kegan Paul.

Milner, Henry
1978. *Politics in the New Quebec*. Toronto: McClelland and Stewart.

Parai, L.
1965. *Immigration and Emigration of Professional and Skilled Manpower During the Post-War Period*. Ottawa: Queen's Printer.

Park, Robert E.
1950. *Race and Culture*. Glencoe, Ill.: Free Press.

Patterson, E. Palmer
1972. *The Canadian Indian: A History since 1500*. Don Mills, Ont.: Collier Macmillan.

Porter, John
1965. *The Vertical Mosaic*. Toronto: University of Toronto Press.

Portes, Alejandro, and John Walton
1981. *Labor, Class, and the International System*. New York: Academic Press.

Reitz, Jeffrey G.
1980. *The Survival of Ethnic Groups*. Toronto: McGraw-Hill Ryerson.

Rex, John
>   1983. *Race Relations in Sociological Theory*, 2nd ed. London: Routledge and Kegan Paul.

Roberts, Lance W., and Rodney A. Clifton
>   1982. "Exploring the Ideology of Canadian Multiculturalism." *Canadian Public Policy* 8:88–94.

Steinberg, Stephen
>   1981. *The Ethnic Myth: Race, Ethnicity, and Class in America*. Boston: Beacon Press.

Tienhaara, Nancy
>   1974. *Canadian Views on Immigration and Population: An Analysis of Post-War Gallup Polls*. Canada: Manpower and Immigration.

Ujimoto, K. V., and Gordon K. Hirabayashi
>   1980. *Visible Minorities and Multiculturalism: Asians in Canada*. Toronto: Butterworths.

Valentine, Charles A.
>   1968. *Culture and Poverty*. Chicago: University of Chicago Press.

Ward, Robin, and Richard Jenkins, eds.
>   1984. *Ethnic Communities in Business*. Cambridge: Cambridge University Press.

Weber, Max
>   1968. *Economy and Society*. New York: Bedminster Press.

Wilson, Willam J.
>   1973. *Power, Racism, and Privilege*. New York: Free Press.

Yancey, William L., E. P. Ericksen and R. N. Juliani
>   1976. "Emergent Ethnicity: A Review and Reformation." *American Sociological Review* 41:391–403.

CHAPTER 10

Gender Relations

PAT ARMSTRONG

JUDITH CRAWLEY.

Introduction

Is it a boy or a girl? This is the first question asked of new parents. The answer is critical because sex assigned at birth has profound implications for an individual's choices and possibilities throughout life.

All known cultures have distinguished between females and males. And in all cultures these distinctions have provided the basis for divisions not only in labour, but also in all kinds of other activities. But the nature of the divisions and the kinds of distinctions that are made vary enormously throughout time and across cultures. They vary because sex distinctions exist within a social environment. They are more a result of social relations and social structures than they are of biologically created differences.

This chapter examines the distinctions that are made between the sexes and the relations among men and women in Canadian society. It begins by examining what we know about biological differences and about the implications of these differences for behaviour and relationships. It then turns to the evidence on sex-specific patterns in behaviour, education and occupations, evaluating alternative explanations for the patterns that have been established. Finally, it outlines some of the strategies that have been developed to alter the patterns and reshape the relations between females and males in our country.

The Relevance of Biology

On a program about sex differences produced for the television series "Man Alive," a young child explained that you could tell the girls from the boys because girls had long hair and boys had short hair. Questioned further, she added that girls and boys had different bottoms. Asked what girls do when they grow up, she said they become mothers. Daddies, on the other hand, work. Pushed to consider whether mommies ever work, the girl replied, "Yes, sometimes they can become the gentleman's secretary." In one short clip, she nicely summed up the kinds of distinctions we often make between females and males in our society. Yet, while the young girl's responses tell us something about popular conceptions, they do not indicate very much about what are often referred to as the "real" differences between the sexes.

For many sociologists, there are clear lines to be drawn between distinctions that are biologically determined and those that are socially learned; between nature and nurture. As Marlene Mackie explains in the introduction to her book *Exploring Gender Relations*: "Sex is the biological dichotomy between females and males. It is determined at conception and is, for the most part, unalterable. Gender, on the other hand, is what is socially recognized as femininity and masculinity" (1983 : 1). By differentiating between sex and gender, sociologists have emphasized the social construction of differences between the sexes. Indeed, gender has become so popular as a non-sexist way of identifying difference that it is often used as the only term.

There are problems, however, with these two terms. First, they imply that biological factors can be separated from social factors and that biological differences have been

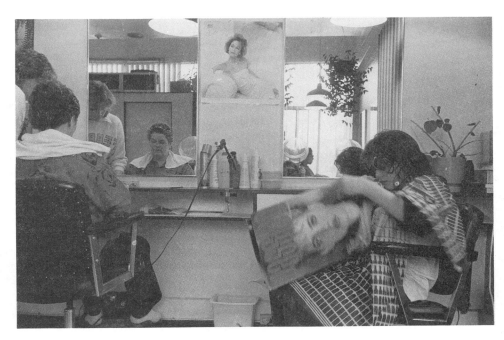

The female gender is what is socially recognized as feminine.

JUDITH CRAWLEY.

firmly established. Second, they imply that biology is unchanging, a category outside human history and influence. Third, the exclusive use of gender suggests that biology is irrelevant to an understanding of distinctions between males and females. The rest of this section will examine each of these problems, explaining why it is not always easy to differentiate between sex and gender, biology and learning.

Separating the Boys from the Girls

Throughout history, there have been debates about the biological differences between the sexes. In spite of extensive research, these debates continue today. Most of us would agree that the hair length used by the little girl on "Man Alive" is a socially created distinction. Fewer would reach a consensus about which aspects of motherhood have biological links. Some would argue that women are naturally secretaries, just as they would claim that men are naturally bosses. And while most would agree with this child that girls and boys have different bottoms, this criterion alone will not divide all people into two clearly distinct sex categories. Indeed, the Olympic Committee considers this criterion so unreliable that they reject it as the basis for determining who shall compete in the women's games.

Science provides us with few definitive answers to this debate. There is little consensus in the vast research done on biological sex differences. The lack of consensus reflects both the problems encountered in conducting the research and the more fundamental problem inherent in the assumption that nature and nurture can be isolated from each other.

Research on biological differences is difficult because children begin learning at birth, if not before. Therefore, we cannot be entirely sure that even the behaviour of the newborn is innate. There are also severe restrictions placed on the kind and amount of experimentation permitted on humans, whatever their age. Moreover, infants have a very limited repertoire that can be studied. As they expand their activities, they also increase their opportunities to learn, and that learning modifies whatever characteristics they may have at birth. In addition, the older the subjects, the more likely they are to respond in ways they think they should or in ways they think the researchers expect them to behave. Perhaps most important, the researchers themselves cannot escape their own learning, and this learning helps structure how they do research as well as how they interpret results and what they accept as evidence (Jacklin, 1981; Messing, 1987).

Research on biological differences in other species also presents problems. Although there are fewer restrictions placed on this research, animals, rodents and even birds also learn. There is enormous variety in behaviour from one species to another, and it is extremely difficult to determine which traits are most likely to be those inherited by humans in a predetermined form. Here, too, researchers' values come into play, often guiding them to select behaviour that best supports their hypotheses. While there are many things we can learn from the study of other species, we cannot be confident that anything innate in another species will also be inherited by humans; humans are, after all, qualitatively different from other species.

An analysis of the difficulties encountered by researchers who try to separate nature from nurture has led many to argue that an answer can never be found because the wrong question is being asked. It is impossible to discover which aspects of our behaviour are biologically determined because "an individual's capacities emerge from a web of interactions between the biological being and the social environment. . . . Biology may in some manner condition behaviour, but behaviour in turn can alter one's physiology. Furthermore, any particular behaviour may have many different causes" (Fausto-Sterling, 1985 : 8). People cannot exist outside a social environment, and what are often called biological processes are influenced by that environment. Jogging or stress may delay a menstrual cycle and tight jeans or a radio carried too frequently below the waist may reduce sperm counts. The more often women run in marathons, the closer they come to matching the speeds of men. The more often men spend their days sitting in office chairs, the less musclebound they become.

To argue that nature cannot easily be separated from nurture is not, however, to argue that there are no biological components to people's behaviour or to argue that there are no sex differences that can be related to biological factors. Rather, it is to argue that biological components have no predetermined meaning or value and that biological components are not unchangeable.

The Sexes: What's the Difference?

Researchers do agree on some biological differences. While both sexes have twenty-two pairs of chromosomes that are not differentiated by sex, the additional pair in normal females is made up of two x chromosomes. Normal men have one x and one y in their twenty-third pair. The y chromosome must be present if the embryonic sex glands are to develop in a male direction. And hormones must be present for either males or females to reach sexual maturity. While estrogens are often called female hormones and androgens are frequently referred to as male hormones, both "sexes secrete both types of hormone; what differs is the ratio of estrogen to androgen in the two sexes" (Rose, Kamin and Lewontin, 1984:151). These chromosomes and hormones are responsible for the different reproductive capacities of women and men. Women gestate, menstruate and lactate. Men produce semen and impregnate.

This, though, is where agreement ends. Debates continue over the implications of these differences in chromosomes, hormonal ratios and reproductive capacities for male and female behaviour and possibilities.

Genetic Determinism   Those convinced that biology determines a wide range of behaviour believe that the lonely y chromosome in men has a very powerful impact. At different times, those working from this perspective have argued that the genetic makeup of men makes them more intelligent than women, superior in visual-spacial abilities and mathematical skills, more aggressive and dominant. Such theorists have also argued that women's double x chromosome creates a maternal instinct and makes females more intuitive, tricky, nurturing and moral than men. According to these theorists, the hierarchical structure of society and the sexual division of labour are the natural and inevitable result of biological differences.

Such theorists also believe that what is often called the double standard in sexual practices has biological roots—that the different sexual patterns attributed to men and women have biological origins. These theorists have claimed that men have a natural sexuality. This sexuality results, David Barash explained in *Psychology Today*, from the "biologically based need to inject their sperm into as many women as possible" (in Messing, 1987:112). This perspective has led some to conclude that rape and violence against women is the result of male physiology. The men cannot help themselves any more than women can stop being nurturant and deceitful. According to these theorists, the child on "Man Alive" was merely describing a natural phenomenon: women are destined to be mothers and secretaries. And in both jobs, they should expect to be dominated and sexually harassed.

Study after study has challenged each of these notions (for summaries, see Fausto-Sterling, 1985; Mackie; 1983, Richardson, 1988). Research on sex differences in other countries reveals an astounding variety in gender relations that seem to deny that gender differences are determined by genetics. In Caribbean countries, for example, at least a third of the households are headed by women, and women provide most of the regular household income (Redclift, 1988:435). In Senegal, there is a rigid division of labour by sex for non-agricultural tasks, but not for agricultural tasks (Mackintosh, 1988). And in New Guinea societies, as Mead's (1935) classic study indicated, there are considerable differences among the three societies she studied in terms of what are considered to be typical male or female traits. Both sexes in Arapesh society are characterized as mild and responsive, while in the Mundugamor society both sexes are considered aggressive and volatile. Tchamuli men, on the other hand, are expected to be dependent and nurturant; Tchamuli women competent and detached.

While most of the research and writing on changing relations between the sexes has focused on women, in recent years there has been a flurry of publications that look at emerging patterns for men. Analysis of advertising offers just one example of this trend. In her examination of the representation of males in advertising, Judith Posner (1987) found that the new male is smaller, has a less pronounced jaw and is more likely to smile. He is also more likely to be found undressing or partially dressed, and he appears more vulnerable. Yet, Posner (1987 : 188) concludes that this does not reflect a move toward equality, but rather demonstrates "the increas-ing commercialization of sexuality" for both men and women. In his analysis of advertising, Andrew Wernick (1987 : 279) argues that as women have moved into the labour force, men have become more involved in private consumption. This move has been reflected in "a steady drive to incorporate male clothing into fashion, and mounting efforts to sell men all manner of personal-care products, from toothpaste and bath oil to hair dye and makeup." He suggests that men are being subjected to the same kind of "intense consumerization as women and are no longer defined as breadwinners."

Within our own society, there are considerable differences in gender behaviour evident when we look back over history. Mitchell (1981 : 48) examined Prairie house-holds at the turn of the century and concluded that "there is no question at all of inequality, the partners have several departments, equally important, and the husband is the first to admit how much he owes his wife, and to own that the burden falls on her heaviest." But she maintained that city life created inequalities among women and made them subordinate in ways we see today.

Research has not revealed any simple dichotomy between the sexes or any direct link between genes and the behaviour patterns attributed by many theorists to each sex. Research has not demonstrated "that a genetically based human nature or genetically based sex differences exist" (Lowe, 1983 : 13). The variability in patterns across cultures, the small differences between sexes in any particular culture and the variations in patterns within sexes all deny any simple genetic determinism.

Hormones   Instead of attributing sex differences to genes, other researchers have looked to hormones as causal agents in what are seen to be predetermined differences between females and males (Dalton, 1983; Goldberg, 1977). From this approach have come arguments that different levels of hormones have an impact on the brain, which in turn results in higher intelligence in males, more ambition and drive, more aggressive behaviour and different sexual patterns. The impact on women is seen to be much more negative. Menstruation and menopause are thought to incapacitate women, making them unsuitable for many kinds of work.

But here, too, research has provided very little support for these theories. Although hormones might influence a rodent brain in ways that encourage mating behaviour, in non-human primates the injection of hormones does not create the same results (Lowe, 1983 : 14). "The evidence that male hormones control aggression in humans and other primates ranges from weak to non-existent" (Fausto-Sterling, 1985 : 45). A survey of current studies concludes that "there is no known causal relationship between sex hormone levels and other traits, such as intelligence, intuition, and creativity" (Richardson, 1988 : 149).

Reproduction as a Determinant of Behaviour

Some feminist theorists have looked to reproductive capacities, rather than to genes or hormones, for explanations of differences between the sexes. Canadian Mary O'Brien (1981 : 59), for example, argues that the very different parts women and men play in reproduction lead to different forms of consciousness and to men's efforts to control women. "Women's reproductive consciousness is a consciousness that the child is hers, but also a consciousness that she herself was born of a woman's labour, that labour confirms genetic coherence and species continuity. Male reproductive consciousness is splintered and discontinuous, and cannot be mediated within reproductive process." Men experience reproduction mainly as alienation of their male seed, and this, it is argued, motivates them to seek control over both mother and child.

This kind of theoretical argument is much more difficult to examine through scientific research than are those that attribute sex differences to genes or hormones. What is clear is that, as is the case with genetic and hormonal influences, the impact of reproductive capacities cannot be understood outside of their time and place.

How women experience childbirth is related to the technology and medical care that is available, to nutrition and to social support. These factors can transform not only how women feel about giving birth and how the birth is evaluated, but also the very biology of the birth process itself. Women's reproductive capacities mean that, without contraceptives, the consequences of sexual intercourse are different for women and for men (Armstrong and Armstrong, 1983a; Hamilton, 1978). Moreover, they are different today than they were in our grandmother's time not only because women have a better chance of avoiding giving birth, but also because they have a better chance of surviving giving birth. The development of better methods for birth control has made the implications of sexual intercourse more similar for both sexes and has contributed to changes in the double standard and in sexual practices. These many social changes have had a profound impact on the way our bodies work and the meaning that is attached to what we often call biological processes.

Biology and Social Environment

Recently, the identification of AIDS and its methods of transmission have altered sexual practices for men, making them more vulnerable to long-term consequences from their sexual activities. Moreover, the syndrome can only be controlled, at this time, by changes in social relationships and social practices, not through biological means. AIDS thus provides a timely example of the complex interrelationship between biology and social environment.

In the end, we are left to conclude that biology cannot be separated from the social environment that influences both its meaning and its structure. Biology is not an independent variable. Moreover, females and males do not constitute opposite sexes.

They share both genes and hormones. They differ mainly in terms of reproductive capacities, and the significance of these differences is primarily socially rather than biologically structured. This does not mean that biology is irrelevant. It does mean, however, that difference cannot be attributed to biology alone.

Growing Up Feminine or Masculine

When parents answer the question about the sex of their child, they trigger a range of social responses that have very little to do with genes, hormones or reproductive capacities. Gender distinctions are a central part of the content and structure of child-rearing practices in the home. They are just as integral to the content and structure of the formal education system and the mass media. They are reinforced by the dominant ideology that is reproduced in all these places. This is not to suggest that children and adults are merely passive recipients or transmitters of ideas and practices. Through interaction with their social and physical world, people alter these worlds and their ideas about them. But child-rearing practices, educational systems and dominant ideologies have a powerful influence on the pace and nature of change, as well as on the distinctions made between males and females.

Influences at Home

Once the child's sex has been identified, we know what toys to bring, what clothes to buy, what colour to paint the baby's room, what stories to read, what games to play, how rough we can be, how much we should talk to the newborn and what kind of name the child will have (see Greenglass, 1982: chs. 3 and 4; Mackie, 1987). But important changes are taking place. Unisex clothes, toys and hair styles have become popular, and many parents are attempting to raise their children in what is often termed a non-sexist manner, trying to treat boys and girls in the same ways.

However, most boys still do not wear dresses and most girls do not get footballs or guns. Boys are more likely to have computers and to be shown how to operate them so they can play their adventure games. Parents tend to spend more time interacting with little girls, while they not only leave boys alone more, but also punish them more often. Girls are more closely supervised, especially when they reach adolescence. Boys are still more likely to be taught physical and rough games such as hockey, and girls to be taught how to play house and dress Barbie in negligees (Richer, 1984). When tasks are assigned in the house, boys are more likely to be told to take out the garbage and shovel the walk; girls to clean the toilet and wash the floor, even if more boys are helping with the dishes and operating the microwave.

These child-rearing practices help shape the behaviour, the physiology and perceptions of both sexes. Girls and boys learn different skills and grow in different ways. Playing with computers and construction equipment encourages males to develop their visual-spatial and mathematical skills. Playing hockey encourages boys to be aggressive and dominant. Shovelling snow and lugging garbage develops strength and helps muscle growth. At the same time, playing with Barbie dolls encourages verbal and relational skills in girls. Dresses discourage a range of physical activities, and washing toilets contributes little to muscle growth. Close supervision limits adventure and encourages passivity or trickery.

These different experiences also lead children to view themselves and the other sex in particular ways. Research undertaken for the Royal Commission on the Status of Women (Lambert, 1971:69) found that children "were more certain about the meaning of masculinity and femininity when they thought in terms of potential jobs or relations than when they thought in terms of personality dispositions." What they experience in terms of jobs is a division by sex in which the tasks assigned to females have less value, are less interesting and have less potential than those done by men. What they experience in terms of relations is that males have more freedom, more choices and more power than females.

These divisions and relations between men and women are most evident in the structure of child care. Even though a majority of women now work in the labour force and even though men are more involved with their children, women still bear the primary responsibility for child care (Bassett, 1985; Michelson, 1985; Luxton, 1983). Some theorists (see, for example, Chodorow, 1978) have argued that being raised predominantly by women has profound implications for the psyche of females and males. Women, as child-rearers, can continue to identify with their mothers and can feel comfortable with intimate or nurturant relations. Males, on the other hand, can

Little girls learn who performs child care tasks at home.

JUDITH CRAWLEY.

only find identity by separating themselves from the caregiver. This painful separation, some theorists (Chodorow, 1978) claim, helps create the urge to dominate women and to repress intimate or nurturant behaviour.

Bonnie Fox (1988 : 173) has argued that this approach oversimplifies the complex process involved in the development of the unconscious and the complex relationship between conscious and unconscious thought or behaviour. Nevertheless, the theory does emphasize how important the division of labour is to the reproduction of sex distinctions in children. It also suggests how profound the implications are for the perceptions of males and females throughout their lives.

Schools and the Media

Even if parents try to raise their children in a non-sexist social environment, once children enter the school system or come in contact with the media, they are exposed to sex distinctions and relations in which women are subordinate. On the basis of research she did in Canadian classrooms, Susan Russell (1986 : 343) concludes that school personnel encourage girls "to believe that their exclusive role is or ought to be childbearing and rearing, and that work that they take on in the labour force is secondary to their role in the family. School personnel exert these pressures through job counselling and through undermining the academic ability of girls while focusing on their domestic futures."

These practices are reflected in, and reinforced by, the content of books, video games, music and television programs. Women are much less likely than men to be portrayed as the initiators of adventures or as the rescuers in the action. Women are more likely to be evaluated primarily in terms of their youth, beauty and ability to attract men, while men are more likely to be evaluated in terms of their skills, courage and ability to capture women (Robinson and Salamon, 1987 : 126–27). In many television programs and in music, women are preoccupied with being attractive to men, even when the women are elderly.

The place of women in the school system influences the young. Most principals are men. While most elementary school teachers are women, the higher the level of the education system, the greater the number of male teachers. Until relatively recently, some university programs had a quota on the number of female students that would be admitted, and many other, less visible barriers remain. Women's proper place is evident.

Schools also reinforce the idea that women are subordinate. The school system structures classes in ways that encourage girls to focus on a domestic future, while it structures sports in ways that encourage boys to be dominant. As former Olympic runner Bruce Kidd (1987 : 255) makes clear: "By giving males exciting opportunities, preaching that the qualities they learn from them are 'masculine,' and preventing girls and women from learning in the same situations, sports confirm the prejudice that males are a breed apart. By encouraging us to spend our most creative and engrossing moments as children and our favorite forms of recreation as adults in the company of other males, they condition us to trust each other more than women."

Various women's groups have exposed and attacked these practices. They have had some success in altering them. More women are principals and more men teach in elementary school, although this latter trend is probably more a reflection of higher wages and scarce employment than it is of feminist action. More girls take shop and more boys take home economics. The content of some textbooks and of some television programs has changed. Women are much more likely to be portrayed as employed outside the home, a change that also reflects a new reality. Quotas on female enrolments have been removed and women have rushed to take places in faculties of law and medicine. Indeed, in some institutions women constitute the majority of those enrolled in these traditionally male programs. Career counselling texts talk about non-traditional work for women, and special courses are offered to counsellors to introduce them to new alternatives for women.

Despite some encouraging changes, many of the old practices remain. In colleges and universities, women remain concentrated in health, education and the social sciences, while the number of women in the technologies has not increased significantly (Statistics Canada, 1985). In textbooks, men are still portrayed as more powerful than women. That portrayal reflects the reality of the social system.

Ideology   The practices of the school, the home or the media cannot avoid being influenced by the dominant system of ideas, or ideology. Nor can males and females avoid this influence in their everyday lives. However, ideology is not static. It is constantly being transformed as experiences and interests change. Ideas that do not coincide with people's experiences or that make little sense do not last.

As feminist sociologist Dorothy Smith (1975 : 353) made clear in her classic article on ideology, women "have historically and in the present been excluded from the production of forms of thought, images, and symbols in which their experience and social relations are expressed and ordered." Women, she goes on to argue, "have never controlled the material or social means to the making of a tradition among themselves or to acting as equals in the ongoing discourse of intellectuals."

While many would argue that women have developed some specifically female ideologies, few would challenge the notion that men have been in a far better position than women to express their views of the world and how they should prevail. This is the case even in the home, the woman's sphere, because it is men who have most often provided the primary financial support. Men's views of women and men's place are more likely to be dominant. Moreover, that view is likely to hold that men should be dominant, reflecting their current position in the home, the school and the media. Nevertheless, although women do not control what Smith (1975 : 355) calls "the means of mental production," they do develop their own ways of viewing the world, ideas that grow out of their everyday experience. As women gain more power in the market and the media, these views are becoming more visible. Older ideas that place women solely in the home no longer make sense of women's experience.

The dominant ideology, child-rearing practices, the division of labour by sex for adults and children, the education system and the media all help shape those small infants born with different bottoms into feminine and masculine adults. They help create female secretaries and male bosses; mommies and daddies. At the same time, as children and adults, both sexes are in turn altering these practices and ideas as their daily experiences and the structure of their lives change.

The Division of Labour by Sex

Sex distinctions are also obvious in the workplace. For the most part, males and females do different work, in different places, for different wages. This work not only creates both limits and possibilities; it also helps shape each sex's ideas about itself. This work is in turn shaped by the ideas people bring with them to the job, as well as by their responsibilities outside paid work and by employers' demands.

Paid Work

As is the case with clothes and with hair styles, women's and men's paid work has become increasingly similar in recent years. More and more women have been moving into the labour force, and the gap between male and female participation rates has been narrowing.

In 1976, 45.2 percent of the women and 77.6 percent of the men were counted as part of the labour force (Statistics Canada, 1985: Table 11). Just ten years later, the official labour force participation rate was 55.1 percent for women and 76.7 percent for men (Statistics Canada, 1986: Table 56), and these figures underestimate the number of women who were employed at some time during the year. According to recent estimates, two-thirds of women fifteen years of age and over had been employed for at least a brief period during 1986 (Statistics Canada, 1988a: Table 1). Most of the increase in the percentage of females in the labour force is accounted for by married women entering the labour market. Even married women with young children are keeping paid jobs. By 1987, almost 60 percent of the women with pre-school-age children were in the labour force. Furthermore, a growing number of women have moved into jobs traditionally done by men. This trend is most obvious in some of the more popular professions. "During the 1971–1981 period, the proportional representation of women increased in all but 1 of the 34 professions identified as male-dominated." The largest percentage increases were in management, law, veterinary work and engineering. The largest numerical increases were in management, pharmacy, law, post-secondary teaching and medicine (Marshall, 1987: 8). Moreover, women's invasion of male-dominated domains was not limited to the professions. They also took on jobs in construction, agriculture, mining and forestry. A few even acquired licences to operate their own fishing boats.

As more women entered the labour force and followed labour force participation patterns similar to men, more of them joined unions. Indeed, the unionization rate for women has been growing while the rate for men has been declining. In 1971, 22 percent of employed women, compared to 40 percent of employed men, belonged to unions. A decade later, 24 percent of women with paid jobs were union members, but men's unionization rate had dropped to 37 percent (Statistics Canada, 1985: Table 8).

TABLE 10-1
Occupations by Sex, Canada, 1986

Occupation	Female % of Occupation	% of All Female Workers	% of All Male Workers
Managerial	31.5	7.8	12.6
Natural Sciences	17.5	1.4	5.1
Social Sciences	57.8	2.6	1.4
Religion	24.1	0.2	0.4
Teaching	61.8	6.2	2.8
Medicine & Health	78.8	8.9	1.8
Artistic, Literary & Recreational	42.1	1.6	1.7
Clerical	78.7	33.5	6.8
Sales	44.4	9.4	8.8
Service	54.1	16.1	10.2
Farming	24.5	2.3	5.3
Fishing	9.4	0.1	0.6
Forestry	6.9	0.1	1.2
Mining	2.0	0.0	0.9
Processing	24.6	2.0	4.6
Machining	7.0	0.4	3.6
Fabricating	24.1	4.2	9.9
Construction	2.4	0.3	10.1
Transportation	7.8	0.7	5.9
Materials Handling	23.0	1.0	2.5
Other Crafts & Equipment Operating	22.8	0.6	1.6
Occupations not elsewhere classified	17.9	0.7	2.4

CALCULATED FROM STATISTICS CANADA, 1986 CENSUS SUMMARY. TABULATIONS OF LABOUR FORCE, MOBILITY AND SCHOOLING. OTTAWA: MINISTER OF SUPPLY AND SERVICES CANADA, MARCH 1988.

In spite of these widely publicized gains, however, most women still do women's work at women's wages, and few have a choice about taking on paid employment. As Table 10-1 indicates, a third of the employed women still did clerical work in 1986. Another 9.4 percent had sales jobs, and 16.1 percent did service work. In other words, close to 60 percent of employed women were segregated into traditionally female clerical, sales and service employment. By contrast, only 26 percent of the men did this kind of work.

Furthermore, while some women moved into traditional male areas, "the vast majority of professional women work in the 12 occupational groups that were not male dominated. In 1981, 78 percent of professional women, compared to just 30 percent of male professionals, were employed in one of these occupations" (Marshall, 1987 : 8). In fact, women's movement into professional jobs was not as great as that of men. The "concentration of women in the professions actually declined between 1971 and 1981. For men, on the contrary, the concentration in the professions increased, and at a faster rate than in the technical jobs" where women made their most significant gains (Armstrong and Armstrong, 1984 : 41).

TABLE 10-2

Full-time and Part-time Employment, Canada, 1986

	Women	Men
Employed entirely full-time	55.2%	73.1%
Employed entirely part-time	28.1%	12.5%
Average weeks employed in 1986	29.1	39.9

CALCULATED FROM STATISTICS CANADA, CANADA'S WOMEN: A PROFILE OF THEIR 1986 LABOUR MARKET ACTIVITY, TABLES 8 AND 16 AND STATISTICS CANADA, CANADA'S MEN: A PROFILE OF THEIR 1986 LABOUR MARKET ACTIVITY, TABLES 8 AND 16. OTTAWA: MINISTER OF SUPPLY AND SERVICES CANADA, MAY 1988.

Not only do women and men do different jobs; they also often do them in different places. Three-quarters of those employed in the goods-producing industries in 1986 were male, while more than 60 percent of those working in community, business and personal services were female (calculated from Statistics Canada, 1986 : Table 71). In addition, women are more likely than men to work in small firms (Statistics Canada, 1988a and c : Table 17). Women are also much more likely than men to do paid work in their homes (Johnson and Johnson, 1982). If men do work in their homes, they are much more likely than women to be their own bosses.

Women are also much more likely than men to work part-time or part-year. As Table 10-2 indicates, while 73.1 percent of men who were employed during 1986 worked entirely full-time, this was the case for only 55.2 percent of the women. Moreover, women worked fewer weeks during the year. Men averaged almost forty weeks of employment, compared to less than thirty weeks for women.

Women's shorter work weeks and the fewer years of paid employment help account for women's lower wages. In 1985, women's average wages were 55.5 percent of men's average wages. Women who worked full-time, however, still averaged only 65.6 percent of male full-time wages. Table 10-3 offers a graphic illustration of the significant wage gap that remains in each occupational category. Although large numbers

TABLE 10-3

Wage Gap in Average Weekly Occupational Earnings, Canada, 1986

Occupation	Union	Non-union	Total
Managerial & Professional	$171	248	209
Clerical	110	46	90
Sales	134	186	183
Service	173	64	117
Primary Occupations	157	171	190
Processing, etc.	196	163	192
Construction	87	—	185
Transportation	209	187	225
Materials Handling, etc.	137	67	122

CALCULATED FROM STATISTICS CANADA, CANADA'S MEN: A PROFILE OF THEIR 1986 LABOUR MARKET ACTIVITY, TABLE 20 AND STATISTICS CANADA, CANADA'S WOMEN: A PROFILE OF THEIR 1986 LABOUR MARKET ACTIVITY, TABLE 20. OTTAWA: MINISTER OF SUPPLY AND SERVICES CANADA, MAY 1988.

of women have moved into what are classified as managerial and professional work, they earn significantly less than the men in this occupational category. Indeed, the only occupational group with a larger dollar income difference is the male-dominated transportation category. Although unions have helped close the wage gap in some occupational groups, this is not the case for the majority of occupational categories listed in Table 10-3.

Women's paid work increases their chores, but women's lower wages usually mean that, in and out of the household, they have less power than men. Women's lower wages also mean that they are much more economically dependent on marriage than men. Indeed, many women are only a man away from poverty. In 1986, 56 percent of female single parents, compared to 22.9 percent of male single parents, lived below the poverty line (National Council of Welfare, 1988 : 31). At the same time, however, there are now more women who can leave an unhappy marriage because they have a job that pays them enough to survive on their own.

More and more women are taking on paid work in addition to their domestic work. The most recent data indicate that two-thirds of married women had paid work at some time during the year. This second job has important consequences for women and for their relations with men. Research conducted by Graham Lowe for the Canadian Advisory Council on the Status of Women concluded that 80 percent of women's illness can be attributed to the stress caused by their double day of paid and unpaid work. This stress may have an impact on relationships with men. When asked if her husband helped at home, one secretary replied: "Are you kidding? That's why I had a big fight with my husband last week because I was fed up. He was complaining about this and that and I turned around and gave it to him. I said, 'I work seven hours a day. I come home, I make supper, I clean up.' I said, 'I do work before I leave in the morning. All weekend I'm working like crazy to get the house clean.' I said, 'You've got the nerve to tell me not to use the bathroom because you want to use it in the morning' " (Armstrong and Armstrong, 1983b : 207).

Different jobs with different wages mean that women and men often have different experiences and possibilities. Women are more likely than men to work in jobs that are dull, repetitive and boring, with little opportunity for training or advancement (see Armstrong and Armstrong, 1983b and 1984). Because they do different jobs, women and men tend to face different health hazards in their paid work. Men are more likely to suffer from a clear, visible, physical injury; women to suffer from cumulative, invisible hazards that are difficult to trace directly to employment and that tend to create effects such as nervousness, headache and irritability that are often blamed on female physiology rather than on working conditions (Armstrong and Armstrong, 1983b : 183–95). Women are also much more likely than men to face sexual harassment on the job (Backhouse and Cohen, 1981). "Sexual harassment is almost expected in job ghetto areas where women represent the service and clerical occupations. Here women are most vulnerable to a supervisor's or a co-worker's explicit or implicit demands" (Kadar, 1989 : 337). They are more vulnerable because they are less likely to be unionized, more likely to have direct contact with their employer and to have fewer other workers around to witness the harassment. In one important characteristic, however, women's and men's jobs are very similar. While both girls and boys are likely to have female caregivers, both men and women are likely to have male bosses.

Research in both the United States (Kantor, 1978; Rubin, 1976) and Canada has shown that the structure of men's jobs can have a significant impact on family life and on gender relations. Luxton's (1983) Flin Flon interviews, for example, show how shift work disrupts social life, making it very difficult for couples to participate together in regularly organized community activities. The frustrations these men felt with their mining jobs were often brought home and "taken out" on their wives or were reflected in their disrupted sleep.

Very little research, however, has been done on how the structure of women's work influences gender relations in the home. A Toronto study suggests that when women enter the labour force to do full-time work, there are profound consequences for relationships. One woman explained: "My husband works evenings, from 5 p.m. until 1 : 30 or 2 a.m. My work hours are from 7 a.m. until 4 p.m. We avoid child care expenses and it gives the kids enough time to spend with both parents." Such arrangements may mean children spend more time with their parents, but they also mean that these parents have very little time to spend with each other. At the same time, however, as women enter the labour force, they share more of men's experiences with paid jobs. This sharing may serve to bring a couple closer together. Much more research is necessary before we have a clear idea about how the conditions of women's work are reflected in how they relate to men.

Unpaid Work

Unpaid work is also segregated. Study after study has shown that women not only do unpaid work that is different from that of men; they also do more unpaid work than men. In a Vancouver study, Meissner et al. (1975 : 431) concluded that "most married women do the regular, necessary and time-consuming tasks in the household every day." They also found that "when men's workload and regular housework are plotted against their own job hours . . . and compared with the data for women, men always work less than women" (1975 : 429).

Luxton's (1983 : 36) research in Flin Flon, Manitoba, indicates that when husbands do take over tasks in the home, they tend to do ones with clearly defined boundaries or ones that are the least boring or monotonous. Moreover, men's contributions to domestic tasks do not seem to reduce women's workload significantly. For example, men now have more involvement with the children. But the father frequently "plays with them and tells them stories and other nice things," while the mother does most of the personal service work and other tasks that accompany children (Luxton,

1983 : 37). Women, for example, provide the meals, brush the teeth and wipe the bottoms.

Even when women have paid jobs outside the home, they still do most of the domestic work. In his Toronto study, Michelson (1985 : 65) found that wives do three times as much household work as their husbands. "In families where the wife has a part-time job, this ratio is approximately 5 to 1, and it increases to 6.7 to 1 when the wife is employed full-time." In other words, when women take on paid work, they take on an additional job and get very little help from their husbands. Clark and Harvey's (1976 : 64) Halifax research indicates that when women work outside the home, "it appears that the wife does most of the adapting; she reduces her household work and leisure hours quite significantly and is more likely than her husband to hold a part-time job."

Although women with relatively high-paying career jobs can afford to hire other women to do much of the domestic work, the tasks that remain to be done are still divided by sex and still done disproportionately by women. In her study of career women, Bassett (1985 : 144) reports that "close to half the career women polled say cleaning the house, grocery shopping, and doing the laundry are their responsibility, and over half say the same about cooking. This traditional division of labour applies also to the so-called 'male' jobs: two-thirds of career women say household repairs and maintenance are their husband's duties in their households."

Women take primary responsibility for the sick, disabled and elderly as well. According to a study conducted for the Canadian Advisory Council on the Status of Women (Heller, 1986 : 12), 79 percent of the women who do part-time paid work and 73 percent of those with full-time employment are mainly responsible for family health care. If elderly relatives need home care, it is also usually women who sacrifice their paid employment or make compromises in their market jobs in order to do this unpaid work (Rogers, 1986 : 7).

When women and men provide support to people outside the home, women are much more likely to do the regular and time-consuming chores such as housework and baby-sitting, while men are more likely to help with yardwork and transportation (Statistics Canada, 1987 : Table Q). Similar divisions appear in volunteer work. Women work longer hours than men in their volunteer jobs, and they are more likely than men to provide personal care. Men who do volunteer work are most likely to coach male teams or to raise funds and handle the money (Armstrong, 1984 : 130–32).

As is the case for paid work, women's and men's unpaid work is often done in different places, under different conditions, giving them different experiences. Women's work is more likely to be dull, repetitive and boring. The health hazards women face are less visible, and here, too, they are sexually harassed or worse. "Although husband battering does exist one cannot compare its incidence to that of wife beating" (Canadian House of Commons, Standing Committee on Health, Welfare and Social Affairs, 1982 : 3). While the extent of violence is difficult to measure with any accuracy, Macleod (1980 : 21) estimates that "every year, 1 in 10 Canadian women who are married or in a relationship with a live-in lover are battered" (see also Macleod, 1987). The women's movement has succeeded in making this problem more visible and in offering some alternatives to battered women, but they have not succeeded in making the problem go away. Given the differences in men's and women's domestic work, it is not surprising that American sociologist Bernard (1972) could talk about "his" and "her" marriages to indicate that women and men often experience very different marriages. She argued that marriage is good for men. It makes them physically, socially and psychologically healthy, while it makes many women sick.

Women's labour force participation rates have been rising steadily in recent years while those of men have been declining. Some women have moved into traditional male occupations and some men are doing more around the house. There are signs that women's and men's work experiences are becoming more similar. However, most women are still doing women's work at women's wages or for no wages at all. Moreover, while women's increasing participation in the labour force has broadened their experiences and increased their access to financial resources and perhaps to some kinds of power, it has also meant more hours of work for women.

Community and Social Life

While home, school and paid work are the primary locations for male and female relationships, there are, of course, other places where females and males meet. Relations in these places, too, are characterized by both change and lack of change, by ambiguity and by the persistence of older patterns of behaviour. What was once called the dating game, what is still called the political game and what are collectively labelled medical services all provide examples of emerging new and lingering old patterns in relations between the sexes.

Although females are now more likely to pay their own way and to open their own doors, males still are much more likely to do the asking, and thereby take the risk of rejection (Allgeier, 1981). Women are also, as far as we can tell from the research, more likely today to engage in premarital or extramarital sex than they were in the past. Young females, however, are still more likely to defend sexual relationships on the basis of love, while young men are much more likely to justify premarital sex on solely physical grounds (Herold, 1984). The old double standard for female and male sexual behaviour has weakened but not disappeared with the advent of better contraceptives and new ideas about women's place.

The persistence of different rules for male and female sexual behaviour may be related to our failure to develop birth control techniques that are entirely effective in preventing conception and that are safe to use. It may also reflect our failure to properly educate young people about contraceptive use. The response to AIDS may serve to alter these relations, however. Males and females are now being taught about, and encouraged to use, condoms. Moreover, men now have to worry more than they used to about the consequences of casual sexual relationships. This may serve to make men's sexual practices more similar to those of women, given that women have throughout history had to worry about the consequences of sexual contacts.

Women's participation in the labour force and the use of contraceptive devices also mean that women have more choices about when and whom they will marry. At the same time, men have more choices as well because they do not have to assume the main financial burden of maintaining a household when they marry or have children. These changes may help explain why more and more couples are living together without what was once termed "the benefit of marriage." On the basis of her Canadian research, Fels (1981 : 19) argues that living together "is a symbolic gesture of rebellion against social conformity and rigidity of thought." Living together without marriage does not necessarily mean a rejection of marriage, however, given that couples who live together often marry eventually. Couples live together because they need to save money, because they cannot, for a variety of reasons, marry or because they want to see if they are compatible. Whatever their reasons, this pattern has become more acceptable in recent years.

Women and men also meet in the political arena. Women have gained many legal rights since the turn of the century, including the right to vote and to be elected or appointed to political offices. These rights, in turn, have helped change laws related to equal pay, equal property rights and equal opportunity to paid employment, to name only a few (Burt, 1988). The number of women who hold political office has grown enormously, altering significantly the relations within legislatures and in regulatory bodies as well as in the laws themselves. Women's concerns and perspectives have to be taken into account.

But here, too, the sexes often remain segregated. Although women have entered all levels of government, the largest proportion of women is found in municipal politics, the lowest level of decision making. On the basis of her study on municipal politics, Kopinak (1988 : 385) concludes that "women candidates and elected officials occupy positions of greater strength than men on several political dimensions," but suggests that this may be related to their smaller numbers at the higher levels. Within municipal politics, the political dimensions dominated by women tend to be traditional areas such as school boards, where they can oversee what is happening to the children. The balance of power is altering, but the seats at the top are still mainly reserved for the men.

In medical services, relations between the sexes are also changing, but very slowly. There are still significant differences in terms of how women are treated within the health care system, a pattern that reflects old ideas about relations between the sexes and about women's proper place. Men are much less likely than women to use health care services, and when they do, they are much more likely than women to be treated as if they have a "real" biological medical problem. "Women consistently receive twice the proportion of prescriptions for tranquillizers as do men" (Cooperstock and Lennard, 1987 : 314). These prescriptions have been justified as a way of supporting social relationships, especially women's subordinate position in the family. The prescription of tranquillizers to women is "consistent with the culturally accepted view that it is the role of the wife to control the tensions created by a difficult marriage." Valium is used "as an aid in the maintenance of a nurturing, caring role" (Cooperstock and Lennard, 1987 : 318). Women's greater use of the health services, which is largely related to their reproductive capacities, also serves to reinforce the idea that women are weak and fragile. Birth has become a medical process, managed by doctors who justify their practices by arguing that they are merely protecting women's health. However, this management by doctors may do more harm than good and certainly serves to reduce women's control over their bodies.

But as more women move into the labour force and as they extend their years of education, the old medical approaches are coming under increasing attack. Men, too, are challenging old medical procedures. More and more men are present at the births of their children, and many are attending prenatal classes. These changes also influence relations between the sexes, often serving to bring women and men closer together as they share aspects of the birth experience.

These three areas—sexual practice, politics and medicine—indicate how patterns between men and women are changing. Women's and men's experiences are becoming more similar; however, men still take the primary initiative in sexual relationships, retain the significant decision-making positions and many still think of women primarily as mothers who must be managed.

Making Connections

There is at least one female and one male in every occupational category, and there are some female bosses and even some female sexual harassers. There are at least some males who stay at home and take responsibility for household chores and child care. There are many men who never harass women and who have never beaten their wives. These facts suggest that biology is not a major factor determining the division of labour by sex or other behaviour patterns associated with each sex.

This does not mean that biology is irrelevant, however. That women, and not men, have babies does make a difference in our society. Because women bear the children and because we have created a separation between child rearing and paid work, women are limited, to some extent, from participating in the labour force in the same way as men do. This difference is exaggerated by the scarcity and high cost of child care and by women's low wages.

Licensed day care regulated by government standards "is available to fewer than nine per cent of the core population needing it" (Status of Women Canada, 1986 : 72). Not only is good child care difficult to find, it is also expensive. Consequently, the families most likely to enjoy access to such care have "either an income high enough to pay for the service or an income low enough to qualify for subsidy" (Status of Women Canada, 1986 : 72). Many families are left in the middle, unable to afford day care. In 1988, the yearly cost of keeping an infant in day care was over $5000 in Ontario. This would be more than half the take-home pay of a woman working a forty hour week, fifty-two weeks a year at $5.00 an hour—a rate higher than the minimum wage in most provinces. For those many families who cannot afford or find day care, it only makes economic sense in most cases for the woman to stay home, because she earns the lower wages. A Statistics Canada study (Burch, 1985 : 26) found that the "exigencies of marriage, pregnancy and childcare had a major impact on the continuity of work for a majority of women, but almost no impact on men."

But women's reproductive capacities and the social arrangements that turn this ability into a liability are not the only factors in the continuing division of labour by sex. Ideas and the dominant ideology also play a role. A large number of Canadians were reared in a time when most women cared for their young children full-time. Most Canadians still feel that women should stay home with young children (Boyd, 1984 : 12). Many employers are convinced that women are physically and mentally suited to some jobs and not others. Career women surveyed by Bassett (1985 : 22) cited sex discrimination as the most important factor contributing to their failure to win top jobs. Furthermore, many women have learned by example and by experience that women and men do different work, and this has become part of their world view.

Women's economic need and employers' demands for employees, however, often overcome the ideas that women should be in the home or in jobs suited to women, and often change these ideas in the process. Most women have moved into the labour force because they need the money (Armstrong and Armstrong, 1984 : ch. 6). Single women have, for most of this century, relied on their own employment for economic survival. The increasing number of women who parent alone have also had to depend on either what they could earn or on welfare, because the majority of their children's fathers do not provide support payments (Dulude, 1984). Increasingly, married women as well have had to contribute to their families' economic support. Between 1971 and 1981, the income of wives "was the significant factor in preventing family income from declining in real dollars," and family economic resources have continued to deteriorate (Pryor, 1984 : 102). "By 1979–81, increases in wives' income were no longer able to offset the decline in husbands' average income" (Pryor, 1984 : 102). Although the decline was reversed in 1985, "the overall average real family income in Canada was 3.5% lower in 1985 than it had been in 1980" (Lindsay, 1986 : 15).

At the same time as women's economic need was growing, employment was expanding in traditionally female areas. The demand for people with the skills women had traditionally learned and for cheap, often part-time, labour increased (Armstrong and Armstrong, 1988). Women responded to the demand because they needed the income and because their family responsibilities often prevented them from searching for alternative, and better, work. Women provided what Connelly (1978) describes as a reserve army—a large number of workers who were available and who competed with others in their group for jobs available to them.

Women's subordinate position in the labour market reinforced their responsibility for domestic work. At the same time, women's domestic responsibilities reinforced their subordinate position in the market. However, as women gained both experience and income with their paid jobs and as they suffered from the tensions created by the competing demands of their paid and unpaid work, their ideas changed and their protests increased in both numbers and strength. Although major differences remain, male and female experiences have become more similar in recent years. These shared experiences open up new possibilities for more egalitarian relationships at the same time as they create new areas of tension.

Strategies for Change

Women, and some men, have developed a number of demands and strategies for change. Individually, women have pushed men to do more domestic labour. They have increasingly charged men who commit abuse and rape, sexual harassment and discrimination.

Collectively, women have worked to create the conditions in which such individual efforts are possible and effective, and they have worked to alter the structures that keep women in their place. Laws have been changed to recognize women's equal contribution to marriage and their equal entitlement to the financial assets of the household, to make sexual harassment an offence under the law, to make unequal pay for work of equal value illegal and to make maternity leave available to employed women. Women have developed education programs to expand women's skills, to provide them with information on birth control and on self-protection. They have opened homes for battered wives, rape crisis centres and day care centres. They have fought for affirmative action programs and for women's right to be heard in union affairs.

Preparing early for nontraditional work.

JUDITH CRAWLEY.

Some of these programs have been successful in altering patterns and relations; many have not. The change has been slow, and both men and women have resisted. Men in general and employers in particular have too much at stake to change the current relations willingly, and men, as we have seen, still have more power. Nevertheless, relations between women and men have been fundamentally altered. Some men have learned to enjoy caring for children and working for female bosses and to assume responsibility for the consequences of sexual relations. It is no longer as easy to assume, when the parents answer that question about the sex of the child, that the girls will be mommies and secretaries and the boys will be bosses and daddies who leave the home each day.

Summary

While there are clearly some biological differences between females and males, there is little evidence to show that these biological differences predetermine two distinctly separate behaviour patterns. Yet, males and females usually do quite different jobs in and out of the labour force, have different sexual practices, own different toys and play different games, are differently involved in politics and are treated differently by doctors. And, in many areas, what males do is more highly valued than what females do and males have more access to resources, as well as more power, than females. The images and relations portrayed in the media, the practices at home and school, the division of labour in the household and in the formal economy, the legislation that regulates marriage, work and property all contribute to the maintenance of these patterns.

The argument for biological determinism has been severely challenged in recent years by the major changes that have been taking place in both female and male behaviour patterns and in relations between the sexes. Female and male experiences have become more similar as many more women have entered and remained in the labour force, as more men help with child care and other household chores and as birth control and the threat of AIDS reduce the strength of the old double standard in sexual practices. Women have gained some power along with their paid jobs and have had increasing success in opposing male privilege, sexual harassment and unequal pay. However, many differences in access to resources and in acceptable practices remain.

Suggested Readings

Armstrong, Pat, and Hugh Armstrong
1984. *The Double Ghetto: Canadian Women and Their Segregated Work*. Toronto: McClelland and Stewart. This book looks at women's paid work in the labour force, their unpaid work in the home and the connections between these two kinds of labour. The three major theoretical explanations for women's position are examined in turn, with the authors arguing that historical materialism offers the most useful approach to understanding women's work.

Kaufman, Michael, ed.

1987. *Beyond Patriarchy*. Toronto: Oxford University Press. This edited collection brings together a range of perspectives on male domination in society and offers some suggestions on what can be done to change this situation. Unlike most books on patriarchy, this book is written from a male perspective.

Luxton, Meg

1980. *More Than A Labour of Love: Three Generations of Women's Work in the Home*. Toronto: Women's Press. Based on a year's participant observation and on interviews done in Flin Flon, Manitoba, this book provides rich material on domestic relations and domestic work. Full of revealing quotations, the book offers a unique study of women's life in the home.

Mackie, Marlene

1987. *Constructing Women and Men*. Toronto: Holt, Rinehart and Winston. Using a symbolic interaction perspective, this book integrates a wide range of literature on relations between females and males. The focus is on socialization, but on socialization understood as a lifelong process.

MacLeod, Linda

1987. *Battered But Not Beaten*. Ottawa: Canadian Advisory Council on the Status of Women. In this, her second book on wife abuse, the author examines the recent increase in reported cases of wife battering and considers the causes, consequences and solutions to this ancient problem.

Michelson, William

1985. *From Sun to Sun: Daily Obligations and Community Structure in the Lives of Employed Women and Their Families*. Totowa, N.J.: Rowman and Allenheld. This recent study of Toronto households documents the daily lives of men, women and children. Although there are certainly differences between these families and those Flin Flon families recorded in the early 1980s by Luxton, there is much that remains the same in domestic relationships across time and place.

Discussion Questions

1. Are you bothered when you cannot easily determine a person's sex? Why or why not?

2. Why is it difficult to separate nature from nurture, biology from culture?

3. Do unisex clothes and hair styles mean unisex behaviour?

4. Do we expect the same behaviour from a black man and a white man, a rich woman and a poor woman?

5. What implications does AIDS have for the double standard in sexual behaviour?

6. How can we explain women's continuing responsibility for domestic work as well as for the care of the young and the old, even when they take on full-time paid employment?

Data Collection Exercises

1. Using Statistics Canada labour force or census data on occupational distribution, determine the proportion of males and females in each of the major occupational groups in Canada in both 1981 and 1986.

2. Do a time-budget study of the division of labour by age and sex in your household.

3. With data from Statistics Canada's *General Social Survey*, develop a table indicating the kinds of support offered and received by each sex after they reach the age of sixty-five.

4. Using Statistics Canada data, compare the occupational distribution of women and men who come to Canada from Greece, Portugal and Italy to that of women who came to Canada from Britain and France.

Writing Exercises

1. Sexual harassment is a form of social control. Discuss.

2. Compare what a sociology text written before 1975 says about relations between the sexes with what a sociology text written in the 1980s says about these relations.

3. "The workplace is organized according to male rules" (Mackie, 1987 : 170). Discuss.

4. As women have moved into labour force work, their power relative to men has increased both inside and outside the home. Discuss.

Glossary

Gender: *a term usually used in sociology to refer to the cultural and behavioural differences between the sexes. Gender is the social distinction between masculinity and femininity.*

Sex: *a term usually used in sociology to refer to physiological differences between the sexes. Sex is the biological distinction between males and females.*

References

Allgeier, E. R.
1981. "The Influence of Androgynous Indentification on Heterosexual Relations." *Sex Roles* (7) : 321–30.

Armstrong, Pat, and Hugh Armstrong
1983a. "Beyond Sexless Class and Classless Sex." *Studies in Political Economy* 10 (Winter) : 7–43.

1983b. *A Working Majority: What Women Must Do For Pay*. Ottawa: Supply and Services Canada for the Canadian Advisory Council on the Status of Women.

1984. *The Double Ghetto: Canadian Women and Their Segregated Work*: Toronto: McClelland and Stewart.

1988. "Taking Women into Account: Redefining and Intensifying Employment in Canada," pp. 65–84. In Jane Jenson, Elizabeth Hagen and Ceallaigh Reddy, eds., *Feminization of the Labour Force*. Cambridge: Polity Press.

Backhouse, Constance, and Leah Cohen

1981. *Sexual Harassment on the Job*. Englewood Cliffs, N.J.: Prentice-Hall.

Bassett, Isabel

1985. *The Bassett Report*. Toronto: Collins.

Bernard, Jessie

1972. *The Future of Marriage*. New York: Bantam Books.

Boyd, Monica

1984. *Canadian Attitudes Toward Women: Thirty Years of Change*. Ottawa: Supply and Services Canada for Labour Canada.

Burch, Thomas

1985. *Family History Survey: Preliminary Findings*. Ottawa: Supply and Services Canada.

Burt, Sandra

1988. "Legislators, Women and Public Policy," pp. 129–56. In S. Burt, L. Code and L. Dorney, eds., *Changing Patterns*. Toronto: McClelland and Stewart.

Canadian House of Commons, Standing Committee on Health, Welfare and Social Affairs

1982. *Report on Violence in the Family: Wife Battering*. Ottawa: Supply and Services Canada.

Chodorow, Nancy

1978. *The Reproduction of Mothering*. Berkeley: University of California Press.

Clark, Susan, and Andrew S. Harvey

1976. "The Sexual Division of Labour: The Use of Time." *Atlantis* 2(1, Fall): 46–65.

Connelly, Patricia M.

1978. *Last Hired: First Fired*. Toronto: Women's Press.

Cooperstock, Ruth, and Henry Lennard

1987. "Role Strain and Tranquilizer Use," pp. 314–32. In Coburn, D'Arcy, Torrance and New, eds., *Health in Canadian Society*, 2nd ed. Markham, Ont.: Fitzhenry and Whiteside.

Dalton, Katherine

1983. *Once a Month*. Claremont, Cal.: Hunter House.

Dulude, Louise

1984. *Love, Marriage and Money . . . An Analysis of Financial Arrangements Between the Spouses*. Ottawa: Canadian Advisory Council on the Status of Women.

Fausto-Sterling, Anne

1985. *Myths of Gender*. New York: Basic Books.

Fels, Lynn

1981. *Living Together* Toronto: Personal Library.

Fox, Bonnie
1988. "Conceptualizing 'Patriarchy.' " *Canadian Review of Sociology and Anthropology* 25 (2, May): 163–82.

Goldberg, Steven
1977. *The Inevitability of Patriarchy*. London: Temple Smith.

Greenglass, Esther
1982. *A World of Difference*. Toronto: Wiley.

Hamilton, Roberta
1978. *The Liberation of Women*. London: Allen and Unwin.

Heller, Anita Fochs
1986. *Health and Home: Women as Health Guardians*. Ottawa: Canadian Advisory Council on the Status of Women.

Herold, Edward
1984. *Sexual Behaviour of Canadian Young People*. Markham, Ont.: Fitzhenry and Whiteside.

Jacklin, C. N.
1981. "Methodological Issues in the Study of Sex-Related Differences." *Developmental Review* 1:266–73.

Johnson, Laura, with Robert E. Johnson
1982. *The Seam Allowance: Industrial Home Sewing in Canada* Toronto: Women's Press.

Kadar, Marlene
1989. "Sexual Harassment as a Form of Social Control," pp. 337–46. In Arlene Tigar McLaren, ed., *Gender and Society*. Toronto: Copp Clark Pitman.

Kantor, Rosabeth Moss
1978. "Jobs and Families: Impact of Working Roles on Family Life." *Children Today* 7(2):11–15, 45.

Kidd, Bruce
1987. "Sports and Masculinity," pp. 250–65. In Michael Kaufman, ed., *Beyond Patriarchy*. Toronto: Oxford University Press.

Kopinak, Kathryn
1988. "Women in Canadian Municipal Politics: Two Steps Forward, One Step Back," pp. 372–89. In Arlene Tigar McLaren, ed., *Gender and Society*. Toronto: Copp Clark Pitman.

Lambert, Ronald D.
1971. *Sex Role Imagery in Children*. Ottawa: Information Canada.

Lindsay, Colin
1986. "The Decline of Real Family Income, 1980 to 1984." *Canadian Social Trends* (Winter):15–17.

Lowe, Marion
1983. "Sex Differences, Science and Society," pp. 7–17. In Jan Zimmerman, ed., *The Technological Woman*. New York: Praeger.

Luxton, Meg
1983. "Two Hands For the Clock: Changing Patterns in the Gendered Division of Labour in the Home." *Studies in Political Economy* 12(Fall): 27–44.

Mackie, Marlene
1983. *Exploring Gender Relations*. Toronto: Butterworths.
1987. *Constructing Women and Men*. Toronto: Holt, Rinehart and Winston.

Mackintosh, Maureen M.
1988. "Domestic Labour and the Household," pp. 392–406. In R. E. Pahl, ed., *On Work*. Oxford: Basil Blackwell.

MacLeod, Linda
1980. *Wife Battering in Canada: The Vicious Circle*. Ottawa: Supply and Services Canada for the Canadian Advisory Council on the Status of Women.
1987. *Battered but Not Beaten*. Ottawa: Canadian Advisory Council on the Status of Women.

Marshall, Katherine
1987. "Women in Male-Dominated Professions." *Canadian Social Trends* (Winter): 7–11.

Mead, Margaret
1935. *Sex and Temperament in Three Primative Societies:* Chicago: University of Chicago Press.

Meissner et al.
1975. "No Exit for Wives: Sexual Division of Labour and the Culmination of Household Demands." *Canadian Review of Sociology and Anthropology* 12(4, November): 424–39.

Messing, Karen
1987. "The Scientific Mystique: Can a White Lab Coat Guarantee Purity in the Search for Knowledge about the Nature of Women?" pp. 103–16. In Greta Hofmann Nemiroff, ed., *Women and Men*. Markham, Ont.: Fitzhenry and Whiteside.

Michelson, William
1985. *From Sun to Sun: Daily Obligations and Community Structure in the Lives of Employed Women and Their Families*. Totowa, N.J.: Rowman and Allenheld.

Mitchell, Elizabeth
1981. *In Western Canada Before The War*. Saskatoon, Saskatchewan: Western Producer Prairie Books. (First published 1915.)

National Council of Welfare
1988. *Poverty Profile 1988*. Ottawa: National Council of Welfare.

O'Brien, Mary
1981. *The Politics of Reproduction*. London: Routledge and Kegan Paul.

Posner, Judith
1987. "The Objectified Male: The New Male Image in Advertising," pp. 180–88. In Greta Hofmann Nemiroff, ed., *Women and Men*. Markham, Ont.: Fitzhenry and Whiteside.

Redclift, Nanneke
1988. "Gender, Accujulation and the Labour Process," pp. 428–48. In R. E. Pahl, ed., *On Work*. Oxford: Basil Blackwell.

Richardson, Laurel
1988. *The Dynamics of Sex and Gender*. New York: Harper and Row.

Richer, Stephen
1984. "Sexual Inequality and Children's Play." *The Canadian Review of Sociology and Anthropology* 21: 166–180.

Robinson, B. W., and E. D. Salamon
1987. "Gender Role Socialization: A Review of the Literature," pp. 123–42. In E. D. Salamon and B. W. Robinson, eds., *Gender Roles*. Toronto: Methuen.

Rogers, Judy
1986. *Attitudes Towards Alternative Work Arrangements: A Qualitative Assessment Among Employers in Metropolitan Toronto*. Toronto: Social Planning Council of Metropolitan Toronto.

Rose, Steven, Leon J. Kamin and R. C. Lewontin
1984. *Not In Our Genes*. New York: Penguin.

Rubin, Lillian Breslow
1976. *Worlds of Pair*. New York: Basic Books.

Russell, Susan
1986. "The Hidden Curriculum of School: Reproducing Gender and Class Hierarchies," pp. 343–60. In Roberta Hamilton and Michele Barrett, eds. *The Politics of Diversity*. Montreal: Book Centre.

Smith, Dorothy
1975. "Ideological Structures and How Women are Excluded." *Canadian Review of Sociology and Anthropology* 12(4, November): 353–69.

Statistics Canada
1985. *Women in Canada: A Statistical Report*. Ottawa: Supply and Services Canada, March.
1986. *The Labour Force*. Ottawa: Supply and Services Canada, December (Cat. No. 71-001).
1987. *Health and Social Support 1985*. Ottawa: Supply and Services Canada, December.
1988a. *Canada's Women: A Profile of their 1986 Labour Market Activity*. Ottawa: Supply and Services Canada, May.
1988b. *1986 Census Summary: Tabulations of the Labour Force, Mobility and Schooling*. Ottawa: Supply and Services Canada, March.
1988c. *Canada's Men: A Profile of their 1986 Labour Market Activity*. Ottawa: Supply and Services Canada, May.

Status of Women Canada
1986. *Report of the Task Force on Child Care*. Ottawa: Supply and Services Canada.

Wernick, Andrew
1987. "From Voyeur to Narcissist: Imaging Men in Contemporary Advertising," pp. 277–97. In Michael Kaufman, ed., *Beyond Patriarchy*. Toronto: Oxford University Press.

CHAPTER 11

Formal Organizations and Bureaucracy

R. JACK RICHARDSON

Introduction

Wherever we turn these days, we are confronted by organizations; they are the most pervasive structures in modern life. We work, study and teach in organizations, and perhaps we play and pray in them too. From the time we wake up with our orange juice and coffee until we leave the pub or watch the late show on television, organizations almost continually invade our daily lives.

Organizations provide many of the good things in life: houses, food, clothing, concerts, air conditioning, television sets, health care and so on. But they also cause many of our greatest frustrations. In our jobs, our classes, in the constraints we face in the courses we can take or add or drop and in countless other ways, organizations seem to run our lives. Indeed, in virtually everything we do outside the privacy of our own homes we seem to be at their mercy. What can we do, for example, when the airline refuses to honour our ticket because it has overbooked and we are late for an important date? This chapter aims to help us understand the structures that wield such enormous power in every realm of modern life.

Opposite page:
In a bureaucracy customers and clients often become highly frustrated: in this case, while waiting for service.

DICK HEMINGWAY.

Organizations

What is an organization? It can be a giant multinational corporation such as General Motors or a small corner variety store, a political party or a government, a church, a school, a sports club or a search party. There is an endless variety of organizational forms and millions of specific examples. What do all these specific examples have in common?

To begin with, we can define an *organization* as a group of people participating in a division of labour that is co-ordinated by communication and leadership to achieve a common goal or goals. But this social group may be spontaneously or deliberately formed. The division of labour may be crude or complex. The communication and leadership may be informal or formal. There may be one goal or several goals. One important distinction to make is between spontaneous and formal organizations. Both types fit our general definition, yet they are different in significant ways.

Spontaneous
Organizations

Perhaps the most commonly cited examples of *spontaneous organizations* are a bucket brigade and a search party. Each has but a single goal—keeping a barn from burning down or finding a lost child. They both arise spontaneously, and their leaders emerge through an informal process. They have a relatively crude division of labour: for example, filling buckets, passing them along, emptying them on the fire. Nevertheless, they are infinitely more likely than an unco-ordinated mob to achieve their goals. Imagine the chance of a mob running off in random directions as compared to a group conducting a co-ordinated search pattern of finding a lost child. Spontaneous organizations will disband as quickly as they form. This happens when their goal is achieved or perceived to be beyond reach or when they become absorbed by a formal organization. Our bucket brigade disperses when the fire is quenched, the barn has burned down or the fire department arrives on the scene.

Spontaneous organizations clearly show how the various elements of our definition of organizations develop in an ad hoc way. But they are hardly the kind of structure that dominates modern societies. Therefore, we will direct our attention for the rest of this chapter to the predominant, formal (or complex) organization.

Formal Organizations

In contrast to spontaneous organizations, formal ones emerge as a result of deliberate planning. Their communication and leadership (which co-ordinates their division of labour) consist of relationships between consciously developed and formalized statuses and roles. They often have multiple goals, and they usually have a long life span. The Roman Catholic Church, for example, is a formal organization that has lasted nearly 2000 years. Furthermore, formal organizations normally have access to far greater resources and more complex technologies than spontaneous organizations.

Consequently, we can define a *formal organization* more specifically as a deliberately formed social group in which people, resources and technologies are consciously co-ordinated through formalized roles, statuses and relationships to achieve a division of labour that is intended to effectively achieve a specific set of objectives. This is very similar to our broader definition of organizations in general. The differences, however, are important. The broader definition omits any reference to deliberate and conscious intent. It omits the formalized roles, statuses and relationships. It also refers to a commonality of goals, implying that goals are shared by all members of the organization. These broad goals are not the same as the "specific set of objectives," which will be set by those filling authoritative roles within a formal organization.

This latter point is contentious. Indeed, most definitions of formal organizations refer to common goals. Allan Fox (1966), an English social psychologist, calls this the unitary view of organizations. He cites a football team as an appropriate example, where all of the organization's members pull together toward the common goal of winning the game. However, he persuasively argues that the greater the degree of formalization in an organization, the less we can assume there is a single set of common goals and the more appropriate is the pluralistic view of the organization. Clearly, a formal organization will have an overarching set of goals that its leaders formulate and its members more or less accept. But we cannot assume that these are the only goals of the membership. Workers, professionals and managers will all have their own occupational goals as well.

Why are some formal organizations more successful and powerful than others? There is a huge literature addressing this question. Although this literature contains many lively debates, the most common explanations include the degree to which an organization:

1. fills a social need (either real or successfully promoted by the organization itself);
2. controls or has access to needed resources and technologies;

3.   tailors its goals to match the goals of its members;

4.   adapts to, or causes changes in, its environment.

Finally, the predominant form of the large, powerful and long-lived formal organizations of the twentieth century is the bureaucracy.

Bureaucracy

The Emergence of the Bureaucratic Form of Organization

Bureaucracy is a pejorative term to most people. It evokes thoughts of red tape, overemphasis on rules and regulations, inefficiency and ponderous government organizations moving at a tortoise-like pace. To sociologists, though, a bureaucracy is merely a particular type of formal organization that thrives in both the public and the private sector and in capitalist and socialist societies alike. The very fact that bureaucracy is the predominant organizational form that competitive corporations take indicates that it can be very efficient.

The modern form of bureaucracy exists in a money economy in which the members are paid salaries and wages. Yet, earlier forms of bureaucracy existed. In fact, bureaucratic organizations in various forms have a history almost as long as civilization itself. They existed in ancient Egypt and China, in the Roman Empire and the Inca and Aztec empires in America. However, the modern form owes its prominence to the development of capitalism and the modern state. In turn, the rise of modern bureaucracy facilitates the growth of capitalism and the state.

On a broader scale, Max Weber (1968) traced the rise of bureaucracy, capitalism and the modern state to the rationalization of human activity. "Rationalization" is central to Weber's general conception of history. For Weber, rationalization refers to the movement away from mystical and religious interpretations of the world to the development of human thought and belief based on the systematic accumulation of evidence. Associated with rationalization is the emergence of impersonal authority based on the universal application of a codified set of rules and laws.

The value system associated with rationalization prizes efficiency and effectiveness in administration and in the production of goods and services. These values spurred the growth of bureaucracy, in Weber's analysis, because bureaucracies organize activity in a logical, impersonal and efficient manner.

The Division of Labour

In earlier eras, individuals generally handcrafted an article from start to finish to produce a society's goods. Gradually, though, this type of production process gave way to specialization and the division of labour. The overwhelming production superiority of specialization was noted by Adam Smith as long ago as 1776. Specialization became the foundation of modern industry and bureaucratization. An automotive assembly line is a modern instance of this division of labour. Workers may perform one highly specialized operation every thirty-six seconds of the working day (Garson, 1972).

Adam Smith and the Division of Labour

The greatest improvement in the productive powers of Labour, and the greater skill, dexterity, and judgment with which it is anywhere directed, or applied, seem to have been the effects of the division of labour. . . . To take an example . . . a workman could scarce, perhaps, with his utmost industry, make one pin in a day, and certainly could not make twenty. But in the way in which this business is now carried on, not only the whole work is a peculiar trade, but it is divided into a number of branches, of which the greater part are likewise peculiar trades. One man draws out the wire, another straightens it, a third cuts it, a fourth points it, a fifth grinds it at the top for receiving the head: to make the head requires two or three distinct operations; to put it on is a peculiar business; to whiten the pins is another; it is even a trade by itself to put them into the paper; and the important business of making a pin is, in this manner, divided into about eighteen distinct operations, which, in some manufactures, are all performed by distinct hands, though in others the same man will sometimes perform two or three of them. I have seen a small manufactory of this kind where ten men only were employed, and where some of them consequently performed two or three distinct operations. . . . Those ten persons, therefore, could make among them upwards of forty-eight thousand pins in a day. But if they had all wrought separately and independently . . . they certainly could not each of them have made twenty, perhaps not one pin in a day; that is, certainly, not the two hundred and fortieth, perhaps not the four thousand eight hundredth part of what they are at present capable of performing, in consequence of a proper division and combination of their different operations.

Adam Smith. 1894. *The Wealth of Nations*, Book 1. London: Macmillan, p. 57. (Originally published in 1776.)

The Characteristics of Bureaucracy

The particular characteristics of the bureaucratic form of organization were first analysed by Weber in this century. In his study of the major organizations of his day, he identified six essential characteristics of bureaucratic organizations (Weber, 1958). These are: 1. a division of labour; 2. a hierarchy of positions; 3. a formal system of rules; 4. a separation of the person from the office; 5. hiring and promotion based on technical merit; and 6. the protection of careers. We will examine each of these.

Division of labour. As we have seen, a specialized division of labour is the fundamental underpinning of all formal organizations. In a bureaucracy, every member performs clearly specified and differentiated duties (like the workers in Adam Smith's pin factory). The bureaucracy itself provides the facilities and resources to carry out these duties. So workers work with the equipment they do not own; that is, workers are separated from the means of production. Furthermore, administrators administer what they do not own. The objectives of this combination of task specialization based on technical competence and the centralized provision of resources are efficiency and productivity.

Hierarchy of positions. We can visualize the organizational structure as a pyramid, with authority centralized at the top. This authority filters down toward the base through a well-defined hierarchy of command. Within this hierarchy, each person is

FIGURE 11-1

Organization Chart of a National Corporation

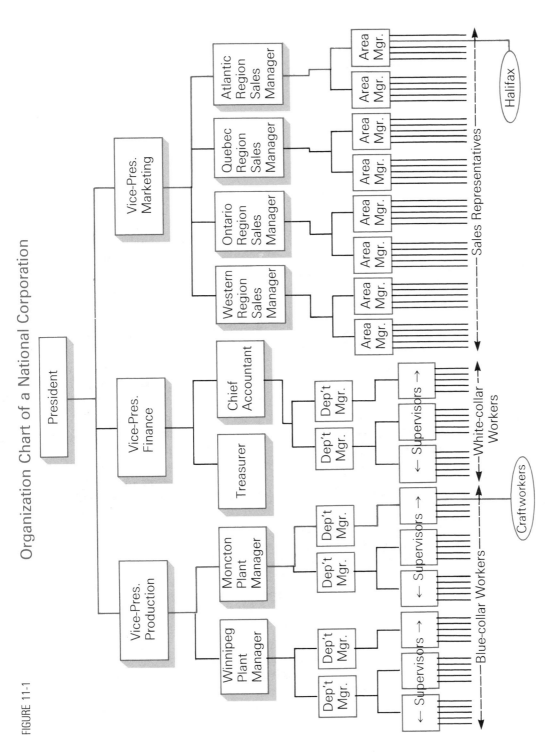

This organization chart exhibits the hierarchy of offices that exists in every bureaucracy. In a bureaucratic hierarchy, power and authority flow down from the top. The division of labour becomes increasingly specialized as one moves toward the base of the hierarchy. All of this—together with the other characteristics of bureaucracy—serves to increase efficiency. Note, however, that formal communication within a bureaucracy can be extremely cumbersome in many instances. This chart shows the *formal* lines of communication involved if a Halifax sales representative wants to discuss a special order with a craftsman in the Moncton plant. Obviously, in real life, people work to avoid such unwieldy communication channels—often forming informal communication networks.

responsible to a specific person one level up the pyramid and for a specific group of people one level down. Thus, the structure explicitly identifies the range and the limits of authority for each position.

Rules. Bureaucracies are run according to written rules. These rules permit a bureaucracy to formalize and classify the myriad circumstances it routinely confronts. For each of these, a rule can be developed, which provides for an objective and impersonal response. These rules, aside from providing objectivity, ensure predictable responses to specific situations by the bureaucracy's members, and this will promote the achievement of the organization's objectives.

Separation of the person from the office. In a bureaucracy, each person is an incumbent of an office in a hierarchy. The duties, functions and authority of this office are all explicitly defined. The relationship between positions in a bureaucracy is one of impersonal relationships between roles, not personal relationships between people. This separation of person and office means that people are replaceable functionaries in the organization. People come and go, but the organization remains intact. It also means that personal feelings toward other office holders must be subordinated to the impersonal demands of the office. Furthermore, these relationships are confined to the official duties of office holders and do not invade their private lives.

To illustrate: Charlie Brown, as sales manager, is empowered to issue specific orders to his sales force. Salespeople follow these orders because they come from the sales manager, not because they come from Charlie. And they follow them only to the extent that they relate to the salespeople's official duties. Next week, if Charlie is transferred to a different job, he can no longer issue the same orders to the same people, because he now holds a different office.

Hiring and promotion based on technical merit. A bureaucracy hires on the basis of impersonal criteria, such as technical competence, and not because of ascribed characteristics such as gender, race or ethnicity. Promotion is also based on technical competence (or sometimes on seniority). People are neither discriminated against nor favoured because of such personal criteria as their personalities or their kinship with someone at the top of the hierarchy.

Protected careers. People can look forward to long careers in a bureaucracy, because they are not subject to arbitrary dismissal for personal reasons.

This description of the characteristics of bureaucracy is, in Weber's terminology, the description of an ideal type. It is a model, an abstraction from reality. Does any bureaucracy in the real world completely match all of these characteristics? Of course not! People in bureaucracies often bypass the hierarchical chain of command to gain some personal advantage. Rules are bent or broken or simply not applied. Bosses (and indeed whole organizations) often invade the private lives of their subordinates. They may demand total commitment and see people's life styles as reflecting on the credibility of the organization. Women and minority groups are perhaps more often discriminated against than judged by objective criteria for hiring and promotion.

Furthermore, while twentieth-century bureaucracies all exhibit the six elements of

Weber's model, they also exhibit important cross-cultural differences (Crozier, 1964). The degree to which they match each individual characteristic reflects the culture in which they exist. For example, many developing societies maintain elements of traditional authority in their cultures. The universal application of rules, the separation of the person from the office and the application of impersonal criteria in hiring and promotion are usually much less pronounced in these societies (Eisenstadt, 1965). Currently, the success of Japanese industry has been attributed to the adaptation of bureaucracy to an important element of Japanese culture: the primacy of the social group over the individual (Ouchi and Jaeger, 1978).

However, because of its complexity, the real world is hard to analyse. It is much easier to construct a model, as Weber did, and then adjust it to reality. Weber's concept of bureaucracy, then, is a very useful model for the study of these complex organizations. We can, however, identify real problems and benefits of the bureaucratic form of organization.

Problems and Benefits

Perhaps the most commonly voiced criticism of bureaucracy is the way it can stifle individuality, human freedom and dignity. The rigidity of the hierarchy and the rules contribute to this oppression. So does the pressure to conform that seems to be part of bureaucracy. Another problem is the inflexibility and "red tape" that results from the universal application of rules. The bureaucracy classifies its members, customers

While impressed by the technical efficiency of bureaucracy, Max Weber and modern sociologists are concerned about bureaucracy's capacity to stifle individuality. Note that these bureaucrats are all the same sex, are all dressed in a similar fashion, all have similar hairstyles, and so on.

IMPERIAL OIL LIMITED.

and clients into categories. It rarely treats them as people with unique needs, desires and personalities. This same inflexibility can also make it difficult for a bureaucracy to react quickly and effectively to changes in its environment. Finally, protection from arbitrary dismissal often becomes protection of mediocrity, to the detriment of organizational effectiveness.

On the other side of the coin, these same factors can also produce efficiency and control. Most situations that bureaucracies face are routine and repetitive. They can classify these and develop effective responses in advance. The resulting rules eliminate the need to reinvent the wheel every time one of these situations develops. This enhances organizational efficiency and centralizes bureaucratic control. The one big danger is that bureaucrats may misclassify situations they face.

Weber was ambivalent about bureaucracy. The superiority of bureaucracy over other organizational forms greatly impressed him. He concluded that it is an extremely powerful tool for whoever controls it. On the other hand, he expressed great concern over the immense power a bureaucracy can wield in society—for example, the power of the state bureaucracy over German parliamentary institutions (Weber, 1968). The fate of "grey-faced bureaucrats" concerned him, and he wrote about the "iron cage" of bureaucracy.

Some Modern Perspectives on Bureaucracy

Modern sociologists have studied this "iron cage" intensively. Most have concluded that it is an oppressive structure that has detrimental effects on the people it touches. Here, we will briefly review a few representative studies.

Merton's "Bureaucratic Personality"

Robert Merton's analysis (1957) of bureaucracy focused on the pressures it places on those within it to act in ways that work against the organization. He compared bureaucrats to overtrained athletes. Bureaucracies place immense pressure on their members to conform. This pressure, combined with their intensive training, overemphasizes their knowledge of the bureaucracy's rules. The emphasis on rules makes it comfortable for bureaucrats to habitually act in routine ways. They follow rules in a "methodical, prudent and disciplined" way. Inevitably, these routines become like blinders on a horse. They prevent the bureaucrat from recognizing new situations in which the old rules are inappropriate. Thus, Merton argued, bureaucrats develop a "trained incapacity."

Furthermore, the routine application of rules requires that all situations must, somehow, be classifiable by objective criteria so they can be made to fit into an appropriate pigeonhole. This means that bureaucrats cannot see their clients as people with unique wants and needs, but only as impersonal categories. The result is, of course, detrimental to the organization since it fails to meet the unique needs of individual clients.

Blau and Perrow on Rules

Peter Blau's many case studies of bureaucracies included an analysis of an American employment agency (1963). In the branch office of this agency, bureaucrats were to interview job-seekers, record their qualifications, search the agency's files to match these candidates with jobs and contact potential employers to arrange job interviews. These procedures were aimed at finding employment for clients. Blau concluded that members of the bureaucracy did this effectively until the agency developed new procedures for appraising their performance. Under the new system, they were judged on the number of interviews they conducted each day. The bureaucrats' rational response was to rush through each interview, make a cursory search of the job files and eliminate the time wasted by contacting potential employers. This maximized their performance under these new rules. However, the organization's fundamental objective was to place people in jobs. The bureaucrats' application of the new rules severely limited the agency's ability to achieve this goal. Bureaucratic rules should be a means to the end of organizational efficiency; however, Blau's studies showed that rules often become ends in themselves.

On the other hand, Blau found automatic compliance with some rules to be beneficial to bureaucracies. Perrow also provides a spirited defence of rules in his essay "The Bureaucratic Paradox" (1977). He argues that control by impersonal rules is both more effective and less demeaning than control by obtrusive and personal direct orders. He also demonstrates (1972) that bureaucratic rules provide protection against arbitrary abuse of power.

The Informal Organization

Although bureaucracy is intended to be an impersonal form of organization, it is people who fill bureaucratic roles. And people resist becoming faceless cogs in the bureaucratic machine (replaceable cogs, at that). Consequently, they develop complex personal and informal networks that function within the formal organization. Collectively, these networks comprise the informal organization of bureaucracy's human face.

These informal networks, which develop among those who interact on the job, serve many purposes. First and foremost, they humanize the organization. They also provide support and protection to those at the lower levels of the hierarchy, serve as active channels of information (the grapevine) and become mechanisms for exchanging favours and exerting influence.

The Hawthorne Studies   The famous Hawthorne studies were conducted between 1927 and 1932 at the Western Electric plant at Hawthorne, Illinois, under the direction of Elton Mayo. Mayo was a Harvard organizational psychologist who propounded the view that workers were non-rational and emotional beings. The Hawthorne studies provided a massive data base that is still being used by social scientists to test a wide variety of hypotheses. They also spawned a huge literature, of which the account of Homans (1951) is probably the most readable. The Hawthorne studies first revealed the importance of the informal organization.

The studies consisted of four phases. Phase I began as a simple experiment to test the effect of light intensity on productivity. That initial research produced some surprising results. For example, when the researchers implied that they were replacing light bulbs with stronger ones, but in fact replaced them with identical bulbs, productivity increased. The researchers concluded that the psychological and emotional states of the employees were acting as an intervening variable, confounding the simple relationship between lighting and productivity.

To eliminate these intervening variables, the researchers proceeded to Phase II, the "relay assembly test room" experiment. They isolated six female workers in a workroom, along with a "test-room observer" in lieu of a regular supervisor. This phase lasted for five full years. The observers kept daily records of the productivity, health and conversations of each worker. They even recorded how many hours of sleep each worker reported to have had the previous night. Imagine the sheer volume of these records in the days before microfiche and the computer!

Before the test began, the women were conducted to the office of the plant superintendent (next only to God, at Hawthorne) where he explained the importance of the experiment. Later, whenever the researchers planned a change in working conditions, the plant superintendent recalled the workers to his office to discuss, approve or propose revisions to the plan. These changes involved implementing rest periods and snacks and reducing the workday and the work week. There were a total of twelve stages of change. Periodically, and for a substantial period at the end of the experiment, the workers were told to revert to the original, less liberal, working conditions.

The results confounded the researchers. No matter what change they implemented—whether positive or negative from the workers' point of view—productivity continued to rise until it gradually levelled off at a very high rate. The researchers realized that these results could not be the outcome of physical changes in working conditions. Mystified, they fell back on Mayo's view of the non-rational and emotional worker. After all, these workers frequently reported that "work was fun." The researchers also realized that an unusual type of supervision was in place (the test-room observer) and decided to investigate the effects of supervision on productivity.

This led to Phase III, a massive program of 21 000 worker interviews that concentrated on worker attitudes toward supervision. The researchers noted that, during these unstructured interviews, workers would usually keep returning to whatever topic was uppermost in their minds. They attributed this behaviour to "compulsive neurosis," a pathological condition popularized by Freud. By this time, the workers were viewed not only as non-logical, but as emotionally and even mentally ill. The research team was nearly ready to give up. "The comments elicited from the employees were of only limited use in improving working conditions and methods of supervision" (Homans, 1951: 229).

Then George Homans and Lloyd Warner (a Harvard sociologist and anthropologist, respectively) were consulted. They suggested that the results of the experiments and interviews needed to be interpreted in the context of social relationships among groups of workers, not as merely the responses of isolated individuals. This insight changed the direction of the studies and ultimately became an important foundation of the human relations school of organizational studies. Hence, Phase IV began; it was another study of a work group similar to the women in the relay assembly test room.

This fourth phase studied fourteen men who were put to work in a separate room, again with a test-room observer in lieu of a formal supervisor. However, there were three important differences between Phase II and Phase IV: meetings with the plant superintendent were not instituted for the men; comments that "work was fun" were never voiced by the men; and the men's productivity did not climb to unprecedented heights, as the women's did. In fact, the men went to great lengths to keep production constant and in line with the normative conception of "a fair day's work" that the group developed. They developed various punitive measures to bring "speed kings" and "chisellers" (those who worked too fast or too slowly) back into line.

The Influence of Hawthorne on Organizational Theory	Early conclusions drawn from the Hawthorne studies provided the foundation of the human relations school. One of the first conclusions became known as the *Hawthorne effect*. This proposition holds that when people know they are subjects of an experiment and they receive a lot of special attention, they tend to behave the way they think the researchers expect them to. Organizational theorists of the day used this effect to explain the anomalous results of the lighting experiments and the women's increased productivity in the relay assembly test room. It has also influenced the design of social psychological experiments ever since, as researchers try to control for this distortion.

The other conclusions drawn from the studies dealt with the social aspect of work, the relationships among the members of the informal group, the norms that informal groups develop and types of supervision. The relationships among the women in Phase II were happy and supportive, while those among the men in Phase IV were not. This led human relations theorists to conclude that happy group relationships are directly related to productivity. Both the women and the men were paid on the basis of a modified group-piecework incentive scheme. That is, once productivity exceeded a given standard, part of their earnings were determined by the productivity of the group. In this respect, the women appeared to act rationally, but the men did not. Human relations theory then tried to determine the group processes involved in developing non-rational norms. Finally, they noted the absence of formal supervision in the relay assembly test room. This led them to conclude that freedom from rigid supervision was as important in increasing the women's productivity as all of the other factors combined. This idea produced decades of intensive research and theorizing on the efficacy of various leadership styles.

Of course, in retrospect, we can see that supervision was similar in both the men's and women's groups while productivity varied dramatically. We can also speculate that the special attention paid to the women by the plant superintendent could have created the Hawthorne effect on their group. Nevertheless, assuming that happy group relationships and rational norms produce high productivity, theorists focused on the type of supervision (that is, the leadership style) that would foster happiness and rationality in group members.

Decades later, reanalyses of these Hawthorne studies (Perrow, 1972) have modified the original conclusions. In fact, they produced a substantially different conception of informal groups.

Starting from the premise that people will respond rationally to the constraints organizations place on them, Perrow and others investigated the objective conditions surrounding the studies. They found that the Hawthorne plant, like most others, had a long history of raising the productivity standard once it had been consistently attained. This meant that, over the long term, workers had to achieve an increasingly fast pace to maintain their incomes. It is also significant that the female workers' productivity climbed during the boom of the late 1920s. It gradually levelled off as the Depression of the 1930s set in. The study of the male workers in Phase IV started only after the plant began to lay off workers in response to bad times. On both counts, then, the male workers' norm of holding to "a fair day's work" seems eminently rational. It is entirely logical that they would attempt to maintain a balance between productivity and earnings and to protect their jobs by not producing too much. This analysis compels organizational theorists to reject the early human relations conception of non-rational workers and group norms.

We can learn important principles from these reanalyses of the Hawthorne studies that help us to understand the behaviour of informal groups. First, let us assume (as a working hypothesis) that group members act rationally, in their own collective best interest. Then, examine the objective situation from the perspective of the group members. This should enable us to understand why they act the way they do. Finally, organizational success can be directly related to (among other factors, of course) the degree of compatibility between the rational goals of the informal group and of the organization itself.

The informal organization can either help or hinder the attainment of the goals of the formal organization. This will largely depend on the quality of the relationship between the two. Frequently cited examples of hindrance are the British coal industry and the Canadian post office. Both of these have a long history of bitter labour-management conflict. Perhaps the most dramatic example of the results of compatible informal and formal goals is Team Canada's victory over the Soviet Union in the eight-game hockey series of 1972. Experts conclude that the intense will to win generated by the team members themselves was the predominant cause of the Canadian team's victory.

The Evolution of Organizational Theory

Organizational theory has developed, somewhat erratically, over the twentieth century. These developments are partly due to the operation of the research cycle, which was explained in Chapter 2. Theories are developed and then empirically tested. The results

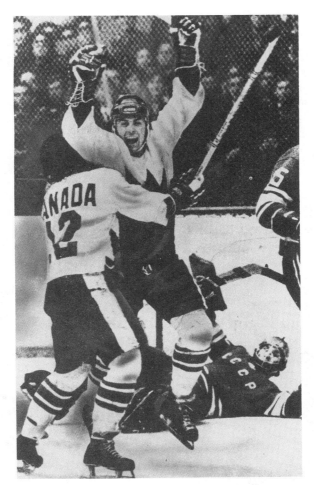

Paul Henderson (with stick raised) scores, with 34 seconds remaining in the final game, to win the Canada–U.S.S.R. hockey series of 1972. Hockey experts conclude that it was the will to win developed by the players themselves (i.e., the informal organization) that resulted in this victory.

TORONTO STAR SYNDICATE.

may support the theory, support a theoretical modification, or lead to efforts to develop a new theory that will better explain the research findings. Developments in organizational theory are also partly due to developments in sociology as a whole. These resulted from changes in the influences of different propositions concerning the nature of human action and from changes in the relative importance of the micro-sociological focus on people versus the macro-sociological focus on social structure.

Taylorism: Homo Economicus and the One Best Way

One of the earliest approaches to organizational theory was Frederick W. Taylor's *Scientific Management* (1911). It attracted great attention in North America and Western Europe during a period of industrial strife. Taylor's intention was to end labour-management conflict over "shares of the pie" by providing a bigger pie. Taylor saw the worker as *Homo economicus*—an economically rational being who works solely for economic rewards. Therefore, reasoned Taylor, if we show workers how to produce more and pay them more as profits increase, everyone will be happy—workers, managers and corporate shareholders alike.

To accomplish this, Taylor and his followers rigorously trained time-and-motion-study experts to break down every task into its essential motions. In the process, they hoped to strip away all the non-essential ones. These experts then trained each worker to perform specific tasks in the precise way their studies showed was the most efficient. Then they timed them with a stopwatch to develop a "standard time," which became the basis of their piecework rates. Workers were then paid (at least partly) on the basis of these rates. The result was often a spectacular, but short-lived, increase in productivity.

Taylorism developed the specialized division of labour to the fullest. It produced an extreme vertical division of labour, within which workers repeated their narrowly defined tasks over and over again. It also introduced a new, horizontal division of labour. No longer could workers use their experience to improve the efficiency of their

The modern assembly line, developed under the influence of scientific management principles, has increased productivity enormously, but at tremendous cost to workers' humanity.

CAMERIQUE STOCK PHOTOGRAPHY.

task performance. Instead, the workplace was now divided into thinkers (managers and experts) and doers (workers). The mindless, repetitive work that scientific management advocated and the alienation it produced was one reason it gradually faded from prominence. The underlying reason was that human beings are too complex to be defined simply as *Homo economicus*. Perhaps a more pressing reason was that "many employers regarded his methods as an unwarranted interference with managerial prerogatives" (Bendix, 1956 : 280).

Classical School: The Functions of Management

The classical school of organizational theory focused on the functions of management. These theorists provided managers with a series of proverbs on managerial effectiveness that were ahead of their time. Chester Barnard was an important classical theorist. He developed the idea that a successful organization must maintain a balance between the inducements it offers its members and the contributions it expects from them. On the other hand, one facet of Barnard's work led organizational theory astray for decades.

Barnard, assuming that co-operation is the basic mode of human existence, defined organizations as "co-operative systems." Yet, his most influential work (1938) included a treatise on management techniques designed to rid organizations of conflict. Barnard resolved the paradox of conflict in co-operative systems by proposing that only unbalanced people became embroiled in conflict. He argued these people existed only among the working classes. Barnard saw rational managers dragging humanity forward into modernity against the resistance of the non-rational, emotional and almost subhuman workers. One reason for the profound influence of Barnard was the legitimacy that he provided to the emerging managerial class.

Human Relations and Behavioural Schools: The Happiness Era

In the early 1930s organizational theory shifted away from seeing organization as structure (in the tradition of Weber and Taylor) to seeing it as *people*. This new focus dominated the field through the 1960s.

Growing out of the famous Hawthorne studies, the early human relations school focused on relationships within informal groups. It assumed that happy group relationships produced job satisfaction, which in turn produced high productivity. This school studied the effects of supervision on this equation. Since it saw workers as emotional and non-rational, management's task was to instil both happiness and rationality in these work groups. The fundamental objective, though, was productivity. Happiness and rationality were viewed as means to this end.

Then in the 1940s and 1950s, Abraham Maslow (1954) developed his hierarchy of needs, which changed our view of workers forever. No longer were organizations seen to be composed of just two groups—workers and managers. They were associations of complex human beings, who responded to inner drives that Maslow ranked in a hierarchy of needs (physiological, security, social, esteem and self-fulfilment).

Douglas McGregor developed and popularized Maslow's path-breaking work. His *The Human Side of Enterprise* (1960) is probably the most influential book ever written

---

A Misguided Cohort

During the 1960s and early 1970s, the influence of the behavioural school was so strong that virtually every large bureaucracy sent their managers to training courses designed to change leadership styles from "task centred" to "employee centred." Many of these courses were badly conceived, and attempted to change managers' personalities to fit the new style. Many managers tried, but failed, to make this change. Others, who had enough confidence in their own self-worth, refused to attempt it.

However, as they returned to their jobs, they came under intense pressure to fit the new behavioural mould. In self-defence, they went through the motions. Managers throughout North America began to keep card files on their subordinates containing personal information such as their spouse's health and occupation, their children's names and ages and the birthdates of every member of the family; a secretary could check the file and send out birthday greetings over the boss's signature.

It became the ritual for managers to look over the file before calling a subordinate into the office. Then the subordinate would be greeted with a, "Hi Joe, how's Mary? I hope she's fully recovered from her operation last year. And how is little Cynthia getting along, and Joe Jr.? Say, he must be nearly ready to start school." Then, the ritual over, boss and subordinate would get down to business.

Well, people on the whole are fairly intelligent, and the insincerity of this misguided approach was soon apparent. Those bosses who had a sincere concern for the well-being of their subordinates were well liked, but those who were insincerely going through the motions in self-defence soon became disliked and even detested.

It seems that, through the inappropriate application of the tenets of the behavioural school, we systematically trained a whole cohort of North American bosses in the art of insincerity.

---

for managers. McGregor and other members of the behavioural school concluded that the predominant leadership style of their era was autocratic and task centred. They proposed that managers should adopt a participative/employee-centred leadership style instead.

The cumulative result of these two schools was the burgeoning of management-training programs aimed at improving superior-subordinate relationships and workers' happiness. However, subsequent research has shown that happiness and job satisfaction are a function of much more than these relationships, and the correlation between them and productivity is tenuous and indirect at best.

Systems Theory: The Organization as Organism	Sociological influence on organizational theory re-emerged with systems theory. This approach saw organizations as complex systems of interconnected parts. More than that, it saw them as open systems, because organizations are also part of the larger social system within which they operate. They receive inputs from their environment, process them and produce outputs for consumption. These outputs must be acceptable to the environment if the organizations are to survive. In fact, survival is a basic theme

of systems theory. It sees organizations and their goals as shaped by the interests of their participants and their environments. Systems theory stressed the effects of the environment on organizations. However, as critic Charles Perrow (1972) correctly charges, it tended to ignore the effects of large and powerful organizations on their environments.

Systems theory also saw organizations as analogous to organisms, that is, as intricately interdependent systems of functional parts. To use an apt analogy: just as blood poisoning from an infected cut on the hand affects the whole human body, so can an ineffective sales department or a hostile work force endanger the success of an entire organization. The view produced an emphasis on the uniqueness of organizations. It also often focused on the "ripple effect"; that is, how changes in one part produce (often unforeseen) changes in other parts of an organization.

The Contingency Approach: "It Depends"

Evolving out of both systems theory and the behavioural school, the contingency approach combines sociological and psychological approaches to organizational theory. It criticizes earlier organizational theories for trying to develop universal principles, whether about the virtues and vices of bureaucracy or the leader-follower relationship. When we try to apply these principles, contingency theorists argue, we run smack up against reality with all its complications. The watchword of the contingency approach is *it depends*. It holds that the essential function of organizational theorists is to specify *upon what* it depends and *in which* ways.

Proponents have applied the contingency approach to organizational topics ranging from structural design to leadership. Perhaps its greatest contribution has been to analyse the effects of the situational contexts within which leader-follower relations are embedded. For example, contingency theorists conclude that in a situation as alienating as the assembly line, autocratic and task-centred leadership is the only style that has a hope of success. Note that this contradicts the conclusions of the behavioural school. Fred Fiedler (1965), a prominent contingency theorist, proposes that it is impractical to get managers to change their leadership style dramatically. Much better, he suggests, to match managers' styles to the jobs they fit.

Some highly influential work straddles the boundary between the contingency and structural approaches. (The structural approach is discussed in a later section of this chapter.) A group of British sociologists have done intensive empirical studies on the differences between mechanistic and organic organizational structures. Mechanistic structures conform most closely to Weber's concept of bureaucracy. Organic structures conform least (Burns and Stalker, 1961). The latter are much more fluid and personal. They contain more lateral than vertical communication. Furthermore, this communication is more likely to include advice, co-ordination and problem solving than the giving and receiving of orders. These studies also suggest that organic structures are more effective in rapidly changing environments, while mechanistic organizations perform best in stable environments. Joan Woodward's (1965) studies of one hundred British corporations suggest that the type of technology an organization employs strongly affects its optimum structure. She found that the most effective firms using mass production technology employ a mechanistic structure. This facilitates the standardization and cost efficiency essential to their success. However, the most successful firms employing unit production (that is, one of a kind) and process production (for example, chemical plants) have organic structures because these take advantage of the innovative capacity of their members.

Labour Process Theory: Worker Exploitation

Arising in the 1970s, labour process theory is a neo-Marxist approach to the organization and conduct of work. It focuses on the alienation of the worker and on power relationships between capitalists and workers.

Alienation is an important concept in Marx's analysis of capitalism. His concept comprises four elements, which are concisely depicted by Rinehart (1987):

1. *Alienation of workers from the products of their labour.* As soon as workers sell their capacity to work to their employers, they receive wages in return rather than any interest in the products they produce. These products belong solely to the employer.
2. *Alienation of workers from the labour process.* Wage workers must surrender to their employer the control of how and when a product will be produced.
3. *Alienation of workers from themselves.* Because of the first two elements of alienation, work no longer becomes a central life activity or a means of self-expression. It becomes, instead, merely a means to the end of obtaining income for life satisfaction *off* the job.
4. *Alienation of workers from others.* Under capitalism, workers are separated from their employers. This is because they hold opposing interests in the control of, and benefits from, the labour process. Workers are also alienated from each other as they compete for jobs.

From these premises, it logically follows that rational workers will resist efforts by capitalists and management to convert the labour time they purchase into increased effort. This perspective sees the "human engineering" of the behavioural school as a misguided and superficial effort. It does nothing to change the power relations of the wider society or at the point of production (Braverman, 1974). Indeed, the ultimate solution would be worker control within a socialist economy (Rinehart, 1987).

An important strand in this perspective is the intensification of management control over the workplace that has taken place since the turn of the century. This is exemplified by Taylor's scientific management, the introduction of assembly lines and the use of technology to convert workers into machine tenders. This perspective sees all these as elements of a strategy to replace the skilled craftsman of a bygone era with a modern unskilled and easily replaceable counterpart (Braverman, 1974). There have been many historical studies that generally support the decline of craft workers. However, the deskilling process is a very complex one, with new skills replacing old ones in many instances (Clement, 1988).

Another central element in this perspective has been an analysis of the evolution of different forms of control that capitalists have exercised over the workplace. Edwards's influential study (1979) concludes that the first of these was the simple, person-to-person domination of the owner or foreman over the worker. As firms grew, this became impractical. Edwards concluded that capitalists then consciously developed technology that enhanced their ability to control the pace and execution of work. Thus, technological control replaced face-to-face domination. The automotive assembly line that Henry Ford first implemented in 1913 would be a clear example of technological control. This made power relations more impersonal, but did nothing to motivate the workers. So, increasing worker resistance led to the advent of today's *bureaucratic control*. This represents the "institutionalization" of control. Rules and procedures now govern the conduct of each specific task, the penalties for poor performance and the rewards for good performance. In this form of control, the power relations became impersonalized and embedded in the structure of the organization. Still, however, "top-echelon management retain their control over the enterprise through their ability to determine the rules, set the criteria, establish the structure, and enforce compliance" (Edwards, 1979: 173).

FIGURE 11-2

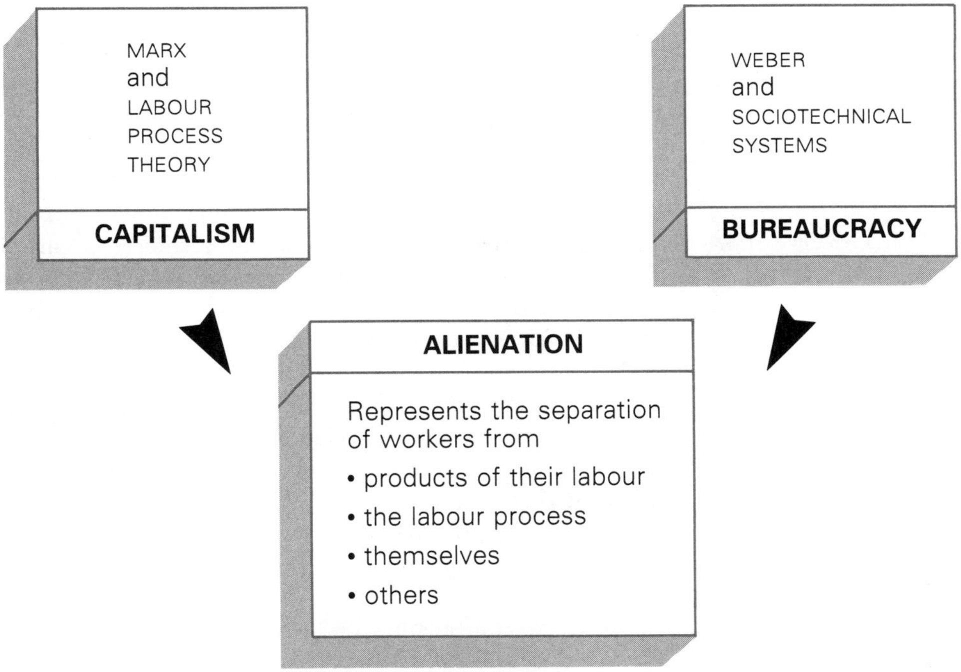

Edwards proposes that this transformation of forms of workplace control has been driven by the capitalists' imperative to extract the maximum possible effort from the wage worker. Critics of labour process theory argue that "deskilling" and the advent of bureaucratic control occur in socialist and capitalist societies alike. While deplorable and even demeaning, they are really specific aspects of Weber's more general concept of bureaucracy. There may be some validity to the critique. Nevertheless, we can learn much from labour process theory about the reality of work and the problems faced by workers in repetitive, mind-numbing jobs.

Robert Blauner's (1964) studies of the effects of bureaucracies were from a Weberian perspective. Nevertheless, they focused on their capacity to alienate workers. He concluded that the technology a bureaucracy employed largely determined the degree of workers' alienation. He classified the four basic technologies used by the industries he studied as assembly line (automobiles), machine tending (textiles), continuous process (petrochemicals) and craft (printing). Then he studied the impact of each on workers' powerlessness, sense of meaninglessness, self-estrangement and social isolation. Not surprisingly, he found that technology powerfully affected alienation. It was highest among assembly-line workers, diminished through the intermediate technologies in his typology and was lowest among craft workers who enjoyed much more control and self-expression in their work. This raises a real dilemma. Do we really want to reduce worker alienation badly enough to eliminate assembly-line work and machine-tending jobs by automating them out of existence? Should we expand the number of jobs in relatively inefficient craft production? Conversely, can we reduce alienation by transcending technological determinism, as the sociotechnical systems approach proposes?

Sociotechnical Systems: Beyond Technological Determinism

Sociotechnical systems theory shares elements of the labour process perspective's critique of the management-oriented scientific management and the human relations schools. Both charge that the social engineering of human relations and behavioural professionals merely aims to make the technical engineering of Taylor's time-and-motion experts more palatable to workers. Both share a worker-oriented perspective. Yet, sociotechnical systems theorists *assume* the continuation of capitalist industry and propose solutions attractive to capitalists and workers alike.

This theory proposes that we have blindly let technology shape our whole concept of work. Engineers, working in the scientific management tradition, follow the technological imperative. They develop the most efficient technology, completely ignoring its dehumanizing effect on the people involved. "To the engineer the perfect machine is the one that an imbecile could operate; he is surprised if the result is a machine only an imbecile is happy operating" (Cherns, 1980 : 112). Proponents of this theory argue that this use of technology will ultimately lead to the collapse of the capitalist industrial system.

The sociotechnical approach sees industrial activity as a sociotechnical system comprising social and technological subsystems that can interact positively or negatively.

Therefore, it proposes that the social and technological subsystems be developed *simultaneously*. This approach contrasts with other paradigms. They assume that technology takes priority in development. Thus, technology will determine the nature of the social system. The sociotechnical approach has produced the quality of work life (QWL) movement, which tries to implement sociotechnical concepts in practical situations.

The principles of QWL, developed initially by the British Tavistock Institute in 1949, are as follows:

1. The social and technical subsystems should be jointly and coincidently developed.
2. Representatives of the social system—workers—should be heavily involved in this development.
3. The basic unit of the organization should be the work group (as a social system), not the individual. Thus, tasks should be formally allocated to work groups, which will set productivity standards jointly with management.
4. The work group should control its own work activities and the way these are distributed to individual members. This would provide some worker autonomy. It should also make work "variety increasing" and reverse the dehumanizing modern trend toward an excessive division of labour.
5. The role of the foreperson changes dramatically. In lieu of the traditional supervision of individual workers, he or she now oversees the boundaries between work groups and co-ordinates their efforts.

Trist (1981) shows that QWL has had a spotty history. Early successes in the British coal and auto industries were short lived. In each case, management terminated the program and reverted to the traditional bureaucratic system. Another highly successful trial in an American coal mine died an early death when the union became split between the workers involved in the project and those who were not.

Eventually, however, the movement took off in Scandinavia, where it was particularly congruent with social values. Norskhydro (Norway's largest employer) and Volvo (who found it impossible to recruit Swedes to work on conventional assembly lines) both achieved notable success. In the past decade or so, hundreds of successful QWL projects have been set up in Western Europe, the United States and Canada. These projects have clearly improved the quality of work life, as evidenced by such empirical evidence as substantial reductions in labour turnover, absenteeism, wildcat strikes and sabotage. They have also provided substantial benefits to the corporations involved in increasing labour productivity.

How can we explain the difficult birth and retarded development of an approach to industrial organization that seems to offer so much to both management and labour? Trist (1981) charges that management is more interested in power than in profits. Because the power of middle management and first-line supervisors is clearly diminished by QWL, management has not been enthusiastic about its success. Nor have unions been universally supportive. Many quasi-QWL projects have attempted to obtain the corporate benefits of the approach without disturbing the traditional organizational

Adapting to a Changing World

Alienation, a sort of non-work ethic, has been increasing in the postwar period, especially among the younger generation whose expectations and experiences are different from those that arose under the conditions of scarcity that characterized the Depression years. Attitude surveys in several countries indicate that only the older worker continues to be willing to trade off dehumanizing work simply for good wages and employment security. . . .

The human individual has work-related needs other than those specified in a contract of employment (such as wages, hours, safety, security of tenure, and so on). These "extrinsic" requirements . . . form the legacy of the old work ethic. In addition, a variety of . . . "intrinsic" factors must also be met if the new work ethic is to develop. These intrinsic factors . . . include:

1. The need for the job to be reasonably demanding in terms other than sheer endurance and to provide a minimum of variety (not necessarily novelty, which is too much for some people though the spice of life for others). This is to recognize enfranchisement in problem-solving as a human right.

2. The need to be able to learn on the job on a continuing basis. Again, this is a question of neither too much nor too little, but of matching solutions to personal requirements. This is to recognize personal growth as a human right.

3. The need for some area of decision-making that the individual can call his own. This recognizes the opportunity to use one's own judgment as a human right.

4. The need for some degree of social support and recognition in the workplace, from both fellow workers and bosses. This recognizes "group belongingness" as a human right.

5. The need to be able to relate what one does and what one produces to one's social life. That is, to have a meaningful occupational identity which gives a man or woman dignity. This recognizes the opportunity to contribute to society as a human right.

6. The need to feel that the job leads to some sort of desirable future (not necessarily promotion). It may involve training or redeployment—a career at shop floor level leading to the development of greater skill. This recognizes hope as a human right. . . .

What have we learned about diffusing a higher quality of working life into the organization as a whole? And what lies ahead?

From Eric Trist. 1977. "Adapting to a Changing World," pp. 4–7. Reproduced by permission.

structure of the corporation. Consequently, they have been soundly criticized by labour process theorists. Many unions argue that if QWL is really as successful as its proponents claim, then surely its very efficiency will ultimately throw their members out of work. Finally, some unions oppose QWL because of its fundamental principle of direct consultation and co-operation between labour and management. They are concerned that this undermines an important source of union power—the role of intermediary between workers and management.

Nevertheless, despite these important obstacles, the sociotechnical systems approach is an exciting and promising new development in organizational theory. It has the potential to combine a degree of workplace democracy with industrial efficiency.

Structural
Approach: The
Organization
Makes the Person

Another prominent recent approach seems to offer great promise. It is the structural approach. In the Weberian tradition, it focuses on the structural characteristics of organizations and the effect of these on the people within them. One objective of contemporary structural analysis is to devise changes in organizational structures that will make bureaucracies more effective by making them more humane. Charles Perrow (1972), for example, concludes that structural analyses of the famous Hawthorne studies show that bureaucratic effectiveness depends on the degree to which a bureaucracy can implement structural changes that will increase the congruence between the goals of the formal and the informal organizations.

Herbert Simon, the Nobel laureate, is an important pioneer of the structural approach. Noted primarily for his work on decision theory, Simon also pointed out the importance of structural constraints on organizational decision making. In doing so, he provided "the muscle and flesh for the Weberian skeleton" (Perrow, 1972:146). His studies led him to conclude that Weber's six elements of bureaucracy define the situation for decision makers and shape the premises upon which they make organizational decisions. Thus, bureaucratic structures influence their members to make decisions that are consistent with those made at the top of the hierarchy.

An influential structural analysis of modern bureaucracy is Rosabeth Kanter's *Men and Women of the Corporation* (1977). Kanter uses three key variables to explain the behaviour of people in organizations: the structures of power, of opportunities for advancement and of proportional representation. Those who have *power*, her evidence suggests, make good leaders. This is not because of the nature of their relationship with subordinates, but because they can obtain for their whole group a favourable share of the organization's resources. On the other hand, "accountable but powerless" people react rationally to their unfortunate situation in ways detrimental to both the organization and their leadership. Those who are upwardly *mobile* support the organization and its goals. Those whose mobility is blocked salvage their dignity by withdrawing their support from the organization and attempting to gain recognition elsewhere (for example, from subordinates or from sources outside the organization). Finally, Kanter proposes that those who make up a small *proportion* of a group, such as women and ethnic minorities among managers, are treated as tokens. The results (exclusion from leaders' networks, stereotyping and intense scrutiny) produce a self-fulfilling prophecy. Tokens perform moderately well, at best, because of structural constraints, not individual deficiencies. Thus, their numbers fail to become large enough to break the bonds of tokenism. Not surprisingly, Kanter advocates modifying the structures of power, mobility and proportions.

Conclusions

Bureaucracy pervades our daily lives; and large bureaucracies wield enormous power in our society. Large business bureaucracies can ruin their smaller competitors, and governmental bureaucracies often prevail over parliaments. Weber (1968) analysed

The advent of the micro-computer makes it entirely feasible for a significant proportion of clerical and technical work to be done at home rather than in the office.

DICK HEMINGWAY.

how the bureaucracy of Bismarck's Germany dominated the weak parliament of the day. Lipset (1950) found that the entrenched bureaucracy aborted many of the newly elected CCF government's reform programs in Saskatchewan in the 1940s. And Campbell and Szablowski (1979) found that Ottawa's "super-bureaucrats" frustrate and circumvent members of our Canadian Parliament.

Indeed, Peter Blau (1963), drawing on the work of Michels (1962), points out a paradox in the relationship between two fundamentally different forms of social organization: bureaucracy and democracy. Bureaucracy is an organization formed to achieve predetermined objectives. Its organizing principle is efficiency, and its organizing structure is the hierarchical relationship of dominance and subordination. Democracy, on the other hand, is an organization established to determine the objectives of a human group. Its organizing principle is the freedom of dissent necessary to permit majority opinions to form, and its organizing structure is essentially egalitarian.

Democratic forms of social organization are well suited to making choices between alternative policies. But they are *not* well suited to implementing them. This is the role bureaucracy fills so efficiently. So, the two forms of organization complement each other. Democracy depends on bureaucracy to implement its policies. But paradoxically, as Blau recognized, by concentrating power in the hands of a very few, bureaucracy is a constant threat to the very survival of democratic institutions.

Summary

To a considerable extent, the evolution of organizational theory parallels changes in social values and ideologies. Taylorism, the classical theorists and the human relations school can be seen as holdovers from the time of the Industrial Revolution. This was an era when the workers were viewed as children (which, indeed, they often were). The behavioural school focused on more enlightened relations between superiors and subordinates in bureaucratic structures. It thrived as the values of North America and Western Europe changed in the 1960s. The systems and contingency approaches reflected the growing complexity of the modern world. Labour process and sociotechnical perspectives reflected disillusionment with the naive optimism of the 1960s. In the 1970s and 1980s, attention also turned to structural theories to explain organizational behaviour. Studies began to show that the "happiness era" was over. People would rather work for a powerful boss than a nice one, because a powerful boss can obtain a larger share of the organization's resources for the whole group (Kanter, 1977).

In fact, if we are in the midst of a prolonged period of moderate economic growth and restricted economic rewards for workers, the critical issue of the next decade may concern our ability to change organizations structurally to make them more effective and more humane.

Suggested Readings

Gross, Edward, and Amitai Etzioni
1985. *Organizations in Society*. Englewood Cliffs, N.J.: Prentice-Hall. A very readable survey of the organization literature, containing many interesting examples and studies of the public sector. Although less comprehensive and incisive than Perrow's book, it has the advantage of being easily accessible to a first-year university student.

Kanter, Rosabeth Moss
1977. *Men and Women of the Corporation*. New York: Basic Books. A study of managers and white-collar workers in a large American conglomerate. An excellent example of the structural perspective.

Krahn, Harvey J., and Graham S. Lowe
1988. *Work, Industry and Canadian Society*. Scarborough, Ont.: Nelson. A superb introductory text to the sociology of work, occupations, labour markets and organizations. Applies classical and contemporary theories within a Canadian context.

Lowe, Graham S. and Harvey J. Krahn, eds.
1984. *Working Canadians: Readings in the Sociology of Work and Industry*. Toronto: Methuen. An excellent collection of forty-seven short articles dealing with various aspects of work in the Canadian context.

Mills, C. Wright
1951. *White Collar*. New York: Oxford University Press. A classic study of the work world of the American "middle classes." Covers small entrepreneurs, managers, professionals and white-collar workers.

Perrow, Charles
1986. *Complex Organizations: A Critical Essay*, 3rd ed. New York: Random House. An excellent survey of organizational sociology from the perspective of an important sociologist who has been influential in the development of several perspectives, most currently the one we label in this chapter the "structural" perspective.

Rinehart, James W.
1987. *The Tyranny of Work*, 2nd ed. Toronto: Harcourt, Brace, Jovanovich. A compelling study of worker alienation in Canada from the perspective of labour process theory.

Discussion Questions

1. What personal experiences can you recall that illustrate the virtues of bureaucracy?

2. What personal experiences can you recall that illustrate bureaucracy's vices?

3. The larger an organization, the more likely it will conform to the ideal typical characteristics of bureaucracy. Why?

4. Assuming that you are headed for a managerial career, rather than for blue-collar or clerical work, why should you bother to learn to look at work and organizations from the perspective of the worker?

5. Given the critiques of the human relations and behavioural schools found in this chapter, account for the influence and longevity of these approaches.

6. "Bureaucracy contains the seeds of its own destruction." Comment.

Data Collection Exercises

1. Design and conduct a participant observation research project to assess the differences with respect to efficiency and personal versus impersonal employee-customer relationships between a bureaucratic fast-food outlet (e.g., McDonalds, Burger King, etc.) and a small non-bureaucratic "greasy spoon" type of local restaurant/coffee shop. Relate your findings to some of the characteristics of bureaucracy and the modern perspectives on bureaucracy discussed in this chapter.

2. Written rules are an important characteristic of bureaucracy. In large organizations these are often contained in "procedures manuals." Visit a small, independent variety store and a large department store and ask the owner or a member of management how many written rules (or pages in a procedure manual) they have for employees to follow. Try to find out some examples of these rules and procedures. What can you conclude about bureaucracy from your findings?

3. Consult the earliest and latest available editions of the *Canada Year Book*. Find the number of people in occupations classified as managerial, administrative, professional and technical. Then find the total number of people in blue- and white-collar occupations *excluding* the above and farming and fishing occupations. Take the ratio of the former group to the latter for each year. Develop a plausible explanation for the change you find in these proportions.

4.   Consult the earliest and latest available editions of the *Canada Year Book*. Calculate the number of employees per establishment and per million dollars of value added for total Canadian manufacturing activity for each year. What conclusions can you draw from this? Can these findings complement the explanation you developed in Question 3?

Writing Exercises

1.   Compare and contrast a successful organization that you know with an unsuccessful one. What major factors account for these differences in effectiveness?

2.   Organizations can be seen as *structures* (in the tradition of Weber and Taylor) or as *people* (in the tradition of Maslow and McGregor). What are the relative merits of these opposing viewpoints? Can they be integrated? If so, how? If not, why not?

3.   What changes in the structures of power, opportunity and proportions would the structural approach propose? How (if at all) would these make bureaucracies more effective and humane?

4.   Under what conditions would you expect QWL programs to work well? to work poorly? Why?

Glossary

Alienation: *a concept derived from Marx's analysis of the position of workers under capitalism. It refers to the separation of workers from the products of their labour, the control of the work process, owners, managers and other workers and even from themselves.*

Bureaucracy: *a specific type of formal organization that contains these characteristics: a division of labour; a hierarchy of positions; a formal system of rules; a separation of the person from the office; hiring and promotion based on technical merit; the protection of careers. May be found in both government and private industry and in both capitalist and socialist societies.*

Classical school: *an approach that focuses on the functions and social importance of management.*

Contingency approach: *an approach that evolved out of both systems theory and the behavioural school. It rejects universal solutions to organizational problems and holds that the essential function of organizational theorists is to specify the critical variables that affect any given organizational situation.*

Formal organization: *a deliberately formed social group in which people, resources and technologies are consciously co-ordinated through formalized roles, statuses and relationships to achieve a division of labour that is intended to effectively achieve a specific set of relationships.*

Hawthorne effect: *a proposition derived from the Hawthorne studies. It holds that when people know they are subjects of an experiment and receive a lot of special attention, they tend to behave the way they think the researchers expect them to.*

Human relations and behavioural schools: *assuming that people are social beings who will be more productive if they are happy, these schools studied different leadership styles to find which would best produce these desired results.*

Informal organization: *complex personal and informal networks that develop among people who interact on the job.*

Labour process theory: *a neo-Marxist approach to organizations and the conduct of work that focuses on alienation and power relationships.*

Mechanistic structures: *organizational structures that closely conform to the bureaucratic form; see Organic structures.*

Organic structures: *organizational structures that are more fluid and personal and that contain more horizontal communications than the mechanistic form.*

Organization: *a group of people participating in a division of labour that is co-ordinated by communication and leadership to achieve a common goal or goals. Includes both spontaneous and formal organizations.*

Sociotechnical systems: *an approach that emphasizes the simultaneous development of both the social and the technological systems of the workplace as a means of combining a degree of workplace democracy with industrial efficiency.*

Spontaneous organization: *an organization that arises quickly to meet a single goal and then disbands when the goal is achieved or perceived to be beyond reach or when it becomes absorbed by a formal organization.*

Structural approach: *an approach that focuses on the structural characteristics of organizations and the effects of these on the people within them.*

Systems theory: *an approach that sees organizations as (a) complex systems of interrelated parts and (b) parts of a complex social system. It studies the intricate relationships between these roles.*

Taylorism: *sometimes called "scientific management." An approach, derived from the assumption that workers perform solely for economic rewards, that develops the division of labour to the extreme. The workplace becomes divided between thinkers (efficiency experts) and doers (workers). The latter's tasks become highly specialized, routine and repetitive.*

References

Barnard, Chester
    1938. *The Functions of the Executive.* Cambridge: Harvard University Press.
Bendix, Reinhard
    1956. *Work and Authority in Industry.* New York: Harper and Row.
Blau, Peter M.
    1963. *The Dynamics of Bureaucracy.* Chicago: University of Chicago Press.
Blauner, Robert
    1964. *Alienation and Freedom.* Chicago: University of Chicago Press.
Braverman, Harry
    1974. *Labor and Monopoly Capital.* New York: Monthly Review Press.
Burns, Tom, and G. M. Stalker
    1961. *The Management of Innovation.* London: Tavistock.
Campbell, C., and G. Szablowski
    1979. *The Superbureaucrats.* Toronto: Macmillan.

Cherns, A. B.
1980. "Speculations on the Social Effects of New Microelectronics Technology." *International Labour Review* 119(6): 705–22.

Clement, Wallace
1988. "The Labour Process," pp. 161–84. In James Curtis and Lorne Tepperman, eds., *Understanding Canadian Society*. Toronto: McGraw-Hill Ryerson.

Crozier, Michael
1964. *The Bureaucratic Phenomenon*. Chicago: University of Chicago Press.

Edwards, R.
1979. *Contested Terrain: The Transformation of the Workplace in the Twentieth Century*. New York: Basic Books.

Eisenstadt, S. N.
1965. *Essays on Comparative Institutions*. New York: Wiley.

Fiedler, Fred E.
1965. "Engineer the Job to Fit the Manager." *Harvard Business Review* 43(5).

Fox, Alan
1966. "Management's Frame of Reference," pp. 2–14. In A. Fox, ed., *Industrial Sociology and Industrial Relations*. London: H.M.S.O.

Garson, Barbara
1972. *All the Livelong Day*. New York: Doubleday.

Homans, George
1951. "The Western Electric Researchers," pp. 210–41. In S. D. Hoslett, ed., *Human Factors in Management*. New York: Harper.

Kanter, Rosabeth Moss
1977. *Men and Women of the Corporation*. New York: Basic Books.

Lipset, S. M.
1950. *Agrarian Socialism*. Berkeley: University of California Press.

Maslow, Abraham
1954. *Motivation and Personality*. New York: Harper and Row.

McGregor, Douglas
1960. *The Human Side of Enterprise*. New York: McGraw-Hill.

Merton, Robert
1957. *Social Theory and Social Structure*. New York: Free Press.

Michels, Robert
1962. *Political Parties*. New York: Free Press.

Ouchi, William G., and Alfred M. Jaeger
1978. "Type Z Organization: Stability in the Midst of Mobility." *Academy of Management Review* 3 (April): 35–44.

Perrow, Charles
1972. *Complex Organizations: A Critical Essay*. Glencoe, Ill.: Scott, Foresman.
1977. "The Bureaucratic Paradox." *Organizational Dynamics* (Spring).

Rinehart, James W.
1987. *The Tyranny of Work*, 2nd ed. Toronto: Harcourt Brace Jovanovich.

Smith, Adam
1894 [1776]. *The Wealth of Nations*. London: Macmillan.

Taylor, Frederick W.
1911. *Principles of Scientific Management*. New York: Harper.

Trist, Eric
1977. "Adapting to a Changing World." Paper presented at the 6th International Conference. Montreal (November).
1981. *The Evolution of Socio-Technical Systems*. Toronto: Ontario Ministry of Labour.

Weber, Max
1958. *From Max Weber: Essays in Sociology*, trans. H. H. Gerth and C. Wright Mills. New York: Oxford University Press.
1968. *Economy and Society*. Edited by Guenther Roth and Claus Wittich. New York: Bedminster Press.

Woodward, Joan
1965. *Industrial Organization*. London: Oxford University Press.

part 4

Central Institutions of Society

This section is about institutions: sets of values, activities, structures and resources that meet important social needs. It builds on what we have covered in earlier sections. In doing so, it illustrates how basic social processes come together to produce order and change. Within the central institutions of society, larger structures contain smaller ones; formal structures, informal ones; complex structures, simpler ones; and permanent structures, temporary ones.

For example, though small, the family is a major social institution. The modern nuclear family is a fairly simple social organization that contains three main relationships: parent and child, husband and wife and sibling and sibling. A less temporary social organization than some (say, a school class), the family dissolves itself with the passage of a generation. In time, the parents die, leaving their children to marry and build families of their own.

Some families last even less than a generation, dissolving through divorce or early death and reconstituting through remarriage. Other families may contain many generations. In such families, grandparents and grandchildren often form alliances to undermine and complicate child/parent relationships. Some households may also contain aunts, uncles and other extended kin. These added relationships make the family and household a more complex social unit.

Remarriage certainly increases family complexity. More and more households today contain unmarried or temporarily married spouses and children of different parents. Conflicting rules and role expectations result, further complicating the family's functioning. Much of the change in family life is due to the easing of divorce laws. This, in turn, is a result of changing ideas about gender and gender relations, discussed earlier.

Male and female rights and responsibilities are far from equal today, but they have changed enough to modify family roles a great deal. Women are more able, economically and socially, to maintain their own households today. Thus, household forms and composition come to vary more than in the past.

Other central institutions include the economy, the political system, religious institutions, mass media and the educational system. These institutions differ in important respects, and they also share many similarities. For this reason, sociologists typically ask similar questions about them.

Institutional
Outputs

The study of a central institution often begins by specifying the institution's parts, or member organizations. Then, it often analyses interactions among the parts. Of prime interest are processes of control and co-operation, information flow, and communication and mutual awareness. The chapters in this section address all of these issues as well as others.

Institutional output includes what the institution is *supposed* to accomplish: its stated goals and what members expect of it. Typically, sociologists will ask: "Are the goals met, and if not, why not?" Institutional output is also what the institution *actually* accomplishes. The sociologist is likely to ask: "Is the institution achieving some unstated, unintended or hidden goal? If so, what is it?"

How do the actual outputs of the institution—whether they are programs, laws, decisions or degrees—affect people? How, for example, do television programs influence family life, peer group relations, literacy and mass behaviour? How do government policies influence public life, belief in the state and trust among citizens? How do economic decisions shape material prosperity, class conflict and technological development? How does formally organized religion in Canada affect morality? And how effectively does the educational system shape intellect, character, job skills and political outlook?

The stated (or supposed) goals of an institution are usually rooted in a society's dominant values. Every institution claims a strong cultural foundation and, therefore, the right to command large numbers of people and massive resources. However, an institution's actual goals and practices often threaten this right. The institution's image must be continuously repaired and trust regenerated.

To do this, central institutions support one another against attack. For example, the media support the political system; the educational system supports the economy; and the legal system supports all of these. At various times and places, organized religion has also supported the "establishment"—the current economic and political structure. Much sociological research is devoted to understanding how this co-operation comes about and how it is maintained.

Institutional
Co-operation

The *polity*, or political system of a society, is also discussed in this section. The state, a part of the polity, plays a major role in protecting and controlling other institutions. As Weber pointed out, the state enjoys a monopoly of legitimate force or authority. It has the right to give or take away freedoms, confiscate property, tax and redistribute wealth and force compliance with rules by punishing deviance.

For example, the state spells out the conditions under which economic organizations may operate, buy and sell, hire and fire labour. From the state, educational institutions get the largest part of their operating revenue. At the primary and secondary levels, provincial governments give strong direction to curriculum and other schooling policies. Not surprisingly, all the other central institutions want to control, co-opt or win the favour of the state.

The economy also plays a major part in protecting and controlling other institutions. Indeed, Marxists assert that all social and political institutions rest on an economic base: namely, the relations of production. People's relations to the means of production determine their opportunities for health, security and self-fulfilment. And an institution's linkages to the economy determine its life chances, too. Therefore, in studying any institution, one must understand its economic basis and relations with the economic system.

Sociologists have studied the linkages between church and state, and between religious and economic institutions for over a century. Karl Marx called religion the "opiate of the masses," meaning that it served to pacify the lower classes and prevent rebellion against economic inequality. Max Weber saw an "affinity" between certain forms of Protestantism and the rise of capitalism in northwestern Europe. Conversely, religion played an important role in preventing, or at least delaying, the rise of capitalism in China, India and elsewhere.

More recently, sociologists have taken note of the growing size and significance of born-again Christian movements. In the United States the political lobbying of fundamentalists has narrowed the traditional distance between church and state. In other parts of the world, such as Quebec, the Catholic Church has continued to lose its influence over political, familial and cultural life. In yet other parts of the world—in Eastern Europe and South America, for example—the Catholic Church has supported some anti-government movements and opposed others. Religious organizations, then, become more or less involved with other central institutions as time passes.

Top religious leaders, or *elites*—the Pope, the Archbishop of Canterbury, Billy Graham, Oral Roberts and Jerry Falwell, for example—use their institutional bases to influence both religious and secular activities. Any elite position offers the potential for influence and control. So in studying any institution, we want to know who makes up its elite: What group, class, tribe, region or other social unit is in control, and how do they use that control?

This question, in turn, raises a variety of interesting issues. How does the institution advance or protect the interests of its controlling group? How does the elite keep control? Who else is vying for control, and how are they kept out? Finally, does the institution promise to aid social change, yet actually help to maintain class, ethnic or gender inequality? The astonishing ability of elites to hold on to their power has led sociologists to carry out a great deal of research on "power elites" and upper classes.

Maintaining the Institutional System

Too narrow a focus on elites may mislead us, however. It is not individuals, or even groups of individuals, who determine the structure of central institutions. In time, all individuals go, but structures persist.

What sets the pattern is modern capitalism itself. Private property, a grossly unequal distribution of wealth and a nominally free market in capital, political decision making and ideas define the capitalist society. These features bring most benefit to the already powerful. Central institutions that reproduce the existing order are bound to result, whoever the elite may be.

Some sociologists hold that the key actors in society are neither elites nor institutions, but dominant organizations within institutions: within the economy, banks; within the polity, political parties; within the media, networks and publishing chains. From this perspective, organizations compete to ensure their own survival, as well as benefit institutional elites (owners, board members) and dominant social classes.

Again we must listen to the conversation between Marx and Weber: Does one institution and one elite, or class, dominate society, as Marx holds; or, as Weber says, do many sources of domination co-exist and compete? If we accept the former, we would expect society to change through conflict between the dominant and subordinate classes; if the latter, through shifting power relationships within the dominant class.

Both Marx and Weber recognize the importance of legitimacy, for controlling society is easier if the public co-operates. What, then, shapes people's awareness of, participation in and perceptions about central institutions and their right to control? Does the "Doublethink" and "Newspeak" George Orwell wrote about in *Nineteen Eighty-Four* distort our ability to tell truth from falsehood? Or are people genuinely committed to the stated goals of the central institutions: to educational "excellence," political "good citizenship," media "awareness," religious "good works" and so on? Nothing is harder than sorting out such questions from inside a society, yet this is precisely what sociologists try to do. How, then, can we see what an institution is really doing for, or to, a society?

The Value of Comparative Analysis

Comparative analysis may help us answer this question. By definition, each central institution is an intimate part of its social environment. To see the unique contribution a particular institution is making, sociologists use a variety of strategies.

One is to study a given kind of institution (for example, a capitalist economy, multiparty political system or adversarial legal system) in different cultural, social and economic settings. Another strategy is to study how an institution has changed historically, in relation to earlier (therefore, potentially causal) changes in other institutions. A third is to compare institutions within the same society, to see how they have adapted differently to the same historical (that is, cultural, social and economic) changes.

Still, we should not underestimate the importance of studying a central institution within its own time and place: for example, in Canada, in the late twentieth century. Many of the generalizations the authors make in this section will hold true for all Western, capitalist, industrial societies. But some will need modifying in the light of Canada's peculiar history: its economic dependency, the dominant role of multinational organizations, regional conflict, the twin British and French cultural traditions, high rates of immigration and the resulting multiculturalism, among others.

History provides a useful backdrop against which to assess contemporary society. Chapters in this section refer to broad historical transformations, such as the shift from pre-industrial to industrial society, or early to late (mature) capitalism. Questions asked include: How are changes in one institution related to changes in other institutions, and how are they related to social change overall?

The sociologist may want to complete the analysis by considering proposed alternatives to present arrangements. The sociologist may ask what prospects there are for future change and what dynamics are likely to bring such changes about. How can we bring about a better fit between actual and intended outputs?

Together, these questions and the answers they receive make up the study of central institutions in society.

F*amilies*

MAUREEN BAKER

Introduction

Despite frequent reports by the mass media about high rates of marriage breakdown and family violence, most Canadians highly value their family relationships. Families provide a vehicle for companionship, sexual expression and reproduction. Children are socialized and taught moral values within families. Parents usually share a common residence, provide important services for each other and their children and co-operate economically. Intimate relationships give life meaning and help children and adults to develop their personalities, self worth and values.

As a social institution, the family regulates sexual behaviour and reproduction, provides a setting for rearing children and takes care of sick and disabled people. Governments tend to encourage people to marry and reproduce because employers need a continual supply of young people to work in the labour force. Furthermore, employers count on families to socialize young people to be law-abiding and to want to work, and to provide workers with an opportunity to recuperate from their workday so that they will be able to return to the job the next day. Governments try to strengthen families because they assist their members to fit into society and help control anti-social behaviour.

Although the family remains an important institution both to individuals and to society, family life for most Canadians has changed considerably throughout the past century. More young people are living together, marriages have a greater chance of ending in separation or divorce and children are less often cared for by family members since their mothers work outside the home. More people are living alone, especially before marriage, after separation and divorce, and after widowhood.

In this chapter, we will outline some historical changes in family life, and then discuss several recent issues in Canadian families: cohabitation, childlessness, child care, family violence, divorce and the feminization of poverty. But before we do this, it is necessary to define more clearly what we mean by the term "family," and to outline some cultural variations in family structure and relationships.

Defining Families and Households

In popular usage, the term "family" can refer to those who live with us (our parents and siblings, or spouse and children) or to our entire kin group (including aunts, uncles, grandparents, cousins and in-laws). We also use the term to refer to children, in contexts such as, "Do you have a family yet?" But in order to analyse and research family life, we need to specify exactly who we will include in our analysis.

Sociologists generally clarify the meaning of family by designating the type of family unit. For example, a husband and wife living with their children has been called the *nuclear family*. One parent living in the household with his or her children has been labelled a *one-parent family*. The *extended family* refers to all those considered to be related by blood or marriage. Sociologists have further differentiated between *families*, which involve mating relationships and offspring, and *households*, which include all persons sharing a common residence, whether or not they are related.

The term "household" refers to all those sharing a dwelling whether they are related or not.

NATIONAL ARCHIVES OF CANADA/PA 128761.

Different activities, such as carrying out social science research, defining who will benefit from a social program, and gathering census data, require different definitions of "family." Although the nuclear family has been the typical arrangement for most Canadians in the past, one in five families now includes only one parent in the household. There has also been an increase in the number of couples remaining childless and more people are living in households that are not based on marriage and family. Typical definitions of family are now being challenged in an attempt to create theories more reflective of social reality and to expand social benefits to common-law and homosexual couples. Historical and cross-cultural comparisons further illustrate the many variations in the way people organize their personal and family lives.

Cultural Variations in Families

In a culturally diverse society such as Canada, it is inaccurate to talk about the family as though a single type of family exists or ever did exist. In actual fact, cultural groups tend to organize their family lives differently, depending on such factors as socio-economic background, immigrant status, historical experiences in Canada, relations with dominant groups and religious beliefs.

Nuclear versus Extended Families

According to some researchers, there has been a convergence throughout the world toward the nuclear or *conjugal family* structure as societies and regions become industrialized (Goode, 1963). In the conjugal family, more importance is placed on the marital relationship than on ties with parents or kin group.

The extended family, however, remains important in Canada and elsewhere as a support group, even when members do not live together. For example, many southern Europeans, Latin Americans and Chinese living in Canada and abroad maintain close ties with siblings and parents after they marry. Even when they do not share a residence, relatives may live in the same neighbourhood, visit regularly, telephone daily, assist with child care, provide economic and emotional support and help find employment and accommodation for one another. Close physical and emotional ties with extended family are also more apparent for working-class than middle-class families. Furthermore, women from all social classes tend to maintain closer family relationships throughout their lives than men.

Sociologists in the 1950s lamented the isolation of the modern nuclear family, implying that extended families used to be more prevalent prior to industrialization (Parsons and Bales, 1955). Historians, however, have found that nuclear families were always more typical in terms of living arrangements both in Europe and North America (Goldthorpe, 1987). Neither has it been common for married couples to live with their parents at any time in Canadian history, except for short periods when the parents were widowed and unable to live alone. Nuclear families were more prevalent because life expectancies were short and parents often died before their children reached maturity. Furthermore, young people had to leave home to find work, as only one child could take over the family farm or outside wages were needed to support all family members.

Monogamy versus Polygamy

In Canada and most industrialized countries, *monogamy*, or having one legal spouse at a time, is the social custom and the law. Yet, many Canadians marry, divorce and remarry, and have more than one spouse over their life span. This lifetime pattern has been called *serial monogamy*. Having more than one spouse at a time (*polygamy*) is illegal in all Westernized countries due to the assumed difficulties in providing adequate financial and emotional support for more than one partner, and due to religious ideas of sexual exclusivity.

In some Moslem countries, however, polygamy is still practised, but is usually reserved for wealthy men who can afford to support more than one wife. Polygamy is generally viewed as a status symbol in those societies, but it has also existed in hunting and gathering societies where there were fewer males due to hunting accidents or warfare. Throughout the world, *polygyny* (more than one wife) is much more common than *polyandry* (more than one husband). This probably relates to the fact that only one male is needed to impregnate several wives, to concerns about paternity, and to men's higher status, which allows them to organize society to suit their preferences.

Arranged versus Free-Choice Marriage

In many parts of the world, especially among the upper classes, marriages are arranged by people other than the couple in order to protect family solidarity, reputation or inheritance. Some marriages continue to be arranged in Middle Eastern nations, in Japan and in Moslem countries. The family of either the bride or the groom may make the initial arrangements, but marriage brokers or intermediaries are occasionally used to find a suitable mate. The potential bride and groom are often given veto power in case they object to their parents' choice, but family pressure encourages them to abide by the judgment of the elders.

In countries in which arranged marriages are common, more importance is placed on extended family solidarity, financial security and potential heirs than on love between the young people. Marital partners are urged to respect each other, and it is hoped that love will develop after they marry and share a home. In actual fact, arranged marriages are more stable than free-choice marriages because both families have a stake in marriage stability, divorce is often legally restricted and women cannot always support themselves outside of marriage. The process of modernization and Westernization, however, encourages young people to value "falling in love" and to seek a more intensive marital relationship.

In societies such as pre-modern India and medieval and Renaissance Europe, where women's labour force participation was low and they were unable to live independently from their families, dowries were used to attract a husband and to insure that women had some money in case of divorce or widowhood. Under the dowry system, a family with a daughter must show the family of a prospective groom that they can provide money or property upon marriage. If a woman has a large dowry, she can find a better husband than she might otherwise be able to do. A good husband is usually a man who is wealthy, well educated, healthy and from a respected family. The dowry system has been a great burden for poor families, especially if they have several daughters, and encourages families to prefer sons.

In other pre-industrial societies, such as eastern Indonesia, the groom's family was expected until recently to pay the bride's family a bride-price for permission to marry their daughter. If the bride was beautiful or came from a wealthy or respected family, the price was high. If the groom did not have enough assets, the bride-price could sometimes be paid in labour rather than money or property. Dowries and bride-prices are associated with arranged marriages, yet even in free-choice marriages, symbols of dowries (such as the trousseau) and the bride-price (a gold wedding band) remain.

In most Canadian families, young men and women choose their social and marital partners without formal assistance. It is not uncommon for siblings or friends to introduce two people to each other, but there is certainly no expectation of marriage after such a meeting.

Patterns of Descent and Inheritance

When Canadians marry, they consider that their primary relationship is with each other, rather than with their parents, siblings or in-laws. In some cases, they have little contact with their partner's family, but more often, they are considered to be part of

Magazine Says Girls Killed to Avoid Dowry Demands

Associated Press

NEW DELHI—Almost 80 per cent of baby girls in a caste of poor laborers in southern India are killed by their parents because of the burden of marriage dowry demands, India's leading news magazine reported yesterday.

India Today said that members of the Kallar community in Tamil Nadu state usually kill female babies with poisonous berries.

"Over the last 10 to 15 years, female infanticide has come to be increasingly accepted among the Kallars as the only way out of the dowry problem," the article said. A dowry is the price a woman's family pays to a man and his family in return for marrying her.

In India, women have less status than men. A son is considered an asset in poor families because he will be another wage earner, but a daughter is dismissed as a liability because of the expense of educating and marrying her.

The magazine quoted one woman, identified only as Chinnammal, as saying she killed her infant daughter just after birth with poison berries.

"I killed my child to save it from the lifelong ignominy of being the daughter of a poor family that cannot afford to pay a decent dowry," she was quoted as saying.

"A mother who has borne a child cannot see it suffer even for a little while, let alone kill it," she said. "But I had to do it because it was better to let our child suffer an hour or two and die than suffer throughout life."

The problem of female infanticide is not limited to one community. Families in other parts of India have been known to commit female infanticide, and the problem now is related to growing dowry demands triggered by increasing consumerism.

From *The Globe and Mail*, June 4, 1986. Reprinted courtesy of Associated Press.

---

both extended families or kin groups. This is called a *bilateral descent* pattern.

In some societies, the bride and groom are considered to be members of only one kin group. This pattern is called *patrilineal descent* if they belong to the groom's family and *matrilineal descent* if they belong to the bride's. Patterns of descent may determine where the couple lives, how they address members of each other's family, from whom they inherit and what surname their children will receive. In some countries, only males can inherit; in others, only first-born males can. An inheritance in a Canadian family is usually divided among close relatives from both sides of the family.

In Canada, we have bilateral descent for kin membership and inheritance, but patrilineal descent for surnames. The surname taken by a man's wife and their children has traditionally been the name of the husband's family, which symbolized that he had become the head of the new household. This tradition has recently changed in the province of Quebec, where the law requires brides to retain their family names. They may hyphenate their names to their husband's, but their children must use both names. In Ontario, women have the choice of taking their husband's name or retaining their own. Legal battles have been fought in other provinces over the legal requirement that brides change their names after marriage, which some see as a loss of continuity with their past.

Canadian Cultural Variations

The socialization of children varies considerably by the ethnic origin and religious affiliation of parents, and the family rather than the classroom is the place where cultural values tend to be learned and reinforced. Many parents make a special point of teaching their children the language, customs and traditional values of their cultural group. Some even insist that their children attend special language classes outside school hours. With sufficient pressure from ethnic groups, schools in multicultural communities may offer "heritage" language classes as part of the regular curriculum. These classes teach children to write and speak their home language or their parents' mother-tongue.

Whether or not children are permitted to be taught in their mother-tongue has been controversial in Canada for over a century. Many groups, such as Hutterites and Doukhobors, immigrated to Canada with the promise of language and cultural rights, but these promises were often rescinded within a few years of their arrival. Francophones outside the province of Quebec are still fighting for language rights.

Ethnic and cultural differences in family life used to be more pronounced than they are today. Before urbanization, transportation improvements, radio and television, cultural groups more often lived in isolation from the dominant culture. Thus, they were more likely to maintain distinct family structures. With urbanization and modernization, ethnic groups, especially second-generation adolescents and younger adults, have been more integrated and assimilated into the dominant culture. Nevertheless, some groups, such as Hutterites and isolated indigenous groups, have managed to resist outside influences and maintain their distinctiveness.

In the case of reserve Indians, however, family life has suffered in a transitional period. Prior to the 1960s, most native people lived within extended families in isolated regions. Among many aboriginal groups, child care was traditionally the responsibility of the extended rather than nuclear family. Elders also instructed young children in language and traditions, but as contact with European culture increased, these traditional patterns were eroded. Especially in western Canada, native children were taught in English in residential schools and were encouraged to reject their own culture.

After the Second World War, social workers argued that legal and social protection was being denied to native children and their families. They condemned placing neglected children in residential schools and recommended an extension of the provincial services of health, welfare and education to residents of reserves. Despite some modifications to the Indian Act in 1951, no major changes were made in social services or living conditions of reserve families (Johnston, 1983 : 23). The proportion of native children taken into care by social service workers during the 1960s grew quickly for a variety of reasons. These included the placement of native children in residential schools, alcohol abuse among their families, widespread poverty, cultural misunder-standings, jurisdictional disputes and policies of colonialism.

The demand for child care services is increasing faster among the native population than among the rest of the Canadian population. This trend is due to several factors, including the rapid growth of the native population, rising rates of poverty and family disintegration and the large percentage of one-parent families. Aboriginal women, especially those living on reserves, have had extremely high unemployment rates and much lower participation rates in the labour force than non-native women. Further-more, aboriginal families have experienced severe social and economic problems requir-ing a variety of social services, including child care and family support programs. But a major issue concerning aboriginal families has been past practices that have allowed so many native people to become alienated from their culture through placement in non-native foster homes.

In recent years, aboriginal people have protested against such policies and have attempted to take control of their own social services. Aboriginal people now expect family and child care services in their own language, controlled by their own people, and based on traditional values such as the importance of the extended family and elders. Some native groups, such as those in Manitoba, have negotiated tripartite agreements with the provincial and federal governments that allow them to control their own child welfare and child care services with money from both levels of government.

Some Theories of Family Development, Interaction and Change

Social scientists have not only analysed cultural variations in family structure, but have also investigated the interaction between family members, and relations between families and political, legal and economic systems. All social science studies are based on certain underlying philosophical assumptions about how society is organized, what motivates human beings, which behaviours are biologically based, and the "best" way to discover patterns in human behaviour. These assumptions cannot be proven or disproven but serve as starting points for research. Some of the more popular perspec-tives or conceptual frameworks from which to study the family are structural functional-ism, conflict theory, systems theory, symbolic interactionism and exchange theory. In the following sections, we will briefly explain each of these perspectives as they relate to the study of families.

Structural Functionalism

Since the nineteenth century, structural functionalism has been used by anthropologists and sociologists to explain variations in family structure in pre-literate cultures. But it has also provided the framework for studies of modern industrialized societies. Within this perspective, the *structures* of society, which include laws, the political system, educational institutions and the family, are the focus of study, rather than interpersonal relations or unique individual behaviour.

The basic assumption of structural functionalism is that behaviour is governed not by personal choice, but by laws, rules, regulations and expectations of behaviour that help maintain a cohesive and stable society. Individuals cannot behave any way they want, but must abide by social expectations and rules that they are taught early in life. Although structural functionalists do not deny the existence of free will, they argue that family and cultural upbringing to a large extent determine future attitudes and behaviour.

Within this perspective, the family is an important contributor to the maintenance of social order because it provides individuals with emotional support and companionship, protection from outsiders, economic co-operation and a setting for sexual expression, reproduction and the socialization of children. Furthermore, individuals often relate to the outside world through their families, and are controlled and disciplined by them. If a young child gets into trouble with the law, for example, the police and social workers go to the parents, who are then expected to discipline the child.

The structural functionist view of the family is essentially a conservative one because it views behaviour as being largely determined by social expectations and family upbringing. Structural functionalists have also implied that a certain type of family structure (such as husband as breadwinner and wife as homemaker) was maintained throughout history because it was "functional" for society (Thorne, 1982). Change is seen as disruptive rather than normal, progressive or beneficial, and individual opposition to social pressure is viewed as "deviance." Consequently, the functionalists have not dealt with conflict and change as well as other approaches, nor have they focused on social class differences or the dynamic nature of interpersonal relations.

Conflict or Political Economy Approach

The conflict or political economy perspective is also a structural approach, but emphasizes the link between family patterns and changes in the type of work people do, how well they are paid for this work, the location of their work and the national and international economy. For example, the Industrial Revolution led to major changes in families because husbands began to work outside the home where they could no longer maintain the same level of authority over their wife and children. Furthermore, goods that were once made at home could be manufactured more cheaply in factories, and families became units of consumption rather than of production.

As more wives and mothers enter the labour force during this century, the division of labour in the family is continuing to evolve. Housework and child care are no longer the exclusive domain of mothers, divorce is more feasible economically, reproductive control is seen as a right and husbands and wives have equal legal rights.

While structural functionalists have discussed the family as though it existed in a political and economic vacuum, political economists have emphasized historical changes in family life, social class differences in family interaction, family violence and the effect of government policies on personal choices. Interpersonal relations and family dynamics are studied only from the viewpoint of how they are influenced by work patterns or the family's economic situation.

Systems Theory

Systems theory defines the family as a system of relationships in which anything that happens to one member affects all others. The focus is on recurring behaviour, triggered by similar situations or responses. For instance, systems theorists have studied the cyclical nature of family violence. A boy is physically abused by his parents, for example, and when he grows up, he beats up his wife and children. The behaviour may be triggered by low self-esteem and heavy drinking. Although he regrets his actions afterward and vows that he will never again mistreat his wife and children, he does. They lose respect for him and verbally abuse him and each other, which accentuates his feelings of worthlessness and his need to drink to forget his unhappy family life. When his children grow up, they also express their feelings of inadequacy and aggression by abusing their children. Social work practitioners have used systems theory in treating clients to show how the entire family can become involved in an apparently personal problem such as being an abusive parent or an alcoholic. Since a person's life is interrelated with the lives of other family members, dealing with the individual's problem may involve treating the entire family.

Systems theory defines the family as a set of relationships in which anything that happens to one member affects all others.

NATIONAL ARCHIVES OF
CANADA/PA 111390.

The family can be viewed as an open or closed system, depending on how much input is received from friends, neighbours, social workers, employers or the outside world in general. Although viewing the family as an open system takes into consideration social and economic influences on family interaction, the systems approach is generally ahistorical and limited to one culture. It has been most useful in psychiatry, psychology and social work, in focusing attention on how the behaviour of individuals is interrelated with that of other family members.

Symbolic Interactionism

Symbolic interactionists also look at the family as a group, in which each individual influences all others. This approach assumes that we are all "actors" who play a part in "creating social reality." Life does not just happen to us, but we make things happen by exerting our free will. While the structural functionalist approach assumes that people are, at least to some extent, passive recipients of societal rules and regulations, symbolic interactionism emphasizes the active participation of people in their own destiny. How people define and interpret reality affects their behaviour, and this process of interpretation is aided by non-verbal as well as verbal cues. People modify their behaviour depending on how "significant others" react to them, but may also influence, in turn, the behaviour of friends, family and co-workers.

Symbolic interaction studies often take place in a small-groups laboratory, using simulations of family behaviour. Researchers observe from behind windows, which appear to the "subjects" as mirrors. Interaction between mothers and their children, among children in a play group, and between husbands and wives has been studied in this kind of setting. Sometimes researchers will ask the subjects to comment on their behaviour, and compare these remarks with their own observations. In a Canadian laboratory study of family decision making, for example, Turk and Bell (1972) found that husbands overestimated and wives underestimated their own power, compared with the observations of the researcher.

While symbolic interactionism does not focus on historical or cultural change, it can explain social interaction within families and provide considerable insight into the dynamics of marriage and marital satisfaction. The interactionist approach became popular in the United States with the work of Charles H. Cooley (1902) and George H. Mead (1934) and has formed the basis of research on topics such as childhood socialization and marital adjustment.

Exchange Theory

Social exchange theory is derived from symbolic interactionism. Using economic analogies from cost-benefit analysis, marriage and family relationships are assumed to involve a process of negotiation and bargaining (Scanzoni, 1982). Social behaviour is influenced by the anticipation of a reward, such as social approval, an improved standard of living or freedom from responsibility. Recently, this kind of theory has been used to explain why some relationships break up and others last. When one partner contributes more time or emotional energy than the other to a relationship, he or she becomes resentful and starts looking elsewhere for gratification. For example, Huber and Spitze (1980) found that among a variety of subject groups, married women who worked for pay and whose husbands did not share the housework were most likely to consider divorce.

Historical Changes in Families

The idea that "a man's home is his castle" has become far less true over the centuries. Under Roman law, a father held the right to life or death over his children and considerable power over his wife. In medieval England, men were considered to be guardians of their wives and children. Major changes in family structure and legal improvements for women and children accompanied industrialization both in Europe and in North America.

In pre-industrial society, most families lived on subsistence farms and produced goods and services for their own consumption. Adults and children worked at home and contributed to the economic maintenance of the family, but the husband/father was considered to be the legal head. With industrialization, however, men, older children and wives from poorer families began to work for wages away from home, as they could no longer make a living on the farm. When working-class families moved to towns or cities to find factory jobs, all family members pooled their wages.

During the nineteenth century, trade unionists and women's groups fought to improve the gruelling working conditions for women and children. Advocates for women's rights further argued that if women were going to be in the labour force, they needed more education. If they worked alongside men, they should receive equal wages, the right to vote and the opportunity to participate in public policy making. Critics of economic and legal equality for men and women focused on women's role and on the decline of the family. They argued that family roles should be complementary—that women's place was in the home raising children and helping their husbands.

When family members began to work outside the home, patriarchal authority within the family was gradually eroded. Legislation was passed to protect women and children both in the workplace and at home. For example, children were granted the right to an education until the age of sixteen, and were protected from certain kinds of exploitative work and parental abuse. After 1872, Canadian married women won the right to retain their own wages or property without requiring their husbands' permission. Women could vote in federal elections after 1918, and during the years 1910 to 1922 women's right to retain custody of their children in the event of separation was gradually introduced. Yet, husbands were still considered to be the "heads" of the household, and wives had to live wherever their husbands wanted, unless the location would be injurious to their health. Responsibility for child care and housekeeping was part of wives' legal duties, while husbands were expected to support their wives and children financially.

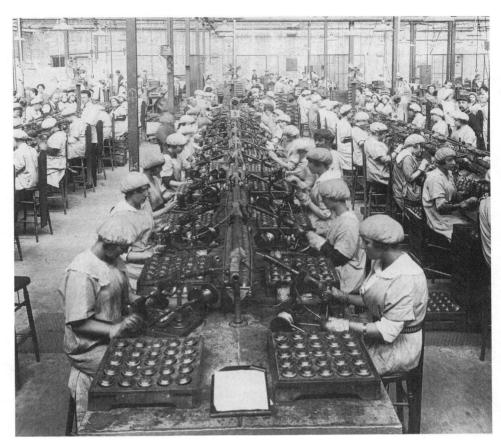

Workers solder fuses during the First World War in the British Munitions Company Ltd. at Verdun, Quebec.

NATIONAL ARCHIVES OF CANADA/C 18734.

In the early twentieth century, new manufacturing and office jobs with fixed hours and greater personal freedom made domestic servants scarce. While large houses with servants' quarters were built for the middle classes until about the 1920s, the decline in household size led to the construction of smaller homes. Developments in household technology and the rising cost of servants encouraged middle-class wives to clean their own houses, care for their own children and volunteer any extra time to charitable organizations. Poorer wives continued to take in sewing, laundry or boarders to make ends meet. But post-war inflation and the expansion of the service sector of the economy eventually pushed even middle-class women with young children into the labour force. Laws equalizing pay, grounds for divorce, division of property after divorce and the custody of children were gradually introduced.

These economic and legal changes affected not only the structure of family life, but also the way members related to one another. For example, children were treated more affectionately and were protected from adult life when families became smaller.

Children were legally required to stay in school until age sixteen. Wives became more confident in asserting their needs. When they obtained university education or began to earn their own living, they began to expect more from life than child rearing. Families remained protective of their privacy, but at the same time grew to expect state assistance with problems and crises.

Although laws have changed to give both partners legal responsibility for the support and care of children, women are still expected to give priority to housework and child care. At the same time, men are pressured to focus on paid work. Women's "double burden" of paid work and housework, however, lowers their motivation and ability to improve their economic status.

Over the years, marriage has become less of a sacred bond and more of an institution for personal fulfilment. Young people increasingly choose their own partners, unsatisfying marriages are dissolved, and new liaisons combine children from former marriages. This makes the boundaries of families more fluid and kin relationships more complex. Less often is tradition the guideline for organizing personal and family life. Instead, new rules for relationships and new ways of relating are being invented.

Recent Issues in Canadian Families

Cohabitation With the availability of more reliable birth control, sex can be more easily separated from marriage. Furthermore, a more permissive society has removed some of the legal discrimination against unmarried couples and their children. Consequently, more Canadians are now living together without being legally married.

Statistics Canada's *Family History Survey* of 1984 found that 22 percent of adult Canadians between the ages of twenty and twenty-four had been a partner in a common-law union. In comparison, fewer than 1 percent of those born before 1940 had been involved in such a relationship in their early twenties (McKie, 1986). The survey also found that 63 percent of first common-law unions end in marriage, while 35 percent end in separation and 2 percent with the death of one of the partners. According to the 1986 census, the cohabitation rate (or the percentage of unmarried adults living common-law) rose from about 9 percent in 1981 to over 11 percent in 1986 and as high as 15.5 percent in Quebec (Turcotte, 1988). Some have referred to the trend of living together before marriage as a new courtship pattern or trial marriage.

For some people, cohabitation is an alternative to legal marriage, especially if they are separated but not divorced. In countries where divorce is impossible, people may leave their legal spouse, live common-law and raise children with a new partner as though they were married. Common-law living, however, may also indicate ideological opposition to marriage; some couples feel that the state has no right to meddle in their personal or sexual lives. Other people perceive that legal marriage involves strict gender roles and expectations of behaviour that they would like to avoid. Despite these attitudes, most common-law relationships are temporary arrangements leading to marriage.

While many people like to test a relationship before they commit themselves to legal marriage, there is no evidence that people who have lived together before the wedding have more stable marriages. In fact, the opposite is the case. What this may indicate is that people who believe that living together before marriage is acceptable are also likely to believe that divorce is an option. Those who accept traditional ideas about premarital chastity may also believe that marriage must be permanent, regardless of how unsatisfying it may be.

Childlessness

There have been childless couples in every society, but people used to assume that childlessness was due to physiological problems. Childlessness is still stigmatized, and is viewed as an indication of ill health, sexual inadequacy, immaturity, gender identity problems or selfishness (Veevers, 1980). Furthermore, sex without procreation also violates some religious beliefs. The presence of children in a marriage not only confirms adult status, but is viewed as an indication of social responsibility, mental and physical health, and selflessness.

Childlessness was not really a viable option for many Canadians until the development of more effective birth control technology in the 1960s and until abortion was legalized in 1969. However, contraception, birth control and infanticide have been practised for thousands of years to prevent unwanted children.

As birth control technology improved and women's roles expanded, more married couples postponed childbearing or decided to remain childless. The percentage of childless couples has not increased dramatically, however, because medical technology has also enabled low-fertility couples to reproduce. If women who previously could not become pregnant are now having children, and others are deciding not to, the two groups cancel each other out in the statistics. Yet, there has been a slight rise in childlessness in Canada in the past two decades. In 1984, for example, about 17 percent of ever-married women were childless compared to about 14 percent in 1961 (Rao and Balakrishnan, 1986:26).

Jean Veevers (1980) found that voluntarily childless couples in Canada tend to perceive that their parents, especially their mothers, lived unsatisfying lives because they sacrificed other activities for child rearing. These couples also associate pregnancy with illness and lack of erotic appeal, and motherhood with dependency and incompetence. They felt that having children would interfere with career plans, travelling or the stability of their marriage. Some childless people lacked child care skills because they were only children, while others were first-borns who experienced too much child care responsibility as children.

Childless couples report various satisfactions with their life style, including spontaneity and avoidance of routine, time to seek out new experiences and develop their skills and opportunities to travel. In industrialized countries, low marriage rates and childlessness have been correlated with high education, continuous employment and high career involvement for women. Childless men tend to emphasize the freedom from having to work to support children, low career involvement or a varied career history. These couples are also likely to enjoy an egalitarian division of labour in the household and similar incomes in their paid jobs. Furthermore, childless married couples (especially men) report more satisfaction with their marriages than married couples with children (Veroff and Feld, 1970).

At the same time, we know that childless couples have higher rates of divorce than couples with children. This can probably be explained by the practical difficulties of divorcing when children are involved, and the relative ease in a childless marriage. Now that couples have expanded life-style options, more may choose a childless marriage.

Yet, there remains considerable social pressure to have children, especially from older relatives and policy makers. Many countries, such as Canada, have promoted pronatalist values, encouraging people to have children and maintain population growth. An example can be seen in Quebec, where the birth rate is the lowest in Canada and among the lowest in industrialized countries. The Quebec government has recently introduced financial incentives to encourage larger families.

In countries without the available technology to test fertility, people usually assume that if a couple is childless the woman is infertile. A wife's infertility has been a ground for divorce or a reason for her husband to take a mistress in some countries. Where fertility is particularly important, a childless woman is pitied and expected to care for her relatives' children or to take on community work. In developed countries, such as Canada, where childless women are usually involved in a career, there is slightly less social pressure to bear children. Nevertheless, most people still feel that having and raising a child is an integral part of life, and they do not want to miss the experience. In fact, some couples spend years trying to adopt or conceive, and thousands of dollars on medical interventions such as *in vitro* fertilization. Yet, the success rate of this intervention is low, the technique is extremely expensive and the process can take years. Some Canadian feminists are calling for a Royal commission on reproductive technology because they feel that important moral and policy decisions are being left to a small group of male physicians (Eichler, 1989).

A small but growing number of childless couples have contracted fertile women to bear children for them. These "surrogate mothers" are usually poor women who see childbearing as a relatively easy way to earn a living, while the childless couple is usually well-off. In addition to the moral problems that may exist in paying poor people to bear children for the rich, legal complications are also a problem. In the recent "Baby M" case, for example, the surrogate mother decided after the birth that she wanted to keep the child rather than give her to the biological father and his wife, as agreed. The father, however, won custody of the child. This well-publicized American court case has underlined the need for public policy on the legality of surrogate motherhood, the role of women in reproductive technology, the acceptability of profit making or the use of public funds in infertility clinics, and the changing definitions of paternity.

Child Care   Raising children is expensive in urban societies. The Social Planning Council of Metropolitan Toronto estimated that the cost of raising a child from birth to age eighteen in the Toronto area, for example, was $94 500 in 1987 dollars. Day care can more than double the annual cost of raising younger children, and is the greatest single child-related expense a family may incur (Mitchell, 1987). With ten years of non-subsidized child care included (pre-school and after-school care), the cost could increase to about $140 100. The authors of this study caution that this was a conservative estimate, and assumed that the family rented an apartment and did not have a car.

In January 1989, 68 percent of mothers with children under sixteen worked for pay—about three quarters of them full-time (Statistics Canada, February 1989 : B—21). The widespread entrance of married women into the labour force resulted mainly from economic considerations. After the Second World War, the expansion of the service sector increased the need for labour. Furthermore, higher education, smaller families, advances in birth control, the removal of legal restrictions, the rising rate of marriage dissolution, changing attitudes about women's role and rising costs also encouraged women to take paid work.

Married women's increased labour force participation is one of the most important social changes of this century, influencing many other aspects of life. Having one's own earnings, for example, can augment confidence, decision-making power and opportunities for personal expansion. The additional income raises the standard of living for two-income families, but also further increases income inequality between one-income and two-income families. Separation and divorce also become viable when both spouses have their own income. In addition, two-income families create the need for new services, such as convenience foods, home cleaning companies, and child care services.

Since 1966, the costs of child care for low-income or one-parent families have been shared between the provincial and the federal governments. Subsidized spaces are set aside in each province, generally in non-profit government-regulated day care centres or licensed homes. Unless they have low incomes, two-parent families requiring child care services must pay the full cost, which ranged from about $4000 to $6000 per child in 1986 (Canada, House of Commons, 1987). Because of the shortage of subsidized spaces and high cost of centre care, most working parents rely on baby-sitters to look after their pre-schoolers.

Because child care is a provincial responsibility, the availability of spaces, the cost and the quality of care vary across the country. Many day care centres have long waiting lists, and the number of families who need child care far outstrips the availability of spaces. In 1987, for example, there were 1 937 163 children under thirteen with parents working or studying, but only 243 545 licensed day care spaces for children in Canada (National Council of Welfare, 1988b : 4).

The quality of child care both in licensed centres and through baby-sitters concerns many parents. Child care workers and baby-sitters are not required to have special training in most provinces, and day care standards usually relate only to health and physical space. Because these jobs generally pay minimum wage, they do not attract educated people. Most working parents do not have the opportunity or time to investigate child care conditions fully, and because they cannot find alternative care, they must accept whatever is available.

Adolescents' Views of Their Future Child Care and Housework Arrangements

"I'll take the kids to nursery school and hopefully go to work. I'll be a child psychologist in a clinic. . . . This is hard, because I want to work and I want to have kids. But I don't like the idea of day care. After lunch, I'd drop them off at Grandma's house or it would be nice to work half-days. . . . "

Faye: 18 years old, Winnipeg

(At age thirty)"I'm married. I have one child aged one or two. I work and my baby-sitter comes to my home every day. She's a woman I know very well. . . . " (translation)

Lise: 15 years old, rural Quebec

"One child will be in school, and the other two will have a sitter . . . but I want six children. I'll take off three months after the birth of each child."

Rhonda: 16 years old, Montreal

"It really wouldn't bother me to do all the housework, because my husband would have a job that involves a lot of work, and he would be tired when he got home."

Betty: 15 years old, rural Nova Scotia

"My wife would work, but if there was no day care she would stay home to look after them (the children). . . . I'll help my wife with the housework, but it'll depend how tired I am when I get home at night." (translation)

Laurent: 17 years old, Montreal

"I go home (at age thirty), pick up my kids, make dinner half the time. . . . My wife gets home same time as me—maybe a little later. . . . "

Jim: 15 years old, Vancouver

"I would have two children—nine and seven—(at age thirty). The children would be at school. . . . I would be reading and watching soap operas, and cleaning a little. . . . I'm trying to remember what my mother does. . . . "

Joanne: 15 years old, rural Ontario

"I have to get my kid ready for school (at age thirty). I'll watch the kid go off to school. As soon as everybody's out, I'd clean up and go back to bed. I'll get up around lunchtime. . . . "

Wanda: 15 years old, rural Manitoba

Excerpts from Maureen Baker. 1985. *What Will Tomorrow Bring . . . ? A Study of the Aspirations of Adolescent Women*. Ottawa: Canadian Advisory Council on the Status of Women. Reprinted with permission.

Child care is important to all mothers working outside the home, but it is particularly critical for recent immigrants who occupy positions with little job control and often do shift work (Seward and McDade, 1988). Most centres operate during regular office hours, but many women need child care that takes into consideration their hours of work and cultural heritage. These women also need child care to enable them to take language training, which may improve their chances of moving to a more lucrative job or assist them to become more independent from their families.

A number of advocacy groups have formed around the child care issue, including the Canadian Day Care Advocacy Association (CDCAA). These groups have demanded better training, fringe benefits and higher pay for nannies and child care workers, who they say are paid less than zookeepers. They also point out the discrepancy between the qualifications and salaries of child care workers and kindergarten teachers, who are essentially doing the same work. CDCAA has asked for improved federal/provincial funding mechanisms for non-profit centres, national guidelines for high quality care, the enforcement of provincial standards and an expansion of services to accommodate all working parents, including shift and seasonal workers. In 1988, the federal government introduced new legislation to alter federal/provincial cost-sharing arrangements for child care services, but the legislation was not passed before the 1988 election.

Whether or not governments should be more involved in child care remains a contentious issue. Some lobby groups, such as REAL Women of Canada, have argued for more taxation support for the one-income family, and wages and pensions for homemakers to enable women to look after their own children. But the amount of these benefits would be much less than the income from working in the labour force, and many families are not able to give up one income.

Family Violence

Over the past decade, the rise in reported cases of family violence has led to a public demand for better laws protecting women and children, and new ways of dealing with abusers. Research has documented the cyclical nature of child abuse and the relationship between early abuse and later emotional problems. Abused children generally develop low self-esteem and are likely to experience future emotional problems. Many "street kids" and young people involved in prostitution were abused throughout their childhood. Battered children also tend to become abusive parents and spouses because they learn violent ways of dealing with frustration within their families.

Parents who abuse their children often feel that they are using justifiable disciplinary measures and that their children are deliberately provoking them. Yet, some parents realize that they cannot control their violent behaviour and join self-help groups with other abusive parents trying to break the habit. But many continue the abuse until the child becomes too big to beat up, leaves home or notifies the authorities.

Although physical abuse remains an issue, recent attention has focused on the sexual abuse of children. The Badgley Report in 1984 concluded that one in two females and one in three males have been victims of "unwanted sexual acts," generally as children. The report noted that sexual abuse tends to occur during the daytime, in the victim's or a friend's home, and is likely to be carried out by a male relative or family friend. While girls are more vulnerable to abuse than boys, a sizable minority of young boys are sexually abused.

Recent incidents of sexual abuse by teachers, youth workers and religious leaders have raised public concern about how to detect potential abusers before an incident occurs and how to deal with those accused of abuse. Insufficient staff and funds and the sheer number of reported cases sometimes prevent intervention even when social workers know a child is at risk. But new federal legislation was passed in 1987 introducing tough penalties to those who sexually abuse children and giving more credence to children's evidence in court (Baker, 1988).

Throughout North America, the number of wife-battering cases reported to the authorities has also grown dramatically. Some researchers have tried to relate this apparent increase in family violence to unemployment, economic recession, alcohol and drug abuse, divorce and working mothers. A large part of the increase, however, has been caused by new laws requiring professionals and ordinary citizens to report such behaviour. Social attitudes that expected victims to tolerate abuse and keep it behind closed doors have changed. Social service workers are becoming more sympathetic and helpful to victims. People charged with family violence are now more likely to be arrested and convicted than in the past, when police and the courts saw such violence as a private family matter. In turn, increased enforcement of the law encourages reporting. These factors have raised the visibility of family violence, but whether there is actually more abuse than before is uncertain. Nevertheless, studies suggest that at least one in every ten women in Canada is abused by her live-in partner (MacLeod, 1987). Although women sometimes physically abuse their husbands, the vast majority of reported cases involve a male abuser.

Some wives continue to tolerate abuse because they feel it may somehow be their own fault. Especially those abused as children may suffer from low self-esteem and feel that they are unworthy of better treatment. Many also fear reprisal from their spouses if they call the police. Others lack money or knowledge about where to turn for assistance. Shortage of temporary and low-income housing prevents many wives and children from leaving an abusive home.

While some people remain in abusive marriages for many years, an increasing number of battered women are leaving and obtaining divorces. But divorce is only a crude indicator of marital conflict, because many couples remain in conflict-ridden marriages, while others separate without legal agreements.

Divorce and the Feminization of Poverty

Canadian divorce rates have been rising since the 1940s, but increased sharply after 1968 when the grounds for divorce were liberalized (see Table 12-1). Before 1925, legal divorce was very restricted, expensive and easier for men than for women to obtain. In 1968, "marriage breakdown" became a ground for divorce. It was strictly defined, but still made divorce more accessible. In 1986, "marriage breakdown" was more liberally defined as a one-year separation.

Numerous factors have pushed up divorce rates in developed societies. With industrialization, many young people moved away from family restrictions and raised their expectations of personal fulfilment. Growing individualism discouraged the view of marriage as sacred or related primarily to family lineage, obligation or procreation.

Shattered Hopes: The Meaning Of Wife Battering For Victims And Survivors

More Than Physical Violence

I was hit plenty by my husband over the years. I had a couple of concussions, broken ribs, and I'm still deaf in one ear from him always hitting on that side of my head. But you can't understand what I went through if you only talk about the beatings. Hitting, punching, kicking—these things hurt your body, and they leave some scars, but mostly your body heals. What hurts me even more now is that with my husband I never had a chance to do anything with my life. I haven't been able to make plans for years. And now I feel like I gave so much love to him but I never even really had love back.

You know what hurts me most? We used to be so happy, so much in love. I want those days back. I want to dream again, to make plans, to see a future for us and our kids. I just ache to feel loved again. It's been so long since anyone's said a kind word to me, been gentle with me, made me feel special. Bruises and bones heal, but this ache never goes away.

I hurt most about my kids. About their future. They'll never feel proud to bring their boyfriends and girlfriends home to meet their parents. They're just little now and they never bring their friends over here. I worry when they see me crying. I worry when I can't play with them because I'm too sore. I worry that one day soon they won't even have a mother. I worry about that a lot—about what will happen to them, about whether they'll end up like me or end up in jail.

Right now, I'm really angry at everything he's done to me and the kids. I'm so glad I finally had the guts to phone the police. It took me so long to phone the police—years and years of hell.

Looking back on it, I feel so silly, but the first few times he hit me I was just shocked, and then he'd be so nice, so loving for a while afterwards, that I'd blame myself and feel sorry for him. The women at the shelter say that just about everyone goes through that. Then I just started to feel numb. Maybe I had a nervous breakdown or something. I just about never went out of the house unless I needed groceries or had to take the kids to the doctor. I didn't want to face anybody asking how things are with Bill and me. For those years I kept going with stupid dreams. I kept hoping that things would change. What else could I do? I couldn't see any other way out.

Linda MacLeod. 1987. *Battered But Not Beaten . . . Preventing Wife Battering in Canada*. Ottawa: Canadian Advisory Council on the Status of Women, pp. 11–12. Reprinted with permission.

People began to feel that they had the right to personal happiness, fair treatment and love in marriage. The entrance of married women into the labour force allowed women to support themselves outside marriage, gave them increased opportunities to meet new people and to compare their personal situations. Improved birth control made it possible to separate sex and marriage, permitting more discreet extramarital relations for both men and women.

Rising divorce rates have led to considerable concern about the social and personal costs of marriage dissolution. The percentage of one-parent families fell from 1931 to

TABLE 12-1

Divorce Rates in Canada, 1921–1986

Year	Rate per 100 000 Population
1921	6.4
1931	6.8
1941	21.4
1951	37.6
1961	36.0
1971	137.6
1981	278.0
1982	285.9
1983	275.5
1984	259.5
1985	244.4
1986	308.3

STATISTICS CANADA (ANNUAL). MARRIAGES AND DIVORCES, VITAL STATISTICS, VOL. II, *CAT. 84-205. OTTAWA: SUPPLY AND SERVICES CANADA. REPRODUCED WITH PERMISSION OF THE MINISTER OF SUPPLY AND SERVICES CANADA, 1989.*

1961 as fewer mothers died in childbirth and life expectancies increased. However, the percentage rose again with high rates of separation and divorce in the 1970s and 1980s. Regardless of the causes of one-parent families, the financial consequences are similar for women and children: poverty.

After the 1971 *Murdoch* case in Alberta, many groups lobbied for changes to divorce laws because they felt that women were receiving a smaller share of matrimonial property and that their unpaid contributions to households were not being considered. In the *Murdoch* case, the wife ran the family farm for several months of each year while her husband worked away from home at another job. The twenty-five-year marriage broke up after he physically assaulted her, but the court gave the farm to the husband because his name was on the deed and most of the money used to purchase it came from him. The wife was given $200 per month alimony, and was allowed to continue to live in the farmhouse (Dranoff, 1977 : 52). This case, and others like it, precipitated legal change in Canada.

Dividing matrimonial property equally after divorce has now become the guiding rule in many Canadian provinces. Yet, because women do not earn equal incomes to men, women often end up living in poverty after marriage dissolution. For these reasons, issues of child support, custody and the division of matrimonial property remain contentious. The American study by Lenore Weitzman (1985) of Stanford University found that the divorced mothers in her study experienced an average drop in household income of 73 percent after marriage dissolution, while divorced men's income increased by 42 percent on average. From an analysis of American divorce settlements over a number of years, Weitzman concluded that "no fault" divorce laws have led to greater financial inequality. Prior to legal reforms, women could be awarded alimony and could delay a hearing until they negotiated a higher settlement. Weitzman argued that present American divorce laws are based on the false assumption of equality between the sexes.

Mother-led one-parent families are much more likely than father-led families to be living in poverty (see Table 12-2). Canadian feminists point out that it is unfair to require the financially dependent spouse (usually the woman) to take the other to court in order to enforce support payments. Most provinces have or are devising enforcement systems in which the provincial government pays child support directly to the custodial parent and retrieves the money from the other parent itself. This may improve the economic status of one-parent families at a relatively low cost to governments. However, since the average amount of these payments is relatively small (less than $200 per month) most one-parent families would still be poor even if court-awarded payments were made regularly. A more effective solution would be seriously and systematically to improve women's status in the labour force. As long as women earn about two-thirds of men's wages, their disposable incomes, their savings and their pensions will be lower, and more women will require social assistance. Governments would save money in the long run by enforcing equal pay for work of equal value, raising the minimum wage and promoting employment equity.

Living in a one-parent family is not the only factor leading to the feminization of poverty. The percentage of elderly persons in the population is rising and the poorest tend to be unattached women, with 46.1 percent living below the poverty line in 1986 (National Council of Welfare, 1988a : 43). In some cases, their husbands died without savings or survivors' benefits. Those few elderly women who were in the labour force for a significant number of years generally earned low incomes, with few fringe benefits such as pension plan membership.

Although governments have responded to the problem of elderly poor by making minor improvements to pensions, a more effective solution would be to address the real reasons for women's poverty. This strategy would involve raising women's wages, providing subsidized child care, implementing employment equity, as well as reforming pension plan regulations. All these actions involve money and political will.

TABLE 12-2
Percent of Canadian Families Living in Poverty, 1981–1986

	Female Single Parents	Male Single Parents	Couples with Children
1981	52.8	5.5	9.5
1982	57.1	22.2	11.2
1983	59.3	27.1	12.0
1984	59.6	27.1	12.4
1985	60.3	26.8	11.1
1986	56.0	22.9	10.4

NATIONAL COUNCIL OF WELFARE. APRIL 1988. POVERTY PROFILE 1988. OTTAWA, P. 31.

The Future of Families

From the trends of the past three decades, we can assume that more married women will enter the labour force. If average paid working hours continue to decrease and the division of labour does not change, only men will have more leisure time because women will retain family responsibilities. But the pressures of women's "double workload" will force more men to share child care and housework. Yet, this transition will not be easy. Parents will have to teach their children that both men and women do household tasks. Wives will have to accept more responsibility for outside work and car maintenance, and husbands will have to take on part of the responsibility for cooking, cleaning and laundry, and total responsibility for their own personal care. It is unlikely that many men will want to become "house-husbands" for the same reasons that many women are rejecting this job—it is unpaid and retains low status.

Living together will probably become more socially acceptable in the future as a preliminary stage, as well as an alternative, to marriage. However, marriage remains popular for the vast majority of the Canadian population. Most couples remain married and derive considerable satisfaction from their family life. Despite high divorce rates, Canadian young people usually expect to marry and to remain with the same partner throughout their lives.

Throughout this century, family size has continued to decline as women bear fewer children and more parents separate and divorce. Most demographers project that declining birth rates will continue in the near future, because children are increasingly costly in urban environments. Furthermore, working in the labour force and caring for children in the evenings and on weekends is very tiring for parents, especially for mothers who perform most of the domestic work.

One-parent families, small families and childless couples will continue to be more prevalent in the future. While more low-fertility couples will be able to reproduce, probably a larger percentage of couples will opt for a childless life style. Already, some couples have postponed childbearing with the result that conception becomes more difficult and the risks of fetal deformities are higher. Increasingly, more couples will postpone childbearing until they can no longer conceive.

Pronatal values encouraging childbearing and domesticity were dominant during the 1950s. Yet, families in the 1980s have been overshadowed by negative publicity relating to child abuse, the high cost of raising children, the probabilities of birth defects after a certain age and women's difficulties in juggling family life and job. After romanticizing family life, we are now focusing on the negative aspects, instead of simply presenting a more realistic picture.

As family size diminishes, there may be increased pressure to create a more conducive social environment for children and to make it easier for women to have children and work outside the home. This could involve creating more subsidized child care spaces in neighbourhoods and workplaces, requiring employers to grant both men and women parental leave for child birth, adoption and illness, and allowing flexible working hours or shared work without loss of benefits. Governments could also increase tax incentives for families with dependent children, provide more generous family allowances and pay parents who choose to care for their own children at home. These reforms, however, will not happen quickly because they involve tax increases and a shift in government priorities. Policy makers are now more concerned about how to encourage families to accept greater responsibility for elderly family members and to pay for the pensions of an aging population.

Summary

Family life is important to the well-being and happiness of most people, and the institution of the family is extremely important to society. The family is significant everywhere, but there are many cultural variations in family structure from one society to another. Several theoretical frameworks and methods have been used in studying families. These perspectives include structural functionalism, conflict theory, systems theory, symbolic interactionism and exchange theory. Many economic, legal and social changes have affected family life throughout this century in Europe and North America. Issues that particularly affect Canadian families are cohabitation, childlessness, child care, family violence and divorce and the accompanying feminization of poverty. However, despite widespread changes in family life, most people still choose to marry and bear children.

Suggested Readings

Armstrong, Pat, and Hugh Armstrong
1984. *The Double Ghetto: Canadian Women and Their Segregated Work*. Toronto: McClelland and Stewart. This book discusses women's work in the labour force and the home and provides three theories to explain trends in these two realms.

Baker, Maureen, ed.
1989. *Families: Changing Trends in Canada*, 2nd ed. Toronto: McGraw-Hill Ryerson. This text examines historical and current trends in Canadian family life, including laws, policies and sociological trends.

Eichler, Margrit
1988. *Families in Canada Today: Recent Changes and Their Policy Consequences*, 2nd ed. Toronto: Gage. This book is a detailed critique of how family life has been studied in social science and how various social policies define and shape families.

Mandell, Nancy, and Ann Duffy
1988. *Reconstructing the Canadian Family: Feminist Perspectives*. Toronto: Butterworths. This book focuses on women's issues and concerns in Canadian families, challenging gender inequalities.

Nett, Emily
1988. *Canadian Families Past and Present*. Toronto: Butterworths. This basic text deals with families in the societal context as well as family relationships and interaction.

Veevers, Jean E.

1980. *Childless by Choice*. Toronto: Butterworths. Based on interviews with couples who remained childless by choice, this book examines decision making about being childless, the childless life style and attitudes about parenthood.

Discussion Questions

1. What do we mean when we say that sociologists use different theoretical perspectives to study family life? What is a "theoretical perspective"?

2. Why does family size tend to decline with industrialization?

3. What initiated widespread family law reform during the 1970s and 1980s in Canada?

4. Why are polygynous marriages more prevalent than polyandrous marriages?

5. Why are more young people living together without legal marriage? Does this indicate a rejection of marriage?

6. Why have reported cases of child abuse increased so much in the past ten years?

7. Consult some studies and books on aging. How is an aging population affecting relationships between adult children and their aging parents? How does widowhood change these relationships?

8. Read several studies about wife battering. Why do women stay with husbands who continue to beat them up?

Data Collection Exercises

1. Prepare a questionnaire that would test the hypothesis that people who come from richer families intend to marry at an older age and produce fewer children. Try out this questionnaire on twenty students, but make sure you include an equal number of males and females in your sample.

2. Prepare a short interview schedule to ascertain the family background and the educational and occupational aspirations of ten of your acquaintances. See if there is any relationship between the education, occupation and incomes of their parents and your friends' educational and occupational aspirations.

3. Consult the 1986 census data on the ethnic origins of Canadian families and compare them with earlier data, perhaps from 1951 or 1961. How has the ethnic composition of Canadian families changed over the years? What implications might these changes have for family life styles in Canada?

4. Consult Statistics Canada or United Nations statistics on divorce rates, and

compare Canada with other countries, such as the United States, the Soviet Union, Sweden, Italy and Ireland. What factors might have influenced Canada's divorce rate to make it different from those of other countries?

Writing Exercises

1. What is the impact of an aging population on families?

2. Why have married women entered the labour force in such numbers from the 1960s to the 1980s?

3. What are the main causes of rising divorce rates?

4. Why do some people intentionally remain childless?

Glossary

Bilateral descent: *relationships and inheritance are traced through both parents' families.*

Conjugal family: *a nuclear family with primary emotional ties between husband and wife rather than other kin.*

Dowry: *money or property provided by a bride's family upon her marriage, to help obtain a husband and to be used by her in case of divorce.*

Extended family: *people related to each other by blood or marriage.*

Feminization of poverty: *the trend for more poor people to be women.*

Household: *people sharing a common residence, but not necessarily related to each other by blood or marriage.*

Matrilineal descent: *relationships and inheritance are traced through the female line.*

Monogamy: *marriage to one partner at a time.*

Nuclear family: *a husband, wife and their children, sharing a common residence and co-operating economically.*

Patrilineal descent: *relationships and inheritance are traced through the male line.*

Polyandry: *marriage to more than one husband.*

Polygamy: *marriage to more than one spouse at a time.*

Polygyny: *marriage to more than one wife.*

Serial monogamy: *several partners over a lifetime, but only one at a time.*

References

Baker, Maureen

    1985. *What Will Tomorrow Bring? . . . A Study of the Aspirations of Adolescent Women.* Ottawa: Canadian Advisory Council on the Status of Women.

    1988. "Child Abuse." Ottawa: Library of Parliament, Research Branch.

Canada, House of Commons
1987. *Sharing the Responsibility*. Report of the Special Committee on Child Care. Ottawa: Queen's Printer.

Cooley, Charles H.
1902. *Human Nature and Social Order*. New York: Charles Scribner's Sons.

Dranoff, Linda Silver
1977. *Women in Canadian Life: Law*. Toronto: Fitzhenry and Whiteside.

Eichler, Margrit
1989. "Reflections on Motherhood, Apple Pie, the New Reproductive Technologies and the Role of Sociologists in Society." *Society/Société* 13(1): 1–5.

Goldthorpe, J. E.
1987. *Family Life in Western Societies*. Cambridge: Cambridge University Press.

Goode, William J.
1963. *World Revolution and Family Patterns*. New York: Free Press (revised with new introduction, 1970).

Huber, Joan, and Glenna Spitze
1980. "Considering Divorce: An Expansion of Becker's Theory of Marital Instability." *American Journal of Sociology* 86(1): 75–89.

Johnston, Patrick
1983. *Native Children and the Child Welfare System*. Toronto: Lorimer.

MacLeod, Linda
1987. *Battered But Not Beaten . . . Preventing Wife Abuse in Canada*. Ottawa: Canadian Advisory Council on the Status of Women.

McKie, Craig
1986. "Common-Law: Living Together as Husband and Wife Without Marriage." *Canadian Social Trends* (Autumn): 39–41.

Mead, George Herbert
1934. *Mind, Self and Society*. Chicago: University of Chicago Press.

Mitchell, Andrew
1987. "The Cost of Raising a Child in the Toronto Area in 1986." *Social Infopac* 6(5): 1–5.

National Council of Welfare
1988a. *Poverty Profile 1988*. Ottawa, April.
1988b. *Child Care: A Better Alternative*. Ottawa, December.

Parsons, Talcott, and Robert F. Bales
1955. *Family Socialization and Interaction Process*. New York: Free Press.

Rao, K. Vaninadha, and T. R. Balakrishnan
1986. "Childlessness as a Factor of Fertility Decline in Canada." Prepared for the Review of Demography and Its Implications for Economic and Social Policy. Ottawa: Health and Welfare Canada.

Scanzoni, John
1982. *Sexual Bargaining: Power Politics in the American Marriage*, 2nd ed. Chicago: University of Chicago Press.

Seward, Shirley B., and Kathryn McDade
1988. "A New Deal for Immigrant Women." *Policy Options* (June): 15–18.

Thorne, Barry
1982. "Feminist Rethinking of the Family: An Overview." In Barry Thorne with Marilyn Yalom, eds., *Rethinking the Family: Some Feminist Questions*. New York: Longman.

Turcotte, Pierre
1988. "Common-Law Unions: Nearly Half a Million in 1986." *Canadian Social Trends* 10 (Autumn): 35–39.

Turk, James, and Norman Bell
1972. "Measuring Power in Families." *Journal of Marriage and the Family* 34: 215–22.

Veevers, Jean E.
1980. *Childless by Choice*. Toronto: Butterworths.

Veroff, Joseph, and Sheila Feld
1970. *Marriage and Work in America*. New York: Van Nostrand-Reinhold.

Weitzman, Lenore T.
1985. *The Divorce Revolution: The Unexpected Social and Economic Consequences for Women and Children in America*. New York: Free Press.

CHAPTER 13

Education and Schooling

NEIL GUPPY

Introduction

Learning is a daily accomplishment. The popular saying, "You learn something new every day," makes this point. Recall that this chapter is included in the section on institutions. The focus, therefore, will be on only a tiny slice of learning—that which occurs in schools. Schooling is a social institution in the sense that formal education is a regular, recurring feature of people's lives. Central to all institutions is patterned, routinized activity, and schooling, as an organized part of our upbringing, possesses this characteristic. Most of what we learn may occur outside the classroom. Still, just under one-quarter of Canada's population are full-time students today, and a substantial portion of each individual's life is spent attending school (about thirteen years on average, or almost one-fifth of a normal, seventy-five-year life span).

As a major social institution, education is relatively young. Although schools have a long history, prior to at least the 1700s it would be impossible to point to a *schooled society*, a society where education was integral to the entire national community. Children of the elite have always received some special instruction, and apprentices often benefited from strict tutelage, but formal education became a regular, core feature of everyone's experience only in the last few centuries.

Because of schooling's early importance in people's lives, sociologists have sought to comprehend its significance in society. Why did mass schooling arise? Why did it expand? In whose interests are schools organized? Who benefits from schooling? How does education relate to other social institutions? A useful beginning in searching for answers to these questions is to consider various claims about the very purpose of education.

Opposite page:
Why are these university students here? What is gained from a university education? Is it just finishing that really matters (getting the degree)? Are skills relevant to work or community service acquired or amplified? Or is university like a warehouse, a place to shelter people from the harsh realities of unemployment?

Why Have Schools?

The Social Functions of Schooling

We know a lot about the world. Certainly our ancestors were knowledgeable, but now we have far more theoretical knowledge than did previous generations. It is difficult to tell exactly how much we know because no one knows everything. Nevertheless, our collective understanding of the world is immense.

Sharing that understanding with successive generations has become a major task. One reason, then, for the growth of formal education is because this wealth of knowledge cannot be passed along efficiently by informal, hit-and-miss operations. To leave all teaching to small, unco-ordinated social units, such as the family or the local community, would result in a cornucopia of standards and curricula. Successful participation in the modern world demands reading, writing, arithmetic and many higher skills, including a rudimentary understanding of subjects from radio waves to infectious diseases. This is one reason for requiring a professional system of education to help in the teaching of each new generation.

Education goes far beyond exposing students to ideas and concepts. Few people need reminding of the importance educators place on examinations. Enormous effort is spent assessing, quizzing, grading, counting, measuring, marking, scoring and testing. This constant evaluation motivates study, but more fundamentally, it serves to sort and select, ostensibly establishing the best and the brightest. "Badges of ability" are a central feature of education.

Classroom activity involves students in more than learning and evaluating of basic knowledge. As part of their schooling, students also learn about authority, deviance, competition, loyalty, personal responsibility, and so on. Below the surface of the formal timetable of academic subjects lies an informal curriculum. Many would argue that it is this implicit learning, this shaping of acceptable and appropriate behaviour, this social control, that lies at the heart of schooling. Another reason, then, for the growth of formal education is to teach us to be good citizens.

Given the importance of these three basic functions of the schooling process—transmission, evaluation and control—it is not surprising to find that formal education is, in almost every country, compulsory. The degree of compulsion varies enormously, but nations invariably provide the broadest education program that they can afford. The right to a basic education is almost universally acknowledged. "Among modern ideals . . . the principle of universal and centrally guaranteed education . . . is virtually unique" in its global fulfilment (Gellner, 1983 : 28).

Controversy About the Social Functions of Schooling

The global emphasis on educating children suggests that schooling plays a strategic role in shaping the economic, political and cultural character of society. Because of this strategic importance, the implementation of education's basic functions often results in conflict, as different interest groups vie to establish their views. What constitutes knowledge? What standards of selection should prevail? What characteristics signify good citizens? Each of these is a controversial issue.

Many people equate knowledge with truth and find it difficult to comprehend disputes arising over what constitutes knowledge. Yet, intense debate continues over the teaching of evolutionary biology in schools. Court cases have raged, and in many jurisdictions both evolutionary and creationist accounts of human origins must, by law, be taught. Controversy over the teaching of sex education continues. Knowledge about sexually transmitted diseases is conspicuously absent from many health curricula. In short, what counts as knowledge is disputed, and what knowledge is considered worthy of being taught is contested.

Appropriate standards of evaluation represent a second area of contention. The abolition of uniform exams, the creation of flexible curricula and the use of open classrooms have all been attacked as instances of schools abandoning traditional values of excellence and achievement. But here, too, debate swirls. Of what value is it for students to list, from memory, six functions of education or fifty causes of chest pain? Memory is surely one component of knowledge, but an ability to think clearly and constructively is another standard. On what criteria, then, should students be judged? For what attributes should badges of ability be awarded? Defining excellence is not easy.

The IQ Controversy

In 1905, the French physician Alfred Binet devised a series of tests to measure an individual's intelligence quotient (IQ), the amount of mental ability a person had. The tests were designed so that graphing people's test scores would produce a bell-shaped curve, with few people at each extreme and the majority around the middle. People who scored extremely well were regarded as geniuses, while those who did very poorly were labelled as retarded. Test scores identified, it was claimed, a fixed, natural allotment of inherited ability. Like eye colour and hair colour, intelligence was taken to be genetically transmitted from parent to child—the genetic makeup of people was the key to their IQ.

Advocates of intelligence testing sought to use the idea of pure intelligence to support a variety of interpretations. Differences in the average scores of blacks and whites were taken to demonstrate that intellect was genetically linked and that whites were naturally more intelligent. In England, Sir Cyril Burt used his research findings on identical twins and adopted children to justify a complete realignment of the British education system. He helped implement a system that streamed children into educational tracks on the basis of their mental ability scores.

IQ research had a major setback when it was discovered that much of Burt's work was fraudulent. Suspicions were roused when Dr. Oliver Gillie, a medical journalist, failed to find any trace of Burt's two research associates (whom Burt claimed had administered the IQ tests). As well, Burt's statistics seemed too perfect. His results were analogous to *always* getting exactly five heads when you flip a coin ten times—a prospect so unlikely as to be implausible.

Other controversy has surrounded the IQ debate. What exactly is intelligence? How adequately can it be measured by paper and pencil tests? How do you interpret the fact that scores improve with study? Perhaps the most frequent charge has been that the tests are biased, reflecting a white, middle-class cultural perspective that disadvantages other groups. A question such as, "Ballet is for a dancer what opera is for a — ?" is not easy for children who have never heard an opera singer or watched a ballet dancer.

A more radical critique questions the purpose, as opposed to the nature, of intelligence testing. IQ testing attempts to legitimize both a hierarchy of ability and each individual's position within that hierarchy. IQ testing provides a "scientific" legitimation for social differences.

Intelligence as a commodity distributed at birth, quantifiable by impersonal tests, is challenged by researchers such as Jean Piaget who believe that the growth of mental ability is a developmental process. Intelligence is not fixed in the first months of life (like eye colour), but is changed by circumstance (like muscle strength or weight).

Like the nature of excellence, the idea of a good citizen is also contentious. Our experiences in school influence our characters, but exactly what issues should receive the greatest stress in the classroom? Should schooling help improve our world by encouraging students to challenge traditional practices and question authority? Or should it push students to learn their places and obediently follow instructions? Likewise, should schools give greater priority to promoting national pride and Canadian identity, or should schooling stress our multicultural, global community? Frequently, definitions of the "good citizen" conflict.

Are open classrooms like the one pictured here useful in a modern school system? Do such classrooms promote the learning of basic arithmetic and literacy skills? Whatever happened to classroom discipline?

Why have schools? To summarize, schools transmit knowledge, evaluate individuals and provide social control. Indeed, these functions are so important that compulsory education is now almost universal. However, because each function is so important and is open to different definitions, struggles over the purposes and effectiveness of schooling are common.

The Development of a "Schooled Society"

Prior to the 1700s, separate, institutional arrangements analogous to the modern school *system* were non-existent. The functions of education were undertaken by the church, the family and the workplace. Nevertheless, formal training was important in specialized areas, such as writing and drawing, for instance. But this very specialized instruction was available to only a few. For example, Rosemary O'Day (1982:25) notes that

> for centuries academic learning had been the preserve of the clergy and potential clergy because only the clergy needed advanced literacy for their work. . . . To the extent that other groups . . . needed book learning, their needs could be satisfied by the father, the master, the churchman.

For sociologists, this raises many questions. How did the schooled society come about? After schooling began, why did it expand? Why was attendance made compulsory? What links schools with other institutions? Historical evidence to answer these questions is gradually accumulating, but various theoretical accounts of the origins of schooling still vie for support.

Functionalist
Accounts

Emile Durkheim, one of the founders of sociology, argued that with the transition to a schooled society, education became the agent of moral regulation in the modern world. The school was the secular equivalent of religion in contemporary society. Durkheim's argument is a functional account—it explains schooling by citing its contribution to the "needs of society." According to Durkheim, education functions to solve a societal need by integrating society. That is, to create a unified society, education must encourage people to accept a set of common beliefs and sentiments.

In the industrialized world, it is true that the historic influence of religion has waned. There is little evidence, however, showing that schooling now contributes to social integration as Durkheim imagined; nor is there good reason to think that mass schooling ever provided such integration. An alternative explanation, often labelled the technical functional approach, is that society requires technically skilled workers to meet the needs of increasingly sophisticated industrial production. Schooling began, the argument runs, because it could best supply the technical skills and expertise demanded by economic growth. Furthermore, as schools produce more skilled workers, this will spur economic development. The key empirical claim of this theory is a strong link between a country's economic growth and its level of education (see Figure 13-1). Schooling functions to satisfy the technical needs of the economy.

A Marxist Account

Marxists also see a linkage between formal education and the economy, but their view is different from that of the technical functionalists. In an economy organized around the profit motive, the accumulation of money, or capital, is paramount. As Samuel Bowles and Herbert Gintis (1976) stress, the imperative faced by owners—to make money or go bankrupt—conflicts with the workers' demand for a share of the accumulated wealth. This conflict is exacerbated by competitive pressures that owners respond to with labour-saving and wage-tightening initiatives. Bowles and Gintis argue that owners sought to resolve threats to the social order by schooling future workers to accept the capitalist system of production and their place within it. For Marxists, schooling was initiated as a means of social control.

A Weberian
Account

The origins of state-supported schooling in Canada do not fit particularly well with either the technical functional or Marxist model. Both theories posit a direct link between industrialization and schooling, but in Canada mass schooling preceded the development of industrial capitalism. Furthermore, the early school promoters were more preoccupied with citizenship than industrial preparation. They saw schooling primarily as a way to civilize society and stem problems of poverty, vagrancy and social and moral decay. Only secondarily did they consider promoting labour productivity and enhancing economic growth.

Samuel Codner in Newfoundland, Egerton Ryerson in Ontario and John Jessop in British Columbia were early school promoters who saw rapid social change, especially increased immigration and urbanization, as root causes of public apathy, moral pollu-

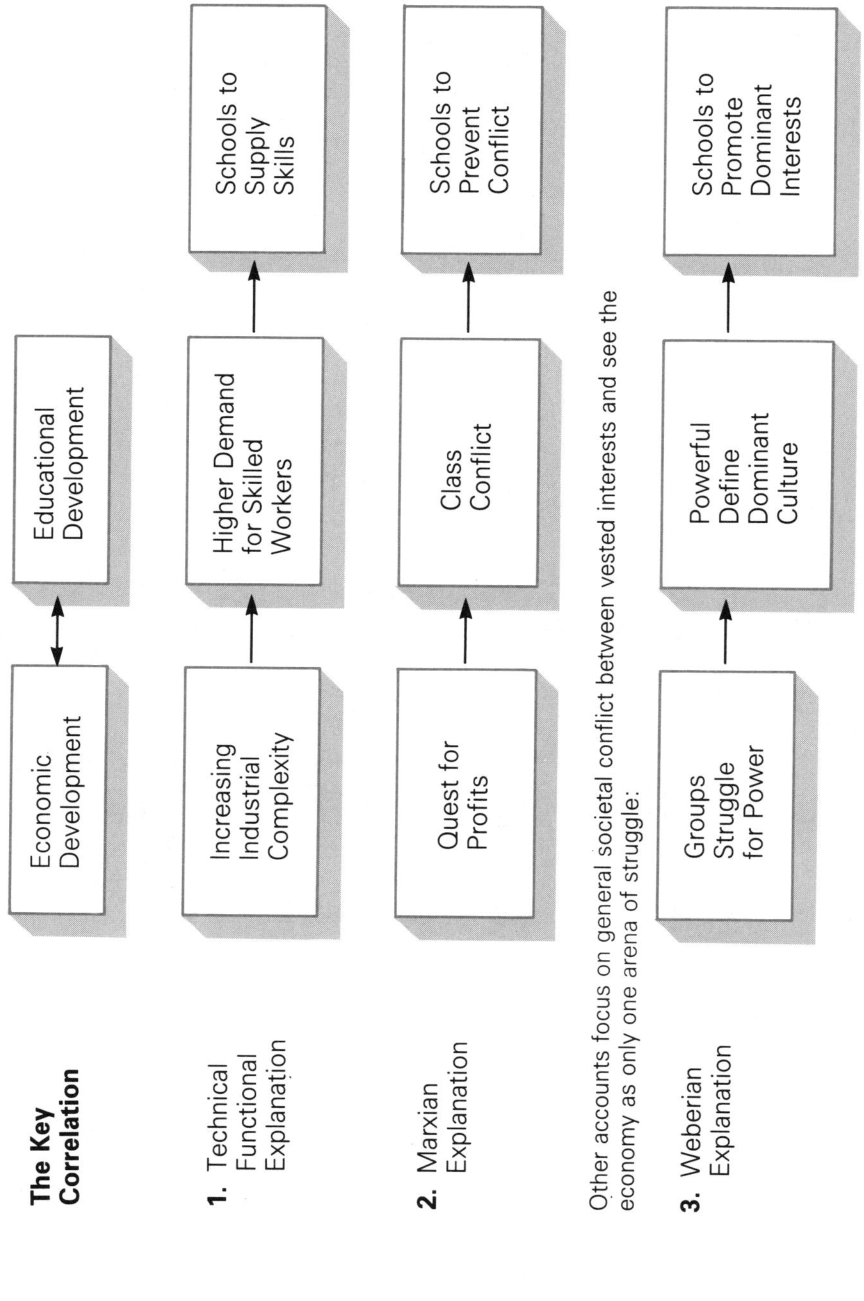

FIGURE 13-1

The Origins of a Schooled Society

Explanations for the origins of schooling are of two general types. Some accounts focus on the link between education and the economy:

The Key Correlation

Economic Development ↕ Educational Development

1. Technical Functional Explanation

Increasing Industrial Complexity → Higher Demand for Skilled Workers → Schools to Supply Skills

2. Marxian Explanation

Quest for Profits → Class Conflict → Schools to Prevent Conflict

Other accounts focus on general societal conflict between vested interests and see the economy as only one arena of struggle:

3. Weberian Explanation

Groups Struggle for Power → Powerful Define Dominant Culture → Schools to Promote Dominant Interests

tion and social disorder. The primary mission of the schools was thus to provide moral guidance and produce good citizens. Human development and character building were of principal concern—moral engineering topped the schooling agenda.

Randall Collins (1977, 1979) provides a theoretical account that fits the historical evidence more closely. He stresses the power of different interest groups in promoting a particular vision of society and in developing education programs that complement this image. In an argument aligned with the Weberian tradition, Collins (1977:4) sees education as "part of a multi-sided struggle among status communities for domination, for economic advantage, and for prestige." By controlling the schools, a powerful status group could work to ensure that what was taught conformed to their values, manners, customs, tastes, interests and experiences.

According to Collins's model, colonial loyalists in Canada instituted schooling as a way of instilling a British model of civilization in order to legitimate and entrench their interests. Everywhere but in Quebec, the impetus for public schooling came largely from white, Anglo-Saxon Protestants. In Quebec, where the church dominated education until well into the current century, the Catholic clergy sought to maintain their dominance. Comparing the historical records in New England, Ontario and Newfoundland, Alan Pomfret (1979) argues that the schooled society was established in each region as small but active middle-class groups tried to impose their definitions of problems and solutions on other groups.

The beginnings of the school system in Canada can thus be traced to the colonial status of the country. Since schooling serves different functions, it is not surprising that theorists have stressed different features. In a way, functionalists such as Durkheim were correct to stress the roles of moral regulation in the origins of a schooled society. But as Collins's model stresses, it was the moral values of one interest group that were at work, not the integration of a shared value system as Durkheim argued. While these three theories help to explain the origins of schooling, the expansion of schooling may have resulted from quite different forces.

Expansion in Education

The absolute size of the school system has expanded and contracted over the years. Expansion was the norm up until the 1970s, but in recent years contraction has resulted in school closures and a decline in the number of teaching positions. Why have these changes taken place? Before reviewing different theoretical explanations, it is useful to understand these patterns of change more clearly.

One measure of size of the school system is the number of students enrolled. Table 13-1 describes the size of the student population over the last four decades, recording the number of students enrolled in kindergarten, elementary school, high school and college or university. The bottom row of the table shows the year in which enrolments in each of the four levels of schooling peaked.

TABLE 13-1

Expansion and
Contraction in
Canadian Education,
Full-time School
Enrolments
(in millions)

| Year | Level of Schooling | | | |
	Kindergarten	Elementary	High School	Post-Secondary
1951–52	.08	2.15	.39	.09
1961–62	.16	3.36	.90	.18
1971–72	.38	3.76	1.72	.50
1981–82	.40	3.07	1.63	.63
1987–88	.44	3.02	1.51	.81
Peak Year	1987–88 (.44)	1968–69 (3.84)	1974–75 (1.81)	1987–88 (.81)

Notes: Figures in millions; for example, 1951–52 kindergarten enrolment of .08 means 80 000 students at this level of schooling.

Peak year—the year in which each level of schooling has experienced the highest enrolment.

ADAPTED FROM EDUCATION IN CANADA. 1989. OTTAWA: STATISTICS CANADA, CAT. 81–229. REPRODUCED WITH THE PERMISSION OF THE MINISTER OF SUPPLY AND SERVICES CANADA.

Kindergarten enrolments have continued to expand from 1951–52 until the present, although the rate of expansion has slowed substantially over the last fifteen years. In both elementary and high school, the size of the student body increased after 1950–51, but decreased at a subsequent point. The bottom row of the table shows that elementary-school enrolments peaked in 1968–69. For high schools, the peak occurred six years later in 1974–75 when 1.81 million students attended high school, and again the numbers have fallen since. Finally, for colleges and universities, the number of students has increased in every year since 1950–51.

The growth and decline in the elementary and high-school populations has a demographic explanation. More children were born in Canada in 1959 than in any year before or after. This population bulge, the baby boom, passed through elementary school in 1968–69 and through high school in 1974–75. The baby boom generation contributed to both the post–Second World War expansion (school construction, teacher hiring) and the more recent contraction.

The constant expansion of kindergarten and post-secondary enrolments is not explicable simply by the total number of children. If only population pressures were at work we would expect kindergarten enrolments to have declined in the early 1960s and college and university student numbers to have dipped by the early 1980s. Neither of these results occurred.

For the youngest group, the enrolment increase is principally a function of the gradual increase in the number of school boards offering kindergarten. Especially in rural areas, it is only in the last decade that kindergarten has become generally available.

Participation in Higher Education

Higher education enrolments have also grown, even after the baby boom generation passed. To remove the effect of fluctuating birth rates on attendance, we can examine

FIGURE 13-2

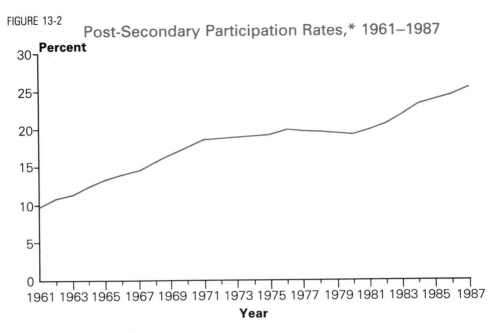

Post-Secondary Participation Rates,* 1961–1987

*Rates for 18–24 year olds.
Statistics Canada, 1989. *Education in Canada* (81-229). Reproduced with the permission of the Minister of Supply and Services Canada.

the percentage of people between certain ages who attend school. This measure is especially meaningful for college and university enrolments where attendance is not compulsory. Figure 13-2 charts the *participation rate*—the percentage of Canadians between eighteen and twenty-four enrolled in higher education—from the 1960s to the mid-1980s. The constant rise reflects the growing proportion of young people attending college or university in the last few decades. Despite the decline in the absolute number of people aged eighteen to twenty-four, the percentage of this age group enrolling in college or university has continued to expand.

The expansion of available spaces accounts for part of the continuing increase in college and university enrolments. Especially with the growth in community colleges, more opportunities to pursue higher education, and in more varied geographical locations, are available now as compared to 1950–51. Most building expansion occurred in the 1970s, however, and so this explanation cannot account for all of the rise in student numbers. In the 1980s, student enrolments have continued to climb, even in the face of government cutbacks in post-secondary funding.

The recent increase in participation rates has occurred mainly because of women's greater participation in higher education. Figure 13-3 shows this growth in women's participation by graphing the number of women and men who receive undergraduate

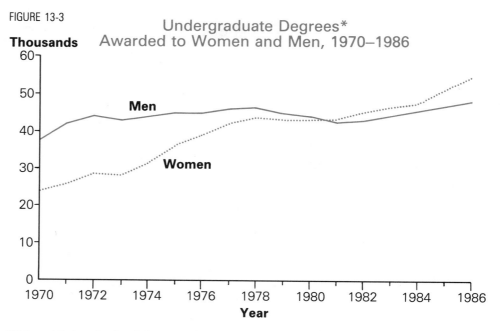

FIGURE 13-3

Thousands   Undergraduate Degrees*
Awarded to Women and Men, 1970–1986

*B.A. and first professional degrees only.
Statistics Canada, 1989. *Education in Canada,* (81-229). Reproduced with the permission of the Minister of Supply and Services Canada.

university degrees each year. University graduating classes have contained more women than men since the early 1980s. Although it is not shown in Figure 13-3, more women than men have been graduating from colleges since the mid-1970s. Several theoretical explanations have been proposed to account for this increasing rate of participation in higher education. Three of these—human capital, equal opportunity and credentialism—are reviewed here.

Human Capital   In 1957, the Soviet Union launched the first satellite to orbit the earth, winning the first leg of the race to space. The Soviet education system was seen by many as a prominent factor in their success. Especially in the United States, reaction was swift—education had to become a national priority in order to withstand the challenge of communist science and technology.

The importance of the link between science and industry was not lost on other Western industrial nations, and education quickly became a political priority. A highly educated work force, with the skills and capabilities necessary to the advanced work in factories and offices, was deemed essential in order to keep abreast of international economic competition. The causal link between education and the economy was once again prominent at two levels. On a national level, success would come to those countries investing in education because their economies would benefit from the infusion of skilled workers. Economic growth was seen as a direct consequence of educational expansion. On an individual level, investments in education would be valuable because job opportunities, promotions and pay would be linked with educational attainment. Just as capital investments in physical machinery were important to production, so too were investments in people. The knowledge and skills that people possess form a reserve of *human capital*.

Under this theoretical model, rising educational attainment is a consequence of growing demands for skilled and responsible workers. A strong version of this human capital model holds that schooling provides the mental skills and abilities necessary for job success. A weaker version claims only that educational attainment indicates an ability to learn that enables workers to do well at their jobs.

Equal Opportunity   A second explanation for expanding college and university enrolments focuses on equality of opportunity. As affluence and economic prosperity grew in the post–Second World War era, popular expression was given to the idea that everyone should be able to share in the new wealth. Pierre Trudeau's concept of a "Just Society," where merit is based on achievement, not birthright, captures the essence of this movement. Schooling should be available to all, and governments have a responsibility to provide at least part of the resources necessary to accomplish this goal.

The equality of opportunity argument and the human capital approach have been combined in a functionalist explanation of educational expansion. In traditional societies, children followed their parents' occupational paths as farmers, fishers or craft workers. However, as the occupational structure grew more diverse, families became less able to train and recruit new job occupants.

The expansion in the types of jobs required that schools replace families as sites for training and sorting. Simultaneously, the criterion for job selection began to shift from who your parents were (*ascription*) to what you were capable of doing (*achievement*). Previously, honour and loyalty made it acceptable (if not mandatory) to advance the interests of family and associates. This system of patronage had to be replaced, the functionalists argued, and the cardinal principle of the new system had to be achievement.

The importance of selection by achievement and equality of opportunity were explained by the human capital thesis. Countries would prosper only if they were able to tap the full potential of *all* their citizens. The best and the brightest individuals must be able to develop their skills and abilities—the cream must be allowed to rise to the top. Talented individuals, no matter what their race, sex or religion, must have the opportunity to contribute. A meritocracy must flourish; competence, achievement and motivation must be rewarded. The expansion of schooling was, according to this combined model, a consequence of efforts to provide equal opportunities for students from all walks of life.

Credentialism   A third explanation for the growth of higher education enrolments focuses upon the competition among young people for economic security. As youth unemployment rises, the pursuit of education credentials grows because people compete to acquire qualifications. College or university attendance comes to be based primarily on the belief that decent jobs are easier to secure with more credentials. A tension results as job opportunities tighten, even for those with education certificates. The demand for education grows; the paper chase, or as Ron Dore (1976) dubs it, the "diploma disease," follows. The quest for credentials results in an "educational arms race" with the further consequence that the attainment of high grades also becomes imperative, leading to the grade inflation now worrying many in higher education (Bercuson, Bothwell and Granatstein, 1984).

Evidence Involving the Growth of Participation in Higher Education

The Politician's Role

Two types of evidence can help sort out what theory best fits the Canadian situation. Since the growth of formal education depends upon government support, it is important to consider what the motives of politicians were in expanding education budgets.

Anisef et al. (1982: 22–30) have documented the extent to which the concept of equality of opportunity permeated legislative debates about education. They show that a stress on meritocracy had high priority in the minds of politicians. Two major government-sponsored reports on education in the 1960s—the Parent report in Quebec and the Hall-Dennis report in Ontario—identified equality of opportunity as a goal for education. Everyone, it was argued, should have the chance to benefit from education, and factors such as race, sex, social class or religion should not impede this opportunity. Efforts were also made to ensure rough equality in the educational facilities of various regions, so that, for example, rural and urban schools, or schools in poor versus rich neighbourhoods, were of comparable quality. The Canada Student Loan plan was also inaugurated as an attempt to provide material support to students who could not rely on family funds to finance their college or university education.

Politicians were quick to employ human capital arguments in justifying an expansion of the school system. Good political mileage could be made by reminding voters that Canada was a rich and prosperous country, and that a strong and healthy education system was crucial to national well-being. Promoting education helps at the ballot box when over a quarter of the population is directly involved in schooling as either students, teachers or administrators and an even larger segment is indirectly connected to education as parents or grandparents. But does the school system actually provide equality of opportunity, and is there a connection between education and skills, as politicians maintain?

Education and Skill

Examination of the link between what students learn and what knowledge and skill employers want is important in understanding the growth of education. This is especially true in human capital theory, where a direct causal tie is made between school learning and job requirements.

Two pieces of evidence favour a sceptical reception for the link between education and job skills. Schools have recently been attacked for failing to teach basic literacy and numeracy skills. Universities have begun to institute remedial courses in communication skills, and English competency exams have been made compulsory at some colleges and universities. Employers, too, have been critical, claiming that students are ill-prepared for the world of business (see Bercuson, Bothwell and Granatstein, 1984).

Empirical tests also suggest there is no link between education and job skills. Ivar Berg's (1970:110) *Education and Jobs: The Great Training Robbery* argues that there is "little concrete evidence of a positive relationship between workers' educational achievements and their performance in work settings."

There is, however, other evidence supporting at least the weaker version of human capital theory (namely, that educational attainment signals an ability to learn). Alfred Hunter (1988) has recently tested this signalling hypothesis by examining whether or not the people in jobs requiring more skill actually have higher levels of schooling. Since this link should be most apparent for entry-level jobs, he focuses upon the initial jobs people attain immediately upon completing their education. He finds that "schooling is quite clearly related to the skill requirements of first jobs" and that this importance has increased over time (1988:763).

The rapid expansion in the numbers of women in higher education (see Figure 13-3) can also be at least partially explained by the signalling hypothesis. Women's labour force participation has risen rapidly in recent decades, and this may have intensified women's desire for the skills developed through education. Hunter's study did not directly test this, but he did find that, over time, schooling has played an increasingly important role in job allocation for women. Had he found the opposite, that the relationship between schooling and job skills weakened for women, then women's growing participation in higher education would have cast doubt on the signalling hypothesis.

Whatever the complete explanation of educational expansion might be, it is clear that the causes for the origins of schooling and the causes for recent growth differ. Each of the postulated causes of educational growth has some support, and as yet no one can point to any full explanation.

Equality in Education

People don't choose their parents. Of all life's unknowns, this randomness of birth is the greatest. It lies at the heart of debates about equality of educational opportunity. Should those born into poverty be given a fair opportunity to escape a life of economic misery? Some see education as a medium for helping people overcome misfortune.

Politicians have argued in favour of this basic fairness and various attempts have been made to provide for equality of educational opportunity. But while the idea of equality may be basic to our value system, the full realization of equality may be quite another matter.

Do we have educational equality? Figure 13-4 displays the percentages of people from different family backgrounds who have and have not participated in post-secondary education. The shaded bar on the left shows that only 31 percent of people whose father had a grade eight or lower education went to college or university.

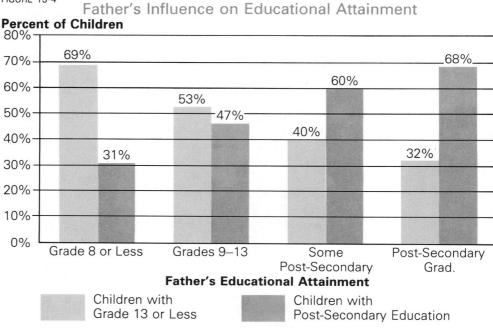

FIGURE 13-4

Father's Influence on Educational Attainment

General Social Survey, 1986.   Sample Size = 11,251.

Conversely, as the bar on the extreme right shows, 68 percent of people whose fathers had a post-secondary degree attended higher education. The basic message of the figure can be summarized as follows: for people with a poorly educated father, the likelihood of attending college or university is one in three; for people with a well-educated father, their chance of going to college or university is two in three. (If the mother's level of education is substituted for the father's, the results are the same.)

Focusing on secondary schools, Porter, Porter and Blishen (1982) have demonstrated that family background has a large effect on the type of educational stream students pursue (another measure of equality of opportunity). They show that students from backgrounds with higher social class are four times more likely to pursue academic streams than students from the lower classes, who are more likely to pursue non-academic courses. While equality of educational opportunity may be a virtue, it is not a reality in Canadian society. Opportunities for those from poorer families have improved little over time (Guppy, 1984).

Why is it that your odds of obtaining a post-secondary education or pursuing an academic high-school program are much higher if you come from a family with well-educated parents? Put another way, what accounts for the consistently replicated finding of *inequality* in education attainment? Is it because intelligence is inherited? Is it because well-educated parents are more likely to have the financial resources needed for children to attend higher education? Is it because children in more educated families receive more encouragement? Is it because the school system favours students from better-educated households? These are the types of questions sociologists explore in attempting to unravel the inequality in educational participation.

Family Origin and Educational Destination

Over a quarter of Canadians between the ages of eighteen and twenty-four enrol in colleges or universities. Figure 13-4 shows that those entering post-secondary institutions are more likely to have fathers with higher educations. This strong, positive association between the levels of education of parents and their offspring has changed little in recent decades (Guppy, 1984). Consequently, the educational advantages of one generation are transferred to the next generation so that education reproduces patterns of inequality across generations—education is not a great equalizer. Explanations for this link between family origin and educational attainment can be simplified as follows:

1. Attainment = Mental Ability

2. Attainment = Mental Ability + Effort

3. Attainment = Mental Ability + Effort + Cultural Capital

The first model views educational attainment as solely the consequence of an individual's intellect. The second model assumes that intellect alone is insufficient and must be complemented by drive and determination; aspirations are as crucial as ability. Under model two, attainment is a strict function of merit—to the able and active go the prizes. The third model views attainment as a function of ability, effort and cultural capital (for example, social skills and graces; impression management abilities), and is the most convincing non-merit explanation of differential educational attainment.

Intelligence The intelligence explanation is hounded by the continuing debate over whether or not mental ability can be accurately measured. Here is a sample question from an IQ test (Eysenck, 1968): "What word goes in the four spaces so as to complete one six letter word and begin another: A M _ _ _ _ E L?" It is not obvious exactly what aspect of intelligence, if any, such a question measures. Furthermore, some people will treat such a task as silly, while others may find it a challenge. If well-educated families were more competitive at games than poorly educated families, students from well-educated families would generally score better on IQ tests. However, these higher scores would be a consequence of socialization, not intelligence.

There is no general systematic evidence showing a link between IQ and family education that would fully explain the educational inequalities of Figure 13-4. However, a classic test of nature (genetic inheritance) versus nurture (social environment) in regards to IQ levels is Harold Skeels's (1966) natural experiment. He studied a group of children who had been labelled as retarded when living in an overcrowded orphanage. Some of the children were moved to a more stimulating setting. He found that children who had moved improved their scores markedly, whereas the scores of the group that were not moved declined further. This is strong evidence that whatever IQ tests measure can be influenced by social environment.

Family Income   Family income is a second explanation for educational inequality. For example, students from families with lower educational backgrounds may not have the economic resources necessary to finance a college or university education. Recent increases in tuition fees and costs of accommodation may have exacerbated economic barriers to higher education. Furthermore, education in expensive private schools is not something all families can afford. Such schooling is, however, an important determinant of a person's future position (Clement, 1975). Aside from elite private schools, the *direct* relevance of family income remains ambiguous.

Families   Robert Pike (1988 : 271) has recently noted that "a growing international body of literature . . . suggests that cultural rather than material factors best explain perceived variations in educational opportunity." Of the cultural factors Pike has in mind, family stimulation and encouragement is one of the most central. Gilbert and McRoberts

(1977) report that the family has the strongest influence on the educational aspirations and expectations of students. For working-class families in which neither mother nor father has a college or university degree, higher education is foreign territory. Working-class families may encourage their children, but they lack the first-hand knowledge that middle- and upper-class parents can use to extol the benefits of post-secondary education.

Even if the importance families place on education is equivalent, their abilities to promote educational success in their children may differ. Many working-class parents have poor educational skills, and they are in jobs with lower occupational prestige than are teachers. This results, Lareau (1987) argues, in working-class parents relying more on teachers to educate their children. Conversely, middle- and upper-class parents see the process of education as something they share with teachers, and so they scrutinize, monitor and supplement their children's education more than working-class parents do. Even when teachers request help from families, working-class parents may be more reticent about complying, more self-conscious about their ability to help their children—they may assist as frequently, but with less confidence.

A more complex appreciation of how the family influences educational attainment focuses not on parental encouragement, but on family socialization. For children who respect the school environment and who strive to perform well, learning to manage

On the right is a private school for girls with decorative landscaping and student uniforms. On the left is a public school with a chain-linked fence and a dumpster. Two different education streams with two different sets of pupils.

the demands of teachers is imperative. They try to tell teachers what they want to hear, in a form they find pleasing. Children with less respect for schooling frequently engage in campaigns of resistance, making life difficult for teachers as a way of signalling their disdain for the schooling process (see Willis, 1977).

These responses to schooling are not random events unconnected with a student's background. Individual responses to any social setting are partly idiosyncratic and personal, but reactions are also the product of a person's cultural background. Many sociologists argue that the cultural experiences of students from working-class homes disadvantage them in the educational setting.

Bernstein   One example of a disadvantage faced by working-class students is studied in the work of Basil Bernstein (1977; see also Atkinson, 1985). Bernstein argues that people differ in the core principles they use to organize written and spoken language. Some people make full use of all the nuances of language, easily manipulating words, meanings and symbols in an *elaborate linguistic code*, which emphasizes impersonal, abstract and referential thinking. Others make use of a more *restricted code*, using only a portion of the communication system, still adept at communicating, but employing a tighter range of techniques.

Bernstein's work is easily misunderstood by assuming that restricted means simpler and more basic, which it does not. It is mistaken, he argues, to confuse surface appearances (that is, written or spoken communication) with the deep-meaning structure (the code), which generates or regulates communication. His research shows that people using the restricted code are more fluent, in the sense of pausing less and using longer phrases, than those relying on elaborate code. Restricted code users are, however, more descriptive and less symbolic, and they rarely employ impersonal pronouns (it, one).

The force of Bernstein's argument comes in linking restricted and elaborated codes, first to social class, and second to schooling. He argues that language use in working-class families tends to rely on restricted code, whereas middle- and upper-class families are more likely to employ elaborate codes. Furthermore, he claims that the school system is concerned with the development and use of elaborate codes. To do well in school, working-class children must adopt a linguistic code that differs from the one they use at home, as well as unlearn a code that is inappropriate in schools.

For Bernstein, then, educational attainment varies by social class because of cultural differences in linguistic codes that distinguish between working-, middle- and upper-class families. There is an opposition between the culture of working-class families and the predominant culture of the school.

Bourdieu   Pierre Bourdieu (1976, 1984) extends the idea of cultural differences well beyond language. Typically culture is regarded as a "design for living" or "shared habits of thought and action." Bourdieu uses culture in quite a different way, more as "cultivation" or "distinction." While economic capital is about money and wealth, cultural capital is about taste, demeanour, style and savoir-faire. It is an ability to manipulate symbols—language, figures, relations and images. Cultural capital means having the skills to influence important people.

Cultural capital is the currency of the education system. Because middle- and upper-class children have more cultural currency, they have greater success in school. As Bourdieu (1976:126) argues: "What the education system both hands on and demands is an aristocratic culture and, above all, an aristocratic relationship with it." Although educational evaluation purports to provide "fair and unbiased" assessments, Bourdieu argues that it favours precisely those skills and abilities that cultural capital provides.

Bowles and Gintis   Both Bernstein and Bourdieu argue that schools are more comfortable settings for children of middle- and upper-class origins. The values taught in school are the very values that middle- and upper-class children experience in their families. Therefore, the inequality of educational attainment is the result of social class differences. The education system reproduces class distinctions by limiting the chances that working-class students will succeed in school. This contention is sometimes referred to as the *reproduction thesis*.

Equality and Education

That schooling is like a race where victory goes to the swiftest is a modern myth. The concept of equality is the banner under which this race is said to be run, but it is a false race, a race where the outcome is known prior to the crack of the starter's pistol. While everyone must enter the race, some come with personalized starting blocks and lightweight track shoes, while others arrive in heavy boots and cumbersome clothing. Some see the race as an exhilarating challenge; others view it with disdain.

There is equality of opportunity in schools only to the extent that everyone has the chance to participate; by law schooling is compulsory. The conditions that entrants bring to schools are, however, unequal. Equality of condition does not exist. Educational outcomes depend on the endowments families are able to provide

to their children (these endowments are explored at length in the text).

Stephen Richer uses the concept of "equality to benefit" as a way of highlighting inequality in the school system. He juxtaposes the "uniformity of schooling" and the "variability in children" (1988:271). Under such conditions, those from advantaged backgrounds benefit the most from schooling, because the values and standards of education favour such children.

It is easy, but incorrect, to dismiss discussions of equality by equating it with sameness. Results or outcomes will differ, but success and failure should be unconnected with such factors as sex, race, nativity or social class. Equality presumes that everyone has equal means for attaining their full potential.

An alternative form of the reproduction thesis is offered by Bowles and Gintis (1976). As you will recall from the discussion of the origins of a schooled society, Bowles and Gintis have a Marxist approach that emphasizes the relationship between schools and the economy. They argue that those in power try to lessen class conflict by schooling workers to accept their place in a capitalist system.

For Bowles and Gintis, the purpose of schools is not to promote equality of opportunity. The knowledge of social relations transmitted as a by-product of schooling is, they argue, far more important than anything learned from the formal curriculum. Rules and regulations, routines and repetitions, experiences of authority and hierarchy—these social relations are basic to instilling in youth the attitudes necessary for the world of work. This harmony of social relations between the school room and the work setting they refer to as the *correspondence principle*. For Bowles and Gintis, schools are explicitly designed to produce obedient workers, not to further opportunities for social mobility.

This correspondence principle has been widely criticized. Critics charge that Bowles and Gintis regard students as "cultural dopes," sponges who absorb uncritically the subliminal messages schools transmit. Jane Gaskell's research (1985a, 1985b) on the occupational choices of working-class females in Vancouver reveals no straightforward correspondence between school and work. The women she interviewed "rejected academic schooling . . . because they believed it was irrelevant. Vocational courses were perceived as less regimented and less confining than academic courses" (Gaskell, 1985a:53). Far from being cultural dopes, these women created personal solutions, adapting to what they saw as their best opportunities.

The correspondence principle of Bowles and Gintis stresses the parallels between school and work. On command, little workers toil away at their set assignments. Do the authority relations of school mirror the requirements of the world of work?

The Hidden Curriculum

The strength of the cultural capital and correspondence principle comes in pointing to what actually happens in schools. By shifting attention away from the formal timetable (math, music, etc.), the informal or hidden curriculum is highlighted. For Bernstein this is communication patterns, for Bourdieu it is cultural capital and for Bowles and Gintis it is the social relations of power and authority. But while each signals the importance of the hidden curriculum, the details of how this informal curriculum operates have been left for other researchers to explore.

The official timetable is a core feature of schooling. Students have their days neatly compartmentalized into a distinct set of classroom lessons—mathematics for forty minutes, followed by physical education, then art class and so on. Within this series of classes, a formal syllabus guides teachers in outlining the content of lessons. This is the formal curriculum, a set of written guidelines and policies formulated by course designers, consultants and school administrators about how the school day should be organized and what should be taught.

The concept of *hidden curriculum* targets what is not explicitly recognized in these formal lesson plans. It reflects both the unwritten assumptions of course designers and consultants, and the unacknowledged, unintended messages of teachers and school administrators.

For example, language, pictures and examples often permit interpretations beyond those intended. Phrases such as "scientists and their wives" or the "businessman's lunch" explicitly identify science and business as masculine activities, even when this was not the purpose intended. Pictures showing male surgeons and female nurses illustrate more than simply people at work. Such images reinforce a familiar perception that nursing is not for men and that women are only patients or nurses in the operating room. This gender stereotyping is often unintentional. It is "hidden" or latent in the sense that gender relations were not the focus of the picture (it was to show people working) or of the discussion (which was about science or business).

Meighan (1981) uses the analogy of ghosts to illustrate the hidden curriculum. Classroom activity is haunted by ghosts, ghosts who reveal ideas that were not originally intended: the timetabling ghost shows that knowledge comes in distinct, forty-minute batches; the textbook ghost reveals unwarranted assumptions; and the school architecture ghost suggests impersonality. It is these covert or veiled messages that the hidden curriculum accentuates. The haunting analogy emphasizes that no conspirators lurk behind the scenes designing these messages—they were not intended.

Stephen Richer's research (1984, 1988) in Ottawa schools demonstrates other dimensions of the hidden curriculum. Show and tell, a school experience many Canadians can recall, is designed to provide children with opportunities to enhance self-confidence and improve verbal skills by encouraging them to speak before their peers. While show and tell may provide these benefits, it also has unintentional consequences (Richer, 1988: 274–75). For children able to display many novelties, show and tell can be an exciting classroom activity. They hold centre stage as their peers and teachers reward them with smiles and attention. They quickly understand that the more novel or unusual their exhibit, the more smiles and attention they receive. Children cannot help but realize the value of material possessions and competition, even though show and tell was not designed to promote this way of thinking.

By observing classroom activities, social scientists have gradually uncovered a "hidden" curriculum that works to the disadvantage of women, ethnic minorities and working-class students. A growing body of evidence shows that schools emphasize competition, obedience to authority, private property and individualism, Christian values, written rather than oral literacy and abstract reasoning. For example, students learn that knowledge is private property. Helping others is not only discouraged, but on many occasions is punished as cheating.

Policy Initiatives

On the basis of our growing understanding of the relationship between school and society, a variety of educational policies have been implemented. For example, school reformers have introduced several types of *compensatory education* programs. These programs involve additional or extra school sessions developed specifically to aid disadvantaged children. "After Four" in Ontario and "Head Start" and "Follow Through" in the United States are examples of programs designed to offset the effects of poverty, deprivation and disadvantage on school performance. Initial research dismissed compensatory education programs as complete failures since frequently only small improvements resulted, and these often "washed out" over time. In the face of widespread social and economic inequalities in the wider society, this is not altogether surprising. Nevertheless, opinion now seems to be shifting and a "more optimistic conclusion about special pre-school intervention programmes" has emerged (Meadows and Cashdan, 1988 : 16).

Other policy initiatives aim at revising school curricula, in both the formal and hidden dimensions. Contemporary school texts are now less likely to denigrate minority groups (for example, by referring to native people as "savages") or to display pictures of a sexist nature. Attempts have also been made to reduce the reliance on a "banking" concept of knowledge (where depositing information in students is seen as the purpose of lessons). Ivan Illich (1971), a former Roman Catholic priest, argues that in schools children are taught, they do not learn. Learning must be made attractive, he argues, and this requires a dramatic shift in policy away from the banking philosophy of many educators.

Education policy will always be contentious. Disputes over the social functions of schooling will persist. No school program can adequately satisfy the range of ideals people may wish to achieve through education (for example, giving their children special opportunities, combatting drug use, increasing skill levels, reducing poverty, developing greater enlightenment, lessening apathy and alienation, instilling moral fortitude and heightening national identity).

Summary

Understanding the relationship between schools and various aspects of Canadian society (the economy, the system of inequality and so on) is a major sociological endeavour. How links between schooling and society are perceived influence education policies, from compensatory education schemes to industry-university ties.

In this chapter various ways of understanding school/society connections have been reviewed by examining debates about the social functions of schools, controversies over why a schooled society developed and arguments surrounding the reasons for the growth of education. Education and society also interact in the way the schooling process relates to the system of inequality in society. Sociologists accept that schooling perpetuates inequalities, but disagree over how this inequality of education operates.

Cultural experiences in education have received overwhelming attention recently. The culture of the home environment—broken homes, orientation to books and learning, child-rearing practices—has been recognized as important. The culture of the school has also been examined, especially the hidden curriculum and the authority relations of the classroom. The opposition between the predominant culture of the school and the cultural experiences of children from different backgrounds is thought to be crucial.

Suggested Readings

Anisef, Paul, Norman Okihiro and Carl James
> 1982. *Losers and Winners: The Pursuit of Equality and Social Justice in Higher Education.* Toronto: Butterworths. A useful review of literature is combined with rich analysis of data. The data focus upon equality by gender, class and ethnicity, using 1971 and 1976 census information.

Gaskell, Jane, and Arlene McLaren, eds.
> 1987. *Women and Education: A Canadian Perspective.* Calgary: Detselig. A collection of essays focusing upon women's experiences in education. The papers cover historical and contemporary debates.

Livingstone, David
> 1985. *Social Crisis and Schooling.* Toronto: Garamond Press. An exploration of social class and the education system highlighting the school-society linkage in the context of contemporary capitalism.

Porter, John
> 1979. *The Measure of Canadian Society: Education, Equality and Opportunity.* Toronto: Gage. One of the best discussions of theoretical and policy issues related to schooling in Canada.

Wotherspoon, Terry, ed.
> 1987. *The Political Economy of Schooling.* Toronto: Methuen. Essays in this collection examine the place of education in capitalist societies. Among other topics, the essays address the politics of schooling, the social control strategies of educators and the reproduction of inequality via education.

Discussion Questions

1. The pace at which ascriptive criteria are replaced by achievement indicators is used by some researchers as a standard for measuring social progress. Starting with the evidence and arguments in this chapter, discuss the degree to which this shift has occurred in the context of Canadian education.

2. By randomness of birth, some people wind up as the heirs of millionaires and others the children of paupers. To the extent that they are able, parents have an interest in seeking positive experiences for their children. Does this mean that education is doomed to fail in any attempt to foster equality because rich families can always buy special advantages for their offspring (private tutors, educational aids)? Discuss.

3. Early in the chapter, it is suggested that the family is not capable of efficiently teaching all the theoretical knowledge now included in the school curriculum. Do you agree with this claim? If the focus were on other functions of education (i.e., evaluation or control) could the family effectively undertake more of the role of education? Would this be a good thing for children, for families and for society? Who might benefit the most and who the least by such a change?

4. Women and men tend to follow different fields in the education system (e.g., men in sciences and women in humanities). A number of causes have been advanced as explanations for this phenomenon: early childhood socialization; biological differences; discrimination; labour market differences; attitudes of peers, parents or teachers; advice of guidance counsellors; mental abilities. Which of these explanations do you consider plausible? Why have the number of women in certain fields, such as law, medicine and engineering, begun to rise, while the number of men entering fields such as nursing has remained small?

Data Collection Exercises

1. The percentage of different age groups enrolled in schools (the participation rate) varies by country. Figure 13-1 provides one set of figures for Canada. Locate comparable data from different countries at one point in time and contrast the percentages between societies (the UNESCO Statistical Yearbook is a good source). Alternatively, find data trends from one country to compare with Canada (for example, compare Statistics Canada figures in *Education in Canada* with data from the U.S. *Statistical Abstracts*—these are both annual government publications). Suggest reasons for the differences you discover.

2. Take a selection of books used either in nursery school or in elementary school and investigate whether or not sexual or ethnic stereotyping can be identified (using pictures might be the most straightforward approach). All libraries have

some children's books and that would be one possible source. You may choose only recent books or you may select from a wide range of years. Before you begin this content analysis, be sure to define what will count as stereotyping. Discuss your findings.

3. Some university programs enrol far more women than men. Women dominate in nursing and home economics, while engineering is overwhelmingly male. Interview both women and men in a selection of these subject areas and ask about the influences on their choices. Explore with them reasons for gender differences. Alternatively, interview members of each sex in those programs in which women's involvement has recently risen (medicine, law, etc.) and ask for their views on the reasons for the change and/or the consequences of the change. Comment on the reasons given.

4. Make arrangements with a toddler's group, a nursery or day care centre or an elementary school class to observe a few sessions. Focus on an aspect of gender differences, such as the activities in which boys and girls are engaged, how boisterous their activities are or who plays with whom. Alternatively, focus on control mechanisms by watching what authority figures do to get children to comply with their wishes. Describe your findings.

5. Interview a selection of teachers and ask them what they see as the purpose of schooling. Be sensitive to any distinctions between the formal aspects of what should, in theory, happen and what they actually think happens. Try to speak with teachers from a range of school levels (nursery up to university). How do the perceptions of teachers compare to the list of social functions identified in this chapter?

6. Find some friends and relatives over the age of sixty and ask them to describe their education experiences. Determine what they recall of their actual classroom sessions. Ask about when and why they left school. Discuss their recollections of teaching methods and examinations. Ask also what they recall of their parents' schooling. Compare their descriptions with your own experiences and comment on what this tells you about social change.

Writing Exercises

1. Find a poem, song or short story that highlights the anti-school subculture found in most high schools (or write your own). Suggest plausible explanations for the existence of this subculture, drawing on the images of the poem, song or story where possible.

2. Compose a letter to your provincial MP or MLA justifying why you should be receiving the benefit of thousands of dollars of taxpayers' money by attending college or university.

3. Draft a policy paper for a political party of your choice outlining a set of

reforms that the Ministry of Education in your province should enact to improve the quality of education.

4. Create a draft document for the president of your student union on ways that students can work to improve the quality of education at your college or university.

Glossary

Ascription and achievement: *ascription refers to judgments about people based on their birthright. Sex and race are ascriptive criteria, as is a very young child's social class (these are individual characteristics fixed at birth). Achievement refers to judgments based on performance and demonstrated merit.*

Compensatory education: *remedial, pre-school or extra education provided to children thought to be disadvantaged within the normal school program. Strenuous debate over the merits of such programs continues (and now many well-off parents seek early educational opportunities for their children).*

Correspondence principle: *a term used by Bowles and Gintis to refer to the harmony of social relations between schools and the workplace.*

Cultural capital: *social polish and style, the display of cultivation and studied elegance are central aspects of Bourdieu's concept of cultural capital. Social profit comes from possessing cultural capital because dominant institutions (such as schools) draw mainly on the cultural resources of privileged groups.*

Equality of opportunity and equality of condition: *equality of opportunity exists when all individuals have similar chances to enter activities or pursue goals. Equality of condition is the availability to all of equal resources in seeking goals. The greater benefits and privileges open to some (unequal conditions) distort the ability of all individuals to achieve just outcomes.*

Hidden curriculum: *the hidden curriculum focuses on the unofficial aspects of schooling. It consists of values learned from the unintended, covert or latent messages and images that exist in official school timetables, curricula and organization.*

Human capital: *human capital refers to the skill and know-how people possess. Investments in human capital can be made by attaining more education, experience and training.*

Linguistic code: *Bernstein refers to regulative principles, which serve as the foundation for communication, as linguistic codes. Restricted code means less use of impersonal pronouns and more context-dependent meanings. Elaborate code generates more expressive symbolism and more impersonal references. The school system favours elaborate code.*

Participation rate: *the percentage of a population that is involved in a specific activity. The higher education participation rate refers to the percentage of eighteen to twenty-four year olds attending college or university.*

Schooled society: *a national community where formal, organized education is a major experience in people's lives is a schooled society. Canada became a schooled society within the last one hundred and fifty years.*

References

Anisef, Paul, Norman Okihiro and Carl James
1982. *Losers and Winners*. Toronto: Butterworths.

Atkinson, Paul
1985. *Language, Structure and Reproduction*. London: Methuen.

Bercuson, David, Robert Bothwell and Jack Granatstein
1984. *The Great Brain Robbery: Canada's Universities on the Road to Ruin*. Toronto: McClelland and Stewart.

Berg, Ivar
1970. *Education and Jobs: The Great Training Robbery*. Boston: Beacon Press.

Bernstein, Basil
1977. *Class, Codes and Control*, 2nd ed. London: Routledge and Kegan Paul.

Bourdieu, Pierre
1976. "The School as a Conservative Force: Scholastic and Cultural Inequalities." In I. R. Dale et al., eds. *Schooling and Capitalism*. London: Routledge and Kegan Paul.
1984. *Distinctions: A Social Critique of the Judgement of Taste*. London: Routledge and Kegan Paul.

Bowles, Samuel, and Herbert Gintis
1976. *Schooling in Capitalist America*. New York: Basic Books.

Clement, Wallace
1975. *The Canadian Corporate Elite*. Toronto: McClelland and Stewart.

Collins, Randall
1977. "Some Comparative Principles of Educational Stratification." *Harvard Educational Review* 47(1): 1–27.
1979. *The Credential Society*. New York: Academic Press.

Dore, Ronald
1976. *The Diploma Disease*. London: Allen and Unwin.

Eysenck, H. J.
1968. *Know Your Own I.Q.* London: Penguin.

Gaskell, Jane
1985a. "Course Enrollment in the High School: The Perspective of Working-Class Females." *Sociology of Education* 58(1): 48–59.
1985b. "Women and Education: Branching Out." *Towards Equity*. Ottawa: Economic Council of Canada.

Gellner, Ernest
1983. *Nations and Nationalism*. Oxford: Basil Blackwell.

Gilbert, Sid, and Hugh McRoberts
1977. "Academic Stratification and Education Plans: A Reassessment." *Canadian Review of Sociology and Anthropology* 14(1): 34–47.

Guppy, Neil
1984. "Access to Higher Education in Canada." *Canadian Journal of Higher Education* 14(3): 79–93.

Hunter, Alfred
1988. "Formal Education and Initial Employment: Unravelling the Relationships Between Schooling and Skills Over Time." *American Sociological Review* 53(3): 753–65.

Illich, Ivan
1971. *Deschooling Society*. New York: Harper and Row.

Lareau, Annette
1987. "Social Class Differences in Family-School Relationships: The Importance of Cultural Capital." *Sociology of Education* 60(2): 73–85.

Meadows, Sara, and Asher Cashdan
1988. *Helping Children Learn*. London: Fulton.

Meighan, R.
1981. *A Sociology of Education*. London: Holt, Rinehart and Winston.

O'Day, Rosemary
1982. *Education and Society: 1500–1800*. London: Longman.

Pike, Robert
1988. "Education and the Schools," pp. 255–88. In L. Tepperman and J. Curtis, eds., *Understanding Canadian Society*. Toronto: McGraw-Hill Ryerson.

Pomfret, Alan
1979. "Comparative Historical School Change: Newfoundland, Southern Ontario and Newfoundland." *Canadian Journal of Sociology* 4(3): 241–55.

Porter, John, Marion Porter and Bernard Blishen
1982. *Stations and Callings*. Toronto: Methuen.

Richer, Stephen
1984. "Sexual Inequality and Children's Play." *Canadian Review of Sociology and Anthropology* 21(2): 166–80.
1988. "Equality to Benefit from Schooling: The Issue of Educational Opportunity," pp. 262–86. In D. Forcese and S. Richer, eds., *Social Issues: Sociological Views of Canada*. Toronto: Prentice-Hall.

Skeels, Harold M.
1966. *Adult Status of Children with Contrasting Early Life Experiences: A Follow-up Study*. Monographs of the Society for Research in Child Development, vol. 31.

Willis, Paul
1977. *Learning to Labour*. London: Saxon House.

CHAPTER 14

Religious Institutions

RAYMOND F. CURRIE

B. BARNETT.

Introduction

The Canadian Charter of Rights and Freedoms, a product of the 1980s, begins as follows: "Whereas Canada is founded upon principles that recognize the supremacy of God and the rule of law. . . ." Just what does this mean? In the minds of our legislators it certainly does not imply a society such as John Calvin's Geneva of the sixteenth century, or the Puritan society of New England. Nor does it imply even more recent examples of religious societies, which may be as different as Duplessis's Quebec and Iran under the Ayatollah Khomeini.

The relevancy of religion differs from one society to another. In 1988, Bangladesh declared Islam the state religion. In India, a number of Sikhs barricaded themselves in the Golden Temple to fight for an independent state based on religious principles. Other countries are involved in wars that may not be directly religious, yet in which religion plays a prominent role. In South Africa, Anglican Bishop Desmond Tutu is prominent in the fight against apartheid. In Nicaragua, a Roman Catholic bishop mediates the dispute between the Contras and Sandinistas. Even in China and the Soviet Union there is a new permissiveness toward religion. China hosted Evangelist Billy Graham in 1988, and in Moscow the foundation stone was laid for a new cathedral in honour of the millennium of Russian Christianity. This is the first cathedral to be built in Moscow since the 1917 Bolshevik Revolution.

In the United States, the born-again phenomenon played a major role in presidential elections in the 1980s. The Moral Majority (founded in 1979 by Jerry Falwell, an evangelical preacher) had an impact on what has become known as the politics of morality. In other words, this evangelical-based political organization attempted to persuade the electorate to support candidates who defended traditional moral values and traditional American foreign policy. Both the Democrats (with Jessie Jackson) and the Republicans (with Pat Robertson) had major candidates for the presidential primaries in 1988 who used a religious ideology for their appeal. One of the reasons the scandals surrounding televangelists received such media coverage is precisely because these religious leaders have a substantial number of followers.

For the past hundred years it has been generally assumed that Canada has been a Christian society. Indeed, a number of institutions, values and norms in our society have religious roots. Our criminal law, based on the understanding that people can be blamed for their behaviour, has its foundation in the Judeo-Christian ethic and the notion of free will (Parker, 1983). Nevertheless, we do not expect the state to punish religious deviance such as heresy, witchcraft and even what some would consider immorality. Most now consider it appropriate to keep the state out of the bedrooms of the nation, as Trudeau put it. Nor do people have to recognize the Christian roots of the society. While it is still the norm to ask people in court to take the Bible in their right hand and "swear to tell the truth . . . so help me God," those who so desire may ask to be "affirmed." This means they "do solemnly, sincerely and truly declare and affirm" to tell the truth. No mention of God is necessary.

The decline in importance of religion to society is usually called *secularization*, a process we will study in more depth near the end of the chapter. A further step in the direction of secularization was taken in 1988 when the Ontario Court of Appeal struck down as unconstitutional a provincial regulation imposing Christian religious exercises in public schools. These legislative trends are supported by the relaxation of traditional individual expressions of religiosity, such as much lower levels of church attendance in recent years.

Nevertheless, significant numbers of religious leaders are challenging these secularizing trends. They are taking an increasingly active public stance on a wide range of social issues that they consider to be moral issues, from abortion to nuclear proliferation, uranium mining and northern development, to revisions of the Bank Act (Williams, 1984). One statement on the economic order in Canada that became the subject of a good deal of public debate was the 1983 letter on the economy by Roman Catholic bishops (see below).

Ethical Reflections on the Economic Crisis

To stimulate economic growth, governments are being called upon to provide a more favourable climate for private investments. Since capital tends to flow wherever the returns are greatest, reduced labour costs and lower taxes are required if countries are to remain competitive. As a result, most governments are introducing austerity measures such as wage restraint programs, cutbacks in social services and other reductions in social spending in order to attract more private investment. And to enforce such economic policies some countries have introduced repressive measures for restraining civil liberties and controlling social unrest.

Moral Crisis

The current structural changes in the global economy, in turn, reveal a deepening moral crisis. Through these structural changes, "capital" is reasserted as the dominant organizing principle of economic life. This orientation directly contradicts the ethical principle that labour, not capital, must be given priority in the development of an economy based on justice. There is, in other words, an ethical order in which human labour, the subject of production, takes precedence over capital and technology. This is the *priority of labour principle*. By placing greater importance on the accumulation of profits and machines than on the people who work in a given economy, the value, meaning and dignity of human labour is violated. By creating conditions for permanent unemployment, an increasingly large segment of the population is threatened with the loss of human dignity. In effect, there is a tendency for people to be treated as an impersonal force having little or no significance beyond their economic purpose in the system. As long as technology and capital are not harnessed by society to serve basic human needs, they are likely to become an enemy rather than an ally in the development of peoples.

Ethical Reflections on the Economic Crisis. 1983. The Episcopal Commission for Social Affairs, Canadian Conference of Catholic Bishops.

Probably the most prominent public debates involving religion today are those over abortion and those involving support for "separate schools," be they Roman Catholic, Christian Reformed, Sikh, Jewish or Buddhist. Are these debates and challenges of importance today? Or is religion in fact declining to the point that it will die away? It should be clear already that the role of religion varies in different societies as it does for different individuals within societies. In order to answer the questions posed here, we will begin by looking at the nature of religion. Following that, we will review sociological evidence on the roles of religion in Canadian society. We will then address the issue of secularization and the sociological controversy over the limits of secularization. By the end of the chapter, you should be in a better position to address the central issues concerning the religious dimensions of social living from a sociological perspective.

The Nature of Religion

Sociologists differ over the definition of religion. It is important to address this issue because it determines the subject matter of the substantive area we call sociology of religion. The definition is also important for politicians and the courts of the country, because it influences what they are willing to legitimize. What does "freedom of religion" mean? Should witches be allowed religious holidays, as a young man in Toronto requested of the courts recently? What groups should receive tax concessions for personal donations? The excerpt by Zaretsky and Leone below highlights the importance of the definition of religion in recent decisions by the U.S. Supreme Court.

There are two major approaches to the sociology of religion—the functional and substantive approaches.

Factors in American Culture Generating the Rise of Contemporary Religions

In our country if a religious innovation incorporated in a church group is to exist and be available to the public at large, it has to avoid continued prosecution. This means that it has to have the support of tax exemption, and its clergy has to have the benefits given to other clergies. It is not that each group innovating seeks this kind of equality, but that it must have it in order to present an attractive alternative to potential members. The direction of Supreme Court decisions has been to *subjectify the definition of religion* and to move from a consideration of a theistic base for religious belief to criteria like sincerity of belief and deeply held convictions applied to individuals. The result of this trend has been to create the ground work for another reformation. *While the essence of the Protestant Reformation was to make every man his own priest,* or to give him unfettered access to the supernatural, *what we are witnessing today, is a second reformation, the essence of which is to make every man his own theologian.* Earlier the channels to God were democratized, but the nature of the deity remained prescribed by the churches. Now it is often up to the individual to define for himself what the nature of the supernatural is. This has been made a possibility within our legal foundations and the individual is now free to decide upon such issues for himself and to act upon them.

Irving I. Zaretsky and Mark P. Leone, eds. 1974. *Religious Movements in Contemporary America.* Princeton, N.J.: Princeton University Press, pp. xxxi–xxxii (italics added).

<table>
<tr><td>Functional
Approach</td><td>In the functional approach, it is, as the name suggests, the functions that religion performs that are deemed important. A very prominent Protestant theologian, Paul Tillich, emphasizes what he considers to be the most important function of religion in the excerpt below. From a sociological point of view, Luckmann, the author of Invisible Religion (1967), is the chief proponent of the functional approach. He does not ask if people are religious, but rather how people are religious. He analyses people's attempts to make sense of their world. While questions of meaning and purpose of life probably occupy everyone at some point in their lives, this perspective does not necessarily assume that everyone has a coherent interpretive system. Luckmann considers that a "world view" as a "universal but nonspecific social form of religion" exists in all societies and for all "normal" individuals. The specific content of that world view, both in the society and as internalized by individuals, is what must be investigated.</td></tr>
</table>

The Lost Dimension of Religion

There are many analyses of man and society in our time. Most of them show important traits in the picture, but few of them succeed in giving a general key to our present situation. Although it is not easy to find such a key, I shall attempt it and, in so doing, will make an assertion which may be somewhat mystifying at first hearing. The decisive element in the predicament of Western man in our period is his loss of the dimension of depth. Of course, "dimension of depth" is a metaphor. It is taken from the spatial realm and applied to man's spiritual life. What does it mean?

It means that man has lost an answer to the question: What is the meaning of life? Where do we come from, where do we go to? What shall we do, what should we become in the short stretch between birth and death?

Such questions are not answered or even asked if the "dimension of depth" is lost. And this is precisely what has happened to man in our period of history. He has lost the courage to ask such questions with an infinite seriousness—as former generations did—and he has lost the courage to receive answers to these questions, wherever they may come from.

I suggest that we call the dimension of depth the religious dimension in man's nature. Being religious means asking passionately the question of the meaning of our existence and being willing to receive answers, even if the answers hurt. Such an idea of religion makes religion universally human, but it certainly differs from what is usually called religion.

Paul Tillich. 1958. From "The Lost Dimension in Religion." *The Saturday Evening Post.* © 1958, The Curtis Publishing Company, pp. 29, 76.

One problem is that in most modern societies there are competing world views. Some of these are overtly "religious" world views, such as competing belief systems (Islam and Christianity). Others are competing religious institutions within a relatively common belief system, usually referred to as *denominations* or *sects*. This situation exists in Hinduism, Buddhism, Islamism and Judaism as well as Christianity. For example, while most Muslims are Sunnite, approximately 95 percent of Iranians are Shi'ite Muslims, a sectarian group of Muslims. Other societal world views are less overtly religious, and perhaps even shy away from the label. Yet, their world view can be the object of investigation for a functionalist, as evidenced in studies of *civil religion*. Civil religion researchers look at the comprehensive value systems of the society and the extent to which a civic value system provides members with a sense of ultimate meaning and purpose. National documents and civic celebrations are common sources of information on civil religion.

Furthermore, there is often a severe confrontation between the *official* model proposed in a society, usually by an established church or a form of civil religion, and the lack of meaning of that model for individuals. Even in those cases, however, Luckmann would argue we must continue to search for the comprehensive symbol systems that give meaning to the lives of those individuals, in other words, to the specific content of their religiosity. Sinclair-Faulkner (1977), with specific reference to Luckmann's work, suggests being a hockey fan or player in Canada is a way of being religious! He describes in detail what he considers to be the symbolic universe that characterizes hockey and the cluster of values that gives meaning to the entire hockey enterprise.

Substantive Approach

In the substantive approach, the focus is on the supernatural belief systems and their embodiment in social organizations. The key word is *supernatural*. It is clear that there are also naturalistic or humanistic belief systems, such as socialism and scientific humanism. But the substantive approach to religion explicitly excludes the analysis of naturalistic or humanistic belief systems in order to focus precisely on those that include other worldly rewards and punishments. However, it is not only the *beliefs* that are important for these sociologists. So also is the degree of formal organization of these beliefs as well as their degree of differentiation, or separation, from other social organizations (Glock and Stark, 1965).

Sometimes we must use both functional and substantive insights to understand social phenomena. The difficulty in distinguishing between magic and religion provides one example. A simple distinction is to suggest that religion is concerned with ultimate meaning, with salvation, while magic is concerned with more immediate goals, such as the end of a drought, or even winning the next hockey or football game. But Weber (1963) points out that the boundary between magical formulas and prayers of petition remains fluid. He argues that two characteristic elements of divine worship, prayer and sacrifice, have their origin in magic. Rituals that include prayer or sacrifice that is carried out in a way that attempts to coerce the gods rather than worship the gods blur the distinctions between prayer and magic.

A second example of the unclear choice between functional and substantive approaches is that some great non-Western religions have somewhat different conceptions of the supernatural than those to which most of us are accustomed. For example, Hinduism has been described as more a way of life than a theology. Both the theist and the atheist may be Hindus if they accept the Hindu system of culture and life (Radhakrishnan, 1961:55). This integration of philosophy and life means that the temples and holy men, although important, are somewhat subsidiary to the diffuse existence of the religious reality throughout the society. Some folk and tribal religions also share this integration of religion and society and do not espouse a dualistic world view, that is, one that isolates the natural from the supernatural. Because it would tend to exclude or misinterpret some religions, a substantive approach, therefore, can be rather ethnocentric and narrow in its perception of what constitutes religion. It is little wonder then, that Luckmann, in his work cited above, argues there is far too much attention paid to church religion and to denominational approaches to the sociology of religion.

A third example of the danger of isolating the two views is the case of astrology. For many people, horoscopes are the first item of reading in the newspaper. Some newspapers now carry disclaimers that their horoscopes are not to be taken seriously, yet there is hardly a major civilization of the world that has not something to say on astrology. One of the original stained-glass windows in the Chartres Cathedral built in the thirteenth century depicts the signs of the zodiac. The prominent theologian of the middle ages, Thomas Aquinas, reconciled Christianity and astrology by suggesting that while the stars had an influence on human affairs by governing bodily appetites and desires, some individuals can indeed rise above their appetites and exercise their free will (McIntosh, 1966:66). McIntosh suggests the current interest in astrology is "not because astrology has made itself scientifically respectable; it is because science itself is beginning to lose its respectability." This is an interesting comment that deserves some attention when we discuss secularization.

Finally, the study of civil religion offers a fourth example of the difficulties in isolating a functional from a substantive approach to religion. At the turn of the century, in his book on *The Elementary Forms of Religious Life* (1965:475), Durkheim asked:

> What essential difference is there between an assembly of Christians celebrating the principal dates of the life of Christ, or of Jews remembering the exodus from Egypt or the promulgation of the decalogue, and a reunion of citizens commemorating the promulgation of a new moral or legal system or some great event in the national life?

His answer is that they do not differ "either in their object, the results which they produce, or the processes employed to attain these results." This thinking has struck a resonant cord in recent times. Robert Bellah took the John Kennedy presidential inauguration speech in 1963 as a key to an understanding of what he came to call *civil religion* (1967). Kennedy began and ended his address with three references to God. These were not references to Christ, to Moses or to any specific great religious person, but to the general concept of God. Kennedy was intentionally vague, in Bellah's view. From the earliest days of the American republic, Bellah sees a collection of beliefs, symbols and rituals with respect to sacred things in American society that have been institutionalized. He does not see American civil religion as "the worship of the American nation, but an understanding of the American experience in the light of ultimate and universal reality."

TABLE 14-1
The Major Religions and Their Distribution

Christianity	995 million followers
Roman Catholicism	580 million followers
Eastern Catholicism	75 million followers
Protestantism	340 million followers
Islam	600 million followers
Hinduism	480 million followers
Buddhism	255 million followers
Confucianism	155 million followers
Shinto	57 million followers
Taoism	31 million followers
Sikhism	16 million followers
Judaism	14 million followers

Figure 14-1 indicates the geographic distribution of major world faiths. Areas of low density of population have been left blank, although this by no means implies that no religious life exists in such places. Similarly, in countries where one religious group predominates, no inference should be drawn that followers of other religions are few in number. Finally, countries where a religion is not recognized by the state have, nevertheless, been included, since there is evidence of religious practice continuing, despite official discouragement.

RICHARD KENNEDY. 1984. THE INTERNATIONAL DICTIONARY OF RELIGION. COPYRIGHT © 1984 BLA PUBLISHING LTD. REPRINTED BY PERMISSION OF THE CROSSROAD PUBLISHING COMPANY.

There are other meanings to the term civil religion, such as Will Herberg's (1960) "American Way of Life," which he considered to be the operative (how people actually act) rather than the normative (how society believes people should act) religion of Protestants, Catholics and Jews in the United States. Religious nationalism is another model of civil religion, epitomized perhaps in the famous saying of a Roman Catholic cardinal of New York when visiting Saigon during the Vietnam war: "My country, may it always be right. Right or wrong, my country" (quoted in Dohen, 1967:1).

Religion in Canadian Society

Religious Institutions in Canada

The Canadian census is one of the few in the world that collects data on religion. On the census questionnaire, religious preference is requested in terms of fourteen specific institutional names that are provided (for example, Anglican, Baptist), a category for "no religious preference" and an open-ended category. Between the 1971 and 1981 censuses, those with no religious preference increased by 93 percent. This significant increase, from 4.3 percent with no affiliation to 7.4 percent, now makes those who report no religious group preference the fourth largest category in the country. We will have occasion to discuss this later. At this point we will examine the 92.6 percent

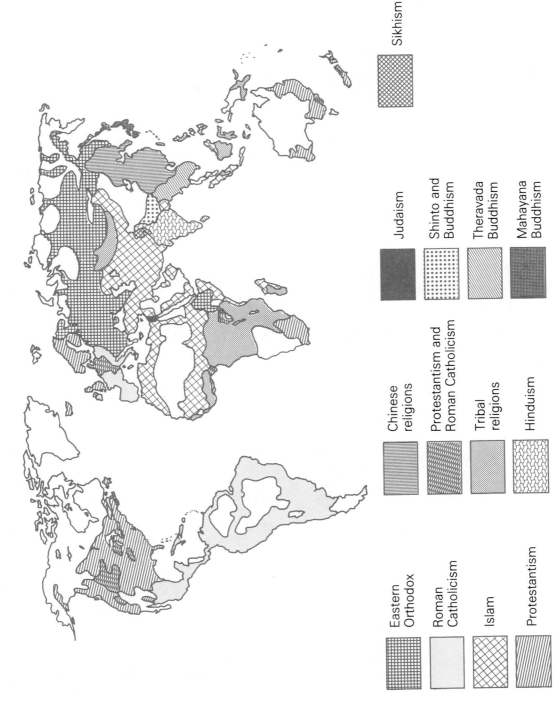

FIGURE 14-1   The Distribution of Major Religions

Sikhism

Judaism

Shinto and Buddhism

Theravada Buddhism

Mahayana Buddhism

Chinese religions

Protestantism and Roman Catholicism

Tribal religions

Hinduism

Eastern Orthodox

Roman Catholicism

Islam

Protestantism

Richard Kennedy, 1984. *The International Dictionary of Religion.* © 1984 BLA Publishing Ltd. Reprinted by permission of The Crossroad Publishing Company.

TABLE 14-2

Population Proportions of Selected Religious Groups, 1871–1981 (percentages)

	1871	1881	1901	1921	1941	1961	1981
ROMAN CATHOLIC	43	42	42	39	42	46	47
UNITED CHURCH	na	na	na	na	19	20	16
Congregationalist	.6	.6	.5	.3			
Methodist	16	17	17	13			
ANGLICAN	14	14	14	16	15	13	10
CONSERVATIVE PROTESTANT	8	8	8	8	7	7	7
Baptist	7	7	6	5	4	3	3
Mennonite	*	*	.6	.7	1.0	.8	.8
Pentecostal	*	*	.0	.1	.5	.8	1.4
Salvation Army	*	*	.2	.3	.3	.5	.5
LUTHERAN	1	1	2	3	3	4	3
PRESBYTERIAN	16	16	16	16	7	4	3
OTHER	1	1	2	5	6	2	7
Eastern Orthodox	*	*	.3	2	3	1	1
Jewish	.0	.1	.3	1	1	1	1
Jehovah's Witness	*	*	*	.1	.1	.4	.6
Mormon	.0	*	.1	.2	.2	.3	.4
Hindu	*	*	*	*	*	*	.3
Islam	*	*	*	*	*	*	.3
Sikh	*	*	*	*	*	*	.3
Buddhist	*	*	.2	.1	.1	.1	.2
Confucian	*	*	.1	.3	.2	.0	.0
NONE	.0	.0	.0	.2	.5	4	7

* Not available; na = not applicable.
Note: Mennonites included with Baptists in 1871 and 1891; Hutterites included with Mennonites.
FROM REGINALD W. BIBBY. 1987. FRAGMENTED GODS: THE POVERTY AND POTENTIAL OF RELIGION IN CANADA, P. 47. REPRINTED WITH PERMISSION OF STODDART PUBLISHING CO. LTD.

who report a religious preference. There are several characteristics associated with religious institutional preferences in Canada that deserve attention.

Religion and Ethnicity

It would be difficult to understand Canadian religious institutions without recognizing the links between religion and ethnicity in Canadian history. A distinct irony of the early development of the nation is that the religion of the dominant English group lost its pre-eminent position, while the religion of the defeated French was given quasi-legal status in Quebec and Manitoba. Following the conquest of Quebec by the British in 1760, an important agreement occurred. In exchange for loyalty to the British Crown on the part of the church, and therefore the assurance of no uprisings from the *habitants*, the English colonial government was willing to acknowledge the Catholic Church's authority in a number of areas, particularly education (Westhues: 1976,

1978). On the other hand, in Upper Canada (later Ontario), Anglicans and Methodists struggled with each other throughout most of the first half of the nineteenth century (Gwynne-Timothy, 1968). Anglicans finally gave up the right to have their church recognized as the official church of the society. (Anglicanism is still the recognized church in England.) They also agreed to support the demand by the Methodists for responsible government—that is, the right of those who pay taxes to have a say in the decisions of society. In exchange, the Methodists promised loyalty to the British Crown rather than to the United States.

The critical point is that both the English and the French charter groups were unable to establish total dominance of either their religion or ethnicity and that this has left its mark on the development of the country. This absence of a common Canadian identity allowed the large number of immigrants the option of retaining their own cultural and religious identities without drawing undue attention to themselves. Thus, both the ethnic and denominational identities of people in Canada continued to mirror those of their countries of origin. Some immigrant groups consider ethnicity and religion to be inseparable. This has been facilitated by the fact that some immigrant groups have been almost totally identified with one religion. For example, virtually all Italians, Portuguese and Philippine immigrants have been Roman Catholic. The Christian Reformed Church in Canada has grown by facilitating the settlement of Dutch immigrants and then by retaining as members the children born to the immigrant community. Thus, one may not have to be Dutch to be in the Christian Reformed Church, but the association is very strong (Bouma, 1984). Herberg writes of "religious monopoly," the degree to which members of an ethnic origin belong to the same religion. He argues that, while there have been important changes in the level of religious monopoly within particular groups, "for the most part, the same ethnicities that were highest in Religious Monopoly in 1871 or 1931 were still at that level in 1981" (1989 : 153).

Hierarchical Nature of the Canadian Churches

Unlike the United States, which is dominated by churches of a congregational nature, the major religious bodies in Canada are hierarchical. *Hierarchical religious bodies* have central authorities, such as bishops (Anglican, Lutheran, Roman Catholic) or national synods (United Church). *Congregational religious bodies*, on the other hand, recognize little authority beyond the local level. National bodies of these latter groups (Baptists, Christian Missionary Alliance, Mennonites) are, above all, voluntary associations of local congregations. Approximately 83 percent of those who state a religious affiliation in the 1981 Canadian census report they are affiliated with a hierarchical religious body. This distinction between hierarchical and congregational bodies has important consequences. For example, congregational bodies have difficulty co-ordinating national tasks such as missions, catechetical programs and seminary training, given that theologically, each congregation is virtually autonomous. Central bodies must strive to gain some power to perform these national tasks while recognizing they have little authority to do so (Harrison, 1959). A difficult situation can also arise if a local pastor decides to take a particularly bold stance on social issues. Since the local church hires and fires, pastors looking to comfort rather than to challenge are likely to be in more demand. Women clergy are less likely to receive positions, or they receive less desirable positions. On the other hand, the more democratic processes of these churches, as well as their strong sense of community, can often make the congregation much more meaningful for the individual member.

Effects of Women's Exclusion on Theological Culture

The exclusion of women from leadership and theological education results in the elimination of women as shapers of the official theological culture. Women are confined to passive and secondary roles. Their experience is not incorporated into the official culture. Those who do manage to develop as religious thinkers are forgotten or have their stories told through male-defined standards of what women can be. In addition, the public theological culture is defined by men, not only in the absence of, but against women. Theology not only assumed male standards of normative humanity, but is filled with an ideological bias that defines women as secondary and inferior members of the human species.

Rosemary Ruether. 1984. "The Feminist Critique in Religious Studies," pp. 265–72. In Patrick H. McNamara, ed., *Religion: North American Style.* Belmont, Cal.: Wadsworth. Reprinted from *Soundings* 64 (Winter 1981).

In the Catholic Church, women, such as Mother Teresa, have risen to prominence in positions that are of service to the larger community, but take a back seat in ritual situations.

J. KELLY.

Women in the Churches

There is little doubt that the relevance of religion in the future will depend to a significant degree upon the ability of the religious bodies to respond to the changing role of women in society. Rosemary Ruether, a theologian, emphasizes the cultural consequences of the traditional institutional treatment of women. Some changes are occurring. By the year 2000, close to 25 percent of pastors in the United States may be women. Even now, women comprise one-fourth of Protestant seminarians, and as much as 50 percent of Harvard Divinity School. Given the much greater dominance of the Catholic Church in Canada, growth in the proportion of women clergy will be much slower here. However, within the United Church, women seminarians now number close to 50 percent and the Anglican Church also has a significant proportion.

Seminary enrolment, however, is only one step. The call to be pastors is significantly less frequent for women than men. It tends to occur more quickly in specific Protestant denominations, such as the United Methodists, where the church leaders appoint the clergy rather than have the local congregation choose their pastor. Even then, however, the more urban and prestigious pastoral positions are rarely accessible to women. Within the United Church of Canada, two women have been elected Moderators. While no Anglican women have been consecrated bishop in Canada, a woman was recently consecrated bishop in Massachusetts in the Episcopal Church.

Another major shaper of religious culture is, of course, the professor of theology, either in a seminary or university. Interestingly, Catholic women have often been leaders in theological thinking, but their input has yet to have any impact on the ordination policies of the church.

As women role models increase in numbers in these various leadership positions in the churches, one can hypothesize that the nature of God, the church, its rituals and its traditions likely will be modified.

A recent issue of the *Review of Religious Research* (1987) provides an important overview of research on women in ministry.

Furthermore, the demands placed upon the members of congregational religious bodies are likely to be more carefully monitored. Many people want to know exactly what is expected of them. Those congregational bodies that are evangelically aggressive and hold to strict theological positions are often called conservative churches. Dean Kelley's thesis, *Why Conservative Churches Are Growing* (1972), states that firm authority and gate keeping is the critical reason for the rapid growth of conservative churches at the same time that more mainline churches report declining membership. However, this viewpoint has been hotly challenged (Bouma, 1979; Bibby and Brinkerhoff, 1983).

Concentration of Membership

Over 70 percent of those who belong to churches in Canada belong to one of only three hierarchical religious bodies: Roman Catholic (47 percent), United (16 percent) or Anglican (10 percent). It takes over twenty denominations in the United States to equal 70 percent of the society, and most of these denominations are congregational rather than hierarchical. Therefore, Canada, while ethnically pluralistic, is from a religious point of view much less so than the United States. Bibby (1987) calls this "a monopolized mosaic." Given our discussion of the links between ethnicity and religion discussed above, this seems a particularly appropriate description.

This highly monopolistic religious environment is distinct from, but associated with, geographic concentration. Roman Catholics provide a good example. The organizational unit of Roman Catholics is a diocese, a geographic area under the direction of a bishop. The province of Alberta, for example, is divided into three dioceses, with headquarters in Edmonton, Calgary and Peace River. Westhues (1978) points out that 32 percent of Catholics in Canada live in dioceses where the total population is more than 90 percent Catholic. In other words, Roman Catholics are not randomly distributed across the country. This concentration, which exists primarily in Quebec but also in some regions of the Maritimes, as well as pockets in southern Saskatchewan and northern Alberta, has several social consequences. It has facilitated a privileged legal status for the Roman Catholic Church in Quebec. It also facilitates ethnic identity retention, marriage between people in the same denomination and loyalty to a particular denomination.

The geographic concentration of those Canadians reporting no religious affiliation, 7.4 percent of the population, increases significantly as one moves westward across the country. In fact, 21 percent of British Columbia's population report no religious

FIGURE 14-2

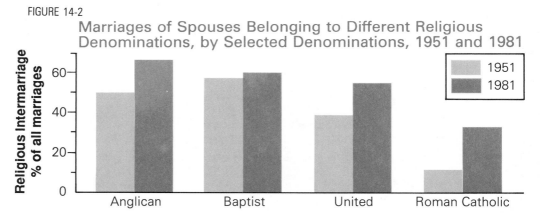

Marriages of Spouses Belonging to Different Religious Denominations, by Selected Denominations, 1951 and 1981

Given the size and geographic concentration of the Roman Catholic community, as well as its strong stand on raising children as Catholics, it is not surprising this group reports the lowest percentage of religious intermarriage among the largest religious bodies in Canada. The relatively high rate of Baptist religious intermarriage is partly a reflection of the lack of eligible partners in the same denomination. Marriage to a partner with a religious preference, and even more so, to a partner with the same religious background, is considered a significant deterent to divorce in research on marriage and the family.

Statistics Canada, 1989. *Marriages and Divorces,* Catalogue 84-205. Reproduced with the permission of the Minister of Supply and Services Canada.

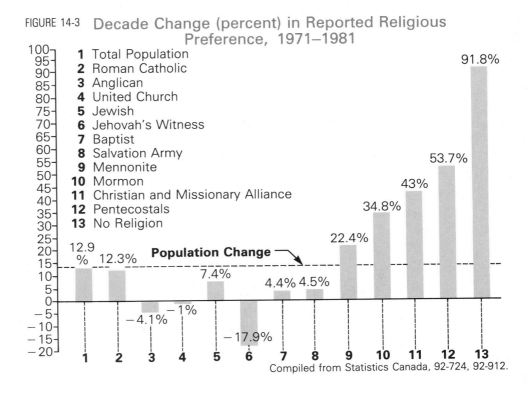

FIGURE 14-3   Decade Change (percent) in Reported Religious Preference, 1971–1981

1 Total Population
2 Roman Catholic
3 Anglican
4 United Church
5 Jewish
6 Jehovah's Witness
7 Baptist
8 Salvation Army
9 Mennonite
10 Mormon
11 Christian and Missionary Alliance
12 Pentecostals
13 No Religion

Population Change

91.8%
53.7%
43%
34.8%
22.4%
12.9%
12.3%
7.4%
4.4% 4.5%
−4.1%
−1%
−17.9%

Compiled from Statistics Canada, 92-724, 92-912.

preference, as do 12 percent of Alberta's people. Together these two provinces contain only a fifth of the total Canadian population, but they account for almost half (46 percent) of those reporting no religious preference. While it has a small population base, the Yukon also reports a very high percentage with no religious affiliation (20 percent). People in Canada with no religious preference are also concentrated in urban areas. This concentration of people with no affiliation has an important bearing on cults and secularization, which will be discussed later in the chapter.

Conservative Protestants (Baptists, Christian and Missionary Alliance, Pentecostal) are found in relatively small groups in Canada. While they are often found in pockets of our society, such as Atlantic Canada, what is more significant is that their expansion, indeed survival, has required a high degree of "continentalism" (Hiller, 1978). In other words, touring evangelists, TV religious personalities, Bible college accreditation and Sunday-school materials often reflect a very significant degree of structural integration in both the United States and Canada.

The Lack of New Religious Movements

The preceding description of the religious climate in Canada has stressed three elements: strong ties between religion and ethnicity, the hierarchical nature of Canadian religious bodies and the geographic concentration of certain religious groups. These factors help explain why Canada has not been a hotbed of institutional religious innovation. Contemporary religious movements do exist in Canada, but few have their origins here. First, Canada's social structures hinder the rise of such movements. For example, the relatively strong religious monopoly that exists in Canada stifles the ability of charismatic individuals to attract followers and thus initiate new movements.

The hierarchical (rather than congregational) nature of the existing religious groups also inhibits the formation of new religious movements. These large, structurally integrated bodies are often able to respond to threats by absorbing them. The charismatic movement provides an excellent example. The word "charisma" means gift. The charismatic movement, also called neo-pentecostalism, highlights the gifts of the Holy Spirit that individuals can receive, giving them a powerful, personal experience of being born again and of feeling the "signs and wonders" that the Acts of the Apostles describe. By the late 1970s, these charismatic or pentecostal experiences, which had been the almost exclusive domain of denominations known as Pentecostals, became acceptable and even encouraged somewhat in mainline Protestantism and Catholicism (Quebedeaux, 1983). This deterred Lutheran, Anglican and Catholic individuals from having to leave their churches to join this exciting new movement. Such external or internal threats within congregational, discrete religious units are more likely to lead to further division and ultimately a new religious body.

Finally, the value system in Canada, both in political and cultural terms, has been much more of a hybrid of conservatism, socialism and liberalism than is the case in the United States. Individualism has had far less free reign in the Canadian context. This also has been a restraining force on the development of new religious movements.

Church Union   There has been one area of religious innovation in Canada, namely church union. The United Church of Canada, formed in 1925 by a union of the Congregational, Methodist and most of the Presbyterian churches, has been called "the first large scale achievement of organic union of separate denominational families since the Protestant Reformation" (quoted in Clifford, 1977). While there is some disagreement over why this union might have occurred in Canada, several factors appear to have been important (Clifford, 1977; Campbell, 1987). First, because none of these religious bodies had their origins in Canada, the conflicts in Europe that gave birth to these Christian churches had less compelling power over their Canadian adherents. Second, the sparsely settled western regions of the country could ill afford the expense and the organization of competing denominations. Lay people who had important decision-making roles in these churches supported this religious merger just as they would support business mergers in small markets. Finally, a united church was viewed as being helpful to create a united country, since the new immigrants would be less likely to retain their Old World ties in a new, homogeneous Christian body.

Individual   Our discussion up to this point has centred on religious institutions. The religiousness,
Religiosity   or religiosity, of individuals is also of significance to sociology. This area is best understood in terms of the dimensions, or components, of religiosity.

In their early study, Stark and Glock (1968) list five dimensions of religiosity: belief, practice, knowledge, experience and consequences. Stark and Bainbridge (1985) prefer to consolidate the dimensions into three, while other authors use still other summary measures of religiosity. Whatever the categorizations used, religion has several components. Usually one or two dimensions are more prominent than the rest in the life of an individual. These differences in prominence also appear in specific religious traditions. For example, the role of theology is much more important in Western than Eastern religions, while the reverse is true for meditation. Individuals and religions may differ in the stress they place on faith, rituals and ethical norms. We will look at the expression of four dimensions of individual religiosity in Canadian society: belonging and commitment, church attendance, religious experiences and conversion and commitment.

Belonging and Commitment

The relationship between belonging and commitment varies from one group to another. While many Jews and Roman Catholics lose their religious commitment over time, they are more reluctant than members of other religious groups to give up their sense of belonging, or affiliation, to the group. They remain culturally identified, if not religiously committed to the group (Currie, 1976). Evangelicals, who do not baptize infants, aspire to a more voluntary religious tradition. When they lose their commitment they are more likely to also drop their membership in the group (that is, their belonging) and pick up a new membership and commitment. Bibby and Brinkerhoff (1973, 1983) call this "the circulation of the saints." These differences between belonging and commitment are important to recognize when trying to interpret the Canadian census data. Over 90 percent of Canadians in 1981 report a religious preference, yet this tells us little about the level of religious commitment of the population.

Church Attendance

The most frequently used measure of religious commitment in Canada is the frequency of attendance at church or synagogue. Data are gathered in Gallup polls as well as in almost all survey research projects interested in the religious commitment of Canadians. This measure, of course, is not appropriate for all religions. Muslims offer five daily prayers individually, if they cannot be present at the mosque. A Hindu makes daily offerings of fruit or flowers before a small shrine in the house. Lay worship in Buddhism is also primarily individual, even though often in the temple.

The general expectation of weekly attendance at religious services in Canada is probably somewhat influenced by the large size of the Roman Catholic population in the country, and the traditionally strict requirement in that church. This expectation is clearly not the "operative" norm. In 1985, the General Social Survey of Canada found that only 30 percent of Canadians with a stated religious preference attended a religious service on a weekly basis, 17 percent attended at least once a month and 20 percent never attended a religious service in the year (Mori, 1987). These data highlight again the important distinction between belonging and commitment.

Bibby (1987) has presented data that reveal a dramatic decline in attendance at religious services in a relatively brief period of time, particularly for the three largest groups, Roman Catholics, United and Anglicans. Among Catholics, the decline has been the sharpest in Quebec. Based on church attendance twice a month or more, data from 1965 to 1985 show a decline from 88 percent to 38 percent among Quebec Catholics, while non-Quebec Catholics declined from 69 percent to 49 percent. It has been suggested that the church's restrictive policy on the use of artificial means of birth control, which was announced during this period, is one of the major reasons for this decline. In the same period, Protestants declined from 32 percent who attended in the last seven days (a more severe requirement than that asked Catholics) to 27 percent. In contrast, about 12 percent of Jews attended a synagogue in the past seven days, which is a slight increase from 1975 to 1985, according to the General Social Survey.

Perhaps because so much attention has been given to the frequency of attending religious services, this decline has been taken as a clear indication of the dwindling significance of religion for many Christians. While some will argue they can be religious without attending services, in fact the percentage reporting devotional prayers on a fairly frequent basis almost equals those who attend services regularly, and there is every reason to believe that these two groups are comprised of the same individuals.

Religious Experiences   One dimension of religion that has become more significant in recent times is unmediated religious experience. This can take many forms. Canadian youth have reported a sense of being in the presence of God, a sense of being saved in Christ and even a sense of having been sent by God to carry out a mission (Currie, Klug and McCombs, 1982). While not unique to our time, there is evidence that a conscious search for these direct, personal religious experiences is rather common today, and that these experiences are much more salient than doctrinal belief for many. There is institutional support, indeed broad cultural support, for the desirability and efficacy of direct experiences and for basing one's life decisions on such experiences. We have noted, in the quotation from Zaretsky and Leone, that the United States Supreme Court has moved to "subjectify the definition of religion." The charismatic movement, which is often interdenominational in character, is fuelled by these personal experiences. The born-again movement, as part of evangelical Christianity, has stressed the experiential dimension more than Anglicanism or Roman Catholicism. It is also a prominent component of the *human potential movement*. The human potential movement can be described as a consciousness-raising movement that is interested in the liberation of the individual from the constraints of an oppressive culture. Devotees believe that only when the individual reaches his or her potential can a society flourish. The movement is composed of a tremendous variety of groups and training methods, including EST, gestalt therapy, biofeedback and Esalen (Stone, 1976). All these movements have in common the quest for direct experience through expanded consciousness, personal insight or bodily awareness.

Personal religious experiences are often viewed as the unique source of truth, in place of tradition, authority or even the Scriptures. In this context, the individual must have the assurance, usually by the religious body promoting personal experiences, that he or she can be sure of having such experiences and that they will be comforting experiences. There are difficulties, however, as well as comforts. It is hard for individuals to live between the highs of such experiences, in other words, to maintain a high level of commitment to the movement. It is also difficult to avoid spiritual anarchy. The more personal the experience, the less it can be shared, and therefore the more narrow the basis for the formation of a spiritual community that can be long lasting.

Conversion and Commitment

It would not be appropriate to conclude this section on individual religiosity without a comment on religious conversions. A *conversion* is a significant break with one's former identity, such that the past and the present are antithetical in some important respects. One can be converted to non-religious as well as religious world views. The study of conversion to religion has been intense in recent years in North America and Western Europe, particularly because of the attractiveness of studying new religions' movements. In fact, a common perception among the public, and certainly one dwelt upon by the media, is that anyone who is converted to a fringe religious group must have been brainwashed. How otherwise could 6000 strangers marry each other the day after they meet, as has happened several times in the Church of the Unification (commonly referred to as the Moonies)? If brainwashing has occurred, then it is logical to assume it is quite permissible to kidnap the converts and deprogram them for their own good. Yet, Eileen Barker (1984) asks the important question why it is that over 90 percent of those who go to Unification Church workshops do not fall victim to the alleged brainwashing techniques. If brainwashing does occur, a careful examination of a large number of new religious movements suggests it is rather ineffective (Hill, 1980).

The Rev. Sun Myung Moon, founder of the South Korean–based Unification Church, has officiated at several mass wedding ceremonies of his followers. This picture was taken in 1982 in Madison Square Garden in New York, where he performed the ceremony for 2200 couples. In 1988, more than 6500 couples were married in South Korea in a mass wedding complete with matching bridal gowns and bouquets, a day after the couples were introduced. Rev. Moon matched the couples personally. He purposely chose to unite more than 2000 Japanese and Koreans "to heal and spiritually cleanse bad feelings left over from the Japanese colonial rule of Korea." He told the newly-weds: "You will overcome international barriers to create one world of the heart and a blessed race for the future."

UPI/BETTMANN
NEWSPHOTOS.

In fact, sociologists suggest that one is often converted to the beliefs of one's friends. In other words, the ideology of a group, or its belief system, initially may not be the most attractive feature of a group. Rather, the potential convert may initially feel that he or she simply wants to belong to a group of people who have become friends. These interpersonal ties are important components in conversion to contemporary religious movements (Lofland and Stark, 1965). Of all the criticisms of new religious movements, the excessive emotional emphasis, which has been referred to as "love bombing" because it inundates prospective members with love and approval (Lofland, 1977), appears to be the most accurate (Hill, 1980). However, interpersonal ties also play a role in conversions to more mainline churches, for example, when one spouse decides to convert to the religion of the other.

The strength of these interpersonal ties also has a major impact on the likelihood of sustaining the commitment once the conversion has been achieved. We should note carefully, however, that the two processes of conversion and commitment are not the same. In fact, conversion to a new religious group is relatively easy compared to the task of maintaining a high level of commitment. Furthermore, the process of conversion tells us little about the ability to maintain the commitment that has been achieved. Converts do not always make the most committed Christians (Barker and Currie, 1985).

The maintenance of commitment has also been the subject of much research, and evangelical churches are particularly proficient at developing mechanisms for this maintenance. These include the conscious attempt to increase the tasks in the congregation so that a relatively high proportion of the members have specific responsibilities.

While the religiosity of individuals has clearly declined on some dimensions, it brings a sense of belonging that many do not wish to discard. Life cycle events such as births, baptisms, marriages and funerals are still celebrated in a religious context by the majority of Canadians. Furthermore, certain religious institutions cater to some dimensions of religiosity more than to others. Yet, there is a clear sense in our time of a greater separation of religion from the daily lives of Canadians, and that this is associated with the declining significance of religion. In the next two sections, we will discuss these two areas more thoroughly.

Impact of Religion on Daily Life

There are many areas where researchers have attempted to assess the impact of religion on daily life. Three examples will be used here. In each case the example has been chosen because it reflects the development, in recent times, from an initial concern about the impact of religion that was voiced by one of the classical sociologists. It is interesting to note that in spite of the lack of religious commitment on the part of many of the classical thinkers, they felt it was essential to look at religion in order to understand human behaviour. The three questions we will address (and the classical theorists who addressed them in the past) are the following: Does religion inhibit deviant behaviour (Durkheim)? Does religion have an impact on economic achievement (Weber)? Does religion inhibit or foster social change (Marx)?

Religion and Deviant Behaviour

At the turn of the century, Emile Durkheim was very concerned about the moral conscience of society being weakened by rapid social change, especially through the division of labour and economic growth. Faith is disturbed, he argued, tradition has lost its sway and individual judgment is not at the beck and call of collective judgment. Our first obligation today, he wrote, is to forge a morality for ourselves (1964 : 408–9). In his analysis of religion (1965), Durkheim suggested that the attitude of respect toward sacred things was identical with the respect shown toward moral obligations and authority. He suggested that *positive rituals* (that is, things one must do as part of one's religion) as well as *negative rituals* (taboos, or things one must not do) highlight the disciplinary function of ritual life.

The disciplinary component of religion seems to be appreciated in our society. Church attendance often increases as children in a family reach school age, when the parents want the support of outside agencies to help them in their socialization and social control efforts. Judges have been known to tell young offenders to attend church as part of their court sentences.

Modern sociologists have analysed the relationship between religion and deviance. In 1969, Hirschi and Stark reported in a paper on "Hellfire and Delinquency" that youth who attend church frequently and who have a strong belief that hell awaits sinners were as likely to engage in deviant behaviour as their irreligious counterparts. This provocative and unexpected finding led to a multiplicity of other studies testing the impact of religion on delinquency rates. Researchers realized that religion is only one institution among many that provides a social control function in society. Furthermore, religion may have a different impact depending on the type of deviance being observed. Following these insights, more recent tests of the hypothesis have consistently found that religion tends to have its *greatest* effect when there is a certain ambiguity in society over the appropriateness of a particular form of behaviour. For example, because virtually everyone in society (heroes of society, mass media, family, etc.) is opposed to stealing, the impact of religion in this area is difficult to isolate, as it is only one of many factors imposing social control on stealing. If, however, there is controversy in society over appropriate behaviour, such as use of marijuana or premarital sex, yet a particular religious institution clearly frowns on the behaviour, then the specific impact of religion appears more clearly to be seen to deter such forms of deviance for its followers.

In fact, it would appear that the more unique the religious regulations are for a specific group (for example, prohibition of caffeine use, lotteries, dancing, drinking, smoking, playing cards, etc.), the more the members and the leaders both have visible signs of highly successful religious commitment. They can easily see who is following the rules and who is not. Members are then more constrained to follow the rules or leave the group.

Religion and Economic Achievement

A second area of research that has looked at the impact of religion on daily life can be summarized as "The Protestant Ethic and the Spirit of Capitalism." This is, of course, the title of the best known of the writings of Max Weber (1930). The spirit of capitalism can be captured in what Weber called rational asceticism. Weber defines *asceticism* as the pursuit of salvation by the mastery over creaturely interests within one's own personality, as well mastery over the whole human condition. He argued that the beliefs and norms of Protestantism, particularly Calvinism and Pietism, were conducive to this rational asceticism.

The God of Calvinism was transcendant, distant from the world. Humans stood in complete submission to the divine will and had to become instruments of God on earth. This doctrine of the calling made hard work a positive virtue and demanded high standards of honesty, both distinct assets for economic success. It also promoted asceticism, or disciplined control, as befits an instrument of the divine. The doctrine of predestination assumed that some people were elected from birth to enter heaven. Calvinists longed for a sign that they had indeed been chosen by God. The best sign would be the material success achieved as a result of the ascetic living. Finally, the doctrine of sanctification demanded of Calvinists not occasional, individual good deeds, but rather a life of good works. This "rigorous rational control over all aspects of life" (Bouma, 1973 : 143), motivated by Calvinist doctrines, is the heart of Weber's understanding of the Protestant ethic.

Weber did not suggest that Calvinism directly caused capitalism. While he was definitely interested in the impact of ideas, he recognized that ideas "without material

Business people across the country meet regularly to inform each other of their efforts in business dealings to keep within the realm of Christian principles.

Many professional sports teams also have a sufficient number of players to constitute local chapters of Athletes for Christ. While such groups are more common to the evangelical tradition, other religious groups often emulate this practice.

CHRISTIAN BUSINESS MEN'S COMMITTEE.

interests are impotent." He suggested, rather, an "elective affinity" between Calvinism and the spirit of capitalism, a gradual convergence of a religious ethic and a materialistic spirit. "Ideas have, like switchmen, determined the tracks along which action has been pushed by the dynamic of interests," he asserted (Gerth and Mills, 1948 : 280).

Gary Bouma (1973) has done a comprehensive review of research initiated by the Weberian thesis. He highlights three general propositions that have been derived from the Weberian thesis. First, ascetic Protestantism should give Protestants greater social mobility than those of other religious faiths, thus resulting in higher social status. Second, ascetic Protestantism should produce higher achievement motivation among these Protestants than members of other religious groups. Finally, ascetic Protestantism should lead to more effectual use of educational opportunities.

Research testing these theses has paid much more attention to the religious *affiliation* than to the beliefs of respondents. One major reason is the cost of doing research that depends on personal interviews. One can usually classify countries or sections of countries as predominantly Protestant or Catholic without much research expense. We have seen that in Canada the census includes a question on religious affiliation, but not on religious beliefs. This provides relatively inexpensive access to information on affiliation and thus facilitates the comparison of this measure of religion with the income, occupation and education of respondents, which are also census questions. Using these data, John Porter, for example, found that higher incomes are related to Protestantism and lower incomes to Catholics in Canada. But he also noted the difficulties of separating the influences of ethnicity and religion on class structure.

In general, there has been little support for the Weberian hypotheses. Bouma's most important finding, however, is that it is in fact difficult to draw conclusions when religion is measured by affiliation. Weber argued that *ideas* have importance. Therefore, to ask simply if someone is Protestant, or even Calvinist, without inquiring whether or not Calvinistic theology is essential to their beliefs is to ignore the catalyst that Weber felt would best predict the impact of religion on economic behaviour.

Religion and Social Change

We may learn from these two examples (deviance and the Protestant ethic) that one should always be wary of the *single factor fallacy*, an attempt to explain behaviour by simply one cause, be it religion or any other variable. A more useful approach is to focus upon the conditions under which religion has an impact on behaviour, so that we can analyse the conditions under which religion can be an agent of social change.

One of the reasons this kind of research has been undertaken is precisely because Karl Marx wrote so forcefully. He viewed religion above all as an agent of social control. He called religion "the sigh of the oppressed creature," the "opium of the people" (1964 : 42), supported on the one hand by those in a position of power because it justified their situation, and on the other hand by those who felt they needed it to make sense of their world of suffering. "Blessed are the poor, for theirs is the kingdom of heaven," has certainly been interpreted in this manner. In a powerful image, Marx compared religion to flowers on a chain that holds people bound. Criticism of religion plucks the imaginary flowers from the chain, he said, not in order to leave people to wear the chain without consolation or illusion, but so that they will shake off the chain and gather living flowers.

In view of Marx's criticism of religion, a paradox of our time is what has become known as the Marxist-Christian dialogue. This dialogue has had a profound impact on the social change possibilities in Central and South America.

The Catholic Church in Haiti until very recently was usually tolerant of, if not identified with, the government and its military force. The lavish church wedding of dictator "Papa Doc" Duvalier's son was a good indicator of the alliance of the church with the powerful. Yet, at present, in Haiti as well as in many other Central and South American countries, radical forces of Christendom have given rise to a *theology of liberation*—a Marxist-Christian struggle for justice that has put the church in a confrontation with governments. This theology argues that there can be little spiritual liberation through baptism unless people have already attained economic liberation from poverty and political liberation of human and civil rights. The pivotal turning point in the adoption of a liberation theology was in 1968, when a general conference of South American bishops held at Medellin, Colombia, critically attacked the socio-economic and political conditions of the region, including poverty, institutionalized violence, oppression and colonialism. Since that time, over 1000 religious, clergy and bishops have been arrested, tortured, expelled or murdered. Some 200 000 Christian grass-roots communities exist as centres for social change (Hornosty, 1988).

Why the change from the silent complicity of the church to confrontation with government? The question is even more interesting given that the church in question is not a sectarian, anti-establishment institution, from which one might expect confrontation with government, but precisely the established church of the area. Hornosty points to the "increased capitalist penetration, failed reformist policies, intensive militarization and state repression" in Central and South America. These factors have increased the inequality between the classes and severely damaged the legitimacy of the civilian and military authorities.

Westhues's (1973) analysis of Paraguayan society suggests four propositions that can help understand the conditions under which a church can be an agent of change in such social circumstances. First, the church must be sufficiently powerful to make a difference in that society. An established church is more likely to have such power. It is unlikely that even all the churches acting in concert would have such power in Canada. Second, it must adopt a change-oriented ideology and mobilize its resources to put the ideology into effect. The theology of liberation espoused at the Medellin conference has fulfilled this critical condition. Third, if the established church is a subunit of a wider, hierarchically organized religion, as is the case for Roman Catholicism, adoption of the change-oriented ideology occurs mainly when that ideology is proposed to it by the central authority. In other words, the ideas emanating from the parent body allow the local church to evaluate itself in the light of international social trends and place the local church in an innovative role. This occurred in two stages

A Nobel Prize winner in 1984, Anglican Archbishop Desmond Tutu is the titular head of his church in South Africa and the leading anti-apartheid religious leader. Anglicanism is certainly not the official church in South Africa as it is in England. But its international stature helps this charismatic leader express his outrage at the injustices of apartheid, especially to the international community, whose pressure, Tutu argues, is essential if the discrimination is to end.

REUTERS/BETTMANN NEWSPHOTOS.

in Central and South America. First, the Medellin conference of bishops took up some of the themes on social justice developed at the council of all Catholic bishops in the world held in Rome earlier in the 1960s. Second, the Medellin conference further developed the themes specifically in light of the economic conditions in Latin America and encouraged the bishops to pursue social change in their own countries. The fourth proposition suggests that acceptance of a change-oriented ideology will be facilitated if the national church perceives the ideology as organizationally rational, that is, for the long-term good of the organization. The bishops of Latin America were well aware of the Cuban experience, where the church lost most of its influence by siding with the reactionary forces at the time of the revolution. Acceptance of the change-oriented ideology, therefore, although likely to result in short-term persecution of the church by government, in fact reduces the likelihood of secularization and therefore increases the long-term survival and relevancy of the church in Latin America.

Secularization

As we have seen above, religion involves several dimensions. Therefore, we should not be surprised that the process of secularization is similarly complex. There are three aspects of secularization that are particularly important to highlight (Shiner, 1972): (1) the desacralization of the world; (2) the gradual removal of society's institutions from religious control; and (3) the complete substitution of secular functions for religious ones.

Desacralization of the World

For some authors, *desacralization* of the world means a loss of the sense of the sacred. Max Weber called it "disenchantment." It is a *rational* interpretation of events that views the world as self-contained without the need to call on supernatural explanations. Mysteries are replaced by problems. The individual who used to interpret events as "the will of God" may now see them as rooted in genetics, psychological attitudes or a corrupt political system. Wuthnow calls this change a "consciousness reformation" (1976).

A good deal of research is now being done on the meaning systems that people use to interpret the world, and the secularization thesis is that the importance of religiously rooted meaning systems is declining. Durkheim, for example, speaks of a shift from religious beliefs to scientific knowledge. He argues that because science moves more slowly than life, and for many individuals the problems of life often cannot await science for answers, a minor speculative role for beliefs will continue to exist, but only as a handmaid or precursor of science. In other words, "scientific thought is only a more perfect form of religious thought" (1965 : 477). McIntosh (1969) is somewhat more sceptical of this position. He views the rise of interest in horoscopes to be directly related to the inability of science to offer any more convincing answers to life's problems than religion does.

Differentiation

A second aspect of secularization is the gradual disengagement of institutional aspects of society from religious domination. This is called differentiation. When Napoleon crowned himself in the presence of Pope Pius VII, this was a dramatic symbol of the differentiation of politics from religion.

In Canada at the turn of the century, virtually all colleges and universities were founded by religious groups. In Quebec, the government did not have a Ministry of Education until the 1960s. Education was administered by the church. Many hospitals and social services likewise have had religious origins. Most of these institutions have now been taken over by government. These are examples of the increased differentiation of religion from other institutions in society.

The greater the religious monopoly in a society, the more slowly differentiation is likely to occur. Slow differentiation often leads to the oppression of minority religious groups in a society, if not to a religious civil war. James Penton's study of the Jehovah's Witnesses (1976) provides important documentation of the legal difficulties faced by a minority religious group in Canadian society. Only since 1943 has this religious group been deleted from the Canadian government list of subversive organizations. As Canada becomes more multicultural, differentiation is bound to increase. The courts are ruling that it is not appropriate to associate Christian religious practices with public functions that include more and more non-Christian participants.

There are, however, two examples of continuing conflict over the degree of differentiation of religion from other social institutions in Canada. One is the abortion issue. Religiously affiliated hospitals almost universally refuse to perform abortions. The issue becomes a public debate, particularly in small communities where the only hospital in town is religiously affiliated and there are no abortion clinics. A second example is the issue of government support for religiously affiliated schools. While most provinces have legislation permitting public funding for religiously affiliated schools, Manitoba and Ontario both have been engaged in heated conflict over the principle as well as the extent of such funding.

Transposition of Religious Beliefs and Institutions

In this aspect of secularization, the society has taken over *all* of the functions traditionally performed by religious institutions. Proponents of differentiation would argue that many of those functions never should have been under the influence of religion in the first place. There should have been separation of church and state. In this expression of secularization, however, not only knowledge and patterns of behaviour but also institutional arrangements are viewed as of purely human creation and human responsibility.

In the three aspects of secularization we have discussed, it would seem that slowly and surely there has been a decline of religion from a situation where it was a "sacred canopy" (Berger, 1969) covering virtually all human behaviour and institutional arrangements, to a society in which religion plays only a small role. Not all sociologists agree that this is an inevitable process. That is what we will now reflect upon.

The Limits of Secularization

The most articulate opponents of the secularization thesis are Stark and Bainbridge (1985). They argue that secularization is a self-limiting process that does not so much lead to irreligion as it does to a shift in the sources of religion. In their view, secularization is only one of three interrelated processes. One countervailing process is *religious revival*. In the Middle Ages in periods when Christianity was declining, religious orders (such as the Benedictines, founded in 529; the Franciscans, 1209; and the Jesuits, 1534) were founded as revival groups within the one Christian church at the time. Since the Protestant Reformation, breakaway sects (for example, Seventh Day Adventists, 1863; the Salvation Army, 1865; Jehovah's Witnesses, 1870; the Assemblies of God, 1914) have performed the same functions. Sects are revival groups because they claim to purge the religious body from which they have split from its weaknesses and to present a cleansed, refurbished version of the existing faith. A second countervailing process is *religious innovation*. In this case, conventional faiths are not revived, but new religions are formed. These are best described as cults in their early stages because they spring from roots other than the religious tradition of the society. They may originate in a host society, but tend not to have a prior tie with another established religious body in that society. Baha'i (1844), the Unification Church (1954) and Scientology (1955) are the best-known examples of cults in Canada. The Church of

Jesus Christ of Latter-Day Saints (1830), often called the Mormons, is included in Tables 14-3 and 14-4 as a cult, but the group is difficult to classify. Although it did emerge out of the Christian-Judaic tradition, there is so much novel doctrine that many classify it as a cult. Sects (examples of religious revival) and cults (examples of religious innovation) tend to recruit from different population bases because they offer different solutions to the meaning of life.

To test their theory of the limits of secularization, Stark and Bainbridge argue that if secularization is inevitable, then new religious movements should only arise in areas where religion is still relatively strong. To state this in terminology familiar to the marketplace, the target population for new religious groups should only be people who still have a religious world view. In areas where religion is weak, secularization theory would lead one to believe that people have humanistic world views and therefore would not be suitable candidates for religious conversion and commitment.

Using ingenious data such as the number of subscriptions to *Fate* magazine and the number of listings per million of each province in the *Spiritual Directory Guide*, Stark and Bainbridge (1985) have shown support for their thesis that there are limits to secularization. The proof is that cults flourish in Canada above all in areas where religion is weakest. The hypothesis is also supported by similar research they conducted in the United States and Europe.

TABLE 14-3

Canadian Cult Rates Per Million Population by Province, 1981

	1	2	3	4	5	6	7	8	9
Newfoundland	0	70.9	0	0	354.8	17.7	0	35.5	17.7
Prince Edward Island	0	247.5	0	0	1,154.9	0	0	0	0
Nova Scotia	17.9	494.2	11.9	0	1,869.5	65.4	23.8	131	17.9
New Brunswick	0	145.1	21.8	0	1,174.9	21.8	0	87	0
Quebec	17.3	101.3	14.1	9.4	37.6	27.4	8.6	117	11
Ontario	116	380.8	152.9	46.9	2,354.6	93.1	49.8	651	51.6
Manitoba	64.1	162.8	172.6	0	1,815.1	123.3	34.5	582	34.5
Saskatchewan	5.2	480.9	20.9	5.2	3,220.3	73.2	10.4	627.3	47
Alberta	74.5	352.3	262	13.6	19,415.9	151.3	58.7	716	51.9
British Columbia	217.4	668.8	696.5	123.5	6,168.9	267.2	117.9	1,520.1	106.9
Canada	80.5	331	170	34.7	3,736.6	95.3	41.3	558.5	42

1 = Spiritualists
2 = Baha'i
3 = New Thought-Unity-Metaphysical
4 = Theosophy
5 = Mormons
6 = Pagan
7 = Fourth Way
8 = Parareligious Groups*
9 = Other Parareligious Groups

*Parareligious groups are those groups that use some traditional religious language and rituals even if some members do not wish the group to be labelled as religious.

FROM DAVID NOCK. 1987. "CULT, SECT AND CHURCH IN CANADA." CANADIAN REVIEW OF SOCIOLOGY AND ANTHROPOLOGY 24(4).

Nock (1987), using the more reliable source of census data, substantiated their findings by showing that areas in Canada of high irreligion tend to be the regions of considerable cult receptivity. Specifically, eight of the nine cults that Nock analysed had their highest rates of membership in British Columbia (Table 14-3). As can be seen from the data in Table 14-4, this province has the highest percentage reporting no religious preference. On the other hand, the lowest rates were found in all nine cases to be in Quebec and the Atlantic provinces. "The hypothesis that cults benefit from irreligion and apostasy from the conventional religions seems to be strongly sustained" (1987 : 519).

Bibby and Weaver (1985) dispute three assumptions of the Stark and Bainbridge theory on the limits of secularization. First, they suggest there is little evidence that humans have desires that require supernaturally based answers. This is an area of research we alluded to earlier in the chapter when discussing the functional approach to religion. In other words, it is important to test the assumption that people *are* religious, as well as *how* they are religious. Second, they believe it is an unfounded assumption that religions provide the desired supernatural answers. On the contrary, Bibby's book *Fragmented Gods* (1987) hypothesizes that people are very eclectic in their approach to religion, choosing a fragment here and there to cope with the crises of life. Some of the fragments are specifically supernatural, while others are not, such as astrology. Finally, they argue that while cults may arise where conventional religions are weak, one should not conclude that cults are necessarily "flourishing." In Canada, less than 1 percent of the population are attracted to cults. Among the people with no religious preference who decide to become affiliated, far more tend to join a mainline church than a cult. They conclude that cult concentration in areas of high non-affiliation provides only a necessary, but not a sufficient, condition for the significant growth of these movements.

TABLE 14-4 **Ranking Comparison of "No Religious Preference" and Cult Receptivity by Province, 1981**	No Religious Preference	Cult Receptivity
British Columbia	1	1.1
Alberta	2	2.6
Manitoba	3	3.3
Ontario	4	4.7
Saskatchewan	5	5.7
Nova Scotia	6	5.6
New Brunswick	7	7.8
Prince Edward Island	8	8.6
Quebec	9	7.1
Newfoundland	10	9.1

COMPUTED FROM CANADIAN CENSUS, 1981, 92–912. REPRINTED FROM DAVID NOCK. 1987. "CULT, SECT AND CHURCH IN CANADA." CANADIAN REVIEW OF SOCIOLOGY AND ANTHROPOLOGY 24(4).

Summary

Is religion relevant to contemporary societies and to individuals? From an individual point of view, it appears accurate to state that most Canadians are reluctant rather than true believers, not committed to full involvement in their religious traditions, as indicated by the minority that attend religious services on a regular basis. Yet, they are reluctant to switch from one group to another, so the oligopoly of the same religious groups continues over time. Also, they are reluctant simply to give up a religious preference, for cultural if not religious reasons, so less than 10 percent report that they have none.

From an institutional point of view, the differentiation of religion from other social institutions has progressed dramatically in this century. There is, therefore, less institutional support for the public expression of religious beliefs and practices than there used to be. How much is differentiation followed by desacralization? How much public support is necessary for individuals to be spiritually nurtured sufficiently? Many cults and sects suggest little public support is necessary, and create comprehensive social networks that intentionally isolate the membership from the rest of society and allow for intensive interaction within the group. These groups, however, represent only a small body of the religious institutions of Canada. Will they flourish even more if the mainline churches are unable to stem the tide of secularization? We have seen that researchers are divided on this point. On the other hand, will the multicultural policy of government foster the strong existing links between ethnicity and religion and thus inhibit the decline of religion? If so, will this same policy also inhibit religious innovation?

These and many other research questions remain. The most fruitful research will surely come from those who understand not only the religious traditions of the society, but also have a firm grasp of the importance of culture, of social movements and of ideology and social change.

Suggested Readings

Barker, Eileen

   1984. *The Making of a Moonie, Choice or Brainwashing*. Oxford: Basil Blackwell. The Unification Church is the most studied religious cult of our times, and this is the most comprehensive and enlightening of these studies. It provides insights into a religious movement, the conversion process of individuals and, as well, many insights into why so many of those exposed to the movement do not join.

Bibby, Reginald W.

   1987. *Fragmented Gods, The Poverty and Potential of Religion in Canada*. Toronto: Irwin. This is the most comprehensive sociological treatment of religion in Canada. Professor Bibby has based his book on three national surveys that he conducted in 1975, 1980 and

1985. In addition, he has integrated a vast amount of other research on religion in Canada. It is a portrait of religion, particularly from the point of view of the individual, but also a projection of religion's future in the Canadian context.

Canadian Journal of Sociology 3(2) (Spring 1978)

This special issue of the journal analyses the similarities and the important differences between Canada and the United States with respect to the social situation of six religious groups. These include mainline Protestantism, Mormonism, Evangelicalism, Judaism, Mennonites and Roman Catholics.

Durkheim, Emile

1965. *The Elementary Forms of Religious Life*. New York: Free Press. This is the classic study of religion from a functionalist point of view. Durkheim's discussion of beliefs, his treatment of positive rituals as well as taboos and his reflections on the relationship of religion and society is masterful.

Mann, W. E.

1955. *Sect, Cult and Church in Alberta*. Toronto: University of Toronto Press. The study looks at the social factors (including geography, history and socio-economic structure) associated with the differential growth of fundamentalist sects, the occult and healing cult religions between the 1920s and 1940s in Alberta. It is one of the first sociological analyses of religion in Canada and has had a significant impact on more recent studies of sectarian religion in Canada.

Stark, Rodney, and William Sims Bainbridge

1985. *The Future of Religion, Secularization, Revival and Cult Formation*. Berkeley: University of California Press. This very provocative book is much more optimistic about the survival and saliency of religion than is Bibby's book. Stark and Bainbridge have used a multiplicity of data collection methods to study religion throughout the centuries in cross-cultural settings. The result is a readable analysis of the environmental conditions under which religious movements (particularly sects and cults) are born, die, break up and are revived.

Weber, Max

1963. *The Sociology of Religion*. Boston: Beacon Press. First published in 1922, these writings on religion represent a broader perspective than Weber's more well-known and easier work *The Protestant Ethic and the Spirit of Capitalism*. The work is so insightful on so many aspects of religion that it cannot be ignored by any serious student of religion. Weber discusses, among other things, the idea of God, prophets, relationship of religion to social classes, theodicies, asceticism and mysticism.

Journal for the Scientific Study of Religion
Review of Religious Research
Sociological Analysis

These three journals are the most important North American publications of research on the sociology of religion. They are usually available in all university libraries. The first is the most interdisciplinary of the three journals. The second includes more studies of a practical nature involving congregational studies as well as church planning issues. The last journal tends to deal with more theoretical issues as well as specific research reports. Students interested in the impact of religion on society, or of society on religion, will find exciting research studies in these journals.

Discussion Questions

1. Under what conditions would a functional rather than a substantive approach to the sociology of religion appear to be more useful?

2. Give some examples in the Canadian context where religions and/or specific religious bodies have been an agent of the status quo and an agent of change.

3. Discuss the major factors that influence people's conversion to a religious group and their relative importance.

4. How do religion and ethnicity mutually reinforce each other for the Ukrainian, Mennonite and Jewish communities?

5. Does "continentalism" help a religious group to grow more rapidly?

6. How can a "church" in one society be a "sect" in another?

7. Why do the media treat so many new religious movements not only as deviant but dangerous?

Data Collection Exercises

1. Contact an evangelical religious body in your area and ask the pastor to enumerate the principle mechanisms he/she uses to maintain a high level of commitment among members.

2. Contact female members of three different religious groups to discuss the role of women in these religious groups. The discussion should include the actual leadership positions of women in their churches as well as the impact of feminism on the theology of their churches.

3. Using data from the 1981 and 1971 censuses, calculate changes in the rates of "no religion" for census metropolitan, urban and rural areas of your province.

4. Using a major city newspaper, take a random sample of ten issues from a given month and analyse the treatment of religion in all first-page articles using several criteria, including presence or absence, major or minor role in the article, religion supporting or opposing change, positive or negative reflection on religion. Add other criteria you wish to examine. Summarize your findings.

Writing Exercises

1. Using the data from Figure 14-3 (Decade Change in Reported Religious Preference), write a short essay comparing a religious group that has grown faster than the Canadian population with one that has grown more slowly.

2. Write a short essay on the future of secularization in Canadian society.

3. Write a brief essay highlighting the institutional and cultural supports for religious experiences in our society.

4. Examine the impact on Canadian society of one or other of the various church statements on social issues, reprinted in Williams (1984).

Glossary

Asceticism: *Weber defines it as the pursuit of salvation by the mastery over creaturely interests within one's own personality, as well as mastery over the whole human condition.*

Church: *a religious group that accepts the social environment in which it exists. While this is a most simple and general definition, it should be recognized that the concept has been the subject of great debate among sociologists.*

Civil religion: *a study of the overarching value system of a society and the extent to which that civic value system integrates the society by providing it with a sense of ultimate meaning and purpose. National documents and civic celebrations are common sources of information on civil religion.*

Commitment: *the extent to which an identity (in this case, a religious identity) pervades the organization and interpretation of one's life.*

Congregational religious bodies: *religious bodies that stress the independence of the local church and the democratic administration of church affairs without appeal to a higher church organizational chart, even if several congregations voluntarily associate with one another as part of a larger religious body.*

Conversion: *a significant break with one's former identity such that the past and the present are antithetical in some important respects.*

Cults: *deviant religious movements that spring from roots other than the religious tradition of the society.*

Denomination: *a religious group that accepts the social environment within which it exists. Unlike the church, the denomination is accepting of "religious pluralism," the co-existence of other religious bodies without an overt attempt to dominate or change these others.*

Desacralization: *the world is deprived of its sacred character and is now the subject of rational explanations and human manipulation.*

Differentiation: *a process whereby social institutions become distinct from one another in organizational structure, accountability, values and goals.*

Established church: *a religious group that receives official or quasi-official recognition and special privileges from the state.*

Hierarchical religious bodies: *Religious bodies that include a number of local churches integrated into a larger system by an authority structure above the level of the local unit.*

Human potential movement: *a consciousness-raising movement that is interested in the liberation of the individual from the constraints of an oppressive culture. Devotees believe that only when the individual reaches his or her potential can a society flourish. The movement is composed of a tremendous variety of groups and training methods.*

Magic: *the attempt to manipulate aspects of the universe for specific goals.*

Negative rituals: *taboos, or things that one must not do if one is religious.*

Positive rituals: *actions that must be performed as part of a religion.*

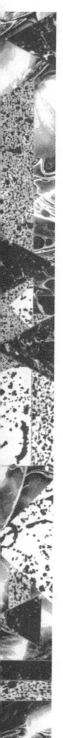

Religious innovation: *a process whereby a new religious group springs from religious roots other than those common to the society in which the activity is taking place.*

Religious revival: *a process whereby an existing religious body recovers new life after a period of stagnation or corruption.*

Sects: *deviant religious movements that have usually broken off from an existing religious body that is within the mainstream of the religious tradition of the society.*

Secularization: *the erosion of faith in supernatural explanations of reality, and the organization of society on the basis of this-worldly explanations.*

Supernatural: *while the nature and meaning of supernatural can vary significantly, it is used here to refer to belief systems that include otherworldly rewards and punishments.*

Theology of liberation: *a theology that stresses there can be little or no spiritual liberation through baptism until people have attained economic liberation from poverty and political liberation of human and civil rights.*

References

Barker, Eileen
1984. *The Making of a Moonie, Choice or Brainwashing*. Oxford: Basil Blackwell.

Barker, Irwin R., and Raymond F. Currie
1985. "Do Converts Always Make the Most Committed Christians?" *Journal for the Scientific Study of Religion* 24:305–13.

Bellah, Robert H.
1967. "Civil Religion in America." *Daedalus* (Winter).

Berger, Peter L.
1969. *The Sacred Canopy: Elements of a Sociological Theory of Religion*. New York: Doubleday.

Bibby, Reginald W.
1987. *Fragmented Gods, The Poverty and Potential of Religion in Canada*. Toronto: Irwin.

Bibby, Reginald W., and Merlin B. Brinkerhoff
1973. "The Circulation of the Saints: A Study of People Who Join Conservative Churches." *Journal for the Scientific Study of Religion* 12:273–83.
1983. "The Circulation of the Saints Revisited: A Longitudinal Look at Conservative Church Growth." *Journal for the Scientific Study of Religion* 22:253–62.

Bibby, Reginald W., and Harold R. Weaver
1985. "Cult Consumption in Canada: A Critique of Stark and Bainbridge." *Sociological Analysis*.

Bouma, Gary D.
1973. "Beyond Lenski: A Critical Review of Recent 'Protestant Ethic' Research." *Journal for the Scientific Study of Religion* 12(2):141–56.
1979. "The Real Reason One Conservative Church Grew." *Review of Religious Research* 20(2):127–37.
1984. *How the Saints Persevere: Social Factors in the Vitality of the Christian Reformed Church*. Clayton, Australia: Monash University.

Campbell, Douglas F.
1987. "The Canadian and Australian Church Unions: A Comparison." *International Journal of Comparative Sociology* 26(3–4): 181–97.

Clifford, N. K.
1977. "The Interpreters of the United Church of Canada." *Church History* 46(2): 203–14.

Currie, Raymond F.
1976. "Belonging, Commitment and Early Socialization in a Western City." In Stewart Crysdale and Les Wheatcroft, eds., *Religion in Canadian Society*. Toronto: Macmillan.

Currie, Raymond F., Leo F. Klug and Charles R. McCombs
1982. "Intimacy and Saliency: Dimensions for Ordering Religious Experiences." *Review of Religious Research* 24(1).

Dohen, Dorothy
1967. *Nationalism and American Catholicism*. New York: Sheed and Ward.

Durkheim, Emile
1964. *The Division of Labour in Society*. Glencoe, Ill.: Free Press.
1965. *The Elementary Forms of the Religious Life*. New York: Free Press.

Gerth, H. H., and C. Wright Mills
1948. *From Max Weber: Essays in Sociology*. London: Routledge and Kegan Paul.

Glock, Charles, and Rodney Stark
1965. *Religion and Society in Tension*. Chicago: Rand McNally.

Gwynne-Timothy, John
1968. "The Evolution of Protestant Nationalism." In Philip LeBlanc and Arnold Edinborough, eds., *One Church, Two Nations*. Don Mills: Longmans.

Harrison, Paul M.
1959. *Authority and Power in the Free Church Tradition: A Social Case Study of the American Baptist Convention*. Princeton, N.J.: Princeton University Press.

Herberg, Edward N.
1989. *Ethnic Groups in Canada: Adaptations and Transitions*. Toronto: Nelson.

Herberg, Will
1960. *Protestant, Catholic, Jew: An Essay in American Religious Sociology*, rev. ed. Garden City, N.Y.: Anchor Books.

Hill, Daniel G.
1980. *Study of Mind Development Groups, Sects and Cults in Ontario*. A report to the Ontario Government, June.

Hiller, Harry H.
1978. "Continentalism and the Third Force in Religion." *Canadian Journal of Sociology* 3: 183–207.

Hirschi, Travis, and Rodney Stark
1969. "Hellfire and Delinquency." *Social Problems* 17: 202–13.

Hornosty, Jennie
1988. "Marxism and Liberation Theology." Paper presented at the annual meeting of the Society for Socialist Studies, Windsor.

Kelley, Dean
1972. *Why the Conservative Churches Are Growing.* New York: Harper and Row.

Lofland, John
1977. *Doomsday Cult.* New York: Irvington Publishers.

Lofland, John, and Rodney Stark
1965. "Becoming a World-Saver: A Theory of Conversion to a Deviant Perspective." *American Sociological Review* 30 (December): 862–74.

Luckmann, Thomas
1967. *The Invisible Religion.* New York: Macmillan.

Marx, Karl, and Friedrich Engels
1964. *On Religion.* New York: Schocken Books.

McIntosh, Christopher
1969. *The Astrologers and Their Creed: An Historical Outline.* New York: Praeger.

Mori, George A.
1987. *Religious Affiliation in Canada: Canadian Social Trends.* Ottawa: Statistics Canada.

Nock, David A.
1987. "Cult, Sect and Church in Canada: A Re-examination of Stark and Bainbridge." *Canadian Review of Sociology and Anthropology* 24(4): 514–25.

Parker, Graham
1983. *An Introduction to Criminal Law,* 2nd ed. Toronto: Methuen.

Penton, James M.
1976. *Jehovah's Witnesses in Canada: Champions of Freedom of Speech and Worship.* Toronto: Macmillan.

Quebedeaux, Richard
1983. *The New Charismatics: How a Christian Renewal Movement Became Part of the American Religious Mainstream.* Cambridge: Harper and Row.

Radhakrishnan, S.
1961. *The Hindu View of Life.* London: George Allen and Unwin.

Shiner, Larry
1972. "The Concept of Secularization in Empirical Research." In Joseph E. Faulkner, ed., *Religion's Influence in Contemporary Society.* Columbus: Charles E. Merrill.

Sinclair-Faulkner, Tom
1977. "A Puckish Reflection on Religion in Canada." In Peter Slater, ed., *Religion and Culture in Canada.* Ottawa: Canadian Corporation for Studies in Religion.

Stark, Rodney, and William Sims Bainbridge
1985. *The Future of Religion.* Berkeley: University of California Press.

Stark, Rodney, and Charles Y. Glock
1968. *American Piety.* Berkeley: University of California Press.

Stone, Donald
1976. "The Human Potential Movement," pp. 93–115. In Charles Y. Glock and Robert N. Bellah, eds., *The New Religious Consciousness.* Berkeley: University of California Press.

Weber, Max

1930. *The Protestant Ethic and the Spirit of Capitalism.* London: George Allen and Unwin.

1963. *The Sociology of Religion.* Boston: Beacon Press.

Westhues, Kenneth

1973. "The Established Church as an Agent of Change." *Sociological Analysis* 34(2): 106–23.

1976. "The Adaptation of the Roman Catholic Church in Canadian Society," pp. 290–306. In Steward Crysdale and Les Wheatcroft, eds., *Religion in Canadian Society.* Toronto: Macmillan.

1978. "Stars and Stripes, the Maple Leaf and the Papal Coat of Arms." *Canadian Journal of Sociology* 3(2): 245–63.

Williams, John R., ed.

1984. *Canadian Churches and Social Justice.* Toronto: Lorimer.

Wuthnow, Robert

1976. *The Consciousness Reformation.* Berkeley: University of California Press.

Zaretsky, Irving I., and Mark P. Leone, eds.

1974. *Religious Movements in Contemporary America.* Princeton, N.J.: Princeton University Press.

*T*he Mass Media

GRAHAM KNIGHT

People spend hours on end doing things that have nothing to do with TV viewing while the set is on.

Introduction

A lot of our leisure time is taken up with the mass media in some form or other. More and more the split between public and private life is blurred by the mass media. We listen to the radio as we drive to work. We watch TV in bars as well as at home. We read magazines and newspapers as we ride the bus or subway, and wear a "walkman" as we walk, or jog, the streets. Similarly, the boundaries between the media are themselves continuing to blur more and more. We watch the latest movie on TV. We listen to the latest music hits on radio, and watch them on rock videos on television. We can sample excerpts from the latest bestseller in newspapers and magazines that now look like "print television." And the TV game-show assistant, who turns the letters and seldom speaks, is featured in the supermarket tabloids, has starred in a made-for-television movie, written a book and very likely will cut a record, all the while insisting how ordinary she is. As one media critic has recently observed, we are living in an "ecstasy of communication" (Baudrillard, 1983).

But what do we mean when we talk about communications and mass media? The term *mass* has two distinct social and political meanings. On the one hand, it is associated with the conservative reaction to industrialization and urbanization. Here, mass is used to characterize people as socially uprooted and isolated, and politically volatile and manipulable (Williams, 1976: 158–63). On the other hand, mass is associated with the radical response to modernization. In this context mass refers in a positive way to the collective potential people have to bring about social change and make society more egalitarian and democratic (Williams, 1976). The term mass media usually evokes the first sense of mass as a large body of people lacking any definite character except low status and taste, and the capacity to be easily manipulated and deceived. For this reason, some use the term popular, rather than mass, to avoid the negative connotations, and to stress the non-elitist aspects of television, music, film and print that have widespread popular appeal.

The terms media and communication have less politically loaded meanings. *Media* is the plural of medium, meaning middle. Hence the idea of intermediary, something acting as a means of connection between two points. We now use the word in a number of different ways. In the technical sense, we speak of sound, vision or print as different media. In the symbolic sense, on the other hand, the word refers to modes of representation, such as language, music or visual images. And we use it to refer to social agencies or institutions, such as television, radio or newspapers, that act as media for particular kinds of content, such as news, entertainment or advertising.

Communication means literally "to make common, to bring together or unite." Hence the idea of communication as a process whereby people exchange and share something. It is only in the twentieth century, however, that communication has come to refer to the distribution, exchange and sharing of information, messages, meanings, ideas or knowledge. Communication now denotes the object or function of the mass media as the latter have come to play a more and more significant cultural role in the way social meanings and social pleasures are produced and shared.

Theoretical Perspectives on the Mass Media

The various theories of the mass media fall roughly into three groups: functional theories, technological theories and critical theories. Each of these provides a different perspective, though what they all share in common is an attempt to understand and explain the development and role of mass communications in modern society.

Functionalism   Functionalism focuses generally on the ways in which the various elements of social life—social roles, institutions, belief systems, etc.—are integrated together to form relatively stable and orderly societies. These elements are seen in terms of the function that they perform in maintaining what Emile Durkheim (1964) called "social solidarity." Durkheim and later functionalists have put particular emphasis on the role of cultural values in generating social solidarity by providing shared beliefs that unite people. Although Durkheim did not discuss the role of the mass media, he did recognize the role of communication in establishing shared values and beliefs. In his discussion of religion, for example, Durkheim (1965) stressed the important function of rituals and ceremonies as situations in which central values and beliefs are acted out and communicated collectively.

Also central to Durkheim's functionalism was the view that deviant behaviour can actually strengthen social solidarity by creating greater awareness of and commitment to norms and values. This occurs through the outrage people feel when those norms are broken or challenged. "Crime," Durkheim wrote, "brings together upright consciences and concentrates them" (1964 : 102). This relates to the mass media, since much media content is about deviance and the social reaction to it. Themes about wrongdoing, crime, disruption, violence and (illicit) sex recur frequently in the media, from news to comics to drama to popular song lyrics. These themes usually involve an equal if not greater focus on how normality is restored through the intervention of the police or some other agency of authority and moral good. News reports, like many novels and dramas, use a narrative form that usually begins with some disruption of the normal state of affairs, followed by a course of events in which normality is finally restored, the deviant punished, justice (seen to be) done, and upright consciences concentrated.

Drawing on Durkheim's insights about the functions of deviance, Erikson (1965) has noted that public displays of punishment, such as executions, began to disappear when the daily newspaper began to grow in circulation and impact. The implication of this is that the newspaper, with its diet of crime news, has now taken over a social solidarity function by publicizing the penalties of crime and deviance. The news media routinely treat some groups and types of behaviour as deviant, and promote others, particularly the agencies of law and order, as positive and good. In this way, one-sided, idealized images are built up that function implicitly to reinforce central values and beliefs (see Knight and Dean, 1982).

A detailed attempt to spell out the particular functions of the mass media for social solidarity is provided by Wright (1975). He identifies four main functions: (1) surveillance of the environment, that is, gathering and distributing information; (2) correlation of the parts of society, that is, interpreting that information and prescribing social behaviour; (3) transmission of the social heritage, that is, communicating information, social values and norms; and (4) entertainment, or providing pleasure. Some media may perform more than one of these functions. Television soap operas, for example, act not only as a form of entertainment, but also as a source of normative references, images and information about social life (see Ang, 1985). Similarly, television news has become increasingly concerned not only with communicating information, but also with entertaining.

The strength of the functional approach is that it directs attention to the ways in which modern society depends on forms of mass communication for its overall functioning. Modern society cannot operate without a rapid and efficient flow of information; nor does it operate without the large-scale social organization of leisure and pleasure.

Technological Theories

The focus on mass media as technologies has been particularly strong in the Canadian tradition of communications research. Two writers stand out as particularly influential—Harold Innis and Marshall McLuhan.

Innis was concerned with the way changes in communications technology affect social structure and values. In *The Bias of Communication* (1951), he develops his earlier interest in orality (speech) and literacy (writing) by distinguishing between time-biased and space-biased media. *Time-biased media* are means of communication that are durable, but relatively immobile, such as stone carvings or clay tablets. *Space-biased media* are more mobile but less durable, for example, paper.

Different media give rise to different configurations of institutions and belief systems. Time-biased media promote a strong sense of tradition and history, which favour religious and mystical forms of authority and culture. Space-biased media, on the other hand, are conducive to quicker communication over larger distances, fostering an orientation to territorial expansion or empire building and to the emergence of secular forms of authority such as are embodied in military institutions and the state. These different forms of power shape the secondary institutions of society and create elites that strive to control the media out of self-interest. Those excluded from control come into conflict with these elites and try to develop alternative means of communication to undercut elite power. This conflict results in social change and the development of the means of communication away from time-biased to space-biased media.

Innis's ideas had an important influence on Marshall McLuhan (1964, 1969). Among other matters, McLuhan was interested in the effects of communications media on our physical senses and psychology. For example, the invention and spread of printing, McLuhan argues, brought an end to oral culture, with its emphasis on hearing, and introduced a new, more visually oriented culture. Printed words are visually separate, yet organized together in a linear way. This encourages us to see the world as composed of separate objects and to interpret reality in terms of linear, cause-and-effect sequences of actions and events. Print removes the process of communication from actual situations of social interaction. As a consequence, information becomes more abstract. This fosters greater individualism, specialization and a weakening of social ties to small-scale, local communities. Larger-scale, national communities develop where social attachments are reinforced by the ability of print to visualize and standardize the national language or mother-tongue in an abstract way.

For McLuhan, the dominance of print is now coming to an end with the growth of electronic media, which make communication instantaneous. TV in particular makes print culture secondary, as it offers a wholly new form of mental and social experience by reintegrating our senses. Sight and sound are joined together, and this makes TV a tactile medium. Touch becomes the overall effect of the senses combined, as in the sense of being "touched" by some experience or other: all our senses, feelings and thoughts are engaged in and by that experience.

McLuhan was criticized by some sociologists for reducing social relations and forces to technology. In response, he maintained that media are the technological extensions of our own senses. When he said that "the medium is the message," he meant that the content of a medium is simply another medium.

Critical Theories

Influenced by Marxism, critical theories have concentrated on the relationship between the mass media and the structure of power and economic inequality. The media are seen as ideological institutions responsible for the production and circulation of meanings, ideas, values and pleasures. They are also seen as economic institutions that are part of the wider marketplace and profit-making system.

Critical theories have taken two approaches to the mass media. The first has focused on the factors shaping media structure and development. The debate here is over how directly the dominant centres of social power—the state and private enterprise—exert their influence over the media. Some argue that the relationship is a fairly direct one, largely because the media are owned and controlled by one or the other of these two power centres. The kind of media available are limited by financial dependence on advertising or government grants. Because they are owned by governments and large corporations, the media develop the bureaucratic structures characteristic of these organizations. And because of their financial dependence, their content tends to be supportive of the interests of advertisers or governments (Golding and Murdock, 1979). The audience has limited influence since it is socialized to want what the media provide. It is seen as an effect or product of the media rather than a determinant (Smythe, 1981). Others criticize this view as too deterministic since it implies that media are only an expression of dominant economic interests and power. They argue that economic pressures and constraints have an indirect effect that is channelled through other social institutions, such as the class system (Hall, 1977).

The second approach taken by critical theorists has been more concerned with the ideological functions of the media. Theorists of the Frankfurt school, notably Adorno,

Horkheimer and Marcuse, argued that the media served dominant political and economic interests by creating an ideology of false consciousness that prevents people from recognizing the real character of capitalism as an oppressive system. This ideology reinforces the power structure by manipulating people and creating passivity through the "culture industry" of information and entertainment media (Horkheimer and Adorno, 1982). When culture is turned into a product made and sold for commercial profit, content becomes standardized at the level of the lowest common denominator (Marcuse, 1964).

This suggests the existence of an all-pervasive system of ideological control in which conflict and opposition are no longer possible. This conclusion has been criticized by those who see ideology and the media as aspects of social life where conflicts do occur, but unevenly and without any permanent conclusion as contending groups struggle to make their perspectives and values socially dominant. Shared values and beliefs do exist, constructed and disseminated by the powerful through their control of institutions such as the media. Yet, because power and inequality generate opposition and conflict, the powerful must continually *work* to establish and maintain their primacy by countering resistance, controlling conflict, legitimizing their power and achieving the consent and participation of those they dominate (see Hall, 1977).

These three perspectives have implications for different areas of empirical research. In the remainder of this chapter we will examine three of these: media effects, control of the media and media content.

Media Effects

Our fascination with the media stems from the belief that they easily manipulate our thoughts and actions. This has been responsible for a lot of popular talk about media effects, mostly from a sceptical if not hostile perspective. The scientific literature does give some grounds for concern about media effects, but the conclusions of much research are far from unconditional. The earlier concern to identify the effects of media exposure in immediate, direct terms has been tempered by a more cautious view that media interact with their broader social context and that there is a two-way flow of influences. Any assessment of media effects has to specify what media are being examined and how effects are being defined. With this in mind, we can identify three main areas of research: agenda setting, television effects and imitation.

Agenda Setting   Agenda-setting studies have looked primarily at the effects of news media on the formation of public opinion, particularly about political and current affairs issues. As a conduit for the passage of information between the dominant political and economic institutions and the general population, media are seen to be in a position to select, rank and define the salient issues and events of the day. They establish the *agenda setting*, the priority list of concerns for public awareness and discussion, emphasizing the significance of some issues and views, while playing down and excluding others. The question is: How great an effect does this have on what people actually think?

The evidence suggests that the media are successful in telling people what to think *about*, but not necessarily what to think (McCoombs, cited in Winter et al., 1982). The extent of influence, moreover, varies according to the issues in question—how specific they are, how "obtrusive" or direct their impact and how immediate and lasting (Winter et al., 1982). The effect of the media on public opinion is not direct and automatic, but mediated by existing social frameworks of understanding and experience.

The influences on the agenda-setting process come from the public as well as political and economic elites. Although these elites have easier and more effective access to the media, their views have to be represented in ways that are intelligible and have some general point of reference and significance that takes account of existing public sentiments and beliefs. This is done increasingly through public opinion polls, which are commissioned by political parties, governments, corporations and media alike, and through the kind of feature journalism that is concerned with how ordinary people feel about what the powerful say and do.

The influence of public opinion on the media was shown in the handling of the free trade issue in the 1988 federal election campaign. The media strategies of the different parties, the news coverage of the leaders' campaigns, the televised leaders' debates and the opinion polls publicized by the media all interacted in a way that established free trade as the dominant issue in the election, creating in the process uncertainty about the eventual outcome. This happened, however, because the parties, the media and the polls reacted to public concerns that were already partly formed, though in varied and contradictory ways.

An election campaign, however, is an atypical context, as the relationship between political elites, the media, the polls and the public agenda is particularly intensified. At other times, issues have to vie with one another in a less orderly fashion, and the need for the media to generate new angles and stories weakens the ability of any one source or cluster of sources to control the agenda-setting fit between elites, media and general public.

Television Effects   More than other media, television has been the subject of effects research, much of it focused on children, violence and sexual stereotyping. One of the most exhaustive studies is by Williams et al. (1986) on the introduction of television reception into a small town in British Columbia in the early 1970s. Their findings generally support the "negative" view of television's impact, although the strength and structure of the effects varied. Williams et al. argue that television works its effects indirectly as well as directly, by displacing other activities as well as by providing models for learning attitudes and behaviour.

For psychological and cultural skills development among children, Williams et al. suggest that this *displacement effect* is indirect. They found, for example, that fluent readers usually had higher IQs and watched less TV. They hypothesize that television may slow down the acquisition of literacy by taking time away from reading. This, in turn, may be influenced by the family's socio-economic status, since higher-status families tend to put more positive emphasis on reading. At the same time, other studies in the United States and Australia indicate that the negative displacement effects of TV on reading affect comics and pulp magazines rather than books (Schramm et al., 1961; Murray and Kippax, 1978).

Television provides standardized resolutions to problems, and does not challenge the imagination or broaden children's experience. Moreover, the convenience and ease of TV viewing may take time away from other activities that are more conducive to the development of problem solving and other creative skills, particularly among less intelligent children for whom creativity-oriented pastimes require greater effort. In this respect, the displacement and content effects of TV may be self-reinforcing: the routineness of TV makes it easily and effortlessly absorbed, and this makes it an attractive alternative to other activities that require more thought and imagination.

For aggression and sexual stereotyping, Williams et al. posit a more direct relationship between content and effect. What makes children particularly susceptible to TV is that their knowledge and experience of the world are still restricted. They have limited points of reference against which to process, compare and judge what they see and hear on the screen. Television images tend to be highly repetitive and formulaic, offering few points of divergence and contrast. In the case of sex roles, the stereotypical character of TV is generally reinforced in the wider society, presenting the child with few alternatives by which to compare reality and media image.

With aggression, the situation differs slightly. Cultural attitudes toward aggressiveness are ambiguous: aggression is negatively valued, yet it is commonly used as a means to achieve goals, in everyday life as in TV. On TV the "bad guys" who initiate violence usually suffer as a consequence. But the nature of TV narrative is such that violence is separated temporally from its consequences, the necessary delay that gives the TV drama its plot. Children, however, watch TV in a more immediate fashion, and so this connection between the use of violence and its punishment may be lost. "Good guys" also use aggression, and this can legitimate its use as a defensive reaction to the aggression of others.

The effects of TV on social participation work through displacement rather than direct learning. For older adults particularly, Williams et al. found that public or community forms of social participation declined with the advent of TV. These are the kinds of activities that take place outside the home and cannot be time-shared with TV. Despite its recent popularity in bars, TV in our culture is still primarily a domestic, family affair. In one sense, this gives it a definite privilege and power since we admit it to the most intimate, familiar sphere of our social existence. On the other hand, the familiarity of TV weakens its impact since it must share this space with other activities that also occur when the TV is on.

In the United States, research by Anderson (cited in Williams et al., 1986), for example, showed that a sample of children spent an average of 1.3 hours a day actually watching the TV screen, and 1.9 hours in the same room with the TV on. This contrasted to an average of 3.3 hours a day of TV watching that their parents estimated beforehand. This suggests that people think of TV viewing in terms of the amount of time the set is on, rather than the amount of time spent paying attention to it. Research in the United Kingdom by Collett et al. (cited in Root, 1986) came up with comparable results: "People spend hours on end doing all kinds of things that have absolutely nothing to do with TV viewing while the set is on" (Root, 1986:26).

There are also social differences in how TV is watched. Morley (1980), for example, found that men preferred to watch attentively, in silence and without interruptions, whereas women treated TV watching as a social activity accompanied by conversation and comments on the programs. This points to still prevalent differences in the domestic roles of men and women. Looking after the material and emotional needs of the family continues to be primarily the responsibility of women. Not surprisingly, they do other things—ironing, cooking, cleaning, etc.—when "watching" TV (see Hobson, 1982).

Any attempt, then, to understand the effects of TV must take into account the social and psychological context, even where TV seems to have a direct effect.

Imitation: Emotions and Economics

The third area of effects concerns what seems to be a direct and immediate pattern of imitation. This may take the form of an irrational copying of particular acts or incidents that have been in the media. In Britain in the early 1980s, for example, the media were blamed for provoking an increase in street rioting among unemployed youths simply by playing up incidents of civil disturbance in the news. Some people charged that this sparked further rioting and amplified the problem (Tumber, 1982). Another example is the series of incidents of Rambo-style violence reported after the success of Sylvester Stallone's movies about the lone avenger seeking private, vigilante justice for wrongs done to him.

What these incidents indicate is a possible triggering effect that media images have. But how systematic is this? Phillips (1979, 1982) and Bollen and Phillips (1982) found that the rate of suicide increased after newspaper stories of suicides, and that the increase varied with the amount and prominence of the news coverage. Working on the assumption that some suicides may have been classified as accidental deaths, they also looked at car crash fatalities and private airplane crashes, finding that these, too, rose after front-page suicide or murder-suicide reports. The rate of suicides and car crash fatalities also increased after the depiction of suicides in soap operas, peaking on the first and sixth days afterward, which suggests impulsive rather than planned behaviour.

A less serious area where imitative behaviour occurs is the effect that media images have on everyday life-style fads such as clothing fashion—the "Annie Hall" look for women in the late 1970s, or the "Miami Vice" look for men in the mid-1980s, for example. While these instances of imitation often arise spontaneously, they are quickly exploited by the clothing and marketing industries in search of opportunities for profit and expanded consumption. And no longer are these instances confined to clothing fashion.

Babette's Feast Fit for a Fling

Viewers of *Babette's Feast*, this year's winner of the Academy Award for Best Foreign Film, may fancy quail stuffed with foie gras baked in a puff pastry nest with truffles.

This is one of the courses in the sumptuous repast that is the core of the movie's story. Toronto movie-going gourmets can enjoy the meal of the movie at the Harbour Castle Westin's Chateauneuf Restaurant.

Babette's Feast opened in Toronto last week and the hotel will feature the special menu until Christmas. At the inaugural feast, **Ulrich Wall**, managing director of the hotel, welcomed guests.

Those enjoying the culinary efforts of executive chef **Rudolph Blattler** included: Danish Consul **Jorgen Jensen** and his wife, **Lily**; **Michael Rechtshaffen**, Canadian correspondent for The Hollywood Reporter, the Los Angeles-based entertainment daily, and **Ron McCluskey**, president, creative exposure, the movie's distributor in English Canada.

The Financial Post, December 9, 1988, p. 15.

The economic exploitation of media culture is probably most developed in the area of children's television, where the whole relationship between programming and the marketing of toys and other products has now been turned around. Up to the early 1980s the program came first, leading later to the marketing of related products such as toys, logos or images of the program's characters. What happens now is that the marketing aspect is integrated into the conception of the program from the outset, turning the latter into an extended commercial for the associated products. Between 1983 and 1985, for example, the number of U.S. licensed-character cartoons rose from fourteen to forty, and 1985 U.S. toy industry revenues from character products were up one billion dollars, to $8.5 billion, over 1984 (Engelhardt, 1986 : 78–79).

The immediate effects of this are often short-lived as new programs and character toys replace old ones. What is of more lasting effect, however, is the general integration of mass consumption into the mass media, and vice versa. The boundary between media as cultural and as economic institutions has never been sharply defined, and it is now becoming even more blurred.

Control of the Media

The question of media control can be examined on two levels. At the institutional level is the issue of economic and political control, which falls within the approach of political economy. At the organizational level, there is the question of the control structure of the media as bureaucratic and professional workplaces, and this falls within the perspective of occupational and organizational sociology.

The Political Economy of the Media

Political economy studies the relationship between power and economic organization, issues such as ownership, government regulation, economic and historical development. While the media are viewed much like any other business, as enterprises producing commodities for the marketplace, there is also an important difference, since the product has cultural as well as economic value and function. Media messages are symbolic goods, which set them apart from other commodities, part of the reason why the so-called "cultural industries"—arts, entertainment and information media—were formally exempted from the free trade agreement with the United States.

Historically, this difference has an added dimension because the original *mass* media were primarily news media that developed in Western society within the context of a democratic ideology of freedom of speech and expression. This context makes the question of political economy problematic. How can freedom of speech and expression be ensured when the media operate as either private profit-making businesses or state owned and funded institutions?

This becomes even more problematic when we look at how media ownership has developed, especially for daily newspapers where ownership has now become concentrated into a small number of corporate hands. In the second half the nineteenth century, when the daily newspaper became the norm, ownership was diversified. Most newspapers were owned and operated by a proprietor-publisher on an independent basis, and a competitive marketplace promoted variety, to some extent at least (see Rutherford, 1979, 1982). Circulation levels were limited, and revenue came primarily from subscriptions. Organizational size was small, with the proprietor often relying on family members or partners for additional labour. And like small businesses generally, there was a high degree of turnover, with new papers being started and existing ones dying at a fairly high rate. Between 1875 and 1900, for example, Montreal alone saw the birth of twenty-three new dailies and the demise of twenty-five (Rutherford, 1982). The economic priority was survival, rather than making large profits, and most proprietors started and ran newspapers to promote a cause or realize a political ambition or religious commitment, not to make money.

Toward the end of the nineteenth century, the business aspect of newspapers gradually became more prominent and decisive. Ownership concentration began to develop, giving rise to local market monopolies and oligopolies—today, for example, only eight cities in Canada have two daily papers in the same language that have different owners. A number of factors were involved in this change. The technology of newsgathering and publishing became more mechanized, costly and capital intensive. This increased the pressure to expand circulation and find new sources of revenue, resulting in greater competition for readers and a growing dependence on advertising as the primary source of income and profit. The reader ceased being the direct source of revenue from subscriptions and became the indirect source through advertising:

advertisers wanted to reach large audiences, and papers competed with one another to deliver these and attract advertising dollars.

Concentration has given rise to the *chain ownership* of newspapers, which combines "horizontal" and "vertical" integration. Horizontal integration occurs when a proprietor owns and operates more than one newspaper, usually in different communities. The effect of this is that locally and independently owned and operated papers disappear. Vertical integration occurs when the newspaper chain owns and controls the various stages of the overall production process, from pulp mills to paper making to printing to distribution, as well as the actual newsgathering process. Today, most newspaper chains have become corporate conglomerates. The Thomson group, to cite one example, have extended their holdings far beyond the newspaper industry and far beyond Canada's border to become the world's fourth largest media corporation, with an annual revenue of almost $6 billion.

By 1980, advertising accounted for about four-fifths of total revenue for the average daily paper in Canada, a sum of almost $1 billion annually (Audley, 1983 : 18). Chains accounted for over three-quarters of daily newspaper circulation, an increase of more than 20 percent from ten years previously (Audley, 1983 : 19). Two chains, Southam and Thomson, owned almost half of all the daily newspapers, and accounted for half of total daily circulation, 60 percent of anglophone circulation. In 1985, the effect of concentration was further enhanced when Southam entered into a share-swap arrangement with Torstar Corporation, which publishes *The Toronto Star* (the largest circulation daily in Canada). The two companies combined have over 30 percent of Canada's daily circulation. For francophone papers, almost 90 percent of circulation was controlled by the three dominant chains—Quebecor, Gesca (part of Paul Desmarais's Power Corporation) and Unimedia—by 1980 (see also Canada, 1981).

Unlike print media, which are privately owned, radio and television have developed in a dual system of private and public control. State involvement in broadcasting has taken the form of both regulation and production. Regulation is now in the hands of the Canadian Radio-television and Telecommunications Commission (CRTC), which has the power to issue and review broadcasting licences. Production is primarily in the hands of the CBC/Radio-Canada, which was created in 1932 in response to the 1928 Aird Commission on radio broadcasting. The Aird Commission had recommended a public monopoly over radio broadcasting and the expropriation of existing private broadcasters by the state. Instead, a compromise was made, and the Canadian Radio Broadcasting Commission (changed to the Canadian Broadcasting Corporation in 1936) was established as a publicly funded institution to produce programming that would contribute to Canadian culture and national identity. Lip-service was paid to the ideal of creating a unified broadcasting system, but existing private broadcasters were allowed to continue in business.

After the Second World War, the relationship between the CBC and private broadcasters became more conflictual as the economic power of private broadcasters grew, especially after the introduction of private television in the early 1960s. For private broadcasters, radio and TV are primarily ways to make money, most of which comes from advertising. Private broadcasters want to minimize costs, and advertisers want to reach large, affluent audiences rather than promote national culture and identity. These two sets of interests have coincided to create a strong pressure to rely on imported American content.

Ownership concentration reduces the kind of competition that might promote more and more varied Canadian content. Competition from the CBC and government regulations are the only sources of pressure on private broadcasters to provide Canadian content. But the CBC has operated in an uncertain financial situation, and has been vulnerable to cutbacks in government funding. Government regulations requiring minimum levels of Canadian content are loosely defined, and have often been weakly enforced in practice. No private TV station, for example, has been refused a request for licence renewal, despite frequent instances of failure to live up to the spirit of providing more and better Canadian programming.

Quebec is a partial exception, since private broadcasters do produce more franco-phone programming. Despite the smaller size of the audience, private francophone broadcasters spent almost as much money in 1985 producing TV entertainment and arts programming (excluding sports) as their English-language counterparts, $32.8

TABLE 15-1

Percent Breakdown of Television Programming Costs, 1984–85

Programming:	Private Broadcasters		CBC/Radio-Canada	
	Canadian	Foreign	Canadian	Foreign
English Language				
Information	42.1%	1.4%	52.6%	—
Children's	0.6	0.4	4.0	—
Films & series	4.9	30.8	2.3	4.3
Other entertainment	5.4	2.9	11.7	0.1
Sports	9.0	1.3	8.7	—
Other	1.0	0.2	16.3	—
Total %	63.0	37.0	95.6	4.4
Total $ million	225.9	132.9	336.6	15.6
French Language				
Information	40.1%	—	47.1%	—
Children's	0.2	—	6.2	—
Films & series	14.5	10.9	4.0	3.4
Other entertainment	29.3	1.0	17.4	0.2
Sports	3.9	0.1	10.2	—
Other	—	—	11.5	—
Total %	88.0	12.0	96.4	3.6
Total $ million	65.8	9.0	203.6	7.6

COMPILED FROM REPORT OF THE TASK FORCE ON BROADCASTING POLICY. *1986. OTTAWA: MINISTER OF SUPPLY AND SERVICES CANADA, TABLE 17.9, PP. 434–35.*

million versus $40.3 million (Canada, 1986) (see Table 15-1). While private English-language broadcasters spend more money producing their own programming than buying imported material—in 1984–85, $225.9 million versus $132.9 million—they can purchase imported programming at about 1 to 5 percent of the production cost. That $132.9 million bought programming that cost anywhere from $3 to 5 *billion* to make, and that adds up to a lot of foreign programming.

Despite the original commitment to a unified broadcasting system, there are really two separate systems, one public the other private, one trying to produce Canadian content, the other resisting pressures to do so since the economics of profit making make ready-made, foreign material highly attractive. Canada's media operate in a continental, if not global, marketplace where considerations of national culture are easily compromised by economic forces and the dominance of the American communications and cultural industries.

The Social
Organization of
the Media

The political economy of Canadian media has been shaped by conflicts brought about by a number of related factors—ownership concentration, Canadian versus foreign (American) content, public versus private control. These various areas of conflict come down to a general confrontation between culture and economics.

When we shift to the level of social organization, we find a similar pattern of conflict, but one that takes on a different complexion as a conflict between professionalism and bureaucracy. Media organizations have a dual structure. On the one hand, they are workplaces for people using professional skills and pursuing goals that usually have a broader cultural significance, such as providing accurate, unbiased information or realizing artistic and aesthetic values. On the other hand, media are workplaces that have to fulfil the administrative needs of any bureaucratic organization: a division of labour, an authority hierarchy, a system to supervise personnel relations, costs and productivity, etc. Where these two aspects clash is over the question of control. Professionals such as journalists, producers and actors expect some degree of autonomy to make decisions and work in a relationship of collegiality with their peers. Bureaucracies, however, usually ensure efficient administration by centralizing and formalizing control, by taking decision making out of the hands of individuals and embedding it in rules and procedures that reduce autonomy. How, then, are the two reconciled?

One of the earliest studies of this problem was by Warren Breed (1955), who was interested in the ways in which newspapers dealt with the potential conflicts between the values and goals of journalists as individuals and professionals, and those of the organization as a private enterprise. Newspapers generally have an editorial slant that represents the beliefs and interests of proprietors and management, and often this tends to be politically and economically more conservative than the views of individual journalists. Breed was interested in how conflict was avoided, and what he found was that the formal exercise of authority was rare because control functioned indirectly and pre-emptively through the process of socialization. Newcomers to the newsroom learned informally, by being immersed into the newsroom as an ongoing work process, the everyday rules and routines and the amount and kind of scope they had for making decisions on the job. Control was internalized, and journalists became self-censoring, learning from co-workers what would be acceptable.

Breed also recognized that this process of control was reinforced by the newsroom structure. The authority hierarchy acted as a promotion system, encouraging those below to conform in the interests of their future career prospects. The organization of the work process around a tight deadline timetable reduced the opportunity to depart from routine ways of producing and presenting news stories. The newsroom had its own informal subculture that acted as a source of control over its members and as an informal status system that provided newcomers with professional role models. There was no strong union to represent reporters' interests and act as a counterweight to management. And, finally, there was a system of formal sanctions that could be used if the more informal methods of control failed.

Later studies of news organizations have generally confirmed Breed's findings, but they have also pointed to a number of additional factors that influence the structure of control. Particularly important are technology, the division of labour and news sources.

Technology is especially important when comparing organizational differences between print and television. Warner's (1971) replication of Breed's study in a TV newsroom found that, because of the greater role of technology (film and video), production was more team oriented. Television reporters need to co-operate with camera operators, film and videotape editors and, very often, field producers who also go out on assignment to make the editorial judgments about story coverage. In print, on the other hand, the reporter usually works on a solo basis, consulting intermittently with his or her newsroom editor about story assignment and development. Print reporters can work more easily from within the newsroom, gathering information and interviewing over the phone. When they go out on assignment they usually go alone, gathering the information and writing the story before submitting it to the desk editor who vets it for publication.

The division of labour in newsrooms occurs within as well as between occupational groups. Its most important form is the distinction made between general and specialist reporters. Generalists cover different types of news stories from day to day, depending on what their editor assigns—a fire one day, a community gathering the next, etc. Specialists, on the other hand, cover the same type of story, their beat, on a continuous basis. This *beat system* is usually defined in territorial terms that coincide with some major institution, often connected with the state—politics, business and industry, labour, education, health, environment, police, courts, etc. Beats are usually more extensive in newspapers than in radio or TV, mainly because newspapers employ more reporters.

The logic behind the beat system is that specialization allows the reporter to acquire greater familiarity with and knowledge of a particular area of news. But it also operates as part of the control system inasmuch as it allows for the delegation of decision-making power. As specialists become more familiar with their beat, they are able to make decisions about story topics and angles to a greater extent than general reporters. For this reason, beat reporters tend to be the more senior members of the newsroom, and the beats themselves are ranked informally in terms of their status, depending very much on the status of the people reporters deal with, and on their own reputation in the newsroom. Familiarity with the beat, however, can also allow the reporter to develop a degree of independence that management finds threatening, or can lead to reporter assimilation and loss of objectivity and balance. To avoid these, newsroom managers regularly rotate reporters through the beats, and editors often play down the need for specialized knowledge, preferring instead to rely on stock reporting formulas and "common-sense" interpretations (see Ericson et al., 1987 : 125–29).

Most newsgathering is done through interviewing sources, and this creates a situation of mutual, if sometimes uneasy, dependency (Ericson et al., 1987). The interests of reporters and sources may be at odds when the former want accurate, important information while the latter want good publicity. Choice of sources may accentuate the potential conflict in the relationship. Reporters prefer to rely on authoritative sources who are thought to be more credible and impressive, such as senior officials or politicians. The authority and credibility of these sources, however, also translates into the power to be selective in how much and what kind of information they provide.

Reporters can counter this power to some extent by using alternative or opposing sources—political coverage is a good example. Politics is, in fact, the principal model for news reporting generally: it enables some semblance of objectivity (telling both sides of the story), and it gives the reporter some leverage over powerful or reluctant sources by giving access to different or opposing views. This becomes more difficult when the reporter is faced with a source monopoly over information supply—crime reporting, for example, where information comes almost exclusively from the police. The police are more immune to the obligation to disclose information than other public agencies, on the grounds that this might compromise their work, and are often suspicious of the media; one Toronto TV reporter once likened the police beat to covering the Kremlin! The reporter is put in a dependent position that calls for management skills to ensure that information does flow. This dependency also makes coverage of negative police stories difficult because of the likelihood of alienating a powerful source (Chibnall, 1977; Altheide, 1976).

Organizational structure, and the balance between professionalism and bureaucracy, varies ultimately from medium to medium. TV production, for example, is more routinized and bureaucratic than movie production because the unit of production is the series or serial, and this allows for a more industrial work process. Movies, on the other hand, are produced on a one-off basis. This makes for a more craftlike work process where the production team is assembled to produce just a single, custom-made item (Ellis, 1982). This difference has an effect on the division of labour, control and status. The serial nature of TV production puts creative as well as financial and organizational control in the hands of the producer; in movies, the two sides remain separate, with the producer in charge of finance and administration and the director in charge of the creative and artistic aspects (Tunstall and Walker, 1981).

Content and Ideology: Two Current Issues

The interest in media content has recently taken a new direction as the result of developments in the critical perspective. For critical theorists, the mass media are ideological institutions that both construct and represent social experiences in meaningful and intelligible ways, but ways that also distort the real effects of power and inequality on social life. We shall take a look at two areas where the ideological character of media images has become particularly controversial: bias in the news and sexism in advertising.

Bias in the News   News bias is a salient issue because we expect the news media to be objective and unbiased. The concern with objectivity, however, has only developed as a result of the changes in the political economy of the media discussed above. As the news media became more dependent on advertising and mass markets, the commitment to objectivity—balanced, fair and factually accurate reporting—developed as a way of appealing to larger audiences. Before the growth of dependency on advertising, most newspapers reported the news in a slanted and partisan way, catering to the particular interests and opinions of their select readership (see Rutherford, 1978, 1982). Objectivity became a way of broadening circulation to a larger, more diverse audience by trying to appeal to all tastes and offend none. In this respect, objectivity was itself ideological, part of the redefinition of news that resulted from the growing concentration of ownership and power.

The ideological biases of news derive from the interaction of two factors: the criteria that news media use to select and report events and issues—criteria that are largely left implicit as natural and obvious—and the sources they use to acquire and present information. The primary news criteria include an emphasis on what is unusual or deviant, an emphasis on dramatic presentation that accentuates conflict and confrontation, an emphasis on immediacy (the "here and now") and the representation of issues and events in terms of personalities (see Knight, 1982).

The effect of these criteria is to produce accounts of reality that usually reinforce dominant social perspectives and exclude or play down alternative ways of understanding. The emphasis on what is unusual or deviant, for example, takes for granted what is ordinary and normal. The assumption here is that there is a natural consensus of values and norms from which certain events deviate. At the same time, not all forms of deviance get equal attention in the news: street crime or political corruption and incompetence, for example, recur more frequently than, say, white-collar crime or business corruption and incompetence. This bias in the structure of news helps to reproduce that consensus as natural and timeless rather than socially and historically conditioned.

Sources play into the biasing of news in the way they are distinguished by role and importance. There are primary sources who effectively define the parameters of the event or issue in question. These are normally the sources with official or expert status, such as politicians, government or business spokespeople, police, scientists, etc., who have the best access to the media as authoritative and credible spokespeople. And there are secondary sources who respond to the event or issue, but usually on the basis of the parameters set by the primary definers. Secondary sources give reactions, the other side of the story, often its more emotional aspect(s). Secondary sources may have some kind of official or expert status, for example as spokespeople for organized groups such as the environmental or peace movements, or may be simply representatives of the woman or man in the street (Knight, 1988). These differences in access and role reinforce one another, with the effect that news tends to reflect the perspectives of the upper middle class, its primary source of information (see Gans, 1979).

Here's a Small Test to Find Out What the Media Really Tell Us

By Gerald Caplan

Can I recommend a fascinating little exercise for you? It's based on Edward Herman and Noam Chomsky's latest book, *Manufacturing Consent*, which argues that under the guise of a free and feisty press, the American mass media actually serve to reflect the special interests of the elites that run the United States.

Through their choice of topics and sources, the way they frame issues, through tone and emphasis, and by keeping debate within the bounds of certain acceptable premises, the actual role of the media is "to inculcate and defend the economic, social and political agenda of privileged groups" that dominate life in America.

This is no batty left-wing conspiracy theory: The authors know that "the U.S. media do not function in the manner of the propaganda system of a totalitarian state. Rather, they permit—indeed encourage—spirited debate, criticism and dissent, as long as these remain faithfully within the system of presuppositions and principles that constitute an elite consensus, a system so powerful as to be internalized largely without awareness."

This, needless to say, is a somewhat disturbing assertion, which Herman and Chomsky massively document analyzing coverage over the years of Central America and Southeast Asia by highly influential American media: The New York Times, Time, Newsweek and CBS News. For my money, they demonstrate a pattern of distorted news coverage so systematically, consistently and blindly pro-American as largely to validate their terrifying hypothesis.

But you can test it yourself today with this paper which, given commercial realities, will inevitably be chock-a-block with American news reports and comments.

The Toronto Star, for example, carried a post-Christmas column by David Broder, a popular American political commentator, that could serve admirably as the text for Herman and Chomsky's next book. "The Sandinistas and the Contras have stopped killing each other on the borders of Nicaragua," Broder wrote, for all the world as if two morally equal groups were at play here. In fact, of course, the Contras are nothing but agents of the mighty American government attempting to overthrow the legitimate government of a tiny Third World country that refuses to kow-tow to American interests.

"Yasser Arafat," Broder went on, "acknowledged the existence of Israel, clearing the way for the first direct talks between the U.S. government and the PLO." Well, literally that's so, but the clear implication is that Arafat, not Washington or Israel, has till now prevented peace, a routine American value judgment but not self-evidently objective reality.

Or take the long article in The Globe and Mail the same day by an American historian, "Viet Nam's road to recovery looks like a long trudge." The obstacles to economic development in Viet Nam, we learn, "are substantial . . . Viet Nam is in desperate economic straits that reduce it to one of the poorest nations on earth." All because—you guessed it—of its incompetent, dogmatic Communist government. No doubt. But what of the simple truth that Viet Nam endured 30 years of devastating war, first against France and then against the invading Americans, ending only 13 years ago?

We all know over 50,000 American boys died in Viet Nam. But did you know some 3 million Vietnamese did too? Or that "the combined ecological, economic and social consequences of American wartime defoliation operations," according to one report, "have been vast and will take several generations to reverse"? Or that 9,000 of the south's 15,000 hamlets were damaged or destroyed, while all six industrial cities in the north were damaged, three of them razed to the ground.

Yet, the Globe article, astoundingly but typically, contains only a single bizarre reference to the war: "Having just fought a 30-year war for independence, many upper-echelon veterans of the struggle are loath to move towards capitalism."

The Toronto Star, January 8, 1989.

By the way, the U.S. massively and routinely used chemical and environmental warfare across Southeast Asia in those ghastly years, which brings us to the evil Colonel Gadhafi. Of all the stories you read last week about the alleged Libyan chemical weapons plant, how many have noted that such peace-loving Canadian allies as the U.S. certainly, and Israel probably, themselves possess great stores of chemical weapons? Or that Libya is in fact offering on-site inspection of the plant, which the U.S. has flatly rejected?

And how many stories have reported the many previous American accusations against Gadhafi that proved to be utter lies and deliberately concocted disinformation?

Herman and Chomsky would assert that the media are manufacturing consent for Ronald Reagan's macho determination to leave office with American guns blazing against Libya. Let's pray they're wrong.

Gerald Caplan is a former national secretary of the New Democratic Party and a public affairs consultant.

Ideological news bias is illustrated in Voumvakis and Ericson's (1984) study of newspaper coverage of a series of sexual assaults in Toronto in 1983. They found that *The Globe and Mail* relied more heavily on official and expert sources, while *The Toronto Star* and, especially, *The Toronto Sun* gave more play to individual citizens as sources. In all three papers, however, the police were used as the primary definers of the story, with ordinary citizens, particularly women, giving emotional reaction—the "fear and loathing" angle (Voumvakis and Ericson, 1984:30–40). These reactions also reaffirmed the definition of the assaults as a threat to women's safety, but in a way that located the problem with the victims themselves. In all three papers, the single most common theme to recur in the coverage had to do with the behaviour and circumstances of the victims at the time of the attacks, presented "in ways which suggested that if the victim had taken care not to place herself in perilous circumstances she could have avoided victimization" (1984:46–47). The implication in all three papers was that the victim, not the offender, was to blame.

Sexism and Advertising   Blaming the victim is a common response to sexual violence committed by men against women. From a woman's perspective, however, it speaks to the much larger issue of inequality, power and gender relations. The representation of women as sexual objects is one important aspect of this, but it is only half of the picture. As many feminists have argued, the ideological oppression of women consists in their being represented in terms of one of two stereotyped images—either the mother or the sex object—that are more the product of male fantasy than of women's own realities. In either case, women are defined in terms of their relationship to and dependency on men. Both images of women are made by men, but they are images women are encouraged to internalize and make their own (see Davies et al., 1987).

Advertising is especially important for the internalization of dominant imagery and ideology because it is the place where culture and symbolism overlap and interact with economics. This interaction occurs through association and identification: desire for the product is created through its association with a desirable social image, an image the consumer can identify with, but recognize as something she has yet to achieve. For identification to occur, the social image must be close enough to be recognizable, yet different enough to create a sense of inadequacy or lack. Purchasing and possessing the product is offered as the way to close this gap between reality and desire (see Dickey, 1987; Williamson, 1978, 1986a, 1986b; Winship, 1980). A strategy that advertisers have long used, for example, is an appeal to being the "new," modern woman.

Female imagery figures prominently in the symbolism of consumption for at least two reasons. First, women are major consumers, at least of products designed for everyday household and personal use. Second, women have traditionally symbolized desire and desirability, specifically in its sexual form. In this respect, images of women in advertising stand side by side with women's images in everything from classical painting to modern media such as news, pornography or romance fiction (see Berger, 1972). Women are depicted as objects of desire for both males and females to look at, but with a crucial difference: when women look at sexualized images of women, they are effectively looking at themselves being looked at by men (Berger, 1972 : 46–47).

The appeal to women as consumers works through both sides of the dichotomy. Advertising for household products, for example, confronts women with images of themselves as competent homemakers—wives and mothers—able to reconcile the demands of sick spouses, messy children, hungry pets, dirty ovens, etc. Yet, the advertiser's woman still has the time and energy (not to mention money) to look and stay attractive (if only because she is now pursuing a professional career outside the home as well). If not exactly depicted as a sex object, the competent homemaker still conforms to its implications—never too old or too young, never visibly disfigured, usually cheerful, willing, smiling, middle class, safely heterosexual and white.

These connotations of attractiveness are made most explicit when women are portrayed openly as sexual—in ads for health and beauty care products and clothing fashion, and also as made-up accessories to products pitched at male consumers, such as alcohol and cars. In these images of desirable femininity, women are often put outside the world of culture and history and their sexuality represented as if it were inherent and natural, yet made simply with men in mind. Advertising plays off themes

"I AM AS WELL AS I WISH TO BE."

Miss Blake of Hamilton, Ont., After Using Paine's Celery Compound, is a Picture of Womanly Vigor and Beauty.

A Story For All Who Stand in Need of Perfect Health.

"I am now a new woman. Can enjoy life, and am as well as I wish to be."

THE GLOBE AND MAIL, SATURDAY, NOVEMBER 2, 1895.

of nature and naturalism a good deal, but usually through some accompanying association with feminine sexuality. Women, like nature, are portrayed as mysterious, exotic, alluring, *different* (Williamson, 1986a, 1986b).

While these images may not seem realistic, they are powerful nonetheless because they speak to and feed off the ideological expectations and ideals that women confront daily. Advertising does not invent its contents from scratch, but takes up values, desires, images and symbols that already exist and circulate in the broader culture. What it does with these raw materials is to accentuate them, and open up the gap between the ideal and the actual. Advertising isn't realistic in the literal sense—if it were, it wouldn't work—yet it has to work with reality in mind.

Conclusion

There is a tendency to speak of the mass media, unlike other social institutions, as if they were separated from the rest of social life and suspended ambivalently above it. The conclusion that emerges from this overview of perspectives and issues, however, is that this image of the media is a misleading one. In whatever respect we examine—effects, content or organization—the media are fully implicated in the flux of social life, not only as a source of influence, but as a recipient as well. Most major developments in the history of modern society have been related in some way to technological and social changes in communications that have extended the scope of "mass" culture by intensifying the movement or passage of goods, people and information—from the railway, telegraph and telephone to the automobile, radio, TV and computer. It is this movement or flow that is the literal "ecstasy"—the *ex stasis*, or putting out of place—of mass communication.

Summary

The term mass communications media is generally used now to refer to newspapers, magazines, radio, television and movies in a way that combines both the institutional and cultural aspects. Mass media are organizations oriented to the goal of producing cultural products (symbolic goods and services) for mass consumption. As such, the media play a central role in both the economic and cultural life of society, and this dual role has given rise to a number of different theories about their structure and functions. Functional theories, for example, focus chiefly on the way the media contribute to social integration. This contrasts with critical theories where the focus shifts to the way the media perpetuate the economic, political and ideological power of dominant groups and interests. Technological theories, on the other hand, emphasize the effects of media as technologies of communication on individual perception, social institutions and processes of social change.

Whatever the theoretical perspective, one of the dominant questions that continues to be asked about the mass media concerns their *effects*. In the case of the news media, the main perspective has been that of agenda setting, which examines the way the media influence public opinion about the salience of current social issues. The research supports the argument that the media are effective in telling people what to think about, rather than what to think. But the area where the study of media effects has been the most prominent, and controversial, is television, which is properly seen as the most powerful mass medium. The study of television's effects has concentrated especially on children, and the research to date does suggest that TV slows down the development of literacy and problem-solving skills. It may well do this, however, through the way it displaces other activities that promote the development of these skills, rather than through the process of learning and role model identification. These account more for the effect of TV on violent behaviour and sex-role stereotyping.

Research on the structure of the media has fallen into roughly two perspectives. The political economy of mass communications focuses on the question of media ownership and control, and particularly on the relationship between the state and private capital as the two dominant centres of media power. All of the main media in Canada have high degrees of ownership concentration, but none more so than newspapers, where a system of chain ownership has gradually developed over the last hundred years. Chain ownership usually entails both the horizontal and vertical integration of corporate assets. Horizontal integration refers to the ownership of various media outlets, often in different media industries, by the same proprietor. Vertical integration means unified ownership and control of all the various stages of media production and distribution. In the case of broadcasting (radio and TV), the involvement of the state, primarily through the CBC, has done little to reduce the overall effect of concentrated media power.

The second perspective on media structure is organizational and occupational: the study of the media as formal work organizations with a division of labour and systems of bureaucratic control and co-ordination. Much of the researchers' attention has been directed to news media and to the potential for conflict between the bureaucratic and professional aspects of the work system. Like other large bureaucracies that employ professionals, news organizations develop structures that have to allow for the exercise of individual decision making about the work process. At the same time, the commitment to organizational goals is ensured in a variety of ways, particularly through the informal socialization process that new journalists undergo. This is reinforced by the way the formal structure of the newsroom serves as a potential career system that allows the individual opportunity for promotion and advancement through the beat system and into management ranks. Constraints on the work process also come from the pressure of meeting deadlines, and the need to rely on outside sources of information for the development of news stories.

The various pressures that operate on news reporting mean that news coverage is necessarily partial and limited in its perspective. The actual structure of this bias has been the subject of a great deal of attention, and much recent research has been concerned with the way news bias has a more systematic *ideological* character to it. Ideological news bias refers not to the conscious attempt to distort information, but to the deeper, taken-for-granted ways in which news acquires a definite perspective or point of view that excludes alternative or even opposing ways of understanding social reality. Most news coverage of sexual violence against women, for example, pays more attention to the whereabouts and state of the victim than the offender, but does so in a way that *implicitly* points the finger of blame at the victim for not policing her behaviour carefully enough. This bias isn't intentional. It results, rather, from the conjunction of a number of factors, such as taken-for-granted assumptions about the need for women to be careful, reporter reliance on the police as the primary source of information and the absence of any "hard" information about the offender. Nonetheless, the overall effect is to reinforce cultural stereotypes and prejudices about women who are the victims of sexual assault.

The area where sexism in the media has been most prominent, however, is advertising. The image of women in advertising gets split in two: woman as nurturer and mother figure and woman as sex object. In the first respect, advertising generates and plays off a desire to conform to the ideal standards of middle-class consumption and its association with the happy life of domesticity and the nuclear family. In the second respect, women are portrayed as the image of sexual desirability whose femininity, while clearly a social construction, is depicted as natural—yet at the same time made simply with men in mind. In both respects, advertising strives to create idealized images that are close enough to reality to be recognizable, yet distant enough to provoke the sense of inadequacy that motivates desire. The product being advertised is then set up as the means to fill this gap between the actual and the ideal.

This effect of advertising, of being at the same time both realistic and yet unreal, is characteristic of all mass media to some degree. It accounts for the way in which we tend to see the media as separated from the rest of social life and suspended above it. What are the media doing to us is the natural question we ask, rather than what we are doing to the media. The conclusion that emerges from this survey, however, is that this attitude is one-sided. Whatever aspect we examine—effects, content, structure—we find that the media are fully integrated into the flux of social life as both a source and recipient of influence.

Suggested Readings

Ellis, J.
1982. *Visible Fictions: Cinema, Television, Video.* London: Routledge and Kegan Paul. A conceptual and theoretical comparison of audio-visual media—the differences (and some similarities) in the structure of their images, the relationship between sight and sound, the structure of narrative, the role of the audience and the social structure of production. Uses mainly British and some American examples, but applicable in general terms to the Canadian context. Useful for essay topics 1, 2 and 4 (see ''Writing Exercises'').

Ericson, R., P. Baranek and J. Chan
1987. *Visualizing Deviance: A Study of News Organization.* Toronto: University of Toronto Press. A comprehensive and detailed study of the social organization of news production in a newspaper and local television newsroom. It discusses, analyses and illustrates the structural and ideological factors that come to bear on the process of news production through the various stages of story development—assignment, newsgathering and reporting and editing. Useful for essay topic 3.

Harrison, D.
1985. ''The Terry Fox Story and the Popular Media: A Case Study in Ideology and Illness.'' *Canadian Review of Sociology and Anthropology* 22(4):496–514. An interesting study, using a critical perspective, of news coverage of the final stages of Terry Fox's run across Canada to raise money for cancer research. The study shows how the news coverage ignored totally the links between cancer and environmental and social structural factors, emphasizing instead dominant ideological themes of life style, individual heroism and medical treatment. Useful again for essay topic 3.

Postman, N.

1985. *Amusing Ourselves to Death: Public Discourse in the Age of Show Business*. New York: Viking/Penguin. Critical analysis of American media culture (much of which is transported wholesale into Canada), especially TV, for trivializing politics and culture by turning them into forms of entertaining spectacle. Interesting contrast to Root (below). Useful for essay topics 1, 2 and 4.

Root, J.

1986. *Open the Box: About Television*. London: Comedia. A provocative and very readable extended essay on television that takes seriously the need to account for and respect the medium's genuine popularity. It defends TV against the middle-class armchair critics who dismiss the medium from an elitist or high-culture perspective as catering to bad taste and the lowest common denominator, yet it is also aware of the relationship between TV and dominant ideology. Uses British examples, but the general ideas are applicable to the Canadian context; good contrast to Postman (above). Useful for essay topics 1, 2 and 4.

Williamson, J.

1986. *Consuming Passions*. London: Marion Boyars. A very readable and thought-provoking collection of essays on various aspects of popular culture and media—movies, advertising, women's magazines, the women's movement, photography—from a critical feminist perspective. The essays stress the connections between sexism and other forms of power and inequality such as social class. The empirical examples are British and American, but the ideas are general enough to be used in other contexts. Useful for essay topic 4.

Discussion Questions

1. Usually an event is "news" only if it emphasizes deviance, conflict and disorder. Why is this? Are the news media giving us what we want or what they want? Are there any media that don't follow this pattern? Discuss this also with respect to violence in TV drama.

2. One of the implications of McLuhan's remark that "the medium is the message" is that social life is determined by technology. How true is this? If technology determines society, then what determines technology?

3. Discuss the ways in which sexual stereotyping occurs in the mass media. What do we mean by a stereotype? Is it only women who are the victims of sexist imagery? What are the negative effects of sexist imagery? How do we eliminate sexist imagery?

4. Assume you are the court reporter on a local newspaper and that you hear off the record that a judge, who also happens to be a good friend of your paper's publisher, has a serious problem with drug and alcohol abuse, and that this may be harming the way he or she does the job. What would you do with this information? How would you go about turning it into a news story that your editor would accept for publication? What are the moral, legal and practical problems involved in doing this?

5.   The boundaries between the different media and between the media and other social institutions and processes seem to be breaking down and becoming more and more blurred. Why do you think this is happening? What do you think the end result will be?

Data Collection Exercises

1.   Choose an American and a Canadian women's magazine (for example, *Cosmopolitan*, *Chatelaine*) and compare the advertising in them in terms of amount; size; product type; the number and social status (social class, gender, age, race/ethnicity) of people in the ads; the social setting and relationship of the people in the ads. How often do the words "new" and "natural" appear in the ads, and for what types of product?

     If you have access to a library that carries back copies of your magazines, repeat this exercise for an earlier point in time (for example, the 1950s). What changes and continuities do you find for the two time periods?

     What does your analysis of the data tell you about how advertisers define the consumer?

2.   Watch at least fifteen minutes of an episode of your favourite TV soap opera and drama show with the sound turned off, and analyse the visual images in terms of the frequency of facial close-up shots; the types of facial gesture people make to show emotion (happiness, uncertainty, disgust, anguish, distress, etc.); the number of times actors use each of these gestures; the number and contents of long shots; the ratio of indoor to outdoor scenes; the extent of camera movement (for example, zooming in or out of the same image, panning sideways or up and down). Compare the results for the two shows. What are the similarities and differences? How do you explain them? What do they tell you about how visual images create meaning? What do they tell you, by default, about the role of sound?

3.   Spend a couple of hours as a participant observer during an afternoon and again during the evening in your local TV tavern or bar. Observe the interactions between people and the TV set—how people watch and listen to TV in a public setting. Make field notes immediately afterwards on your observations, focusing on how attentive people are to the TV, and how this varies (if at all) in terms of such things as the gender, age and social status of the clientele, the size of the group people are seated with, the level of conversation noise, the type of programming on the TV set, or any other social variables that seem to be significant. Are there any major differences in the way people watch in the afternoon as compared to the evening?

4.   Choose a major news story and compare the way two newspapers have covered it. Pick at least five news reports (this can include editorials and feature articles) from each paper and break the coverage down in terms of which

sources are cited, how frequently they are used and in what order (primary, secondary, etc.); what angles are emphasized (Does the coverage concentrate on why an event occurred or on what its effects are; does the coverage play up elements of conflict and disorder or of co-operation?); what kinds of metaphors are used to describe the events (for example, incidents of violence and conflict are usually said to "erupt" or "break out," whereas co-operation and agreement are said to "take place" or be "reached"). Compare the data for the two papers, and give your interpretation of the differences and similarities, and what these imply.

Writing Exercises

1. Critical theorists from the Frankfurt school have been criticized for being elitist because they argue that the culture industry (especially the mass media) creates false consciousness and bland conformity through mass deception. The implication of this is that the masses are incapable of resisting or seeing through the manipulative nature of mass culture. How appropriate is this criticism?

2. The finding of Tannis MacBeth Williams and her colleagues in their study of the impact of television in a small town in British Columbia was that television works its effects through displacing other activities as well as through direct learning. Discuss why television seems to be able to displace other activities so easily.

3. How do you think the level of ownership concentration affects the content of the mass media? Discuss with respect to the question of Canadian content in TV programming and ideological bias in news reporting.

4. Outline and discuss how you would construct a non-sexist television advertisement for (a) beer, and (b) facial makeup. How would you deal with the problem of the broader social and cultural context of sexism in which the ads will exist? Would you try to portray the product in a sexually neutral way, or would you use reverse sexism to make an impact on the viewer?

Glossary

Agenda setting: *this refers to the ways in which the media establish different social, political and economic issues as priorities for public concern and discussion.*

Beat system: *denotes the division of labour among news reporters between generalists and specialists. The latter cover a regular beat, that is, a specific area of interest, usually defined in some way in relation to the state, for example, politics, crime, education, courts, health. Generalists cover all kinds of topics and issues, differing on a day-to-day basis. Beat systems are usually more elaborate in newspapers than TV or radio news.*

Chain ownership: *usually used in reference to newspaper ownership, but can be used with respect to* *other media. It refers to the ownership of several different media outlets, located in different places, by the same proprietor.*

Communications: *from the Latin term meaning to unify, it evolved into a word meaning to move or transfer something, initially physical goods, then later information, ideas and knowledge.*

Displacement effect: *denotes the effect of the media in taking time and interest away from other activities such as reading or socializing, and the subsequent effect this may have on attitudes and behaviour. It contrasts with the direct learning or modelling effects of the media. Usually used to refer specifically to the effects of TV.*

Mass: *Latin origin meaning a large, dense, amorphous body of material that could be easily shaped and reshaped. Its meaning has developed along two opposite political lines: a conservative, pejorative sense referring to the working and lower classes as rootless, dangerous and easily deceived and manipulated, and a radical, positive sense referring to the working and lower classes as the bearers of democratic and/or socialist principles and values. The conservative sense carries cultural connotations of bad taste, whereas the radical sense implies popular appeal and involvement.*

Media (pl. of medium): *channels or means of communication. The term is used now, often indiscriminately, to denote the senses (sight, sound, etc.), technology (print, electronic media, etc.), symbolic systems (painting, sculpture, music, etc.) and social institutions (radio, TV, cinema, etc.).*

References

Altheide, D.
> 1976. *Creating Reality: How TV News Distorts Events*. Beverly Hills: Sage.

Ang, Ien
> 1985. *Watching Dallas: Soap Opera and the Melodramatic Imagination*. New York: Methuen.

Audley, P.
> 1983. *Canada's Cultural Industries*. Toronto: Lorimer.

Baudrillard, J.
> 1983. "The Ecstasy of Communication." In H. Foster, ed., *The Anti-Aesthetic: Essays on Postmodern Culture*. Port Townsend: Bay Press.

Berger, J.
> 1972. *Ways of Seeing*. London: Pelican Books.

Bollen, K., and D. Phillips
> 1982. "Imitative Suicides: A National Study of the Effects of Television News Stories." *American Sociological Review* 41:34–51.

Breed, W.
> 1955. "Social Control in the Newsroom: A Functional Analysis." *Social Forces* 33:326–35.

Canada
> 1981. *Royal Commission on Newspapers*. Ottawa: Minister of Supply and Services Canada.
> 1986. *Report of the Task Force on Broadcasting Policy*. Ottawa: Minister of Supply and Services Canada.

Chibnall, S.
> 1977. *Law-and-Order News*. London: Tavistock.

Davies, K., et al., eds.
1987. *Out of Focus: Writings on Women and the Media*. London: Women's Press.

Dickey, J.
1987. "Women for Sale: The Construction of Advertising Images." In K. Davies et al., eds., *Out of Focus: Writings on Women and the Media*. London: Women's Press.

Durkheim, E.
1964. *The Division of Labour in Society*. New York: Free Press.
1965. *The Elementary Forms of Religious Life*. New York: Free Press.

Ellis, J.
1982. *Visible Fictions: Cinema, Television, Video*. London: Routledge and Kegan Paul.

Engelhardt, T.
1986. "Children's Television: The Shortcake Strategy." In T. Gitlin, ed., *Watching Television*. New York: Pantheon Books.

Ericson, R., et al.
1987. *Visualizing Deviance: A Study of News Organization*. Toronto: University of Toronto Press.

Erikson, K.
1965. *Wayward Puritans*. New York: Wiley.

Gans, H.
1979. *Deciding What's News*. New York: Vintage.

Golding, P., and G. Murdock
1979. "Ideology and the Mass Media: The Question of Determination." In M. Barrett et al., eds., *Ideology and Cultural Production*. London: Croom Helm.

Hall, S.
1977. "Culture, the Media and the 'Ideological Effects.'" In J. Curran et al., eds., *Mass Communication and Society*. London: Edward Arnold.

Hobson, D.
1982. *Crossroads: The Drama of a Soap Opera*. London: Methuen.

Horkheimer, M., and T. Adorno
1982. "The Culture Industry: Enlightenment as Mass Deception." In *The Dialectic of Enlightenment*. New York: Continuum.

Innis, H.
1951. *The Bias of Communication*. Toronto: University of Toronto Press.

Knight, G.
1982. "News and Ideology." *Canadian Journal of Communication* 8(4):15–41.
1988. "Stratified News: Media, Sources and the Politics of Representation." In P. Bruck, ed., *A Proxy for Knowledge: The News Media as Agents in Arms Control and Verification*. Ottawa: Carleton International Proceedings.

Knight, G., and T. Dean
1982. "Myth and the Structure of News." *Journal of Communication* 32(2):144–61.

Marcuse, H.
1964. *One Dimensional Man*. Boston: Beacon Press.

McLuhan, M.
1964. *Understanding Media: The Extensions of Man.* New York: Mentor Books.
1969. *The Guttenberg Galaxy.* New York: Mentor Books.

Morley, D.
1980. *The Nationwide Audience.* London: British Film Institute.

Murray, J., and S. Kippax
1978. "Children's Social Behaviour in Three Towns with Differing Television Experience." *Journal of Communication* 30(4): 19–29.

Phillips, D.
1979. "Suicide, Motor Vehicle Fatalities and the Mass Media: Evidence Toward a Theory of Suggestion." *American Journal of Sociology* 84: 1150–74.
1982. "The Behavioural Impact of Violence in the Mass Media." *Sociology and Social Research* 66: 560–68.

Root, J.
1986. *Open the Box: About Television.* London: Comedia.

Rutherford, P.
1979. *The Making of the Canadian Media.* Toronto: McGraw-Hill Ryerson.
1982. *A Victorian Authority: The Daily Press in Late Nineteenth-Century Canada.* Toronto: University of Toronto Press.

Schramm, W., et al.
1961. *Television in the Lives of Our Children.* Stanford: Stanford University Press.

Smythe, D.
1981. *Dependency Road: Communications, Capitalism, Consciousness, Canada.* Norwood, N.J.: Ablex.

Tumber, H.
1982. *Television and the Riots.* London: British Film Institute.

Tunstall, J., and D. Walker
1981. *Media Made in California.* Oxford: Oxford University Press.

Voumvakis, S., and R. Ericson
1984. *News Accounts of Attacks on Women.* Toronto: University of Toronto Centre of Criminology.

Warner, M.
1971. "Organizational Context and Control of Policy in the Television Newsroom: A Participant Observation Study." *British Journal of Sociology* 12: 283–94.

Williams, R.
1976. *Keywords.* London: Fontana.

Williams, T. M., et al., eds.
1986. *The Impact of Television.* Orlando: Academic Press.

Williamson, J.
1979. *Decoding Advertisements.* London: Marion Boyars.
1986a. *Consuming Passions: The Dynamics of Popular Culture.* London: Marion Boyars.
1986b. "Woman Is an Island: Femininity and Colonization." In T. Modleski, ed., *Studies in Entertainment.* Bloomington: Indiana University Press.

Winship, J.

    1980. "Sexuality for Sale." In S. Hall et al., eds., *Culture, Media, Language*. London: Hutchinson.

Winter, J., et al.

    1982. "Issue-Specific Agenda-Setting: The Whole is Less than the Sum of its Parts." *Canadian Journal of Communication* 8(2) : 1–10.

Wright, C.

    1975. *Mass Communication: A Sociological Perspective*. New York: Random House.

CHAPTER 16

Political and State Institutions

PETER SINCLAIR

The House of Commons, Ottawa. In the centre of the picture is the speaker's chair; the seats to his or her right are filled by members of the government; to the left are the seats of the opposition parties.

NATIONAL ARCHIVES OF CANADA/PA 67522.

Introduction

How can some people control others? Why do some people consistently have a greater say in decisions? Why do people accept authority? What makes people vote as they do? Such questions have long fascinated political sociologists. This chapter will introduce you to some of their ideas and set out important issues.

Social Power and Authority

What is social power? For Max Weber, *power* is "the probability that one actor within a social relationship will be in a position to carry out his own will despite resistance" (Weber, 1968 : 53). Weber also recognized group power: "We understand by 'power' the chance of a man or *a number of men* to realize their own will in a communal action even against the resistance of others" (1968 : 180, emphasis added). Power in this sense is a component of all social relationships. Sometimes, as in friendship groups, the participants appear more or less equal in their ability to achieve their wishes; in others, such as master-servant relationships, inequality is more evident. Yet, power relationships are not fixed; they may change when those involved change their strategies or objectives, and when the resources that provide the basis for power (such as money, weapons, information, organization) are distributed differently.

Types of Authority

For Weber, domination "is the probability that a command with a specific content will be obeyed by a given group of persons" (Weber, 1968 : 53). This domination may be based on purely material interests, custom or idealistic motives, but normally it is accompanied by a belief in legitimacy. Thus, legitimate domination or *authority* exists when people accept that the person making a command has the right to do so.

Authority is power considered legitimate by those subject to it. Weber identified three types of authority according to the source of this legitimacy. Authority is *traditional* when people obey because that is the way things have always been done—according to "the sanctity of immemorial traditions" (Weber, 1968 : 215). As long as the ruler does not try to extend his or her traditional rights, he or she is unlikely to meet with opposition. The power of chiefs and elders in tribal societies would be a good example, and so too would be the power of the husband or father in patriarchal families in which his rights have not been challenged. Some wives accept that their husbands have a right to ask for meals on the table at specific times, or perhaps to change house and community without opposition from others in the household. This is traditional authority in practice.

Charismatic authority rests on "devotion to the exceptional sanctity, heroism or exemplary character of an individual person, and of the normative patterns or order revealed or ordained by him" (Weber, 1968 : 215). The person with charisma is thought able to resolve problems beyond the capacity of ordinary people. Belief in such exceptional powers is the source of obedience. Charismatic authority does not require that the dominant person really possess such capacity, although it would be normal for the charismatic figure to point to some signs of success as proof of charisma. Weber saw charisma as a revolutionary force, arising in troubled times, that permits the bonds of tradition to be broken. However, he did not clearly specify the circumstances under which charismatic authority will appear or decline. Some examples of charismatic figures who have wielded enormous political power are Hitler, Mao Tse-tung and Gandhi. In various ways, each challenged the status quo and persuaded millions to commit themselves to movements for change.

Weber's third form of authority is a feature of contemporary industrial societies. *Rational-legal* authority is based on "a belief in the legality of enacted rules and the right of those elevated to authority under such rules to issue commands" (Weber, 1968:215). A person is obeyed because the request is associated with that person's office or position and is permitted by the rules of that office; it is not personal authority. The rules would apply to anyone in that office. Generally, the organization of modern bureaucracies, both state and private, best reflects this kind of authority, because those in higher-ranked positions may command those in lower offices within the limits of their jurisdiction. For example, managers may expect secretaries to type reports during the working day because they have the authority to make such requests. Demands for sexual services, however, would lie outside the boundaries of the manager's rational-legal authority. Another example of rational-legal authority is the professional-client relationship. It is considered appropriate by most people that those who possess

A bureaucratic work setting.

DICK HEMINGWAY.

specialized knowledge should be able to exercise control within their sphere of competence. The physician, for example, can persuade most patients to endure unpleasant and undignified procedures even when the patients do not fully understand the reason for them.

Decisions, Actions and Power

Weber's contribution has been immense, but recent theory should not be overlooked. Steven Lukes (1974) stands out among modern theorists for his challenge to most earlier authors, especially those who focus on overt decision making. What might be called the standard view in political sociology was that a person exercised power when his or her objectives were reached despite open opposition, or when another person was compelled to do something he or she would not otherwise do. To identify power, the sociological investigator must find issues on which opposing preferences have been stated and then determine who won. It is assumed that people's stated preferences represent their actual interests and that silence on any matter means consensus. Thus, authors such as Dahl (1961) studied power by observing behaviour in actual decision-making situations.

Dissatisfied with this approach, Bachrach and Baratz (1970) pointed out that controversial or threatening topics might be kept off the agenda for public debate. They focused on a special kind of decision—those through which "demands for change in the existing allocation of benefits and privileges in the community can be suffocated before they are even voiced" (Bachrach and Baratz, 1970:44). Their focus is on opposition that is manipulated and stifled in the political process. Lukes's approach (1974) is more radical. The crux of his argument is that even people's perceptions of their interests (and thus what they take to be an issue) can be controlled. If this happens, people accept the existing state of affairs as legitimate, or at least they see little point in challenging it in public. Working-class Tories, for example, believe that privileged people are best suited to make national decisions and thus ought to have political power. To have one's position of control identified as legitimate by those subject to it is the most effective way of exercising power. There is no open conflict, but such situations nonetheless involve domination. Consequently, in studying political power from this perspective, we should focus not only upon open disputes, but also on the control of information and on how people acquire the values that lead them to accept authority, to become participants in a *culture of silence*. This evocative concept, coined by Paulo Freire, refers to a passive acceptance of inequality and lack of power in which people appear to acknowledge the legitimacy of their own subordination.

John Gaventa's (1980) work on Appalachia demonstrates the utility of this approach in a practical research situation: the investigation of the culture of silence among Appalachian miners over a prolonged period (from the late nineteenth century until 1975), despite a high degree of evident poverty. Apart from brief periods when their position was weakened by recessions, landowners and mine operators wielded effective power through a combination of power mechanisms. In particular, the poor miners and their families accepted the existing conditions because (1) their opponents controlled the vital resources of jobs, houses, land, stores, access to medical facilities and even the local electoral process; and (2) the elite controlled the opinion-forming institutions of the area, that is, the schools, mass media and churches.

Political Institutions

It should now be clear that one of the most fascinating and important tasks for sociologists is to uncover the distribution of power in society and the mechanisms by which it is maintained. Our particular focus here is on power and authority in political institutions, that is, the typical patterns of behaviour and values associated with decisions affecting society as a whole. These political institutions form a network of power relationships that we can analyse in terms of their internal structure and how they are linked to the surrounding society. Sociologists try to understand the character of any society's political institutions by describing them in terms of key sociological dimensions. The most important are the degree of centralization of power, the extent to which the institutional structure is viewed as legitimate (and on what basis) and the pattern of connection between the political and other centres of social action.

Key Questions for Political Sociology

1. Is the political organization open or closed, democratic or authoritarian?

2. To what degree are political office holders independent actors in the decision-making process?

3. What groups are best placed to influence political decisions?

4. By what means is political power maintained?

5. How are policies implemented?

6. Under what conditions has the political system developed and how may it change in the future?

Usually sociologists attempt to classify political institutions by relating them to a general theory of society and social development, but most contemporary investigators would deny the existence of any single, linear path of political change. At most, it is possible to discern several general trends, such as the increasing scale of government, more political intervention in social affairs, the rise of the nation-state and various forms of bureaucratic administration (Bottomore, 1979). But these developments proceed at varying paces in different locations and are so general as to allow wide variety in practice. In recent years, the state has been the institution at the centre of attention in political sociology as many thinkers have struggled with the problem of how to explain its emergence and its practices.

The Idea of
the State

To Max Weber (1946:78), "a state is a human community that (successfully) claims the monopoly of the legitimate use of physical force within a given territory." This is not to imply that force is the normal means of administration, but it is available when needed. The claim to legitimacy rests on one or more of the three types of authority previously described; yet, that claim may be challenged both internally and externally. Weber's definition, however, is silent on the routine politics of the state. In contrast, this chapter will treat the *state* as that set of procedures and organizations concerned with creating, administering and enforcing decisions that are binding on the inhabitants of a specified territory. It encompasses government, the military, police, the judiciary and public bureaucracy.

The state should not be regarded as a coherently unified structure. In practice, the parts of the state are loosely integrated and often work at cross-purposes. The Department of Finance, for example, may be trying to reduce taxation and state spending, while the Department of Defence is trying to promote modernized but costly armed forces. The state is a vital part of the *political system*, which in addition to the state includes interest groups and political parties. *Interest groups*, or pressure groups, are organized expressions of special interests that attempt to achieve their objectives by exerting political pressure on governments through lobbying the Cabinet and members of Parliament, by influencing senior officials and by building visible public support for their causes. A *political party* is a voluntary organization that aims to win political power by controlling the institutions of government. These interest groups and parties attempt to influence or control the state to which they are closely connected. The links are most obvious with reference to the political parties that govern states, though we should remember that many states are under military rather than civilian control.

Emergence of the
Modern State

The emergence of new forms of political organization from the eighteenth century to the present time is the subject of an enormous literature. Political development and nation-building (the emergence of nation-states in which the boundaries of state and national community coincide) are two of the most frequently used terms to capture the theme. Some authors focus on individual societies, such as Lipset (1963) on the United States, while other studies are comparative (Almond and Powell, 1966; Moore, 1969). Scholars have faced a great challenge in answering the question of why societies developed the different types of institutions that characterize their political lives. Why should liberal democracy appear so entrenched in Sweden or the United States, yet so weak in Germany and Italy that it was overthrown by fascism between the two world wars? What accounts for Chinese or Soviet socialism in contrast with India's capitalist, democratic route? Why have so many attempts at nation-building in the Third World ended in military dictatorship and other forms of authoritarian government? And what is to count as political development? What values are embedded in the concept?

Nobody has been able to deal successfully with every question, but such authors as Moore (1969), Bendix (1977) and Skocpol (1979) have written major stimulating studies. Among the finest works of political sociology is Barrington Moore's (1969) seminal investigation of the conditions that led to the major forms of the modern state—democracy, fascism and communism. His achievement is based on a comparative assessment in which the key examples of the capitalist path to democracy are Britain, France and the United States, followed, less securely and more recently, by India. A second path led to fascism in the cases of Germany and Japan, while China and the Soviet Union are the critical cases of communist development. To understand the routes taken, Moore directs us to the relationships among the major agrarian classes.

Rather than try to review all Moore's complex work, this chapter will only summarize the critical conditions he identified for the emergence of democracy, which he takes to involve the elimination of arbitrary rule and mass participation in the making of rules. The conditions are as follows:

1. Neither the monarchy nor the landed aristocracy should be able to dominate each other consistently. A central power must bring some semblance of order to the nobility; yet, where the Crown holds absolute power for too long, democracy cannot flourish. The histories of China, Russia and Germany make this point.
2. Without urban dwellers to counteract the landed aristocracy when it challenges royal power, democratic impulses falter. "No bourgeois, no democracy" (Moore, 1969:418). For example, the weakness of German towns meant there was no pressure to expand the scope of aristocratic demands in a democratic direction.
3. The development of commercial agriculture by the landed aristocracy is a key to democratic resistance to monarchy. In England, the aristocracy became commercial farmers and displaced the peasantry. This provided the basis of common interest with the urban bourgeoisie. Where landowners maintain an agrarian labour force in conditions resembling serfdom (as in Prussia), the result is more likely to be fascism if an alliance with the bourgeoisie develops. French and American experiences show that different forms of commercial agriculture are associated with different paths to democracy.
4. As capitalism develops there should be no massive reservoir of peasants that might be mobilized for fascist-type ends or form the base of communist movements. The United States never had a "peasant problem," and English peasants were drastically reduced in number. French democracy was more unstable in the nineteenth and twentieth centuries partly because of the large size of the French peasantry.
5. Finally, a revolutionary break with the past should occur. In this context, Moore points to the importance of the English Civil War, the French Revolution and the American Civil War as vital components of democratic development.

Moore is reluctant to generalize from these conditions to evaluate the fate of contemporary societies because he is sensitive to the fact that the early development of some societies necessarily changes the circumstances that others encounter (Moore, 1969:413–14). Still, his is a major achievement.

Another outstanding work is Theda Skocpol's study of *social revolutions*, which are "rapid, basic transformations of a society's state and class structures" (Skocpol, 1979:4). Her theory is based on an examination of the French, Russian and Chinese revolutions, with additional reference to Germany, Japan and England. She explains change as a result of how society is structured, and states are treated as key parts of the social structure that contribute to bringing about change. Skocpol also stresses a society's international environment much more than Moore does. Thus, she argues that modern social revolutions occur only in countries situated in disadvantaged positions in the international arena.

Like Moore, Skocpol places great weight on the actions of the peasant masses as a factor in the political outcome. She demonstrates that France, Russia and China were each characterized by conditions favourable to both political crisis and peasant revolt. Prior to 1917, Russia (to give one example) was a bureaucratic, absolutist state with a politically weak nobility and inadequate development of backward agriculture. (*Absolute states* were states dominated by monarchs who claimed to rule by divine right and were not bound by rule of law.) Conflicts with other societies placed Russia under pressure by showing up its military and economic weakness. Despite the land reforms of the nineteenth and twentieth centuries that eliminated feudalism, peasants remained impoverished by rents and redemption payments. Through their close-knit village communities, they could be mobilized against the existing order. Peasant revolts against private landed property, although rarely organized by the Bolsheviks, contributed to the defeat of the old state in 1917 and helped bring the Bolsheviks to power. The czarist state could not be defeated by internal pressure alone, but stumbled into its final crisis as a result of its military defeats during the First World War.

Wisely, Skocpol does not conclude her analysis with the rise to power of a new regime, but recognizes that the process of "revolutionary state-building" can last for decades. In the three cases she examined, popular mobilization against counter-revolutionaries and foreign powers facilitated revolutionary state-building. The outcome has consistently meant that new states are larger, more centralized, more bureaucratic and more concerned to mobilize the masses than was true of the old states.

Despite the majestic sweep of Skocpol's analysis and the range of evidence that she musters in support, she leaves room for argument and extension. First, the differences in origin and outcome of the three main cases are considerable. One must recognize, for example, that the success of the Chinese communists depended on their mobilization of the peasantry, whereas the Russian Bolsheviks had no significant rural organization. Indeed, Skocpol pays too little attention to the urban, industrial roots of the Russian Revolution. Another point (recognized by the author) is that general theories of nation-building are difficult to square with the historically specific factors that condition each case. Finally, Skocpol leaves almost no role for creative human action because she emphasizes so much the general structural conditions of change. It would be better to pay more attention to how those conditions have been judged and acted upon by organizational leaders.

The Modern State I: State Socialism

The Russian Revolution gave rise to a type of industrial society often called *state socialism*. It is socialist in that most productive property is publicly owned through the state, and state socialist in that control is centralized in the state bureaucracy (effectively in the Communist Party) rather than decentralized to collectives of workers. At best, working people have been consulted before decisions are made; at worst, they have been merely subjected to decisions of party leaders in a one-party state.

Although the Soviet state and those modelled on it are highly centralized, they are not monolithic entities from which all debate and dispute has been excluded, even in the years before Mr. Gorbachev's leadership. Interest groups and factions have struggled for control within the party. There has, for example, been a long-standing competition between advocates of a more decentralized economic system and those who believe that modern information-processing technologies can permit centralized planning to a high degree, even in a complex industrial economy. Until recently, the latter position has been dominant, but with the rise of Mikhail Gorbachev and his commitment to a more decentralized structure, it will be interesting to discover whether state socialism can be reformed from within.

Do Communist Party leaders form a ruling elite? Strictly speaking, the answer should be negative. Soviet rulers should not be considered the equivalent of corporation owners and managers in capitalist societies. The economy is not organized with the prime objective of private profit, and state property cannot be inherited by the children of Soviet leaders. Labour does produce wealth that is appropriated by the state, but allowing for some corruption and parasitic living, it is generally appropriated for subsequent public investment. Officials who occupy the higher circles of the state

Perestroika

Mikhail Gorbachev, in his address to the special Nineteenth Communist Party Conference in Moscow, spoke for almost four hours. Below follow extracts from the Soviet leader's speech.

"The basic question facing us, delegates to the 19th All-Union Party Conference, is how to further the revolutionary restructuring launched in our country on the initiative and under the leadership of the party and make it irreversible . . . .

"It is a fact, and we have to admit this today, that at a certain stage the political system underwent serious deformations. This made possible the omnipotence of Stalin and his entourage, and the wave of repressions and lawlessness.

"With state structure bureaucratised and the people's social creativity impaired, society became accustomed to single-option and static thinking. It is this ossified system of government, with its command and pressure system, that the fundamental problems of perestroika are up against today.

"We are learning democracy and glasnost, learning to argue and conduct a debate, to tell one another the truth. In raising the question of cardinally reforming the political system, we must proceed above all from a clear understanding of which of its qualities have stood the test of time and are needed today, and which have to be reduced to a minimum or overcome completely . . . .

"Perestroika has brought the question of people's political rights into sharp focus. Their implementation was affected particularly painfully by the command methods of administration and associated restriction of democracy. All this retarded and inhibited the process of overcoming the people's alienation from government and from politics . . . .

"I would like to dwell particularly on the political freedoms that enable a person to express his opinion on any matter. The implementation of these freedoms is a guarantee that any problem of public interest will be discussed from every angle. And there is no need to fear the novel, unconventional character of some opinions, there is no need to overreact and lapse into extremes . . . .

"We have defined the functions of the CPSU as the political vanguard. But to perform these functions, the Party should remodel its activity, the style, methods and forms of its work—from the grassroots level up to the Central Committee.

"The matter is, in the first place, that the principle of democratic centralism, which underlies the structure and activity of the CPSU, was at a certain stage largely replaced by bureaucratic centralism.

"The task now is fully to restore in the party an atmosphere of fidelity to principle, openness, discussion, criticism, and self-criticism, unconditional personal responsibility and efficiency. The main criterion of appraising the merits of a person applying for party membership is his stance and the part he really plays in perestroika. This demand should concern all people . . . . Openness, a critical approach and efficiency should reign in all elective bodies."

Manchester Guardian Weekly, July 10, 1988, p. 8.

apparatus may be able to offer educational and political advantages to their kin, but their families cannot simply inherit their positions in the state or the wealth accumulated and invested in the name of the state.

Unfortunately, this introduction can provide no more than a glimpse of the fascinating history and structure of states such as the Soviet Union. We must now turn to the institutions associated with capitalist industrialization and to Canadian society in particular.

The Modern State II: Industrial Capitalism

During the early period of capitalist development in Europe, up to the late eighteenth century, the core powers were characterized by absolutist monarchies in which the rulers were advised by aristocratic elites, leaving ordinary people without voice. This system began to crumble, first in seventeenth-century England with the Civil War, later in France and other parts of northern and western Europe, as the demands of the rising capitalist class and the ideology of government by consent of the governed proved increasingly irresistible. Despite violent opposition, the remnants of feudalism collapsed before the ideological and economic force of the new order. Political change was part of a process that went hand in hand with the expansion of industrial capitalism, which could not flourish where the factors of production (land, labour and capital) were restrained by feudal practices. Capitalist development required a radical political break with the past, as well as a technological and economic transformation.

Several general features of the modern states that emerged with industrialization were as follows. First, the political process became increasingly complex and housed in special institutions—the legislature, governing executive and administrative apparatus—that were now separate from the personal entourage of the Crown. Second, government was no longer the personal right of any individual. Action was justified increasingly according to the principle of rational-legal authority. Third, the new states rather quickly expanded the scope of their involvement in the regulation of social life to an unprecedented level. Fourth, as the means of force became ever more sophisticated and destructive, they were more effectively monopolized within the state apparatus by the formation of standing armies and "professional" police. Fifth, the boundaries of states and the concept of a national territory were increasingly associated. Finally, in liberal democratic states, rights of citizenship have been slowly extended to encompass the adult population as a whole (Hechter and Brustein, 1980; Poggi, 1978; Tilly, 1975).

Despite these common features, the states of the advanced capitalist world exhibit marked variation. Some are *constitutional monarchies*, which means that the formal head of state is a hereditary ruler advised by an elected legislature. Britain, Denmark and Canada (where the governor general represents the monarch) are examples. Others are *republics* with elected heads of state, for example, the United States and France. Some states are *unitary*, that is, formal power rests with a single central authority (Sweden or Italy), while others are *federations* in which powers are formally divided between a central authority and smaller territories within the state (Canada and the United States).

Electoral systems also vary; the most important distinction is between *proportional representation* and *single member, simple majority constituencies*. In the former, political parties are entitled to be represented in the legislature in proportion to their support among the electorate. Thus, a party with 15 percent of the votes would expect about

15 percent of the seats, although to avoid excessive fragmentation in the legislature a party must usually obtain a minimum percentage of votes cast to qualify for any seats. Italy, Sweden, Israel and Germany use proportional representation. The single member, simple majority system is the one familiar to Canadians. Here the electorate is divided into constituencies from which a single member is elected. An absolute majority of votes is not required. Hence, if more than two parties take part, the elected member may have less than 50 percent of the vote. In such a system, a party whose representatives obtained about 15 percent of the vote in all constituencies would not be represented in Parliament, in contrast with the result under proportional representation.

State Theory   Sociologists have attempted to explain the politics of the modern bureaucratic state by analysing the connection between the state and the social groups of which society as a whole is composed. Some have described the advanced capitalist societies, particularly the United States, in a way closely corresponding to the ideology of representative democracy in that they find no clear centre of power. Rather, it is dispersed among a wide range of competing groups, none of which consistently gets its own way. This perspective is often called *pluralism* (Lipset, 1960). In a more cynical interpretation, C. Wright Mills (1956) identified a *ruling elite* (composed of the highest levels of the military, political and economic structures) that holds sway on all matters of truly national importance. Some Marxists have viewed the state as a conservative force, in effect the instrument of the bourgeoisie, because of its dependence on the major capitalist corporations and the roots of so many officials in middle- and upper-status backgrounds (see Miliband, 1969). Other Marxists (Poulantzas, 1973) claim some independence or *relative autonomy* for the state in its relationship with capital because the state may have to resist certain short-term demands of capitalists (for example, reduced taxes and public spending) to meet the long-term needs of capitalism as a whole (for example, maintaining an appropriately educated labour force). Thus, the expansion of public welfare against capitalist opposition is sometimes interpreted as a move to shore up the future of capitalism by smoothing over some of the discontent engendered by unemployment, poor health care and unequal access to education. Finally, there has emerged a theory that claims a genuinely independent source of power for state officials based on the resources of the state that they control themselves (see Skocpol, 1979). Some evidence relevant to evaluating these theories will be presented in the following section. Whereas most state theory has focused on class issues, feminist analysis is beginning to bring attention to the state as a contributor to the subordination of women and as an institution permeated by gender inequality.

Canadian Political Institutions

Canada is a federation with a complex state structure in which the powers of legislation are divided between the federal and provincial levels. Although sociologists should analyse the social relationships within legislatures and governments, especially how decisions are actually made, they have generally left this work to political scientists. Sociologists usually link political institutions and the structure of society as a whole. The comments that follow present some central issues in the sociology of the contemporary Canadian state.

State and Social Structure

This analysis paints a rather black picture of unequal participation and social domination, although the situation is by no means peculiar to Canada. The Canadian circumstance differs in detail from other mature capitalist societies, but the general pattern of control has also been recognized in such countries as the United States and Britain (Dye, 1983; Guttsman, 1974; Useem, 1984).

Gender

Whether or not a particular social group is well represented in the state apparatus may not be decisive for the achievement of its objectives, but groups that are underrepresented are in a weak position to press their interests. The most extreme bias in the state's structure is the inadequate representation of women. While there is no reason to expect women to behave differently than men on many issues, it is more likely that the interests of women will be more effectively represented if they are present in decision-making positions. Regardless of whether or not women would be better protected by greater political participation, their absence for so long from positions of power is unacceptable, since it seems to rest purely on the ascriptive criterion of gender. Women did not achieve federal voting rights until 1918; and in Quebec, not until 1940. The sixty-five women elected between 1921 and 1984 amount to 0.8 percent of all elected members of the House of Commons in the same time period. In 1984, 9.6 percent of MPs were women, 15 percent of the Cabinet. In 1983, women constituted 6 percent of the provincial legislatures and held 5 percent of Cabinet positions (Brodie, 1985 : 2–4). Generally, in Western democracies, the more powerful the position, the fewer the women to hold office (Bashevkin, 1985). No woman has ever been a Canadian prime minister or provincial premier.

The position of Canadian women is echoed elsewhere in advanced industrial societies. At the national level, about 1980, less than 10 percent of the legislators of Britain, France, Italy and the United States were women. Margaret Thatcher's prime ministership of Britain remains an exception. Only in the Scandinavian countries did women fare much better, holding about 25 percent of the elected seats (Bashevkin, 1985 : 144). Women are cracking the bastions of male political dominance, but it is an exceptionally slow process, one that will contribute to, and yet depends itself upon, a general reorientation of attitudes toward gender roles in society. The socialization process must change before this incipient discrimination will disappear.

Class

The class bias of the Canadian state is only slightly less severe than the gender bias. The extent to which Canada's tiny capitalist class also occupies the pinnacles of state power has been the subject of considerable research (Porter, 1965; Clement, 1975; Olsen, 1980; Fox and Ornstein, 1986). In the nineteenth century, the wealthy were

TABLE 16-1
Female Candidacy and Legislative Office Holding, National Level

Country	Year	% Candidates	Year	% Legislators
Britain	1918	1.2	1929	2.3
	1929	3.9	1975	4.4
	1979	8.2	1980	3.0
Denmark	1979	21.8	1945	5.4
			1970	11.8
			1979	23.0
Finland	1948	12.1	1907	9.5
	1970	17.3	1948	12.0
	1978	26.0	1970	21.5
			1979	26.0
France	1968	3.3	1945[a]	5.5
	1973	6.7	1981[a]	5.9
	1978	15.9	1981[b]	2.3
Italy	n/a		1948	7.8
			1968	2.8
			1979	8.2
Norway	1945	13.2	1969	9.3
	1957	18.0	1975	16.1
	1969	19.7	1979	23.9
Sweden	n/a		1971	14.0
			1977	22.9
			1980	27.8
United States	1979[c]	5.3	1975[d]	4.4
			1979[d]	3.7
			1983[d]	5.0

[a]represents National Assembly members only.
[b]represents Senate members only.
[c]represents major party candidates only for House of Representatives.
[d]represents House of Representatives members only.

SYLVIA B. BASHEVKIN. 1985. TOEING THE LINES: WOMEN AND PARTY POLITICS IN ENGLISH CANADA. TORONTO: UNIVERSITY OF TORONTO PRESS, P. 145.

often directly represented in the state apparatus; in the late twentieth century, this is less common, but connections are still close.

For the years 1946 to 1977, Fox and Ornstein (1986) examine the extent to which persons in leading state positions also sat on the boards of Canada's largest corporations, universities and hospitals. The federal positions examined included Cabinets, deputy ministers, major Crown corporations, the Senate, senior courts and the governor general. At the provincial level, they considered Cabinets, deputy ministers, major provincial Crown corporations and lieutenant-governors. A link or tie was established if the same person held a position in both state and corporate organizations between 1946 and 1977. "Overall, more than 3300 ties connect the 148 state organizations and 302 private organizations" (1986:489–90). Manufacturing and finance firms were especially well connected to the federal Cabinet, the Senate and the federal bureaucracy. Provincial governments were much less likely than the federal governments to be linked to the corporations. Overall, the number and density of interlocks (that is, the actual number of interlocks as a proportion of all possible interlocks) increased substantially over three decades. An *interlock* occurs when any individual occupies a top-level position in more than one organization. When the number of individuals rather than organizations who are linked is considered, the number of ties rises to over 5000. We find that about 20 percent of members of the federal Cabinet, the Senate, senior courts and university and hospital boards held corporate positions at some time (see Table 16-2). These links are substantial, certainly enough to permit direct input of capitalist interests into the state arena, but "the data demonstrate nothing like a fusion of state and capital" (1986:502). Power can also be exercised indirectly through powerful interest groups that lobby government and appeal to popular opinion. Recently, Langille (1987) claims that the most powerful corporate group, the Business Council on National Interests, has been the effective architect of Canada's free trade policy. Still, a simplistic view of the state as the instrument of capital will not hold, but the data are consistent with interpretations that see the state as structurally connected to the interests of capital.

Even if they are not major capitalists, the Canadian state elite probably hold similar values as a result of common social origins and socialization. Olsen (1980) collected biographical data on federal and provincial politicians, senior officials and judges for the period 1961 to 1973. Representing about 1 percent of the general population, the upper class in Olsen's account provided 22.4 percent of the state elite in 1973; the middle class accounted for 69 percent; and the working class only 8.6 percent, a slight decline over the previous decade. These figures are based on the class position of fathers of the 1973 elite. Considering the previous occupations of Cabinet ministers, we find that 86 percent were lawyers, business people, doctors or other independent professionals.

Ethnicity   The composition of the federal state elite is also biased in relation to the ethnic divisions in Canadian society. In 1973, those of British origin were overrepresented in both the political-juridical and bureaucratic segments of the state, although the situation was more equitable than it had been in earlier decades (Olsen, 1977:204–10). Francophones were only slightly underrepresented by 1973. Thus, the preponderance of those of British origin was mainly at the expense of Canadians who belonged to ethnic groups other than the French.

State elites are not mere tools of capitalists (consider the bitter opposition to the Canada Energy Policy in 1979), in part because capitalists are seldom united on specific policies, in part because the state elites control key resources, such as legal authority, force and information, which provide scope for independent action. They are compelled

TABLE 16-2
Percentage of State and Business Organization Office Holders Ever Holding Any Corporate Position by Type of Office by Time of Corporate Office Holding

State or Business Organization		Percentage with Any Position in Corporation						Number of Persons
		Positions Not Concurrent		Positions at Least Partly Concurrent			Ever Hold Corporate Position*	
		Corporate Position First	State Position First	Corporate Position First	State Position First	Begin at Same Time		
Federal	Cabinet	4.5	14.7	0.6	1.3	0.0	17.9	156
	Deputy Ministers & ADMS	1.2	5.1	0.7	0.2	0.2	7.3	413
	Crown Corporation Executives	3.0	7.8	1.1	0.7	0.7	12.6	435
	Crown Corporation Directors	7.0	9.6	10.2	8.7	3.9	27.2	541
	Royal Commissions	10.0	17.1	10.6	1.2	1.2	27.1	170
	Senate	2.2	0.7	5.9	8.5	5.9	19.2	271
	Supreme and Federal Courts	18.4	2.0	0.0	2.0	0.0	22.4	49
	Governors General	33.3	33.3	0.0	16.7	0.0	66.7	6

						Total*	N
Provincial Cabinet	0.5	3.1	0.4	0.5	0.1	4.7	768
Deputy Ministers	0.9	1.8	0.6	0.2	0.2	3.1	650
Crown Corporation Executives	4.7	2.6	0.5	3.1	0.5	13.5	193
Crown Corporation Directors	9.0	3.8	6.0	3.6	0.3	18.1	365
Lieutenant-Governors	7.0	10.5	1.8	7.0	1.8	31.6	57
University Boards	6.7	5.3	10.1	8.8	4.1	25.5	1862
Hospital Boards	4.2	5.0	6.6	5.5	3.2	18.6	1386
Wartime Federal Bureaucracy	—	44.0	—	—	—	44.0	277
CMA and CCC	9.3	16.7	23.0	8.1	9.1	43.3	418
Business Policy Organizations	21.5	4.3	35.4	12.7	9.0	49.8	675

*Since a state or business organization office holder may hold more than one corporate position, the values in this total column are generally lower than the sum of the figures in the first through fifth columns.

JOHN FOX AND MICHAEL ORNSTEIN. 1986. "THE CANADIAN STATE AND CORPORATE ELITES IN THE POST-WAR PERIOD." CANADIAN REVIEW OF SOCIOLOGY AND ANTHROPOLOGY. P. 500.

to accommodate deprived groups to some degree to ensure the legitimacy and stability of the political structure in which their own careers are located. But having said that, the ideological compatibility of state elites and Canadian capitalists and the complementarity of their interests in maintaining the social structure from which they benefit inhibit the possibility of radical institutional change. Years ago, Presthus argued that the unequal distribution of political resources permits those with a vested interest in the status quo to enjoy more meaningful and successful political participation. His crisp conclusion remains valid: "The perhaps inevitable inequalities of political resources among interest groups mean that government, to some extent, is pushed into the anomalous position of defending the strong against the weak" (Presthus, 1973 : 349).

Political Parties and Elections

Do elections matter? Pluralists would suggest that even if the state appears biased in favour of privileged classes, men and anglophones, other classes and marginal groups may still hope to be represented through political parties on the grounds that politicians must be responsive to the population as a whole in order to receive their support at elections. Political parties in liberal democratic systems require success in general elections, thus they are closely tied to the state. We will now examine the pluralist position more closely.

Organizations and the Expression of Interests

One problem for the recognition and expression of interests is that the main political parties have usually adopted similar positions on most potentially divisive issues (Winn and McMenemy, 1976), although the clash on free trade in the 1988 election campaign is a striking exception.

Looking specifically at social inequality, only the New Democratic Party (NDP) persistently raises questions in this sphere, although the proposals of the NDP leadership have seldom gone beyond advocating the regulation of capital and the introduction of improved welfare measures. But the NDP has never enjoyed federal political power (except during the minority Liberal government of 1972–74) and has never received more than 20 percent of the popular vote. For the most part, the dominant Liberal and Conservative parties have been able to submerge issues of inequality by tinkering with the rough edges of a system they claim to be basically sound, especially because it protects the basic rights of personal freedom. Political campaigns have been run successfully as a matter of leadership or people, rather than principle.

How can many social issues be suppressed by the political parties, given that leaders are now elected and that conventions pass all manner of policy resolutions? A possible answer lies in the social composition of parties, particularly the people who attend conventions and hold office. Do they represent the structure of society as a whole, or are they drawn from a narrow segment? Lele et al. (1979) demonstrated the limited democracy of conventions. They found neither the Liberal, Conservative nor NDP conventions to be representative of the Canadian population. Moreover, convention procedures ensure advantages to party elites by permitting party officials to appoint a large number of delegates. When 30 to 40 percent of delegates fall into these categories, it is difficult to challenge the party leadership. At the constituency level, the possibility of packing meetings with "instant" members or conducting meetings with minimal publicity offers opportunities for manipulation, although the extent to which such practices occur is hard to estimate.

A person's social background is no guarantee that she or he will either understand or support the interests that are typical of that social group (as Williams [1989] recently demonstrates for Canada's political elite), but it is a disadvantage for any group to have to rely on the sympathetic perceptions of others. We should also note that Canadian parties try to incorporate representatives from regions and cultural groups where the party as a whole is weak. However, since class and gender issues are downplayed, they do not recruit on the basis of class or gender.

In the House of Commons, there has been a "modest increase" in how representative candidates are when their economic backgrounds are compared with the general population over the period 1965 to 1984, but the backgrounds of those actually elected are more unrepresentative than ever. By the 1980s, 87.9 percent of MPs came from the top two socio-economic groups, which encompassed only 19.5 percent of the total population (Guppy et al., 1987).

FIGURE 16-1   Occupations of Federal Cabinet Ministers

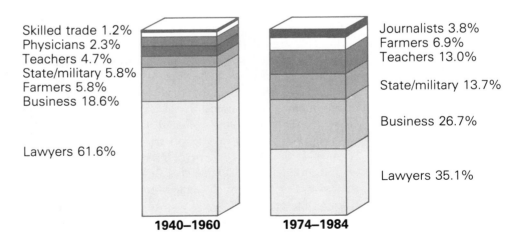

Skilled trade 1.2%
Physicians 2.3%
Teachers 4.7%
State/military 5.8%
Farmers 5.8%
Business 18.6%

Lawyers 61.6%

Journalists 3.8%
Farmers 6.9%
Teachers 13.0%

State/military 13.7%

Business 26.7%

Lawyers 35.1%

1940–1960   **1974–1984**

Neil Guppy, Sabrina Freeman and Shari Buchan. 1987. "Representing Canadians: Changes in the Economic Backgrounds of Federal Politicians." *Canadian Review of Sociology and Anthropology* 24:426.

Regardless of the party, party elites and activists come from more privileged social backgrounds. The typical party delegate to a convention is a male businessman or lawyer of above-average income and education. The same can be said for candidates for election to the House of Commons, and we know it to be valid for the higher levels of the state apparatus. Thus, "men, and higher SES [socio-economic status] groups, are grossly overrepresented in politics" (Guppy et al., 1987 : 427). The NDP does nominate and elect more people from lower-status groups than the Liberal or Conservative parties do, but middle-class people still predominate (Guppy et al., 1987 : 424). Of course, the connection of the NDP with the Canadian labour movement ensures some representation of organized labour in the inner circles of the party, while big business is hardly visible.

Canadian parties do not "speak" in class terms, which is one factor explaining low levels of class consciousness and the lack of expression of class interests despite widespread concern about economic matters. In 1979, less than half of Canadians identified spontaneously with a social class or thought that class conflict was inevitable. More Canadians identify with the middle class than with the working class. Only 3 percent of this sample maintained a spontaneous working-class identity over a five-year period (Pammett, 1987 : 274–79).

Voting

Voting is the most common form of mass political participation, the only one in which most people take part at the national level. Does a person's social position influence his or her vote? It was once believed that Canada constituted an exception to the predominant voting patterns of the Western democracies in which the main line of cleavage was based on class position (Alford, 1963). In Canada, ethnicity, region and religion (in the past) have been considered of far greater importance than class. However, the importance of class in Canada's elections has been underestimated.

Ogmundson (1975) did not accept that class is unimportant in explaining Canadian voting. He argued that we should know how voters, rather than experts, label the class orientation of the parties and did a survey to support his view. First, parties were classified according to whether people saw them as "for the working class" or "for the middle class." Then, the respondents were grouped by whether they worked in manual or non-manual occupations. Social class was found to be related to party support in Canada during the 1960s. Manual workers who perceived the Liberals as "for the working class" tended to vote Liberal, and so on. Using 1960s data, Ogmundson and Ng (1982) also show that the difference in class voting between Canada and Britain is substantially reduced when class images of the parties are introduced. Nevertheless, the association between class and voting in Canada was still only half as strong as in Britain. Hunter (1982), using data from 1974, found that socio-economic status and Marxist measures of class are also poor predictors of the voting patterns in Canada at federal and provincial levels, with the exception of Quebec.

Recently, Lambert et al. (1987) have again explored class voting, this time for the 1984 national election. With the class orientation of the parties defined by the respondents, socio-economic status accounted for only a small part of variation in

FIGURE 16-2   Canadian Political Parties, Popular Vote (percent), 1921–1988

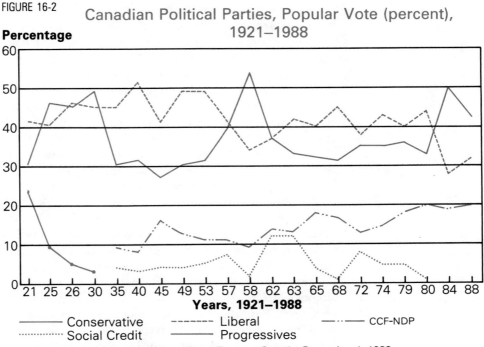

Thorburn. 1985:349. *Canadian News Facts*. Toronto, Canada, December 4, 1988.

voting at the national level, but the relationship was stronger in western Canada. Class voting was also more common in provincial than in federal politics. If the respondents' identifications with a social class and political ideology are also taken into account, the ability to predict party voting patterns is much better, but still modest. In particular, people who subscribed to a "left" ideology would tend to choose a party identified as "for the lower social classes."

The region in which voters live is frequently considered a decisive factor in Canadian elections. In the 1970s and early 1980s, the Liberal Party had only a handful of seats west of Lake Superior, whereas it dominated Quebec and battled for supremacy with the Conservatives in much of Ontario and Atlantic Canada. The NDP enjoyed strength in Manitoba, Saskatchewan, British Columbia and parts of Ontario, but was a minor political force east of the Ottawa valley. The Conservative Party in 1984 surged to the forefront in Quebec and became the only national party in that it elected MPs from coast to coast. Although a region can be associated with support for particular parties in Canada, one should hesitate to identify regionalism as a cause of the structure of representation. According to Matthews (1983 : 17–18), regionalism is best understood as the sense of identification that inhabitants of a particular area feel toward it. It is not a region as such, but the economic and social dimensions of life experience, which happen to vary geographically, that are likely to have some causal impact on politics.

Social factors do not allow us to predict accurately how individual Canadians will vote. In their analysis of the 1974 national election survey, Clarke et al. (1979) demonstrate that class, ethnicity, religion, region, community size, sex and age all have some effect, but much less than political variables such as prior voting record, concern about immediate issues and the image of the party leader. Should we then conclude that a sociological approach has relatively little to offer in this field? Perhaps not. A crude theory in which voting behaviour inevitably follows from social experience is obviously untenable. However, a more useful sociological account might start from the assumption that voting is an interpretive action. Voting is one way in which people respond to political situations in which they usually have incomplete information and inadequate understanding of the operation of the political system. As Lukes (1974) might argue, they are not fully aware of their interests and of how those interests can or should be acted upon. Social divisions and conflicts of interest are not unimportant. However, they are well camouflaged by political debates that imply a broad social harmony. Disputes are usually limited to the preferred means and individuals to run the country. Rarely is there any debate about what kind of society Canadians want, although free trade and the Meech Lake constitutional accord are important recent exceptions. Basically, the structure of society does not encourage adequate political involvement. Also, voters are less concerned with issues than with personalities, making it easier for the elite to dominate. The conclusion follows that voting does not really determine state policy; it provides legitimization for those who do control it.

Opposition and Change

At this point, the attentive reader may wonder how change is possible at all if the avenues to the decision-making core of the state are structured in such a way as to favour the dominant classes and other groups in society, especially men and those of British ethnic origin. However, it is important to remember that these groups do not have complete authority and domination. People are not doomed to be the passive objects of political manipulation, for the powerful can be weakened by internal division, by the intervention of international forces, by economic failures and by a general loss of legitimacy, while the "powerless" can mobilize to challenge for change. This has occurred on numerous occasions as disaffected Canadians have formed protest movements on a wide range of issues including labour rights, the status of women, Quebec nationalism, native peoples, agrarian interests, prohibition and poverty. The point is that the existing structure of political institutions is biased and tends to suppress dissent or to channel it into relatively innocuous activities; the structure, however, does not emasculate people's capacity to act in their own interests.

The continuation of economic insecurity, the massive changes related to the new micro-electronic technologies, environmental dangers and the threat of nuclear disaster may threaten the established political institutional structure. The impact of free trade with the United States, if it harms basic social programs and regional development policy to the extent critics have argued, may raise social issues to the fore and change political allegiances. The resurgence of a new Quebec separatist movement following the failure of the Meech Lake accord cannot be discounted. The conservatism of so many states, including Canada, may be only temporary. The probable failure of the new right politicians and of radical policies of economic austerity that are socially divisive (under a rhetoric of national unity and the national interest) may raise the level of polarization and open the door to a period of conflict that the existing institutional structure cannot contain or restrain.

Summary

This chapter began by introducing several key concepts for the analysis of political institutions. The most general concept is power, which enters into all social relationships in one way or another. Power often takes the form of authority, which itself displays several often overlapping patterns. The most important of these patterns for us is rational-legal authority, often considered a distinctive feature of contemporary industrial societies. Several contemporary sociologists have studied the ways that power is exercised without those subject to it being fully aware of what is happening.

Political sociologists are especially interested in political institutions and how they are connected to the rest of society. Foremost among contemporary political institutions is the state, whose emergence and varied structure has been analysed by several outstanding sociologists, including Barrington Moore. In his theory, whether the state takes a democratic or dictatorial form depends on the class relationships in the countryside and the possibility of revolutionary break with old, authoritarian forms of power as capitalism develops. Focusing on the French, Russian and Chinese revolutions, Skocpol found that revolutions occurred when states were weak in comparison with international competitors and internal peasant revolts could not be repressed.

The two most important forms of the modern state are state socialism and industrial capitalism. The most interesting recent feature of state socialism is how, beginning in the late 1980s, major decentralizing reforms are taking place in response to the economic stagnation and inefficiency associated with extreme central planning. In industrial capitalist societies, the scale and scope of the state have expanded, and in the liberal democratic states, rights of citizenship now include most adults. State structures vary from monarchies to republics, from dominant central authorities to looser federations, from those with simple majority electoral systems to others that use proportional representation.

We find our own state, Canada, organized to serve the interests of certain social groups—men, the capitalist class and those of British ethnic origin—more than others. Through political parties and elections, Canadians may hope to have their concerns adequately voiced, yet the social structures of parties do not coincide with the structure of society as a whole. Class and gender issues have usually been downplayed by politicians. Perhaps the avoidance of class by party elites is one reason that Canadians do not vote according to their class position to the same degree as West Europeans. With some notable exceptions, such as the 1988 "free trade" election, personalities have been more salient than class issues in Canadian elections.

Suggested Readings

Barrington Moore, Jr.'s *Social Origins of Dictatorship and Democracy: Lord and Peasant in the Making of the Modern World* (London: Peregrine, 1969) is a tour de force, an exciting, complex book on the main paths to contemporary state structures. From a more structural and international perspective, and equally important, is Theda Skocpol's *States and Social Revolutions* (Cambridge: Harvard University Press, 1979) in which she compares the French, Russian and Chinese revolutions.

John Gaventa, in *Power and Powerlessness: Quiescence and Rebellion in an Appalachian Valley* (Urbana: University of Illinois Press, 1980), manages to bring the abstract theories of social power vividly to life by portraying the domination of poor miners and their communities.

A number of important books have appeared on state theory in the last ten years. Few are easy to read, but one of the most thorough and provocative is Robert R. Alford and Roger Friedland, *Powers of Theory: Capitalism, the State, and Democracy* (New York: Cambridge University Press, 1985).

Somewhat dated, but still a valuable reference on the Canadian state, is the collection of essays edited by Leo Panitch, *The Canadian State: Political Economy and Political Power* (Toronto: University of Toronto Press, 1977). The growing attention to gender in politics is well reflected in Janine Brodie, *Women and Politics in Canada* (Toronto: McGraw-Hill Ryerson, 1985), while an interesting historical and sociological approach to Canadian politics is provided in Janine Brodie and Jane Jensen, *Crisis, Challenge and Change: Party and Class in Canada Revisited* (Ottawa: Carleton University Press, 1988).

Students interested in keeping abreast with the literature, especially on Canada, should consult the articles and book reviews in *Canadian Public Policy*, *Canadian Journal of Political Science*, *Studies in Political Economy* and the major Canadian sociology journals.

Discussion Questions

1. Discuss the ways in which authority can be exercised. Give examples.

2. What are some common features and some sources of variation in the advanced capitalist states?

3. What sources of bias, if any, can we observe in the organization of the Canadian state?

4. Electoral institutions ensure that political leaders are responsive to the interests of the population as a whole. Discuss.

5. To what extent is class a factor in explaining Canadian voting?

6. Why do you think women are so underrepresented in the state's decision-making organizations?

Data Collection Exercises

1.   Select an issue that has been important during the last year in the province or municipality where you live. Using media sources and interviews with key persons (if possible) try to determine who was able to exercise power and why.

2.   Collect information on the size of public sector employment relative to private sector employment in Canada's provinces. Try to explain any variations among the provinces.

3.   Discover the gender composition of your provincial legislature in 1950, 1960, 1970, 1980 and 1990. What differences are there? How would you explain the change or stability?

4.   Attend a court and describe the people who represent the state. What occupational roles are they performing and why?

5.   Select any five Western democracies. Find out the percentage of electors who voted in at least three general elections since 1970. Try to explain any differences you observe.

Writing Exercises

1.   Write a letter to the editor of a newspaper in which you set out your views of the social impact of a political decision or an issue that interests you.

2.   Review Denis Olsen's *The State Elite* (Toronto: McClelland and Stewart, 1980). What would a pluralist have to say about it?

3.   Imagine that a Royal commission into the current status of women was established. Write a brief in which you argue for or against changes in the political process with regard to promoting women's involvement in politics.

4.   Imagine that you have the chance to contribute to a survey of the Canadian electorate. What questions would you ask in order to find out if they voted in the last federal election, for which party's candidate they voted and why?

Glossary

Charismatic authority: *a relationship in which a person is obeyed because of a belief in his or her extraordinary or even supernatural capacity to solve problems.*

Culture of silence: *a passive acceptance of inequality and lack of power with the result that those who exercise control are not challenged.*

Interlock: *in this context, an interlock occurs when any individual occupies a top-level position in more than one organization.*

Pluralism: *a view of contemporary political life that sees power based on open competition in which there are no inevitable winners and in which any person or group can take part.*

Political party: *a voluntary organization that aims to win political power by controlling the institutions of government.*

Power: *the capacity to achieve objectives, even when opposed.*

Rational-legal authority: *a relationship in which a person is obeyed because he or she occupies a particular position and commands according to the rules associated with the position.*

Relative autonomy: *applied to the state, it suggests that the state has the freedom to reject immediate demands of capital when the longer-term interests of capitalism require other actions.*

Revolution: *a rapid transformation of the organizational structure of society, which is often but not necessarily accomplished through violent means.*

Ruling elite: *a small group, based at the apex of political and economic structures, that makes all critical decisions.*

State: *the set of procedures and organizations concerned with creating, administering and enforcing decisions that are binding on the inhabitants of a specified territory.*

State socialism: *a type of society in which the productive property is collectively owned, but economic control is exercised through centralized state institutions.*

Traditional authority: *a relationship in which a person is obeyed because the command reflects established practice.*

References

Alford, R. Robert
1963. *Party and Society*. Chicago: Rand McNally.

Almond, Gabriel, and G. Bingham Powell
1966. *Comparative Politics: A Developmental Approach*. Boston: Little, Brown.

Bachrach, Peter, and Morton S. Baratz
1970. *Power and Poverty*. New York: Oxford University Press.

Bashevkin, Sylvia B.
1985. *Toeing the Lines: Women and Party Politics in English Canada*. Toronto: University of Toronto Press.

Bendix, Reinhard
1977. *Nation-Building and Citizenship*. Berkeley: University of California Press.

Bottomore, Tom
1979. *Political Sociology*. London: Hutchinson.

Brodie, Janine
1985. *Women and Politics in Canada*. Toronto: McGraw-Hill Ryerson.

Clarke, H. D., J. Jensen, L. Leduc and J. H. Pammett
1979. *Political Choice in Canada*. Toronto: McGraw-Hill Ryerson.

Clement, Wallace
1975. *The Canadian Corporate Elite*. Toronto: McClelland and Stewart.

Dahl, Robert
1961. *Who Governs? Democracy and Power in an American City*. New Haven: Yale University Press.

Dye, R. Thomas
1983. *Who's Running America? The Reagan Years*. Englewood Cliffs, N.J.: Prentice-Hall.

Fox, John, and Michael Ornstein
1986. "The Canadian State and Corporate Elites in the Post-War Period." *Canadian Review of Sociology and Anthropology* 23 : 481–506.

Gaventa, John
1980. *Power and Powerlessness: Quiescence and Rebellion in an Appalachian Valley*. Urbana: University of Illinois Press.

Guppy, Neil, Sabrina Freeman and Shari Buchan
1987. "Representing Canadians: Changes in the Economic Backgrounds of Federal Politicians." *Canadian Review of Sociology and Anthropology* 24 : 417–30.

Guttsman, W. L.
1974. "The British Political Elite and the Class Structure." In P. Stanworth and A. Giddens, eds., *Elites and Power in British Society*. Cambridge: Cambridge University Press.

Hechter, M., and W. Brustein
1980. "Regional Modes of Production and Patterns of State Formation in Western Europe." *American Journal of Sociology* 85 : 1061–94.

Hunter, Alfred A.
1982. "On Class, Status, and Voting in Canada." *Canadian Journal of Sociology* 7 : 19–39.

Lambert, R. D., J. E. Curtis, S. D. Brown and B. J. Kay
1987. "Social Class, Left/Right Political Orientations, and Subjective Class Voting in Provincial and Federal Elections." *Canadian Review of Sociology and Anthropology* 24 : 526–49.

Langille, David
1987. "The Business Council on National Interests and the Canadian State." *Studies in Political Economy* 24 : 41–85.

Lele, J., G. C. Perlin and H. G. Thorburn
1979. "The National Party Convention." In H. G. Thorburn, ed., *Political Parties in Canada*, 4th ed. Scarborough: Prentice-Hall.

Lipset, S. M.
1960. *Political Man*. London: Heinemann.
1963. *The First New Nation*. Garden City, N.Y.: Doubleday.

Lukes, Steven
1974. *Power: A Radical View*. London: Macmillan.

Matthews, Ralph
1983. *The Creation of Regional Dependency*. Toronto: University of Toronto Press.

Miliband, Ralph
1969. *The State in Capitalist Society*. London: Quartet.

Mills, C. Wright
1956. *The Power Elite*. New York: Oxford University Press.

Moore, Barrington, Jr.
1969. *Social Origins of Dictatorship and Democracy: Lord and Peasant in the Making of the Modern World*. London: Peregrine.

Ogmundson, Rick
1975. "Party Class Images and the Class Vote in Canada." *American Sociological Review* 40 : 506–12.

Ogmundson, R., and M. Ng
1982. "On the Inference of Voter Motivation: A Comparison of the Subjective Class Vote in Canada and the United Kingdom." *Canadian Journal of Sociology* 7 : 41–59.

Olsen, Denis
1977. "The State Elites." In L. Panitch, ed., *The Canadian State*. Toronto: University of Toronto Press.
1980. *The State Elite*. Toronto: McClelland and Stewart.

Pammett, Jon
1987. "Class Voting and Class Consciousness in Canada." *Canadian Review of Sociology and Anthropology* 24 : 269–90.

Poggi, G.
1978. *The Development of the Modern State*. Stanford: Stanford University Press.

Porter, John
1965. *The Vertical Mosaic*. Toronto: University of Toronto Press.

Poulantzas, Nicos
1973. *Political Power and Social Classes*. London: Left Books.

Presthus, Robert V.
1973. *Elite Accommodation in Canadian Politics*. Toronto: Macmillan.

Skocpol, Theda
1979. *States and Social Revolutions*. Cambridge: Harvard University Press.

Tilly, Charles, ed.
1975. *The Formation of National States in Western Europe*. Princeton: Princeton University Press.

Useem, Michael
1984. *The Inner Circle*. New York: Oxford University Press.

Weber, Max
1946. *From Max Weber: Essays in Sociology*, trans. and edited by H. H. Gerth and C. W. Mills. New York: Oxford University Press.
1968. *Economy and Society*, vol. 1. Edited by G. Roth and C. Wittich. Berkeley: University of California Press.

Williams, A. Paul
1989. "Social Origins and Elite Politics in Canada: The Impact of Background Differences on Attitudes Towards the Welfare State." *Canadian Journal of Sociology* 14 : 67–87.

Winn, Conrad, and John McMenemy
1976. *Political Parties in Canada*. Toronto: McGraw-Hill Ryerson.

CHAPTER 17

Economic Institutions and Power

R. JACK RICHARDSON

Economic institutions produce and distribute a society's wealth. Toronto's skyline is dominated by the headquarters of many of Canada's economic institutions.

DICK HEMINGWAY.

Introduction

What are economic institutions? How are they related to other types of social institutions and to society in general? How do they affect our daily lives? This chapter will examine the significance of economic institutions to society and to ourselves as individuals. First, we will examine general theories of economic institutions and their relationship to society. Then, we focus more specifically on North American and then Canadian issues of economic influence and power.

Defining Economic Institutions

Societies consist of people, their relationships with one another, their activities and their values. But the groups people form are not randomly created, nor are their activities or the values they develop arbitrary. In fact, these all are shaped by the central elements of social organization in any society. We call these institutions.

More specifically, institutions are collections of organizations or groups that mobilize people and resources in ways consistent with the values of a society. Institutions, in turn, reinforce these values. Every society contains familial, political, religious, educational and economic institutions in one form or another. In some societies, these institutions are highly integrated. For example, the Bushmen of the Kalahari subsume virtually all of them under the institution of family and kinship. In others, such as modern Canada, these institutions are highly differentiated. Although they are interrelated in various ways, they each take on a concrete form of their own.

This chapter will focus on *economic institutions*, which we may define as the set of organizations, groups and processes by which people in a society produce and distribute goods and services. Between societies, these economic institutions may vary substantially, depending on: the society's basic mode of existence (for example, hunting and gathering versus manufacturing); the technology available (for example, Stone Age tools versus nuclear power and the microchip); the central values of the society (for example, co-operation versus competition and the primacy of the individual versus the primacy of the group).

Nevertheless, despite this diversity, economic institutions in any society provide the basic social organization for satisfying the material wants of the society's members. These wants include the necessities of life such as food, clothing and shelter. They also include all of the goods and services that form part of the society's culture.

Economic institutions perform two basic material processes—production and distribution. The production process combines land, labour, capital, technology and organization to produce goods and services. The distributive process recognizes the claims of the members of the society to share in the benefits of production. In other words, economic institutions produce and distribute a society's wealth.

Economic institutions are the central focus of the discipline of economics, so one might ask why sociology should study them too. Is it just empire-building on the part of sociologists? To this, we can answer with a firm no. Just as war is too important to leave to the generals, so the economy is too important to leave to the economists.

We will see in this chapter that economy and society are intimately related and that economic sociology tends to focus on relationships that cross the boundaries of disciplines. For example, economists study market and sociologists *non*-market relationships in economic enterprise. (Market relationships are those between buyers and sellers. Non-market relationships include a wide variety of connections between firms, such as common ownership, having the same individual sit as a director on their boards, membership in lobby groups, etc.)

Economic Power

When we think of power, we often think in terms of personal characteristics, as in the statement, "He is a powerful man." So, to many of us, power is perhaps merely an abstract form of physical strength. But to sociologists, power is a *relationship*, not an attribute. Weber, for example, defined power as "the probability that one actor in a social relationship will be able to carry out his own will despite resistance" (1968 : 53). Since power is a relationship, it can also be the inverse of dependence (Emerson, 1962). Thus, your power over me depends on how much I am dependent on you.

Power can be wielded within any of society's institutions. *Economic power* is, of course, wielded in economic institutions and originates in economic relations. It is an aspect of the economy that economists tend to ignore because of their focus on competitive markets and the impersonal laws of supply and demand. But power arises in the economic realm wherever an individual or group controls a significant share of a particular resource. This creates dependence in others who want or need that resource.

Weber (1958) proposed that the distribution of benefits in an economic exchange depends on the relative market power of the parties involved. *Market power*, in turn, rests on two interrelated factors in Weber's analysis. The first is how much the control of a commodity is concentrated in a few hands. The second is how effectively one party to an exchange can withhold a commodity from the market.

We can see these principles at work in the labour market and the wheat market. The labour market contains few capitalists and many workers. Thus, individual workers cannot affect wages by withdrawing their services. A major reason for the rise of unions has been the unionized workers' collective ability to use the strike to try to reduce this imbalance in economic power. (For a comprehensive analysis of strikes, see Chapter 21.)

Canadian wheat farmers, from the 1880s to the Second World War, participated in a competitive world market containing millions of independent producers. Throughout this period, wheat prices fluctuated violently. This happened because no individual farmer (or group of farmers) could affect the price by withholding wheat from the market. The central Canadian suppliers of their agricultural equipment and machinery, on the other hand, were few in number. Consequently, these suppliers could maintain a substantial degree of price stability in agricultural equipment by reducing production in times of falling demand. This vast difference in market power between the wheat farmers and their suppliers has been an important element throughout the history of Prairie society. While Weber analysed economic power mainly in terms of the relations of exchange, Marx focused on the relations of production. Marx (1954) proposed that those who control the means of production (the bourgeoisie) dominate and exploit those who do not (the proletariat). Nevertheless, these different analyses of economic power are complementary, not incompatible. For both, economic structures determine the distribution of economic power. We can view much of Weber's work as a debate with the ghost of Marx (Zeitlin, 1968), or as a positive critique and extension of Marx.

Classifying Economic Institutions

The types of economic institutions that have existed throughout human history are virtually endless. They range from the primitive communism of many tribal societies, through agricultural societies based on slavery and serfdom to modern industrial capitalism and socialism. Here, we will examine only a few examples to demonstrate the principal variables that differentiate types of economic institutions. These variables are the technologies employed, the division of labour, the ownership or control of the means of production, the principles for distributing society's wealth, and the degree to which economic institutions are separate and distinct.

Tribal and industrial societies differ in all of these variables. Tribal societies based on hunting and gathering or primitive agriculture employ restricted technologies suitable to producing what they need. Production is usually based on the kinship unit, which is relatively self-sufficient. The unit contains a rudimentary gender- and aged-based division of labour. Yet, there may still be some in the society who specialize in producing specific items, such as weapons, so there is a limited amount of exchange.

A Bushman of the Kalahari brings home a porcupine. Tribal societies based on hunting and gathering meet their needs (often very effectively) by employing restricted technologies.

IRVEN DEVORE/ANTHRO-PHOTO.

However, this exchange is based on *who* is involved and what roles they play. Property, such as the land used for hunting, gathering and tilling, is usually communal. Distribution of the products of the society's labour is relatively egalitarian. Any surplus produced is distributed on the basis of non-economic criteria, such as military prowess and tradition. In these societies, economic activity is densely interwoven with kinship obligations and religious belief, and so economic institutions are not distinct from other institutions.

In contrast, industrial societies use an extremely diverse application of machine technology. They have an intensive division of labour that results in workers being slotted into formal occupations. Whereas in tribal societies the available technology severely restricts the choice of what to produce, this choice is virtually unlimited in industrial societies. Yet, resources are not unlimited. Therefore, choices must be made, and how these are made varies between capitalist and socialist industrial societies.

Under capitalism, there is private ownership of the means of production. Those who own or control these means will make productive choices aimed at maximizing their profits. The forces of supply and demand largely determine these profits. Consequently, production is generally geared toward the goods and services in highest demand. Economic criteria determine the distribution of wealth generated by economic activity. These criteria include the ownership of the means of production, the market price of specific types of labour, expertise and technology and Weber's market power. Clearly,

In industrial societies, the diversity of technology permits an almost unlimited choice of what to produce. Here, a complex refinery produces hundreds of energy products, lubricants, and petrochemicals.

IMPERIAL OIL LIMITED.

in capitalist industrial society, economic activity is secularized, rationalized and distinct from other activities. Economic institutions are much less interwoven with other institutions, such as religion, the family and the political order.

Socialist industrial societies substitute public for private ownership. Productive decisions are based on centralized planning that aims to meet the consumer demand and political objectives, such as development and defence. They are not based on economic criteria. Economic wealth is distributed (at least in part) according to people's needs, rather than according to their position in the economic structure. There may be more links between political and economic institutions here than in capitalism. However, the economic institutions are distinct and well developed.

We have seen that economic institutions can take many forms. But what shapes them? Clearly, they are affected by technology, but we have seen important differences between capitalist and socialist economic institutions that share similar technologies. Furthermore, the Greek, Roman and Chinese civilizations developed many important technologies that were never widely used for economic purposes. Perhaps, then, technology both affects and is affected by the economy. On a broader scale, we might ask: Does the economy shape society, or is it the other way around?

Economy and Society

Marx, Weber and Durkheim all addressed the relationship of economy to society and the transformation from one set of institutions to another, for example, the transformation from a feudal to a capitalist society. A brief and somewhat oversimplified summary of their analyses follows, working from the simplest to the most complex.

The Transformation of Economic Institutions

Emile Durkheim (1965) proposes that economy shapes society but that economy, in turn, is shaped by the demographic variable of population density. Primitive societies, he argues, have a sparse population and a rudimentary division of labour. Nearly everyone fills similar occupational roles. Because of this common base, the members of society behave alike and share a set of beliefs or a "collective conscience." Hence, there is an idealistic basis for maintaining social order. However, the economic base of self-sufficient production fosters little interdependence among people. Therefore, there is no structural basis for social integration. The society will lose its identity if it tolerates deviance or even individuality. The collective conscience, then, must be maintained and reinforced by repressive and punitive laws. Durkheim calls the economically determined basis for this type of social order *mechanical solidarity*.

The population density may increase to the point where a simple division of labour no longer allows the society's members to survive. Then, Durkheim believes that a much more complex division must develop. This high degree of specialization produces a similarly high degree of interdependence among a society's members. Consequently, a new structural basis of social order develops, which Durkheim calls *organic solidarity*. This new, stronger basis of social integration no longer requires repressive law to maintain the collective conscience. In fact, the individualism and uniqueness of personality resulting from specialization is now desirable. Hence, in Durkheim's view, economy shapes society and economic institutions change in response to population pressures.

Marx (1970, 1978) also holds that the economy shapes people and society. "The nature of individuals thus depends on the material conditions determining their production" (1978 : 150). In his analysis, not only human nature, but also human ideas, laws, religion and social institutions arise from how people conduct their economic activities. These, in turn, occur within a specific set of economic institutions, which he terms a mode of production.

This *mode of production* is the foundation of Marx's concept of history, and changes in it represent distinct historical epochs. It comprises two elements. The *forces of production* represent the interaction between human producers, tools, technology and the material environment. The *relations of production* are the class, property and power relationships in a society (Zeitlin, 1968). Marx proposes that the relations of production are relatively static in any given epoch. The *forces* of production, however, are dynamic. They change with population pressures, the division of labour, technological developments and so on. The friction between these dynamic forces and the static relations of production causes class conflict. This eventually becomes severe enough to produce the objective conditions for social change (that is, change from one mode of production to another). For change to actually happen though, workers must come to think of themselves as an oppressed class and become determined to take action (Zeitlin, 1968). (For a much more comprehensive account of Marx's concept of history, see Cohen, 1978.)

Karl Marx on the Relationship between Economy and Society

The general conclusion at which I arrived and which, once reached, became the guiding principle of my studies can be summarised as follows. In the social production of their existence, men inevitably enter into definite relations, which are independent of their will, namely relations of production appropriate to a given stage in the development of their material forces of production. The totality of these relations of production constitutes the economic structure of society, the real foundation, on which arises a legal and political superstructure and to which correspond definite forms of social consciousness. The mode of production of material life conditions the general process of social, political and intellectual life. It is not the consciousness of men that determines their existence, but their social existence that determines their consciousness. At a certain stage of development, the material productive forces of society come into conflict with the existing relations of productions or—this merely expresses the same thing in legal terms—with the property relations within the framework of which they have operated hitherto. From forms of development of the productive forces these relations turn into their fetters. Then begins an era of social revolution. The changes in the economic foundation lead sooner or later to the transformation of the whole immense superstructure.

From Karl Marx. 1970. *A Contribution to the Critique of Political Economy*. Moscow: Progress Publishers, pp. 20–21.

Marx's analysis of economic institutions and the relationship of economy to society is much more complex and conditional than Durkheim's. Nevertheless, they agree that economy shapes society. In Weber's analysis, the causal direction is unclear.

Some of Weber's analyses suggest that the economic base shapes society. For example, Weber (1976) analysed the decline of the slave-based economy of the Roman Empire and its evolution into a feudal society. He concluded that the disintegration of the empire was an inevitable political consequence of the decline of commerce. Elsewhere, Weber (1961) proposed that the political structure of agricultural societies and their systems of land tenure depend on their economic institutions.

On the other hand, he argued that military and religious motives affect economic developments. For example, he cited the need for large armies in continental Europe as a factor favouring peasant agriculture, which maximized population per acre. England, on the other hand, was protected by the English Channel and its navy and had much more modest military needs. This favoured capitalist agriculture, which maximized profits, rather than population. It also permitted the expropriation of peasants to meet the labour demands of the Industrial Revolution. Elsewhere, Weber (1930, 1958) identifies motives as the "switchmen" directing social and economic change.

To this point, we have examined the general classical perspectives on the transformation of economic institutions. Now, we turn to Marx's and Weber's specific analyses of the emergence of capitalism as the dominant economic institution in the modern Western world. Figure 17-1 depicts how Durkheim, Marx and Weber relate the economy to society in respect to social change.

FIGURE 17-1

The Relationship Between Economy and Society with Respect to Social Change

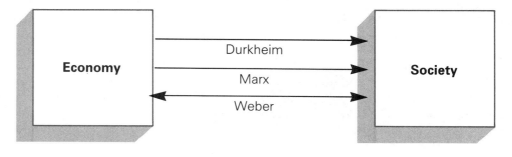

The Emergence of Capitalism

How and why did capitalism arise when and where it did? These questions were central to the sociology of both Marx (1954) and Weber (1958, 1961). There are many similarities in their conclusions, as we should expect, but also some important differences.

Both held that an essential precondition for capitalism was the separation of the labourer from the means of production. This occurred when feudal tenure was replaced by capitalist agriculture and the majority of English agricultural workers were thrown off the land between the sixteenth and eighteenth centuries. That trend was accompanied by new laws that created a class of labourers free, indeed *compelled*, to sell their labour-power on the market. Labour-power, then, became a commodity like potatoes.

Both Marx and Weber attributed the rise of the prosperous capitalist farmer to European inflation, which was induced by Spain's importation of gold from the New World. Both saw the manufacturing capitalist emerging via two routes. One was a slow process, where independent artisans employed more and more wage labourers. The other, faster one involved merchants and financiers expanding into manufacturing. Hence, both agriculture and manufacturing increased commodity production for an expanding market.

Marx (1954) concentrated on analysing capitalism as an economic system producing commodities and surplus value. Weber's analysis was more diverse. For one thing, although Marx certainly did not ignore the emergence of a mass market, Weber focused much more on it. To Weber, the rise of the mass market was as essential to the emergence of capitalism as the decline of commerce was to the end of the Roman Empire. He also extended Marx's analysis by placing it within a broader sweep of historical dynamics (Zeitlin, 1968). The first of these dynamics was the rise of rationality. This became institutionalized through technology, the marketplace, economic enterprise and the law. The second was the coincident development of bureaucracy, which separated the producer from the means of production, administration, science and war. Third, Weber (1930) examined the influence of religion on the rise of capitalism. He proposed that early Protestantism encouraged the self-discipline, hard work and individualism that fostered competition and investment. It also contained prohibition against conspicuous consumption. This combination produced the investment in and growth of industry that were the dynamic elements of capitalism.

As capitalism emerged in England, so did the doctrine of *laissez-faire*. This doctrine derived from the philosophy of Adam Smith (1894). Smith proposed that the greatest good for the greatest number was served when individuals pursued their own selfish objectives, constrained only by the "unseen hand" of competition. So government, other than acting to bolster capitalism *as a system*, left business alone.

It was from observing laissez-faire capitalism that Marx (1954) formulated his laws of capitalist competition. Marx concluded that competition forced capitalist enterprise continually to adopt the latest technology. Firms that did prospered; those that did not failed. Thus, there is a tendency for the economy to be dominated by ever fewer and ever larger firms. Not only is capital concentrated in fewer and fewer hands, but employment is also increasingly concentrated in the few large establishments. Dense concentrations of impoverished wage labourers then provide the conditions for developing the class consciousness and cohesion necessary to overthrow capitalism. Thus, ultimately, "the expropriators are expropriated" (1954:715). Marx correctly forecast the increasing concentration of capitalist enterprise. However, the inevitable revolution by the working class that he predicted has not occurred because of several factors he could not have foreseen. Small-scale enterprise survives to this day in labour-intensive sectors of the economy. We also find it in new industries where the entry of small, new firms offsets, for a while, the process of concentration. We have also seen that the increased productivity accompanying new technology has reduced living costs. This produces a higher standard of living for the working class than Marx forecast. Furthermore, concentration has reduced price competition among the few large firms in each industry. This has permitted wages to rise, because firms can recover the cost of higher wages by raising prices. Finally, laissez-faire capitalism has gradually given way to the welfare state.

The modern welfare state evolved out of the massive depression of the 1930s. Since then—until the advent of President Reagan and Prime Minister Thatcher, at least—there has been ever-increasing government involvement in the economy. The welfare state reduces the economic impact of unemployment, becomes a major employer in its own right and sets minimum wages for the working class. It also provides welfare for businesses through tax breaks and subsidies.

Large modern corporations have immense power. However, their power is not unfettered, for they are subject to significant constraints imposed by governments and the judiciary.

How the Economy Shapes Modern Society

The massive unemployment of the last decade shows the effect of economic institutions on society. In fact, some claim that robotics and the microchip will make chronic unemployment endemic in future decades as well. The unemployed are protected from complete financial ruin by unemployment insurance and other social safety nets. But they are often robbed of their *raison d'être*. If work is central to life, as many sociologists conclude, is it any wonder that unemployment breeds psychological disorders, marital break-up, drunkenness, violence, crime and suicide? Truly, private troubles are public issues (Mills, 1959), as the economy affects so many private lives.

The economy affects us all as consumers, as well. The dramatic growth in consumer credit since the Second World War has induced us to buy more and sooner than we otherwise would. This has produced economic growth and material prosperity. But it has also made us more dependent than ever on economic institutions as we struggle to pay later for what we buy now. It is also a factor in the dramatic growth of the number of families having both parents working outside the home.

Why should so many get caught in the credit trap? Duberman and Hartjen (1979) attribute this largely to the effectiveness of modern advertising. We are bombarded with images of the affluent society dozens of times every day. The accumulative result

In order to "keep up with the Joneses," North Americans contribute to Alvin Toffler's "throw-away society." Yet, what would happen to unemployment if planned obsolescence were eliminated?

MILLER COMSTOCK INC.

may not induce us to buy a specific product, but it makes affluence seem desirable and achievable. So, we buy our way into it. Vance Packard (1960) and Alvin Toffler (1970) espouse a closely related argument. They propose that economic institutions, through advertising, lobbying, influence on the school system and so on, have created the throw-away society. One element of this tinsel world is planned obsolescence. Industries design products—anything from light bulbs to pantyhose—that have deliberately limited life spans. Or they persuade consumers to replace their outmoded clothes, even through they are still perfectly functional. Many of us with a closet full of clothes still claim we have nothing to wear.

Until the late 1970s, the North American automobile provided an excellent example of industrial success in promoting Toffler's throw-away society. European cars have an average life span of about twelve years, and they rarely undergo superficial changes in styling. North American car manufacturers, on the other hand, used to make major style changes about every two years. They also used to make enough trim changes in the intervening years to make last year's car out of date. It was essential for people— if they were going to keep up with their neighbours—to trade in their cars about every two years. This had two results, just as the automakers planned. First, it increased the demand for cars. Second, cars were built a lot more cheaply because they were only expected to last a few years.

In the last few years, the throw-away ethos seems to be declining. Perhaps this is a result of changing values. If so, it suggests that society can affect economy. On the other hand, sales of paper plates and drinks in non-returnable cans continue to grow exponentially. Perhaps the process is circular. Recent hard economic times have affected our values. This has reduced the influence of the throw-away ethos, which has made times even harder by reducing demand and thus employment.

Economic Organizations and Society

Sociologist Charles Perrow argues that societies adapt to economic organizations more than organizations have to adapt to societies.

"Society is adaptive to organizations, to the large, powerful organizations controlled by a few, often overlapping, leaders. To see these organizations as adaptive to a 'turbulent,' dynamic, ever changing environment is to indulge in fantasy. The environment of most powerful organizations is well controlled by them, quite stable, and made up of other organizations with similar interest, or ones they control. Standard Oil and Shell may compete at the intersection of two highways, but they do not compete in the numerous areas where their interests are critical, such as foreign policy, tax laws, import quotas, government funding of research and development, highway expansion, internal combustion engines, pollution restrictions, and so on. Nor do they have a particularly turbulent relationship to other powerful organizations such as the auto companies, the highway construction firms [and] the Department of Defense."

From Charles Perrow. 1972. *Complex Organizations: A Critical Essay.* Permission granted by Random House, Inc.

Issues of Economic Power

Not only does the economy affect society, but many scholars have noted the pervasive economic base of social conflict. Peasants struggling against landowners, workers against employers, the poor against the rich, even racism and wars contain elements of such conflict. The First World War was a struggle for access to markets, materials and food—in short, for world economic dominance. From this viewpoint, the Second World War was merely the second round.

To Marx (1978), the essence of history is the class struggle. This economically based struggle is over the control of property—whether that property is human beings, land or capital.

The relationship between economic power and the state has been the subject of intensive debate. To Weber (1958) and modern Weberians, it is a complex relationship in which each element affects the other. On the other hand, Marx (1978) held that all struggles within the state are class struggles. At stake is the political power to represent the economic interest of one class as the general interest. It does happen, of course, that *segments* of a particular class also struggle for political power (Marx and Engels, 1950).

Modern neo-Marxist theory of the state is split between the *instrumentalist* (Miliband, 1969) and the *structuralist* views (Poulantzas, 1978). The former proposes that a cohesive capitalist class (or its dominant element) is able to manipulate the state into supporting its economic interests. The latter view gives limited autonomy to the state. It can respond to working-class demands while maintaining the long-term economic interests of the capitalist class. For excellent reviews of these positions, see Gold, Lo and Wright (1975) and Cuneo (1979).

However, in a critique of these views, Brym (1985) grants further autonomy to the state. He argues that one source of this autonomy is the simple fact that politicians and bureaucrats want to keep their jobs. To do so, they must not offend any class or group to the point that their re-election or reappointment is jeopardized. Although he grants that economic power greatly influences the state, Brym persuasively argues that it is not the only influence. (For a much broader discussion of the state and political authority, see Chapter 16.)

Multinational Enterprise

An important recent controversy about economic power concerns the emergence of multinational enterprise as the paramount economic fact of the present epoch. Many sociologists argue that these giant conglomerates, which operate in many countries, cannot be effectively controlled by any government. Vernon (1971) argues that the international operations of American multinational corporations are so vast that they have become a power unto themselves. They can defy the attempts of their own government to prevent them from exporting jobs. At the same time, they can export American economic and political power around the world. As a result of the rapid growth and incredible power of multinational enterprise (MNE), "suddenly, it seems, the sovereign states are feeling naked. Concepts such as national sovereignty and national economic strength appear curiously drained of meaning" (Vernon, 1971:3).

TABLE 17-1
Foreign Control of Canadian Industry, Selected Years, 1926–1975

Sector	% Foreign Controlled					
	1926	1939	1948	1958	1967	1975
Manufacturing	35	38	43	57	57	56
Petroleum and natural gas*				73	74	74
Mines and Minerals	38	42	40	60	65	60
Railways	3	3	3	2	2	1
Utilities	20	26	24	5	5	4
Total of these industries plus commerce	17	21	25	32	35	33

*included in mines and minerals prior to 1958.

STATISTICS CANADA, CATALOGUE 67–202, VARIOUS YEARS. ADAPTED FROM JORGE NIOSI. 1982. LES MULTINATIONALES CANADIENNES. MONTREAL: BOREAL EXPRESS.

The pervasiveness of MNE has concerned many Canadian sociologists and economists. Since the Second World War, well over half of Canadian manufacturing and other key industrial sectors have become foreign controlled (see Table 17-1). Although the degree of foreign control has declined slightly in the past decade, it is still the highest among the world's industrialized economies. This has prompted serious concern about the nature of our economy, our society and even our national sovereignty. Scholars such as Clement (1975), Watkins (Canada, 1970) and Brym (1985) have identified the "branch plant" nature of the Canadian economy. They propose this kind of economy has consequences as diverse as the serious drain dividend payments place on our foreign exchange; the retardation of Canadian industrial research; and the barriers to Canadian social mobility created by foreign-controlled branch plants.

A second aspect of the relationship between MNE and Canadian society has, until recently, gone unnoticed. Niosi (1982) points out the startling fact that Canada ranks sixth among the nations that are *home countries* for MNE. In fact, on a per capita basis, it ranks first! So, in two ways—as a host country for foreign MNE and as a home country for our own multinationals abroad—Canada is intimately linked to the world economy. To the degree economy shapes society, we are more a world than a national society.

Two further issues involving MNE are important to the relationship between economy and society. These are the questions of extraterritoriality and of values. Extraterritoriality concerns the application of the home country's laws in the host country. Since the laws of the countries involved often conflict, they can generate a "catch-22" situation for MNE. To obey the law of one country requires breaking the law of another. The Royal Bank of Canada was in such a situation. It refused to break Panamanian banking laws by releasing banking records of an important client to a Canadian tribunal. The Bank of Nova Scotia found itself in an even more painful situation. It refused to break Bahamian law by releasing client records to a federal grand jury in Florida. It was hit with a $25 000 per day fine. Ford of Canada and M. L. W. Worthington both risked breaking Canadian law and offending Canadians. They declined to fulfil orders for trucks to China and locomotives to Cuba respectively. To do so might have resulted in jail terms for the top executives of their American parent firms for breaking the United States' Trading with the Enemy Act. Such circumstances raise questions for both governments and MNE. Governments must ask: How can nations protect their sovereignty? And multinational enterprises must ask: How can MNE avoid catch-22 situations?

Should a multinational firm be guided by the values of its home society or of the society in which it is operating? Bata found itself in this dilemma in South Africa. The position of that legally constituted government and the values of the dominant white society concerning blacks are diametrically opposed to the values and laws of Bata's home country, Canada. Similarly, Northern Telecom restricted the employment of women to the most menial of jobs in Saudi Arabia. It did this in keeping with that country's values and laws concerning gender relations, which are different from our own. Both of these Canadian companies followed the values and laws of their host country, to the chagrin of many Canadians. But an American multinational, ITT, followed the values of its strongly anti-communist American *home* country by helping to overthrow the democratically elected Marxist President Allende of Chile (Bosk, 1974). This, too, offended many Canadians.

Who Controls Economic Institutions? We have seen that economic power is wielded not only within and between economic institutions, but also over other sectors of society. In the early days of capitalism, the owners of capital wielded this power. Many of these were *nouveaux riches*. The rise of this new and powerful class of capitalists was a revolutionary development in rigidly stratified societies. We need only recall the names of Rockefeller, Carnegie and Morgan, for example, to comprehend the extent to which those controlling the rapidly consolidating American corporations wielded economic power. Gradually, this control passed to the descendants of the economically powerful through inheritance. Then, capitalism became more of a conservative than a revolutionary influence on social stratification. And so, a self-perpetuating capitalist class wielded increasing power from the command post of the economy.

Then, Berle and Means (1967) argue, this power began to break down because of the very growth in size and power of the major corporations. This growth required massive infusions of new capital. This produced a wide dispersion of stock ownership and loss of control by the original owners. Management acquired control of (that is, was able to direct the activities of) the economy's largest corporations. This separated ownership from control. Berle and Means found that 58 percent of the top two hundred American corporations were management controlled in 1929. This proportion rose to 85 percent by 1963. Several other studies supported Berle and Means's proposition that, as a corporation grows, the likelihood of management control also grows.

Many social scientists applauded this development. They believed that management control of the economic power wielded by these dominant corporations would benefit society at large. It would break down the rigid class system and replace it with a new, more flexible system of stratification. Economic power would now be based on achievement and occupation, not inheritance. This would produce greater social mobility.

In the 1970s, however, many sociologists began to refute Berle and Means's findings. They argued that a family can retain control of a corporation with even a small minority ownership, if the remaining shares are widely dispersed. In a reanalysis of Berle and Means's data, Zeitlin (1974) claimed that roughly two-thirds of the top American corporations were retained under ownership control.

A recent study shows that a mere seventeen huge enterprises control over three-quarters of the assets of large Canadian corporations (Richardson, 1990). Furthermore, it shows that eleven of these are controlled by their owners. Two examples will provide an indication of the power wielded by some of these families.

The Bronfmans own and control the world's largest distilling company. They also own and control Canada's largest diversified financial corporation, our largest real estate company, our largest dairy, mining and forest products firms. They also control Canada's second-largest brewery, third-largest independent oil and gas producer and over two hundred other large Canadian firms—many of them among the largest half-dozen in their industry. This same family is the largest shareholder in one of the world's largest chemical companies, which in turn is the largest shareholder in the world's largest automaker.

But this family is far from the richest in Canada. That honour belongs to K. C. Irving—the *world's* third-richest person (*Forbes Magazine*, October 1988). Besides Irving's huge fortune, the Bronfman wealth is surpassed by the Reichmanns (property development, oil and gas, railways, etc.), the Thomsons (publishing, The Bay, Simpsons, Zellers, etc.) and the Weston food and supermarket empire. Irving's empire is centred on his control of most of the economic activity of New Brunswick. In fact, "New Brunswick is really just a company town and Irving owns the company" (Francis, 1986).

The concentration of economic power in the hands of so few families raises serious concern. On the other hand, many of these examples display outstanding social mobility and exemplify the opportunities available to risk-taking entrepreneurs in Canadian society. The Bronfmans, for example, are sons of Saskatchewan small-town merchants, and K. C. Irving's father was the Scottish-Canadian owner of a small general store in Restigouche, New Brunswick.

Canadian Economic Institutions

Are all industrial capitalist societies about the same, or is Canadian society unique? If so, how is it unique? Canadian sociologists who ask these questions see Canadian society as very wealthy. It has a per capita production of goods and services among the top half-dozen in the world. Furthermore, they note the flood of American television programs, movies, books and magazines across the border and wonder if a distinct Canadian culture is possible.

On the other hand, several interrelated characteristics of our society distinguish Canadian society from others. These include the degree of foreign control of our economy; the effect of the regionalism that fragments our society; our unique (and even contradictory) combination of bilingualism and multiculturalism; and our weak sense of national identity.

Even Canadian sociology differs from American sociology in its emphasis and approach. An important focus of Canadian sociology is the attempt to explain the nature of our society by determining the effect of our economic institutions on the rest of our social institutions. American sociologists put less emphasis on exploring the uniqueness of their society. When this *is* the topic of their investigations, there is an understandable urge to explain their dominance in terms of the desirable psychological traits of Americans. They contrast these characteristics with the less desirable traits they ascribe to the members of less "advanced" societies (Lipset, 1970). Other societies, such as Canada, are naturally less than receptive to explanations based on the shortcomings of their own members. Hence, rather than looking for psychological explanations, we seek institutional ones, such as those developed by economic sociology and political economy.

Innis and the Staples Perspective

Harold A. Innis (regarded by many as Canada's greatest scholar) developed the staples perspective to explain the nature of Canada's economic and social development. He studied Canada's trade in *staples* (that is, primary products such as cod, fur, lumber, wheat and minerals) within the context of the world market.

In essence, Innis (1930, 1956) proposed that the Canadian economy was driven by the demands for raw materials of the metropolitan markets of France, then Britain and then the United States. Canadian exploitation of these raw materials stimulated manufacturing in Europe and the United States, but not in Canada. Indeed, the entire energy of the Canadian economy has been expended in producing raw materials and in providing the infrastructure necessary to process, transport and market them. Furthermore, the demands of other countries for these staples have been highly erratic

Innis persuasively argues that the Canadian economy has been driven by the foreign demand for staples, such as wheat (pictured here) and oil. The events of the past two decades have supported Innis's explanation for the "boom-bust" nature of our regional economies. In the 1970s, prices of wheat and oil skyrocketed, bringing prosperity, people, and investment to Alberta and Saskatchewan. Then, demand and prices fell, bringing a regional economic depression, unemployment, farm abandonment, and an exodus of people. In the case of wheat, this was magnified by the drought of 1987–88.

SASKATCHEWAN ARCHIVES BOARD.

and beyond our control. The demand for these staples develops, peaks and then declines. This has produced a "boom-bust" Canadian economy. Since different staples are produced in different regions of Canada, regional economic peaks and valleys are even more pronounced than national ones.

Why did Canada not diversify out of its concentration on staples production? Because of the *staples trap*. During good times, there is capital to diversify, but not the will to do so. After all, why meddle with prosperity? In bad times, the will to diversify is present, but not the capital.

Innis and others have used this staples perspective to explain many characteristics of Canadian society. Regionalism is seen to be the result of the different economic interests of Canadian regions. They are all tied more strongly to foreign economies than to each other. The lifeblood of British Columbia is the American market for lumber and the Japanese demand for coal. Is it not natural, then, that British Columbians are more concerned with political and economic developments abroad than at home?

The boom-bust nature of the Canadian staples economy has historically influenced the Canadian pattern of immigration. As the demand for a particular staple in a specific region boomed, it attracted a flood of immigrants. Each wave came from a particular part of Europe. These waves of immigrants could settle together in blocks large enough to develop their own institutions and maintain their culture. Thus, our staples economy is a cause of the Canadian multicultural society.

It is also a cause of our weak sense of national identity. Identity, like culture, is passed on by tradition carriers—those who have acquired the identity and the culture of the society. However, the staples perspective suggests that the nature of our economy influences Canadians to focus outward. It also draws a flood of new arrivals during boom periods. Then, as boom turns to bust, there is a surge of emigration. For example, during the last quarter of the nineteenth century, 500 000 more people left Canada than arrived here. This erratic population pattern has produced one of the lowest ratios of tradition carriers to new arrivals of any nation in the world (Bell and Tepperman, 1979). Even had we begun with a strong national identity (and many argue that we did not), this low ratio would weaken it over the course of our history.

The staples perspective, then, attempts to explain the particular nature of the Canadian economy. It suggests how Canadian economic institutions have affected other elements of our society. It has had, justifiably, a strong influence on Canadian scholarship, both directly and by influencing the development of subsequent approaches. However, we must be careful to neither oversimplify nor exaggerate its message. There are other persuasive explanations for Canadian regionalism, multiculturalism and weak national identity that draw on a variety of approaches (Bell and Tepperman, 1979; Hiller, 1976; Marsden and Harvey, 1979; Matthews, 1983). Nor are Canadians all hewers of wood and drawers of water in contrast to our highly industrialized American cousins, as the staples perspective suggests. In fact, the contribution of manufacturing to the gross national product has been nearly as high in Canada as in the United States ever since Confederation (see Table 17-2). On

TABLE 17-2

Manufacturing as a Percentage of Gross National Product, Canada and the United States, Selected Years, 1870–1979

Year	Manufacturing % of GNP United States	Canada	Ratio U.S. : Canada
1870	23.0	20.5	1.1 : 1
1880	23.2	21.9	1.1 : 1
1890	27.2	25.4	1.1 : 1
1900	26.4	23.2	1.1 : 1
1910	24.6	24.6	1.0 : 1
1919	28.3	27.0	1.1 : 1
1929	29.7	27.9	1.1 : 1
1933	25.2	26.2	1.0 : 1
1939	27.1	27.1	1.0 : 1
1947	32.1	26.2	1.0 : 1
1950	31.5	33.0	1.0 : 1
1960	32.6	28.6	1.1 : 1
1970	30.7	25.4	1.2 : 1
1979	30.0	24.6	1.2 : 1

COMPILED FROM UNITED STATES DEPARTMENT OF COMMERCE, HISTORICAL STATISTICS OF THE UNITED STATES. WASHINGTON: U.S. GOVERNMENT PRINTING OFFICE, 1975 : 201, 203, 224, 231, 666, 667, 1984 : 431, 746; M. C. URQUHART AND K. BUCKLEY. 1965. HISTORICAL STATISTICS OF CANADA. TORONTO: MACMILLAN, PP. 130, 141, 463; STATISTICS CANADA, CANADA YEARBOOK. OTTAWA: INFORMATION CANADA, VARIOUS YEARS. (THESE SOURCES REFER TO THE TECHNICAL TERM "VALUE ADDED IN MANUFACTURING.")

the other hand, Canadian industry has traditionally emphasized the production of semiprocessed goods for export and the assembly of imported components.

Political Economy: Beyond the Staples Perspective

When Innis wrote, political economy was the dominant perspective within economics. Political economy is the study of economic processes and political policies, their interrelationship and their mutual effects on society. It later became eclipsed by econometrics (the use of mathematical methods) within the discipline of economics, but it continues to make a major contribution to sociology. Innis set the initial agenda for this research by analysing the divisive effects of the new staples (for example, minerals, newsprint, petroleum) on Canadian society. He concluded that, in moving from the orbit of British to American imperialism, "Canada moved from colony to nation to colony" (1956 : 405). Canadian sociologists then began to try to explain this return to colonial status.

The staples perspective assumed that Canada was a passive hinterland unable to control its own destiny. The political economy of the 1970s, however, produced a Canadian ruling class that was an active agent in the takeover of Canadian industry. Naylor (1972) and Clement (1975) developed the most influential analysis. They proposed that the Canadian staples economy fostered the development of merchant capital to finance the production, transport and export of staples to Britain and the United States. It was not in the interest of the descendants of the early import-export merchants to divert capital from the staples trades into domestic manufacturing. American manufacturers filled this void by expanding into Canada with the blessings of the Canadian merchant capitalists. Perhaps the most forceful proponent of this view is Clement, who declares: "Canadian manufacturers could not survive because the commercial ruling class would not allow them to" (1975 : 80).

The sociological implications of this analysis are enormous. First, it implies that a small group of merchant capitalists operating in the fields of finance, trade, transportation and utilities shaped Canadian economic development to serve its own selfish ends. This, in turn, suggests that this group wielded enormous economic and political power. In fact, studies have shown that the economically powerful have had close ties to the political system and held many important political posts ever since Confederation (Smith and Tepperman, 1974; Clement, 1975). Second, the resulting invasion of American manufacturing enterprises ultimately led to the establishment of American economic power in Canada. Thereafter, the power of Canadian governments was constrained by the economic power of American MNE and the need to maintain good relations with the United States (Levitt, 1970; Marchak, 1979). In all of this, we can see the influence of the Marxist perspective, which argues that economy shapes society and economic power affects other institutions.

However, this explanation of Canadian economic development (known as the *merchants-against-industry argument*) has not been universally accepted. One study finds, on the contrary, that there was no historical cleavage between Canadian merchants and industrialists. In fact, they were often the same people (Richardson, 1982). This same study also contests the alleged dominance of merchants over industrialists.

Another extensive analysis compares industrialization in Canada and several other nations. It finds, in all but Canada, that the landholding and agricultural classes helped shape the political and financial institutions to promote industrialization. To a significant degree, then, this study suggests that the defeat of the Canadian farmers in the Rebellions of 1837–38 shaped the Canadian economy because it removed the farmers' influence from the political realm (Laxer, 1985). On the other hand, Carroll (1985) proposes looking beyond internal class dynamics, and even beyond the relationships between Canadian and American capital, to explain the degree of foreign control of Canada's economy and society. Adequate explanation, he contends, will only come within the context of a Marxist theory of imperialism.

Economic Institutions and Regionalism

Innis's staples perspective partly explained the high degree of Canadian regionalism in economic terms. More recently, Canadian sociologists have built upon Innis's theory to extend significantly our understanding of Canadian regionalism.

"The most significant feature of Canadian social organization is not its unity, but its regional diversity" (Matthews, 1980 : 51). Why should this be? Why should Canadian society be more regionally divided than the societies of Britain, France and the United States? The most persuasive explanations focus on the development of Canadian economic institutions.

There are many objective indicators, such as income and educational attainment, of profound regional differences in Canada. For example, Ontario's per capita personal income has remained almost exactly double the personal incomes in Prince Edward Island and Newfoundland over the past fifty years (Matthews, 1980). These dissimilarities are the result of the different economies of our provinces and regions. The economy of central Canadian society is based on foreign-controlled manufacturing. In fact, nearly three-quarters of all Canadian manufacturing is located within the narrow Montreal–Windsor corridor (Brym, 1985). On the other hand, the Atlantic provinces base their economies on fishing and other primary industries, the Prairies depend on agricultural products and oil for export and British Columbia on forestry and mining.

Regional specialization is partly the result of geography, of course. But it is also partly the result of political action, such as the National Policy of the late nineteenth century. These policies helped open Canada's western agricultural frontier as an internal economic colony of central Canada, largely because of the need for a new market for central Canadian industry, which was facing bankruptcy at the time.

It should be easy to understand that a wheat farmer, an autoworker, a fisherman and a banker all see the world differently. They earn their daily bread in very different ways, they live in different types of communities and the institutions they are connected with take different forms. Thus, Canadian regionalism is both an economic and a social phenomenon (Matthews, 1980).

Canadian regionalism can, perhaps, be analysed best in terms of dominance and dependency. Canada itself is dominated by the United States, and this limits our ability to forge stronger interregional ties (Marsden and Harvey, 1979). Within Canada, the economic dominance of the central provinces has been reinforced by the political dominance of Ontario and Quebec. Those occasions where the location of economic and political power did not coincide, such as the period of the Albertan oil boom, have been turbulent times of regionally based social change.

Summary

This chapter has shown that economic institutions produce and distribute the wealth of a society. Although these functions are common to all societies, they have been fulfilled in very different ways throughout human history. Sociologists are interested in the different forms economic institutions may take, of course, but most of all sociological curiosity seeks to learn how economic institutions relate to the other institutions of a historically specific society. In other words, sociologists differentiate themselves from economists by setting out to explain the relationship between economy and society. This has been the major objective of this chapter.

Readers may be discouraged, perhaps, by the lack of agreement among Canadian sociologists on a topic as important as the development of the Canadian economy. But actually, this controversy only shows that sociologists are willing to search for answers to extraordinarily complex puzzles. Indeed, it is disagreement that provides excitement in any developing science.

Suggested Readings

Clement, Wallace

1975. *The Canadian Corporate Elite*. Toronto: McClelland and Stewart. The most intensive analysis of Canada's economic elite, which extends and reinterprets Porter's work of a decade earlier. The book also contains a historical analysis of the causes of extensive foreign control of the Canadian economy.

Grant, George

1965. *Lament for a Nation*. Toronto: McClelland and Stewart. A philosophical examination of the Americanization of Canadian values, culture and politics caused by the ever-increasing dominance of modern technology.

Innis, Harold A.

1956. *Essays in Canadian Economic History*. Toronto: University of Toronto Press. Some of the essays in this collection provide an excellent depiction of the staples perspective. Others portray Innis's approach to the relationship between economy and society.

Marchak, Patricia

1979. *In Whose Interests*. Toronto: McClelland and Stewart. An intensive critical examination of multinational enterprise in Canada, and of its effects on Canadian society.

Matthews, Ralph

1983. *The Creation of Regional Dependency*. Toronto: University of Toronto Press. A superb analysis of the relationship between economic institutions and culture that provides a compelling explanation of the various dimensions of regionalism in Canadian society.

Porter, John

1965. *The Vertical Mosaic*. Toronto: University of Toronto Press. The classic study of the Canadian elite structure. Includes a substantial analysis of the economic elite, of relations between elites, and of the social implications thereof.

Discussion Questions

1. What are economic institutions? How do they differ between tribal and industrial societies?

2. Using the development and the possible decline of the "throw-away" society as an example, show how the economy and society affect each other.

3. Why should Canadians study the impact of multinational enterprise?

4. How does the study of Canadian economic development help us to understand regionalism in Canada?

5. Does it matter who controls the major economic institutions of a society? If so, why? If not, why not?

6. How do you think that the kind of job you hold would affect the way you view the world?

Data Collection Exercises

1. From the *Canada Yearbook* and *Statistical Abstracts of the United States*, calculate the proportion of the gross domestic product that is comprised of exports for each country for a comparable year in the 1980s. Speculate on the social and cultural implications of these contrasting economic statistics.

2. From various issues of the *Canada Yearbook*, obtain the following information for Canada, by year, 1971 to 1985:
   (a) cash receipts from farming operations (excluding supplementary payments);
   (b) value of shipments of goods of own manufacture.
   Plot these data and comment on the *social* significance of your findings.

3. From the latest available issue of Statistics Canada's *Intercorporate Ownership*, list the agribusiness (i.e., food) corporations controlled by Weston. (Look for "Weston Group" in the index.) Speculate, from your findings, on the degree of price competition you would expect to find in this industry.

4. Go to the largest shopping mall in your community and obtain the names of all the ladies' and men's clothing stores situated there. Find out who controls each of these stores by examining Statistics Canada's *Intercorporate Ownership*. What is the significance of your findings?

Writing Exercises

1. Marx, Weber and Durkheim all studied the conditions under which one form of economic institution will be transformed into another. What are the key elements of the explanations developed by each of these classical sociologists?

2. Carefully identify the relationships between economy and society that we find in the works of Durkheim, Marx and Weber.

3. The predominant issue in the 1988 Canadian federal election was free trade with the United States. In this debate, economists tended to support free trade, while political scientists and sociologists tended to oppose it. Why? What does this tell us about the positions that these disciplines take with respect to the relationship between economy and society?

4. The Soviet Union has recently taken the initial steps in the move toward a capitalist economy. Assuming it is successful in this respect, speculate on the *social* implications of this economic policy.

Glossary

Capitalism: *a socio-economic system. Socially, it is based on the nominal freedom of a society's citizens and their division into two main classes: those who own or control the means of production and those who do not. Economically, it consists of profit-seeking production and the predominance of a (more or less) free market.*

Economic institutions: *the set of organizations, groups and processes by which people in a society produce and distribute goods and services, that is, by which they produce and distribute a society's wealth.*

Economic power: *the power that arises in the economic realm wherever an individual or group controls a significant share of a particular resource. This creates dependence in others who want or need that resource; see also Market power.*

Instrumentalist theory of the state: *neo-Marxist view stating that the state is merely the instrument of the capitalist class (or its dominant element).*

Market power: *a factor that influences the distribution of benefits in an economic exchange. It rests on the control of a significant share of a particular resource combined with the ability of the controlling group to withhold that resource from the market; see also Economic power.*

Mechanical solidarity: *Durkheim's term for the basis of social integration in primitive societies, which contain a rudimentary division of labour. It rests on shared beliefs (a "collective conscience"), which are maintained by repressive laws; contrast with Organic solidarity.*

Merchants-against-industry argument: *an explanation for the high degree of foreign control in Canadian manufacturing. It holds that the powerful group of Canadian merchants concentrated Canadian economic investment and activity in the staples trades—to the detriment of Canadian manufacturing development.*

Mode of production: *Marx's term for the combination of the "forces of production" and "relations of production" within a set of economic institutions. The former represent the interaction between human producers, tools, technology and the material environment; the latter are the class, property and power relationships of a society.*

Organic solidarity: *Durkheim's term for the integrative basis of modern societies that contain a complex division of labour. It rests, fundamentally, on a high degree of interdependence among a society's members; contrast with Mechanical solidarity.*

Staples: *primary industries such as (in the case of Canada) the exploitation, processing and distribution of fish, furs, lumber, wheat and minerals.*

Staples trap: *a condition that tends to retard diversification of staples economies into finished manufacturing. It occurs because, during good times in the staples trades, capital is available to diversify, but the will is lacking; while in bad times, the will to diversify is present, but the capital is lacking.*

Structuralist theory of the state: *a neo-Marxist view that holds that the state, while serving the interests of the capitalist class in the long run, has some degree of autonomy to consider the interests of other classes.*

References

Bell, David, and Lorne Tepperman
1979. *The Roots of Disunity*. Toronto: McClelland and Stewart.

Berle, Adolphe A., and Gardner C. Means
1967. *The Modern Corporation and Private Property*, rev. ed. New York: Harcourt, Brace and World.

Bosk, P. G.
1974. "The Transnational Corporation and Private Foreign Policy." *Society* (January/February): 44–49.

Brym, Robert J.
1985. "The Canadian Capitalist Class, 1965–1985." In Robert J. Brym, ed., *The Structure of the Canadian Capitalist Class*. Toronto: Garamond Press.

Canada, Privy Council Office
1970. *Foreign Ownership and the Structure of Canadian Industry* (The Watkins Report). Ottawa: Information Canada.

Carroll, William K.
1985. "Dependency, Imperialism and the Capitalist Class in Canada." In Robert J. Brym, ed., *The Structure of the Canadian Capitalist Class*. Toronto: Garamond Press.

Clement, Wallace
1975. *The Canadian Corporate Elite*. Toronto: McClelland and Stewart.

Cohen, G. A.
1978. *Karl Marx's Theory of History*. Oxford: Clarendon Press.

Cuneo, Carl
1979. "State, Class and Reserve Labour: The Case of the 1941 Canadian Unemployment Insurance Act." *Canadian Review of Sociology and Anthropology* 16(2): 147–70.

Duberman, Lucille, and Clayton A. Hartjen
1979. *Sociology*. Glencoe, Ill.: Scott, Foresman.

Durkheim, Emile
1965. *The Division of Labour and Society*. New York: Free Press.

Emerson, Richard M.
1962. "Power-Dependency Relations." *American Sociological Review* 27: 31–41.

Francis, Diane
1986. *Controlling Interest*. Toronto: Macmillan.

Gold, David, Clarence Lo and E. O. Wright
1975. "Recent Developments in Marxist Theories of the Capitalist State." *Monthly Review* 27(5): 29–43.

Hiller, Harry H.
1976. *Canadian Society*. Scarborough: Prentice-Hall.

Innis, H. A.
1930. *The Fur Trade in Canada*. New Haven: Yale University Press.
1956. *Essays in Canadian Economic History*. Toronto: University of Toronto Press.

Laxer, Gordon
1985. "Class, Nationality, and the Roots of Foreign Ownership." In Robert J. Brym, ed.,

The Structure of the Canadian Capitalist Class. Toronto: Garamond Press.

Levitt, Kari
1970. *Silent Surrender.* Toronto: Macmillan.

Lipset, S. M.
1970. *Revolution and Counterrevolution.* New York: Anchor Books.

Marchak, Patricia
1979. *In Whose Interests.* Toronto: McClelland and Stewart.

Marsden, Lorna, and Edward Harvey
1979. *Fragile Federation.* Toronto: McGraw-Hill Ryerson.

Marx, Karl
1954. *Capital*, vol. 1. Moscow: Foreign Languages Publishing House.
1970. *A Contribution to the Critique of Political Economy.* Moscow: Progress Publishers.
1978. "The German Ideology." In R. C. Tucker, ed., *The Marx-Engels Reader.* New York: Norton.

Marx, Karl, and Friedrich Engels
1950. "The Class Struggles in France." In Karl Marx and Friedrich Engels, *Selected Works,* 2 vols. Moscow: Foreign Languages Publishing House.

Matthews, Ralph
1980. "The Significance and Explanation of Regional Divisions in Canada: Toward a Canadian Sociology." *Journal of Canadian Studies* 15(2):43–61.
1983. *The Creation of Regional Dependency.* Toronto: University of Toronto Press.

Milibrand, Ralph
1969. *The State and Capitalist Society.* London: Quartet Books.

Mills, C. Wright
1959. *The Sociological Imagination.* London: Oxford University Press.

Naylor, R. T.
1972. "The Rise and Fall of the Third Commercial Empire of the St. Lawrence." In Gary Teeple, ed., *Capitalism and the National Question in Canada.* Toronto: University of Toronto Press.

Niosi, Jorge
1982. *Les Multinationales Canadiennes.* Montreal: Boreal Express.

Packard, Vance
1960. *The Waste Makers.* New York: David McKay.

Perrow, Charles
1972. *Complex Organizations: A Critical Essay.* Chicago: Scott, Foresman.

Poulantzas, Nicos
1978. *Political Power and Social Class.* London: Verso.

Richardson, R. Jack
1982. " 'Merchants Against Industry': An Empirical Study of the Canadian Debate." *Canadian Journal of Sociology* 7(3):279–95.
1990. "Economic Concentration and Social Power in Contemporary Canada," pp. 341–51. In James Curtis and Lorne Tepperman, eds., *Images of Canada: The Sociological Tradition.* Scarborough: Prentice-Hall.

Smith, Adam
1894. *The Wealth of Nations*. London: Macmillan.

Smith, David, and Lorne Tepperman
1974. "Changes in the Canadian Business and Legal Elites, 1870–1970." *Canadian Review of Sociology and Anthropology* 11(2):97–109.

Statistics Canada
Canada Yearbook. Ottawa: Information Canada, various years.

Toffler, Alan
1970. *Future Shock*. New York: Bantam.

United States Department of Commerce
1975. *Historical Statistics of the United States, Colonial Times to 1970*. Washington: United States Government Printing Office.

Urquhart, M. C., and K. Buckley
1965. *Historical Statistics of Canada*. Toronto: Macmillan.

Vernon, Raymond
1971. *Sovereignty at Bay*. New York: Basic Books.

Weber, Max
1930. *The Protestant Ethic and the Spirit of Capitalism*. London: Edward G. Allen.
1958. *From Max Weber: Essays in Sociology*, trans. H. H. Gerth and C. Wright Mills. New York: Oxford University Press.
1961. *General Economic History*. New York: Collier.
1968. *Economy and Society*. Edited by Guenther Ross and Claus Wittich. New York: Bedminster Press.
1976. *The Agrarian Sociology of Ancient Civilizations*. London: New Left Books.

Zeitlin, Irving M.
1968. *Ideology and the Development of Sociological Theory*. Englewood Cliffs, N.J.: Prentice-Hall.

Zeitlin, Morris
1974. "Corporate Ownership and Control: The Large Corporation and the Capitalist Class." *American Journal of Sociology* 79 (March):1073–119.

part 5

Processes of social change deserve a separate section because they are a key to understanding social organization. Some see the construction of theories about social order as sociology's central task; many others think it is the construction of theories about change that is of paramount importance. In fact, the two tasks must go hand in hand.

Theories of change are usually either *evolutionary* or *revolutionary*. Theories of social evolution first appeared in sociology over a century ago. Here, the early work of Emile Durkheim (1858–1917) and Herbert Spencer (1820–1903) is most important. These authors focused on continuity in change: how things stay the same while changing and how early changes lay the groundwork for later ones.

Durkheim examined the social change from primitive, pre-industrial to modern, industrial conditions. He noted two main correlates of this process. First, work and all aspects of life associated with work become specialized, and a division of labour develops. Second, with a division of labour, the basis of social cohesion changes from mechanical to organic solidarity.

With mechanical solidarity, people lead similar lives and tend to hold identical views and values. Violation of their values is punished harshly. Conversely, organic solidarity permits many different roles. People lead very different kinds of lives from one another. For this reason, they develop different views and values. Deviance is harder to define, and punishment is less uniform, harsh and automatic. Without moral uniformity, societies must find new ways of integrating people. Otherwise, a state of *anomie* (normlessness) exists, which leads to psychological distress and even to higher rates of suicide.

The institutions of a society characterized by mechanical solidarity are typically undifferentiated. Religion, science, law and government may be jumbled up together in a small body of received wisdom, perhaps in a holy book, in legends or folktales. The society lacks mechanisms for revising or rejecting this wisdom. Such a social system has a limited capacity for change.

The emergence of freedom to contract, rather than duties based on tradition or kinship, is a major development. Yet, early contractual relations are ultimately rooted in tradition or kinship. These "primitive" elements provide the trust without which rational, voluntary economic activity is impossible. Only later, with strong state protections against contract violation, do such traditional elements become unnecessary. Thus, modern practices rise on the shoulders of older ones.

Theories of dialectical change, or revolution, are theories of discontinuity. They are about radical shifts in social organization. Georg Hegel (1770–1831) and Karl Marx (1818–1883) first used the notion of dialectic in social analysis. For Marx, the dominant characteristic of a society is its class structure, which arises out of its relations of production. Accordingly, the change from one type of society to another involves a change in relations of production and class structure. This fundamental change is typically accomplished through the revolutionary overthrow of a ruling class and its replacement by a new ruling class. Such change gives birth to a new order, but not without upheaval and revolution. As Mao said, there is no omelette without broken eggs.

A variety of theorists, of whom Max Weber (1864–1920) is the most eminent, have attempted to combine these two approaches to social change. According to Weber, certain social forms, such as bureaucracy or the city, radically shift the course of later social development. In that sense, they are revolutionary changes. Yet, what typically follows is a return to some kind of routine and evolution at a higher level of complexity. A new social order emerges, then begins to differentiate and integrate again.

Weber gives us the example of a charismatic social movement. A fiery, persuasive leader gathers his followers and proclaims new values, smashing tradition and its guardians. Followers are swept forward by their excitement and the belief that their leader is right. They risk and share and suffer in ways quite out of the ordinary. Eventually, after the prophet dies, this charismatic phase passes. People return to ordinary lives, transformed by the charismatic experience. Disciples organize to carry out the ideals the prophet had proclaimed. In the process, they create new traditions: a new structure and order. Despite their different goals, both revolutionary (sectarian) religious and political movements follow this pattern.

Social differentiation is a common process of social change. By "differentiation" we mean that all social organizations, from roles up through central institutions, tend to become more specialized, more different from one another, over time. Economy, polity, the legal system and other central institutions become more distinct from one another. They develop their own operating rules, agendas, resource bases and patterns of socialization.

Another common process of social change is *integration*, or *co-ordination*. Without integration, differentiation leads to confusion and a waste of organizational resources—the state that Durkheim called anomie.

In discussing social change so generally, there is the danger that students will start to think that societies change themselves. But processes of change such as differentiation and integration, evolution and revolution, are not societal actions. Nothing could be further from the truth. In fact, people, not societies, make social change. People are both the acted upon and the actors whenever society changes. Thus, when discussing social change, we must be careful to link changes at the macro (or societal) level with changes at the micro (or individual) level. Failing to do so makes for an incomplete, even misleading, explanation.

The connection between societal and individual changes is most evident when sociologists study social movements. As members of social movements, individual people have their greatest impact on societal structure. Understanding the formation and mobilization of social movements is, therefore, key to understanding social change at both the macro and micro levels.

We are, then, only writing in shorthand when we write that *societies* evolve, differentiate or integrate; or that change is caused by population pressures, new technology or economic development. In each instance, a huge number of people created and experienced an enormous variety of new opportunities and dangers. Their experiences and reactions constitute society's change.

Where Does Change Begin?

To a large degree, all theories of social change are really variations on these few themes. Yet, theories differ in what they see as the cause of change. If all the parts of a society are tied together, it follows that they will tend to keep one another from changing much. This is precisely why many planned attempts at social change fail. An intervention that is intended to produce change in one subsystem may be offset by counterforces or shifts in a connected subsystem. So what kinds of change break this self-stabilizing pattern?

On a descriptive level, the question is easily answered. We know, for example, that capitalism transformed the social life of Western societies from what they were five hundred years ago. As well, we can relate the rise of capitalism to changes in religion, warfare and colonization, monetary and economic practice, political organization and other factors. If anything, we have too many explanations, but no widely accepted, single theory about the rise of capitalism in the West and its effects on society.

During the nineteenth and twentieth centuries, Western societies grew and urbanized. Their populations relocated geographically; the ratio of young to old altered; and the presence of males and females, old and young, in particular relationships also changed. These population shifts put great pressure on social institutions such as marriage and the family, education and the workplace. New kinds of people had to be assimilated into ongoing social organizations. New organizations were established to accommodate the new population groups. The flood of immigrants that filled North American society and its institutions made keeping the social order a problem.

New communities formed; cities grew rapidly and people experienced new kinds of problems. Urban sociology developed to explain the patterns of observable change and study ways that people could deal with new "social problems" such as delinquency, racial conflict and overcrowding. Exposure to the opportunities, pleasures, dangers and hardships that city life made available generally transformed social relationships.

In historical analyses, theorists tell their story from many different starting points. Some begin with the economy, others with religion, still others with the nation-state. A Marxist theory typically sees economic conflicts as basic and value conflicts (for example, in religion) as secondary. A Weberian analysis, by contrast, will consider value conflicts just as basic as economic or political ones. We can only judge these theories by their thoroughness, economy and agreement with the evidence. Theories of societal change, especially theories aimed at explaining the past, can rarely be verified by prediction and testing. However, not all theories of societal change focus on the past. Increasingly, theories of change aim to predict the future.

Theories about the future are not confined to sociology. They come out of a new, interdisciplinary field called "futures research," to which sociologists contribute both methods and substance. A major work in this area, *The Coming of the Post Industrial Society*, by sociologist Daniel Bell (1970), describes a society that is already in sight, though far from completion. In this society, knowledge (especially information) creates power, and educational institutions have even more importance than they do today.

Other theorists, such as Alvin Toffler, whose ideas are similar in many respects to Bell's, predict that technological changes will continue to alter society dramatically. Our lives will become more prosperous, varied and secure as new micro-electronic gadgets revolutionize our homes and workplaces. Yet, this technology-driven approach to prediction is largely on the wrong track: specifically, it confuses "the possible" with "the likely." It makes this error because it fails to consider power and belief.

Power and Belief

Amid all the competing sociological theories about past and future, two major concerns emerge time and again—power and belief. They come together in the study of ideology and its effect on social change and order.

Changes to a society are largely determined by *who* controls technology, knowledge and the other agents of change already mentioned. No theory of change can validly ignore the way power is actually used in a society. For example, the fact that computers could free people from mindless toil tells us little. To predict the future, we must know who actually controls the computers and what they plan to use them for. The fact that knowledge is becoming an ever more important social resource does not ensure that educated people will become more powerful, only that people in power will make more use of the educated.

Even so, the possession of power is not everything. We need to know what people in power are thinking, how they understand the world and what their goals are. How do they exercise their power? How effective are they in projecting their goals and world view into the minds of people they rule? Power is, and will always be, exercised as much by persuasion as by force.

Max Weber directed our attention to the continuing contest between power and belief. Century after century, we witness people in power attempting to control the thinking of the masses. We also witness the tendency for disaffection, and the rise of prophets with a power to unite and inspire trust among the masses. And, century after century, we see disciples of the prophet consolidating the achievements of their leader and becoming new, powerful rivals to the existing order. History shows us that belief and leadership play an important role in social protest and change.

Under what conditions will people in power be able to keep their control over the thinking of the masses? When and why will ordinary people become disaffected and rebellious? How do charismatic leaders emerge and succeed in challenging the people in power? Some of these questions will be answered in this section.

Sociology is a science of social relations. It has already taken significant steps toward understanding social relations. Much more thought and research is needed. This introductory volume merely outlines the sociologist's aims, tools and achievements to date.

CHAPTER 18

Social Change

ANTON ALLAHAR

*A wonderfully preserved
Indian longhouse built
some five hundred years ago
to house an extended
family.*

*A modern condominium
complex that will accommodate close to fifty nuclear
families.*

Introduction

One definition of sociology is the study of social order, social disorder and social change. According to this definition, the topic to be discussed in this chapter comprises one-third of the discipline. *Social change* is a ubiquitous and permanent feature of every society and is best conceived of as a shift in broad, institutionalized patterns of interaction. It involves significant alterations of social behaviour and occurs on countless different levels. For this reason, it is impossible to give it a comprehensive treatment in any single publication, lecture or film. As a consequence, those sociologists who address the subject of social change must break it down into smaller, more manageable sub-areas.

Discussions of change have to include three elements: magnitude, temporality and spatiality. Some things change more than others, faster than others, and have a wider impact than others. Thus, sociologists can speak of slow evolutionary change, quick revolutionary change, micro and macro change, short-term and long-term change and so on.

One of the most common divisions is between micro- and macro-level change. The first involves small-scale changes that are not likely to have wide or major implications for society. Micro-level changes might involve reducing the highway speed limit from 65 km to 60 km, increasing the amount of spousal support to be paid by husbands to wives, or even something as trivial as changes in clothing style. Macro-level change, on the other hand, occurs on a larger scale and affects whole societies, cultures and civilizations. A socialist revolution, granting the vote to women or prohibiting migration between provinces would each be a macro-level change.

No one study can reasonably be expected to address the entire field of social change, so this chapter will be restricted to a discussion of change at the macro level. Some theories have been proposed that try to describe and explain how human societies have changed from traditional, pre-industrial groupings to modern, industrial entities. In this context, industrialization and advancement are closely linked with the idea of progress: more industrialized societies are deemed to have progressed further than less industrialized ones. And even within a given society or country, industrialization and development are very uneven processes. Not all parts of the society in question will exhibit the same levels of industrial development. In other words, not all parts will have changed to the same degree and at the same pace.

Sociology and History

In his now-classic monograph entitled *The Sociological Imagination*, C. Wright Mills wrote that "all sociology worthy of the name is historical sociology" (1959:146). What this means is that many of the essential insights of sociology are drawn from history. Increasingly, a great number of macro-sociologists have looked to history as a source for understanding social change. They try to answer the question: Why does the world look as it does today?

Recognizing the fact that our basic modes of interaction, our social institutions and our cultural patterns are tremendously history-laden, a new sub-area of sociology has been created: historical sociology. Two of today's leading historical sociologists are Immanuel Wallerstein and Charles Tilly. Wallerstein's major contribution to understanding historical change and the emergence of the present international order is the concept of *world system*. He describes three types of world systems. The first, which he refers to as "world empire," is based on political and military domination, with war and territorial expansion taking precedence over economics and the production of goods. World empire is best represented by ancient Rome. The second type of world system he calls the capitalist "world economy," in which economic domination is the distinguishing feature, production for profit is paramount and those with economic power dominate the state. And the third, which Wallerstein foresees as a distinct possibility, is a socialist "world government," a reintegration of the political and economic moments (or spheres) that were separated in the first two world systems (Ritzer, 1988 : 280–84).

In Wallerstein's schema, the capitalist world economy resulted from three related historical processes. The first concerned geographical expansion and entailed such phenomena as colonialism, slavery and imperialism. The second dealt with the development of an international division of labour between core, peripheral and semiperipheral nations, depending on the economic contributions of each to the global market. Core countries are the advanced industrial ones, such as the United States and Britain. The peripheral countries are generally those of the Third World, whose economies are underdeveloped and dependent on the core countries. Semiperipheral countries are those such as Australia and Spain, which fall somewhere in the middle—neither totally dependent nor totally independent economically. Thus, some countries came to specialize in the production of different raw materials and goods (mineral, agricultural or industrial) and others in services (labour or expertise) for the world market. The third process involved the consolidation of strong national states, which represented and promoted the interests of powerful economic groups.

According to Wallerstein, then, social change from world empire to world economy is to be understood as the triumph of economic exploitation over political and military dominance. The economic exploitation is less cumbersome and more efficient because it makes it possible to increase the flow of surpluses and profits from the peripheral nations to the core nations (Wallerstein, 1974 : 15). And it does so purely on the basis of economic necessity, without having to insist on political unity or political coercion as was the case with world empire.

Although he applauded the basic historical thrust of Wallerstein's work, Charles Tilly (1981 : 37–46) criticizes it for being overly descriptive and insufficiently analytical. Focusing principally on the causes and consequences of the rise of capitalism and the changes that it has wrought, Tilly argues that more attention should be paid to class relations, instead of purely economic exchanges between countries, as the defining feature of capitalism (1981 : 41). For Tilly, the historical-sociological enterprise revolves around studies of large-scale structural change and patterns of collective action: "a quest for regularities in the collective action of particular historical eras" (1981:44).

In this context Tilly, like Wallerstein, identifies two "master change processes" that are of central importance: the expansion of capitalism and the growth of national states. When discussing the expansion of capitalism, he focuses on such issues as proletarianization and capital accumulation, urbanization and secularization and the fate of the peasantry in the industrial age. Bound up with these changes was the growth of national states in Western Europe. States struggled with one another, borrowed from one another, contested and co-operated with one another "creating new states, containing old states, and realigning the weaker states to meet the interests of the stronger. In short, not only states, but systems of states came to dominate the world" (1981:45).

By contrast with Wallerstein, Tilly places greater emphasis on the role of social classes in the broad sweep of historical change. He is interested in the process by which economically dominant classes came to control the state and the implications of this for the study of riots, rebellions and revolutions. Tilly's work serves as an ideal complement to that of Wallerstein as far as defining *contemporary* thinking on social change. But to appreciate fully the intellectual path that such thinking has traversed, we must examine chronologically some of the theories and explanations of socio-historical change against which today's theorists are reacting.

Social Evolutionary Theory

During the nineteenth century, when sociology was a fledgling science and when the full force of the Industrial Revolution was beginning to exert itself on Western Europe, various social theorists on the Continent became interested in industrialism. They wanted to understand, first, how societies changed from a pre-industrial to an industrial order, and second, what the essential characteristics of the new order were that set it apart from the old. On this score, the works of Sir Isaac Newton, Charles Darwin and Herbert Spencer served as important points of departure.

This is not to say that Newton, as a physicist, Darwin, as a biologist, and even Spencer, who worked as a railway engineer, were explicitly concerned with explaining social change. Newton's contribution stemmed from his work on the laws of motion (published in 1687) that showed "how the universe ran of its own accord like a clock" (Collins and Markowsky, 1984:21), and not according to some plan laid down by God. This "discovery" led thinkers to embrace science and rationality as a means of identifying those natural laws that governed the universe, with a view to putting society in step with them. Building on the idea that the universe was rationally intelligible and that it unfolded in keeping with natural processes, thinkers began to look outside of religion for an explanation of natural and social phenomena.

Charles Darwin, in his *Origin of the Species* (1859), challenged the biblical account of Creation and postulated that the human being was not descended from Adam and Eve, but rather represented a higher form of life that evolved out of previously existing

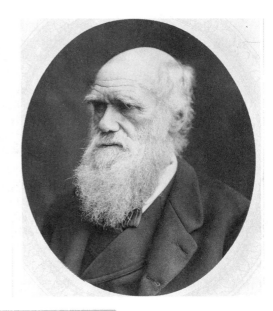

Top left:
Sir Isaac Newton, 1642–1727. English physicist and mathematician.

Top right:
Charles Robert Darwin, 1809–1882. English naturalist.

Bottom:
Herbert Spencer, 1820–1903. English philosopher.

THE GRANGE COLLECTION, NEW YORK.

lower forms. In his highly controversial *The Descent of Man* (1871), he argued that man shared a common ancestor with animals, most probably the great apes. It is thus said that Darwin, "at a stroke, set the natural world in order, just as Newton had done two centuries earlier in physics" (Collins and Markowsky, 1984:87).

Building on the theme of evolution, which saw all species as evolving from common ancestors, Herbert Spencer talked about the evolution of societies along a continuum of primitive to ancient to modern forms. And just as the principles of "natural selection" and "survival of the fittest" were used to describe the evolution and development of the living organism, they were also applied to human societies. Such societies were said to be like living organisms, and the various parts (or institutions) were compared to the parts of the body (heart, liver, lungs, etc.) that functioned to maintain the whole or to ensure its survival. Those social theorists who applied the *organismic analogy* to the study of how societies change were called *social Darwinists*.

A great many sociologists have sought to adapt the basic ideas and assumptions of evolution to the study of how societies change and develop. Among these, Ferdinand Tönnies's (1957) "community" versus "society" and Emile Durkheim's (1933) "mechanical" and "organic" solidarity and perhaps the best known. For Tönnies, "community" represented a simple, even rural way of life in which spontaneity and intimacy characterized the interaction between people. Within "society," on the other hand, social relations were more complex, impersonal and formal. Durkheim, in talking about "mechanical solidarity" or "mechanical society," posited a fundamental "likeness" or similarity among people, based on a common "collective conscience" and morality. Organic solidarity, conversely, describes contemporary society based on an intricate division of labour and increasing social dissimilarity, differentiation and complexity. In both cases, the move from community to society, and from mechanical to organic solidarity, implied evolutionary changes from one stage to another.

Social Evolutionism and the Pattern Variables

To give more concrete content to the defining features of traditional and modern societies, several social evolutionary theorists seized upon the "pattern variable scheme" developed by Talcott Parsons (1954). Although Parsons himself did not initially conceive of the pattern variables in this context, they were adopted by people such as Hoselitz (1960) and Chodak (1973) in their descriptions and explanations of social change. But before getting to those descriptions and explanations, we should clarify what the pattern variables are, and how it was possible to adapt them to the study of social change. As a central feature of both the social evolutionary and the "value-orientation" (to be discussed next) theories of change, the pattern variable scheme has coloured much of the work in the sociology of development.

The idea of the pattern variables came to Parsons during a study of the doctor-patient relationship. He observed that in such a highly specialized relationship, the doctor's behaviour toward the patient is guided by the same principles that inform the patient's behaviour toward the doctor. Their interaction is patterned. The patient expects the same degree of concern, dedication and professionalism from the doctor as he or she affords to *all* other patients. No favouritism or prejudice should come into play. And the doctor, for his or her part, expects to be judged on the basis of competence and according to the same universalistic criteria by which all other doctors are judged. No exceptions or personal considerations should enter the picture.

It thus occurred to Parsons that our patterns of social interaction in modern society increasingly reflect the highly specialized conditions under which we live. Not only the doctor-patient relationship, but teacher-student, employer-employee and other contacts occur in institutional and bureaucratic settings that more than anything else serve to define contemporary living. And in the *public domain* we expect, and are expected by others, to act in certain specific and patterned ways as established by social convention or accepted practice. This was the context in which Parsons identified four *variable sets of interaction patterns* among people, known in sociology as the "pattern variables."

Briefly stated, the four sets of pattern variables or the four sets of continua along which our social behaviour tends to vary, are: (a) particularism-universalism; (b) ascription-achievement; (c) diffuseness-specificity; and (d) affectivity-affective neutrality. In contemporary society, our formal, public behaviour, for example, at work or at school, tends to be universalistic, achievement-oriented, specific and affectively neutral. This means we expect, and are expected by others, to be judged according to impersonal criteria that are equally applicable to all other members of society. We expect, and are expected by others, to move ahead on the basis of merit and knowledge or skills acquired in fair competition with all co-competitors. We expect, and are expected by others, to interrelate on the basis of specific roles such as doctor, student, employee and so on, and finally, we expect, and are expected by others, to interact, not merely on the basis of emotion, but according to reason, following our "heads" rather than our "hearts."

Conversely, our informal, private behaviour, for example, within the family or peer group, will follow more particularistic, ascriptive, diffuse and affective lines. We do not expect our mothers to treat us as our teachers or bosses do. Parents or friends usually take into account the particular attributes of individuals and respond on a more personal level. Further, our status within the family is ascribed, we occupy diffuse roles such as son, brother, cousin, part-time worker and so on, and we are sensitive to the emotions and moods of other family members. Moreover, homes are supposed to exude love and warmth in a way that offices and schools do not.

As was indicated above, the pattern variables were quickly adopted by several sociologists and applied to the study of social change. Criticizing Hoselitz (1960), who saw the pattern variables as representing the "sociological aspects of economic growth" (the title of his book), Portes (1976:62) argues that it is highly ideological to view the underdeveloped, traditional or backward societies as causing their own problems, and to portray those problems as being related to roles that are ascribed, functionally diffuse and oriented toward narrow, particularistic goals. The developed, modern or advanced societies, however, are characterized by clearly delineated specific roles, acquired through achievement criteria and oriented toward universal norms. This is ideological because it distorts the root causes of underdevelopment by deflecting blame away from the advanced countries.

As far as the actual dynamics of change and development are concerned, social evolutionary theorists focus on two related processes that affect the internal dynamics of specific societies: *social differentiation* and *social integration*. Accepting the Durkheimian view that the developing division of labour simultaneously erodes mechanical solidarity and promotes an integrated organic solidarity, these theorists explain change in traditional society as a constant interplay between forces that, on the one hand, increase social differentiation, and on the other, produce structures that enhance social integration. For example, in a typical agricultural community, there may be food scarcity owing to war, drought, famine, flood or overpopulation. This situation causes social differentiation since some people will give up attempting to produce food as farmers and will become fishermen, hunters, gatherers and so on. If the community is to remain intact, however, the splintering that results from increased specialization and differentiation will have to be reintegrated *at a higher level*. Networks of interdependence will develop (such as organizations for distributing or sharing food) that lead to ever-growing societal complexity and more and more systems.

> If this process of differentiation into increasingly specialized units were to continue without other structural modifications, the system would disintegrate. However, the tendencies toward disintegration are counteracted by the evolution of more sophisticated integrative mechanisms [for example] the development of bureaucratic forms of organization. (Wilson, 1983 : 96)

For Neil Smelser (1968 : 138), therefore, change and development are conceived as a "contrapuntal interplay between differentiation (which is divisive of established society) and integration (which unites differentiated structures on a new basis)"; and for Eisenstadt (1964 : 376), social differentiation is a process of "continuous development from the 'ideal' type of primitive society." According to these social evolutionary theorists, societies change and develop as a result of the gradual, qualitative passage from less to more differentiated social forms. And in the process, ever more complex structures of specialization and functional interdependence are generated.

Modernization Theory and Value Orientation

Evolutionary thinking has also had a marked influence on other theories of change and development. Emphasizing social-psychological processes, writers such as David McClelland (1963; 1964), Daniel Lerner (1965), Alex Inkeles (1966; 1973) and Seymour Martin Lipset (1967; 1985) have developed value-orientation or *modernization theory*.

Modernization theorists have identified themselves as the intellectual heirs of Max Weber because of his insistence on the primacy of ideas and motives as key elements of human conduct. Reacting to Marx's view that much of social life is economically conditioned, Weber attempted to show where, in some instances, ideas, as opposed to material interests, have become effective forces in history. This is the central theme he traced in *The Protestant Ethic and the Spirit of Capitalism* (1958). In essence, Weber was able to link the emergence of capitalistic behaviour with the religious teachings and ideas of Protestantism, particularly in its Calvinist form. Though not arguing that Protestantism caused capitalism, he showed where people's ideas, motives and values, their outlooks on the world, religious and otherwise, have a significant impact on the daily conduct of their lives and their economic dealings.

It is in this context that McClelland seeks to cement the link between Weber and modernization theory, when he asserts (1963 : 17) that there is a

> growing conviction among social scientists that it is values, motives or psychological forces that determine ultimately the rate of social and economic development.

However, the connection is tenuous, for the modernization theorists are far less sensitive to historical and structural analysis of change than Weber was. Nevertheless, they do draw our attention to some of the non-economic determinants of human action.

Compared to the "pure" social evolutionary thinkers, modernization theorists are less concerned with detailed descriptions of traditional or modern social structures. Rather, they stress the actual character of the individuals living in particular societies. Their aim is to assess, in social-psychological terms, how those individuals come to understand their actions, and how they may bring about or retard change. As Myron Weiner (1966 : 9) observed, the modernization theorists believe "attitudinal and value changes are prerequisites to creating a modern society, economy, and political system."

The modernization school is more analytical than descriptive in its approach because it seeks to answer the question "why." It does not content itself with merely describing traditional and modern society, but attempts to explain why some remain backward and why others advance. Hence, as Chodak (1973 : 11) put it:

> Instead of asking "What is development?" or "What happens in its course?" modernization theorists ask *why* it happened, and what specifically *caused* the breakthrough from traditional into modern societies. Thus such theories start with the question "What are the *causes* of industrialization?" (Emphasis added.)

In answering such queries, modernization theorists look to the sphere of value orientations—the values and attitudes held by members of a given society. Adopting an approach that is more *analytical* than that used by the earlier evolutionary school, these theorists reason that it is possible to identify certain factors that, when present, lead to development and industrialization, and when absent, cause stagnation. The key factors identified relate to value orientations. Implicitly, therefore, Western Europe developed and advanced on the basis of its people's value and attitudinal structures. In underdeveloped countries, the people are somehow devoid of similarly progressive values and attitudes.

As McClelland argued, too much attention has been paid to the *external* causes of development, such as favourable trade opportunities, abundant natural resource endowment and conquest of markets. He was more interested in *internal* factors—the "values" and "motives" that lead people to exploit favourable opportunities and

FIGURE 18-1

How Development Happens

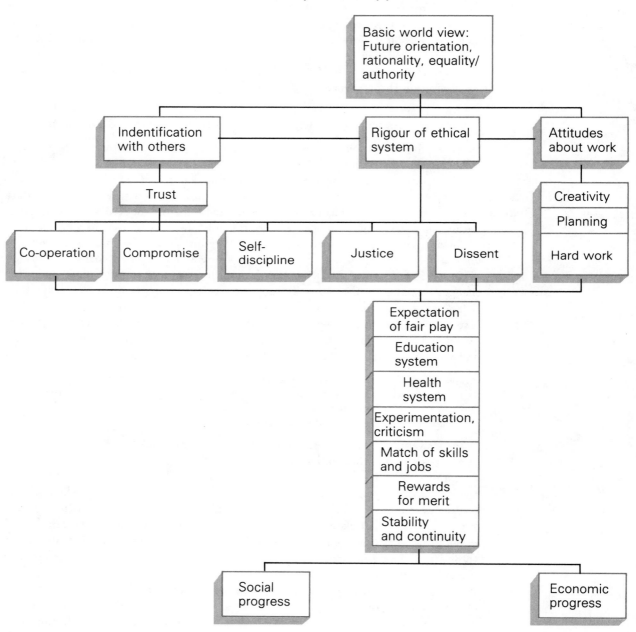

Lawrence Harrison. 1985. *Underdevelopment Is a State of Mind*. Landham, Md.: Center for International Affairs, Harvard University and University Press of America, p. 5.

conditions and "to shape their own destiny" (1964:179–80). In this respect McClelland examines two related factors that are supposed to lead to development: a need for achievement and entrepreneurship. Societies in which people demonstrate a high need for achievement are more likely to develop than those in which traditional values and non-progressive attitudes and orientations prevail. As a psychological factor promoting modernization, the need for achievement is defined by McClelland as a desire to do well, not so much for social recognition, but to attain an inner feeling of personal accomplishment or self-satisfaction. It is thus like an internal force that drives individuals

> to work harder at certain tasks; to learn faster; to do their best work when it counts for the record, and not when special incentives like money prizes are introduced; to choose experts over friends as working partners, etc. (McClelland, 1964:180–81)

Arguing that people who have a high need for achievement usually make the most successful entrepreneurs, McClelland goes on to show where those societies that encourage entrepreneurial behaviour and competitiveness tend to be more developed than those in which people "act very traditionally on economic matters" (1964:183). For McClelland, then, entrepreneurs possess the "strategic mental virus" that leads to the establishment of businesses, economic rationality and market innovation so crucial to developing any society.

Building on these assumptions, another modernization theorist, Daniel Lerner (1965), spoke of modern man as having a "mobile personality" that prepares him for dealing with new and challenging situations. For Lerner, "modern man" and "Western man" are one and the same. And among those features that make Western man modern are his mental adaptability to change, his rationality, his ability to make independent choices regarding his individual destiny and his disposition to forming and holding political opinions (1965:47–52).

In a similar vein, Alex Inkeles more or less duplicates Lerner's list of the attributes of modern man (1973:345). Like McClelland and Lerner, he is concerned with the social-psychological import of values and attitudes, and the roles they play in "making men modern" (the title of his study). To this end, he constructed a questionnaire to measure the range of "attitudes, values and behaviours conceived as relevant to understanding the individual's participation in the roles typical for a modern industrial society" (1973:343). From that questionnaire, he went on to assert (1973:345):

> Evidently the modern man is not just a construct in the mind of sociological theorists. He exists and can be identified with fair reliability within any population which can take our test.

Lipset and the Latin American Value Structure

With his study entitled "Values, Education and Entrepreneurship in Latin America," Seymour Martin Lipset (1967) does for Latin America what he was to do later for Canada. To explain the underdevelopment of Latin America, Lipset sought to combine Parsons's pattern variable scheme with the value orientation approach of McClelland

Modernization in a Nutshell

The enormous gap in well-being between the low-income and the industrialized countries is apparent from the following summary table, the source of which is the World Bank's *World Development Report, 1982*.

	Low-income countries	Industrialized countries
Total population (mid-1980)	2.2 billion	.67 billion
Annual average population growth rate (1970–80)	2.1%	.8%
Average per capita gross national product (1980)	$260	$10 320
Average life expectancy at birth (1980)	57 years	74 years
Average adult literacy (1977)	50%	99%

What explains the gap? What have the industrialized countries done that the low-income countries have not? What makes development happen or not happen?

There are those who will say that what the industrialized countries have done that the low-income countries have not is to exploit the low-income countries; that development is a zero-sum game; that the rich countries are rich because the poor countries are poor. This is doctrine for Marxist-Leninists, and it has wide currency throughout the Third World. To be sure, colonial powers often did derive great economic advantage from their colonies, and U.S. companies have made a lot of money in Latin America and elsewhere in the Third World, particularly during the first half of this century. But the almost exclusive focus on "imperialism" and "dependency" to explain underdevelopment has encouraged the evolution of a paralyzing and self-defeating mythology.

I believe that the creative capacity of human beings is at the heart of the development process. What makes development happen is our ability to imagine, theorize, conceptualize, experiment, invent, articulate, organize, manage, solve problems, and do a hundred other things with our minds and hands that contribute to the progress of the individual and of humankind. Natural resources, climate, geography, history, market size, governmental policies, and many other factors influence the direction and pace of progress. But the engine is human creative capacity.

From Lawrence Harrison. 1985. *Underdevelopment is a State of Mind*. Landham, Md.: University Press of America, pp. 1–2.

and others. Focusing on culture as the embodiment of societal values, Lipset begins his study by noting that whereas "structural conditions make development possible, cultural factors determine whether the possibility becomes an actuality" (1967 : 3).

In Latin America, where particularism and ascriptive criteria are emphasized, Lipset says underdevelopment is the natural result. He thus focused on the predominant value systems in the region that foster behaviour antithetical to the systematic accumulation of capital. For the United States, by contrast, the pattern variables of "universalism" and "achievement orientation" are the norm. And this specific combination is "most favourable to the emergence of an industrial society since it encourages respect or deference toward others on the basis of merit and places an emphasis on achievement" (1967:6).

Therefore, in social systems united around kinship and local community, one does not tend to find people who exhibit those characteristics associated with "modern man." Power and authority are decentralized, roles remain diffuse, expressive rather than instrumental behaviour is common and traditional values are perpetuated. According to modernization theorists, these precise value orientations are symptomatic of backwardness and underdevelopment.

In trying to explain the *origins* of these ideas and values among Latin Americans, Lipset is even more explicit. He argues, for example, that we can trace them back to the very institutions and norms the Spaniards and Portuguese took to Latin America during colonial rule. At the time of colonial conquest, we are reminded, both Spain and Portugal were engaged in a long struggle to expel the Moors, who were Muslims, and the Jews, who had for centuries occupied part of the Iberian peninsula. Apart from being non-Christians, the Moors and the Jews were also engaged in economic activities that at the time were seriously frowned upon by the Catholic Church. They monopolized commerce and banking, and the latter particularly was viewed as sinful for it represented institutionalized usury and a crass preoccupation with material possessions.

Thus, Lipset observes that during the colonial period the roles of soldier and priest were glorified, while commercial and business pursuits were denigrated (1967:8). As a result, the dominant culture and value system that emerged in Latin America "was not supportive of entrepreneurial activity" (1967:23), which the modernization theorists view as the cornerstone of economic development. Because the leading political and economic institutions in the society did not encourage pragmatism, materialism and rational business dealings, there was little or no opportunity for the emergence of modern men with modern ideas to direct the development of a modern society.

| Canadian-American Value Differences | In a recent update of an earlier study Lipset (1985) applies the pattern variables to an analysis of cultural differences between Canada and the United States. He begins his comparison with the American Revolution and goes on to discuss differences in the religious, political, legal, socio-economic and ecological spheres of both societies. Unlike the Americans, who embraced the liberal democratic traditions of the French Revolution, Canadians, he says, opted for continued colonial dependence on Britain. As a result, Canadian society and institutions came to exhibit a definite European bias, complete with a conservative political orientation and a healthy respect for the established European churches (Roman Catholic and Anglican). In the United States, conversely, one can see a greater emphasis on the separation of church and state, and the growth of non-conformist Protestant sects that opposed organized state religions. |

Politically and philosophically, we are told, Canadians and Americans differ greatly. The former tend to be more elitist and resigned to accepting governmental intervention in their lives; the latter are more strongly committed to egalitarian thinking and clearly try to limit state interference in the private lives of citizens. Canadian conservatism contrasts sharply with American liberalism and individualism.

Cultural Imperialism, Eh?

Some years ago, Mordecai Richler gave The New York Times a fascinating interview to help promote his novel *Joshua Then and Now*. The patronizing interviewer wanted to know why Americans think Canada is so boring. "Maybe," Richler suggested slyly, "it's a failure of American imagination. What you fail to grasp is that in our own sneaky way we have been infiltrating your country for years and we are a far greater threat to you than the Communist Party." He rhymed off a list of prominent Canadian infiltrators, among them, presidential adviser John Kenneth Galbraith; novelist Saul Bellow; Abe Rosenthal, executive editor of The New York Times; Mary Pickford, "America's sweetheart"; and Superman.

Richler dug his dagger deep: "Even as we pretend to be a self-effacing bunch, we are manipulating the cultural life of your country."

How true! I don't want to gloat, but here's more incontrovertible evidence. Canadian nationalists, take note: who's acculturating whom?

Cutting a swath south of the border among TV anchors, count Peter Jennings, ABC; Robert MacNeil, PBS; and Morley Safer, CBS. A couple of years ago, Alan Thicke, of Kirkland Lake, Ont., gave Johnny Carson a creditable run for his money on late-night TV. And don't discount daytimers Monty Hall and Alex Trebek.

Among actors, the names are legion: Lorne Greene, Christopher Plummer, Donald Sutherland, Kate Nelligan, William Shatner, Margot Kidder, *Dynasty's* Gordon Thomson and Michael J. Fox, the kid from Burnaby, who is so convincing on *Family Ties* as the reactionary son of hippie parents that Ronald Reagan's office asked him to be an official spokesman in the last reelection campaign.

In pop, early infiltrators included Paul Anka, Joni Mitchell, Neil Young and The Band; top of the pops now are Corey Hart and Bryan Adams. In opera, Teresa Stratas and Jon Vickers have dazzled at the Met. Among writers, Earl Pomerantz has come up with funny lines for Mary Tyler Moore and Bill Cosby; Tom Hedley conceived *Flashdance*; and playwright Bernie Slade has wowed 'em on Broadway.

In architecture, Frank Gehry is a trailblazer in L.A. In business, Elizabeth Arden is a cosmetics legend; while today's high rollers include the Bronfman brothers (Seagram) and the Reichmann brothers, who by now must own half of New York.

It's also probably no accident that Allan and Sondra Gotlieb are the hottest diplomatic couple in Washington right now.

One of life's petty annoyances is how Americans co-opt but don't duly credit. In the August *GQ*, in an article purporting to track the genealogy of American humor, John Candy, David Steinberg, Rich Little, Mort Sahl, *Saturday Night Live* and *SCTV* figure prominently. Homegrown all right . . . in Canada. Elsewhere, an American writer claims Glenn Gould's daring and originality as "quintessentially in the American grain." *Harrumph*. And even Trivial Pursuit, which everybody knows is a made-in-Canada board game, was marketed in the U.S. as an inalienable right: "Every American is entitled to Life, Liberty and the Pursuit of Trivia." *Double harrumph*.

Who's afraid of Canadian cultural imperialism? Certainly not self-confident Americans. If you've got it, come on down and flaunt it.

Canadians are dull, boring and unimaginative . . . and they have no hustle?

Says who?

In economic matters these differences are crucial. Reflecting the classic biases of modernization theorists, Lipset (1985 : 42) argues:

> The United States, born modern, without a feudal elitist, corporatist tradition, could create . . . the purest example of a bourgeois society. Canada, as we have seen, was somewhat different, and that difference affected the way her citizens have done business.

Describing Canadian capitalism as "public enterprise" (as opposed to "private enterprise" American capitalism), Lipset implicitly criticizes public or state ownership of parts of the Canadian economy. Because Canada has not experienced "a pure laissez-faire market capitalism," he affirms, Canadian capitalists have grown dependent on government for precisely those things that make American capitalists strong. Canadian capitalists, in comparison to their American counterparts, are less aggressive, less innovative and less willing to take risks. These are exactly the same terms used by McClelland and Lipset himself to describe underdevelopment in Latin America.

Such a situation, we are told, is clearly related to the fact that Canada lags behind the United States in developing a modern society. Stated according to the pattern variables, Canadians are more elitist, ascriptive and particularistic, whereas Americans are more committed to egalitarianism, achievement orientation and universalism: "Canada's economic backwardness relative to the United States is primarily a function of her value system." (See the sections of this chapter on Dependency Theory for a critique of this perspective.)

Post-Industrial Society

As we have seen, modernization theorists concern themselves mainly with the changes encountered in the passage from a pre-industrial to an industrial society. Implicit in their approach is the idea that industrialism represents the end point of development— that there is nothing beyond the present stage in which the advanced countries find themselves. New or recent changes within the industrial societies themselves, however, have led to a reconsideration of that position, and the outcome has been a set of analyses and predictions concerning future trends toward a *post-industrial society*; trends leading to the emergence of "the service society, post-industrial society, technetronic society, post-modern society, post-cultural society and even post-civilized society" (Giddens, 1974 : 255).

The best known exponents of the post-industrial thesis are Alain Touraine (1971) and Daniel Bell (1971; 1973), who identified several key areas in which post-industrial society differs from its industrial forerunner. Basic to this trend to a post-industrial society are the technological advances that have led to a marked shift away from an economy based on the production of goods in factories, to one in which the provision of services becomes central. Accompanying this basic change, four other features of post-industrial society are identified: an increasing importance of professional and technical workers; emphasis on theoretical knowledge as opposed to manual skills; planning and control of technological growth; and the enhanced use of intellectual technology such as computers.

In the post-industrial society, growing numbers of people are occupied in service sectors, such as restaurants and fast-food chains, law and real estate, banking and insurance, sales, appliance repairs and clerical jobs. Unlike industrial society, therefore, where emphasis was placed on "blue-collar" factory workers who produced the bulk of goods and commodities, post-industrial society is the result of a pronounced shift to "white-collar" workers who are largely engaged in distribution operations (for example, sales) and the provision of services (for example, social workers).

Changes of this nature are viewed favourably by Bell. He assumes the most serious problems of industrial capitalism, for example, high levels of unemployment, will be overcome once post-industrialism becomes entrenched. Rinehart (1975 : 83–84) sums up Bell's position by noting that as a growing number of the labour force

> is engaged in cleaner, more complex and more desirable white collar jobs, problems growing out of the nature and organization of work subside. Manual jobs, the traditional source of work dissatisfaction and conflict, are scheduled for near extinction.

Because the new post-industrial society is one in which possession of technical knowledge becomes more important than the owning of property, Touraine believes the "technocrats" (those who possess technical expertise, for example, the computer analyst) have become the new dominant class in such societies. As the major forms of decision

As a key part of today's intellectual technology, computers are now commonplace in schools, universities, businesses, and regular offices.

making take on an increasingly technical character, industrialists and business leaders give way to technical specialists who occupy key positions of power in the large, formal bureaucracies. Theorists of post-industrialism single out the university for special attention, for in the knowledge society, the university is the main locus of knowledge production:

> Both Bell and Touraine argue that the university, which is the main locale in which theoretical knowledge is formulated and evaluated, becomes the key institution in the newly emerging society. (Giddens, 1974 : 256)

The glowing optimism of post-industrial theorists is thus premised on the belief that the knowledge society will eliminate the bulk of the conflicts associated with industrial society. As white-collar jobs increase in number relative to blue-collar jobs, as scientific knowledge and information become more widely disseminated, intrinsic job satisfaction will grow and traditional problems related to inequalities in the workplace will disappear. Such optimism, however, has proven to be largely illusory. As Blumberg (1980 : 74) has argued, the majority of white-collar jobs in the tertiary or service sector are neither high paying nor of high status. There may be more professionals, managers, executives and accountants,

> but a moment's thought is sufficient to realize that the mass of employees in "finance" are bank tellers, not bank presidents; that the majority of employees in retail trade are low paid sales people, not chief executives; that the bulk of employees in insurance are clerical workers, not company executives.

And even if it is true that labour strife has been minimized (a contentious claim), this is probably due to the fact that in the tertiary sector (finance, insurance, real estate, trade and services) unions are either very weak or non-existent.

Political ideology is another reason for the optimism that greeted the post-industrial thesis. Coming out of the Cold War era, governments and business leaders in the West were anxious to repudiate the teachings of Marx, and to distance themselves from the incisive criticisms that he levelled at industrial capitalism (Blumberg, 1980 : 217). What better way to deal with the situation than to claim that the type of society of which Marx spoke had been transcended? If we have in fact moved to a post-industrial society, the theory implies, we have also solved the problems and contradictions that Marx identified in industrial society.

In this context, it is instructive to examine Bell's argument in "The Social Framework of the Information Society" (1979). Bell directly challenges Marx's central idea that labour is the source of all value when he contends that knowledge is (intellectual) property. Although knowledge is produced, Bell argues, it cannot be treated as a commodity in the traditional sense of that term. For unlike a commodity that can be produced, sold to, and consumed by another, knowledge, "even when it is sold, remains with the producer" (1979 : 74). From Bell's point of view, then, the knowledge society produces knowledge as a "collective good" that is *available to all people*.

Because the production, processing, storage, retrieval *and sharing* of knowledge are such central features of post-industrial society, Bell is convinced that economists can no longer afford to ignore their role in market and exchange relations. Knowledge has become an important commodity or asset, making it indispensable to the functioning of modern, post-industrial society:

> When knowledge becomes involved in the applied transformation of resources, then one can say that knowledge, not labour, is the source of value. . . . Just as capital and labour have been the central variables of industrial society, so information and knowledge are the crucial variables of postindustrial society. (Bell, 1979 : 168)

Bell claims to have transcended Marx's labour theory of value. However, he does not specify the details of how the *labour* that produces knowledge is organized, and he fails to provide an adequate definition of knowledge (Weizenbaum, 1979 : 443–45). Despite these weaknesses, a challenging set of questions remains to be answered. How, for example, do we know when a society ceases to be industrial and enters its post-industrial phase? Does the logic of capitalism (the pursuit of profit) associated with industrial capitalism disappear in post-industrial society? And very centrally, in the knowledge society, is it a fact that the knowledge produced is equally accessible and beneficial to everyone?

In sum, it seems that the most important attribute of post-industrial theory is that it sensitizes us to new and significant societal trends in the advanced countries. It alerts us to the potential problems and social consequences of the information explosion, but does not go very far toward proposing solutions.

Dependency Theory

While the theorists of post-industrialism accepted and extended the assumptions of the evolutionary and value-oriented perspectives, another school of thought was radically opposed to those perspectives and their implications. Known generally as the *dependency* school, theorists of this persuasion rejected the ideas of people such as Hoselitz, Harrison and McClelland, and argued that societal development results from neither natural nor evolutionary processes. Dependency theory—advocated by theorists such as Gunder Frank (1972), dos Santos (1970), Cardoso (1972), Sunkel (1972) and many others—states that the overall structure of the world capitalist system makes development possible for some countries, but renders it highly unlikely for others. As the very label attached to this school of thought suggests, those countries that are dependent on others, for whatever reasons, are disadvantaged. As dos Santos notes (1970 : 231):

> By dependence we mean the situation in which the economy of certain countries is conditioned by the development and expansion of another economy to which the former are subjected.

Implicit in this definition is the idea that the dominant countries can expand their economies and become virtually self-sustaining, while the dependent ones can only develop *in a limited or restricted way* within the confines imposed by the overall context of the dominant-subordinate relationship.

Although there are many varieties of emphasis among dependency theorists, they all agree on one key point. Underdevelopment is *not* the original state or stage in which all societies once found themselves. There is a firm distinction between *underdeveloped* and *undeveloped* societies. Whereas all countries were at one point undeveloped, not all of them were underdeveloped. For the dependency theorist, *underdevelopment* is the *active* socio-economic and political process of promoting dependence, which in turn leads to the establishment of structures and institutions that pre-empt development. Hence, some countries moved from undevelopment to development, while others moved from undevelopment to underdevelopment.

But why do some countries move to development and others to underdevelopment? Is is because, as McClelland and Lipset believe, some undeveloped countries fostered entrepreneurial behaviour and progressive values and attitudes in their populations, while others did not? Is it because some countries have naturally evolved more or further than others? According to Paul Baran (the precursor of dependency theory), the answer to these questions is an unequivocal no. In developing his argument that underdeveloped countries also possess an abundance of talented and enterprising individuals, Baran is in clear disagreement with McClelland and Lipset. He tells us that in all countries and at all different times in history, we could find "ambitious, ruthless and enterprising men who had an opportunity and were willing to innovate, to move to the fore, to seize power and to exercise authority" (1957 : 235).

It seems, therefore, that although they possessed many "strategic ingredients" that make for modernization (according to the stipulations of Lerner, Inkeles and McClelland), certain countries have nevertheless failed to realize economic development. Most dependency theorists concur that the underdevelopment of the so-called Third World is the result of the economic and political consequences of colonialism and imperialism. The subordination of countries in Asia, Africa, Latin America and the Caribbean by those in Western Europe and North America caused dependence. Beginning with the voyages of so-called "discovery" and the capture of colonial territory, entire countries were brought into the orbit of world capitalism and relegated to the status of satellites. In the process, the institutions of slavery and the slave trade were firmly established as the economic and political structures of the colonies were deformed or distorted to meet the needs of capitalist colonizers.

In contemporary times, the countries of the Third World are not permitted to develop in an *autonomous* fashion. They are viewed solely as producers of raw materials destined for export in foreign-owned ships to the metropolitan centres of manufacturing and industry. Once exported, the raw materials are converted into finished products and re-exported to the Third World at greatly inflated prices. In the process, jobs are created for workers in the advanced countries where most manufacturing and industrial operations are located, and where capital is accumulated. Within the centres of advanced capitalism, a thriving internal market develops, wages are increased, and the spread of commercial activity results in higher demand for various other goods and services, greater economic differentiation, "modernity" and higher societal complexity.

Within the mining and plantation colonies, however, the picture is quite different. There, one finds rather backward techniques of land cultivation, low levels of technological and scientific development, a reliance on raw or unfinished agricultural and mineral exports, very few centres of industrial production and highly labour-intensive methods of work (Allahar, 1982 : 32–33). Major decisions regarding what to produce, how much to produce and what prices to charge are made outside the countries in question, thus depriving them of any say in determining the structure of their main economic and income-generating sectors. The economies of the Third World countries are thus distorted or biased toward activities that favour development in the centres of advanced capitalism. And, as the dependency theorists point out, although the mining and plantation sectors may employ better technology, pay higher wages and afford their workers a generally higher standard of living than the rest of the society in question, the vast bulk of the population in that society continue to live in backwardness with low levels of skill, education, health care, housing and so on.

By tailoring the economies of these countries to meet the needs of the advanced countries, the former become dependent on the latter for supplies of capital, credit, technology, expertise and the very market demand that makes possible continued production. Hence, local needs and local markets tend to be neglected, for the better part of all economic activity is directed toward external markets and consumers. In the process, a crippling foreign debt is amassed by the dependent countries. Table 18-1 conveys a sense of the magnitude of the foreign-debt problem in Central America.

Such a situation is perpetuated, dependency theorists argue, because political leaders in the dependent countries are generally mere pawns of international capitalism. Because of the economic and/or political pressure used against them, these leaders come to see their class interests as bound up with those of foreign capital. Hence, as Gunder Frank states, they "accept dependence consciously and willingly," and as "junior partners of foreign capital" they impose policies that increase dependence on the imperialist nations (1972 : 3–15).

TABLE 18-1
**Central American
External Debt
(in millions)**

	1960	1970	1978	1980	1984
Costa Rica	55	230	1870	2520	4050
El Salvador	33	130	990	930	2300
Guatemala	51	180	820	1050	1910
Honduras	23	144	970	1720	2250
Nicaragua	41	220	960	2150	3900
Panama	59	290	1770	2850	3550
Central America	260	1190	7380	11220	17960

DERIVED FROM DATA IN STATISTICAL ABSTRACT OF LATIN AMERICA, *VOL. 23, 1984;* CEPAL REVIEW, *JANUARY 1985.*

Marxism and
Dependency
Theory

Although Marxists agree with the general spirit and thrust of dependency theory, they find it too descriptive and generally lacking in class analysis. Taking account of the *political* aspects of underdevelopment, Zeitlin, for example, argues that the "full and unhampered" industrial development of the colonies was not in the interests of the imperialist forces; hence it "became the cardinal principle of every imperialist's policy to prevent and retard" such development (1972:96). Realizing that industrial development would eventually lead to the development of national consciousness, a working-class movement, opposition to both the imperialist presence and domination by local capitalists, and ultimately to calls for independence, none of which was in the interests of the imperialists, international capitalists cultivated allies among the locally dominant landlord class. And as Zeitlin (1972:97) writes:

> The imperialist-landlord alliance contributed further to the economic stagnation of the colonies because both groups had a powerful interest in preventing industrialization and the profound changes that inevitably would follow.

From the Marxist perspective, therefore, the development of capitalism is closely bound up with the ways in which specific social classes historically have come into contact with each other, sometimes working together, sometimes working against each other. It must be pointed out, however, that as an economic system, capitalism developed *unevenly* throughout the world. That is to say, a country such as Jamaica is *no less capitalist* than the United States, although it may be *less economically developed*. Like the United States, Jamaica boasts a free enterprise economic system and a liberal democratic political system; but nevertheless, the two countries are at polar extremes of the development continuum.

Underdevelopment, then, according to the Marxists, is accounted for in class terms. The dependent countries are sources of cheap raw materials and viable markets to which finished goods can be re-exported. Therefore, specific commercial, manufacturing and industrial classes within the advanced countries are keenly interested in gaining access to those raw materials and markets. During the early colonial period, such access was secured by outright plunder and conquest. The politically and economically powerful classes in the colonizing countries thus benefited at the expense of the indigenous inhabitants of the colonies. In more contemporary times, however, the imperialist connection is cemented by the multinational corporation (MNC).

Acting through their respective MNCs, the commercial, manufacturing and industrial classes represent *imperialist interests*, which "work out deals" with local governments and the powerful dominant classes in the dependent countries, and establish operations within restricted sectors of those countries. Along with the exploitation of cheap labour, the MNCs also manage to secure attractive concessions from local governments, for example, tax incentives, relaxed customs duties on imported technology and certain monopolistic privileges. Whatever changes to the infrastructure they promote are limited generally to transportation and communication networks that link the mines and plantations with the sea ports, thus yielding a very lopsided picture of local industrial development.

TABLE 18-2		
Major Canadian Multinationals in the Caribbean	Banks	Royal Bank of Canada
		Bank of Nova Scotia
		Canadian Imperial Bank of Commerce
	Tourism	Scott's Hospitality (Holiday Inn)
		Canadian Pacific
		Air Canada
	Manufacturers	Bata
	Insurance	Sun Life Assurance
		Imperial Life Assurance
		Dominion Life Assurance
	Agriculture	Maple Leaf Mills
		Quaker Oats of Canada
		Global Food Processors
		Seagram
	Minerals	Alcan Aluminum
		Falconbridge

TOM BARRY, DEB PREUSCH AND BETH WOOD. 1984. THE OTHER SIDE OF PARADISE. *NEW YORK: GROVE PRESS, P. 221.*

An important consideration in this context is the nature of the link between the economic and political aspects of imperialism. When Marxists speak of U.S. imperialism, for example, they refer not merely to the economic exploits of American MNCs abroad, but *also* to the fact that those economic interests are fully supported by U.S. governmental foreign policy. Hence, when *private* American foreign investments are threatened by local uprisings in a dependent country (for example, Cuba in 1959–62), the American government, *not* the MNCs, dispatches the armed forces to that country in an effort to safeguard those private investments.

Such domination, they say, may create the conditions for revolutionary change in the backward countries. Objectively, imperialist exploitation produces increased misery and poverty for the bulk of the population, very few of whom are employed in the foreign-controlled sectors. The constant draining away of national wealth, the monopolization of the best lands by foreign corporations, the recruitment of trained experts from abroad and the underdevelopment locally of health and educational facilities all accentuate social and economic disparities between the mass of the workers and peasants and the tiny core of privileged classes that benefit from the imperialist connection. Subjectively, this leads to a growing sense of nationalism as local parties, opposition interests and lobby groups see the possibility for change and start mobilizing for more responsible government, better wages and working conditions, greater self-determination and so on. Depending on the extent of such mobilization and the degree of political education and consciousness that develops, government repression is increased, and this deepens the social discontent.

According to the Marxists, then, when the objective condition of poverty and the subjective condition of consciousness reach the correct mix, a revolutionary situation is created. This is not to say that revolution is a mechanical affair, for other factors can always militate against the effective combination of these two sets of conditions. For example, the Marxists often talk of "false consciousness," which occurs when workers fail to recognize the true source of their oppression. Certain religions promote false consciousness by making a virtue of poverty ("the meek shall inherit the earth") and counsel conservatism ("turn the other cheek"; "you will be rewarded tenfold in the next world"). Nevertheless, when the objective and subjective conditions are ripe, and when the oppressed no longer view their oppressors as legitimate, the former will rise up against the latter. And tracing the source of their discontent back to the structures of imperialist exploitation, the workers will seek to abolish private property and capitalism, and create a workers' state or socialism.

In summary, both dependency theorists and Marxists view underdevelopment, poverty and backwardness as products of imperialism. They are diametrically opposed to the evolutionary and value-orientation schools, which see greater capitalist development as the solution to the problems of pre-modern or traditional societies. The debate between these perspectives must thus be judged on the basis of the evidence. Some relevant questions are: Why does capitalism lead to development in some countries and not in others? Which classes benefit from such development and which classes don't? Can imperialism enhance the possibility for development in the Third World, or does it exacerbate the problem and create the conditions for revolutionary transformation?

Dependency
Theory Applied
to Canada

In her book *Silent Surrender*, Kari Levitt (1970) describes Canada as the world's richest underdeveloped country. Citing numerous examples of American MNCs operating within Canada, Levitt argues that the Canadian economy has become a branch-plant economy, playing host to a wide variety of U.S. business interests. These branch-plant subsidiaries of parent firms located in the United States serve to drain Canada's wealth south of the border and have yielded a very lopsided pattern of industrial development in this country—development that is not locally directed. As Hiller (1976:93) has argued, MNCs are not necessarily concerned with the local problems or priorities of a given country.They are not compelled to reinvest profits locally, and if pressured by local governments to do so, they often threaten to move their operations elsewhere:

> It is the very nature of corporations to make decisions according to the norms of capitalism and their desire for profit; national sentiments are rarely able to change these norms.

And it was precisely this type of situation that led Levitt (1970:58) cryptically to remark:

> Some sixty years ago Sir Wilfrid Laurier declared that the twentieth century belongs to Canada. By the middle of the century it had become clear that Canada belongs to the United States.

In a recent study, Jorge Niosi (1985:33–60) agrees that the Canadian economy has been subject to external control and dependence on foreign influences, but he does not go as far as to claim that Canada is underdeveloped. He speaks of Canada's "dependent industrialization" and outlines in very clear detail the processes by which American corporations literally have "invaded" the Canadian economy and have established controlling interests in areas such as transportation equipment manufacturing, mining and smelting, oil and gas, lumber and electronics, among many others. Although in recent years various Canadian governments (federal and provincial) have sought to buy back control in several of these areas, the Canadian economy continues to exhibit traits of dependence on foreign technology, foreign markets, foreign capital and foreign expertise:

> Canada, after a century of pursuing a liberal policy towards foreign direct investment and the transfer of technology, now finds itself with half of its technology under outside control—one of the highest percentages of foreign control in the world. (Niosi, 1985 : 30)

How do the dependency theorists account for this situation? In recent years, a large body of literature has grown around the themes of dependency, regionalism, colonialism and internal colonialism in Canada. Focusing on the questions of regionalism and uneven development *within* Canada, writers such as Clement (1980; 1983), Phillips (1982) and Veltmeyer (1978) have looked to the disciplines of economics, geography, history and sociology for answers. Their basic argument is that historically Canada's dependence on foreign powers stemmed from its status as a colony of Britain. Being politically, culturally and economically dominated by the mother country (Hiller, 1976 : 84), Canadian society came to exhibit a pronounced European orientation, whereas American society did not (Lipset, 1985). In economic terms, the Canadian economy was geared to the production and export of raw materials to Britain, where they were processed and manufactured, thus creating jobs in that country and boosting its industrial development. And as we saw in the previous section, the host country (Canada) traditionally served as a ready market outlet for the manufactured goods produced in the *metropole* or the developed core countries (Clement, 1983 : 55–56).

While sympathetic to this basic line of argument, Gordon Laxer seeks to refine our historical understanding of dependence and underdevelopment in Canada by pointing to the structure of internal class forces. Specifically, he contends that the very high foreign ownership of the Canadian economy must not necessarily be blamed on the bourgeoisie alone, or that fraction of it that favoured free trade. For in addition to the bourgeoisie's pursuit of its own interests, two other factors militated against the development of a truly independent state in Canada: the weakness and political fragmentation of the agrarian classes and the French-English divisions in Lower and Upper Canada. In other words, the absence of effective political opposition to the big business interests and their alliances with foreign capital had repercussions that went beyond the bourgeoisie itself:

> Ethno-national appeals led only to national conflict, not to national unity. . . . The forces of big business were politically ascendant and faced little challenge because

the class that could have ousted them—the farmers—was seriously divided by ethno-national issues. (Laxer, 1989 : 140)

Over the years, when the United States replaced Britain as Canada's foremost trading partner, Canada's external dependence increased greatly, and the internal disparities between regions were accentuated. The dependency notion of a chain of metropoles and satellites is useful for explaining the processes involved. As Clement (1980 : 276) asserts, "regional economies are tied to national economies and national ones to international ones." This is the idea of the chain. Canada is neither strictly developed nor underdeveloped. Some regions are more developed than others. The less developed are linked to the more developed, and the latter in turn are tied to even more developed international centres:

> Canada is not unequivocally an industrial country. Part is industrialized—but the rest [is] a resource hinterland. Most of Canada's industrial capacity is located below a line starting at Windsor, encompassing Toronto and moving to Montreal. This is industrial Canada. (Clement, 1980 : 276)

When one speaks of the underdeveloped regions of Canada, one automatically thinks of the Atlantic provinces (Nova Scotia, New Brunswick, Prince Edward Island and Newfoundland). As the *hinterland* of Ontario and Quebec, the Atlantic provinces are not centres of banking, industry and commerce. Because they are resource-based economies, they are sources of wealth; but that wealth is traditionally accumulated and reinvested outside, bringing jobs to outsiders (Ontarians and Quebeckers, for example) and providing those outsiders with a generally higher standard of living than those in Atlantic Canada.

The economies of the Atlantic provinces are said to be underdeveloped not because they lack resources, but because they are dependent on outsiders for technology, expertise, capital and markets. Because such "outsiders" usually present themselves in the form of MNCs, and because they do not necessarily have local interests at heart, it is understandable that the peripheral areas and single-industry towns are seriously disadvantaged. Whatever development of the economy or infrastructure does occur is highly resource specific and does not lead to integrated development for the region as a whole. Hence, *social* development is neglected; schools, hospitals and housing are substandard; and general life chances of the population are not as promising as those of Canadians who live in the "golden triangle" (Toronto–Montreal–Ottawa).

To explain further the dynamics of underdevelopment and dependency in Canada, theorists such as Clement, Niosi, Carroll, Laxer, Veltmeyer and Smucker have argued for a class analysis. Specifically, they direct our attention to the structure of the Canadian capitalist class, which is concentrated largely in the golden triangle area. This class exerts a growing dominance in matters of finance, transportation and utilities nationally. Internationally, they are able to compete effectively with the most powerful capitalist enterprises for profits and markets.

Within the underdeveloped regions of the country, the economic structures do not provide much opportunity for the advancement of the local populations. The jobs that are usually available tend to be of an unskilled or semi-skilled variety, and the general content of school curricula reflects the demands of that job market. Housing conditions, health and welfare provisions and overall life styles often lag behind those that one encounters in the more developed parts of Ontario and Quebec. But even within Ontario and Quebec there are numerous pockets of backwardness in single-industry towns and rural areas. A very clear picture of dependence and uneven development in single-industry towns is painted by Rex Lucas in his classic study entitled *Minetown, Milltown, Railtown* (1971).

Although he would probably resist the label of "dependency theorist," William Carroll does not appear to be in serious disagreement with the descriptive thrust of dependency theory. What he does add to this perspective, however, is a concern for class analysis and detailed historical research. For example, in seeking to explain the reasons behind major U.S. control of industries such as automobiles, petroleum and electrical equipment in Canada, he asked:

> What class-structured conditions made these investments more attractive to American capitalists than possible investments elsewhere, while limiting the extent to which Canadian capitalists could directly compete in the same industries? (Carroll, 1986 : 200)

His answer is threefold. First, owing to its geographical proximity to the United States and the fact that Canada's was a high-growth capitalist economy, U.S. investors were naturally attracted. Second, we are told that since Canada's working class developed in the late nineteenth century as a relatively high-wage proletariat, Canadian capitalists were unable to compete effectively with the larger and more technologically advanced U.S. firms. And third, because Canadian finance capitalists had tied up such large amounts of capital in the construction and operation of a domestic transportation system (CPR, CNR), they had even less capital to invest in competition with American capitalists in other sectors. As a consequence, both Canadian capitalists and Canadian capitalism were rendered weak (Carroll, 1986 : 200–201).

TABLE 18-3
Canadian Banks in the Caribbean (1982)

	World Assets ($ billions Canadian)	No. of Caribbean Branches	International Earnings as % of Total Earnings
Royal Bank of Canada	$89.6	109	37%
Canadian Imperial Bank of Commerce	69.4	58	36%
Bank of Montreal	63.5	3	32%
Bank of Nova Scotia	54.7	143	49%

COMPILED FROM BANK ANNUAL REPORTS; POLK'S BANKING DIRECTORY.

From the foregoing, we can get an idea of how dependency theory and class analysis can be applied to an understanding of change and development in certain regions of Canada. One must not get the impression, however, that Canada is an underdeveloped society as Levitt implied. A far more accurate view is that supplied by Niosi and Carroll, who argue that today Canada is a major imperialist country whose MNCs have extensive control of banking (see Table 18-3), mining, transportation and communications in many Third World countries. The Canadian capitalist class is allied internationally with other capitalist classes, and together they are responsible for much of the underdevelopment that characterizes large parts of Canada and the Third World.

Summary

In this chapter we have examined several approaches to the questions of social change and development. First, we looked at the social evolutionary and value-orientation perspectives, which depict change as slow, evolutionary and cumulative. Value-orientation theory, however, emphasizes psychological factors as the key to explaining change and development. Members of this school thus examine the values and attitudes held by individuals in particular societies in order to determine whether those values and attitudes are likely to produce behaviour that will lead to development. Finally, dependency theorists and Marxists are not convinced that underdevelopment is an original or natural state in which all societies once found themselves. Nor are they convinced that underdevelopment results merely because a given population lacks progressive values and attitudes. Rather, these theorists consider underdevelopment to be the social, political and economic outcome of colonialism and imperialism. They believe the problem can only be overcome by the reorganization of the society and economy along socialist lines.

Suggested Readings

Allahar, Anton

> 1989. *Sociology and the Periphery: Theories and Issues*. Toronto: Garamond Press. A discussion and amplification of the theories of social change presented in this chapter. Special attention is focused on the politics of change and the relationship between theory and ideology. Numerous examples from both the developed and underdeveloped countries are analysed.

Gunder Frank, André

> 1972. *Lumpenbourgeoisie: Lumpendevelopment*. New York: Monthly Review Press. This is a very clear presentation of dependency theory by its most famous exponent. Combining a wealth of historical and contemporary data for Latin America, the author is able to underscore the dynamics of backwardness. Of special interest is the attempt to introduce class analysis to dependency theory.

Harrison, Lawrence

> 1985. *Underdevelopment Is a State of Mind*. Boston: University Press of America. Just when

we thought that modernization theory was dead, this new publication by Harvard's Center for International Affairs proves the reverse. Citing evidence from several underdeveloped countries, the author is able to drive home his point concerning the crucial role played by values and attitudes in promoting or retarding social change. This study is in striking contrast with that of Gunder Frank.

Kitching, Gavin

1982. *Development and Underdevelopment in Historical Perspective*. New York: Methuen. A survey of development studies from the 1940s to the present. The central question posed is as follows: How do the intellectual origins and historical background of Western and other theories of social change affect their relevance to contemporary conditions in the Third World (China and Tanzania). The central focus is on populism and neo-populism, which are seen as the basis for all recent thinking on change and development. Populism is understood as a political movement of the masses inspired by appeals to "the people."

Rinehart, James

1987. *The Tyranny of Work*, 2nd ed. Don Mills, Ont. Harcourt, Brace, Jovanovich. An excellent discussion of the themes of alienation, technology and post-industrialism in Canadian society. Combining a historical and critical perspective, the author addresses the growth of the factory system and scientific management in the context of social change in Canada. Of special interest is the class analysis of blue- and white-collar workers and the change in the Canadian economy from agriculture to industry.

Veltmeyer, Henry

1987. *Canadian Corporate Power*. Toronto: Garamond Press. This study looks at corporatism as a central element in the structure of Canadian capitalism. It stresses the importance of economic analysis and draws attention to the degree of concentration of corporate power in Canada. The study covers a variety of issues treated in this chapter: multinational corporations; dependency theory; and colonialism.

Discussion Questions

1. In what sense do the social evolutionary and value-orientation schools promote a conservative approach to change and development?

2. Why do dependency theorists think it is important to make a distinction between undeveloped and underdeveloped societies?

3. What do students of social change have to gain from an understanding of Marxism?

4. Which parts (regions) of Canada are best described by the post-industrial thesis? And where is that thesis least applicable?

5. Why is an understanding of history indispensable to the study of social change?

6. Which of Parsons's pattern variables are most applicable to a description of Canadian society? And which are least applicable?

Data Collection Exercises

1. Select two groups of immigrants to Canada and analyse the changing circumstances in their own countries that led to their migration. For purposes of comparison, you may want to make these groups as dissimilar as possible (i.e., one group from a developed and one from an underdeveloped country).

2. The women's movement of the 1960s and 1970s, we are told, has resulted in a major change in female employment patterns. Focusing on the professional level, do a comparative investigation of the changing numbers of female faculty members at Canadian universities. Examine a selection of university calendars from the 1960s, 1970s and 1980s to see whether or not there has been any change in the proportions of women hired, and if so, which faculties have changed most/least.

3. By consulting the relevant sources such as census data, historical tracts, literary works and so on, construct a picture of a typical Canadian family at the turn of the century (number of children, type of employment, place of residence, level of education, etc.), and compare it to a typical family today. What are some of the major changes that can be noted? How can they be accounted for sociologically? The processes of industrialization, urbanization and secularization are relevant here.

4. In this chapter we have said a fair amount about economic development and dependency. Within the Canadian economy we are told that foreign corporations have had a strong ownership influence ever since colonial times. Investigate this claim with a view to showing any key changes that have occurred with particular reference to U.S. corporations. Are there any areas in which Canadian ownership was once weak and is now strong, or vice versa?

Writing Exercises

1. Pretend you are a columnist for *The New York Times* and write a critical response to Harrison's basic argument in *Underdevelopment Is a State of Mind*.

2. You have been hired by the prime minister as a speech writer and your first assignment concerns an address by the prime minister to the Canadian Civil Liberties Union. The topic is abortion and the changing attitudes toward it.

3. Go to the library and select two journals devoted to the publication of articles dealing with some aspect of macro-social change. Choose any two articles that argue from opposing points of view and write an abstract of three hundred words for each.

4. Write a two-page critique of the present chapter indicating its strengths and weaknesses, with suggestions for remedying the latter. At least two weaknesses should be discussed.

Glossary

Dependency: *a condition that characterizes the relationship between two economies (countries) whereby the one grows and expands at the expense of the other.*

Hinterland: *a term commonly used in the dependency literature to describe the periphery or the countryside. It is often used in opposition to the "core" or "centre," which designates the urban, industrial capitals.*

Imperialism: *the expansion of capitalism across national boundaries. It involves both the political and economic penetration of one country by another.*

Labour theory of value: *arguably the crux of Marxist analysis. The view that labour is the source of all value and its exploitation constitutes the basis of capitalist profits.*

Modernization: *the approach to development that stresses the importance that values and attitudes have on social change. Backwardness is caused by the lack of appropriate values and attitudes.*

Organismic analogy: *the same as social Darwinism. An attempt to view and analyse society as if it were a living organism with needs and prerequisites for survival.*

Post-industrialism: *a view that the advanced societies have left the industrial era of factory production behind and have entered a new era where knowledge production in universities is a more defining characteristic of those societies.*

Social Darwinism: *the ideas of biological evolutionism applied to the study of how societies change and develop. Herbert Spencer was the chief exponent of social Darwinistic thinking.*

Social differentiation: *the process whereby a homogeneous social entity becomes more heterogeneous or splintered. As societies or social groups become more complex, dissimilar or internally divided, they are said to be socially differentiated.*

Social evolutionary theory: *the approach to understanding social change that employs the basic Darwinian principles of "natural selection" and "survival of the fittest," applying them to an understanding of how societies come into existence, grow, mature and then die.*

Social integration: *the opposite of social differentiation. It is a state described by Durkheim as mechanical solidarity in which all parts or units are very similar or homogeneous. A village community, for example, is generally thought to exhibit a high level of social integration: most people do similar jobs, have similar levels of education, worship the same god(s), have similar aspirations and so on. That pervasive sameness produces a sense of commonality and sharing that one does not find in a differentiated, heterogeneous social setting.*

Underdevelopment: *a state that usually characterizes the economies and countries of the Third World. It speaks to the widespread poverty, unemployment and grossly inefficient social services that accompany dependence.*

World system: *a concept developed by Immanuel Wallerstein to discuss macro-historical change. He used it specifically to analyse the capitalist world economy, which is made up of core, semi-core and peripheral economies. The modern world system is to be distinguished from ancient world empires and socialist world government.*

References

Allahar, Anton
1982. "Colonialism and Underdevelopment." *Two-Thirds* 3(2).

Baran, Paul
1957. *The Political Economy of Growth*. New York and London: Monthly Review Press.

Bell, Daniel
1971. "Technology and Politics." *Survey* 16.
1973. *The Coming of Post-Industrial Society*. New York: Basic Books.
1979. "The Social Framework of the Information Society." In Michael L. Dertouzos and Joel Moses, eds., *The Computer Age: A Twenty-Year View*. Cambridge, Mass.: MIT Press.

Blumberg, Paul
1980. *Inequality in an Age of Decline*. New York: Oxford University Press.

Cardoso, Fernando Henrique
1972. "Industrialization, Dependency and Power in Latin America." *Berkeley Journal of Sociology* 18.

Carroll, William K.
1986. *Corporate Power and Canadian Capitalism*. Vancouver: University of British Columbia Press.

Chodak, Szymon
1973. *Societal Development*. New York: Oxford University Press.

Clement, Wallace
1980. "A Political Economy of Regionalism in Canada." In John Harp and John R. Hofley, eds., *Structured Inequality in Canada*. Toronto: Prentice-Hall.
1983. *Class, Power and Property*. Toronto: Methuen.

Collins, Randall, and Michael Markowsky
1984. *The Discovery of Society*, 3rd ed. New York: Random House.

dos Santos, Theotonio
1970. "The Structure of Dependence." *American Economic Review* (May).

Durkheim, Emile
1933. *On the Division of Labour in Society*. New York: Macmillan.

Eisenstadt, S. N.
1964. "Social Change, Differentiation and Evolution." *American Sociological Review* 29 (June).

Giddens, Anthony
1974. *The Class Structure of the Advanced Societies*. London: Hutchinson University Library.

Gunder Frank, André
1972. *Lumpenbourgeoisie; Lumpendevelopment: Dependence, Class and Politics in Latin America*. New York: Monthly Review Press.

Harrison, Lawrence
1985. *Underdevelopment Is a State of Mind*. Lanham, Md.: University Press of America.

Hiller, Harry
1976. *Canadian Society: A Sociological Analysis*. Toronto: Prentice-Hall.

Hoselitz, Berthold F.
  1960. *Sociological Aspects of Economic Growth*. Glencoe, Ill.: Free Press.

Inkeles, Alex
  1966. "The Modernization of Man." In Myron Weiner, ed., *Modernization: The Dynamics of Growth*. New York: Basic Books.
  1973. "Making Men Modern." In Amitai Etzioni, ed., *Social Change: Sources, Patterns, and Consequences*. New York: Basic Books.

Laxer, Gordon
  1989. *Open for Business: The Roots of Foreign Ownership in Canada*. Toronto: Oxford University Press.

Lerner, Daniel
  1965. *The Passing of Traditional Society*. New York: Free Press.

Levitt, Kari
  1970. *Silent Surrender: The Multinational Corporation in Canada*. Toronto: Macmillan.

Lipset, Seymour Martin
  1967. "Values, Education and Entrepreneurship." In S. M. Lipset and Aldo Solari, eds., *Elites in Latin America*. New York: Oxford University Press.
  1985. "Canada and the United States: The Cultural Dimension." In Charles F. Doran and John H. Sigler, eds., *Canada and the United States*. Toronto: Prentice-Hall.

Lucas, Rex
  1971. *Minetown, Milltown, Railtown*. Toronto: University of Toronto Press.

McClelland, David
  1963. "Motivational Patterns in Southeast Asia." *Journal of Social Issues* 29(17).
  1964. "The Achievement Motive in Economic Growth." In David Novack and Robert Leckachman, eds., *Development and Society: The Dynamics of Economic Change*. New York: St. Martin's Press.

Mills, C. Wright
  1959. *The Sociological Imagination*. New York: Oxford University Press.

Niosi, Jorge
  1985. *Canadian Multinationals*. Toronto: Garamond Press.

Parsons, Talcott
  1954. *Essays in Sociological Theory*. Glencoe, Ill.: Free Press.

Phillips, Paul
  1982. *Regional Disparities*, 2nd ed. Toronto: James Lorimer.

Portes, Alejandro
  1976. "On the Sociology of National Development: Theories and Issues." *American Journal of Sociology* 82(1).

Rinehart, James W.
  1975. *The Tyranny of Work*. Toronto: Academic Press.

Ritzer, George
  1988. *Sociological Theory*, 2nd ed. New York: Knopf.

Smelser, Neil
  1968. *Essays in Sociological Explanation*. Englewood Cliffs, N.J.: Prentice-Hall.

Sunkel, Osvaldo
　　1972. "Big Business and 'Dependencia,' " *Foreign Affairs* 50(3).

Tilly, Charles
　　1981. *As Sociology Meets History*. New York: Academic Press.

Tönnies, Ferdinand
　　1957. *Community and Society*. East Lansing: Michigan State University Press.

Touraine, Alain
　　1971. *The Post-Industrial Society*. New York: Random House.

Veltmeyer, Henry
　　1978. "The Underdevelopment of Atlantic Canada." *Review of Radical Political Economics* 10(2).

Wallerstein, Immanuel
　　1974. *The Modern World System*. New York: Academic Press.

Weber, Max
　　1958. *The Protestant Ethic and the Spirit of Capitalism*. New York: Charles Scribner's Sons.

Weiner, Myron, ed.
　　1966. "Introduction." In *Modernization: The Dynamics of Growth*. New York: Basic Books.

Weizenbaum, Joseph
　　1979. "Once More: The Computer Revolution." In Michael L. Dertouzos and Joel Moses, eds., *The Computer Age: A Twenty-Year View*. Cambridge, Mass.: MIT Press.

Wilson, John
　　1983. *Social Theory*. Englewood Cliffs, N.J.: Prentice-Hall.

Zeitlin, Irving M.
　　1972. *Capitalism and Imperialism*. Chicago: Markham.

Population Processes

LORNE TEPPERMAN

SUMMARY

Westerners visiting China come face to face with a population of over one billion people. Recent government efforts to discourage childbearing have enjoyed some success. Even so, a birth rate of less than 2 percent produces nearly as many new Chinese babies each year as there are people of all ages living in Canada today.

Introduction

Many of the things sociologists write about are hard to understand and impossible to see. When did you last look at a norm, a social class or a self? On the other hand, this chapter is about things that are easy to see and understand; in fact, things that comprise the absolute minimum for any society.

This chapter relies on your knowledge that societies contain different "kinds" of people—male and female, young and old—and that, over the course of time, people come and go. What you may not have realized is that these comings and goings have a pattern and have social consequences. The study of different kinds of people, their comings and goings, and the resulting social consequences is called *demography*, or *population studies*. The "comings and goings" themselves are usually called *population processes*, and the stock of people at a given moment is called a *population*.

According to economist Kenneth Boulding (1981 : 55), a population is merely "the stock of a species with throughput." This somewhat obscure definition applies to any "species," such as people in Canada, professors at the University of Manitoba, trees in Algonquin Park or used cars in Quebec City. However, sociologists study the throughput of *human* populations: the addition and subtraction of people through births and

FIGURE 19-1

A Simple Throughput Model

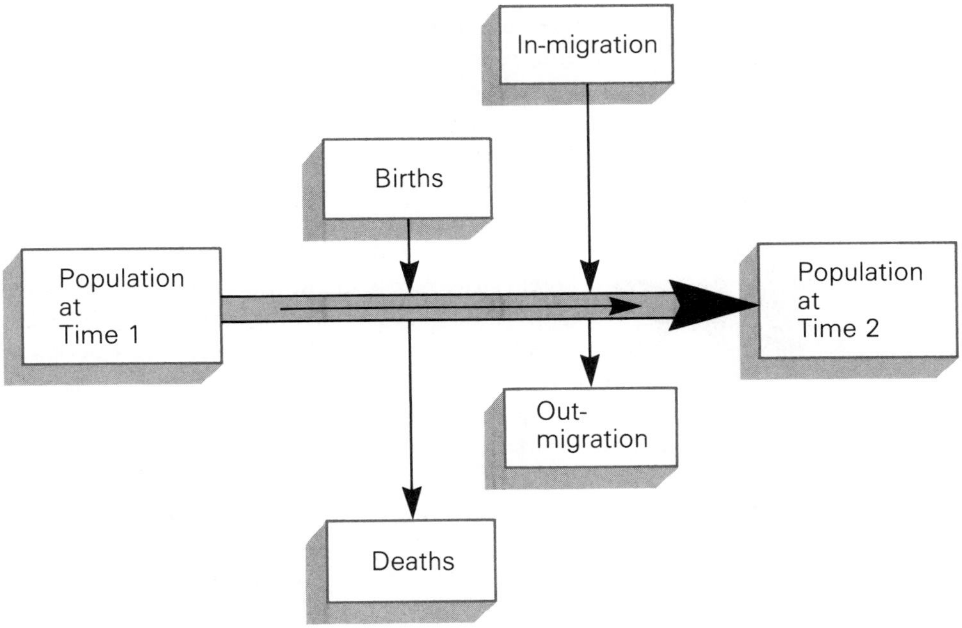

deaths, in-migrations and out-migrations and relocations. Figure 19-1 shows some of these throughput factors affecting the total size, or "stock," of the human population.

The study of human population is more complicated than the study of other "species." Humans think, communicate, plan and take purposeful action, thus influencing birth, death and migration rates. Moreover, their thoughts and actions influence the social structures through which they move. Any social role or institution through which people move in a predictable way can be studied from a "population perspective." For example, a study of *social mobility* concerns the movement of people from one social class to another, and study of careers concerns the movement of people through a series of jobs or organizations.

Social relationships often keep the same form despite the individuals involved in them. Take the relationship between parents and their children. Naturally, families differ due to class, ethnic background and other variables. But if a foreigner asked how average Canadian parents interact with their children, sociologists could answer with considerable accuracy. The answer would reveal important similarities among Canadian families, as well as differences between Canadian families and, for example, Chinese families.

Many factors contribute toward making family relationships predictable: laws, such as those against child abuse; social values learned and relearned throughout life; role expectations parents and children hold about one another; and social pressures brought to bear by outsiders, such as friends, relatives and teachers.

No pattern is altered *suddenly* when individuals enter into the roles of parent or child. Children are born daily, grandparents die and adults become parents; yet, it is remarkable how little this continuous flow of people in and out of roles affects the parent-child relationship as a cultural ideal.

That is not to say, however, that population processes have *no* effect whatever on the stability of social processes. If the numbers of people flowing through social roles change, the social structures themselves may be affected. Think of society as a large, fully furnished hotel. Ordinarily, people check in and out of the hotel in an orderly procession. But what if the rate of movement sped up, if twice as many people crowded into the same number of rooms or if people arrived who lacked knowledge of, or respect for, the hotel rules? People might move the furniture around, perhaps even vandalize or destroy the building. Certainly, the hotel would change. How much it might change is partly decided by the size, composition and distribution of the hotel population. The study of the relationship between a social structure and its population, whether in a hotel or in a national sample, is the study of how each changes the other over the course of time.

Let's look back at family roles. The flow of people through these roles has been changing. Today, people are slower to become parents than they used to be and many more are choosing not to become parents at all. People are also slower to leave the role of parent, due to an increase in average life expectancy, or quicker to leave it through divorce. And fewer people are enacting the role of child, because families are becoming smaller.

These changes are altering the number of "conventional" families, and this trend weakens predictable family relations. Traditional patterns are dying out, and traditional expectations do not apply as well as they once did (Eichler, 1981). But we have not yet formed new expectations. We feel confused about what "proper" family relationships are. We are passing through a period of social change induced, in part, by population change.

Consider the change that has taken place in Quebec. Fifty years ago, large families were the norm in Quebec. Since the 1960s, however, francophone marriage and childbirth rates have fallen rapidly and are currently the lowest in Canada. Worried by these cultural and political implications, the Quebec National Assembly has enacted incentives to encourage more people to have more children.

Two principles for studying population emerge from these concepts. First, the best way to study population processes is historical (change over time). Second, the best way to study population change is to relate it to a study of social change.

The Study of Population Change

Good theories about population processes demand good historical data, including censuses, vital statistics and national and international migration records. A *census* of the population is the collection of demographic, economic and social data about all the people within the boundaries of a country or any other geographical unit. In

A large family has become a rarity in this country; this was much less the case in previous decades, as suggested by this Quebec family from the early 1940s.

NATIONAL ARCHIVES OF CANADA/PA 112893.

Canada, censuses are conducted every ten years (for example 1971, 1981, 1991), and mini-censuses are conducted in between (for example, 1976, 1986). The scientific study of these records is called demography. The most accurate records are available in modern Western societies. As a result, population theories often reflect the experiences of these societies. Even after the Second World War, population data were drawn almost entirely from European and North American sources, leading sociologists to believe that population changes in the Third World would follow the patterns that they had observed in Europe for several centuries. By collecting better data in developing countries, we have changed our theories. Demographers, people who study population scientifically, have helped governments improve the quality of their data and interpret this information more effectively. Demographers have even developed techniques for judging and correcting flawed data (United Nations, 1967; Shyrock and Siegel, 1973).

Recent advances in methodology and data quality have also improved historical analysis. For example, parish records can now be analysed by computer in order to study the populations of historic communities and tell us about family life, household membership and population processes hundreds of years ago. The work by Peter Laslett and his Cambridge (England) group (Laslett, 1971, 1972; Wrigley, 1966) is especially notable in this area. Quebec demographers have used similar techniques to study the entire population of seventeenth-century New France (Legare, 1988). This ongoing project will eventually reveal a lot about the demographic history of French Canada, through parish records, early censuses, genealogies and other archival materials.

A great many demographers and historians make creative use of historical censuses. Perhaps the most advanced and systematic work has been done by researchers associated with Princeton University's European Fertility Study, under the guidance of Ansley Coale. Already, volumes have been published on the demographic histories of seventeen European countries (see Coale and Watkins, 1986, for a complete listing of these publications).

With reliable statistics, we can begin to chart past and future trends. Social planners are especially interested in a population's growth rate. A *growth rate* is the number of people added to (or subtracted from) a population in a given period of time, expressed as a percentage change over that same period. Demographers also measure population growth rates in terms of *doubling time*, or the number of years in which a population will double in size if it continues to grow at its current rate. An easy way to estimate doubling time is to divide the growth rate into .69. For example, the current growth rate of the world's population is about 2 percent per year—the population is increasing by .02 of the total every year—so the world's population will double in less than thirty-five years (.69 ÷ .02 = 34.5) to a total of more than 8 billion early in the next century. This technique works only for areas where net migration is zero, such as the earth as a whole.

According to demographer Philip Hauser (1964:17), if growth continues at the present rate, by the year 3530 the human population will outweigh the earth it stands on. This hypothetical result is clearly absurd, but it illustrates the speed at which our species is approaching its territorial limits on earth. Sooner or later, growth must stop. But when and how? Will the change be sudden or gradual, chosen or forced upon us? Will it be accompanied by a drastic decline in childbirth or a rise in the number of deaths? The world population increases when the rate of births (*fertility rate*) is higher than the rate of deaths (*mortality rate*). This excess is called *natural increase* (as distinct from increase due to migration). There are only two ways for world population growth to slow (or stop): the fertility rate falls or the mortality rate rises. A good theory about the causes and cures of rapid population growth is essential when planning for our future as a species on earth.

The Population of the World

It is possible quickly to summarize the remarkable acceleration of his growth rate which man has experienced. It took most of the millennia of man's habitation of this planet to produce a population as great as one billion persons simultaneously alive. This population was not achieved until approximately 1850. To produce a population of two billion persons simultaneously alive required only an additional seventy-five years, for this number was achieved by 1925. To reach a population of three billion persons required only an additional thirty-seven years, for this was the total in 1962. Continuation of the trend would produce a fourth billion in about fifteen years and a fifth billion in less than an additional ten years.

If man's precursors prior to the old Stone Age are ignored, it has been estimated that since the beginning of that era there have been perhaps 77 billion births. Of this number only 12 billion, or less than 16 percent of the total, occurred during the approximately 8000 years encompassing the Neolithic period and history up to the middle of the seventeenth century. Some 23 billion births, or 30 percent of the total, occurred during the three centuries of the Modern Era. Of the total number of persons that have ever been born, according to these estimates, about 4 percent, therefore, are now living.

Excerpt from "The Population of the World," by Philip M. Hauser from the book *Population: The Vital Revolution* by Ronald Freedman. Copyright 1964 by Doubleday & Company, Inc. Reprinted by permission of the publisher.

Three Theories of Population Growth

There have been many theories proposed to explain population growth, as to explain every other social phenomenon this book discusses. Below, we discuss only three of these: Malthusian theory, Marxian theory, and demographic transition theory. They share a common concern with connecting population processes and social change. As such, they are historical theories. Malthusian and demographic transition theories have been widely debated and vigorously researched by demographers. Marxian theory, though less influential, is included because it is part of a more general theoretical and philosophical outlook often discussed in the course of this book.

Malthusian Theory

One of the earliest and most influential theories about population growth was put forward by Thomas Robert Malthus (1766–1834), an English clergyman and economist. In 1798, Malthus published an *Essay on the Principle of Population* (1959; originally 1798) in which he argues that over time a population grows faster than its means of food production. At best, Malthus claims, food production increases only arithmetically, as in the series 1, 2, 3, 4, 5; but population increases geometrically, as in the series 1, 2, 4, 8, 16. The gap between these two series gets wider and wider if population growth goes unchecked.

Malthus bases his ideas on the assumption that people want sex, and sex results in childbirth. But as more children are born, the total need for food increases. People will respond to food shortages by having fewer children, but once more food becomes available again, they will resume having more children. The population, Malthus argues, will always increase to the limit of subsistence, catching up to and consuming any food surplus. Thus, material progress—in the production of food and other areas—can have no lasting effect. Population will always increase when the means of subsistence increases, unless kept from doing so by powerful checks—either *preventive* or *positive*.

Preventive checks are actions individuals take to limit births. Because birth control by artificial means was considered to be immoral in Malthus's time, he recommended postponing marriage. In a society without contraception, the later a woman begins bearing children, the fewer children she will bear in total. Malthus did not believe that people were capable of being abstinent within marriage. *Positive checks* are such population-reducing events as wars, famines, plagues or other disasters. Malthus thought these disasters were inevitable, since humans, like other living creatures, reproduce beyond their means of subsistence.

In his early works, Malthus stressed the inevitability of positive checks and the value (especially for the poor) of religious faith in helping people accept life's inevitable hardships. But in his later work, Malthus emphasized preventive checks as a means of avoiding positive checks. Thus, his name became associated with birth control, even though Malthus did not favour birth control by artificial means. In later editions of *Essay on the Principle of Population* (1970; originally 1830), he was more and more optimistic that general education would result in preventive checks to population growth. For this reason, Malthus pushed for general education in an era when even enlightened people thought it might prove dangerous to the social order.

Criticisms of the Malthusian Theory

The debate about Malthusian theory rages on, because history proves Malthus was partly right and partly wrong. He was right to suggest that positive checks would wreak havoc in societies without adequate preventive checks. He was wrong to believe that food supplies increased only arithmetically or population only geometrically; that people would consume their entire food surplus to produce more babies; or that love, sex, marriage and reproduction always had to go together.

On one hand, Malthus's most dire predictions have not yet come to pass, even a century after his death. On the other hand, this could be explained by three recent social changes: the opening of new land for food production and improved agricultural methods; the increasing use of contraception as a preventive check; and the shift from an agricultural to an industrial economic base, which has proven better able to bring prosperity. However, as some observers point out pessimistically, population figures are swelling, there are recurring famines in many parts of the world and there are growing shortages of non-renewable resources (such as water) in the developed world (Meadows et al., 1972; Higgins, 1980). These may be signs that the alarm Malthus raised was well founded. After all, he did not say when disaster would strike, only that it was inevitable.

When Malthus introduced his theories nearly two centuries ago, he was vilified by the English intellectual establishment. Even the popular press parodied Malthus as cold and calculating, inhumane and indifferent to the needs of the poor. Interestingly, similar criticisms are voiced when Western scientists and governments urge industrializing countries to control their population growth and rate of environmental destruction. Like Malthus, these observers remain convinced that the planet earth can only take so many people and so much punishment. Surely, earth does not have an unlimited "carrying capacity." To ignore this fact, however cruel to those who are poor today, may destine the human race to extinction tomorrow. The earth's *carrying capacity* is the number of people it can support. It is limited by the planet's resources, our technology and the standard of living people will accept. At our present levels of population and technology, all the world's people cannot possibly enjoy the level of affluence North Americans enjoy today. There is not enough wealth to go around. To raise the average standard of living on earth, we must find many more resources—an unlikely event—or improve our technology. Technology will probably continue to improve, but it produces its own harmful social and environmental side effects. In any event, we cannot know in advance what technology will be able to do for us.

Population control is the most cautious type of social planning. Limiting the number of births to ensure at least a minimum standard of living for everyone is a more reliable means than a reliance on technological innovation and new resources. This emphasis on controlling population to prevent disaster leads some people to equate all cautious social policy making with "Malthusianism."

Malthus's theory marks the beginning of scientific thinking about population. His *Essay on the Principle of Population* was important in two ways. First, he was an early social planner, using data to develop and defend his policy positions. He recognized that the population was growing rapidly and that fertility would have to be controlled in order to avoid higher mortality rates. Second, Malthus reminded us that we are biological as well as social beings. We cannot improve our societies without taking our sex drives and our need for food into account.

The Marxist Perspective   Malthus showed that our standard of living is determined by the ratio of resources (especially food) to population, and the ratio is declining rapidly (Wrigley, 1969). But did Malthus demonstrate a law of population that held true at all times and places? Or was it the result of historically specific conditions and, primarily, of a capitalist economy?

In his first essay, Malthus attacked the socialist doctrine that stated that if the world's wealth were shared equally, everyone would have plenty. Marx and Engels, writing two generations later, abandoned that view (Meek, 1954). They argued that a capitalist economy is the system most likely to produce an excess of population and a shortage of food. It is in the interest of the capitalist employer to have a large, impoverished reserve army of the unemployed, since an increased labour supply results in lower wages. As a seller, it is in the capitalist's interest to maintain scarcity and thereby ensure the highest possible prices. Therefore, capitalism produces a population crisis: many mouths to feed, too little food to feed them all.

A capitalist economy exaggerates the disastrous effects of overpopulation by further decreasing the percentage of resources available to most of the population. Two trends contribute to this inequity. Over time, capital becomes concentrated in fewer hands. The demand for workers may continue to grow, but much more slowly than the demand for new technology. In effect, the proportion of capital invested in workers, compared with that invested in technology, falls faster and faster. Jobs are eliminated; workers are displaced. There seem to be too many workers for the available jobs, but according to this theory, the problem comes from capitalistic competition creating ever fewer jobs, not from too many people.

Marxists today use their arguments to analyse relations between capitalist countries and the Third World. They show that economic colonialism has forced poor nations to produce mostly cash crops intended for export, in order to benefit rich nations. In the short run, poor countries deprive their own people of needed food, and in the long run, they fail to develop their economies (Gunder Frank, 1966; Wilber, 1973). Furthermore, an underdeveloped economy based on manual labour and a low level of technology encourages people to have large families so they can achieve some measure of material security. Marxists claim that overpopulation is not the cause of poverty; instead, poverty and exploitation cause overpopulation.

Criticisms of the Marxist Theory

Marxist theory has many strengths. For example, it identifies the replacement of humans by machines as a central and continuing cause of "overpopulation." Moreover, the theory has a great deal of appeal to modern scholars, siding as it does with the underdog, calling for justice and equality among peoples of the world, and offering an apocalyptic vision—"the Fire of Revolution, the Judgement of Proletarian Dictatorship and Terror, the Second Coming, when the Golden Age of primitive communism will return unimaginably glorified in a new kingdom of brotherly love and divinization of man" (Rexroth, 1986: 178–79).

Regrettably, as a theoretical system it has not yielded testable hypotheses, or where testable, correct predictions at least where population is concerned. Even in the homelands of capitalism, poor people have escaped overpopulation, just as they have

Regional Perspective on Agricultural Development

Africa

- a drop in per capita food output of about 1 per cent a year since the beginning of the 1970s
- a focus on cash crops and a growing dependence on imported food, fostered by pricing policies and foreign exchange compulsions
- major gaps in infrastructure for research, extension, input supply, and marketing
- degradation of the agricultural resource base due to desertification, droughts, and other processes
- large untapped potential of arable land, irrigation, and fertilizer use

West Asia and North Africa

- improvements in productivity due to better irrigation, the cultivation of high-yielding varieties, and higher fertilizer use
- limited arable land and considerable amounts of desert, making food self-sufficiency a challenge
- a need for controlled irrigation to cope with dry conditions

South and East Asia

- increased production and productivity, with some countries registering grain surpluses

- rapid growth in fertilizer use in some countries and extensive development of irrigation
- government commitments to be self-reliant in food, leading to national research centres, development of high-yielding seeds, and the fostering of location-specific technologies
- little unused land, and extensive, unabated deforestation
- growing numbers of rural landless

Latin America

- declining food imports since 1980, as food production kept pace with population growth over the last decade
- government support in the form of research centres to develop high-yielding seeds and other technologies
- inequitable distribution of land
- deforestation and degradation of the agricultural resource base, fueled partly by foreign trade and debt crisis
- a huge land resource and high productivity potential, though most of the potentially arable land is in the remote, lightly populated Amazon Basin, where perhaps only 20 per cent of the land is suitable for sustainable agriculture

World Commission on Environment and Development. 1987. *Our Common Future*. New York: Oxford University Press, p. 21.

escaped progressive impoverishment and revolutionary fervour. Even outside the imperial reach of capitalism, poor people have had to struggle against overpopulation, often with the help of capitalist institutions such as the World Bank and International Monetary Fund.

Marxist theory helped to understand pre-industrial and industrializing countries of the West, but it does not seem to help us understand those—or any other—countries today. Today, neither a capitalist nor a communist government sees a great deal of advantage in overpopulation; and both are alert to the problems of "technological displacement"—the unemployment of people by machines.

The Theory of
Demographic
Transition

When Marx and Engels were criticizing Malthus in the mid to late nineteenth century, industrial capitalism was still in its early stages. Low wages and high subsistence costs seemed likely to continue. Yet, later capitalists realized that it would be profitable to create a large market of affluent consumers. Creating such a market meant paying higher wages and charging lower prices.

In the mass consumer society and welfare state of the twentieth century, families do not depend on having many children to achieve financial security, so the "Malthusian problem" seems to have taken care of itself. Population growth has declined, and the standard of living has risen as people limited the sizes of their families. World fertility rates have been declining for the last twenty years, despite general improvements in health and material well-being. To understand this change, we must turn to the theory of the demographic transition. This theory is based on observed changes in Western European societies. It relates historical changes in population to social and economic modernization.

According to this theory (Davis, 1945; Stolnitz, 1964), the transition from a traditional to a modern population pattern passes through three stages. In the first stage, called *pre-transition*, a population's fertility and mortality rates are both high. However, both rates are greatly affected by such Malthusian positive checks as famines and epidemics, resulting in little, if any, population growth. In stage two, the *transitional stage*, the mortality rate begins to fall while the birth rate remains high, so the population grows rapidly. In stage three, *post-transition*, fertility rates also fall, while

FIGURE 19-2

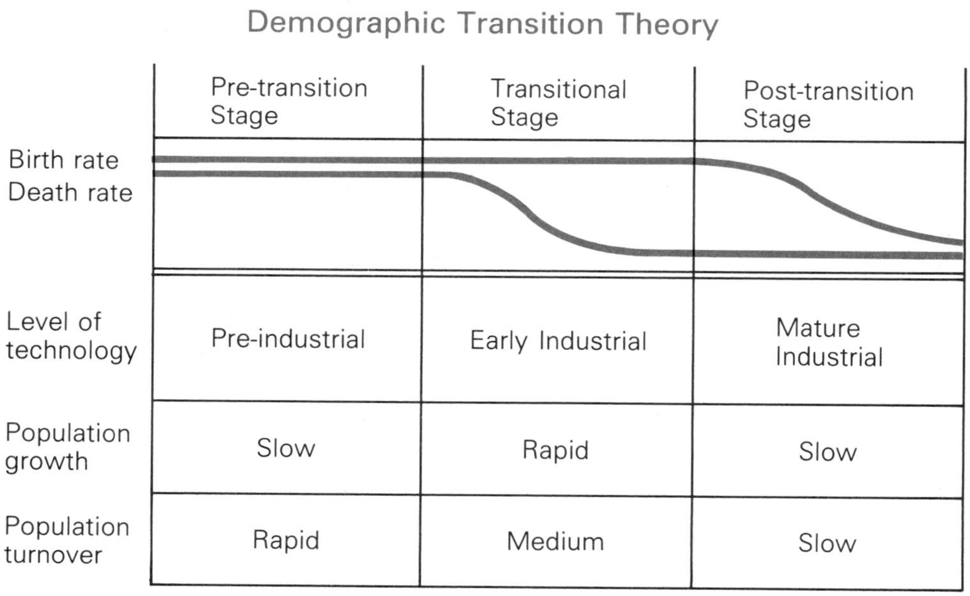

Demographic Transition Theory

	Pre-transition Stage	Transitional Stage	Post-transition Stage
Birth rate Death rate			
Level of technology	Pre-industrial	Early Industrial	Mature Industrial
Population growth	Slow	Rapid	Slow
Population turnover	Rapid	Medium	Slow

mortality rates stay low. As a result, population growth slows dramatically. Both the pre-transition and the post-transition populations are stable. But in the first case, population turnover is very rapid, in the second, very slow. Figure 19-2 summarizes the characteristics of the three stages.

Another difference between the pre-transitional and post-transitional stages is that in the former, the death rate fluctuates widely and the birth rate is relatively stable, often near a biological maximum. However, in post-transition, the death rate is relatively stable: public health, improved medical techniques, better housing and nutrition all but eliminate epidemics, famines and many infectious diseases. Now fertility rates fluctuate widely because of changes in desired family size, which in turn are influenced by changes in prosperity. Shifts in economic opportunities influence career decisions, the timing of marriages and the timing and frequency of childbearing. For example, fertility in the prosperous baby boom years of the 1950s was much higher than that in the austere 1970s and 1980s, when couples delayed childbearing and often avoided it altogether.

According to this theory, demographic transition is irreversible. Societies differ in when they begin the transition, how fast it proceeds and which factors start the process. But no society returns to high mortality or high fertility after reaching post-transition. The reasons are plain: no society would willingly accept higher death rates; and no society can long afford high birth rates once it has lowered its death rate.

How Population Change Is Related to Socio-economic Change

Demographic transition theory relates population changes to social and economic changes, a relationship that has been especially interesting to sociologists. Each demographic stage has its own social and economic context.

Pre-transition, with high fertility and mortality rates, is typical of a pre-industrial society. Such societies cannot ensure the survival of the individual, due to the unpredictability of crops, the lack of a regular food surplus and the absence of a market where food can be bought if necessary. Contagious diseases are also a problem, especially in cities. For example, the bubonic plague of 1348–50 killed approximately one-quarter of Europe's population. Under such unpredictable circumstances, death rates cannot be controlled. High fertility is essential; any population with a low fertility rate would simply die out.

The transitional stage is associated with the Industrial Revolution, which began in England in about 1775. New technology increased productivity and improved transportation and communication, helping to create mass markets, mass literacy, a mass culture and the modern nation-state. Improved medicine and public sanitation caused a rapid decline in mortality, particularly among infants and children, upsetting the balance between birth and death rates.

In the post-transition stage, fertility begins a long, steady decline, although it changes more slowly than mortality because it is affected by social mores and traditional values. The economic reasons for having large families disappear; in cities, children are more costly and less useful than on farms. Fewer children need to be born to ensure that one or two will survive. More and more, the state steps into family life, requiring that children be educated and preventing child labour. The state also ensures the security of the elderly, undercutting another reason for having large families. Parents shift from having children for financial gain to having children for pleasure.

Criticisms of Demographic Transition Theory

A theory that so closely mirrors English and European historical change has obvious strengths. But a closer analysis of pre-industrial parish records and other historical artifacts and an observation of demographics in the Third World has raised strong doubts about its validity.

First, the demographic transition theory is not universally valid. It does not explain current changes in the Third World. There, availability of Western technology has cut the link between modernization and population change (Kirk, 1971). In the West, new medical treatments to reduce sickness and mortality often developed after massive advances in public sanitation and preventive medicine had already taken place. Likewise, new techniques of contraception became available after people had already been trying for several generations to reduce their childbearing rates with existing knowledge and techniques. But in the pre-industrial nations today, modern medicine and contraceptive technology are made instantly available without the same infrastructure of public health, government involvement or motivation to change behaviours that one found in Europe and North America a century ago. This cuts the link between technological readiness and attitudinal, social and cultural readiness to use that technology.

Since the Second World War, better medicine and inexpensive birth control have been available worldwide. This has given rise to an international debate over whether birth control must be preceded by modernization or whether Third World nations should control births more effectively before getting economic aid from developed countries (Coale and Hoover, 1958; Coale, 1963).

Second, the theory may not provide a valid explanation of historical experience even in Europe. Pre-industrial societies vary widely in the average age at which people get married (Hajnal, 1965). Fertility rates also vary. Each pre-industrial society seems to have uniquely combined preventive checks to control its population growth.

It is not clear whether the burst of population growth during the transitional stage was primarily due to a decline in the death rate (McKeown and Brown, 1965) or a rise in the birth rate (Habakkuk, 1965). Births may have risen as a result of factors such as the breakdown of traditional social controls on childbearing and increasing prosperity. Probably, birth and death rates were rising and falling in different parts of the same population. Certainly, to prove that a transitional population always begins to grow because of declining mortality requires more reliable statistics than we have.

Finally, no simple, reliable correlation has been found between modernization and fertility decline in post-transitional societies. Fertility did decline in the West, but the causes and timing of this decline seem to vary from one locale to another.

Because population processes today are very similar throughout the West, it is easy to believe that they were always similar. The European Fertility Study, which compared

FIGURE 19-3

Evolution of Total Fertility Rate and Expectation of Life at Birth in Seventeen European Countries, 1870–1980

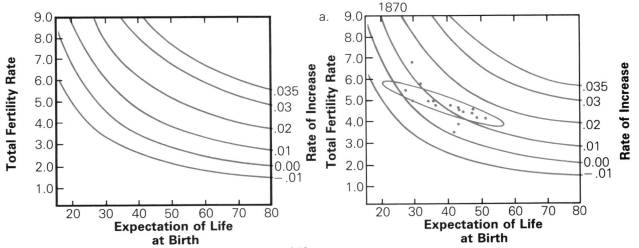

Combinations of total fertility rate and expectation of life at birth that produce long-run growth from −1 percent to 3.5 percent.

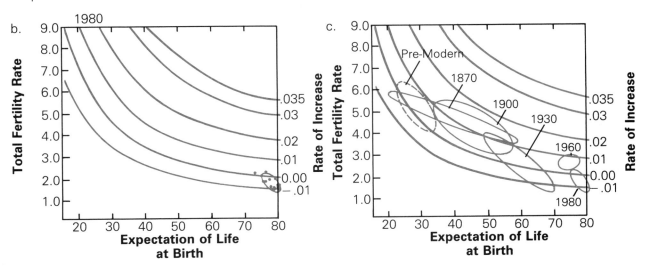

Ansley J. Coale and Susan Cotts Watkins, eds. 1986. *The Decline of Fertility in Europe.* Princeton: Princeton University Press, pp. 3, 27.

birth and infant mortality rates in seventeen European countries over time, shows that demographic transition theory has vastly oversimplified the historical record. The data in Figure 19-3 show that countries relatively similar in economy and social organization had very different rates of fertility, mortality and natural increase only a century ago. What these differences suggest is that there was no single, simple path from the high fertility and mortality rates of pre-industrialism to the low fertility and mortality rates of modern industrialism. At present, local variations in mortality and fertility patterns are impossible to summarize in any simple scheme.

These failings in the theory of demographic transition suggest that, in the past, demographers may have exaggerated the importance of economic factors and under-played the cultural ones. New ways of thinking about family structure and behaviour may significantly influence childbearing without being related directly to economic change, as Philippe Ariès (1962) has shown in his classic study of changing European conceptions of childhood (see also van de Walle and Knodel, 1980). For example, family living (and procreation) will be greatly affected by the way children are perceived. When children were thought of as miniature adults-to-be, they were continuously integrated into adult activities and tasks until they became full-fledged adults. How-ever, when people came to think of childhood and then adolescence as distinct developmental stages requiring special teaching and caring—overall, insulation from adult life—induction into adult tasks was delayed. Children remained "useless" and became costlier for a longer period than before; no wonder, then, that childbearing started to decline among the wealthy in France after 1750 and thereafter in other parts of Europe and America.

Despite its difficulties, demographic transition theory is an ambitious, wide-ranging attempt to explain a large mass of historical detail. It is, in effect, a theory about history. Also, it is a sociological theory that tries to find social, rather than biological, factors at the root of our problems. Finally, the theory appeals to our optimism. Its story of change proceeding from one condition of stability (high fertility/high mortality) to another (low fertility/low mortality) is quite different from the story Malthus told, for it has a happy ending. Material progress not only takes root, it solves the Malthusian problem of overpopulation and scarcity. Unfortunately, this story seems to have got some of the facts wrong.

Population Growth in Canada

Canada's population has grown a lot in some periods and very little in others. Times of rapid growth include the decade before the First World War and the decade after the Second World War; times of slower growth include the later nineteenth century, the 1930s, and the 1970s and 1980s. These shifts are a result of changing patterns of natural increase and international migration. (For a good overview of these changes, see Beaujot and McQuillan, 1982.)

When Europeans "discovered" North America in the early 1600s, between 200 000 and 1 000 000 people already lived in what is now Canada. Their ancestors had arrived in the Americas from Asia not less than ten thousand years earlier, and possibly as much as fifty thousand years earlier (Farb, 1978). By 1763, European immigrants and their descendants had increased the local population by about 100 000. Over the next two centuries, Canada's population has grown to more than 25 000 000, with a growth rate of about 4 percent in the century before Confederation and about 2 percent after Confederation. Both high rates of childbearing and high rates of immigration contributed to this growth. Children and immigrants are newcomers to a culture. In our society, we have an extremely high ratio of newcomers to *tradition carriers*, adults who were born into and grew up with Canadian culture.

The Wide Fluctuations of Immigration

Almost all Canadians are descended from immigrants, particularly immigrants who arrived in the last fifty to one hundred years. But emigration was sometimes so common in Canada that it largely offset the effects of immigration. In 1982 alone, more than 45 000 people left Canada to live elsewhere. Demographers estimate that between 1851 and 1971, about 9 500 000 immigrants entered Canada while 6 500 000 left, for a net gain through immigration of about 3 000 000 people. Yet, in this same period, 28 000 000 children were born and 11 500 000 people died, for a net gain through natural increase of about 16 500 000. Overall, fertility has influenced Canada's population history much more significantly than immigration (especially in French Canada).

Although natural increase has had a greater effect on the size of Canada's population, the effects of immigration have fluctuated more widely over time. As in Western Europe, birth and death rates have dropped slowly, smoothly and predictably in Canada since about 1851. True, the economic depression of the 1930s pushed birth rates below the expected level, and the post-war baby boom of the 1950s pushed birth rates above it. Overall, however, the downward trend has been slow and steady.

By contrast, migration in and out of Canada has varied a great deal from one decade to another in response to various influences. Canadian economic development has proceeded rapidly, almost crazily, from one resource-driven economic boom-and-bust to another. (For an overview of this "staples approach" to Canadian history, see Watkins, 1963.) With each resource discovery comes the opening of a new portion of the country, creating new communities and new jobs in manufacturing, services, communications and transportation. Often there are not enough natural-born Canadians with the right skills to fill the new jobs. At these times, Canada opens its doors to immigrants, liberalizing legislation, increasing quotas, even searching out immigrants in preferred countries (Kalbach, 1970; Hawkins, 1972). This need for workers lasts only as long as there is foreign demand for the resource at Canadian prices. When the demand dies down, the need for immigrant labour collapses. Immigration laws tighten again and fewer immigrants are admitted. Also, as job opportunities evaporate, more people leave Canada, chiefly for the United States.

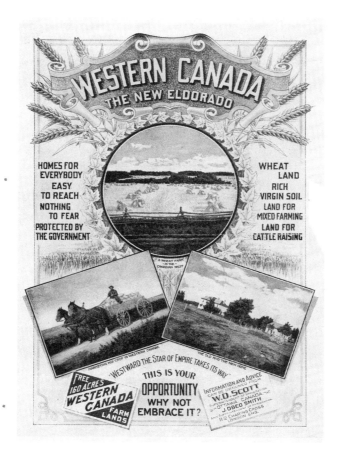

A poster encouraging migration to farm lands in western Canada.

NATIONAL ARCHIVES OF CANADA/C 85854.

Fluctuating migration rates have social as well as population effects. These effects are most striking when confined to a small region. In the 1970s, the population of Edmonton and Calgary grew rapidly, and in the 1980s it slowed down again. More recently, there were massive shifts of migrants away from increasingly separatist Quebec. More dramatic still are the effects of migration on resource-based, single-industry company towns (Lucas, 1972). A psychology of population instability results from (and, in turn, causes) the movement of migrants; its effect is out of all proportion to the number of migrants in the population (Porter, 1965).

On this, John Porter (1965 : 34–35) has written:

Collective efforts to create a Canadian society have been marked by periods of population stagnation and social despair or rapid population growth and the promise of greatness. . . . Canadian society has a brief history, and the traditions and loyalties of its people as Canadians are obscure, or at least lack sufficient clarity and tenacity to produce a cohesiveness which will withstand the grativational pull of the United States.

French Canadians "struggle to retain their identity while the non-French are looking for one," or at least one they can share as Canadians.

> Traditions and social values are carried in the minds of a society's population, but the ebb and flow of migrations make a kind of flotsam of those sentiments which should accumulatively produce a consensus about what Canada is. For example, the events of the pre-Confederation period and the evolution of self-government have little meaning for the European immigrant. Nor can they enter much into the consciousness of the native as he prepares to leave.

Ethnic origin cannot serve as a basis for national solidarity; moreover, because of population instability, neither can social class.

> In Canada there has always been the additional ameliorative condition that the way out was relatively easy and cost little. The choice of leaving or staying was open to all until the 1920s and for the Canadian-born most of the time.

For this reason, class-based politics is unlikely to take hold in Canada as it has in England, Italy or even Scandinavia.

> Class traditions and sentiments, like those which bind the whole society together, develop over time and are carried around in the minds of people who see themselves as members of the same class. Some class consciousness is also necessary for non-violent forms of class-based political behaviour. Only rarely has this type of politics existed in Canada. The migratory character of the Canadian population may help to explain this fact, for large migrations into, out of, and across the country are not likely to be the conditions which give rise to class sentiments. Moreover, this migratory population has been ethnically heterogeneous, thus making it possible for class hostility to be deflected into ethnic hostility. (Porter, 1965 : 36–37)

Fluctuating migration levels have twice been particularly problematic for French Canadian culture. Through the early part of this century, the emigration of French Canadians to the United States (documented by Lavoie, 1972) threatened to diminish the French presence in Canada. More recently, French Canada has had another threat posed by an influx of immigrants from abroad who cannot speak French and are unwilling to learn. This trend, combined with the clear evidence of French-language loss outside Quebec, has led to concern among francophone demographers (Henripin, 1974) and policy makers. However, more recent analysis (Lachapelle, 1980) suggests that the French language within Quebec is alive and well.

The Baby Boom   In recent years, the biggest population change in Canada was caused by the baby boom of the 1950s. The baby boom cohort or generation is a group of Canadians born mainly in the 1950s. After reaching a historic low (about 20 births per 1000 population) in the 1930s, the birth rate climbed to a peak in the period 1945 to 1965. The year 1959 recorded the single highest birth rate (that is, ratio of births that year to population at mid-year) of the baby boom period: 27.4 births per 1000 population. The birth rate has since declined again, falling below even the low birth rate during the Great Depression; by 1986, it stood at 14.7 births per 1000 population.

During the 1950s, parents and government were chiefly concerned with providing adequate primary schooling. In the 1960s and 1970s, concern focused on jobs and housing for the baby boomers. In the early twenty-first century, old age pensions, retirement rules and nursing-home vacancies will probably become of greater interest to most Canadians (see, for example, Foot, 1982).

The Baby Boom

The baby boom is consumer society's R&D division— testing new products, new fads, new drugs, new morality, even new ideas about marriage and children. . . .

Now, as it washes up in the 1980s, the baby-boom generation is experiencing a shift in the way it thinks about itself and its future. Optimism is yielding to pessimism. Altruism is yielding to narcissism. The generation that grew up convinced of its special place in society is not finding it. The maternity wards were too crowded; the schools were crowded; they were sent to Vietnam; they couldn't find jobs; they couldn't get promoted. Instead they found themselves causing booms in crime, in suicide, in divorce, in childlessness, in venereal disease, in housing prices, and in property taxes. . . .

The faith in the future that powered the boom generation through the sixties is shattered.

From Landon Y. Jones. 1980. *Great Expectations: America and the Baby Boom Generation*, pp. 387–89. Reprinted by permission of publisher Putnam Publishing Group.

Finding it harder to get jobs than in the past, members of the baby boom generation are postponing marriage and are having fewer children. Dual-income families are increasingly common. There will be further problems in twenty-five years when baby boomers begin to retire. If our present population growth rate continues, there will not be enough younger workers to support them through contributions to pension and social security funds.

The Composition of the Population

So far, we have paid attention only to the *size* of the population, but the composition and distribution are also very important. *Composition* is the characteristics of people in a population, especially age and sex, but often other "demographics" such as race and ethnicity; education; social class and occupation; work, employment and unemployment; health and illness; place of birth; and religious affiliation. *Distribution* is the geographical location of people—their place of residence: the region, province and (where appropriate) metropolitan area, county, town and census tract they live in.

Two important features of a population's composition are sex and age. Sex and age composition are biologically based in birth and death processes, so sex and age composition theories can hold good for all societies. Also, sex and age are central bases of *social differentiation*. *Differentiation* is a process whereby sets of social activities become split up between different social institutions or groups of people. This represents an increasing specialization of the society, making for greater heterogeneity. But although most social roles are differentiated by age and sex, *how* they are differentiated may vary widely from one role to another. Most social roles in any society are age and sex specific. They are filled by people of one sex, not the other, and by one age group, not others. Thus, social planners will always need to know the number of males and females and the number of young and old in a population.

Sex Composition and Its Effects

The sex composition of a population refers to the ratio of males to females, or the number of males per hundred females. In every human population, more males are born than females. In Canada, the ratio at birth is about 105 males to every 100 females. But this ratio is not found at every age. In Canada, the ratio begins falling almost immediately after birth. In cities, for example, women outnumber men in every age group after age forty. Presently, the longevity gap, or difference in average life expectancy from birth, between males and females is seven years.

Women are hardier than men, as Madigan (1957) showed in his comparative study of nuns and monks. As well, their relative longevity is partly due to differences in behaviour. For example, until recently, men smoked many more cigarettes than women. Also, men typically play more hazardous or reckless roles in society, such as working in mines and getting caught up in the "jock" culture.

For all these reasons, women live longer, and at each age after adulthood the ratio of women to men increases. As a result, women are more likely to die as widows than men as widowers. Also, male companionship is harder for women to find with each passing year. This difficulty is increased by our culture, since women in our society (as in many others) usually marry older men. In general, age is a greater handicap for women than for men in the marriage market.

These problems are often further complicated by events such as wars, where it is usually men who are killed, increasing the imbalance of the ratio of males and females in the population. As well, men usually leave first for foreign lands, causing shortages of males in the home countries and surpluses in the new ones. On the other hand, women today are more likely to migrate within Canada, typically from rural regions or small towns to large cities. This creates an excess of females in cities and a shortage in the less-populated areas.

People respond to such problems creatively. Wherever men suffer a shortage of women, they find ways to deal with it, including importing mail-order brides and patronizing prostitutes. When women suffer shortages of men, they relax the rules about appropriate age, ethnic, racial or other characteristics of potential spouses, or find ways to live comfortably while remaining unmarried.

The Marriage Squeeze

Most recently, imbalances in the sex ratio have stemmed from the baby boom and bust, creating a problem known as the *marriage squeeze*. Between the late 1930s and

The Nose Creek brothels, Calgary, in 1911.

1959, more babies were born each year; after 1959, fewer were born. Because women in our culture usually marry men two to three years older than themselves, a woman born in 1959 would typically select her mate from among men born in 1956. But fewer men were born in 1956 than women in 1959. Women born in 1959 (or any year before 1959) would suffer a marriage squeeze, or shortage of eligible men. On the other hand, a woman born in 1965 would typically select her mate from among men born in 1962, when births had already begun to decline. Thus, more men were born in 1962 than women in 1965 and the women could choose from a relative surplus of men. Conversely, men born after 1959 would suffer the marriage squeeze: a shortage of women of the right age.

The results of such shortages are not fully known. Yet, the "market value," or the attractiveness, of relatively scarce older men is likely to be higher than that of the more common younger men. Were the less-numerous men born before 1960 able to impose their ideas of courtship and marriage? If so, they could create a social climate that favoured free sex, while being against a more general women's liberation.

Such imbalances in the sex ratio also affect family formation. During periods of severe imbalance, fewer than usual families are formed, depressing population growth. One solution is *serial monogamy*, or people entering into and leaving several marriages per lifetime. Extramarital sex, romantic affairs, and divorce and remarriage have also increased in the last two decades. They reflect a change in sexual morality, but they may also represent a solution to demographic imbalance, to the marriage squeeze, since they also make scarce males available (however partially) to a larger number of females.

Personal column from city newspaper.

REPRINTED WITH PERMISSION FROM *THE NEW YORK REVIEW OF BOOKS.* COPYRIGHT 1989, NYREV, INC.

Age Composition and Its Effects

The age composition of a population is harder to describe than its sex composition because ages can be grouped in many ways. Still, *life expectancy*, or the average number of years a person will live, can be predicted from a demographer's life table. The *life table* "is a life history of a hypothetical group, or *cohort*, of people as it is diminished gradually by deaths. The record begins at the birth of each member and continues until all have died." To simplify the calculations, it is assumed that "(a) the cohort is closed against migration in or out. Hence, there are no changes in membership except the losses due to death. (b) People die at each age according to (an empirically based) schedule that is fixed in advance and does not change. (c) The cohort originates from some standard number of births (always set at a round figure like 1,000, 10,000, or 100,000) called the 'radix' of the life table. . . . (d) At each age (excepting the first few years of life), deaths are evenly distributed between one birthday and the next. . . . (e) The cohort normally contains members of only one sex" (Barclay, 1958:94).

Calculations resulting from these assumptions produce the number of annual deaths expected at each age, the number of people alive at each age and the mean expectation of life (or life expectancy) at each age. In a population without migration, demographers can perfectly predict the numbers of people at each age, if that population is stable. By *stable*, we mean the birth rate and the mortality rate at each age are unchanging.

Stable population theory tells us a lot about the age composition of a population. The theory was first developed by Alfred Lotka in the 1920s (Dublin and Lotka, 1925; Lotka, 1928). It shows mathematically the relationship between the proportion of people in any age category (for example, the proportion of people who are twenty-two years old), the birth rate, the probability of surviving to a given age and the population growth rate. Thus, we can estimate any of these population factors, as well as the relative size of one age group compared to another. This method helps us to distinguish common from unexpected features of observed populations.

This theory works only in a *stable* population without migration. Since these conditions rarely exist in the real world, why construct such a theory? The stable population theory meets this objection in several ways. First, a theory is not intended to duplicate reality, but to abstract from it the relationships between groups of variables: in this case, between births, deaths and age structure. For example, Newton's laws of motion ignore friction, though in reality friction affects every moving body. Newton's laws are still valid, however. When we formulate a theory, we expect eventually to eliminate, or correct for, the effects of outside factors. Second, many pre-industrial populations *have* been fairly stable; and in future modern societies may be too. Thus, stable population theory will prove useful in studying past populations (or certain bands of hunter-gatherers living today in pre-modern conditions) and in predicting the age compositions of populations that have achieved zero population growth. It is also useful in *smoothing*, correcting data obtained in flawed censuses or in birth or death registries (Keyfitz and Flieger, 1971; United Nations, 1967).

Measures of Age Composition
Measures of age composition include the median age, the dependency ratio and the population pyramid. The *median age* is the age of the middle-ranked person in the population. In Canada, the median age is currently about thirty and should reach thirty-seven by the year 2001. The median age gets higher mostly as a result of falling fertility, not rising life expectancy. The aging of the Canadian population is emphasized by two startling facts. In the near future, the death rate will temporarily overtake the birth rate in Canada; and by the year 2031, the percentage of Canadians over age sixty-five will equal the percentage under age fifteen (Foot, 1982).

The *dependency ratio* is the ratio of dependent-age people (ages 0–17 and 65 plus) to working-age people (18–65). As a population ages, the *youth dependency ratio* (the ratio of people ages 0–17 to those aged 18–65) drops, and the *elderly dependency ratio* (the ratio of people aged 65 and over to those aged 18–65) rises. Taken together, these two ratios give an overall dependency ratio today of about 58 dependants to every 100 persons of working age, the lowest in Canada's history. This means that almost two Canadians in three are of working age. In a population with a higher median age, a larger proportion of the population is of working age and is therefore more productive.

Of course, other factors influence national wealth, including the *participation rate* (the proportion of working-age people actually working in paid jobs) and the *productivity rate* (the dollar-value produced by each worker per unit time). Still, up to a point, an older population is more productive.

Actually, the matter is still more complicated. A successful enterprise—whether a family, a sports team or a society—requires just the right mix of young people and old, youth and experience. Therefore, whichever age group is in shortest supply gains in value and enjoys the most opportunity for advancement. For example, the baby boom generation is at a disadvantage because of the surplus of mid-career workers compared to older, more experienced workers (Easterlin, 1980). Today, experience is in short supply, and older workers are paid more. Teenagers are also in short supply and are starting to receive higher wages. In general, scarcity brings high rewards.

The Population Pyramid   Median age and dependency ratios are two ways of summarizing the age-sex structure of a society. A third way is to use a *population pyramid*. Demographers have distinguished three common forms of pyramid (see Figure 19-4). The *expansive pyramid* has a particularly broad base, indicating a high proportion of children in the population. Such a pyramid results from high fertility levels; it characterizes a young, rapidly growing population. The *stationary pyramid* has a narrower base and nearly equal

FIGURE 19-4

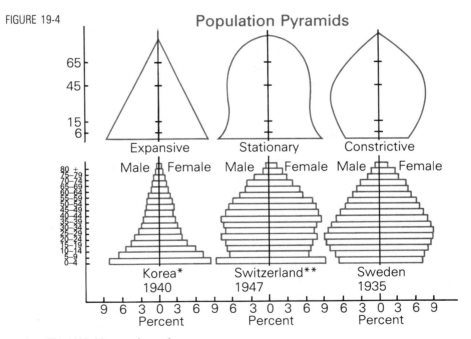

*Most Third World countries today.
**An increasing number of developed (European and North American) countries.

Reprinted with permission of Macmillan Publishing Company from *Population*, 3rd ed., by William Petersen. © 1975 by William Petersen.

proportions of all ages. Such a pyramid results from prolonged low fertility and characterizes an old, non-growing population. Finally, the *constrictive pyramid* has a base narrower than its middle, indicating a recent, rapid decline in fertility.

A population pyramid has several advantages over other methods as a means of describing a population's composition. It readily communicates complex information. We can quickly see the general state of the population. As well, we can readily see gross deviations: age categories that are too large, probably indicating in-migration; or too small, probably indicating a population loss due to war, reduced childbearing or out-migration.

We can also note imbalances between the sexes at particular ages. Fluctuations involving both sexes usually result from changes in prosperity and fertility, while those affecting the numbers of one sex more than another are usually the consequence of migration or war. The timing of major social and economic changes is thus reflected in a modern population's age structure. By contrast, a pre-industrial or transitional population has somewhat more regular, symmetrical demographic features. Sometimes, the age structure shows the effects of positive population checks: a plague or epidemic, a bad harvest or series of bad harvests and so on. In this case, the increased death rate is (more or less) equally shared across ages and between sexes, so the age structure shrinks but keeps a regular shape. Usually, gross distortions point to incorrect age or gender reporting or to administrative confusion and a need for better data collection.

A demographer can read a population pyramid for signs of change the way a geologist reads layers of rock. Each observer is guided by a theory of how process creates structure, of what "normal" structures look like and what changes produce deviations. But population structures do not preserve their history for long. Two populations with very different age-sex pyramids will eventually become identical if subjected to the same birth and death processes. (This remarkable fact is known to us through stable population theory.)

This is quite unlike what we encounter in most other daily experience. Consider a common throughput process in everyday life: consuming calories and burning calories. If we start with two men, one 200 cm tall and 100 kg in weight and the other 165 cm and 57 kg, and submit them to the same throughput—the same number of calories per day (per pound of body weight) and the same exercise to burn those calories—after a week, a year, a lifetime they will *still* differ in height and weight. The throughput will *not* have affected their structure significantly.

But populations are different. Two dissimilar populations exposed to the same rate of throughput will become identical. How quickly they become identical will be determined, first, by how different they were to begin with and, second, by how high the rates of throughput are (higher rates change the structure faster than lower ones). Population *processes* are steadily changing and re-creating population *structures*.

Summary

A good deal more could be written about population processes. Entire books have been devoted to the construction and use of life tables alone. Government, the health professions, educational institutions and the insurance industry all depend on good demographic data and theories to monitor public demand for their services. Their need has been met by a vast number of specialized reports and studies that we have not begun to examine. And the discussion of long-term population policy has occupied a great deal of expert and public attention. Recently, the federal government has even conducted a "demographic review" to acquaint legislators with the interrelations between demographic, social and economic forces.

A lot has been written in sociological literature about the social factors influencing fertility and mortality, topics not dealt with here. We have given no attention in this chapter to fertility decline in Canada. Nor have we thoroughly discussed migration, a topic that will come up again in the chapters on urbanization and social development. This chapter, however, has shown that demography is guided by a few central theories. Some, such as the demographic transition theory, relate population processes to social processes, such as modernization. Others, such as the stable population theory, relate population processes to population structures, such as the age pyramid. Together, these theories enhance our understanding of what Malthus pointed out: the human drives for food and sex have social, cultural, economic and political consequences.

Few social sciences have created as much sustained, international interest and co-operation as demography, yet none of the theories we have explored is complete or above dispute. Demography, like other sciences, is always refining its theories. Demography is a truly interdisciplinary enterprise, yet it is central to sociology, the study of societies.

Suggested Readings

Beaujot, Roderic, and Kevin McQuillan
  1982. *Growth and Dualism: The Demographic Development of Canadian Society*. Toronto: Gage. This is an excellent introduction to the historical development of Canada's population, containing chapters on mortality, fertility, immigration and migration, regionalism, linguistic balance and debates over population issues.

Canadian Social Trends
  This journal, published four times a year by Statistics Canada (Canada's official collector of population information), contains the most recent data on topics of interest to demographers and population students. Articles are written in a style that is accessible to specialist and non-specialist alike.

Coale, Ansley, and Susan Watkins, eds.
  1986. *The Decline of Fertility in Europe*. Princeton: Princeton University Press. Edited by one of the world's most eminent demographers and his colleague, this book brings together the findings of Princeton University's European Fertility Study (mentioned in the chapter). Readers will get a sense of the vast richness of that project and the possibilities for interesting research in historical demography.

Easterlin, Richard

1980. *Birth and Fortune: The Impact of Numbers on Personal Welfare*. New York: Basic Books. Professor Easterlin's book stirred a lot of controversy when it first appeared, because it attributed a great many life satisfactions (and dissatisfactions) to a single "accident of birth": that is, whether you were born in a small or large birth cohort. Some believe he has overstated the case for demographic factors.

Family History Survey

So far, only a few reports (Burch, 1985; Pool and Moore, 1986; Burch and Madan, 1986) have come out of Statistics Canada's *Family History Survey*, conducted in 1984. This ambitious project collected comprehensive marital and childbearing histories from a large sample of representative Canadians. It is hard to imagine a better source of data for studying what happens demographically to ordinary people over an average lifetime.

Statistics Canada

1987. *Report on the Demographic Situation in Canada, 1986*. Catalogue 91-209E, May. This is the most recent in a series of reports on current population processes, including up-to-date information on trends in population growth, population structure, marriage, fertility, mortality and migration. Theories are presented to account for current trends (for example, the lowest-ever rate of first marriages in Canada's history and a divorce rate that seems to have reached its peak).

Discussion Questions

1. The same shortages result if there are too many people or too few resources (food, land, jobs). Marx and Malthus might, therefore, have analysed the same situation in opposite ways. How can we tell who was right?

2. What other countries are likely to have the same "psychology of population instability" as Canada? Do some research on these countries to find out whether the effects on social and cultural organization are also similar.

3. How much do you think the liberalization of sexual norms (for example, premarital and extramarital sex, open homosexuality, easier divorce) has resulted from demographic imbalances, such as the marriage squeeze, and how much from other causes? What might these other causes be?

4. Does Canada need a population policy? If not, why not? If so, should this policy include cash incentives for childbearing, euthanasia or easier migration across the Canada-U.S. border? How should these policies be administered?

5. How will the reduction in family size affect the number of kin (including uncles, aunts, cousins, nephews, nieces and so on) each person has? How will this change affect social, psychological or cultural life, if at all?

6. What do changes in the age pyramid of Vienna (see Figure 19-5) tell you about the past, present and future of that Austrian city? Do you see any war effects? Fertility decline? Emigration? What else?

FIGURE 19-5

Age Pyramids of Vienna

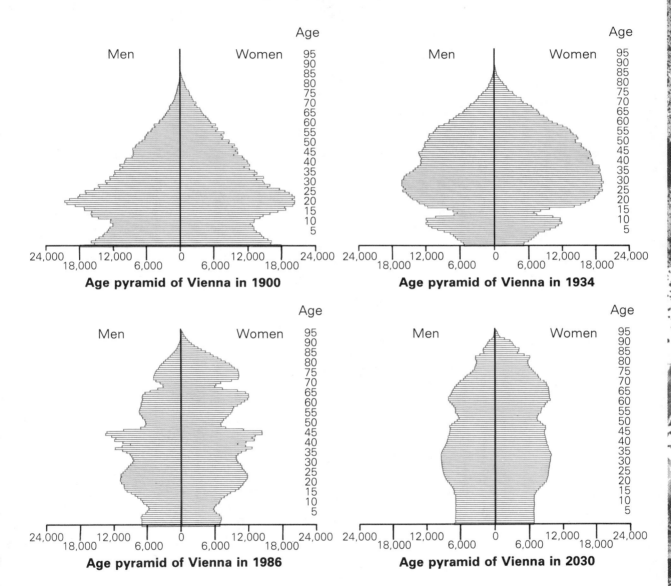

Wolfgang Lutz and Alexander Hanika. 1988. "Vienna: A City Beyond Aging." *POPNET* 14
(Laxwnburg, Austria: IIASA Population Network Newsletter):1–4.

Data Collection Exercises

1. Use published population statistics from 1971, 1976 and 1981 to predict (a) the number of births occurring in 1986; (b) the number of marriages occurring in 1986; and (c) the population of Alberta in 1986. Account for discrepancies between your own predictions and the numbers published in 1986.

2. Select a sample of fellow students. Using a questionnaire you have devised, study their intentions to marry and raise children. What kinds of people seem most inclined to marry young and raise large families?

3. Collect published data on the causes of death among young people (roughly, ages fifteen to twenty-five) since 1880. Measure and explain the changing importance of accidents and suicide as causes of death for this age group.

4. One study shows that Canadian women working in male-dominated professions are less likely to marry, or (if married) less likely to remain married, or (if remaining married) less likely to bear children than women in female-dominated professions or non-professional jobs. Collect data from two or three comparable countries to see if this generalization holds true elsewhere. If it does, try to explain why.

Writing Exercises

1. Select one of the items listed in the Suggested Readings and critically review it in two pages, pretending that you are T. R. Malthus.

2. Draft a letter to your local newspaper editor arguing forcefully in favour of or against a massive increase in (a) immigration to Canada from the Third World; or (b) Canadian economic aid to the Third World. Support your position by referring to population theories discussed in this chapter.

3. Imagine you have been made responsible for planning the 1991 Canadian census. Draft *three* questions that were not on the 1986 form but, in your opinion, should definitely be added. Write your superior (the Statistician-General of Canada) a two-page letter defending your decision.

4. Using data from the 1981 or 1986 Canadian census, make a population pyramid for the census tract you live in and compare it with the population pyramid of Canada as a whole. Explain the differences you observe.

Glossary

Carrying capacity: *the number of people who can survive biologically on a unit of land, or on the earth as a whole.*

Composition: *the proportions of people of different kinds (for example, different ages, sexes, ethnicities,* races, religions, classes, educational attainments, language groups and so on) who are mixed together to form a population.

Dependency ratio: *the ratio of dependent-aged people (young, old or both) to people in the middle of the age span (ages 18–65) who are, typically, working for pay and supporting the rest.*

Life table: *a standard set of calculations for measuring and expressing the risks of death at specific ages.*

Marriage squeeze: *a shortage of (traditionally) desirable mates due to rapid and radical shifts in fertility, mortality or migration.*

Population pyramid: *a visual representation of the numbers of males and females in the population, by advancing age.*

Positive checks: *the disasters that Malthus saw as setting limits to growth in a population that did not limit its fertility.*

Preventive checks: *the practices (chiefly, avoidance of marriage) that according to Malthus helped a population avoid childbearing and excessive population growth.*

Stable population: *a population without any migration whose rates of mortality and fertility (and therefore growth) are unchanging, and whose age structure is therefore also unchanging.*

Transitional stage: *the stage in a population's history when mortality rates are falling more rapidly than fertility rates and, as a result, the population size is growing.*

References

Ariès, Philippe
   1962. *Centuries of Childhood: A Social History of Family Life*. New York: Vintage Books.

Barclay, George W.
   1958. *The Techniques of Population Analysis*. New York: Wiley.

Beaujot, Roderic, and Kevin McQuillan
   1982. *Growth and Dualism: The Demographic Development of Canadian Society*. Toronto: Gage.

Boulding, Kenneth E.
   1981. *Ecodynamics: A New Theory of Societal Evolution*. Beverly Hills: Sage.

Burch, Thomas K.
   1985. *Family History Survey: Preliminary Findings*. Statistics Canada, Catalogue 99-955. Ottawa: Supply and Services.

Burch, Thomas K., and A. K. Madan
   1986. *Union Formation and Dissolution in Canada: Results from the 1984 Family History Survey*. Statistics Canada, Catalogue 99-963. Ottawa: Supply and Services.

Coale, Ansley J.
   1963. "Population and Economic Development," pp. 46–69. In Philip Hauser, ed., *The Population Dilemma*. Englewood Cliffs, N.J.: Prentice-Hall.

Coale, Ansley J., and Edgar M. Hoover
   1958. *Population Growth and Economic Development in Low Income Countries*. Princeton: Princeton University Press.

Coale, Ansley J., and Susan Cotts Watkins, eds.
1986. *The Decline of Fertility in Europe*. Princeton: Princeton University Press.

Davis, Kingsley
1945. "The World Demographic Transition." *Annals of the American Academy of Political and Social Science* 237 (January).

Dublin, L. I., and A. J. Lotka
1925. "On the True Rate of Natural Increase." *Journal of the American Statistical Association* 20(151): 305–39.

Easterlin, Richard A.
1980. *Birth and Fortune: The Impact of Numbers on Personal Welfare*. New York: Basic Books.

Eichler, Margrit
1981. "The Inadequacy of the Monolithic Model of the Family." *Canadian Journal of Sociology* 6(3): 367–88.

Farb, Peter
1978. *Man's Rise to Civilization: The Cultural Ascent of the Indians of North America*, 2nd ed. New York: Bantam Books.

Foot, David K.
1982. *Canada's Population Outlook: Demographic Futures and Economic Challenges*. Toronto: James Lorimer.

Gunder Frank, André
1966. "The Development of Underdevelopment." *Monthly Review* 18(4): 17–31.

Habakkuk, H. J.
1965. "English Population in the Eighteenth Century," pp. 269–84. In D. V. Glass and D. E. C. Eversley, eds., *Population in History*. London: Edward Arnold.

Hajnal, J.
1965. "European Marriage Patterns in Perspective," pp. 101–43. In D. V. Glass and D. E. C. Eversley, eds., *Population in History*. London: Edward Arnold.

Hauser, Philip M.
1964. "The Population of the World." In Ronald Freedman, ed., *Population: The Vital Revolution*. New York: Doubleday.

Hawkins, Freda
1972. *Canada and Immigration: Public Policy and Public Concern*. Montreal: McGill-Queen's University Press.

Henripin, Jacques
1974. *Immigration and Language Imbalance: Canadian Immigration and Population Studies*. Ottawa: Information Canada.

Higgins, Ronald
1980. *The Seventh Enemy: The Human Factor in the Global Crisis*. London: Pan Books.

Kalbach, W. E.
1970. *The Impact of Immigration on Canada's Population*. Ottawa: Queen's Printer.

Keyfitz, Nathan, and Wilhelm Flieger
1971. *Population: Facts and Methods of Demography*. San Francisco: W. H. Freeman.

Kirk, Dudley
1971. "A New Demographic Transition?" pp. 123–47. In National Academy of Sciences,

Rapid Population Growth: Consequences and Policy Implications. Baltimore: Johns Hopkins University Press.

Lachapelle, Rejean
1980. "Evolution of Ethnic and Linguistic Composition," pp. 15–43. In R. Breton, J. Reitz and V. Valentine, eds., *Cultural Boundaries and the Cohesion of Canada*. Montreal: Institute for Research on Public Policy.

Laslett, Peter
1971. *The World We Have Lost*, 2nd ed. London: Methuen.

Laslett, Peter, ed.
1972. *Household and Family in Past Time*. London: Cambridge University Press.

Lavoie, Yolande
1972. *L'émigration des Canadiens aux États-Unis avant 1930*. Montréal: Les Presses de l'Université de Montréal, Collection Démographie canadienne 1.

Legare, Jacques
1989. "A Population Register for Canada under the French Regime: Context, Scope, Content, and Applications." *Canadian Studies in Population* 15(1).

Levine, David
1984. "Production, Reproduction and the Proletarian Family in England, 1500–1851," pp. 87–128. In David Levine, ed., *Proletarianization and Family History*. New York: Academic Press.

Lotka, A. J.
1928. "The Progeny of a Population Element." *American Journal of Hygiene* 8(6):875–901.

Lucas, Rex
1972. *Minetown, Milltown, Railtown*. Toronto: University of Toronto Press.

Madigan, Francis C.
1957. "Are Sex Mortality Differentials Biologically Caused?" *Millbank Memorial Fund Quarterly* 35:202–23.

Malthus, Thomas Robert
1959 [1798]. *Population: The First Essay*. Ann Arbor: University of Michigan Press.
1970 [1830]. "A Summary View of the Principle of Population." In *Malthus: An Essay on the Principle of Population*. Edited by Anthony Flew. New York: Penguin.

McKeown, Thomas, and R. G. Brown
1965. "Medical Evidence Related to English Population Changes in the Eighteenth Century," pp. 285–307. In D. V. Glass and D. E. C. Eversley, eds., *Population in History*. London: Edward Arnold.

Meadows, D. H., et al.
1972. *The Limits to Growth*. New York: Universe Books.

Meek, Ronald L., ed.
1954. *Marx and Engels on Malthus*. New York: International Publishers.

Pool, I., and M. Moore
1986. *Lone Parenthood: Characteristics and Determinants (Results from the 1984 Family History Survey)*. Statistics Canada, Catalogue 99-961. Ottawa: Supply and Services.

Porter, John
1965. *The Vertical Mosaic*. Toronto: University of Toronto Press.

Shryock, H. S., and J. Siegel

1973. *The Methods and Materials of Demography.* Washington: U.S. Bureau of the Census, Government Printing Office.

Stolnitz, George J.

1964. "The Demographic Transition." In Ronald Freedman, ed., *Population: The Vital Revolution.* New York: Doubleday.

United Nations

1967. *Manual 1V. Methods of Estimating Basic Demographic Measures from Incomplete Data.* ST/SOA/Series A/42. Population Studies, No. 42. New York.

van de Walle, Etienne, and John Knodel

1980. "Europe's Fertility Transition: New Evidence and Lessons for Today's Developing World." *Population Bulletin* 34(6).

Watkins, M. H.

1963. "A Staple Theory of Economic Growth." *Canadian Journal of Economics and Political Science* 29(2): 141–58.

Wilber, Charles K., ed.

1973. *The Political Economy of Development and Underdevelopment.* New York: Random House.

World Commission on Environment and Development

1987. *Our Common Future.* New York: Oxford University Press.

Wrigley, E. A., ed.

1966. *An Introduction to Historical Demography.* London: Weidenfeld and Nicolson.
1969. *Population and History.* New York: McGraw-Hill.

Opposite page:

The city is the home, workplace, and locus of consumption. Allocating scarce land among competing priorities provides severe challenges and the potential for huge profits. Urban sociology addresses a variety of urban processes, behaviours, patterns, and outcomes.

CHAPTER 20

Cities and Urbanization

WILLIAM MICHELSON

Introduction

The interests of sociologists in cities run the gamut from the city's role in society to the interiors of dwelling units. The impacts of industrialization, avoidance behaviour among strangers, why suburban youth "hang out" in shopping centres and the rationales of metropolitan government are all valid matters for study within urban sociology. Understanding one concern, however, does not automatically explain others. No single theory is sufficient to describe, explain or solve all problems. A mixture of sociological perspectives is needed to help us understand and deal with the many unique, challenging situations in urban life.

Cities and urbanization will therefore be discussed in this chapter according to four perspectives:

1. *urbanization*—the nature, extent and distribution of cities in the larger society or nation;
2. *urbanism*—behaviour patterns of people living in cities;
3. *ecology*—the internal makeup and physical patterns of cities;
4. *structural analysis*—what functions cities perform in society and who has what bearing on decisions and outcomes.

Urbanization

The First Cities   If the most elementary conception of the city is a settlement containing at least some non-agricultural workers, then its emergence at about 3500 BC was truly something new under the sun. And its impact on the rest of the society was immediate and direct. Members of the rural sector, instead of simply growing enough food for themselves, had to grow a surplus of food to feed the urbanites. Thus, right from the start, urbanization affected whole societies. Creating stable and predictable agricultural surplus required simultaneous developments in technology and social structure (Adams, 1966).

Important technological innovations included irrigation, bronze metallurgy for plowing and cutting instruments, animal husbandry for use in agriculture, stone mortars, selective cultivation of rich, non-perishable foods such as grains and dates, wheeled carts and sailboats for transport and building bricks for permanent settlements.

Social structures also evolved. The division of labour beyond age and sex became a legacy to new cities and to society. One aspect of the increased division of labour was vertical stratification—differential degrees of responsibility and power. Some individuals ensured that the farmers produced surpluses for the non-agricultural workers by providing technological support and controlling delivery. Another aspect was horizontal stratification—specialization at a given stratification level. Full-time soldiers, artists and artisans appeared in the urban settlements, while farmers became even more specialized. Even from the start, therefore, cities had heterogeneous populations with complex, usually coercive relationships with the rest of society. Although farmers did get consumer goods and the often dubious benefits of laws and law enforcement from city administrators, they relinquished some of their produce under terms they did not control.

Although this relationship between urban and rural people may appear familiar from our own contemporary observations, there have been enormous changes in the balance between the two, reflecting developments in technology and social organization. For example, technology was at first barely adequate to create the necessary food surplus. It took fifty to ninety farmers to produce enough surplus food for one urbanite. Now one farmer in a technologically developed country produces food for about nine urbanites.

Social organization also changed. In the first few thousand years of urban life, even the largest cities were very small. Archaeological evidence suggests the largest were between 5000 and 30 000 in population. Their size was limited by how far a labour-intensive transportation technology could bring food from outlying rural areas, by how far coercion could be extended and by the state of sanitation and public health.

With refinements in technology and social structure, some ancient cities grew larger. Athens had about 150 000 residents in 500 BC. Then ancient Rome grew to between 250 000 and a million inhabitants. Despite these city-states, with dominance over vast tributary areas, the kind of urbanization that we know today took many centuries more to develop—until after the Middle Ages.

Industrialization and Urbanization

The development of industry, which is based on inanimate sources of energy, is commonly given credit for shifting the population balance from rural to urban, and for greatly increasing the size of cities. For example, about two hundred years ago, only about 3 percent of the world's population lived in settlements of five hundred or more inhabitants, and a city about the size of the current Vancouver metropolitan area would have been the largest in the world.

Industrialization reflected societal developments in technology and accentuated the division of labour. The same advances in science and engineering that made possible large-scale factories using machines also led to innovations in agricultural technology that enabled fewer farm workers to grow food more intensively and on larger holdings. Thus, in technologically advanced societies, a surplus of agricultural labour was created. These workers took newly emerging, specialized city jobs. There were specialists in housing, food, transportation, financial services, warehousing and distribution and much more.

Technically, observers measure urbanization as the percentage of a nation's population living in settlements of a certain minimum size, usually five thousand and over. After industrialization, advanced nations have swung from urbanization levels of only a few percent to beyond 75 percent.

Canada belongs to a group of industrial nations with reasonably similar, high rates of urbanization. Recent figures show Belgium at the top with 87.1 percent urbanization, and Australia next at 86 percent. Canada, with 76 percent in 1986 (Statistics Canada,

1988 : 1), is close to the United Kingdom at 77.9 percent, the United States at 74 percent and France at 73 percent (Statistics Canada, 1984). In contrast, underdeveloped nations have lower urbanization levels. India and China, despite the presence of some of the world's largest cities, have urbanization levels of 20.1 and 13.2 percent respectively (Statistics Canada, 1984).

The urban population in highly urbanized societies is distributed among a number of reasonably sized settlements rather than concentrated in just one obviously large metropolis in a nation or region. The largest city in the world right now is neither Tokyo nor New York, but Mexico City. Its 1985 population was 18.1 million, and it is projected to grow to 26.3 million by the year 2000, despite severe pollution problems (Dogon and Kasarda, 1988). Most of these extremely large cities, such as Bombay, Calcutta, and Shanghai, were centres from which foreign imperial powers exported the region's raw materials for industrial production back home. Their large size made them obvious destinations for the rural poor, despite the virtual absence of an industrial economic base (Dogon and Kasarda, 1988). Urban populations in such situations are typically underemployed, poor and predominantly male. When more persons reside in

FIGURE 20-1

Urban and Rural Living in the Provinces and Territories, 1986

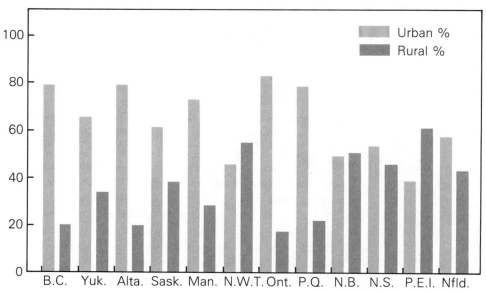

Statistics Canada, 1988.

a city than can be supported by its economic base, the result is called *overurbanization*.

In Canada, high levels of urbanization are not confined to Ontario and Quebec, with their predominant cities. The majority of people in every Canadian province and territory except New Brunswick, Prince Edward Island and the Northwest Territories live in urban areas (see Figure 20-1). In both Canada and the United States, economic factors attract people (especially women) to cities rather than simply pushing them away from rural areas.

Urbanism

Classical Approaches

Does life in an urban context differ systematically from that in a rural context? Many analysts have thought so. Sjoberg (1960), for example, found that job specialization and the complexity of production and marketing that accompanied industrialization required standardization in weights, measures, currencies, pricing and financial interaction. Rational, exact actions became necessary for the system to work.

Nonetheless, the best known ideas on urbanism were attributed to Louis Wirth in "Urbanism as a Way of Life" (1938). Wirth's piece said that cities had three defining characteristics: large numbers of inhabitants, high densities and heterogeneous populations. Large numbers of inhabitants in cities lead to the impossibility of knowing everyone and hence to the relative absence of intimacy in most interpersonal relationships. Human relations become segmented into many largely anonymous, superficial and transitory contacts.

High density fosters human diversification and specialization. Due to the inescapable presence of close physical contact with diverse persons, social distance is established to maintain personal space. Nonetheless, accentuated friction inevitably arises, and formal means of social control (for example, uniformed police) assume prominence in cities. Because of such close proximity, complex patterns of segregation take shape.

Finally, Wirth felt that a heterogeneous population makes it difficult to constrict individuals by rigid social structures. Urban individuals more often find themselves in varied social settings and groups. Both upward and downward mobility, with the resultant greater feelings of instability and insecurity, are more likely in cities.

Other early-twentieth-century observers made similar assessments. Simmel (1950), for example, found that German urbanites were forced to pay continuous attention to contextual signals: lights, signs, footsteps, whistles and the like. The head rather than the heart dictated behaviours, according to principles of rationality, impersonality, exactness and distrust of others. The result was a blasé attitude: people pretend not to care about what's happening around them. Although this classic approach to urbanism was never accepted by everyone (Dewey, 1960), its legacy was sobering: any societal gains coming from greater division of labour, rationality, large scale and personal freedom seemed counterbalanced by unending suspicion, distrust and isolation.

Modern Social-Psychological Approaches

Social psychologists have recently begun to explore urbanism through experimental work. Milgram (1970), for example, developed Simmel's notion of external signals and, using modern systems analysis, described it as sensory overload. According to Milgram, urbanites cope with overload in various ways. First, they tune out what they find overburdening: drunks, poverty and negative consequences of policies and practices that benefit only some. One example of tuning out is not aiding strangers who need help, so as to avoid troubling oneself. Much research followed public shock when a woman named Kitty Genovese was murdered after appealing for help outside the windows of at least thirty-eight onlooking neighbours in a New York City apartment house. The research suggested that the more people are there, the less likely any individual will intervene.

"City life, as we experience it, constitutes a continuous set of encounters with overload, and of resultant adaptations."

–Stanley Milgram, 1970

"Minimize involvement. . . . Maximize social order."
— Karp, Stone and Yoels, 1977

Urbanites also minimize involvement by removing themselves from easy contact with others. They buy telephone answering devices, have unlisted telephone numbers, filter visitors through secretaries and assistants, travel by private automobile and live in segregated (and increasingly guarded) neighbourhoods. In public places, urbanites pretend not to see each other (for example, on beaches). They tolerate other life styles except where these represent clear and present dangers. They follow unspoken but definite rules about how much distance to keep from others in particular situations, where to sit (for example, on buses or in libraries) and how to walk (Hall, 1966; Sommer, 1969).

Styles of clothing, particularly uniforms, provide a basis for secure interaction without previous personal acquaintance. Certain addresses now provide the same kind of instant identification. Not only do clothes make the man or woman, but streets and neighbourhoods help complete the introduction.

The Subcultural Theory of Urban Life

But is it really the city itself that creates such behaviour? Reiss (1959), for example, found that the anonymous, segmented and impersonal relations noted by Wirth reflected occupation more than residence. Men living in rural areas with non-farm jobs had daily contact patterns resembling those of their urban counterparts.

In contrast to the *deterministic* approach of the classical analysts, others employ a *compositional* perspective, in which behaviour reflects the composition of the population

"In Boston, they ask, How much does he know? In New York, How much is he worth? In Philadelphia, Who were his parents?"
    Mark Twain (1899)

In Toronto, Where does he live?

7ORO/EHILL

Clothing provides a basis for secure interaction without previous personal acquaintance. Addresses also provide identification. Clothes make the person, and streets and neighbourhoods complete the introduction.

COSTAIN LIMITED.

(Fischer, 1976). Gans (1967), for example, explained suburban behaviour not in terms of the physical nature of the suburbs, but in terms of the social class background and life cycle characteristics of the population. The nature and extent of their contact with neighbours, their participation in organizations and their interest in schools reflected the fact that they came from middle-class backgrounds and belonged to families with young children. Thus, according to the compositional approach, urban life reflects the most salient features of the particular population groups living in cities: by class, ethnic background or race, religion, age or sex.

In *The Urban Experience* (1976), Claude Fischer attempts to reconcile deterministic and compositional perspectives and to go beyond them. He argues that Wirth is right in stressing the significance of there being large numbers of persons in cities. But rather than the numbers providing *direct* effects, Fischer sees them as providing the nucleus for various specialized subcultures within cities. It is the particular composition of the subcultures that influences the so-called urban life styles.

Fischer calls his approach the *subcultural theory of urban life*. Which subcultures become major in any city depends on many macroscopic characteristics of cities—their

Hong Kong? Lisbon? Athens? Subcultures flourish in Toronto.

economic base, sources of migration, climate and more. Within highly urbanized societies, cities of different sizes and in different locations may be functionally specialized. This does not mean that they are monolithic in their activities or populations; but there are distinct tendencies regarding who chooses to live and work there and hence which subcultures take root. It is unusual for any city to have more than 25 percent of its jobs in manufacturing due to the need for complementary and supportive activities; yet, the difference between 25 percent and 10 percent in manufacturing spells a big difference in the critical mass of a blue-collar subculture. Ways of life in Hamilton, with its huge steel mills, are in many ways different than in nearby London, an insurance and financial centre, not to speak of Victoria with its combination of government, benign weather, retirement and afternoon tea!

The largest national cities, however, are usually economically diverse, and their population size supports varied subcultures and life styles. It takes a city the size of Toronto, not of Truro, to supply the critical mass of people to support a variety of ethnic centres as well as major cultural, youth, yuppy, gay, sports, criminal and endless other subcultures side by side.

Does subcultural theory invalidate the kind of generalizations urban social psychologists have been making about problems such as overload, anonymity and adaptations? Not really. A more recent book by Fischer (1982) shows that the personal interactions of urbanites are concentrated in their specialized group or subcultures. Urbanites are likely to trust their closest neighbours, but not the rest of the city in general. People living in smaller settlements or rural areas are less discriminating in their personal contacts. In cities, selective interaction and avoidance behaviours are two sides of the same coin.

Ecology

We have seen so far that urban behaviour patterns reflect subcultural differences. One would therefore suspect that the physical structure of cities would reflect and reinforce such patterns. Examining the city in ecological terms strongly supports such suspicions.

Cities, Suburbs and Metropolitan Areas

While Canadian urbanization levels show that we live predominantly in cities, they do not tell us where in cities we live or in what kind of settlements. Do most Canadians live in large or small cities, downtown or in the suburbs?

A common pattern in technologically advanced societies has been the buildup of urban populations beyond city limits and into newer municipalities immediately adjacent. These are commonly called suburbs, although the word is often applied to areas that simply look newer and less crowded than the centres of the traditional cities; Montreal, for example, has suburbs around it, while much of Calgary and Edmonton appears suburban without the need to cross municipal borders.

Large cities may have different names from their suburbs, but in terms of everyday behaviour and economic activity, they form an entity. This entity is called a *metropolitan area*. For example, people commonly live in one part of a metropolitan area and work in another; the interchange between, for example, Vancouver and New Westminster is active.

Statistics Canada defines a *census metropolitan area* (CMA) as an area with at least 100 000 inhabitants and one or more large cities at its centre. Municipalities adjacent to the city must have at least 50 percent of their employed residents (minimum 100 persons) working in the city or 25 percent of their own labour force commuting from the city (or cities) (Statistics Canada, 1983 : vi; Statistics Canada, 1987 : vi). Based on these criteria, some CMAs include a centre city and many municipalities extending a considerable distance from the urban core, while others involve only a single municipality. This reflects not only the size of the urban area, but its history and the amount of land suitable for expansion around the centre city. Toronto, for example, extends

TABLE 20-1

Distribution of Canadian Census Metropolitan Areas by Main City(ies) and Suburban Population (1986)

Census Metropolitan Area	Total Population	% in Main City(ies)	% in Suburbs
1. Toronto	3 427 168	18%	82%
2. Montreal	2 921 357	35	65
3. Vancouver	1 380 729	31	69
4. Ottawa–Hull	819 263	44	56
5. Edmonton	785 465	73	27
6. Calgary	671 326	95	5
7. Winnipeg	625 304	95	5
8. Quebec (City)	603 267	27	73
9. Hamilton	557 029	55	45
10. St. Catharines/Niagara	343 258	64	36
11. London	342 302	87	13
12. Kitchener	311 195	67	33
13. Halifax	295 990	38	62
14. Victoria	255 547	26	74
15. Windsor	253 998	76	24
16. Oshawa	203 543	61	39
17. Saskatoon	200 665	89	11
18. Regina	186 521	94	6
19. St. John's	161 901	59	41
20. Chicoutimi–Jonquière	158 468	75	25
21. Sudbury	148 877	60	40
22. Sherbrooke	129 960	57	43
23. Trois-Rivières	128 888	39	61
24. Thunder Bay	122 217	92	8
25. Saint John	121 265	63	37

ADAPTED FROM STATISTICS CANADA. 1987. CENSUS CANADA 1986; CENSUS METROPOLITAN AREAS AND AGGLOMERATIONS. *OTTAWA: MINISTER OF SUPPLY AND SERVICES CANADA.*

almost to Hamilton (through Oakville), while Saskatoon not only includes nearly all the residents in its vicinity, but also controls undeveloped land for future development. Whether they live in small or large municipalities, most urban Canadians live in a CMA—78 percent (Statistics Canada, 1988).

The image many people have of the city is that of an older municipality with high density and buildings that are large and striking or old and grey. They think of suburbs as somehow something else. This view needs revision. Most residents of Canadian and American metropolitan areas are suburbanites. This does not even include the great numbers of people in newer cities (largely in the West) who live in typically suburban conditions. Table 20-1 shows Canada's CMAs by size, indicating the breakdown of the population by residence in central city and suburban municipalities. Overall, 55 percent of city dwellers are suburbanites. They live mostly, but not exclusively, in the largest and oldest of the CMAs. This distribution is essential to understanding the pattern of local areas and life styles in metropolitan areas. Whereas people previously focused on the central city and then spoke in stereotyped terms about the suburbs and suburbanites, now it is essential to recognize that a major share of the population lives outside central cities.

Metropolitan Population and Land-Use Patterns

How, then, are people and their subcultures patterned within metropolitan areas? Burgess (1925) identified from his studies of Chicago an initial land-use and stratification pattern of cities called *concentric rings*. At the heart of this pattern was the *central business district* (CBD), consisting of the major private and public sector offices, department stores and hotels. It is serviced by public transit to make it the most accessible place in the city. Burgess assumed that the central business district would be the only major centre in the city and that it would continue to grow indefinitely.

Because of CBD growth, the land around it would be held speculatively, for future profit. Before upgrading, these areas, called *zones in transition*, would be used, without maintenance or improvement, for rooming houses, transient hotels and other impermanent, out-of-the-way uses. The zone in transition contains the poorest, newest migrants, criminal elements, prostitution and other vices—subcultures requiring short-term, affordable housing and, in many cases, anonymity.

The more regularized sectors of the population are distributed in rings around the zone in transition, depending on their ability to pay for greater amounts of land increasingly far from the CBD and for the cost and time involved in more lengthy commuting. Working-class communities would be in the zone immediately surrounding the zone in transition. Next would be the middle-class and then the upper-class zones. Hence, major land uses would claim, through market competition, the CBD. Residential areas would be distributed at distances from the centre according to income.

Forms of behaviour that arose because birds of a feather flocked together were called *community* (Park, 1925). Within a ring, local communities that were homogeneous by ethnic or religious background would form within boundaries, such as major streets, railways and parks. These communities were called *natural areas* because no one rationally planned their location. They were simply a consequence of urban land values and constrictions of natural features or public works as boundaries.

Unfortunately, the concentric ring pattern was more imageable than universal. It has been demonstrated in few places outside Chicago. Indeed, in many settings outside the United States, the rich occupy the city centres, while the poor are left from the benefit of the urban infrastructure. Ironically, it was in Chicago that a researcher named Hoyt (1939) discovered a rather different pattern in cities: *sectors*. These resembled pieces of a pie, extending from the centre outward without interruption. Hoyt noted that certain amenities and eyesores extend outward, such as waterfront parks and freight railways. People of means tend to live within view of the amenities, while those without tend to live near the eyesores. Others locate in-between. One side of town becomes better than another, if only because it is upwind from centrally located industries.

Another view is called the *multiple nuclei theory* (Harris and Ullman, 1945). It states that the location of each land use or subculture has unique criteria for what is a desirable location. Heavy industry wants to be near railways and highways, but doesn't need to be as accessible to consumers as retailers do. Head offices attract fine restaurants, banks and law offices to their vicinity, while universities attract fast-food chains and bookstores. What emerges are cities with many diverse centres whose locations are not in a fixed geometric pattern.

Based on data from many American cities, Shevky and Bell (1955) found that local residential areas differ mainly in social class, size of family and ethnic and racial characteristics. Another procedure, called *factorial ecology*, is used to analyse the census statistics for local areas in a city to determine what kind of pattern exists there. For example, Murdie's pioneering analysis of Metro Toronto concluded that family size increased with distance from the centre, that social classes were segregated in sectors from the centre outward and that ethnic groups lived in multiple nuclei (Murdie, 1969).

Neighbourhoods and Communities

Does this mean everybody lives in a tightly knit neighbourhood with people similar in social class, family size and ethnicity? Not really. But the concepts of neighbourhood and community help clarify the situation. *Neighbourhood* refers to a specific physical area within a city. It may have formal boundaries, though people may have an image of it even without knowing its exact limits. *Community* refers to interpersonal contact patterns; it has primarily social connotations.

Traditionally, neighbourhood and community were synonymous. In the old days or in small towns, people centred their interpersonal relationships within the physical areas where they lived. The deterministic view of urbanism said this kind of community was lost in the city. Later, however, researchers found extremely strong ethnic subcultures in cities. These subcultures appeared to re-establish the conjunction between community and neighbourhood (Gans, 1962). Community was said to be regained (Wellman and Leighton, 1979).

More penetrating analyses of people's interpersonal networks went on to show that many people in cities have specific types of contact patterns that reflect subcultures, but are not confined to the boundaries of neighbourhoods (Wellman, 1979; Wellman, Carrington and Hall, 1988). Community members might be all over the city, yet could be reached easily by telephone or computer or could be met at work, bars, parties or conventions. This has been called *community without propinquity* (Webber, 1963) or community liberated or unbound (Wellman and Leighton, 1979).

Urban neighbourhoods take various forms, starting from the ideal type, where everybody interacts with everyone else (Hallman, 1984; Wireman, 1984). The most common urban neighbourhoods have been called the *community of limited liability* (Janowitz, 1952). People recognize that they live in a specific area, which has identifiable institutions. Yet, they limit neither their contact patterns nor their everyday activities to this area.

A *conscious neighbourhood* is something that developers and designers work to achieve in newly built areas. They try to construct unifying symbols, so that residents will treat the area well and interact with each other. Clarence Perry (1966) created the *neighbourhood unit plan* in 1927. It was a development of about four hundred homes, surrounded by traffic arteries but with only local roads inside, focusing on an elementary school and community facilities. Though this plan has been shown ineffective in its most grandiose social engineering objectives (because people often have greater interpersonal loyalties elsewhere), it has been highly influential in suburban development.

Some Selected Urban Neighbourhoods

Within the inner cities, planners have noted the crucial differences between actual slums and low-income ethnic subcultural neighbourhoods. The former, typified by the *skid row* (or skid road) is what Burgess had in mind with his zone in transition. People go there to avoid contact, ostensibly (but not always) for short periods of time. Intense personal networks are not common, and there is little or no proprietary interest in buildings or neighbourhood areas apart from their pragmatic function in the short run. Skid rows contrast greatly in their interpersonal communities with other areas that may also have old buildings, poor maintenance and poor people, but where there are well-established kinship and neighbourhood relationships. Gans (1962) and Whyte (1943) have written extremely detailed accounts of the high degree of organization within two Italian-American communities in central Boston. These communities were called "urban villages" by Gans, a term fitting many neighbourhoods in Canadian cities with ethnic communities—for example, Italian (Sidlofsky, 1969), Jewish (Shaffir, 1974) and Portuguese (Anderson, 1974).

A recent phenomenon changing urban neighbourhoods is *gentrification*, which occurs when upper-middle-class professionals move into and transform formerly working-class areas of the central city (Rosenthal, 1980). Gentrification occurs less frequently in new cities, and its extent is highly variable. Yet, it is well developed in Canada, the United States, Britain and other nations. It normally occurs in cities with centralized white-collar and professional jobs, where the suburbs are extending farther and farther out and where the housing stock in one or more central areas is fundamentally sound and with aesthetic potential. At first, on an individual and piecemeal basis, wealthier people purchase, restore and modernize the buildings for personal use or for sale at enormous markups. As more upper-middle-class people move in, the neighbourhood changes. Neighbourhood stores, for example, shift to the tastes of well-heeled adults: trendy restaurants, health food stores, art galleries, computer boutiques and more.

City fathers laud gentrification because it improves the condition of neighbourhoods, the tax values of property and the commercial potential of the residents. But they commonly ignore what happens to the former residents, who must make do in more remote areas of the city, where access to most opportunities and necessities is less available. What former owners receive for selling to the gentrifiers does not go far in newer areas of the city, but their situation is still better than that of displaced tenants facing few or no comparable housing opportunities elsewhere.

The suburbs provide a diversity of urban neighbourhoods. The old suburban stereotypes came from studies of middle- and upper-middle-class areas. Yet, other segments of the population seek suburban residence simply for decent, available housing. Many blue-collar families seek affordable housing away from what some regard as disreputable elements in the central city. Suburban life styles end up reflecting diversity in the composition of their residential populations (Clark, 1966).

Colonies of artists, writers, and wealthy city people are increasingly found even beyond the usual range of everyday commuting. The ideas of these new arrivals often conflict with the economic interests of long-term residents. This was well described in a study of Elora, Ontario (Sinclair and Westhues, 1974) in which newcomers wanted to curtail, in the name of preservation, the town's economic growth, which was desired by the longtime residents. The new residents of one rural area recently passed a by-law preventing farmers from plowing after nine p.m. so as to safeguard rural tranquillity!

Third World nations, whose large cities typically receive in-migrants fleeing rural poverty, add another suburban variation, the *shantytown* (also known as the *favala* or *bidonville*). A shantytown is built very quickly with a miscellany of salvaged materials on found land in poorly accessible areas outside the actual cities. It is an illegal foothold into the city, giving residents some access without the requirements of money, jobs or legitimacy. Planners and other "respectable people" despair of these communities, but development agencies have learned that the most responsible avenue is to try to help install a basic infrastructure, such as sewage, water and electricity. As the economic situation of the population starts to regularize, so too does the quality of life in shantytowns: mobility to the city becomes a possibility (Van Vliet, Huttman and Fava, 1985).

It is evident that there is a wide variety of urban areas, and a wide variety of factors account for their differentiation. This differentiation goes far beyond the assumption of central business district growth that was advanced by Burgess to explain natural areas. Human intervention establishes and changes local areas far more than the invisible hand of land economics does. Developers cultivate new neighbourhood images, and real estate agents help reinforce or change the composition of older ones. Banks and insurance companies can influence who enters, leaves and stays in neighbourhoods by their lending and insuring policies. Planning and zoning activities can influence stability and change, while ratepayers' associations, tenants' groups and trade organizations can influence planning and zoning bodies.

Built Environments and Behaviour
: The elements of our urban pattern are indeed many and complex, as are the influences of this pattern on residents. The social composition of sub-areas of cities is not the only influence on human behaviour within urban areas. The built environment and the organization of its infrastructure are also important factors. In many instances, the ways buildings, neighbourhoods and cities are designed and planned facilitate or constrain behaviours (Michelson, 1970).

Housing and Other Institutions
: Housing is a natural focus for analysis. Families of different ages, compositions, sizes and ethnic backgrounds choose or are forced to live in homes of varying size, tenure, density, layout and amenity. Does it matter who lives where, aside from status and identity connotations?

Enormous amounts of research confirm that housing design does have an effect on people's lives (see Marcus and Sarkissian, 1987). For example, a study of married couples living in high-rise apartments and single-family homes in both downtown and suburban areas of Metro Toronto indicated that behaviour differed because of the respective opportunities in their housing (Michelson, 1977). One Swedish house design attempts to help neighbours keep up their personal contacts during cold and wet weather by putting a glass roof over the space between pairs of row houses.

Intriguing research has suggested that enlightened designs of residential buildings and grounds can mitigate against crimes such as vandalism and muggings that occur where perpetrators believe they can get away with them (Jeffery, 1971; Newman, 1972). For example, apartment houses that have stairways that are out of public view provide opportunities for muggings; those providing glass walls to their stairways take away the intruder's protection. Long, anonymous hallways make it possible for strangers to lurk unchallenged; small apartment groupings, where residents are more likely to know each other and their respective guests, do not. Well-lit, open lobbies situated in view of many apartments are less of a target than those out of sight. The environment of other institutions also affects behaviour. It takes no stretch of the imagination to consider what difference the amount and design of space in schools, hospitals, offices and factories makes to the people there. For a review of the literature on this topic, see Gifford (1987).

Neighbourhood Design
: On a somewhat larger scale, the design of neighbourhoods is of considerable importance to housewives, children and others whose daily routines or resources restrict them to the areas where they live. Consider children. The scope of their world starts with a crib or room and expands slowly; only as teenagers do they typically go beyond their

Year-round protection from the elements provides more opportunity for neighbour contact in the Gardsakra walk-up apartments in Eslov, Sweden.

neighbourhoods for independent activities (and even then only by the grace of adults in the absence of good public transportation) (Michelson and Roberts, 1979).

Urban Design and Organization

It is more difficult to grasp how the design of the city as a whole affects the behaviour of individuals. The Swedish geographer Torsten Hägerstrand provides some insight (1970; Carlstein, 1978). He shows that the spatial dimensions of the greater urban area (that is, the degree of mixture or separation of its land uses, its densities and its private and public transportation) create capability constraints. They make combining different daily activities such as work, shopping and entertainment easier or harder to manage. The time dimensions of community (for example, working hours, school and day care hours, medical and bank hours, the opening and closing times of stores, services and bureaucracies, delivery hours, etc.) likewise impinge on what we can do on a given day; these are called *authority constraints*. These and other constraints combine to limit daily activity and to serve as the basis for habit formation (van Paasen, 1981; Cullen, 1978).

The way our urban areas are laid out and organized can facilitate or frustrate the pursuit of daily life for certain segments of the population (see Popenoe, 1985). With the influx of married women (including those with children) into the paid labour force, many of the arrangements of the city are no longer functional. Problem areas include low density, segregated land uses, day care centres in marginal locations, standard working hours and restricted hours for many public services and stores (Hayden, 1984; Michelson, 1985; Andrew and Milroy, 1988). Other segments of the population that are vulnerable in the greater urban structure include children, the elderly, the handicapped, the poor and many more—indeed everyone at some time in their lives.

Structural Analysis

Cities must take collective action regarding both social and physical policies. Cities must decide what actions to take, at what level of aggregation, serving whose interests and at whose initiative. Cities in North America are formed and get their powers and responsibilities according to the laws and decisions of provincial and state governments. Therefore, determining what cities "do" and how they are organized are functions of higher levels of government.

Schools have traditionally been organized at the municipal level and have always accounted for the greatest portion of municipal spending. Among other long-standing responsibilities of municipalities are police and fire protection, public works (roads, parks, water and sewage) and public health (epidemic prevention, sanitary standards and, more recently, pollution control). In this century, planning, transportation, recreation, child care and welfare are becoming increasingly important municipal responsibilities. Performing these specific functions are central government bureaucracies, where by-laws, records, permits and licences are written, processed and maintained, and where taxes are collected and bills paid.

Conflicts within the System

It is possible to view the functioning of municipal government as a harmonious application of rational laws—but only if you never do more than read descriptions of how the system is formally structured and you never attend a meeting of city council. There are at least two reasons, however, why urban structure should be viewed through a conflict perspective, where disagreements emerge naturally within the system.

First, because cities need money and money is always limited, different functions have to compete for funds. In any given year, a new day care centre may have to compete with a new stadium for the marginal dollar.

Second, while municipalities have a mandate to preserve and enhance health, welfare and safety in terms of the greatest good for the greatest number, specific issues typically carry costs and benefits that affect different segments of the population differently. Employed mothers (as well as their children and spouses) are most interested in new child care facilities, while the construction and hospitality industries are more directly interested in building stadiums. On many issues, one part of town may receive benefits and another the costs. For example, building a superhighway from a suburb to the centre provides greater access for the suburbanites, but gives the problem of providing land for the highway and space for more cars to the centre.

Power

Into this mixture of interests comes the exercise of power—the ability of one person or group to get others to do what they want them to do. The formal structure of government accords power to elected representatives and to those who implement policies and laws. Sociological studies, however, have documented a host of ways in which this formal system is swayed by informal power structures (Hawley and Wirt, 1968; Domhoff, 1980). Power is centralized in the hands of a few in some cities and dispersed among different interest groups in others. Obviously, no two cities are the same in this regard, reflecting a variety of conditions in each. Long (1958) argues persuasively that the city is an "ecology of games." By this, he means that the outcome of any policy issue is never totally predictable. Each will draw a unique combination of protagonists, whose influence and power are cast in different combinations upon the formal decision makers. According to this view, urban politics is kaleidoscopic, forming a different pattern with various combinations of elements each time.

Some persons argue that one should focus primarily in this arena on major actors in the economic system and on associated motives for profit and control (Friedland and Palmer, 1984; Tabb and Sawers, 1984). Logan and Molotch (1987) argue convincingly that there is a coalition of persons promoting and usually benefiting personally from continuous urban growth, which they unflaggingly foster. This neo-Marxist view has been called the "urban growth machine." Analyses of Toronto, for example, have put the interests of large property owners at the centre (Lorimer, 1978). Recent transaction patterns there and in Vancouver have indicated that the urban growth machine is increasingly fuelled from outside Canada.

Ironically, the activities of the urban growth machine to produce increased numbers of new and costly buildings, creating upward pricing pressures throughout the urban real estate market, have been accompanied by an unprecedented increase in the number of homeless persons. Homelessness is even more serious because most people in North America (especially in colder climates) assume it can't happen "here" (Smith, 1988; Bingham, Green and White, 1987).

There is no questioning the presence and impact of economic forces and factors. But they do not always win. Many decisions have been made in recent years in both Vancouver and Toronto, involving so-called reform politicians and citizens' groups, that have gone in opposite directions from what an ideologically pure economic determinist perspective would have predicted.

The Scope of
Urban Functions
and Organization

Many municipalities exist side by side in metropolitan areas. To what extent should decisions and operations be kept "close to home" in one relatively small municipality after another, or to the contrary, be reorganized at the higher level of the metropolitan area?

Many responsibilities of municipal governments transcend their borders. Polluted smoke or water from one municipality has tangible effects in other jurisdictions; pollution is not purely a local concern. Similarly, roads, policing and licensing are chaotic without clear co-ordination or reorganization at higher levels.

Furthermore, the tax money a municipality can gather has traditionally reflected the intensity and wealth of the buildings and activities within its borders. But the needs of a given municipality for money (for education, welfare, police and fire protection, etc.) are not always in line with its tax base. Indeed, the relationship is often an inverse one. Municipalities with poor and aging populations may need greater levels of service, yet have less basis for raising the money. While the different parts of the metropolitan area may function as entities in terms of everyday activity, their historical boundaries divide efforts to solve problems facing urban areas as a whole.

While reorganization into larger metropolitan governments may make economic sense, many people oppose it. Some feel that local control is essential to defending their interests. Affluent people benefit from channelling tax monies to support their own priorities. When, for example, the village of Forest Hill was an independent municipality surrounded by the city of Toronto, it was known for its superior schools and snow removal, which its affluent citizens demanded, unburdened by the welfare needs of surrounding areas.

A purely fiscal solution to the inequitable availability of tax money is to let higher levels of government (national or provincial) collect taxes and then provide grants to municipalities with special needs. However, the idea of such a system can be distorted in its actual operations. School financing, for example, relies more and more on provincial grants to correct local inequities. But the strings attached often limit what the recipients can do with the money. Even when grants have few strings, the benefits from federal-provincial transfer payments do not always go where intended. Federal transfers for higher education, for example, can end up in more mundane coffers.

Metropolitan
Government

One response to the underlying problem of municipal conflicts and inequities is to create a metropolitan government, including all the existing municipalities. This higher level of government carries out those functions where metropolitan co-ordination and financing are instrumental. Which functions are handled at the metropolitan level vary from place to place and from time to time. Metropolitan Toronto was formed in 1953 to care for water, sewage, travel arteries, parks, school financing, welfare, co-ordinated planning, policing, business licensing and air-pollution control. Currently run by a council elected from wards in the various municipalities and a chairperson elected by its members, it collects tax money from the cities and boroughs within Metro and distributes it where needed. Periodic reviews since 1953 have increased the powers of the metropolitan government and decreased those of the municipalities. The metropolitan government of Winnipeg has more responsibility, while that of Montreal has less. The power of the Greater Vancouver Regional District has waxed and waned over the past decades.

In practice, metropolitan governments are not always ideal. The sociological lessons of informal systems should not be lost when evaluating formal solutions such as metropolitan government. Even very rational structures like metropolitan governments are affected by human interests and influences.

Other Structural
Solutions

Where people fear alterations in municipal jurisdictions but urgently require area-wide services, special authorities, commissions or districts are commonly set up. These are charged with building and operating specific functions. Depending on their location, they may have taxation rights or receive public subsidies or they may charge the public for their services. But these bodies are usually shielded from the direct control or scrutiny of city officials. They generally function more efficiently than local municipal services, but are often more remote from constituency demands.

There is obviously no perfect governmental structure to resolve problems. The main factors to consider are what needs to be done, what kind(s) of structures are appropriate to these function(s) and what interests are mobilized in the *de facto* operation.

Urban Planning in
Structural
Perspective

So far, the discussion has failed to mention urban planning where it fits into the perspectives of urban structure and power (Simmie, 1974). Planning is a profession practised by persons hired to municipal staffs or by private consultants hired to contribute services and reports. Planners are not elected. In most municipalities, planning is found in one or more places within city structures. It may be a department of the city, parallel to public works or licensing. It may be advisory to the mayor. It may work under the supervision of an elected or selected commission that reports to city council. Planning activities usually also take place within other organizations, such as transit agencies, school boards and public housing agencies.

What do urban planners plan? They help create long-range, comprehensive plans to facilitate the orderly growth of cities. They also help design transportation networks. In addition, they are highly visible when planning interventions within existing city areas.

False Creek in Vancouver (above) and St. Lawrence in Toronto (below) are examples of new land use for old in the centres of large Canadian cities.

Urban renewal occurs when the nature or use of an area changes. City officials disapprove of areas whose property value and, hence, tax base potential are low. When the current buildings or activities are considered outdated or unusable—and unlikely to change through private-sector initiative—cities often intervene. One form of intervention is *redevelopment*; here, the area is levelled and a new land use is arranged in co-operation with public- or private-sector bodies. Another type of intervention is *rehabilitation*, where buildings are modernized and either resold or rerented at higher levels.

While American cities have seen much publicly planned and implemented renewal of residential and commercial areas, major Canadian projects have turned increasingly to the reuse of old industrial sites and railway yards that are no longer useful. The False Creek area of Vancouver, for example, was built on redeveloped railway lands adjacent to downtown, yet provides housing with considerable amenities to households varying in income and family structure. Similarly, the St. Lawrence area in downtown Toronto was built on outdated industrial land.

Not all planning activities involve such radical intervention. Preventive medicine is preferred to surgery, and much planning activity is devoted to liaison with specific neighbourhoods in hopes that smaller, site-by-site improvements (such as off-street parking) can maintain or upgrade existing areas.

Yet, whatever they do, planners are caught in a difficult structural position. Their recommendations always involve economic benefits to some parties and losses to others. Moreover, they have no political decision-making power. The decision-making process can be influenced from many sources above their heads and from outside the formal decision-making structure (Pahl, 1970). Planners deviate from the wishes of their employers at the risk of their jobs.

Citizen Participation

Many people feel that citizens need to express their interests to those in power in an organized and active way, just as large corporate groups do. The best-known approach is that of the late Saul Alinsky and his many North American followers (Reitzes and Reitzes, 1987). This conflict approach recognizes the difficulty in motivating largely apolitical people to unite in a public stand on technical matters. The answer lies in the way people will join together during a crisis. Activists bring in trained conflict agents to discover (or invent) problems besetting the local community that could bring them into conflict with others (often the city government). Through such a conflict, the latent power of residents is used to pursue planning interests. The problem in this approach is the difficulty of maintaining organizational momentum after resolving the main conflict.

An alternative to the conflict approach is the coalition approach. Here, organizers try to create a local citizens' group, such as a ratepayers' association or a tenants' union. But rather than acting independently, such groups join with other interests and organizations for mutual support. This provides a broader base of support, but it is unclear how broad a coalition can be before the interests of the various groups clash on pending issues.

Canadian planners and municipalities have experimented with many models of citizen participation (Draper, 1971). Halifax, for example, funded a highly successful public encounter on planning issues after more traditional renewal projects had failed (Clairmont and Magill, 1974). Given that planners have technical expertise and that city officials are elected by the people, it may seem surprising that it is so difficult to represent the ordinary Canadian's interests in planning issues. Once again, however, one must recognize the diversity of people and interests in our urban areas, and that many informal processes occur that are not part of the formal institutional structures. Organizational innovation and animation is often necessary to promote the legitimate interests of citizens to the same extent as those of strong economic interests.

Summary

The diversity in nature and scale of urban considerations and problems taxes the scope of the sociological imagination. This chapter is itself a summary. There is no single sociological theory or perspective that addresses all urban problems or phenomena. No two matters are likely to draw on the same combination of factors for their solution or understanding. Yet, it is useful to start thinking through questions about cities and urban living in terms of the logic of four perspectives: (1) urbanization; (2) urbanism; (3) ecology; and (4) structural analysis. Like other forms of sociological inquiry, analyses and research along these lines help clarify what goes on around us and help us shape our contexts and structures in useful ways.

Suggested Readings

Andrew, Caroline, and Beth Moore Milroy, eds.
1988. *Life Spaces*. Vancouver: University of British Columbia Press. Chapters by various authors clarify gender considerations in Canadian urban contexts.

Carlstein, Tommy, Don Parkes and Nigel Thrift, eds.
1978. *Time Geography and Human Activity*. New York: Halstead Press. Definitive explication and illustration of how the temporal and spatial dimensions of urban context constrain everyday life.

Dogon, Mattei, and John Kasarda, eds.
1988. *The Metropolis Era*, 2 vols. Beverly Hills: Sage. A wealth of information on both urbanization and individual cities worldwide.

Karp, David, Gregory P. Stone and William Yoels
1977. *Being Urban*. Toronto: D. C. Heath. A comprehensive and even entertaining examination of how people adapt to the conditions of urban life.

Kennedy, Leslie W.
1983. *The Urban Kaleidoscope: Canadian Perspectives*. Toronto: McGraw-Hill Ryerson. A

pleasingly eclectic introduction to urban sociology rooted in the Canadian urban experience.

Logan, John, and Harvey Molotch

1987. *Urban Fortunes*. Berkeley: University of California Press. A penetrating but not dogmatic analysis of the interests influencing urban land use.

Marcus, Clare Cooper, and Wendy Sarkissian

1986. *Housing as if People Mattered*. Berkeley: University of California Press. Full of examples and illustrations of how to make housing responsive to people's needs.

Phillips, E. Barbara, and Richard T. LeGates

1981. *City Lights*. New York: Oxford University Press. A comprehensive and attractive examination of the issues covered in this chapter.

Smith, Christopher J.

1988. *Public Problems: The Management of Urban Distress*. New York: Guildford Press. A prime example of how multifaceted, contextual thinking can unravel urban problems. This book examines a number of contemporary problems.

Discussion Questions

1. What demands do present-day cities make on the non-urban areas of their own societies? on other societies?

2. What role does technology play in contemporary urbanization? in the growth or decline of specific Canadian cities?

3. How do urbanites avoid personal contact with most other people even in large cities? Can you give examples of this from your own behaviour?

4. What are the most distinct subcultures in your area? How are they reflected in spatial patterns?

5. Name some subgroups in the population that are poorly served by the current arrangements of built environments. How would you improve matters?

6. Explain how the urban growth machine increases homelessness.

Data Collection Exercises

1. Look up census tract information about two or more distinct neighbourhoods in a city with which you are familiar. What do these statistics tell you about the similarities and differences between the two places?

2. Observe and record in a systematic way the population characteristics of a neighbourhood. Compare your impressions with census tract information.

3. Devise an experiment to test how urbanites react to potential communication with strangers.

4. Examine voting records on particular issues in your city council. Can you determine patterns in the interests that particular councillors support?

Writing Exercises

1. Describe the experience of growing up in a city.

2. Read and report on a work of fiction dealing with some aspect of city life. To what extent does this agree or differ from what urban sociologists have to say?

3. How would you improve the design of a building or institution you know by incorporating additional considerations about human behaviour?

4. Describe and explain how you think you might be living if you were born, raised and now living in a particular setting outside Canada. Be specific.

Glossary

Community: *interpersonal contact patterns.*

Ecology: *the internal makeup and physical patterns of cities.*

Gentrification: *piecemeal upscale transformation of working-class urban neighbourhoods by upper-middle-class professionals that restores sound and/or historically interesting buildings.*

Metropolitan area: *the larger area beyond arbitrary city boundaries within which the logical interdependencies of an urban area's everyday life (such as commuting) are contained.*

Natural area: *term given by the Chicago school of urban sociology to local areas with largely homogeneous populations and institutions, situated as a consequence of urban land values and the constrictions of natural features or public works as boundaries.*

Neighbourhood: *specific physical area within a city with a particular social image.*

Redevelopment: *levelling previous buildings in an area and/or changing land use to develop new land uses.*

Rehabilitation: *modernizing existing buildings in an area.*

Urban growth machine: *term given by Logan and Molotch (1987) to the ideology of continuous urban growth, particularly large projects in city centres, espoused by certain commercial interest groups.*

Urbanism: *behaviour patterns of people living in cities.*

Urbanization: *the nature, extent and distribution of cities in the larger society or nation.*

Urban renewal: *a general term for upgrading buildings and land use through redevelopment and/or rehabilitation.*

References

Adams, Robert M.
1966. *The Evolution of Urban Society*. Chicago: Aldine.

Anderson, Grace
1974. *Networks of Contact: The Portuguese and Toronto*. Waterloo: Wilfrid Laurier University Press.

Andrew, Caroline, and Beth Moore Milroy, eds.
1988. *Life Spaces*. Vancouver: University of British Columbia Press.

Bingham, Richard D., Roy E. Green and Sammis B. White, eds.
1987. *The Homeless in Contemporary Society*. Beverly Hills: Sage.

Burgess, Ernest
1925. "The Growth of the City: An Introduction to a Research Project," pp. 47–62. In Robert E. Park, Ernest Burgess and R. McKenzie, eds., *The City*. Chicago: University of Chicago Press.

Carlstein, Tommy
1978. "A Time-geographic Approach to Time Allocation and Socio-ecological Systems," pp. 69–82. In William Michelson, ed., *Public Policy in Temporal Perspective*. The Hague: Mouton.

Clairmont, Donald H., and Dennis W. Magill
1974. *Africville: The Life and Death of a Canadian Black Community*. Toronto: McClelland and Stewart.

Clark, S. D.
1966. *The Suburban Society*. Toronto: University of Toronto Press.

Cullen, Ian
1978. "The Treatment of Time in the Explanation of Spatial Behavior," pp. 27–38. In T. Carlstein, Don Parkes and Nigel Thrift, eds., *Human Activity and Time Geography*. New York: Halstead Press.

Dewey, Richard
1960. "The Rural-Urban Continuum: Real but Relatively Unimportant." *American Journal of Sociology* 66:60–66.

Dogon, Mattei, and John Kasarda, eds.
1988. *The Metropolis Era*. Beverly Hills: Sage.

Domhoff, G. William, ed.
1980. *Power Structure Research*. Beverly Hills: Sage.

Draper, James A., ed.
1971. *Citizen Participation: Canada*. Toronto: New Press.

Fischer, Claude S.
1976. *The Urban Experience*. New York: Harcourt Brace Jovanovich.
1982. *To Dwell Among Friends*. Chicago: University of Chicago Press.

Friedland, Roger, and Donald Palmer
1984. "Park Place and Main Street: Business and the Urban Power Structure." *Annual Review of Sociology* 10:394–416.

Gans, Herbert J.
    1962. *The Urban Villagers*. New York: Free Press.
    1967. *The Levittowners*. New York: Pantheon.

Gifford, Robert
    1987. *Environmental Psychology: Principles and Practice*. Toronto: Allyn and Bacon.

Hägerstrand, Torsten
    1970. "What About People in Regional Science." *Papers of the Regional Science Association* 24:7–21.

Hall, Edward T.
    1966. *The Hidden Dimension*. Garden City, N.Y.: Doubleday.

Hallman, Howard W.
    1984. *Neighborhoods: Their Place in Urban Life*. Beverly Hills: Sage.

Harris, Chauncy, and Edward L. Ullman
    1945. "The Nature of Cities." *Annals of the American Academy of Political and Social Science* 242:7–17.

Hawley, Willis, and Frederick M. Wirt
    1968. *The Search for Community Power*. Toronto: Prentice-Hall.

Hayden, Dolores
    1984. *Redesigning the American Dream*. New York: Norton.

Hoyt, Homer
    1939. *The Structure and Growth of Residential Neighborhoods in American Cities*. Washington, D.C.: Federal Housing Administration.

Janowitz, Morris
    1952. *The Community Press in an Urban Setting*. Chicago: University of Chicago Press.

Jeffery, C. Ray
    1971. *Crime Prevention through Environmental Design*. Beverly Hills: Sage.

Karp, David, Gregory P. Stone and William Yoels
    1977. *Being Urban*. Toronto: D. C. Heath.

Kennedy, Leslie W.
    1983. *The Urban Kaleidoscope: Canadian Perspectives*. Toronto: McGraw-Hill Ryerson.

Logan, John, and Harvey Molotch
    1987. *Urban Fortunes*. Berkeley: University of California Press.

Long, Norton
    1958. "The Local Community as an Ecology of Games." *American Journal of Sociology* 64:251–61.

Lorimer, James
    1978. *The Developers*. Toronto: James Lorimer.

Marcus, Clare Cooper, and Wendy Sarkissian
    1987. *Housing as if People Mattered*. Berkeley: University of California Press.

Michelson, William
    1970. *Man and His Urban Environments: A Sociological Approach*. Toronto: Addison-Wesley.

1977. *Environmental Choice, Human Behavior, and Residential Satisfaction*. New York: Oxford University Press.

1985. *From Sun to Sun: Daily Obligations and Community Structure in the Lives of Employed Women and Their Families*. Totowa, N.J.: Rowman and Allenheld.

Michelson, William, and Ellis Roberts
1979. "Children and the Urban Physical Environment." In W. Michelson, S. Levine, A. Spina and colleagues, *The Child in the City: Changes and Challenges*. Toronto: University of Toronto Press.

Milgram, Stanley
1970. "The Experience of Living in Cities." *Science* 167 : 1461–468.

Murdie, Robert
1969. *Factorial Ecology of Metropolitan Toronto*. Department of Geography Research Paper No. 116. Chicago: University of Chicago.

Newman, Oscar
1972. *Defensible Space*. New York: Macmillan.

Pahl, R. E.
1970. *Whose City? and Other Essays on Sociology and Planning*. New York: Longman.

Park, Robert E.
1925. "The City: Suggestions for the Investigation of Human Behavior in the Urban Environment," pp. 1–46. In R. Park, E. Burgess and R. McKenzie, eds., *The City*. Chicago: University of Chicago Press.

Perry, Clarence
1966. "The Neighborhood Unit Formula," pp. 94–109. In William Wheaton et al., eds., *Urban Housing*. New York: Free Press.

Popenoe, David
1985. *Private Pleasure, Public Plight*. New Brunswick, N.J.: Transaction Publishers.

Reiss, Albert J., Jr.
1959. "Rural-Urban and Status Differences in Interpersonal Contacts." *American Journal of Sociology* 65 : 182–95.

Reitzes, Donald, and Dietrich Reitzes
1987. *The Alinski Legacy: Alive and Kicking*. Greenwich, Conn.: JAI Press.

Rosenthal, Donald B., ed.
1980. *Urban Revitalization*. Beverly Hills: Sage Urban Affairs Annual Reviews, vol. 18.

Shaffir, William
1974. *Life in a Religious Community: The Lubavitcher Chassidim in Montreal*. Toronto: Holt, Rinehart and Winston.

Shevky, Eshrev, and Wendell Bell
1955. *Social Area Analysis*. Berkeley: University of California Press.

Sidlofsky, Samuel
1969. "Post-War Immigrants in the Changing Metropolis, with Special Reference to Toronto's Italian Population." Ph.D. dissertation in sociology. University of Toronto.

Simmel, Georg
1950. "The Metropolis and Mental Life," pp. 400–427. In *The Sociology of Georg Simmel*. Edited by Kurt Wolff. New York: Free Press.

Simmie, J. M.
1974. *Citizens in Conflict: The Sociology of Town Planning*. London: Hutchinson.

Sinclair, P. R., and Kenneth Westhues
1974. *Village in Crisis*. Toronto: Holt, Rinehart and Winston.

Sjoberg, Gideon
1960. *The Preindustrial City*. New York: Free Press.

Smith, Christopher J.
1988. *Public Problems: The Management of Urban Distress*. New York: Guildford Press.

Sommer, Robert
1969. *Personal Space*. Toronto: Prentice-Hall.

Statistics Canada
1983. *Census Metropolitan Areas with Components* 3 (Profile Series B). Ottawa: Minister of Supply and Services Canada.
1984. *Canada Update* 2(4). Ottawa: Minister of Supply and Services Canada.
1987. *Census Metropolitan Areas and Census Agglomerations*. Ottawa: Minister of Supply and Services Canada.
1988. *Urban and Rural Areas, Canada, Provinces and Territories, Part 1*. Ottawa: Minister of Supplies and Services Canada.

Tabb, William K., and Larry Sawers
1984. *Marxism and the Metropolis*, 2nd ed. New York: Oxford University Press.

van Paasen, C.
1981. "The Philosophy of Geography: From Vidal to Hägerstrand," pp. 17–29. In A. Pred, ed., *Space and Time Geography: Essays Dedicated to Torsten Hägerstrand*. Lund: C. W. K. Gleerup.

Van Vliet, Willem, Elizabeth Huttman and Sylvia Fava, eds.
1985. *Housing Needs and Policy Approaches*. Durham: Duke University Press.

Webber, Melvin M.
1963. "Order in Diversity: Community without Propinquity," pp. 23–54. In L. Wingo, ed., *Cities and Space*. Baltimore: Johns Hopkins University Press.

Wellman, Barry
1979. "The Community Question: The Intimate Networks of East Yorkers." *American Journal of Sociology* 84:1201–231.

Wellman, Barry, Peter Carrington and Alan Hall
1988. "Networks and Personal Communities." In S. D. Berkowitz and Barry Wellman, eds., *Structural Sociology*. New York: Cambridge University Press.

Wellman, Barry, and Barry Leighton
1979. "Networks, Neighborhoods, and Communities: Approaches to the Study of the Community Question." *Urban Affairs Quarterly* 14:363–90.

Whyte, William Foote
1943. *Street Corner Society*. Chicago: University of Chicago Press.

Wireman, Peggy
1984. *Urban Neighborhoods, Networks, and Families*. Toronto: Lexington Books.

Wirth, Louis
1938. "Urbanism as a Way of Life." *American Journal of Sociology* 44:1–24.

CHAPTER 21

*I*deology and Social Change

JAMES E. CURTIS AND RONALD D. LAMBERT

The dominant ideology of the legal system in Canada calls for prohibition of capital punishment, but not everyone agrees with this.

Introduction

> Government requires make-believe. Make believe that the king is divine, make believe that he can do no wrong or make believe that the voice of the people is the voice of God. Make believe that the people *have* a voice or make believe that the representatives of the people *are* the people. Make believe that governors are the servants of the people. Make believe that all men are equal or make believe that they are not. (Morgan, 1988:13)

In this quotation, the historian Edmund Morgan points to the edifice of beliefs or fictions, as he calls them, to which people give their assent and which clothe their collective lives with political and social meaning. Calling these beliefs "fictions" does not detract from their validity, for they enjoy people's loyalty and exercise a constraining force on social reality. "The governing few no less than the governed many," Morgan attests, "may find themselves limited . . . by the fictions on which their authority depends" (1988:14). At the same time, these fictions may inspire people to defend the status quo or to pursue far-reaching changes in it.

As we have seen in the preceding chapters of this book, there are many sources of social change. Social change originates in the struggles between powerful economic and political interests, in disadvantaged groups struggling for a larger share of society's limited resources of income and power, in technological change, in inventions and innovations of all sorts, in population dynamics and in cultural diffusion from other societies. Most instances of social change have two factors in common. First, they involve confrontations between different beliefs and values, or ideologies. These ideologies touch on matters of justice, rights, freedom and other core values, and on how society should be organized to achieve these values. Second, most instances of social change involve at least some measure of social conflict between categories of people or groups that subscribe to competing visions of society and how these visions ought to be realized. Thus, it is that ideas clash, and with them, the people whom they inspire.

In social conflict, people's views on their vested interests—or what they feel is best for them and their families—help determine the ideas they support. As might be expected, these same two factors—ideology and social conflict around vested interests—are also involved in most attempts by groups to *resist* social change. Our purpose in this chapter is to describe the interrelated processes of ideological thinking, social conflict, and social change and social order.

What Is Ideology?

Ideologies are emotionally charged descriptive and normative beliefs and values that explain and justify how society is organized or should be organized. In Canada, we are most accustomed to ideological debate around political and economic affairs; ideologies may, however, deal with any area of social life (Mannheim, 1936; Curtis and Petras, 1970). Questions of ideology arise in such widely disparate areas as whether Salman Rushdie's *The Satanic Verses* should be published, whether Canada should admit a greater number of refugees, whether Crown corporations in Saskatchewan should be privatized, whether a fetus is properly regarded as a person entitled to legal rights, whether modern Canada owes a moral, legal and economic debt to its first inhabitants, whether affirmative action is called for to redress past discrimination against women and so on. A review of daily newspapers will remind us of many areas of intense ideological debate. People's positions in these disputes often will be cast in terms of what is most "efficient" and whether it is too "costly"—which are themselves ideological biases—and proposed resolutions of the dispute will be treated as obvious by one side or the other. All the while, there are very important ideological loyalties that give added force to these arguments.

We distinguish between two broad types of ideologies. *Reformist and radical ideologies* rally the forces of change, while *dominant ideologies* support existing social arrangements, or the status quo (Parkin, 1971). Now, there is often dispute about the precise identity of the status quo. Is our economy, for example, "essentially" a mixed economy, made up of public and private sector initiatives, or is it "essentially" a private enterprise economy? How we conceive of our society "in its essence" undoubtedly reflects our ideological commitments. Granting this complication though, *reformist ideologies* seek changes without challenging the basic ground rules, as when medicare, welfare and unemployment insurance were established without eliminating either the unequal distribution of wealth between the owners of capital and workers, or the principle of private property that underlies our economic order. *Radical ideologies* call for a fundamental restructuring of society or one of its institutions, as the Co-operative Commonwealth Federation (CCF, the predecessor of today's New Democratic Party) did at the time of its founding in the 1930s. Thus, the Regina Manifesto, adopted by the CCF at its founding convention in 1933, declared, "No CCF government will rest content until it has eradicated capitalism and put into operation the full programme of socialized planning which will lead to the establishment in Canada of the co-operative commonwealth" (McNaught, 1959:330). The independence movement in Quebec also seeks to restructure the Canadian state. But reformist and radical ideologies may also call for a restoration of former ways—or what are believed to be former ways—of doing things in society. An example would be proposed reforms to social welfare to eliminate its universal coverage, on the grounds that these programs are too costly for taxpayers and the people should assume more of the burden for their own care as they once did.

Ideologies in the second category are called *dominant ideologies* to emphasize their prevailing and ruling character. The institution of private property and capitalism currently prevails in our society. In the context of a socialist state, however, the dominant ideology would be socialist. For example, Boris Yeltsin, a radical democrat by Soviet standards, is said to be opposed by "right-wing" conservative elements in the Soviet Communist Party and government.

Ideologies can be "dominant" in either of two senses. They may be dominant in the sense that most people endorse them. Or they may be dominant in the sense that the most powerful groups in society sponsor them, whether or not most people agree, and

COURTESY OF JACK LEFCOURT,
WATERLOO, ONTARIO.

they are reflected in the way society is run. Belief in private property is an example
of ideology that is dominant in both respects in our society.

Dominant ideologies include sexism, which justifies the unequal treatment of men
and women, and ageism, which justifies the unequal treatment of age categories. We
could coin some additional words to refer to ideological justifications for the unequal
treatment of different religions, occupations, educational categories and so on. These
forms of unequal treatment, however, have not been widely regarded as "problems"
in Canadian society in recent years and have not therefore led to the creation of
distinctive words to refer to them. Education, for example, is widely used as a basis
for the unequal treatment of people in the job market. However, unlike treatment
according to gender or age, there is a widespread presumption in Canadian society
that people who lack certain kinds of education and paper credentials should be
denied access to various jobs (Collins, 1979). Ordinarily, we do not speak of this as
"discrimination" because for most Canadians it seems right that this should be so. In
the case of education, there is no significant counter-ideology that calls into question
the differential treatment of people on the basis of their education.

The reform and radical ideologies in any society are *counter-ideologies*. They are *counter*
inasmuch as they challenge the assumptions and beliefs of dominant ideologies. For
example, they might ask: Why is some level of education demanded for entry into
particular occupations? What is meant by "the top occupations," and why should
people strive for them? Is prestige properly associated with material wealth? What do
sales managers do that make them important, and to whom is their work important?

Why would anyone not work when the penalties for unemployment are so severe? It is the point of counter-ideology to expose ideological inconsistencies and hypocrises and to offer an alternative vision of society (see Marchak, 1988:2).

The Subtle Teaching of Ideology

According to Marchak (1988), "Ideologies are screens through which we perceive the world. . . . They are seldom taught explicitly and systematically. They are rather transmitted through example, conservation, and casual observation." The following example suggests how a dominant economic ideology is conveyed in an otherwise innocent exchange between parent and child:

The child asks the parent: "Why is that family poorer than us?" and receives an answer such as "Because their father is unemployed" or "Because sales clerks don't make as much money as sales managers." The accumulation of such responses provides a ready index to the organization of the society in occupational terms, and with reference to age and gender roles. The child is informed by such responses that some occupations provide higher material rewards than others, that an occupation is essential, and that fathers, not mothers, earn family incomes. The child is not provided with an explanation for the differential between sales clerks and sales managers, between the employed and the unemployed, between families in one income group and families in the other, but some children think to ask. There are, then, additional responses such as: "If you work hard at school, you can go to the top," or "Managers are more important than clerks," or "Well, if people don't work, they can't expect to get along in the world." (Marchak, 1988:2)

Counter-ideologies represent a response to forms of unequal treatment that, for one reason or another, seem problematic to some people. Counter-ideologies have the effect of calling the status quo to account and threatening to delegitimize, at least to some extent, customary ways of treating people. Thus, feminism, for example, represents a counter-ideology whose thrust is to undermine sexist ideology and traditional ways of treating men and women. In a similar way, those ideas that support human rights commissions and the Charter of Rights in this country represent counter-ideologies attacking various forms of discrimination. Calling something "discrimination" represents an acknowledgment that dominant ideology has been called into question.

How many people can be said to think in ways that we would describe as ideological? How well developed are their ideas? These questions have preoccupied many researchers since Converse (1964) showed that very few people, less than 10 percent in the case of Americans, gave evidence of substantial ideological thought. He arrived at this estimate from evidence of low correlations between respondents' attitudes on different social policy issues; few people had consistent views across policy areas. As we will see below, there is little reason to believe that Canadians differ greatly from Americans in this respect.

There is a certain paradox in Converse's findings, however. As he says, few people think ideologically in the one sense; yet, we see all around us evidence of people's ideological thinking, on matters of property ownership, politics, race, gender, language and so on. For this reason, we ought to draw a distinction between two kinds of ideology. One is the kind of ideology that Converse discusses, a set of connected beliefs and attitudes. The other is the stubborn reality of ideology as we encounter it in the street, people's bedrock assumptions about what ought to be or what ought to be done. These assumptions constitute principles that may or may not be "activated" or seen by the people who hold them as relevant to any given situation. When we hold these assumptions, however, it means that they *may* be activated, perhaps by other people who seek to control our behaviour. Both of these phenomena—few people having "connected" ideological beliefs and the widespread distribution of certain specific assumptions—are facts of ideology in Canadian society.

The idea that ideology consists of a set of interconnected beliefs carries with it the implication that people choose or reject beliefs based on some deeply held evaluating principles. This implication is conveyed when we speak of people "subscribing" to or "espousing" an ideology, as though they may choose not to subscribe or not to espouse, if they wish. However, in acquiring ideologies, individuals often have little awareness of the learning process, or that they have "acquired" anything at all. We are exposed to ideological beliefs and values in many subtle ways over our lifetime; the learning of ideology begins in family socialization, where we are taught the values and beliefs of our parents, and it extends to socialization through education and interaction with friends and workmates. Also, the media, in its distribution of the ideologies of government and business, is central to the teaching of ideology.

The Old Order Mennonite life style depicted in this picture reminds us of the ideological commitments contained in any life style.

KITCHENER-WATERLOO
RECORD PHOTO
COLLECTION. THE LIBRARY,
UNIVERSITY OF WATERLOO,
WATERLOO, ONTARIO.

The Several Effects of Ideology

What does ideology accomplish or do, both for those who hold such ideas and for others in society? First, we want to underscore what we are not saying in speaking of the effects of ideology. It is not our contention that elites cynically cultivate beliefs in others from which they profit but to which they themselves do not subscribe, although this is no doubt true in some cases. For example, most people who own private property and who benefit from the dissemination of a belief in the institution of private property probably also place a high value on this institution. Neither is it our position that those who benefit from other people's beliefs necessarily "will" the full range of consequences, some of them costly to the believers, to which these beliefs sometimes give rise. In a sexist society, for example, men may benefit from women's conviction that their vocation is in the home, without at the same time wishing upon them the poverty that often awaits women following divorce (Ontario Government, 1988).

We can examine the effects of subscribing to an ideology at two different levels. The first deals with the consequences of ideology for individual believers. In this case, we are interested in the utility of ideology for individuals. The second level of effects occurs for groups in society, either groups whose members subscribe to an ideology or groups that benefit from other groups whose members do so.

Individual-Level Effects

Self-Congratulation

Ideology in its various forms does not speak to us only about society. It is also has something to say about our place in society and the burden of historical responsibility we bear in our dealings with others. McDiarmid and Pratt (1971) found this when they studied the culture of the citizens of Ontario. They argued that a particularly valuable source of information on ideological statements about who and what we are is contained in textbooks approved for use in the province's senior public and high schools. Such textbooks, insofar as they bear the imprimatur of the provincial Ministry of Education, may be regarded as portraying "official" culture approved for student consumption. It is clear on the basis of McDiarmid and Pratt's analysis of themes having to do with Canadians' treatment of minority groups that these textbooks flatter those of us who are of white descent. Our relations with the native peoples of this country, as well as with more recent arrivals from Third World nations, are generally portrayed as benign. Little of the conflict of race relations in this country is presented in the textbooks. These readings give majority Canadians little cause to ponder their collective role in history and to question their effects on others. They encourage complacency.

Standards of Judgment

Sometimes people label their viewpoints as left or right, liberal or conservative. Many who use these terms find that they offer standards for judging our culture's values and procedures for pursuing them. Sometimes, of course, they may not appreciate the relevance of their viewpoint for the judgment at hand. For example, individuals may place a high value on freedom of choice, and yet fail to discern that freedom of choice is at stake in a given situation. And when they do, there is no guarantee about the direction of the judgments they draw. This should come as no surprise when we consider that the application of any principle or value rarely occurs without regard for other values. It is precisely this failure to "connect" that led Converse (1964) to claim that ideological thought is confined to a small minority of the population.

Frames of Reference

Beyond questions of value judgments, ideology in its various forms offers the individual a frame of reference in terms of which to interpret events. Meaning is not given directly to us by the world; we seek meaning in it, impose meaning on it and negotiate meaning in the company of others.

An example of a frame of reference that we use to assign credit for success or blame for failure is provided by recent research on belief about social class. When asked whether they understood the concept of social class, many Canadians in a national survey denied that they did (Lambert, Curtis, Brown and Kay, 1986b). Yet, when asked how people in different social classes differ from each other, these same respondents singled out personal characteristics such as ambition, intelligence and character. In doing so, they showed that they subscribe to an individualistic or psychological rather than a sociological conception of human behaviour. That is, they account for people's standing in society, not in terms of social forces, but in terms of individual motivation. Many people in our society find the concept of social class to be ideologically offensive, apparently because they believe it diminishes the importance of individuals. For many Canadians "society is merely derivative of the individuals who make it up since it is individuals who act, who are responsible, and who shape history" (Lambert et al., 1986b: 395).

Along the same lines, Johnston (1969) asked teenage Canadians what the factors are that make for people's success. He found that English Canadians were more likely to mention individualistic factors, such as hard work. French Canadians were more likely to explain success in terms of where people are located in the social structure. Similar differences between English and French Canadians were reported by Lambert et al. (1986b).

Empowerment

Ideology embodies ideas. These are not "just" ideas, but ideas that make a difference for people who are committed to them. For those in dominant positions, ideology legitimates their good fortune. When we are socialized into an occupation and its skills, we are also socialized into some conception of the worth of the activities associated with the occupation. People who accept their occupational ideology believe in the value of what they are doing and impute worthy qualities to themselves.

In her book *The Spiral of Silence*, Elisabeth Noell-Neumann (1984) makes the case that people who sense that theirs is, or shortly will be, the majority opinion, are thereby empowered. *Empowerment* refers to an ideology's effect on people's self-esteem, sense of power and comprehension of their position in the social structure of society. Imbued with confidence, they willingly express their views and argue for them. Conversely, people who feel that support for their opinions is ebbing grow silent.

Counter-ideology also has the effect of empowering people, often people in subordinate positions in society. Members of racial minorities that subscribe to counter-ideology are equipped to question what happens to them, to understand the ongoing course of race relations and perhaps even to anticipate significant changes in their status in society. Counter-ideology is a source of self-esteem, as in "black is beautiful." It motivates members of minority groups to promote their personal and collective advancement. "Consciousness-raising" refers to a process of empowerment through understanding the dimensions of one's subordination and the "deceptions" practised by the status quo and its dominant ideology. This empowerment of members of minority groups has a sustaining effect on their ability to survive in the face of unequal treatment based on skin colour, social class, country of origin, language and so on.

Group-Level Effects

Social Control of Subordinate Groups

Dominant ideology aids in the control of subordinate groups by dominant groups. Sometimes this works through the educational system. For example, Bowles and Gintis (1976) have shown that, by attending school year after year, students acquire a conception of social structure and their place in it. Passively taking notes and directions from teachers, they learn a way of relating to authority that will eventually confront them in the workplace. By learning to work for grades, certificates, degrees and the approval of their teachers, they learn to work for extrinsic reasons and rewards, rather than for intrinsic rewards, such as the joy of learning.

McDonald's (1978) analysis of the development of education in mid-nineteenth-century Ontario illustrates further some of the ideological effects of education. Egerton Ryerson, who designed the school system, wanted to ensure that the young people of Ontario would remain loyal to the Crown, that they would never participate in the kind of rebellion that had been put down in Upper Canada in 1837, and that they would learn to co-operate with each other, regardless of their social class backgrounds. He argued that a successful educational system would persuade the working classes that "their interests were also those of the middle and upper classes, and that, as a collectivity, there was a 'common' or 'public good' towards which all must work" (McDonald, 1978:96–97). In short, Ryerson's objective was social control, and he charged the schools with the responsibility of inculcating the beliefs and attitudes of mind that would accomplish this.

Unification of Dominant Groups

If ideology is a means of controlling subordinate groups, and if it is disseminated through the educational system, then how can it control members of subordinate groups if they drop out of school prior to graduation? The answer to this paradox is twofold.

While they may not be fully indoctrinated into a dominant ideological perspective, members of subordinate groups have been taught ideas that offer little promise for understanding their probable station in life in any way that differs significantly from the dominant point of view. In short, such ideology as they have been introduced to is not an empowering ideology. Indeed, it may be argued that they have been taught enough of dominant ideology to immunize them against the efforts of others to introduce them to counter-ideology. Mann (1970) has suggested that social control is

The Schools and Dominant Ideology in the Mid-Nineteenth Century

Egerton Ryerson was superintendent of education in Canada West, later Ontario, from 1844 to 1876. During these years, he placed his imprint upon the province's emerging public school system. Drawing on Ryerson's revealing writings, educational historian Neil McDonald describes the ideological mandate that Ryerson assigned to public education in Ontario.

According to Ryerson, next to legislation and government, social progress depended on the harmonious and sympathetic relations existing among the various classes. Indeed, he characterized it as a "law" that "the interests of the whole society are binding upon each member of it." By this he meant that each member of society, no matter what their occupation or class, must contribute to "the one great end of individual and public happiness." The various classes should not be "rivals, but fellow-helpers, not aliens, but members of the same household, and parts of the same body." He declared, "All arbitrary class distinctions are, then, so many impediments to the social advancement of the country; and as they prevail to a less or greater extent, will the energies of society for the common welfare be crippled and paralyzed."

It was not an argument for the elimination of a class structure, which he considered divinely ordained, but for the elimination or reduction of class conflict. In a society where the visibility of class distinctions and separation were clear and absolute there always loomed the danger of open conflict with ominous potential for serious social strife. Ryerson intended that the common school should play an important part in reducing these traditional class tensions. . . .

Divisiveness was destructive to this common goal. In practice, it was an attempt to impose a set of values on the working class youth that were not particularly helpful for interpreting the social reality with which he was in contact. Indeed, it sought to gloss over the fact that the interests of this class were in conflict with those of the classes above them. As a result it was more likely that the working class would accommodate to the values of the higher classes. Since these values were imposed and not relevant to their experience, it was too much to expect that they actually adopt those values. Their acceptance of the social order was designed to give legitimacy to the dominant ideology, and not to increase feelings of political competence. . . .

The great task of the school, then, was not only to direct intellectual behaviour, but also moral and social behaviour. The safety of the state depended on the "safe" citizen. The ideal state was one in which there was order, stability, and loyalty. Order implied an hierarchical concept of authority as well as the absence of political and social chaos. Citizens know their "places" in this state where issues were decided on a cold, rational basis by a ruling elite, rather than in the heated, emotional political arena of party divisiveness. Once political and social stability had been achieved, the passive but enlightened citizen, whose intellectual, moral, and physical faculties have been "educated" to recognize and to accept legitimate authority, could be relied on to give the social and political order a permanent measure of stability. Moreover, those same citizens could also be depended upon to be loyal to the state, especially in time of crisis. The school, of course, was ideally designed to contribute to this particular state of political and social equilibrium. Through the school, the public mind could be manipulated "in the right direction."

N. McDonald and A. Chaiton, eds. 1978. *Egerton Ryerson and His Times*. Toronto: Macmillan, pp. 95–98.

achieved over people in subordinate statuses, not through ideological compliance, but through what he calls "pragmatic acquiescence." This means that they comply with dominant ideology, not out of conviction, but because they know of no alternatives to compliance. They are uninformed about available counter-ideologies, or if they are aware of them, they have been taught to greet them with scepticism and distrust.

The other part of the answer to the paradox is the suggestion that the effects of ideology are not felt primarily by subordinate people, but by those in dominant statuses. It is individuals who continue through the school system who will in due course exercise power in society's institutions, and it is among these people that ideological correctness matters most. If the more powerful people endorse the status quo, then social control and control of social change are more readily assured.

Definition of Group Boundaries

To talk about groups implies that there are boundaries between a group and what lies outside the group. We mark boundaries in a variety of ways, some more visible than others. Initiations, titles and uniforms are some of the ways in which we declare our membership in groups. Ideological beliefs, where these are supported by groups, announce to others who we are and what groups we belong to. The political spectrum in Canada is populated by a variety of groups from left to right, such as the New Democratic Party, the Christian Heritage Party and the Fraser Institute. We expect people who are members of these groups to espouse particular views, and it comes as no surprise that people who espouse certain views declare membership or allegiance

"Quebec needs jobs not the Army," a protest sign set against the Parliament Building in Ottawa, shows contrasting symbols of counter-ideology and dominant ideology.

NATIONAL ARCHIVES OF CANADA/PA 12647.

to one or other of these groups. Unlike uniforms, however, ideological beliefs are invisible, and so we may feel called upon to declare them in order to establish who we are and with which groups we ally ourselves.

Social Change   Dominant ideology and counter-ideology capture competing visions of society. As we have already observed, dominant ideology consists of ideas that have the effect of defending the status quo, especially with respect to the distribution of economic and political power. Some of these ideas are summed up in assertions and truisms such as "A man's home is his castle," "As you sow, so shall you reap" (referring to the importance of work) and "Economic decisions should be made in the marketplace."

There may be a number of counter-ideologies. A "leftist" counter-ideology in Canada, for example, will employ public enterprise as a tool of public policy, would limit the role of the marketplace, and asserts something like the following: "From each according to his (or her) ability; to each according to his (or her) need." A "green" counter-ideology will declare that "small is beautiful," favour zero-population growth, promote the recycling of waste products, and some vegetarian versions will assert that "meat is murder." It is out of the clashes among proponents of such competing ideas, embodied in political parties, interest groups and social movements, that social change occurs. The change will probably be nothing so simple as the victory of one ideological perspective over other perspectives. Rather, it will be some synthesis of the competing ideas and the several values that inspire them.

Left/Right Ideology in the General Public

A good example of ideology in Canadian society can be found in left/right political thinking. Laponce (1981) has shown how the meaning of these terms differs between societies, and even within a single society in different historical periods. In Canada, for the greater part of this century, *left* has signified "some degree of support for the proposition that institutions in the public sector should promote economic and social equality," while *right* has referred to "a commitment to the marketplace as the appropriate instrument for the achievement of social as well as personal objectives" (Lambert, Curtis, Brown and Kay, 1988:386). This distinction has sometimes been called "liberalism" and "conservatism," but these labels are too easily confused with the two major political parties that bear these names. Also, "conservative" is often used as a synonym for dominant ideology, that is, for ideas supportive of the status quo or that call for a return to an earlier way of doing things. It is these two quite different ways of using the word that sometimes creates problems. Thus, North American conservatives, who think of conservative ideology in terms of economic individualism and the centrality of the marketplace, often object to the description of members of the central committees of the Communist parties of the Soviet Union and China as conservatives or right-wingers to indicate their support for the communist status quo in those countries.

Some students of Canadian politics have objected to the use of "left" and "right" because these terms mean little or nothing to many Canadians, and even for people who use them, they signify many different things (see, for example, Lambert and Hunter, 1979; Ogmundson, 1979). To check on these two observations, a national sample of adult Canadians were asked to define the concepts of left and right, and to rate their own political orientations along a seven-point left/right scale (Lambert, Curtis, Brown and Kay, 1986a). The results showed that only approximately 40 percent of those surveyed could offer definitions for each of the concepts. Half as many again rated their political opinions as "left" or "right" even though they could not define the concepts.

Table 21-1 summarizes the kinds of definitions that people volunteered in their answers. Adding first and second mentions together, a third of the respondents equated the concept of left with "socialism," compared to just under 20 percent who mentioned "communism." Somewhat more than 15 percent gave evaluative judgments, such as "(dis)honest" and "(un)principled." Nearly 11 percent cited orientations toward social change, and about the same percentage embodied the concept in political parties or leaders.

In the case of the concept of right, a quarter of the respondents defined it in terms of "conservatism." (In comparison, only 4 percent equated left with "liberalism.") A

TABLE 21-1

Themes in Canadians' Definitions of the Concepts of Left and Right

Mention =	Left		Right	
	1st	2nd*	1st	2nd*
Communism	13.9%	5.4%	0.8%	0.1%
Socialism	28.8	5.0	1.8	0.3
Liberal	3.7	0.4	2.8	0.3
Conservative	1.8	0.3	23.4	1.8
Fascist	0.1	0.1	2.1	1.0
Change	6.9	3.7	7.5	3.7
Free Enterprise	2.2	3.1	15.3	5.0
Democracy	1.5	0.9	6.2	3.7
Equality	0.7	0.9	—	—
Welfare	6.1	2.3	0.9	1.8
Role and size of government	0.2	0.6	0.4	0.6
Other attitudes, issues	1.5	1.2	2.1	1.0
Parties, leaders, politics	9.1	1.4	9.3	1.2
Interest groups, groups favoured	5.6	3.8	13.3	5.0
Evaluations, feelings	15.0	2.6	10.4	2.1
Other; uncodable	3.0	0.5	3.6	—
N =	(1380)		(1350)	

*Second mentions were coded on the basis of the total number of respondents who provided first mentions, so that total percentages exceed 100 percent of each concept.

1984 CANADIAN NATIONAL ELECTION STUDY.

fifth of the respondents who answered said that the right meant "free enterprise," and nearly as many associated it with groups in society that benefit from right-wing policies. In the latter case, reference was made primarily to the upper classes and to powerful and wealthy groups. "For the most part," in the researchers' opinion, "respondents invoked themes having to do with socialism, communism, conservatism, free enterprise, the economic interests favoured by each tendency, specific political figures and parties, and orientations toward social change—and generally in what might be considered the appropriate directions" (Lambert et al., 1986a:559).

In a later study, the same researchers make the following theoretical observation:

> We are not troubled to find that many people are unable to define left and right because this ability has never been a requirement for using language in everyday intercourse. Neither are we troubled by the fact that people vary in the constructions that they place on these terms. The specific content of left and right is handled as a matter of convention and is commonly the subject of dispute within the political process. . . . Indeed, debate about what and who should properly be regarded as left and right, and to what practical effect, represents an important part of the symbolic side of politics. The mass media, for example, especially the print media, regularly instruct people in the use of these concepts by naming their exemplars—parties, leaders, policies, and ideas—and even the appropriate feelings to associate with them. (Lambert et al., 1988:387)

These authors conclude with the view that "what appears to be 'noise' in people's grasp of left and right, and which academics so often treat as error, is in fact the stuff of politics" (Lambert et al., 1988:387).

For left or right ideologies to be effective, it is not necessary that everyone, or even most people, have a profound understanding of or commitment to them. It is more important to ask who these people are and where they are located in society. We know, for example, that the more educated people are, the more knowledgeable they are about left and right and the more likely they are to employ these terms (Lambert, Curtis, Kay and Brown, 1988). At the same time, more educated people tend also to give greater support to dominant ideology (Lambert and Curtis, 1979; Baer and Lambert, 1982). In general, it is more likely to be the case that more educated people occupy the commanding heights of society's institutions. As we have noted above, and as Abercrombie, Hill and Turner (1980) have argued, one of the more important functions of dominant ideology is to unify and render ideologically dependable those groups and individuals who occupy positions of power in society. It is when these people begin to lose faith in the correctness and moral superiority of the status quo that social change is hastened.

Some idea about the relationship between people's levels of formal education and their beliefs on a number of economic and moral issues is presented in Table 21-2. We can see that the most educated Canadians are less likely than less educated people to believe that government bears responsibilities to alleviate social inequality in a number of areas. In particular, people with the most education are least likely to express the view that the disparity between the rich and the poor is too great.

There is also a relationship between people's education level and their moral beliefs, with one exception. The least educated people are more likely than those who are highly educated to endorse capital punishment for murders and censorship of pornography, and most opposed to permitting homosexuals to teach. Abortion is the exception. About half of the respondents at each level of education strongly support a pregnant woman's right to an abortion. The findings in Table 21-2 confirm the view that left/right or liberal/conservative are complex issues and that there are two dimensions underlying this dichotomy—one economic and the other moral.

TABLE 21-2
Percent Who Strongly Agree with Selected Economic and Moral Positions by Education Level

| Economic and Moral Positions | Highest Education Attained | | | |
	Elementary or Some High School	Finished High School	Some Post-Secondary Education	University Degree
Economic Issues				
Government should ensure adequate housing	49.2	40.9	39.8	35.6
Ban extra-billing by doctors and hospital	69.3	61.7	54.3	49.1
Difference between rich and poor is too great	50.1	43.3	28.3	25.7
People with high incomes should pay more taxes than currently	58.3	52.0	45.9	43.6
Government should increase its job opportunities for women	41.1	37.4	37.0	34.1
Moral Issues				
Endorse capital punishment for murderers	57.3	48.2	39.2	21.4
Censor pornographic magazines and movies	59.0	46.9	45.7	38.1
Pregnant woman's right to an abortion	50.6	53.8	52.5	51.9
Permit homosexuals to teach school	12.8	15.7	25.1	29.9

1984 CANADIAN NATIONAL ELECTION STUDY.

The suggestion has been made by Inglehart (1977, 1979) that the concerns embodied in left/right ideology are themselves undergoing change or may even be superseded by a new set of concerns, at least in Western "post-industrial" societies. Inglehart builds on the theory of Maslow (1970), a psychologist who has proposed that people attend to their mental and social needs once they have taken care of their more basic biological physical needs. Maslow's distinction between two kinds of needs has led Inglehart to distinguish between two broad kinds of values—materialist and post-materialist. *Materialist values* are concerned with questions of social control and economics, and these are the concerns of the traditional distinction between left and right. *Post-materialist* values refer to aesthetic, social and intellectual matters. Inglehart believes that the growth in service sector employment, increasing levels of education, technological innovations, several generations that have been spared a global war and depression, and the growth of mass communications and the global village have ushered in a new kind of society among the Western post-industrial nations, with distinctive post-materialist concerns. Inglehart and his colleagues have reported some evidence for the rise of post-materialism in their cross-national surveys, but there is no clear evidence that this is the case in Canada.

Social Class, Ideology and Political Party Support

Do people put their ideological beliefs to work in voting behaviour? Do people practice *class voting*? Do they vote for political parties that they feel will pursue the interests of their class in promoting social change or in resisting change? It turns out, according to recent research, that these questions have different answers depending on whether we are speaking of the working class or the middle class.

Patterns of class voting for Canadians in three federal elections between 1965 and 1984 are presented in Table 21-3. (These are the three elections for which relevant national survey data are available.) The results in the table are based on a procedure first introduced by Ogmundson (1975, 1976). The survey respondent is asked about what social class he or she belongs to, as follows:

> If you had to pick one, which of the following five social classes would you say you were in—upper class, upper middle, middle class, working class, or lower class?

People who answered upper class, upper middle class or middle class are combined as "middle class" for present purposes, and people who answered working class or lower class are treated as "working class" (Ogmundson, 1975a: 17). The surveys then asked respondents whom they voted for; and in a separate set of questions they were asked to indicate whether each of the federal political parties was biased in favour of the working class or the middle class. This information was then compared with the respondents' reports on their social class self-placement (see Table 21-3).

Table 21-3 also presents information on the associations between the respondents' income levels, occupational statuses and educational attainments on the one hand, and whether they voted for a party perceived as for "their" social class on the other hand. Each measure of social class is categorized so that higher levels of income, occupation or education are assumed to represent "the middle class" and the lower levels "the working class." A percentage difference score is also presented for each election. This represents the percentage of the middle class who voted for middle-class parties minus the percentage of the working class who voted for working-class parties.

As Table 21-3 shows, only about 35 to 40 percent of the working-class people, whether measured by self-definition or by income, occupation or education, voted for parties that they felt were for the working class. The figures for middle-class people voting for parties defined as for the middle class were around 70 percent for each election. Thus, class voting is high for the middle class both in comparative and absolute terms, and it is low for the working class.

The difference scores show that there was a slight change over time in the direction of less class voting in the 1984 election than in the 1960s. Also, both the middle-class

TABLE 21-3

Percentages of Persons in Each Social Class (Various Measures) Who Voted for a Party that Was Seen as "For" Their Class: Data for 1965, 1968 and 1984

Measures of Social Class	Voted for a Party for Their Class		
	1965	1968	1984
Self-definition			
Middle class	72.4	74.7	72.6
	(1023)	(1192)	(1408)
Working class	45.2	42.4	39.7
	(969)	(920)	(754)
% difference	17.6	17.1	12.3
Occupation			
Middle class	70.2	76.0	74.2
	(758)	(749)	(986)
Working class	40.6	38.1	36.8
	(1029)	(1158)	(846)
% difference	10.8	14.1	11.0
Income			
Middle class	70.6	76.8	73.1
	(776)	(1109)	(690)
Working class	39.8	39.7	34.7
	(1219)	(1016)	(1368)
% difference	10.4	13.2	7.8
Education			
Middle class	72.3	76.8	71.9
	(712)	(753)	(987)
Working class	40.1	37.8	34.3
	(1342)	(1470)	(1272)
% difference	12.4	14.6	6.2

1965, 1968 AND 1984 CANADIAN NATIONAL ELECTION STUDIES.

vote for a party "for the middle class" and the working-class vote for a party "for the working class" declined slightly over the preceding years.

The election studies also show that the national samples overall, in each election year, perceived the New Democratic Party as favouring the working class and Liberals and Conservatives as favouring the middle class. The proportion of the working class (by self-placement) who voted for the NDP in 1984 was only 23 percent, though. The figure for voting for the Liberals or Conservatives among the middle class was 88 percent. Similar percentages have been reported for other federal elections of the 1960s through 1980s.

Why is the working class low on voting for a working-class party, even when we take into account the person's own definition of what the party stands for? Ogmundson's answer is that this has little to do with underdeveloped ideological thinking, or with the failure of the working class to translate their class beliefs into class voting. He believes that the answer lies in the limited alternatives that party elites make available to the Canadian working-class voter. The complex of issues that are important to the working class are not well articulated by any of the parties.

In support of this interpretation, Ogmundson cited respondents' answers to open-ended questions in the 1965 and 1968 election surveys, in which respondents were asked what important problems faced Canada. Their answers suggested "that economic/class issues are of far greater importance to the Canadian electorate than the regional, ethnic, and religious issues that have been the staples of our national politics at the federal level" (1976:3–4).

Ogmundson also speculated that working-class Canadians tend to be economically liberal and socially conservative. Perhaps these contradictory tendencies in the working class, without a party clearly articulating this combination of belief, accounts for the low level of support given by the working class to a distinctively "working-class" political party.

> It helps explain the difficulties facing the New Democratic Party as it tries to gain votes for a socially and economically liberal party from working class voters who, though economically liberal, are often socially conservative. It may be that a combination of conservative social values and liberal economic values represents the opinions of the working classes much better than does the traditional Left's combination of liberal economic and social values. (Ogmundson, 1975b:574)

As you will see in Chapter 22, Brym (see also Brym, 1986; Brym et al., 1989) provides us with other explanations for levels of support for the NDP. In his view, provinces vary in their support for the NDP because of differences in the size of the working class, the incomes of workers and the strength of unions. In short, the stronger the working class and the greater their access to organizational resources, the more likely they (and members of the middle class) are to vote for the NDP.

Another explanatory factor worth noting, one that is consistent with Ogmundson and Brym's line of reasoning, is the fact that there is not even one working-class daily newspaper published in Canada. This means that definitions of the class situation and of the NDP are entrusted to print and electronic media owned by people whose interests are inimical to the NDP, if not to the working class. Readers of newspapers such as *The Toronto Sun* encounter the concept of left and democratic socialism in the pages of that paper, but these are generally portrayed in a bad light. And our schools often teach that political "extremism" and labour unions are not to be trusted (McDiarmid and Pratt, 1971).

Dominant Ideology and the Elites

The "dominant ideology thesis" emphasizes that there are dominant classes or elites in society and that the effect of dominant ideology is to justify and unify these groups (Abercrombie et al., 1980). However, there is great debate among Canadian sociologists about which specific groups are dominant.

There are two theories about the kinds of powerful groups in Canadian society: one emphasizes elites that hold top positions in society's major institutions; the other points to the upper class, members of which typically inherited their wealth (along with influence, social standing, respectability) from their parents. The first theory is the accommodating elite theory and the other is the capitalist class control theory.

The key feature of "elite" positions is their tie to organizational control; the key feature of "upper-class" positions is their transmission from one generation to the next within a family. Elite positions are to be found in economic organizations (for example, bank president or executive officer of a manufacturing company), in government (for example, elected prime minister or appointed deputy minister) and in a variety of other organizations such as labour unions, the Red Cross, the Canadian Broadcasting Corporation, universities and so on. Often these organizations are in conflict or fail to share the same goals and interests. If so, we should expect their elites to be in conflict or, at least, to promote opposing goals and interests. But is this what happens? Are elites in open conflict? Or do they "accommodate"—that is, co-operate with one another; and if so, how and why? Moreover, if elites *do* accommodate to prevent or minimize conflict, is it because co-operation is in the best interest of their respective organizations? Or is it because elites, coming mainly from the same (upper) social class background, share similar ideologies, regardless of the organization they work for? Or, finally, is it because some parts of society—especially the economy—dominate other parts of society (for example, universities, labour unions, government), forcing compliance and apparent co-operation?

According to the *accommodating elite theory*, elites in different sectors of society struggle to promote the goals of their own organizations. Each sector and each organization possesses some measure of power in this conflict. However, more often than not, elites must collaborate with other elites because this will further their organization's interests in the long run; because elites have a fundamental commitment to avoid upsetting the social order; and because they share a common ideology. The latter occurs because the elites interact together. Many of these people are acquaintances, friends, members of the same social class (with the same background experiences) and perhaps even kin. Within this theory, class of origin is relatively unimportant. Elites fight to further their organization's interests, rather than the interests of their social class.

The *capitalist class control theory* also assumes that competition and conflict between organizations and elites are less common than collusion and domination. However, it argues that those in control of the economic sector, and within that sector the largest and wealthiest organizations (in Canada, the banks and other financial institutions), will control *all* other sectors of the economy, all other organizations, and thereby all other elites. This is accomplished, in part, by controlling the state: that is, by controlling both elected and appointed officials and, in part, by controlling access to capital, the ultimate source of power. In turn, the dominant economic elite is filled by people from the hereditary upper class and by a very few "new" capitalists. Thus, the elite structure of society simply duplicates the capitalist class structure. What appears to be elite accommodation is simply co-operation among capitalists and their agents.

Porter's work has given the most sustained attention to the accommodating elite model. In *The Vertical Mosaic* (1965), Porter concluded that continuity and change were the product of actions, or failures to act, on the part of the elites. He saw no room for the average person to effect social change except by working through organizations that might ultimately affect the behaviours of the elites. Thus, organizations, such as unions and other lobby groups for vested interests, are essential weapons if average people are to effect change.

Porter also saw a significant role for ideology in producing social change, albeit through the elites. The elites' ideology shapes the behaviours of elites and non-elites, both in the present and in the future. In North America, for example, the elites' ideology includes the notion that capitalism works for the common good. Porter saw a major difference between Canadian and American elites, though. He believed that Canada did not inherit, through its history, an ideology that called for social equality to the same extent as the United States. He observed (1965 : 366) that:

> Canada has no resounding charter myth proclaiming a utopia against which periodically progress can be measured. At the most, national goals and dominant values seem to be expressed in geographic terms, such as from "sea to sea" rather than in social terms, such as "all men are created equal" or "liberty, fraternity, and equality."
> In the United States, there is a utopian image which slowly over time bends intractable social patterns in the direction of equality, but a Canadian counterpart of this image is difficult to find.

In Porter's view, Canada is ruled by five elite groups. These elites consist of people in the top positions in each of five broad areas of social organization in Canada—in major economic corporations, political organizations, government bureaucracies, labour organizations and ideological (that is, church, educational and media) organizations. The dispersion of power among elites is due to the placement of the elites at the tops

The symbols in this photograph remind us of the ideologies underlying and justifying the institutions of religion and commerce.

KITCHENER-WATERLOO
RECORD PHOTO
COLLECTION. THE LIBRARY,
UNIVERSITY OF WATERLOO,
WATERLOO, ONTARIO.

of large organizations, each with its own wealth, power and mandate provided by long-standing values and norms to perform different services to Canadians.

The economic or corporate elite, according to Porter, has been most successful in ensuring that its interests have been served over the years. Holding second place, by the same criterion, was the bureaucratic elite. This elite is made up of high-ranking civil servants, the "mandarins" of government. The most powerful civil servants are in the federal bureaucracy, but this elite was also said to include high-ranking personnel of provincial bureaucracies.

Several reasons were given for the paramount strength of the corporate and (federal) bureaucratic elites, not the least of which are the enormous economic resources each commands, and the fact that these sectors employ major proportions of the Canadian working population. Moreover, these sectors provide better-paying and more stable careers than politicians and labour leaders typically enjoy. For the latter reasons, the corporate and bureaucratic sectors are able to recruit the most talented workers for their bureaucracies. Porter saw a plural set of elites, with two more powerful than the others.

Porter asked how closed the elite groups are by studying the social backgrounds of

The Charter of Rights and Freedoms as Ideology

Since he sought ways of achieving greater equality, Porter would have welcomed the framing of the Canadian Charter of Rights and Freedoms in 1981, but he did not live to see it occur. The Charter proclaims such goals as:

Everyone has a right to life, liberty and security of the person and the right not to be deprived thereof except in accordance with the principles of fundamental justice (section 7).

Every individual is equal before and under the law and has the right to equal protection and equal benefit of the law without discrimination and, in particular, without discrimination based on race, national, or ethnic origin, colour, religion, sex, age, or mental or physical disability (section 15-1).

Subsection (1) does not preclude any law, program or activity that has as its object the amelioration of conditions of disadvantaged individuals or groups including those that are disadvantaged because of race, national or ethnic origin, colour, religion, sex, age or mental or physical disability (section 15-2).

This charter shall be interpreted in a manner consistent with the preservation and enhancement of the multicultural heritage of Canadians (section 27).

Notwithstanding anything in this Charter, the rights and freedoms referred to in it are guaranteed equally to male and female persons (section 28).

Porter would have emphasized that such goals reflect, and will reinforce, the multicultural themes in Canadian culture, and that they should help lead to greater equality across ethnic groups, races, genders and so on. He would also have been quick to point out, however, that the Charter does not contain certain other equality goals that might have been in it if the society's prevailing ideology was different. For example, it does not guarantee equality of opportunity for higher education (the basic avenue to higher incomes in Canada). It does not guarantee free university education for those who wish it but cannot afford it. Nor does the Charter (1) place limitations upon how much wealth one person or group can accumulate to the disadvantage of others, or (2) establish a minimum level of economic well-being and security for the poor. These remain questions of counter-ideology, not dominant ideology.

their members. His procedure was to look at the characteristics (including social class backgrounds, ethnicity, religion and gender) of elite members and compare them with the characteristics of the general adult population. In this way, Porter was able to estimate crudely the extent to which different types of Canadians were over- and underrepresented in the elite. (Porter found the appropriate data on elites in biographies, directories and census data.)

Porter showed that the economic elite is least representative on all of the counts just mentioned, although each of the elites exhibited some form of exclusivity. The economic elite was defined by Porter "as the 985 Canadian residents holding directorship in the 170 dominant corporations, the banks, insurance companies, and numerous other corporations" (1965 : 274). Within this group, a high proportion had fathers who had been in the economic elite; conversely, few worked their way into the elite by establishing their own firms or by taking over existing firms. In addition, over 50 percent of the economic elite had upper-class origins, while only about 1 percent of the general population did. Thirty-two percent of the elite had middle-class backgrounds; and only 18 percent had working-class backgrounds, even though over 85 percent of the general population had such origins. In terms of ethnicity and religion, the vast majority of the economic elite were English-speaking Protestants, even though more than 30 percent of all Canadians were French-speaking Catholics. Less than 1 percent of the elite were Jews, who comprise 1.5 percent of the general population. "Economic power belonged almost exclusively to those of British origin," Porter concluded (1965 : 286). Most dramatically, perhaps, there were *no* women in the corporate (economic) elite, despite their (roughly) 50 percent representation in the population.

The exclusivity of the other elite groups was less marked, but exclusion was always present. People of middle-class and French Canadian backgrounds were found more frequently in the bureaucratic, political and ideological elites, but people with middle-class and upper-class backgrounds and people of British origin were still overrepresented, and people of non-English and non-French backgrounds were seldom to be found. Only the labour elite came close to representing average Canadians on class and ethnicity. But even here, women were seriously underrepresented.

Despite much conflict between elites, Porter concluded that accommodation eventually held sway. He drew this conclusion by studying economic, political and social issues that had faced the country, and assessing how decisions about these issues affected each elite's interests.

The accommodations of the elites are facilitated by a pronounced sharing of values and interests, Porter contended. Each of the elites, he felt, had many members who subscribed heavily to the idea that corporate capitalism was "for the common good"; and they shared in the "Western" values of democracy, nationalism and Christianity. They came to these common views, Porter believed, from the similarities of their social backgrounds, their similar training in upper-class schools, and their repeated interaction on boards of directors and through memberships in the same clubs. These connections resembled "a web of kinship and lineage which provides cohesion to primitive life" (1965 : 304).

Porter stopped short of concluding that there was a dominant capitalist class. He considered this possibility, but rejected it. As he said, he found the Marxist theory of the state, according to which "the economic . . . system is the master" (1965 : 206), too simplistic. He drew this conclusion despite the evidence, which he accepted, of the greater strength of the corporate elite, and despite his belief that the corporate elite interests are entrenched in values shared by the other elites. He was impressed by the "counteracting power" (1965 : 522–23) of the other elites. We must wonder, though, whether this power was more an unrealized potential than an exercised force.

It is on the role of social class, especially, that Porter's work has been most seriously criticized. Many insist that the capitalist class exercises enormous control through the corporate elite and the state (generally including Porter's bureaucratic and political elites, and the judiciary). The other elites, in this alternative theory, are forced to accommodate or simply lose out.

This is just the view that Wallace Clement put forward in his *The Canadian Corporate Elite* (1975) and *Continental Corporate Power* (1977). Clement showed that the corporate elite was often tightly tied into the corporate elite of other countries, especially the United States. He found it necessary, therefore, to distinguish between "comprador elites" and "indigenous elites" within the Canadian corporate elite. The comprador elites were people working for foreign-owned operations in Canada. They administered these organizations as "branch plants," with most major policies likely originating in the foreign-based parent organization. The indigenous elites were people who controlled firms that were Canadian-owned.

In Clement's view (1985 : 562):

> No matter what institution is the most powerful, a society reproduces itself through the production of means of living (food, clothes, shelter), and, therefore, the economy is always a fundamental activity, whether organized by religious, political, military, or business leaders. Those who control the economy are a powerful elite within any modern society.

Thus, Clement sees Canada as a society with capitalist class control, much of it exercised from outside Canadian borders, but operating through a Canadian-based corporate elite. He believes that there is only limited accommodation necessary at the elite level, between the corporate elite and the state elite, because of the great strength of the corporate elite.

Michael Ornstein (1986) has been among the few to study the beliefs of members of different elites (see also Presthus, 1973). Until his study, people often argued that we could not determine whether elites shared a common ideological outlook because their members are not inclined to respond to interviews. Yet, Ornstein found that it

TABLE 21-4

Percent Support for Social Welfare Policies in Four Elites and the General Public

	Desire More Government Effort for Health and Medical Care	Desire More Government Assistance to the Unemployed	Desire More Government Help for the Poor	Agree that Too Much Difference between Rich and Poor	Agree that Unemployment High Because Welfare Too Easy to Get	Agree that People with High Incomes Should Pay More Taxes
	%	%	%	%	%	%
Capitalists	6	16	40	22	65	13
Civil Servants	14	27	40	49	40	34
Politicians	17	35	49	44	38	46
Labour Leaders	72	64	85	88	12	84
General Public	47	38	41	64	68	59

ADAPTED FROM MICHAEL D. ORNSTEIN. 1986. "THE POLITICAL IDEOLOGY OF THE CANADIAN CAPITALIST CLASS." CANADIAN REVIEW OF SOCIOLOGY AND ANTHROPOLOGY *23(2)* : 190.

TABLE 21-5

Beliefs on the
Rights of Workers
in Four Elites and
the General Public

	Desire More Government Effort for Workman's Compensation	Want to Raise Workman's Compensation to Pay Level	Want to Prohibit Employers Hiring Strike-breakers	Want to Put Employee Representatives on Company Boards	Agree that the Power of Unions is Too Great
	%	%	%	%	%
Capitalists	9	16	14	17	89
Civil Servants	12	31	31	50	77
Politicians	21	35	30	57	75
Labour Leaders	63	70	92	42	9
General Public	45	—	55	69	71

ADAPTED FROM MICHAEL D. ORNSTEIN. 1986. "THE POLITICAL IDEOLOGY OF THE CANADIAN CAPITALIST CLASS."
CANADIAN REVIEW OF SOCIOLOGY AND ANTHROPOLOGY *23(2) : 194.*

was not difficult to interview them. He asked members of four different elites questions on social welfare policy and labour relations, foreign investment and taxation. He compared (1) executives of the largest Canadian corporations, (2) top-level federal, provincial and big-city politicians, (3) top-level federal and provincial civil servants, (4) trade union leaders and (5) members of the general public. As might be expected, the trade union leaders were comparatively left-leaning in their beliefs, while corporate leaders gave responses considerably to the right of them. The corporate leaders were also to the right of politicians and the bureaucratic elite (see Tables 21-4 and 21-5). For example, in Table 21-4 corporate executives were more conservative on all six questions on social welfare, union leaders gave the most liberal responses, and politicians, civil servants and people from the general public were somewhere in between. Table 21-5 shows the same patterns for five questions concerning the rights of workers.

At this level of policy beliefs, then, some differences between the elites do appear. There is not the level of elite consensus that Porter and Clement might have expected. On the other hand, Ornstein (1986) also found that different portions of the economic elite (from small and large corporations, from national and international corporations) showed only very small differences in beliefs, suggesting that economic forces tend to unite the capitalist class in their outlook.

We do not know yet whether the accommodating elite model or the capitalist class control model best describes which groups are most dominant in Canada. A clear answer will require more research. However, this research will probably not significantly alter our understanding of the role of dominant ideology because, on this issue, the two theories have much in common. They each see dominant ideology as being promoted by the most powerful groups and distributed to the general public. And these beliefs are said to help the former control the lives of the latter. In addition, each of these theories sees the values of the capitalist economy as central to the dominant ideology. Also, each theory describes the same major ways in which ideology is distributed to the people. The educational system and the government or state are the primary disseminators of dominant ideology and, therefore, the most important social control agents in society.

Our examples to this point have been drawn from electoral politics and elite studies. We would not wish the reader to think that ideology is confined to these areas. As we have noted, ideology can be observed in diverse areas, including race and gender. In the area of race relations, for example, there is convincing evidence that racially discriminatory hiring practices persist among Toronto employers (Henry and Ginzberg, 1988). Given that these practices are proscribed by existing human rights legislation, this suggests that racist ideology has not been supplanted by the efforts of government to promote a more tolerant multicultural ideology among Canadians. Other research, dealing with people's verbally expressed attitudes, however, indicates a marked decline in Canadians' opposition to interracial marriages in the period 1968 to 1983 (Lambert and Curtis, 1984). These findings should not be dismissed as "merely" verbal behaviour. The emergence of this kind of normative constraint on respondents' verbal behaviour in an interview situation is significant in itself. It is surely noteworthy if respondents believe that there are norms forbidding the expression of hostility toward racial minorities.

In the area of gender relations, the critique of dominant sexist ideology has occurred in several waves, with the most recent wave dating from the publication of Betty Friedan's *The Feminine Mystique* in 1963. Gender ideology illustrates well the importance of looking at how groups are socially organized in support of the several ideological positions and the national contribution of government agencies to the contending parties to the struggle. In support of feminist counter-ideology, the National Action Committee on the Status of Women, a coalition of hundreds of women's groups lobbying in behalf of gender equality, is perhaps the most visible such group in Canada. Arrayed against the NAC is REAL (Realistic, Equal, Active for Life) Women of Canada, a more traditionally oriented lobby. This group opposes most of the positions identified with feminist counter-ideology, including equal pay for work of equal value legislation, women's right to abortion, tolerance for homosexuals and support of day care services out of taxes (Vienneau, 1989).

What is also significant about this struggle is the rivalry of these two groups for federal government funding. The attempt of the NAC to block funding to REAL women, and the success of the latter group, for the first time, in obtaining financial support for its conference in April 1989, underscores the fact that ideological struggle depends finally on the access of the contending parties to money and, thereby, access to the public.

The Individual and Social Change

The evidence of elite control and a measure of ideological consensus among the elites lead us to conclude that social change is very much out of the individual's hands. It does not follow, however, that individuals have *no* effect upon their future. It is an axiom of the sociological approach that we affect our social environment and history while being shaped by it, however limited our effect may be. C. Wright Mills put the issue this way (1959:6):

> Every individual lives, from one generation to the next, in some society . . . lives out a biography and . . . lives it out within some historical sequence. By the fact of his living, he contributes, however minutely, to the course of its history, even as he is made by society and by its historical push and shove.

Mills (1959:5) went on to emphasize that one payoff from the "sociological imagination," from coming to have an informed sociological understanding of society, is that:

This labour protest against the Free Trade Agreement reveals ideologies in conflict.

ONTARIO FEDERATION OF LABOUR (CLC).

> the individual can understand his own experiences and gauge his own fate only by locating himself within his period, that he can know his own chances in life only by becoming aware of those of all individuals in his circumstances. In many ways it is a terrible lesson; in many ways a magnificent one.

Mills argued that "knowledge is power," if we choose to act upon it. That is to say, when we know what is going on in society, and then act accordingly, we stand some chance of maximizing our opportunities.

There are two broad strategies to be followed in acting upon sociological understanding: individual-level coping procedures and organization-based action (Tepperman, 1989). Under the individual-level response, people "work the system" to their benefit. For example, if a person learns that some sections of the work force are shrinking while others are expanding, he or she can prepare for a job in one of the expanding sections. We all have some "choices" of this type to make. Social change is not so much involved here, though; it is chances or options in the individual's life that are at issue.

We may also join an interest group and/or political party, and take organization-based action. There are various alternatives here, groups with different policy agendas and ideologies. Social change *may* occur when we participate in such organizations. Social change certainly is made by people acting in groups and organizations. This is especially true of dominant groups and organizations. Political action via organizations often will *not* meet with success, and social change, when the organization supports counter-ideology and subordinate groups. As we have seen, dominant interest groups will oppose unwanted change. They will not likely give ground easily, and they will have considerable organizational and ideological power. Nonetheless, some political struggles are won by subordinate groups working through organizations. There are some recent examples of success by protest movements of subordinate groups—the civil rights movement in the United States, the Quiet Revolution in Quebec, the women's movement and "the revolt of pensioners" that stopped pension change proposed by the Mulroney government a few years ago. Also, an important case in point is the success of the labour movement in Canada and the United States over the decades in securing better wages and job conditions for the working class. There has been some change brought about by subordinate groups. Counter-ideologies sometimes become dominant ideologies.

Summary

Ideologies are emotionally charged beliefs and values that either explain and justify the status quo or, in the case of reformist or radical ideologies, call for and justify alternatives. To speak of discrimination is to call into question the justifying ideology of a society. Ideology can be seen as a sophisticated thought process engaged in by a minority of people, or as powerful but disconnected beliefs and values exhibited by everybody.

In this chapter, we have considered the consequences of ideology both for individuals and for groups within society. At the individual level, ideology flatters and empowers believers and provides frames of reference and standards of judgment. At the group level, ideology unifies dominant groups and contributes to the control of subordinate groups. It also helps to define group boundaries and contributes to or impedes social change. To illustrate the operation of ideology, we have discussed research on left/right ideology, the role of ideology in political behaviour and the use of ideology by elites in Canadian society.

Suggested Readings

Abercrombie, Nicholas, Stephen Hill and Bryan S. Turner.
1980. *The Dominant Ideology Thesis*. London: Allen and Unwin. A systematic and detailed critique of the idea of dominant ideology; describes the properties of dominant ideology in different historical periods, and the factors affecting the dissemination of ideology.

Christian, William, and Colin Campbell
1983. *Political Parties and Ideologies in Canada*, 2nd ed. Toronto: McGraw-Hill Ryerson. Contains an extensive treatment of the ideologies of liberalism, convervatism, socialism and nationalism as manifested in political party activity in this country.

Hardin, Herschel
1974. *A Nation Unaware: The Canadian Economic Culture*. Vancouver. J. J. Douglas. Three central contradictions in Canadian society (class, region and the United States vs. influence of indigenous groups) are shown to be alternative sites of ideological development.

Hartz, Louis
1964. *The Founding of New Societies*. New York: Harcourt, Brace and World. Presents a theory about the ideological origins of the United States and Canada as fragments from Europe's ideological conflicts.

Laponce, Jean A.
1981. *Left and Right: The Topography of Political Perceptions*. Toronto: University of Toronto Press. Discusses the historic transformation of an "up/down" vertical metaphor to a "left/right" horizontal metaphor to describe social relations and ideology and, also, the religious context of left/right.

Marchak, Patricia M.
1988. *Ideological Perspectives on Canada*, 3rd ed. Toronto: McGraw-Hill Ryerson. Discusses the properties of ideology, and the relation of ideology to ruling classes, class protest, nationalism and social change.

Discussion Questions

1. Compare and contrast dominant ideologies and reformist and radical ideologies, and give Canadian examples of each. Show how one of these types of ideologies can become the other type over time.

2. Choose a recent major ideological clash in Canada and describe the elements of the ideologies and groups involved on each side of the clash.

3. Discuss the individual-level and group-level effects of ideology for any example of ideology you care to choose.

4. Define, compare and contrast left ideology and right ideology. Describe each as it applies to the areas of (a) class relations, (b) gender relations and (c) ethnic relations.

5. What does the future hold for class voting in Canada, and why? Be sure to specify the key explanatory processes—of social control, social change and ideology—that you assume will take place.

6. C. W. Mills emphasized that "every individual . . . contributes, however minutely, to the course of . . . history." Discuss and criticize this observation.

Data Collection Exercises

1. Select several issues of a major city daily newspaper and identify every usage of the words "left," "right," "liberal" and "conservative." What are they used to describe? Distinguish among parties, leaders, policies, issues and ideas. What effect or feeling is attached to each of the concepts?

2. Suppose that you were going to conduct a sample survey of people's support for or rejection of dominant ideology. Design a series of statements corresponding to propositions in dominant ideology that you might use as questions.

3. Interview five people about their political ideologies. Show how apparent "inconsistencies" in their views are reconciled or made consistent in *their* thinking.

4. Interview your close friends on their ideologies. To what extent do *you* share their beliefs? Did you discover that they hold beliefs that you did not expect? Finally, analyse the relevance/irrelevance of agreement on ideology for your friendship network.

5. Select a recent issue of a daily newspaper and issues of the same newspaper from the same month and date ten, twenty and thirty years ago. What were the subjects of ideological debate in each of the four issues of the newspaper? Offer explanations for the continuity and change that you observe in the "ideological agenda" contained in the newspapers.

Writing Exercises

1. Choose your favourite and least favourite newspaper columnists. Write an essay showing the differences in their ideological views on politics, religion and culture.

2. Show how the central assumptions of sexist or racist ideology are refuted by feminist or multicultural counter-ideology.

3. Write an essay about how people deal with inconsistencies among their ideological beliefs.

4. Read Jean A. Laponce's chapters on the historical origins of the concepts of left and right in his *Left and Right: The Topography of Political Perceptions*. What claims does he make about the relationship between religion and these concepts?

5. Analyse the amount of ideological overlap between different areas of social life, such as politics, religion, family and so on.

Glossary

Accommodating elite theory: *theory that holds that there are several elite groups in society that collaborate and compete in pursuing their respective interests. Dominant ideology is seen to serve the common interests of the elites.*

Capitalist class control theory: *theory that holds that the dominant group in society is the capitalist class; this class prevails by controlling capital (said to be the ultimate source of power) and the state. Dominant ideology is seen to serve the interests of the capital class and the state.*

Class voting: *the extent to which voters support political parties that favour their respective social classes.*

Counter ideologies: *reform and radical ideologies that challenge the assumptions of dominant ideologies.*

Dominant ideologies: *emotionally charged beliefs that explain and justify the status quo.*

Empowerment: *ideology's effect on people's self-esteem, sense of power and comprehension of their position in the social structure of a society.*

Ideologies: *emotionally charged beliefs and values that either explain and justify the status quo or, in the case of reformist or radical ideologies, call for and justify alternatives.*

Left ideologies: *in Canada, support for the proposition that public sector institutions, including government, should promote economic and social equality.*

Materialist values: *goals and standards having to do with social control and economic matters.*

Post-materialist values: *goals and standards having to do with aesthetic, social and intellectual matters.*

Radical ideologies: *beliefs favouring the fundamental reconstitution of society.*

Reformist ideologies: *beliefs favouring changes in society without calling for a fundamental reconstruction of society.*

Right ideologies: *in Canada, support for the proposition that the private sector, through the marketplace, is the appropriate arena for the achievement of social as well as personal objectives.*

References

Abercrombie, Nicholas, Stephen Hill and Bryan S. Turner
   1980. *The Dominant Ideology Thesis.* London: Allen and Unwin.

Baer, Douglas E., and Ronald D. Lambert
   1982. "Education and Support for Dominant Ideology." *Canadian Review of Sociology and Anthropology* 19(2): 173–95.

Bowles, S., and H. Gintis
   1976. *Schooling in Capitalist America.* New York: Basic Books.

Brym, Robert J.
   1986. "Incorporation Versus Power Models of Working Class Radicalism with Special Reference to North America." *Canadian Journal of Sociology* 11(3): 227–51.

Brym, Robert J., Michael W. Gillespie and Rhonda L. Lenton
   1989. "Class Power, Class Mobilization, and Class Voting: The Canadian Case." *Canadian Journal of Sociology* 14(1): 25–44.

Clement, Wallace
1975. *The Canadian Corporate Elite*. Toronto: McClelland and Stewart.
1977. *Continental Corporate Power: An Analysis of Economic Power*. Toronto: McClelland and Stewart.
1985. "Elites," pp. 562–63. In *The Canadian Encyclopedia*, vol. 1. Edmonton: Hurtig.

Collins, Randall
1979. *The Credential Society: An Historical Sociology of Education and Stratification*. New York: Academic Press.

Converse, Phillip E.
1964. "The Nature of Belief Systems in Mass Publics," pp. 206–61. In D. L. Apter, ed., *Ideology and Discontent*. Glencoe, Ill.: Free Press.

Curtis, James E., and John W. Petras
1970. "Introduction," pp. 1–85. In James E. Curtis and John W. Petras, eds., *The Sociology of Knowledge*. New York: Praeger.

Friedan, Betty
1963. *The Feminine Mystique*. Harmondsworth: Penguin.

Henry, Frances, and Effie Ginzberg
1988. "Racial Discriminiation in Employment," ch. 18. In J. Curtis, E. Grabb, N. Guppy and S. Gilbert, eds., *Social Inequality in Canada: Patterns, Problems, Policies*. Toronto: Prentice-Hall.

Inglehart, Ronald
1977. *The Silent Revolution: Changing Values and Political Styles among Western Publics*. Princeton, N.J.: Princeton University Press.
1979. "Value Priorities and Socioeconomic Change," ch. 11. In Samuel H. Barnes and Max Kaase, eds., *Political Action: Mass Participation in Five Western Democracies*. Beverly Hills: Sage.

Johnston, John C.
1969. *Young People's Images of Canadian Society: An Opinion Survey of Canadian Youth 13 to 20 Years of Age*. Studies of the Royal Commission on Bilingualism and Biculturalism, 2. Ottawa: Information Canada.

Kelley, Harold H.
1955. "Salience of Membership and Resistance to Change of Group-anchored Attitudes," pp. 297–310. In Herbert H. Hyman and Eleanor Singer, eds., *Readings in Reference Group Theory and Research*. New York: Free Press.

Lambert, Ronald D., and James E. Curtis
1979. "Education, Economic Dissatisfaction, and Nonconfidence in Canada Social Institutions." *Canadian Review of Sociology and Anthropology* 16(1): 47–54.
1984. "Québécois and English Canadian Opposition to Racial and Religious Intermarriage, 1968–1983." *Canadian Ethnic Studies* 16(2): 30–46.

Lambert, Ronald D., James E. Curtis, Steven D. Brown and Barry J. Kay
1986a. "In Search of Left/Right Beliefs in the Canadian 1986 Electorate." *Canadian Journal of Political Science* 19(3): 541–63.
1986b. "Canadian Beliefs About Differences between Social Classes." *Canadian Journal of Sociology* 11(4): 379–99.

1988. "The Left/Right Factor in Party Identification." *Canadian Journal of Sociology* 13(4): 385–406.

Lambert, Ronald D., James E. Curtis, Barry J. Kay and Steven D. Brown
1988. "The Social Sources of Political Knowledge." *Canadian Journal of Political Science* 21(2): 359–74.

Lambert, Ronald D., and Alfred A. Hunter
1979. "Social Stratification, Voting Behaviour, and the Images of Canadian Federal Political Parties." *Canadian Review of Sociology and Anthropology* 16(3): 287–304.

Laponce, J. A.
1981. *Left and Right: The Topography of Political Perceptions*. Toronto: University of Toronto Press.

Mackie, Marlene
1987. *Constructing Women and Men: Gender Socialization*. Toronto: Holt, Rinehart and Winston.

Mann, Michael
1970. "The Social Cohesion of Liberal Democracy." *American Sociological Review* 35(3): 423–39.

Mannheim, Karl
1936. *Ideology and Utopia*. New York: Harcourt, Brace and World.

Marchak, Patricia M.
1988. *Ideological Perspectives on Canada*, 3rd ed. Toronto: McGraw-Hill Ryerson.

Maslow, Abraham
1970. *Motivation and Personality*, 2nd ed. New York: Harper and Row.

McDiarmid, G., and D. Pratt
1971. *Teaching Prejudice*. Toronto: Ontario Institute for Studies in Education.

McDonald, N.
1978. "Egerton Ryerson and the School as an Agent of Political Socialization." In N. McDonald and A. Chaiton, eds., *Egerton Ryerson and His Times*. Toronto: Macmillan.

McNaught, Kenneth
1959. *A Prophet in Politics: A Biography of J. S. Woodsworth*. Toronto: University of Toronto Press.

Mills, C. Wright
1959. *The Sociological Imagination*. New York: Oxford.

Morgan, Edmund S.
1988. *Inventing the People: The Rise of Popular Sovereignty in England and America*. New York: W. W. Norton.

Murphy, Raymond
1988. *Social Closure: The Theory of Monopolization and Exclusion*. Oxford: Oxford University Press.

Noelle-Neumann, Elisabeth
1984. *The Spiral of Silence: Public Opinion — Our Social Skin*. Chicago: University of Chicago Press.

Ogmundson, Rick

1975a. "On the Use of Party Image Variables to Measure the Political Distinctiveness of a Class Vote: The Canadian Case." *Canadian Journal of Sociology* 1(2): 169–77.

1975b. "On the Measurement of Party Class Positions: The Case of Canadian Federal Political Parties." *Canadian Review of Sociology and Anthropology* 12(4): 565–76.

1976. "Mass-Elite Linkages and Class Issues in Canada." *Canadian Review of Sociology and Anthropology* 13(1): 1–12.

1979. "A Note on the Ambiguous Meaning of Survey Research Measures which Use the Words 'Left' and 'Right'." *Canadian Journal of Political Science* 12(4): 799–805.

Ontario, Government

1988. *Transitions: Report of the Social Assistance Review Committee.* Toronto: Ontario Ministry of Community and Social Services.

Ornstein, Michael D.

1986. "The Political Ideology of the Canadian Capitalist Class." *Canadian Review of Sociology and Anthropology* 23(2): 182–209.

Parkin, Frank

1971. *Class, Inequality and Political Order.* London: McGibbon and Kee.

Porter, John

1965. *The Vertical Mosaic: An Analysis of Social Class and Power in Canada.* Toronto: University of Toronto Press.

Presthus, Robert

1973. *Elite Accommodation in Canadian Politics.* Toronto: Macmillan.

Tepperman, Lorne

1989. *Choices and Chances: Sociology for Everyday Life.* Toronto: Holt, Rinehart and Winston.

Vienneau, David

1989. "Group Attacks 'Childless' Judge on Abortion Ruling." *The Toronto Star*, Sunday, April 23, p. A2.

CHAPTER 22

Social Movements

ROBERT J. BRYM

Toronto International Women's Day poster, 1979.

DESIGNED BY BARBARA KLUNDER.

Introduction

Social movements are collective attempts to change some or all aspects of society. Participating in social movements may involve rioting, demonstrating, petitioning, striking, forming unions and new political parties or taking part in other types of protest activity.

When masses of people get involved in conflicts with authority, they provide fresh material for one of sociology's traditional areas of study. Why do social movements emerge? Who participates in social movements? How are social movements related to broad changes in the structure of society? What consequences do social movements have for society? These are among the chief questions that have interested students of social movements for close to two centuries, and we will focus on them in the following discussion.[1]

The next section of this chapter outlines the two main explanations of why social movements emerge and who takes part in them. It introduces a number of concepts that will help us understand what social movements are all about. Then, some of these concepts are illustrated in a discussion of the three main social movements in Canadian history: the farmers' movement, the workers' movement and the women's movement. In the process of outlining the growth of these movements, some of the connections between social movements and social change will be examined.

Causes and Composition of Social Movements

Consider the question of why social movements emerge in the first place. Charles Tilly, one of the leading contemporary authorities in the field, has pointed out that two main types of explanations of social movement formation have been proposed over the years (Tilly, Tilly and Tilly, 1975). According to the first type of theory, social movements result from social and personal breakdown. The second type of theory views movements as expressions of new forms of social solidarity.

Breakdown Theories

Breakdown theories are rooted in the thinking of certain nineteenth-century conservatives who were opposed to the French Revolution of 1789. The revolutionaries proclaimed liberty, equality and fraternity as their goals. The conservatives, in contrast, saw the overthrow of the old government and the old ruling class as a great danger to the well-being of the French citizenry. The conservatives emphasized how existing authority, traditional forms of community and rigid social hierarchy constrain human wants and actions, thereby preventing disorganization and anarchy. They thought that the

---

For comprehensive and up-to-date reviews of the entire field, see Marx and Wood (1975), Jenkins (1983) and Roy (1984).

migration of peasants to the cities had the opposite result: traditional community breakdown, erosion of moral and religious standards, increased crime, growing desire for material improvement on the part of the new urban poor and the eventual outbreak of mob violence against authority.

Various aspects of these ideas have found their way into modern sociological thought, albeit stripped of their explicit moral and political messages. One popular modern variant of the breakdown approach holds that social movements emerge when dissatisfaction with the present fuses with hope for the future. This is frequently called a situation of frustration, strain or *relative deprivation* (Davies, 1969; Gurr, 1970). In this view, people revolt when the gap between what they need and what they expect to receive becomes intolerable. For example, great poverty in itself (or *absolute deprivation*) is not enough to spark rebellion. But poor people whose aspirations are not constrained, who want much more than they can get, are likely to act collectively to further their aims.

Such a situation typically arises (according to modern relative deprivation theorists) during periods of rapid industrialization and urbanization. When most people were poor peasants, nearly everyone knew their place in society, were well integrated in village and estate and could rarely hold out hope of improvement. The trouble presumably began only when peasants moved from the countryside to the hectic and unsettling city. There, they experienced a painful clash between traditional and modern values, and they began to hope that they could achieve the living standards of the more wealthy urban dwellers. Frustration at failing to advance as rapidly as they had originally hoped led to widespread crime (an attempt to succeed materially by illegal means), suicide (an admission of defeat) and popular rebellion (collective attempts to change conditions perceived as unjust).

This interpretation of the causes of mass social unrest has not gone unchallenged, especially over the past twenty years. A main criticism of breakdown theories is that they do not fit available facts well. For example, Charles Tilly and his associates (Lodhi and Tilly, 1973; Tilly, 1979; Tilly, Tilly and Tilly, 1975) have collected relevant data on France and other Western European countries for the period 1830 to 1930. For each year and for each region, they measured collective unrest (the number of strikes and demonstrations that took place), individual unrest (crime rates) and the level of strain and frustration (as indicated by urban growth rates). The breakdown interpretation would have been supported if they had discovered that rates of urbanization, collective unrest and crime fluctuated together. But Tilly and his colleagues found no such association. Their research indicates that personal and social disorganization are unlikely to be the main causes of social movement formation because protest actions do not necessarily increase in the wake of such disorganization.

A second problem with theories that emphasize breakdown and disorganization as causes of social movement formation is that they regard social movement members as people who lack attachments to local communities and secondary associations. For example, the *theory of mass society* was once widely used to explain the rise of many movements, notably Nazism in Germany. According to the theory's chief exponent (Kornhauser, 1959), Germany in the 1930s had relatively few voluntary, civic, religious, occupational and other secondary associations. As a result, large numbers of German citizens were easily influenced by extremist politicians such as the Nazis. Presumably, the Nazi appeal would have fallen on deaf ears if more people had been busy attending church, participating in trade unions, running for local office and so forth. If this had been the case, a variety of social cross-pressures would have prevented people from having their attention drawn to only one extremist movement as a solution to the economic and political distress that confronted them in the 1930s.

Subsequent research (well summarized in Oberschall, 1973 : 102ff.) has demonstrated that this portrayal is inaccurate. Studies show that membership in secondary associations may actually *encourage* participation in social movements. Consider, for example, the Co-operative Commonwealth Federation (CCF) of Saskatchewan, a radical farmers' and workers' movement and political party that originated in the 1930s and first formed the Saskatchewan government in 1944. The early joiners and chief activists of this movement/party had been leading members of consumers' co-operatives and trade unions before getting involved in the CCF. They were not socially unattached, but unusually well connected to their communities and to their communities' secondary associations (Lipset, 1968).

These and other similar findings (Pinard, 1971) raise another question. Under what conditions do secondary associations encourage people to get involved in movements for change, and under what conditions do secondary associations suppress such involvement? The answer hinges on how socially diverse the membership of the secondary associations in question is. If members of secondary associations tend to come from a variety of different classes, ethnic groups and so forth, secondary associations really do act as the mass society theorists say. People's class or other group identities and interests get diffused and political behaviour tends to be moderated. However, when secondary associations tend to *segment* the population—that is, when secondary associations contain socially homogeneous memberships—class and other group consciousness is sharpened and radicalism is more likely. *Segmentation* refers to the polarization or clustering of social groups in distinct social organizations. Thus, research now shows that Germany during the rise of Hitler was a society full of socially rootless people. Germans had plenty of organizational ties—but to socially homogeneous organizations that kept major categories of the population separated or segmented. This made extreme conflict among segments of society more likely.

In summary, breakdown theories are oversimplifications. Social movements do not arise simply from the strains and frustrations caused by personal and social disorganization. Nor are new movements socially disorganized collectivities. True, people who press collectively for social change are angry or relatively deprived. But the most recent research on social movement formation demonstrates that only under certain *social structural* conditions can feelings of anger or deprivation be translated into collective protest behaviour (Korpi, 1974).

**Solidarity
Theories**

Two social conditions are likely to lead to social protest:

1.   Social movements are more likely to form where potential rebels are more socially segmented from authorities.
2.   Social movements are more likely to form where potential rebels have more social solidarity among themselves.

These propositions are the core ideas of *solidarity theories* of social movements, the second school of thought distinguished by Tilly. If breakdown theories have conservative intellectual origins, solidarity theories may trace their pedigree back to the socialism of Karl Marx.

Writing in the middle of the nineteenth-century, Marx predicted that capitalist industrialization would forge a large and growing class of workers. Peasants, driven from the countryside to work in factories, and inefficient entrepreneurs, unable to compete with wealthier and more adept business people, would form this proletariat. According to Marx, economic efficiency requires the concentration of workers in huge factories; such concentration encourages workers to think of themselves as a class; and working-class consciousness sparks the creation of working-class organizations, such as trade unions and political parties. Simultaneously, Marx felt, wealth would concentrate in the hands of a small group of capitalists. Consequently, Marx predicted that the class structure would become highly polarized or segmented over time. Marx thought that this would result in sharp and heightening conflict, both in the workplace and in the political arena, between workers and capitalists. He expected that eventually the working class would overthrow capitalism, in most cases violently, and establish a new socialist order (Marx and Engels, 1972).

Most modern solidarity theorists are not explicitly concerned with the political significance of Marx's work. But they have generalized and extended its sociological implications in interesting and fruitful ways. Some of these sociological developments can best be introduced by considering how social movement formation is influenced by the distribution of power in society (Brym, 1979; Korpi, 1974).

Imagine a highly simplified situation in which a society consists of just three groups of people: (a) authorities, who occupy the strategic command posts of the economy, the military, the political system, the educational system and other major institutions; (b) potential partisans of movements for change, who are disadvantaged, conscious of their disadvantaged position and keen to improve their lot; and (c) the uncommitted, who are sought as recruits and allies by members of groups (a) and (b) (cf. Gamson, 1968). What is the likelihood of potential partisans creating a movement to influence or force authorities to improve the position of the disadvantaged? That depends on how powerful group (a) is relative to group (b). The power ratio is the power of group (a) divided by the power of group (b) (or authorities' power over potential partisans' power). The larger this power ratio, the less likely it is that a movement for change will emerge. But as the ratio falls, the probability of social conflict and social movement formation increases. In the extreme and infrequent case where the ratio falls to 1 or less—group (b) is as strong as or stronger than group (a)—a *revolution* takes place. This is a violent and rapid upheaval in which potential partisans are sufficiently powerful to take over positions of authority from the previous ruling group and substantially alter the organization of the whole society.

This raises the further question: On what does the relative power of the two groups depend? One useful definition holds that group power is a function of three factors (Bierstedt, 1974; McCarthy and Zald, 1977; Tilly, 1978). In ascending order of importance, these are: (a) the *size* of the group and its allies; (b) its level of internal *organization*; and (c) its access to scarce *resources*. (Such resources may, in turn, be categorized under three headings. *Normative resources* are the newspapers, schools and other ways of teaching people beliefs acceptable to the authorities. *Material resources* are means of paying people to behave in desirable ways: the ability to withhold or bestow jobs, bribes, etc. Finally, *coercive resources* refer to police and military forces that can be used to compel people to act appropriately.)

These concepts help us understand why the power ratio is the central determinant of social movement formation. Consider, for example, the question of resource control. Where the power ratio is very high, authorities are able to influence heavily the political values taught in churches, schools and in the mass media. The point of view of the authorities will be so firmly ingrained in the public mind that potential partisans of

The Communists promised that they would create a society free of classes and ethnic groups—and therefore free of class and ethnic group conflict. In practice, however, classes and ethnic groups did not vanish under communism, and conflict continues. The photo shows a riot in the Central Square of Lhasa, the capital of Tibet, which is under Communist Chinese rule. On March 5, 1988, some 3000 to 5000 Tibetan demonstrators gathered to demand the separation of Tibet from China. The Chinese People's Armed Police opened fire on the crowd, killing, wounding, and arresting participants. The photo was taken by the Chinese Public Security Bureau in 1988. It was procured and smuggled out of Tibet by Ron Schwartz, and is reprinted here with his permission.

change will scarcely be able to conceive of the possibility of improving their life situation. The result might be something like the totalitarian society depicted in George Orwell's *Nineteen Eighty-Four*, in which a virtually new language was created by the authorities for such political ends. Similarly, where the power ratio is very high, authorities can buy off or co-opt many potentially troublesome people by giving them jobs, or threatening to take away their jobs and preventing them from finding employment elsewhere. In the extreme case, authorities who have full control over coercive resources can also call troops into action and suppress dissent violently. However, where the power ratio drops on one or more of these dimensions, the probability increases that movements for change will develop.

George Orwell's "The Principles of Newspeak," *Nineteen Eighty-Four*

The purpose of Newspeak was not only to provide a medium for the world-view and mental habits proper to the devotees of Ingsoc [English Socialism], but to make all other modes of thought impossible. It was intended that when Newspeak had been adopted once and for all and Oldspeak forgotten, a heretical thought—that is, a thought diverging from the principles of Ingsoc—should be literally unthinkable, at least so far as thought is dependent on words. Its vocabulary was so constructed as to give exact and often very subtle expression to every meaning that a Party member could properly wish to express, while excluding all other meanings and also the probability of arriving at them by indirect methods. This was done partly by the invention of new words, but chiefly by eliminating undesirable words and by stripping such words as remained of unor-thodox meanings, and so far as possible of all secondary meanings whatever. To give a single example. The word *free* still existed in Newspeak, but it could only be used in such statements as "This dog is free from lice" or "This field is free from weeds." It could not be used in its old sense of "politically free" or "intellectually free," since political and intellectual freedom no longer existed even as concepts, and were therefore of necessity name-less. Quite apart from the suppression of definitely heret-ical words, reduction of vocabulary was regarded as an end in itself, and no word that could be dispensed with was allowed to survive. Newspeak was designed not to extend but to *diminish* the range of thought, and this purpose was directly assisted by cutting the choice of words to a minimum.

From George Orwell. 1954 (originally published 1949). *Nineteen Eighty-four*. Harmondsworth: Penguin, pp. 241–42.

These ideas have also been used to explain the level of violence that may develop once conflict erupts between movement partisans and authorities (Gamson, 1975; Oberschall, 1973:242–345; Tilly, Tilly and Tilly, 1975:280–90). On the whole, available evidence indicates that violence has been more frequently and massively used by authorities than by movement partisans. And generally speaking, the less powerful authorities are, the more likely they are to respond violently to challenges from movement partisans; paradoxically, the use of force by authorities is a sign of their weakness. For example, if ruling groups are well organized, they can speak in a binding way, recognize the legitimacy of protesters without feeling threatened, bargain and negotiate with them and act to institutionalize and tame the conflict. But if ruling groups are disorganized, they may not be able to speak authoritatively and they may feel threatened by protest activities. This makes bargaining and negotiating with rebels difficult and undesirable from the authorities' viewpoint. They may then feel it is necessary to apply force to maintain order. Similarly, if authorities have not had access to abundant normative resources and have not been able to teach their values to potential movement partisans, and if authorities have too few available jobs and too little money to co-opt rebels, they will be inclined to put down unrest by force.

Although no society can long rely on force alone to maintain order, if authorities decide to use force it is more effective if it can be applied toughly and consistently. In contrast, if relatively mild doses of force are administered to an aggrieved and unruly population, and if these doses are applied in fits and starts, these actions are likely to increase violence among movement partisans. Partisans will be angered by the violence directed against them, will sense the inability of the authorities to apply force more severely and will therefore take advantage of the perceived weakness.

The violence of movement partisans also depends on how the movement is organized. Two broad types of movement organizations can be distinguished: primitive and modern (Tilly, 1979). The members of *primitive movements* are recruited from kinship networks, villages, ethnic groups or tribes. These movements result in collective violence that is small scale and local in scope and that tends to have inexplicit and non-political objectives. Bread and tax riots, social banditry (robbing from the rich to give to the poor) and movements that anticipate the imminent onset of a messianic age are examples of such forms of social protest (Hobsbawm, 1959).

Modern movements tend to be less violent than primitive movements because they are, in effect, bureaucracies. That is, modern movements are large, specialized associations with well-defined economic and political objectives and routine procedures and patterns of action. The modern trade union movement is a good example of such organizations. Their leaders tend to enjoy privileged positions that they do not want to see endangered, and their bureaucratic staffs need stability if they are to perform their duties effectively. Violence is likely to disrupt the smooth operation of the movement and threaten the interests of its leaders, so it is avoided.

However, if a modern movement happens to consist of a number of competing, decentralized organizations, radicalism and even violence is more likely. As Anthony Oberschall (1973:260–61) points out, the leaders and activists in decentralized movements compete with each other to gain followers and obtain outside resources and allies, and they disagree with each other on goals, tactics and ideology. Conservative tendencies are relatively unlikely to crystallize under such circumstances.

This suggests the following conclusions:

1. The relative power of a social group derives from its comparative size, level of organization and access to politically useful resources.

FIGURE 22-1   Conflict and the Power Ratio

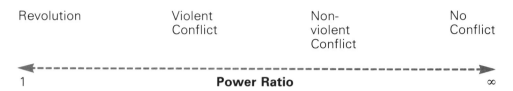

Revolution	Violent Conflict	Non-violent Conflict	No Conflict

1   **Power Ratio**   ∞

As the ratio of authorities' to potential partisans' power falls, the rate and intensity of conflict increases.

2. The frequency of social movement formation varies inversely with the ratio of power between authorities and potential partisans.
3. When a social movement emerges, authorities are more likely to respond violently if they are relatively disorganized and/or if they have access to few normative and material resources (see Figure 22-1).
4. Primitive social movements tend to be more violent than modern social movements because the latter are bureaucratically structured. However, radicalism and even violence may occur in modern movements that are decentralized.

Three Canadian Examples of Social Movements

The discussion to this point has been rather abstract. In order to make these concepts more concrete, let us now briefly examine some aspects of the three most important social movements in Canadian history: the farmers' movement, the workers' movement and the women's movement.

The Farmers' Movement

Since the 1920s, there have been several social movements that have given rise to third parties. *Third parties* are political parties that remained unaligned with the establishment parties (Liberal and Progressive Conservative) and have for the most part stood on the left wing of the political spectrum. Third parties have gained up to about a fifth of the vote in national elections, but have never formed a federal government. They have, however, formed provincial governments in British Columbia, Alberta, Saskatchewan, Manitoba, Ontario and Quebec. At first, farmers were the largest constituency for these third parties. Manual workers also formed an important third-party support base. By the 1960s, manual and non-manual workers were the main (although by no means the exclusive) supporters of the most popular third parties in the country.

The story of Canada's third parties begins on the Prairies in the late nineteenth century (Lipset, 1968; Macpherson, 1962). The Prairies have aptly been called an "internal colony" of Canada. Since the time of Confederation, Montreal and Toronto financiers and industrialists had dreamed about settling Saskatchewan and Alberta with European immigrants. They wished to establish on the Prairies a market for the manufactured goods of central Canada. They also viewed the Prairies as a source of agricultural exports that would earn revenue for the new Dominion. To achieve these aims, they—or, more accurately, the federal government, which they controlled—placed high tariffs on manufactured goods. This protected central Canadian manufacturers and their employees from foreign competition. From the point of view of the Prairie farmer, however, it made ploughs and tractors, saws and hammers, shoes and automobiles, more expensive. Moreover, the federal government set low freight rates to ensure that the West would remain an agricultural frontier: it was inexpensive to ship grain out and to ship manufactured goods into the region. Finally, large business interests in central Canada controlled the marketing of grain and the availability of credit. It was widely felt that this non-competitive business environment enabled eastern businessmen to set low prices for grain and high prices for loans.

The protective tariff, freight rates policy and price setting were the issues that galvanized the farmers into collective action. As early as 1906 they formed the Grain Growers' Grain Company. Its purpose: to collect wheat in a collectively owned grain elevator system and sell it directly to the central wheat exchange without using the services of intermediaries. This was only one of many important marketing and consumer co-operatives that the farmers created in order to lower costs of production and increase incomes.

In the 1910s, however, two developments convinced western farmers that collective economic action was inadequate. The price of wheat fell on the world market. Freight rates and the cost of manufactured goods rose. The farmers, caught in a cost-price squeeze, decided that political action was necessary: they hoped that by electing members of Parliament to represent their interests it might be possible to force the government to lower the tariff on manufactured goods, buy grain that could not be immediately sold, establish a floor price for wheat and take other actions that would ease the difficulties faced by the agricultural sector.

In 1920, the National Progressive Party was formed. In the 1921 federal election it won sixty-four seats, over 25 percent of the total. However, the party had a short life. This was partly because the elected representatives were unsure whether they should remain a separate party or simply try to influence government policy from within by becoming part of an establishment party. In fact, some of the leaders of the National Progressive Party were given important positions in the Liberal Party and were thereby co-opted.

The farmers did, however, learn from this experience the importance of remaining politically independent. To that end, they created the CCF in 1933 in alliance with the small Independent Labour Party. The CCF, the forerunner of the New Democratic Party, became the government of Saskatchewan in 1944.

Originally, the CCF was a democratic-socialist party. It aimed to decrease the level of inequality in society by expanding the state's role in economic ownership and planning. However, in order to appeal to the majority of landowning farmers, it had to weaken and even abandon some of its more radical socialist principles, notably the notion that a CCF government would take control of all land for the benefit of the population as a whole. Most farmers considered this equivalent to robbery and therefore rejected it out of hand. Nevertheless, the CCF remained a party that stood for the reform and humanization of the capitalist system, and it championed progressive reforms at the provincial and federal levels: unemployment insurance, medicare and so forth. It also remained a highly democratic party that stood for the protection of individual and minority rights.

The Regina Manifesto

The CCF is a federation of organizations whose purpose is the establishment in Canada of a Co-operative Commonwealth in which the principle regulating production, distribution and exchange will be the supplying of human needs and not the making of profits.

We aim to replace the present capitalist system, with its inherent injustice and inhumanity, by a social order from which the domination and exploitation of one class by another will be eliminated, in which economic planning will supersede unregulated private enterprise and competition, and in which genuine democratic self-government, based upon economic equality, will be possible. The present order is marked by glaring inequalities of wealth and opportunity, by chaotic waste and instability; and in an age of plenty it condemns the great mass of people to poverty and insecurity. Power has become more and more concentrated into the hands of a small irresponsible minority of financiers and industrialists and to their predatory interests the majority are habitually sacrificed. When private profit is the main stimulus to economic effort, our society oscillates between periods of feverish prosperity in which the main benefits go to speculators and profiteers, and of catastrophic depression, in which the common man's normal state of insecurity and hardship is accentuated. We believe that these evils can be removed only in a planned and socialized economy in which our natural resources and the principal means of production and distribution are owned, controlled and operated by the people.

From the "Regina Manifesto" adopted at the First National Convention of the CCF, Regina, Saskatchewan, July 1933. Walter D. Young. 1969. *The Anatomy of a Party: The National CCF, 1932–61.* Toronto: University of Toronto Press, pp. 304–5.

In this, the CCF differed from a social movement in neighbouring Alberta that experienced a meteoric rise to political power in 1935. The Social Credit Party, like the CCF, railed against eastern business interests and the federal government. At least in its early years, it, too, aimed to reform the capitalist system. However, for reasons too complex to discuss here (see Brym, 1980; Richards and Pratt, 1979), the Social Credit Party eventually lost its reformist zeal. It was never run along particularly democratic lines, and many of its leaders and members had little regard for minority rights, as is evidenced by the anti-semitic propaganda the party occasionally distributed.

The emergence of social movements on the Prairies has been explained in terms that correspond closely to the general principles of solidarity theory. Macpherson (1962), for example, stressed two factors that encouraged the success of Social Credit in Alberta: the nature of the province's class structure and the relationship between its economy and eastern Canadian economic forces. Macpherson described the economic system as quasi-colonial in the sense that it was largely controlled by capitalist interests in the East. The relatively homogeneous class structure meant that a large mass of people in the province faced the same kinds of economic problems, had the same interests, were aware of them and were therefore in a position to act collectively. The fact that the economy was quasi-colonial meant there was a highly visible group in the East that was perceived as the major source of the population's disadvantaged position. In other words, there was a high degree of social cohesion *within* the major disadvantaged class and a high degree of segmentation *between* that class and external powers. This facilitated the emergence of the Social Credit Party.

In his study of the Saskatchewan CCF, Seymour Martin Lipset (1968) also noted the homogeneity of that province's class structure: nearly 60 percent of the Saskatchewan work force was employed in agriculture in 1941. Moreover, Lipset showed how the dense network of ties among farmers in the co-operative movement, and among blue-collar workers in the trade union movement, facilitated their participation in the CCF.[2]

Maurice Pinard (1971; 1973), in a study of the rise of Social Credit in Quebec in the early 1960s, extended Macpherson's and Lipset's arguments. First, Pinard argued that class homogeneity and solidarity among potential partisans of a third party is not the only basis of social cohesion that facilitates protest. Strong social attachments among members of any disadvantaged group—through voluntary organizations, face-to-face contact in small communities, common work contexts and so forth—will have much the same effect. Second, he argued that cleavage between a quasi-colonial economy and a dominant metropolitan economy is not the only form of social segmentation that is conducive to the rise of third parties. Virtually any significant cleavage—between social classes, between ethnic groups, etc.—will suffice.

Pinard also showed that segmentation is enhanced by unrepresentative political party systems, and he paid special attention to systems of one-party dominance. When Pinard wrote of one-party dominance, he referred to a situation where one of the two establishment parties receives less than a third of the vote for some considerable time, or where it suddenly loses popular support as a consequence of, say, the revelation of flagrant corruption among party officials. In either case, only one of the establishment parties has a chance of forming the government. When seriously aggrieved segments of the population face a choice between a dominant establishment party and a very weak establishment party, they will be inclined to vote for neither. The dominant

---

[2] The next two paragraphs are reproduced with slight changes by permission of Butterworth and Company (Canada) Ltd., from R. Brym. 1984. "Social Movements and Third Parties." In S. Berkowitz, ed., *Models and Myths in Canadian Sociology*. Toronto: Butterworths.

party is too closely identified with the sources of the population's grievances, and the other establishment party is not seen as a realistic alternative since it is so weak. A third alternative party is then likely to emerge. Pinard's analysis of Canadian provincial elections offered compelling evidence to support his thesis.

Mention must also be made of the few studies that have tried to explain why different regions or subregions of the country have experienced different rates of social movement and third-party formation (Brym, 1979; 1980; 1984; 1986a; 1986b; Brym and Neis, 1978; Brym, Gillespie and Lenton, 1989). While the rate of third-party formation has been unusually high on the Prairies, it has been unusually low in Atlantic Canada. This is true even though the per capita income and standard of living in Atlantic Canada is the lowest in the country; and though, according to several public opinion polls, Maritimers and Newfoundlanders feel relatively worse off than other Canadians and are less satisfied with governments.

Absolute and relative deprivation are not enough to cause Atlantic Canadians to rebel because the distribution of power in the region has been so highly skewed in favour of ruling circles. Potential partisans of change—traditionally, primary producers (farmers, fishers, etc.) and wage earners—are relatively weak for several reasons. First, it should be borne in mind that employed workers are generally more easily mobilized to participate in social movements than are unemployed workers; and workers employed in large establishments are more easily mobilized than workers in small establishments. This is because employed workers, and especially those employed in settings where they have contact with many people in the same work situation, can easily communicate among themselves, recognize they are similarly disadvantaged and decide to take collective action to improve their conditions. But there are proportionately fewer employed workers in the Atlantic region than elsewhere in the country, and wage earners who are employed tend to work in relatively small establishments. These conditions exist because the region is economically underdeveloped. Low levels of investment result in high levels of unemployment and relatively small-scale industrial establishments. Second, potential partisans of change are relatively weak because they have low incomes: per capita earnings in Atlantic Canada are below earnings elsewhere in the country. This lack of money (a politically useful material resource) makes it more difficult for them to mobilize. Third, primary producers tend to be less socially cohesive in Atlantic Canada than elsewhere. Farmers and fishers in the region tend to produce less for the market and more for their own subsistence than is the case elsewhere in the country. As a result, they have not needed to form many of the economic co-operatives that greatly increased the social cohesion and solidarity of Prairie farmers and served as a vitally important mobilizing force. For all these reasons, Atlantic Canadians have been less likely to form social movements and third parties than westerners.[3]

---

[3] There have been a few instances of third-party candidates winning seats in Atlantic Canada. Significantly, these have tended to occur in areas where atypically high levels of capital investment have created relatively solidary and prosperous classes of blue-collar workers, farmers and fishers at a time when the establishment parties were temporarily disunited.

In summary, the evidence indicates that in Canada there is a positive association between the rate of social movement/third-party formation and the degree of social segmentation. There is also a negative association between the rate of social movement/third-party formation and the value of the power ratio.

The Workers' Movement

On March 22, 1976, tens of thousands of workers demonstrated on Parliament Hill to protest the government's imposition of wage and price controls.

NATIONAL ARCHIVES OF CANADA/PA 169601.

Less than 5 percent of the Canadian labour force are now engaged in agriculture, while more than 75 percent are employed as wage labourers. Reflecting the massive change in class structure implied by these figures, workers, particularly trade union members, have become major forces in such Canadian third parties as the NDP and the Parti Québécois. If third parties were first founded largely as a response to farmers' demands, the subsequent consolidation and growth of third parties has been partly a response to workers' increasingly important role in Canadian society. Through third parties, workers have tried to get their interests established as rights. They have, for example, sought to influence governments to redistribute income more equitably, provide more protection against market forces and make public day care widely available.

This is not, however, to suggest that Canadian workers have sought to achieve their goals only through third parties. A second form of protest—a favourite of Canadian workers—is the strike. By withholding their labour, workers generally aim to extract

higher wages or better working conditions from their employers. Occasionally, strikes have taken on a political character as strikers demand government reform or the overthrow of a government. In extremely rare cases, such as in Russia in 1917, striking workers have demanded revolutionary changes in the way society as a whole is organized.

In order to sketch the pattern and significance of strike activity in Canada, let us first define the *strike volume* as the number of eight-hour days (person-days) lost due to strikes in a year. Let us further define *strike frequency* as the number of industrial disputes resulting in work stoppage in a year. Researchers have shown that, in the post–Second World War period, both these measures of strike activity have been closely related to fluctuations in the business cycle (Hibbs, 1976; Korpi and Shalev, 1980; Smith, 1981). Why? Largely, it seems, because good business conditions lower the power ratio between employers and employees, while poor business conditions increase the power ratio. During times of low unemployment and steady increases in real wages, workers are in a better position to press their demands. Employers are anxious to maintain high production levels since profits are up during booms in the business cycle. At the same time, workers have more personal and union financial reserves to sustain them while on strike, and they are likely to have alternative job

FIGURE 22-2   The Volume of Strike Activity in Canada, 1901–1985

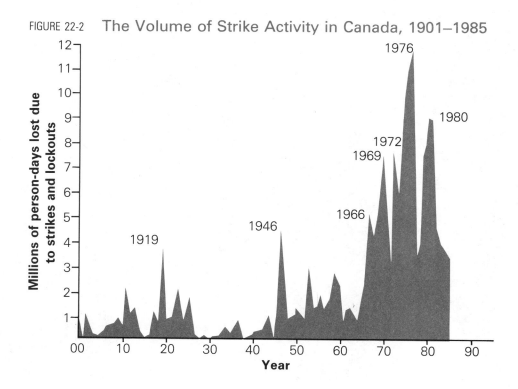

opportunities to which they can turn if they so desire. However, during economic slowdowns, employers are less anxious to settle disputes. Why should they want to produce at full capacity when there is no market for their products? As far as workers are concerned, strikes are less desirable in bad times because they have less money and fewer alternative job opportunities.

Long-run trends in strike activity can be interpreted in similar terms (Hibbs, 1978; Korpi and Shalev, 1980; Shorter and Tilly, 1971). Figure 22-2 shows the volume of strike activity in Canada from 1901 to 1985. Obviously, the graph reveals a strong upward trend. It also shows that peaks in the volume of strike activity have occurred more frequently with the passage of time. Both tendencies may be interpreted as a result of increasing working-class power. The *size* of the non-agricultural labour force has increased greatly since the beginning of the century, both in absolute terms and as a percentage of the entire labour force. (In 1911, 66 percent of the 2.7 million people in the labour force were non-agricultural workers, compared to 95 percent of 9.3 million workers in 1975.) The level of *organization* of the working class has also gone up. Workplaces are on average much larger, and a steadily increasing proportion of the labour force is unionized. (In 1923, 13 percent of the non-agricultural paid labour force was unionized. In 1983, the figure reached 40 percent; see Figure 22-3.)

FIGURE 22-3 Trade Union Growth in Canada, 1921–1988

FIGURE 22-4   The Shape of Strikes in Canada, 1901–1980

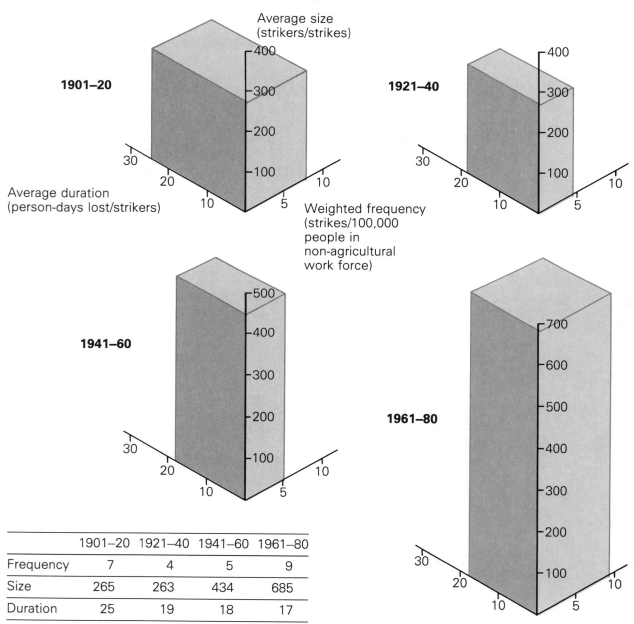

	1901–20	1921–40	1941–60	1961–80
Frequency	7	4	5	9
Size	265	263	434	685
Duration	25	19	18	17

Data taken from *Report on Strikes and Lockouts in Canada, 1901–1916*. Ottawa: Department of Labour, 1918; *Strikes and Lockouts in Canada*. Ottawa: Department of Labour, annual, 1917–81; *Union Growth in Canada, 1921–1967*. Ottawa: Department of Labour, 1970; *Directory of Labour Organizations in Canada*. Ottawa: Department of Labour, annual, 1968–81.

And the *material resources* of workers have also increased markedly. (Allowing for inflation, there was a 199 percent increase in average weekly wages and salaries from 1939 to 1980 alone.)

It is also instructive to examine historical tendencies in the *shape* of Canadian strikes. *Strike shapes* are formed by three dimensions: (a) the *weighted frequency* of strikes, or strike frequency divided by the number of people in the non-agricultural work force per year; (b) the *average size* of strikes, or the number of strikers divided by the strike frequency per year; and (c) the *average duration* of strikes, or strike volume divided by the number of strikers per year. Figure 22-4 demonstrates that, over time, there has been a tendency for strikes to occur more frequently and a strong tendency toward bigger strikes. Strikes also tend to be of shorter duration.

Although there are wide variations from country to country in these patterns of strike activity, there is a universal tendency toward more frequent, bigger strikes of shorter duration. Industrialization and urbanization have universally caused working-class power to grow, so that while strikes used to be tests of endurance, they are now shows of strength.

Despite this general tendency, Canadian strikes tend to last considerably longer than those of any other country in the Western industrialized world. Indeed, that is the main reason why, in the 1970s, Canada placed first among Western industrialized countries in person-days lost due to strikes per 1000 workers, and why from 1980 to 1985 Canada placed second, next to Italy (Ward, 1981; International Labour Organisation, 1987). Here, we arrive at a fascinating paradox. Above, the pattern of strike activity in Canada was interpreted as a sign of how working-class power has *increased over time*. But it may also be suggested that *when Canada is compared to most other Western countries*, its working class is *weak*: a smaller proportion of the working class is unionized and trade union structure is highly decentralized (cf. Ingham, 1974).[4] In many Western countries, strikes by large, powerful and unified trade union movements can so seriously affect the entire nation's economy that disputes are settled quickly and the overall volume of strike activity is consequently low. Not so in Canada, where strikes are more likely to be bitter, protracted affairs.

All this is interesting because there is a strong relationship between strike activity and democratic-socialist party strength. The longer democratic-socialist governments are in power, the lower the volume of strike activity (Hibbs, 1978); that is, over the long run, left-wing governments have the effect of lowering strike levels. The Western industrialized countries with the highest levels of strike activity since the Second World War—Canada, Italy and the United States—are also the countries that have had little or no democratic-socialist representation in federal Cabinets. The countries with the lowest levels of strike activity—the Scandinavian nations—have the longest histories

---

[4] At the same time, the capitalist class in Canada is powerful by international standards, as ownership concentration figures and other indices show. See, for example, Ornstein (1989).

of democratic-socialist rule. This is not to suggest that, when democratic-socialist governments get elected, fights over the distribution of rewards in society cease. They continue; but their locus shifts. They tend to take place in Parliament, or at government-sanctioned negotiating tables, not at the workplace.

The Coyote Condition

Industrial experts call it the "coyote condition"—a Canadian on strike would rather gnaw off his leg than go back to work without a satisfactory settlement.

It's the major reason Canada has racked up the industrialized world's worst strike record over the past decade. . . .

Canada's unenviable distinction as the industrialized world's strike leader was won on the basis of International Labor Office statistics showing strikes cost this country 1,840 working days for every 1,000 employees over the past decade.

We took the dubious honor by nipping Italy in the stretch.

It was the duration of strikes that catapulted Canada to the top. Other countries had more frequent strikes involving more workers—but shorter in duration.

In Canada, a strike is a matter of endurance, says [John] Crispo [an industrial relations expert from the University of Toronto]. "Once a strike starts, it's a struggle of the will. Each side is determined to outlast the other."

Often, millions of workers in several related unions will walk off the job together.

These common-front strikes hit at the solar plexus of small European countries. Because the entire nation is affected, settlements become a top priority.

It's generally accepted that a Canadian strike—because it is isolated—will seldom inconvenience the public to any great degree. . . .

Bruce Ward. 1981. "Coyote Conditions Make Our Strikes Long, Spiteful Battles." *The Toronto Star*, August 5, p. A20. Reprinted with the permission of the Toronto Star Syndicate.

It is, of course, uncertain whether Canada will eventually follow the European model, whether its democratic-socialist party, the NDP, will grow beyond minor party status, form the federal government and eventually exert a dampening influence on strike levels. There are forces leading in that direction, but countervailing tendencies also exist.

Among the major developments pushing Canada toward the European pattern is the "nationalization" of our trade union movement. Until the mid-1970s, the great majority of trade unionists in Canada were members of American-dominated unions with American and Canadian members, usually in the ratio 10 : 1. These "internationals," which began organizing in Ontario before the First World War, were "business unions." They stood for the idea that workers should use their votes to punish their political enemies and reward their political friends without, however, forming an independent labour party. Thus, the idea of an independent labour party was slow to take root in Canada. American labour leaders opposed it, and the right to support such a party was expressly denied in some international union charters. Consequently, the trade union movement in Canada has historically had weak ties to the CCF/NDP.

Over the past fifteen years, this picture has altered considerably. In the mid-1970s, some Canadian unionists who were involved in protracted strikes were angered to watch their co-unionists in the United States work extra shifts to make up for lost production in Canadian plants. The feeling also grew that union funds were being drained from Canadian locals to head offices in the United States. And there was a general rise of nationalist feeling in Canada. These factors all contributed to the so-called "breakaway movement"—the resignation of Canadian members from international unions and the formation of independent Canadian unions. By 1977, for the first time in Canadian history, a majority of trade unionists were not members of internationals, and this trend is continuing. Important gains in Canadianization have also been registered since the mid-1970s because of the continuing first-time unionization of white-collar workers (public service employees, nurses, etc.) (Jamieson, 1973; Laxer, 1976).

The Canadianization movement has brought about a strengthening of ties between trade unions and the NDP: increased financial support, election campaigning and so forth. This is reminiscent of the strong ties that unite European trade unions and labour parties. At the federal level, support for the NDP has risen slowly and unevenly to just over 20 percent of the popular vote in the 1988 election. Over the next few decades the weakening influence of American trade union political practice may result in increased popular support for the democratic left in Canada.

It is important to add, however, that countervailing forces are likely to be unleashed by the free trade deal that Canada and the United States have signed. Consider the following scenario, sketched by one Harvard economist (*The Globe and Mail*, 1988). Let us imagine that, under free trade, a firm wants to build a new plant in North America. Its owners will know that, as a general rule, strong unions are able to extract wage concessions from employers. The owners will also know that proportionately more than twice as many workers belong to unions in Canada as in the United States. They will therefore be inclined to establish the new plant in the relatively non-unionized United States—unless Canadian workers are able to offer concessions by accepting lower wages, a more modest package of social benefits and/or a reduced level of unionization. The likelihood of this scenario is confirmed by some corporate leaders (Cameron, 1988).

In short, some commentators expect that the material resources (wages, welfare state benefits) and level of social organization (unionization) of Canadian workers will decline under free trade. The trade union movement in Canada is thus being subjected to contradictory pressures: while the free trade environment threatens to lead to lower levels of working-class power and therefore less support for the NDP, the Canadianization movement is pushing workers in a more militant direction. Which set of forces will prevail is anybody's guess, since sociologists' long-range forecasts are rarely as good as meteorologists'.

The Women's Movement

The farmers' and workers' movements recruit members of a particular class. To a lesser degree, the political parties that emerged from these movements have also been inclined to speak for specific classes. But the women's movement, the last social movement we will discuss, is different. It recruits members from various classes. Moreover, few feminists believe that they should form a separate political party. Instead, they have generally fought their battles inside established political parties or outside the party system entirely.

The women's movement has been usefully interpreted as a response to four interrelated developments: (1) the declining role of women in domestic production; (2) their entry into the paid labour force; (3) their confrontation with gender inequality in the labour market; and (4) the prospect of freedom from oppressive authority in the family that accompanied their growing economic independence (Strong-Boag, 1986:179). At the beginning of the nineteenth century, women's status derived mainly from their responsibility for a broad range of economic activities in the home and on the farm, such as food preparation and the care and education of children. By the end of the last century, however, these functions were increasingly purchased outside the home. At the same time, women in growing numbers began to work outside the home for a

Socialist feminists argue that women's career progress will be hampered until the state provides free public day care for all.

wage. Their own earnings gave them a measure of economic autonomy and power, but they were accorded less pay and worse working conditions than men. Thus, as women's domestic status declined, their economic freedom increased and their perception of domestic and market inequality sharpened; their demand for social reform grew apace.

We know that formulating a program for social change requires certain resources, such as time, money and education. It is not surprising, therefore, that the *first-wave* feminists were highly educated, urbanized, upper-middle-class, professional women. In 1883, a group of women with that social profile established the Canadian Woman Suffrage Association in Toronto. Their chief aim—to win the right to vote for women—was achieved federally in 1918, in all provinces save Quebec by 1925, and in Quebec in 1940. But suffrage was not the only principle for which the early feminists fought. They also sought equal access to the education that led to better jobs, more equitable pay, receipt of a fair share of family assets and child support in case of divorce or desertion and protection from the domestic violence that was commonly associated with male alcoholism.

None of this, however, detracted from the early feminists' sense that they were mothers above all else. Indeed, in their reformist zeal they tried to extend the maternal role to the public sphere and win greater recognition of that role's full social value. Characteristically, Nellie McClung, one of the most important of the first-wave feminists, referred to the state as "the larger home"; and one feminist political scientist recently characterized the reformist efforts of McClung and her contemporaries as "housekeeping on a grand scale" (Bashevkin, 1986:252).

The main strategy of the first-wave feminists was to seek institutional reform through government action. To that end they petitioned, demonstrated and ran for public office, mainly for the precursors of the NDP and the Liberals. In 1917 in Alberta, the first woman was elected to a provincial office, and in 1921, the first woman was elected as a federal MP. By 1988, however, women represented only 13.2 percent of MPs. At that rate of improvement women can expect to achieve 50 percent representation in the House of Commons by the year 2182!

Partly as a result of that dismal record, the institutional emphasis of the women's movement was augmented twenty years ago by a *grass-roots* approach. The *second-wave feminists* of the late 1960s and early 1970s tried to reform old institutions, too. But they also sought to achieve change "from below" by creating new organizations such as study groups, women's book stores, rape crisis centres, homes for battered women and so forth.[5]

There are two other ways in which contemporary feminists differ from the suffragettes (Adamson, Briskin and McPhail, 1988). First, radical feminists argue that "the

---

[5] In addition, it seems that second-wave feminists are more likely to be academics or wage earners than were the first-wave feminists.

personal is the political." This slogan implies that motherhood and female sexuality are neither natural nor immutable facts of life; instead, they are socially determined, variable and therefore ultimately political issues. It follows that if women are to be free to choose their roles, they must have access to cheap and safe contraception and abortion facilities and they must stop being stereotypically portrayed and treated only as mothers, heterosexuals and sex objects.

Second, while socialist feminists agree that the personal is the political, they also stress that equality between the sexes cannot be assured unless women are accorded economic equality and not merely equal legal rights. In this view, working-class women lack the economic means to take advantage of such equality of opportunity as exists between the sexes. For example, both men and women have close to equal access to higher education today, but working-class women with children often cannot afford to attend university because, given the lack of public day care facilities, they are usually obliged to stay at home with their children. From the point of view of the socialist feminists, then, legal equality is not enough. They demand that the state provide day care and other services to alleviate the economic burdens faced by most women, especially those from the working class.

The validity of this argument is supported by the research of an English economist who examined the degree to which the women's movement in 117 countries gave prominence to child support policies (Reed, 1986). She found that where the movement stressed child support policies, women did better in the labour market. For example, in the United States there is no statutory maternity leave and there are next to no government-sponsored pre-schools. Among full-time workers, the average woman earns less than two-thirds of what the average man earns. In Western Europe, by contrast, maternity leave is on average five months long and government-sponsored pre-schools are very widespread. Consequently, among full-time workers, the average woman earns 70 to 80 percent of what the average man earns. The Canadian pattern is closer to the U.S. model than the Western European one (Fox, 1986).

These findings prompt the conclusion that working women need more than equal treatment in order to achieve equality with men on the labour market. They need benefits and services that ease family responsibilities. In Canada, where such benefits and services are relatively modest, the achievements of the women's movement have been considerable, but middle-class women have benefited more than women from the working class. Compared to the late 1960s, socialization and education are now more egalitarian; men's and women's educational credentials are more alike; more women are employed in traditional "men's" occupations; more women earn income and are less economically dependent on husbands; more have access to day care facilities and maternity leave; and there is equal division of family property in divorce. However, safe, cheap, legal abortion is not widely available. The gap between men's and women's wages has not narrowed. The level of sex segregation in jobs has not changed much. And child care responsibilities continue to be a private concern that handicaps working-class women. As one feminist sociologist recently stated, "Without the social supports women need because they are different than men, most women cannot compete . . . as men can. Ultimately, the crucial battle for change must involve a deprivatization of the responsibility for child care, for that responsibility is what makes women's lives so different from men's, and represents the crucial handicap in the labour market" (Fox, 1986 : 42).

Summary

The three social movements examined above are responses to social change and causes of further social change. When various social developments increased farmers', workers' and women's power, these groups created political and other organizations to correct perceived injustices. To the degree that they succeeded in establishing their aims as rights, these movements helped create modern society as we know it.

These movements are *not* inevitable outcomes of societal and personal breakdown, of economic disadvantage and anger. There is plenty of injustice and rage in the world that never gets translated into collective protest. Society—most importantly, the social organization of power relations—stands between ire and action, and the study of social movements helps us understand the circumstances that make collective conflict a part of everyday life.

Our analysis of the farmers', workers' and women's movements demonstrates how society affects protest activity. In investigating the farmers' movement, we learned that social movements and third parties are more likely to form where farmers are more *segmented* from other categories of the population. We also learned that social movements and third parties are more likely to form when the *power ratio*—the ratio of authorities' to potential partisans' power—is low. In extending our analysis to the workers' movement, we investigated how shifting power relations affect the *form* of conflict. Accordingly, we saw how various dimensions of strike activity—weighted frequency, average size and average duration—are influenced by changes in working-class power. And we noted how increasing worker involvement in parliamentary politics can displace strike action. Our brief sketch of the women's movement also focused on the factors that determine what form protests will take. We saw that the limited successes of the first-wave feminists prompted a turn from an institutional to a grass-roots approach, and the development of more radical and socialist programs.

These considerations permit us to conclude that Marx and Engels clearly over-simplified when they wrote that the "history of all hitherto existing society is the history of class struggles" (Marx and Engels, 1972 : 335). But it is just as surely evident that social movements and the conflict they generate have always been, and continue to be, a normal and pervasive part of social life and that they are among the main forces changing the shape of the society in which we live.

Suggested Readings

For good introductions to the social movements discussed in this chapter, see Seymour Martin Lipset's *Agrarian Socialism: The Cooperative Commonwealth Federation in Saskatchewan*, rev. ed. (Berkeley: University of California Press, 1968; originally 1950); Gad Horowitz's *Canadian Labour in Politics* (Toronto: University of Toronto Press, 1968); and Veronica Strong-Boag and Anita Clair Fellman, eds., *Rethinking Canada: The Promise of Women's History* (Toronto: Copp Clark Pitman, 1986).

Robert J. Brym with Bonnie J. Fox, *From Culture to Power: The Sociology of English Canada* (Toronto: Oxford University Press, 1989) demonstrates in detail how the analysis of power relations has reshaped the analysis of Canadian social movements and Canadian society as a whole since the 1960s.

Two very important and accessible works that document the "resource mobilization" approach to social movements employed in this chapter are Anthony Oberschall's *Social Conflict and Social Movements* (Englewood Cliffs, N.J.: Prentice-Hall, 1973) and Charles Tilly's "Collective Violence in European Perspective," pp. 83–118 in H. Graham and T. Gurr, eds., *Violence in America: Historical and Comparative Perspectives*, 2nd ed. (Beverly Hills: Sage, 1979; originally 1969).

Discussion Questions

1. It is generally agreed that people must be seriously aggrieved in order to rebel. What additional social structural conditions facilitate protest against the social order?

2. What are the strengths and weaknesses of breakdown and solidarity theories of social movements?

3. What is the relationship between the distribution of power and the intensity of conflict in society?

4. What accounts for the high volume of strike activity and the unusually long duration of strikes in Canada?

5. What accounts for regional variations in the strength of Canadian third parties?

6. What is the relationship between economic protest (such as strikes for higher wages) and political protest (such as the formation of parliamentary third parties)?

7. What are the achievements of the women's movement in Canada? What are the major divisions within the movement in Canada?

Data Collection Exercises

1. Using the International Labour Organisation's *Yearbook of Labour Statistics*, diagram the shape of strikes in Sweden, Japan and Canada for the years 1980 to 1985 (see Figure 22-4 for examples of such diagrams). How do you explain the differences in the shape of strikes in these three countries?

2. How much rioting was there in Canada compared to the United States over the last two years? Look up "riots" and other key words in recent *New York Times* and *Globe and Mail* indexes. Read the relevant newspaper articles. Note the number of riots that took place, the number of people who participated in each riot, the property damage caused, the amount of personal injury, the reasons for each riot, etc. Then write up a profile or summary of riots in Canada and the United States and try to account for the differences you observe.

3. Read the biographical sketches in the *Canadian Parliamentary Guide* of women who were elected to Parliament between 1921 and 1930 and between 1981 and 1990. Keep a tally of how many women were elected to each Parliament, what parties they represented, what provinces they came from, their occupations and whether their husbands were previously elected to Parliament. What generalizations does your research allow you to make about the role of women in Parliament?

4. Attend a demonstration outside your provincial legislature or some other public institution. Interview some of the participants to find out who they represent, what they hope to achieve, how they got organized and what their short-term tactics and long-term strategies are.

Writing Exercises

1. Read a contemporary account of the Russian Revolution, such as John Reed's *Ten Days that Shook the World*. Describe the differences between reformist movements (such as the Canadian farmers', workers' or women's movements) and revolutionary movements in terms of goals, strategy, tactics, ideology and level of violence.

2. How would you organize a social movement? Write up a list of grievances against your university. Set out a strategy for achieving a redress of grievances. Who would you try to recruit as movement partisans? What collective actions do you think would be most successful? Against whom would you direct these actions?

3. Write a book report on one of the items listed in the Suggested Readings.

Glossary

Breakdown theories: *theories of social movements that argue that collective protest occurs in the context of high levels of personal and/or social strain.*

First- and second-wave feminism: *refer, respectively, to the liberal, maternal feminism of the turn of this century and to the radical and socialist feminism that originated in the late 1960s.*

Power: *determinants of power include (a) access to political resources (material, normative and coercive); (b) level of social organization; and (c) group size.*

Relative deprivation: *a condition in which people's expectations exceed their capabilities.*

Segmentation: *the polarization or clustering of social groups in distinct social organizations.*

Social movements: *collective attempts to change some or all aspects of society.*

Solidarity theories: *theories that argue that social movements emerge out of newly empowered groups that seek to have their aims accepted as rights.*

Strike shape: *diagrammed by calculating (a) the weighted frequency of strikes; (b) the average size of strikes; and (c) the average duration of strikes.*

Third parties: *political parties that have gained up to about a fifth of the vote in national elections but have never formed a federal government; formed provincial governments in some (mainly western) provinces; remained unaligned with Liberals and Progressive Conservatives; and for the most part stood on the left wing of the political spectrum.*

References

Adamson, Nancy, Linda Briskin and Margaret McPhail
1988. *Feminist Organizing for Change: The Contemporary Women's Movement in Canada.* Toronto: Oxford University Press.

Bashevkin, Sylvia B.
1986. "Independence Versus Partisanship: Dilemmas in the Political History of Women in English Canada," pp. 246–75. In V. Strong-Boag and A. Fellman, eds., *Rethinking Canada: The Promise of Women's History.* Toronto: Copp Clark Pitman.

Bierstedt, Robert
1974. "An Analysis of Social Power," pp. 220–141. In R. Bierstedt, *Power and Progress: Essays in Sociological Theory.* New York: McGraw-Hill.

Brym, Robert J.
1979. "Political Conservatism in Atlantic Canada," pp. 59–79. In R. Brym and R. Sacouman, eds., *Underdevelopment and Social Movements in Atlantic Canada.* Toronto: New Hogtown Press.
1980. "Regional Social Structure and Agrarian Radicalism in Canada: Alberta, Saskatchewan, and New Brunswick," pp. 344–53. In A. Himelfarb and C. Richardson, eds., *People, Power and Process: A Reader.* Toronto: McGraw-Hill Ryerson.
1984. "Social Movements and Third Parties," pp. 29–49. In S. Berkowitz, ed., *Models and Myths in Canadian Sociology.* Toronto: Butterworths.
1986a. "An Introduction to the Regional Question in Canada," pp. 1–45. In R. Brym, ed., *Regionalism in Canada.* Toronto: Irwin.

1986b. "Incorporation Versus Power Models of Working Class Radicalism: With Special Reference to North America." *Canadian Journal of Sociology* 11 : 227–51.

Brym, Robert J., and Barbara Neis
1978. "Regional Factors in the Formation of the Fishermen's Protective Union of Newfoundland." *Canadian Journal of Sociology* 3 : 391–407.

Brym, Robert J., Michael Gillespie and Rhonda Lenton
1989. "Class Power, Class Mobilization and Class Voting: The Canadian Case." *Canadian Journal of Sociology* 14 : 25–44.

Cameron, Stevie
1988. "Post-Election Days Just Full of Coincidences for Canadians to Ponder." *The Globe and Mail*, December 1, p. A2.

Davies, James C.
1969. "Toward a Theory of Revolution," pp. 85–108. In B. McLaughlin, ed., *Studies in Social Movements: A Social Psychological Perspective*. New York: Free Press.

Fox, Bonnie J.
1986. "An Examination of 'The Longest Revolution': Women's Position in Canada, the 1960s to the 1980s." Paper presented at a conference on "Trends in Social Inequality." London: University of Western Ontario.

Gamson, William
1968. *Power and Discontent*. Homewood, Ill.: Dorsey Press.
1975. *The Strategy of Social Protest*. Homewood, Ill.: Dorsey Press.

The Globe and Mail
1988. "Unions May Scare Off U.S. Investment: Harvard." December 1, p. 39.

Gurr, Ted Robert
1970. *Why Men Rebel*. Princeton, N.J.: Princeton University Press.

Hibbs, Douglas A.
1976. "Industrial Conflict in Advanced Industrial Societies." *American Political Science Review* 70 : 1033–1058.
1978. "On the Political Economy of Long-Run Trends in Strike Activity." *British Journal of Political Science* 8 : 153–75.

Hobsbawm, E. J.
1959. *Primitive Rebels: Studies in Archaic Forms of Social Movement in the 19th and 20th Centuries*. New York: Norton.

Ingham, Geoffrey K.
1974. *Strikes and Industrial Conflict: Britain and Scandinavia*. London: Macmillan.

International Labour Organisation
1987. *Yearbook of Labour Statistics, 1986*. Geneva.

Jamieson, Stuart
1973. *Industrial Relations in Canada*, 2nd ed. Toronto: Macmillan.

Jenkins, Craig J.
1983. "Resource Mobilization Theory and the Study of Social Movements." *Annual Review of Sociology* 9 : 527–53.

Kornhauser, William
1959. *The Politics of Mass Society*. Glencoe, Ill.: Free Press.

Korpi, Walter
1974. "Conflict, Power and Relative Deprivation." *American Political Science Review* 68 : 971–84.

Korpi, Walter, and Michael Shalev
1980. "Strikes, Power, and Politics in the Western Nations, 1900–1976." *Political Power and Social Theory* 1 : 301–34.

Laxer, Robert
1976. *Canada's Unions*. Toronto: James Lorimer.

Lipset, Seymour Martin
1968. *Agrarian Socialism: The Cooperative Commonwealth Federation in Saskatchewan*, rev. ed. Berkeley: University of California Press.
1983. "Radicalism or Reformism: The Sources of Working-Class Politics." *American Political Science Review* 77 : 1–18.

Lodhi, Abdul Qaiyum, and Charles Tilly
1973. "Urbanization, Crime, and Collective Violence in 19th-Century France." *American Journal of Sociology* 79 : 296–318.

Macpherson, C. B.
1962. *Democracy in Alberta: Social Credit and the Party System*, 2nd ed. Toronto: University of Toronto Press.

Marx, Gary T., and James L. Wood
1975. "Strands of Theory and Research in Collective Behavior." *Annual Review of Sociology* 1 : 363–428.

Marx, Karl, and Friedrich Engels
1972 [1848]. "Manifesto of the Communist Party," pp. 331–62. In *The Marx-Engels Reader*. Edited by R. Tucker. New York: Norton.

McCarthy, J., and M. Zald
1977. "Resource Mobilization and Social Movements." *American Journal of Sociology* 82 : 1212–241.

Oberschall, Anthony
1973. *Social Conflict and Social Movements*. Englewood Cliffs, N.J.: Prentice-Hall.

Ornstein, Michael
1989. "The Canadian Capitalist Class in Comparative Perspective." *Canadian Review of Sociology and Anthropology* 26.

Orwell, George
1954. *Nineteen Eighty-Four*. Harmondsworth: Penguin (originally published 1949).

Pinard, Maurice
1971. *The Rise of a Third Party: A Study in Crisis Politics*. Englewood Cliffs, N.J.: Prentice-Hall.
1973. "Third Parties in Canada Revisited: A Rejoinder and Elaboration of the Theory of One-Party Dominance." *Canadian Journal of Political Science* 6 : 439–60.

Reed, Christopher
1986. "Today's Woman: Is Equality Enough?" *The Globe and Mail*, November 7, p. A7.

Richards, John, and Larry Pratt
1979. *Prairie Capitalism: Power and Influence in the New West*. Toronto: McClelland and Stewart.

Roy, William G.
1984. "Class Conflict and Social Change in Historical Perspective." *Annual Review of Sociology* 10:483–506.

Shalev, Michael, and Walter Korpi
1980. "Working Class Mobilization and American Exceptionalism." *Economic and Industrial Democracy* 1:31–61.

Shorter, Edward, and Charles Tilly
1971. "The Shape of Strikes in France, 1830–1960." *Comparative Studies in Society and History* 13:60–86.

Smith, Michael R.
1981. "Industrial Conflict in Post-War Ontario or One Cheer for the Woods Report." *Canadian Review of Sociology and Anthropology* 18:370–92.

Strong-Boag, Veronica
1986. "Ever a Crusader: Nellie McClung, First-Wave Feminist," pp. 178–90. In V. Strong-Boag and A. Fellman, eds., *Rethinking Canada: The Promise of Women's History*. Toronto: Copp Clark Pitman.

Tilly, Charles
1978. *From Mobilization to Revolution*. Reading, Mass.: Addison-Wesley.
1979. "Collective Violence in European Perspective," pp. 83–118. In H. Graham and T. Gurr, eds., *Violence in America: Historical and Comparative Perspectives*, 2nd ed. Beverly Hills: Sage.

Tilly, Charles, Louise Tilly and Richard Tilly
1975. *The Rebellious Century, 1830–1930*. Cambridge, Mass.: Harvard University Press.

Ward, Bruce
1981. "Coyote Condition Makes Our Strikes Long, Spiteful Battles." *The Toronto Star*, August 5, p. A20.

Young, Walter D.
1969. *The Anatomy of a Party: The National CCF, 1932–61*. Toronto: University of Toronto Press.

index